13th Workshop on Cognitive Modeling and Computational Linguistics (CMCL 2024)

Bangkok, Thailand
15 August 2024

ISBN: 979-8-3313-0160-6

Printed from e-media with permission by:

Curran Associates, Inc.
57 Morehouse Lane
Red Hook, NY 12571

Printed with permission by Curran Associates, Inc. (2025)

Association for Computational Linguistics
209 N. Eighth Street
Stroudsburg, Pennsylvania 18360

Phone: 1-570-476-8006
Fax: 1-570-476-0860

acl@aclweb.org

Additional copies of this publication are available from:

Curran Associates, Inc.
57 Morehouse Lane
Red Hook, NY 12571 USA
Phone: 845-758-0400
Fax: 845-758-2633
Email: curran@proceedings.com
Web: www.proceedings.com

CMCL 2024

The 13th edition of the Workshop on Cognitive Modeling and Computational Linguistics

Proceedings of the Workshop

August 15, 2024

This workshop was supported by JST, PRESTO Grant Number JPMJPR21C2.

Association for Computational Linguistics (ACL)
317 Sidney Baker St. S
Suite 400 - 134
Kerrville, TX 78028
USA
Tel: +1-855-225-1962
acl@aclweb.org

Introduction

Welcome to the 13th edition of the Workshop on Cognitive Modeling and Computational Linguistics (CMCL 2024)!

CMCL has traditionally been the workshop of reference for research at the intersection between Computational Linguistics and Cognitive Science. After a blank in 2023, we are thrilled to be back, hosting this event once again after two years.

This year, CMCL has experienced multiple *firsts*, making it a landmark edition in its history. First, the organization team has transitioned to a younger generation and adopted modern logistics, such as using OpenReview and allowing commitments via ACL Rolling Review, for the first time. Second, this is the first CMCL held in the age of large language models (LLMs), prompting us to focus on fundamental scientific questions (e.g., their alignment with human cognition/perception) regarding artificial intelligence and cognitive science. Third, this is also the first CMCL held in Asia, marking a new geographical milestone for the workshop. Lastly, we received a record number of 55 submissions (37 regular submissions and 18 cross-submissions, including Findings papers), nearly doubling the submission number in the previous edition, providing a testament to the growing interest in this scientific, interdisciplinary field and the need for the dedicated workshop even in the age of somewhat engineeringly-oriented LLMs.

Out of 37 regular submissions, 34 papers are via direct submission (including 1 paper withdrawn before reviewing), and 3 papers are through the ARR commitment. We accepted 23 papers, resulting in an acceptance rate of 23/36=63.9%, slightly higher than in previous years. Additionally, 12 non-archival, cross-submissions were accepted and will be presented during the poster sessions. We are excited to have a diverse set of topics, including but not limited to, sentence processing, language acquisition, and new investigations powered by modern (multimodal) LLMs, covered in this year's program.

We extend our deepest gratitude to the Program Committee members; their dedication and expertise are the backbone of CMCL's success. We also express our sincere thanks to our invited speakers, Dr. Frank Keller, Dr. Aida Nematzadeh, and Dr. Sandro Pezzelle, for their valuable contributions to this year's program.

Lastly, we are immensely grateful to our sponsor, the Japan Science and Technology Agency. Their generous support allows us to subsidize the participation of our invited speakers.

The CMCL 2024 Organizing Committee

Organizers:

Tatsuki Kuribayashi, Mohammed bin Zayed University of Artificial Intelligence
Giulia Rambelli, University of Bologna
Ece Takmaz, University of Amsterdam
Philipp Wicke, Ludwig Maximilian University
Yohei Oseki, University of Tokyo

Invited speakers:

Frank Keller, University of Edinburgh
Aida Nematzadeh, Google DeepMind
Sandro Pezzelle, University of Amsterdam

Program committee:

Raquel G. Alhama, University of Amsterdam
Afra Alishahi, Tilburg University
Ted Briscoe, Mohamed bin Zayed University of Artificial Intelligence
Christos Christodoulopoulos, Amazon
Claudia Collacciani, University of Bologna
Aniello De Santo, University of Utah
Vera Demberg, Universität des Saarlandes
Dota Tianai Dong, Max Planck Institute for Psycholinguistics
Micha Elsner, Ohio State University
Wenxi Fei, Hong Kong Polytechnic University
Meaghan Fowlie, Utrecht University
Robert Frank, Yale University
Richard Futrell, University of California, Irvine
Shubham Garg, Amazon
John T. Hale, Johns Hopkins University, University of Georgia and DeepMind
Nora Hollenstein, University of Copenhagen
Samar Husain, Indian Institute of Technology Delhi
Go Inoue, Mohamed bin Zayed University of Artificial Intelligence
Cassandra L Jacobs, State University of New York, Buffalo
Carina Kauf, Massachusetts Institute of Technology
Yova Kementchedjhieva, Mohamed bin Zayed University of Artificial Intelligence
Snigdha Khanna, Indiana University
Fajri Koto, Mohamed bin Zayed University of Artificial Intelligence
Sandra Kübler, Indiana University at Bloomington
Yu Xi Li, Hong Kong Polytechnic University and Xi'an Jiaotong University
Tal Linzen, New York University and Google
Ziqian Luo, Oracle
Shrirang Mhalgi, Indiana University
James A. Michaelov, University of California, San Diego
Sathvik Nair, University of Maryland
Ludovica Pannitto, University of Bologna
Tiago Pimentel, ETH Zurich
Laurent Prevot, Université d'Aix-Marseille
Rachel Ryskin, University of California at Merced
William Schuler, Ohio State University, Columbus
Dylan Scott, National Taiwan Normal University

Cory Shain, Massachusetts Institute of Technology
Adina Williams, FAIR
Xinchen Yang, University of Maryland
Ryo Yoshida, The University of Tokyo

Table of Contents

Archival papers

Non-archival papers

So many design choices: Improving and interpreting neural agent communication in signaling games
Timothée Bernard and Timothee Mickus

The Emergence of High-Level Semantics in a Signaling Game
Timothée Bernard, Timothee Mickus and Hiroya Takamura

PUB: A Pragmatics Understanding Benchmark for Assessing LLMs' Pragmatics Capabilities
Settaluri Lakshmi Sravanthi, Meet Doshi, Pavan Kalyan Tankala, Rudra Murthy, Raj Dabre and Pushpak Bhattacharyya

Program

Thursday, August 15, 2024

08:45 - 09:00 *Opening Remarks*

09:00 - 09:40 *Keynote talk by Dr. Sandro Pezzelle*

09:40 - 10:40 *Session 1: Oral Presentations*

Hierarchical syntactic structure in human-like language models
Michael Wolfman, Donald Dunagan, Jonathan Brennan and John T. Hale

Do large language models resemble humans in language use?
Zhenguang Cai, Xufeng Duan, David Haslett, Shuqi Wang and Martin Pickering

Evaluating Vision-Language Models on Bistable Images
Artemis Panagopoulou, Coby Melkin and Chris Callison-Burch

10:40 - 11:00 *Break*

11:00 - 12:20 *Session 2: Poster Presentations*

BAMBINO-LM: (Bilingual-)Human-Inspired Continual Pre-training of BabyLM
Zhewen Shen, Aditya Joshi and Ruey-Cheng Chen

The Curious Case of Representational Alignment: Unravelling Visio-Linguistic Tasks in Emergent Communication
Tom Kouwenhoven, Max Peeperkorn, Bram Van Dijk and Tessa Verhoef

Do LLMs Agree with Humans on Emotional Associations to Nonsense Words?
Yui Miyakawa, Chihaya Matsuhira, Hirotaka Kato, Takatsugu Hirayama, Takahiro Komamizu and Ichiro Ide

Predict but Also Integrate: an Analysis of Sentence Processing Models for English and Hindi
Nina Delcaro, Luca Onnis and Raquel G. Alhama

Transformer Attention vs Human Attention in Anaphora Resolution
Anastasia Kozlova, Albina Akhmetgareeva, Aigul Khanova, Semen Kudriavtsev and Alena Fenogenova

Diachronic change in verb usage statistics predicts differences in sentence processing across the lifespan
Ellis Cain and Rachel Ryskin

How can large language models become more human?
Daphne Wang, Mehrnoosh Sadrzadeh, Miloš Stanojević, Wing-Yee Chow and Richard Breheny

15:00 - 15:40 *Invited talk by Dr. Frank Keller*

15:40 - 16:00 *Break*

16:00 - 17:20 *Session 4: Poster Presentations*

Locally Biased Transformers Better Align with Human Reading Times
Andrea Gregor De Varda and Marco Marelli

Evaluating Lexical Aspect with Large Language Models
Bolei Ma

Analysing and Validating Language Complexity Metrics Across South American Indigenous Languages
Felipe Ribas Serras, Miguel De Mello Carpi, Matheus Castello Branco and Marcelo Finger

Morphology Matters: Probing the Cross-linguistic Morphological Generalization Abilities of Large Language Models through a Wug Test
Dang Thi Thao Anh, Limor Raviv and Lukas Galke

Evaluating Grammatical Well-Formedness in Large Language Models: A Comparative Study with Human Judgments
Zhuang Qiu, Xufeng Duan and Zhenguang Cai

Evaluating Semantic Relations in Predicting Textual Labels for Images of Abstract and Concrete Concepts
Tarun Tater, Sabine Schulte Im Walde and Diego Frassinelli

How Useful is Context, Actually? Comparing LLMs and Humans on Discourse Marker Prediction
Emily Sadlier-Brown, Millie Lou, Miikka Silfverberg and Carla L. Hudson Kam

LLMs' morphological analyses of complex FST-generated Finnish words
Anssi Moisio, Mathias Creutz and Mikko Kurimo

An Eye Opener Regarding Task-Based Text Gradient Saliency
Guojun Wu, Lena Sophia Bolliger, David Robert Reich and Lena Ann Jäger

Improving Language Models for Emotion Analysis: Insights from Cognitive Science
Constant Bonard and Gustave Cortal

Structural Similarities Between Language Models and Neural Response Measurements
Antonia Karamolegkou, Jiaang Li, Yova Kementchedjhieva, Mostafa Abdou, Sune Lehmann and Anders Søgaard

Exploring Spatial Schema Intuitions in Large Language and Vision Models
Philipp Wicke and Lennart Wachowiak

Can You Learn Semantics Through Next-Word Prediction? The Case of Entailment
William Merrill, Zhaofeng Wu, Norihito Naka, Yoon Kim and Tal Linzen

The Emergence of High-Level Semantics in a Signaling Game
Timothée Bernard, Timothee Mickus and Hiroya Takamura

PUB: A Pragmatics Understanding Benchmark for Assessing LLMs' Pragmatics Capabilities
Settaluri Lakshmi Sravanthi, Meet Doshi, Pavan Kalyan Tankala, Rudra Murthy, Raj Dabre and Pushpak Bhattacharyya

17:20 - 18:00 *Invited talk by Dr. Aida Nematzadeh*

18:00 - 18:10 *Closing Remarks*

BAMBINO-LM: (Bilingual-)Human-Inspired Continual Pre-training of BabyLM

Zhewen Shen[1] **Aditya Joshi** [1] **Ruey-Cheng Chen**[2]
[1] University of New South Wales, Sydney, Australia
[2] Canva, Sydney, Australia
zhewen.shen@student.unsw.edu.au, aditya.joshi@unsw.edu.au, rcchen@canva.com

Abstract

Children from bilingual backgrounds benefit from interactions with parents and teachers to re-acquire their heritage language. In this paper, we investigate how this insight from behavioral study can be incorporated into the learning of small-scale language models. We introduce BAMBINO-LM, a continual pre-training strategy for BabyLM that uses a novel combination of alternation and PPO-based perplexity reward induced from a parent Italian model. Upon evaluation on zero-shot classification tasks for English and Italian, BAMBINO-LM improves the Italian language capability of a BabyLM baseline. Our ablation analysis demonstrates that employing both the alternation strategy and PPO-based modeling is key to this effectiveness gain. We also show that, as a side effect, the proposed method leads to a similar degradation in L1 effectiveness as human children would have had in an equivalent learning scenario. Through its modeling and findings, BAMBINO-LM makes a focused contribution to the pre-training of small-scale language models by first developing a human-inspired strategy for pre-training and then showing that it results in behaviours similar to that of humans.

1 Introduction

The recently held **BabyLM** challenge (Warstadt et al., 2023) explores pretraining of language models using a constrained dataset analogous to the linguistic exposure of a 13-year-old English-speaking child. In this paper, we extend the BabyLM challenge to a bilingual setting, drawing inspiration from parent-child interactions in heritage language acquisition (Lohndal et al., 2019). Immigrant children in western societies, who may have acquired their home language at a young age, can sometimes need to re-acquire the same language during the school years when the language becomes a minority. These heritage speakers typically benefit from an extended exposure to the minority language at home or in the community, owing largely to feedback and stimuli provided by parents and family members (Montrul, 2010). This observation about child bilingualism is in line with the behaviorist theory for child language development (Demirezen, 1988).

Inspired by this line of work, we ask the following research question in the context of computational language modeling:

> *Can a small-scale language model trained on the majority language (e.g. English) be continually pre-trained on the minority language, leveraging the feedback of a second model that is fluent in the latter language?*

To address this question, we introduce '**Bilingual language Acquisition Modeling Based on INterleaved Optimization of Language Models (BAMBINO-LM)**', a novel continual pretraining strategy that uses a combination of alternation and proximal policy optimization (PPO) using a reward from a second model playing the parent role (i.e., a large language model pre-trained in the minority language). We experiment with BabyLM trained on *English*, and continually pretrain this model on an assumed second language, *Italian*.In its connection to cognitive processing, our work makes the following contributions:

- BAMBINO-LM draws inspiration from bilingual language acquisition and learns from interactions with a second model by **incorporating a perplexity-based reward for language model pre-training**. To the best of our knowledge, this is the first work to use PPO-based modeling for language acquisition in BabyLM.
- We show that BAMBINO-LM can acquire Italian to a reasonable degree with some expected

Proceedings of the Workshop on Cognitive Modeling and Computational Linguistics, pages 1–7
August 15, 2024

degradation in its English capability. The findings hint at **a common learning trajectories for second language acquisition shared by language models and humans**.

2 Related Work

Pre-training small-scale language models is an emerging field that has garnered some interest from the language acquisition community. BabyBERTa (Huebner et al., 2021) is an early adaptation to this scenario. Warstadt et al. (2023) introduce the BabyLM challenge to provide an atypically small dataset for benchmarking small-scale language models. This shared task enables research in not only language acquisition but also sample-efficient pre-training. In the case of our paper, we do not focus on sample efficiency but instead describe ways to enhance the ability of a second language via continual pre-training.

Our work is conducted in a setup similar to Yadavalli et al. (2023), where a tiered first/second language acquisition process is attempted. Samuel (2023) also experiments with a teacher-student setting but only tests the approach on English tasks. Evanson et al. (2023) is another closely related work, which investigates the learning trajectory of large-scale language models by probing their syntactic and semantic capabilities at each step.

Conventionally in language generation for natural language processing, the design of feedback signals is commonly discussed in the context of knowledge distillation (Calderon et al., 2023). Recently, reinforcement learning from human feedback (RLHF) utilizes human preferences for serving reward signals when dealing with sparse training labels (Christiano et al., 2017; Stiennon et al., 2020), and has been shown successful for generative tasks such as dialogues and summarization. This approach is further extended in Bai et al. (2022) by using AI feedback (RLAIF) to remove the dependency on human preference data, leading to better scalability and signal availability. The approach we take in this paper mostly falls within the latter camp, but generally departs from all prior efforts in the way the parent model's perplexity is used to signal the conformity of the child model's generation. This is in contrast to sequence-level knowledge distillation (Kim and Rush, 2016) where teacher's generation is used to guide the learning process.

3 Methods

Figure 1 shows the two phases of BAMBINO-LM. The learning phase involves continual pre-training a small-scale language model (*baby model* $\mathcal{B}$) whose initial pre-training was originally done on English data, while the feedback phase involves interactions with the Italian language model (*parent model* $\mathcal{P}$). During the learning phase, pre-training for $\mathcal{B}$ is continued by employing causal language modeling on Italian data. Causal language modeling (CLM), also known as next token prediction, is a standard technique to train a decoder-only model. The objective is defined as follows:

$$\mathcal{L}_{\text{CLM}} = -\frac{1}{|x|}\sum_{i=0}^{|x|} \log \mathbb{P}(x_t \mid x_0, \ldots, x_{t-1}).$$

There are two architectural innovations in BAMBINO-LM:

Feedback phase based on PPO We construct prompt x by selecting the first k tokens from the training example and solicit output $y_{\mathcal{B}} = \mathcal{B}(x)$ from the baby model. We then use Proximal Policy Optimization (PPO) where $\mathcal{B}$'s parameters are updated according to a clipped surrogate objective (Schulman et al., 2017). This objective moderates the updates to the policy, facilitating stable and efficient learning by incorporating a clipping mechanism. Its definition is given as follows:

$$\mathcal{L}_{\text{PPO}} = \hat{\mathbb{E}}_t \left[\min\left(r_t(\theta)\hat{A}_t, \text{clip}(r_t(\theta);\epsilon)\hat{A}_t\right)\right],$$

with θ being the model parameters and $r_t(\theta)$ defined as:

$$r_t(\theta) = \frac{\pi_\theta(a_t|s_t)}{\pi_{\theta_{\text{old}}}(a_t|s_t)}.$$

In the autoregressive setting of language modeling, θ controls the generation of tokens based on the given state or context s_t. The probability ratio $r_t(\theta)$ quantifies the change in the likelihood of selecting action a_t (the next token), under the updated policy parameters compared to the previous parameters θ_{old}. This ratio provides understanding on the impact of parameter updates on the policy's behavior, ensuring that changes do not excessively deviate from the previous policy, thereby maintaining training stability. The clipping mechanism, defined by $\text{clip}(r_t(\theta);\epsilon)$, restricts $r_t(\theta)$ within the bound $[1-\epsilon, 1-\epsilon]$, mitigating the risk of large policy updates that could lead to divergence.

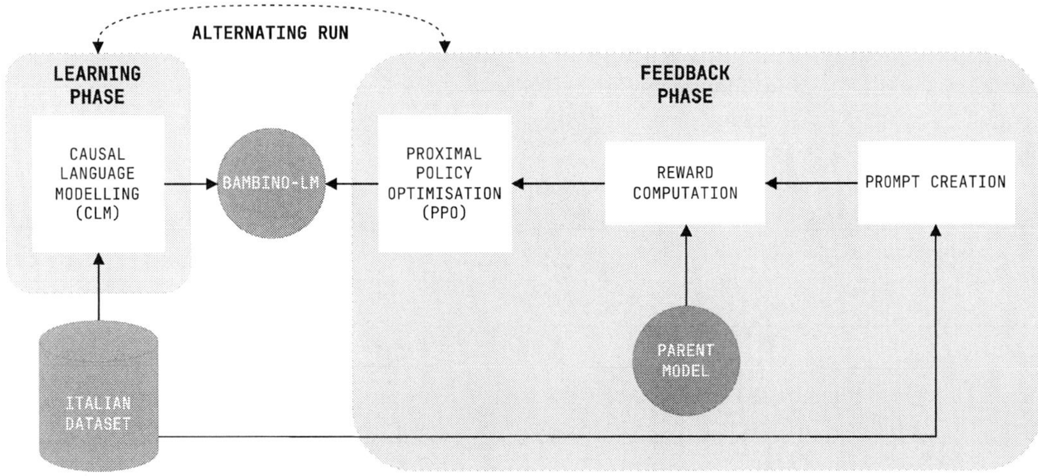

Figure 1: Architecture of BAMBINO-LM.

The advantage function, $\hat{A}_t = R + \gamma V(s_{t+1}) - V(s_t)$, which reflects the relative gains of selecting a_t given s_t. This function guides the optimization process by favoring actions that lead to better than expected outcomes.

The reward R for the advantage function is then calculated using the following function:

$$R(y_{\mathcal{B}}) = \frac{\alpha}{\beta(\text{PPL}_{\mathcal{P}}(y_{\mathcal{B}}) - \tau)}, \quad (1)$$

where α and β are parameters, $\text{PPL}_{\mathcal{P}}$ represents the perplexity of the parent model $\mathcal{P}$ for the sequence $y_{\mathcal{B}}$, and τ is a threshold value for perplexity. We use the following formulation of perplexity:

$$\text{PPL}(x) = \exp\left[\sum_{i=0}^{|x|} \log \mathbb{P}(x_t \mid x_0, \ldots, x_{t-1})\right].$$

Alternating run We adopt an alternating run strategy between the learning and feedback phases, which is summarized in Algorithm 1. The rationale behind this is two-fold: 1) this strategy simulates frequent interactions between a child and its parent through dialogues, which has been our main motivation behind this study; 2) using multiple rewards is shown beneficial for reinforcement learning (Dann et al., 2023). To expand on the second point, our findings further suggest that using perplexity as a reward can lead to exploitation when baby model $\mathcal{B}$ attempts to produce similar utterances to those coming from parent model $\mathcal{P}$. Without this strategic alternation between CLM and PPO, the pre-training tends to produce undesirable behaviours such as repeating words.

Algorithm 1 BAMBINO-LM Training.

procedure TRAIN($\mathcal{D}, \mathcal{B}, \mathcal{P}$)
  Input: pre-training dataset $\mathcal{D}$, baby model $\mathcal{B}$, and parent model $\mathcal{P}$.
  $r_{\text{CLM}}, r_{\text{PPO}} \leftarrow 10, 2$
  $r \leftarrow r_{\text{CLM}} + r_{\text{PPO}}$
  for $i, x \in \text{enumerate}(\mathcal{D})$ **do**
    if $i\%r < r_{\text{CLM}}$ **then**
      perform CLM step
    else
      $y_{\mathcal{B}} \leftarrow \mathcal{B}(x[1..k])$
      reward $\leftarrow R(y_{\mathcal{B}})$
      perform PPO step
    end if
  end for
end procedure

4 Experiment Setup

Mimicking their process to create the BabyLM challenge corpus (Warstadt et al., 2023), we create an Italian dataset that is comparable in size to the *strict-small* track of the challenge, and perform identical preprocessing[1]. Table 1 shows the statistics of the Italian language dataset. A cursory quality check was conducted to ensure that the dataset was in a readable format.

For the choice of the baby model, we use English baseline `OPT-125m` (Zhang et al., 2022) model for the *strict-small* track provided by the BabyLM organizers. For the parent model, we

[1] `https://github.com/babylm/babylm_data_preprocessing`; Accessed on 13th May, 2024.

use `gpt2-small-italian` model by de Vries and Nissim (2021). Using the Italian dataset described above, we conduct continual pretraining over 10 epochs, consisting of 10 learning phase steps followed by 2 feedback phase steps. We use $k = 5$ to solicit the first few tokens for prompting the baby model. All models are trained using HuggingFace's `transformer` (Wolf et al., 2020) and `trl` (von Werra et al., 2020) library.

Dataset	%
CHILDES (MacWhinney, 2000)	2.23
DailyDialog (Li et al., 2017)	4.45
QED (Abdelali et al., 2014)	11.86
OpenSubtitles (Lison and Tiedemann, 2016)	27.58
Standardised Project Gutenberg Corpus (Gerlach and Font-Clos, 2020)	16.19
Children's Story [2]	18.57
Wikipedia [3]	19.10

Table 1: Italian dataset used for continual pre-training.

For downstream tasks, we use four Italian language tasks in UINAUIL (Basile et al., 2023) and four English language tasks in GLUE (Wang et al., 2018). The tasks were selected primarily based on computational constraints for the project. We also include BLiMP (Warstadt et al., 2020) for that it is used in the original BabyLM challenge. All tasks are conducted in a *zero-shot classification* setting.

5 Results

Table 2 shows a significant improvement in Italian downstream tasks for BAMBINO-LM as compared with the BabyLM baseline. Specifically, we achieve an average improvement of 0.1197 ($0.3416 \rightarrow 0.4613$) without substantial differences in English classification tasks. However, we notice an expected decrease of 0.0752 ($0.6255 \rightarrow 0.5503$) in the English language BLiMP dataset. These observations are in line with Yadavalli et al. (2023) which show that native child-directed speech can lead to negative cross-lingual transfer and impede L2 acquisition depending on the choice of L1.

In Table 3 we examine two ablated versions of our model: (a) **w/o PPO:** Trained solely on the CLM objective with no feedback phase; (b) **w/o alternating:** Use BAMBINO-LM with no alternating runs. Instead, it trains with the CLM objective for the first 85% of each epoch and then switches to the PPO objective for the remaining 15%.

[2] https://www.gutenberg.org/ebooks/bookshelf/353

[3] https://dumps.wikimedia.org/itwiki/

Task / Model	BabyLM	BAMBINO-LM
UINAUIL		
HaSpeeDe	**0.4774**	0.4592
IronITA	0.4966	**0.5516**
SENTIPOLC	0.1575	**0.4050**
Textual Entailment	0.4950	**0.5525**
Average	0.3416	**0.4613**
GLUE		
MNLI	0.3472	**0.3530**
MNLI-MM	0.3483	**0.3521**
RTE	**0.5271**	0.5199
SST2	0.5034	**0.5241**
Average	0.4315	**0.4373**
BLiMP		
Average	**0.6255**	0.5503

Table 2: Comparison of BAMBINO-LM with BabyLM.

Removing the interactive feedback mechanism (w/o PPO) and the alternating strategy (w/o alternating) significantly decreases Italian performance compared to our primary model. On UINAUIL tasks, the average score drops from 0.4613 to 0.4000 (w/o PPO) and 0.3513 (w/o alternating). However, we do not observe significant improvements in performance in both the English language task sets (GLUE and BLiMP). For GLUE tasks, the average scores remain consistent, with 0.4373 for BAMBINO-LM, 0.4375 for w/o PPO, and 0.4357 for w/o alternating. On the BLiMP dataset, the average scores are 0.5503 for BAMBINO-LM and 0.5554 for w/o PPO.

These results indicate that PPO modeling and alternating runs are both crucial for improving the bilingual ability of BAMBINO-LM without negatively impacting English performance. Furthermore, the lack of significant changes in English scores reinforces that these strategies enhance bilingual capabilities without compromising performance on existing benchmarks.

6 Conclusion

This paper introduces BAMBINO-LM, a continual pre-training strategy mimicking the process of sec-

Task / Model	BAMBINO-LM w/o PPO	BAMBINO-LM w/o alternating
	UINAUIL	
HaSpeeDe	0.4798	0.4925
IronITA	0.4966	0.4989
SENTIPOLC	0.2775	0.1580
Textual Entailment	0.5500	0.5500
Average	0.4000	0.3513
	GLUE	
MNLI	0.3540	0.3522
MNLI-MM	0.3502	0.3545
RTE	0.5343	0.5271
SST2	0.5115	0.5092
Average	0.4375	0.4357
	BLiMP	
Average	0.5554	0.5268

Table 3: Results of the ablation experiments.

ond language acquisition in an interactive setting. BAMBINO-LM uses a two-phase approach: it incorporates reward from a parent Italian model into a PPO-based mechanism and alternates this procedure together with causal language modeling based on Italian language text. Our experiments demonstrate systematic improvement in Italian with a marginal but expected decrease in English, which echoes the past results in second language acquisition for large language models (Evanson et al., 2023). These findings highlight the efficacy of our approach in enhancing bilingual capabilities while maintaining performance in the original language.

In future work, we aim to explore the effect of alternative metrics and different reward learning mechanisms that better align with human feedback behaviors. This also includes exploring rewards that capture linguistic quality and provide direct, "constructive" corrections to the model output which is commonly known as an effective learning strategy for language development. Although BAMBINO-LM was applied for second language learning with Italian as an example, the method must be validated for other languages, especially languages that are distant from English or those that use a different set of tokens. The degradation in the performance of the first language, English, points to the potential of alternating with language modeling for the first language.

Limitations

The approach relies on the availability of a base model in a language, English in our case. Although we download Italian language datasets from known Italian sources, we do not explicitly validate the language of the text. We use the PPO model as is, and do not experimentally tune its parameters. Similarly, using perplexity as a metric for computing rewards may not be the optimal solution, as perplexity itself is influenced by many factors of the parent model.

Ethics Statement

The paper uses publicly available datasets for training and evaluation that do not possess known harms. The evaluative tasks are typical language learning tasks. However, the resultant models are not tested for harmful or biased content.

Acknowledgment

Zhewen Shen conducted this research as a part of UNSW Sydney's Taste of Research Program.

References

Ahmed Abdelali, Francisco Guzman, Hassan Sajjad, and Stephan Vogel. 2014. The AMARA corpus: Building parallel language resources for the educational domain. In *Proceedings of the Ninth International Conference on Language Resources and Evaluation (LREC'14)*, pages 1856–1862, Reykjavik, Iceland. European Language Resources Association (ELRA).

Yuntao Bai, Saurav Kadavath, Sandipan Kundu, Amanda Askell, Jackson Kernion, Andy Jones, Anna Chen, Anna Goldie, Azalia Mirhoseini, Cameron McKinnon, et al. 2022. Constitutional AI: Harmlessness from AI feedback. *arXiv preprint arXiv:2212.08073*.

Valerio Basile, Livio Bioglio, Alessio Bosca, Cristina Bosco, and Viviana Patti. 2023. UINAUIL: A unified benchmark for Italian natural language understanding. In *Proceedings of the 61st Annual Meeting of the Association for Computational Linguistics (Volume 3: System Demonstrations)*, pages 348–356, Toronto, Canada. Association for Computational Linguistics.

Nitay Calderon, Subhabrata Mukherjee, Roi Reichart, and Amir Kantor. 2023. A systematic study of knowledge distillation for natural language generation with pseudo-target training. In *Proceedings of the 61st Annual Meeting of the Association for Computational*

Linguistics (Volume 1: Long Papers), pages 14632–14659, Toronto, Canada. Association for Computational Linguistics.

Paul F Christiano, Jan Leike, Tom Brown, Miljan Martic, Shane Legg, and Dario Amodei. 2017. Deep reinforcement learning from human preferences. *Advances in neural information processing systems*, 30.

Christoph Dann, Yishay Mansour, and Mehryar Mohri. 2023. Reinforcement learning can be more efficient with multiple rewards. In *International Conference on Machine Learning*, pages 6948–6967. PMLR.

Wietse de Vries and Malvina Nissim. 2021. As good as new. how to successfully recycle English GPT-2 to make models for other languages. In *Findings of the Association for Computational Linguistics: ACL-IJCNLP 2021*, pages 836–846, Online. Association for Computational Linguistics.

Mehmet Demirezen. 1988. Behaviorist theory and language learning. *Hacettepe Üniversitesi Eğitim Fakültesi Dergisi*, 3(3).

Linnea Evanson, Yair Lakretz, and Jean Rémi King. 2023. Language acquisition: do children and language models follow similar learning stages? In *Findings of the Association for Computational Linguistics: ACL 2023*, pages 12205–12218.

Martin Gerlach and Francesc Font-Clos. 2020. A standardized project gutenberg corpus for statistical analysis of natural language and quantitative linguistics. *Entropy*, 22(1).

Philip A Huebner, Elior Sulem, Fisher Cynthia, and Dan Roth. 2021. BabyBERTa: Learning more grammar with small-scale child-directed language. In *Proceedings of the 25th Conference on Computational Natural Language Learning*, pages 624–646.

Yoon Kim and Alexander M Rush. 2016. Sequence-level knowledge distillation. In *Proceedings of the 2016 Conference on Empirical Methods in Natural Language Processing*, pages 1317–1327.

Yanran Li, Hui Su, Xiaoyu Shen, Wenjie Li, Ziqiang Cao, and Shuzi Niu. 2017. DailyDialog: A manually labelled multi-turn dialogue dataset. In *Proceedings of the Eighth International Joint Conference on Natural Language Processing (Volume 1: Long Papers)*, pages 986–995, Taipei, Taiwan. Asian Federation of Natural Language Processing.

Pierre Lison and Jörg Tiedemann. 2016. OpenSubtitles2016: Extracting large parallel corpora from movie and TV subtitles. In *Proceedings of the Tenth International Conference on Language Resources and Evaluation (LREC'16)*, pages 923–929, Portorož, Slovenia. European Language Resources Association (ELRA).

Terje Lohndal, Jason Rothman, Tanja Kupisch, and Marit Westergaard. 2019. Heritage language acquisition: What it reveals and why it is important for formal linguistic theories. *Language and Linguistics Compass*, 13(12):e12357.

Brian MacWhinney. 2000. *The CHILDES project: The database*, volume 2. Psychology Press.

Silvina Montrul. 2010. Current issues in heritage language acquisition. *Annual Review of Applied Linguistics*, 30:3–23.

David Samuel. 2023. Mean BERTs make erratic language teachers: the effectiveness of latent bootstrapping in low-resource settings. In *Proceedings of the BabyLM Challenge at the 27th Conference on Computational Natural Language Learning*, pages 221–237.

John Schulman, Filip Wolski, Prafulla Dhariwal, Alec Radford, and Oleg Klimov. 2017. Proximal policy optimization algorithms. *arXiv preprint arXiv:1707.06347*.

Nisan Stiennon, Long Ouyang, Jeffrey Wu, Daniel Ziegler, Ryan Lowe, Chelsea Voss, Alec Radford, Dario Amodei, and Paul F Christiano. 2020. Learning to summarize with human feedback. *Advances in Neural Information Processing Systems*, 33:3008–3021.

Leandro von Werra, Younes Belkada, Lewis Tunstall, Edward Beeching, Tristan Thrush, Nathan Lambert, and Shengyi Huang. 2020. TRL: Transformer reinforcement learning. `https://github.com/huggingface/trl`.

Alex Wang, Amanpreet Singh, Julian Michael, Felix Hill, Omer Levy, and Samuel R Bowman. 2018. GLUE: A multi-task benchmark and analysis platform for natural language understanding. In *International Conference on Learning Representations*.

Alex Warstadt, Aaron Mueller, Leshem Choshen, Ethan Wilcox, Chengxu Zhuang, Juan Ciro, Rafael Mosquera, Bhargavi Paranjabe, Adina Williams, Tal Linzen, and Ryan Cotterell. 2023. Findings of the BabyLM challenge: Sample-efficient pretraining on developmentally plausible corpora. In *Proceedings of the BabyLM Challenge at the 27th Conference on Computational Natural Language Learning*, pages 1–34, Singapore. Association for Computational Linguistics.

Alex Warstadt, Alicia Parrish, Haokun Liu, Anhad Mohananey, Wei Peng, Sheng-Fu Wang, and Samuel R Bowman. 2020. BLiMP: The benchmark of linguistic minimal pairs for english. *Transactions of the Association for Computational Linguistics*, 8:377–392.

Thomas Wolf, Lysandre Debut, Victor Sanh, Julien Chaumond, Clement Delangue, Anthony Moi, Pierric Cistac, Tim Rault, Remi Louf, Morgan Funtowicz, Joe Davison, Sam Shleifer, Patrick von Platen, Clara Ma, Yacine Jernite, Julien Plu, Canwen Xu, Teven Le Scao, Sylvain Gugger, Mariama Drame,

Quentin Lhoest, and Alexander Rush. 2020. Transformers: State-of-the-art natural language processing. In *Proceedings of the 2020 Conference on Empirical Methods in Natural Language Processing: System Demonstrations*, pages 38–45, Online. Association for Computational Linguistics.

Aditya Yadavalli, Alekhya Yadavalli, and Vera Tobin. 2023. SLABERT talk pretty one day: Modeling second language acquisition with BERT. In *Proceedings of the 61st Annual Meeting of the Association for Computational Linguistics (Volume 1: Long Papers)*, pages 11763–11777, Toronto, Canada. Association for Computational Linguistics.

Susan Zhang, Stephen Roller, Naman Goyal, Mikel Artetxe, Moya Chen, Shuohui Chen, Christopher Dewan, Mona Diab, Xian Li, Xi Victoria Lin, et al. 2022. OPT: Open pre-trained transformer language models. *arXiv preprint arXiv:2205.01068*.

Evaluating Vision-Language Models on Bistable Images

Artemis Panagopoulou[*], **Coby Melkin**[*], **Chris Callison-Burch**
University of Pennsylvania
Correspondence: artemisp@seas.upenn.edu

Abstract

Bistable images, also known as ambiguous or reversible images, present visual stimuli that can be seen in two distinct interpretations, though not simultaneously, by the observer. In this study, we conduct the most extensive examination of vision-language models using bistable images to date. We manually gathered a dataset of 29 bistable images, along with their associated labels, and subjected them to 121 different manipulations in brightness, tint, rotation, and resolution. We evaluated twelve different models in both classification and generative tasks across six model architectures. Our findings reveal that, with the exception of models from the Idefics family and LLaVA1.5-13b, there is a pronounced preference for one interpretation over another among the models, and minimal variance under image manipulations, with few exceptions on image rotations. Additionally, we compared the models' preferences with humans, noting that the models do not exhibit the same continuity biases as humans and often diverge from human initial interpretations. We also investigated the influence of variations in prompts and the use of synonymous labels, discovering that these factors significantly affect model interpretations more than image manipulations showing a higher influence of the language priors on bistable image interpretations compared to image-text training data. All code and data is open sourced [1].

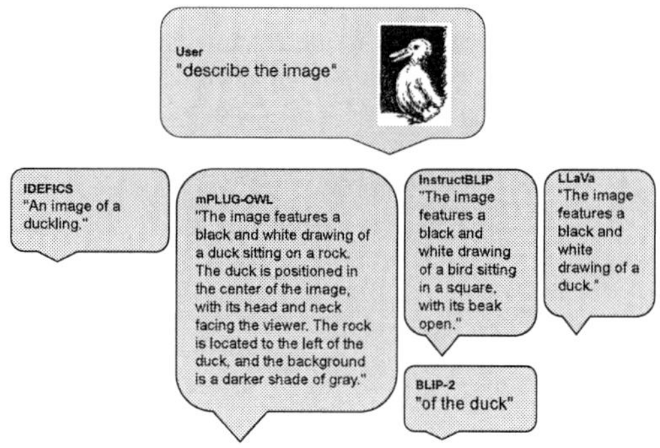

Figure 1: Depiction of generative models' descriptions of a Duck-Rabbit image. Responses are drawn directly from model outputs.

1 Introduction

Bistable images, also known as ambiguous or reversible images, offer unique visual stimuli that present two distinct interpretations, though a viewer cannot simultaneously perceive both (Khalil, 2021). An example of this is depicted in Figure 1, which can be seen as either a rabbit or a duck. The rapid advancements in vision-language models (VLMs) (Ye et al., 2023; Radford et al., 2021; Dai et al., 2023; Liu et al., 2023b; Li et al., 2023a) have sparked interest in testing these models against various types of visual challenges, including optical illusions. While considerable research has been done on how these models interpret geometric and color-varying optical illusions (Guan et al., 2023; Villa et al., 2019; Zhang et al., 2023b; Afifi and Brown, 2019; Benjamin et al., 2019; Sun and Dekel, 2021), exploration into their performance with bistable images remains sparse.

Motivated by this gap, this work aims to conduct a comprehensive investigation into how vision-language models process and interpret bistable images. We assemble the largest dataset of bistable images to date, apply a range of visual transformations, and examine the models' interpretations and their alignment with human perception.

In particular, we collect 29 bistable images from diverse online sources and cognitive science literature. Each image is subjected to 121 transformations affecting brightness, tint, and resolution resulting in a total of 3,509 processed images. We assessed the behaviors of twelve vision-language

[1]https://github.com/artemisp/Bistable-Illusions-MLLMs.git
[*]authors contributed equally

Proceedings of the Workshop on Cognitive Modeling and Computational Linguistics, pages 8–29
August 15, 2024 ©2024 Association for Computational Linguistics

models across six distinct model families in both classification and generative settings. Our analysis shows that, apart from a few exceptions, these models generally demonstrate a preference for one interpretation of bistable images over the other. Notably, models from the Idefics family (Laurençon et al., 2024) and LLaVA1.5-13b (Liu et al., 2023b,a) exhibit more balanced preferences. Additionally, while most model responses show little variation to image manipulations, exceptions include CLIP (Radford et al., 2021) and BLIP2 OPT6.7 (Li et al., 2023a), which are sensitive to such changes.

To further understand the influence of training data, we considered multiple models from the same families, trained on identical datasets but using different base language models (LLMs). This approach revealed that even when trained on the same visual data, the models do not consistently align in their preferences, suggesting that LLM priors play a major role in ambiguous image interpretation. This observation underscores that image-text interaction during training is not the sole determinant of how vision-language models perceive ambiguity, echoing earlier findings on the importance of textual signal in VLMs (Jabri et al., 2016; Goyal et al., 2017a; Agrawal et al., 2018).

Additionally, we explored how variations in prompts and the use of synonymous labels affect model interpretations. These textual modifications significantly influenced the models' interpretations, reinforcing the importance of LLM priors on the VLM processing of bistable images. This finding contrasts with previous research on convolutional neural networks (CNNs) focused on geometric optical illusions (Villa et al., 2019; Gomez-Villa et al., 2020; Afifi and Brown, 2019; Benjamin et al., 2019; Sun and Dekel, 2021), which typically show biases consistent with human perception. The CNNs studied did not utilize language model priors, highlighting a fundamental difference in how traditional vision models and VLMs handle visual ambiguity. Our contributions are as follows:

- We have curated the largest collection of bistable images from various online sources and cognitive studies, consisting of 29 unique images. These images have been modified through 121 transformations, creating a comprehensive set of 3.5k images for analysis.
- We analyze the behavior of twelve different vision-language models across six architectural types in both classification and generative tasks, providing a detailed account of their performance on bistable images.
- We examine the influence of prompt variations and synonymous labeling on model interpretations, finding that these textual modifications significantly impact how models perceive bistable images.
- Through direct comparison with human subjects and reference to established cognitive science studies, we assess the degree to which model preferences align with humans. Interestingly, we find that unlike previous work on CNNs (Villa et al., 2019; Gomez-Villa et al., 2020; Afifi and Brown, 2019; Benjamin et al., 2019; Sun and Dekel, 2021), VLMs do not exhibit human biases in bistable images interpretations.

2 Background

2.1 Bistable Images

Bistable images, a unique class of cognitive illusions, present two or more plausible perceptual states, yet viewers cannot observe multiple percepts simultaneously (Khalil, 2021). Instead, observers typically "switch" between the percepts in a seemingly random manner (Kornmeier and Bach, 2005). This phenomenon prompts two primary questions in Cognitive Science regarding bistable images:

1. What causes an individual to initially perceive a particular percept?

2. What triggers the seemingly random switching between percepts?

The exploration of these questions incorporates both bottom-up and top-down considerations (Wang et al., 2013). Bottom-up explanations focus on how the brain processes visual stimuli, starting from the simplest sensory inputs and moving to more complex interpretations. This process involves the detection of subtle visual cues and the neural computation within the visual cortex that ultimately determines the perceived image. Conversely, top-down explanations emphasize the role of cognitive processes, such as expectations, which heavily influence initial perceptions. For instance, a person's previous experiences, like frequently viewing cubes from above, shape their initial interpretation of a Necker Cube (Kuc et al., 2023).

Regarding the switching phenomenon, the dominant bottom-up explanation involves neural mechanisms like spike frequency adaptation or synaptic depression, where the neural connections producing one percept become fatigued, allowing the alternative percept to emerge (Laing and Chow, 2002). Other bottom-up theories propose that this switching is influenced by the brain's inherent noise or randomness (Moreno-Bote et al., 2007) or by unconscious, subtle cues within the images (Ward and Scholl, 2015). On the other hand, top-down explanations suggest that higher cognitive functions, such as motivation and attention, can also induce switching. Studies have shown that individuals can exert some control over their perceptual focus, which influences the switching between different states (Hugrass and Crewther, 2012; Slotnick and Yantis, 2005).

2.2 Vision-Language Models (VLMs)

VLMs integrate visual information as input and generate text as output. VLMs are categorized into contrastive and generative types. Contrastive VLMs, such as the prototypical model CLIP (Radford et al., 2021), are trained to match visual representations with corresponding textual descriptions by distinguishing between different data points. These models create a latent embedding space where similar text and images are drawn closer together, while dissimilar ones are pushed apart. Generative VLMs extend this by incorporating a vision-to-language connection module that projects visual information into the LLM space. This module can either prepend to the input layer of the LLM or condition deeper layers through cross-attention. The integration allows for flexible and dynamic text generation based on visual inputs. For our experiments, we employed models from various families, including CLIP, Idefics (Laurençon et al., 2024), LLaVA1.5 (Liu et al., 2023b,a), mPLUG-Owl (Ye et al., 2023), InstructBLIP (Dai et al., 2023), and BLIP-2 (Li et al., 2023a). Detailed information on the model architectures and the datasets used for training these models is presented in the appendix, in Tables 1 and 2.

2.3 VLMs and Cognitive Illusions

While prior studies have investigated how Convolutional Neural Networks (CNNs) process optical illusions, showing that they often mimic human perceptual errors (Gomez-Villa et al., 2020; Villa et al., 2019; Afifi and Brown, 2019; Benjamin et al., 2019; Sun and Dekel, 2021), the interaction of VLMs with cognitive illusions, especially bistable images, remains underexplored. In contemporary work, Luo et al. (2024) introduce a benchmark designed to evaluate the performance of VLMs on ambiguous, context-dependent visual inputs. Their findings reveal that VLMs significantly underperform compared to humans in these scenarios. More closely related to this work, Zhang et al. (2023b) evaluated VLMs on optical illusions by soliciting binary Yes/No responses and found that larger VLMs tend to be more susceptible to such illusions. However, their study was limited to 16 root images with 100 manually edited variations, focusing primarily on color, shape, and geometric illusions and did not include bistable images. Furthermore, they experimented with only three families of models, whereas our study encompasses six. Limited resources restricted our ability to test some of the larger models that Zhang et al. (2023b) included. Hallusion-bench (Guan et al., 2023) integrates a subset of these optical illusion images, predominantly sourced from Zhang et al. (2023b), but lacks bistable examples.

3 Methodology

3.1 Data Collection

Our dataset comprises 29 bistable images categorized into seven distinct types, sourced from both online platforms, such as Wikipedia, and academic studies (Schooler, 2015; Trautmann, 2021; Wilson, 2012; Pastukhov et al., 2019; Fields et al., 2013; Di Blasi, 2014). Notably, we source all images from the Takashima et al. (2012) research on face perception illusions to compare VLMs to the results of the human study. Among these, twelve images are organized into four classic categories of bistable illusions: the Rubin Vase, Necker Cube, Duck-Rabbit, and Young-Old Woman. Each category includes several iconic versions of the respective illusion type.

To explore the influence of visual modifications on perception, we created 121 variations for each image through a series of controlled manipulations. These manipulations include adjustments to image resolution, rotation, brightness—both increases and decreases—and the application of color tints. The specific colors used for the tints, along with their RGB values, are as follows: red, green, blue, yellow, magenta, and cyan. The intensity of each tint was varied by 0.1 from 0 (no change) to 1.0 (maximum change), and the brightness was adjusted within a range from -1 (darker) to 1 (brighter). We also applied image rotations from 0 to 360 degrees

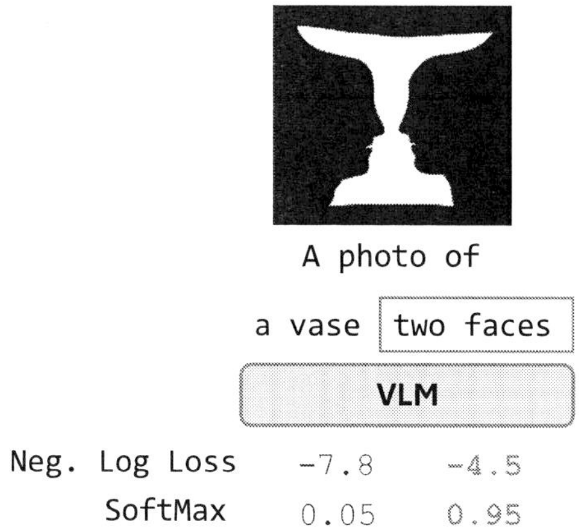

Figure 2: Classification Setup for Generative Models: Each candidate label and corresponding image is forwarded to the model. The prediction is set to be the one with lower loss (higher negative log loss).

every 10 degrees. Finally, we scale the resolution of the images from 0.5 to 1.0 in increments of .1.

3.2 Experimental Setup

We utilized six VLM families, encompassing a total of twelve different models, to evaluate bistable image description. We employed all six VLMs for classification tasks and five for generation tasks (excluding CLIP). The models used and their corresponding implementations on Huggingface Transformers are listed in the footnotes: CLIP (Radford et al., 2021)[2], Idefics 9b (Laurençon et al., 2024)[3], LLaVA1.5 (Liu et al., 2023b,a)[4], mPLUG-Owl (Ye et al., 2023)[5], InstructBLIP (Dai et al., 2023)[6], and BLIP-2 (Li et al., 2023a)[7]. Each model was queried with the default generation parameters and the prompt suggested by their respective model page on Huggingface. All experiments were conducted on a single A100 40GB GPU.

Although all VLMs used, except for CLIP, are generative models, we adapted their outputs to simulate classification. Specifically, we utilized a loss ranking technique (Wei et al., 2022; Li et al., 2021, 2023a; Dai et al., 2023) for classification. As depicted in Figure 2, this technique employs the score to determine the negative log likelihood of each candidate label. In the classification setup, we prompted each VLM with each image along with a pair of strings corresponding to its potential interpretations[8].

In the generative setup, we prompted the models with the format suggested in the HuggingFace documentation for captioning. In addition to model-specific setups, all models were presented with each image and asked to `"describe the image."`

4 Results

4.1 VLMs on Original Images

The models displayed clear preferences between interpretations for the original bistable images. Very rarely were models indifferent between interpretations. The averages between models for our four image categories are shown in Figure 3. We see a strong preference for the 'two faces' interpretation in the Rubin Vase group moderate preferences for 'a cube seen from above' and 'duck' interpretations in Necker Cube and Duck-Rabbit groups. Less classical illusions such at the 'Grimace-Begger, 'Idaho-face', and 'Lion-Gorilla-Tree' also show strong inclinations towards one interpretation. The images with the highest variation across models where the 'Woman-Trumpeter', 'Schroeder Stairs', and 'Raven-Bear' with CLIP variants showing almost consistently opposite preferences to the LLM based generative models.

While the six models generally showed alignment in their interpretation preferences, there was significant variance observed. Figure 4 shows a heat map of model preference correlation coefficients. For more details, refer to Figure 9 in the Appendix which displays the probability distributions for each image category across individual models, revealing some noteworthy model-specific trends. Firstly, all CLIP variants exhibited the exact same probability distributions, with high variance across images within the same category, suggesting a heightened sensitivity to bistability. Secondly, the variants of Idefics 9b and LLaVA 13b demonstrated minimal variance among images of the same category and exhibited relatively moderate preferences, indicating a lower sensitivity to bistability. Moreover, BLIP2-FlanT5, InstructBLIP FlanT5, and mPLUG-Owl showed opposite preferences to CLIP, despite it being used to encode images for these models. This is likely due to the underlying LLM, highlighting the importance of language priors in VLM predictions. Interestingly, all models

[2] openai/clip-vit-base-patch32, openai/clip-vit-base-patch16, laion/CLIP-ViT-B-32-laion2B-s34B-b79K

[3] HuggingFaceM4/idefics-9b, HuggingFaceM4/idefics-9b-instruct

[4] llava-hf/llava-1.5-7b-hf, llava-hf/llava-1.5-13b-hf

[5] MAGAer13/mplug-owl-llama-7b

[6] Salesforce/instructblip-flan-t5-xl

[7] Salesforce/blip2-opt-2.7b, Salesforce/blip2-opt-6.7b, Salesforce/blip2-flan-t5-xl

[8] Image interpretations are found in Appendix C

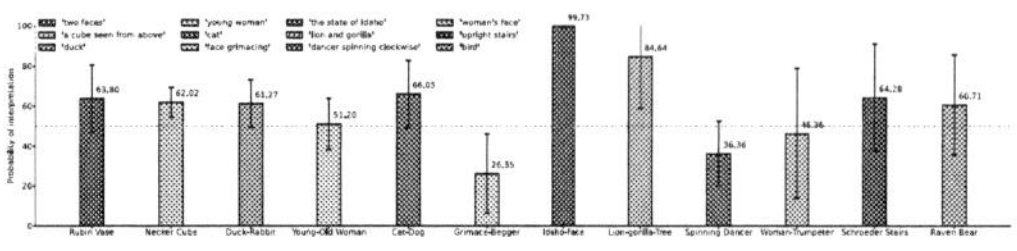

(a) Original Labels

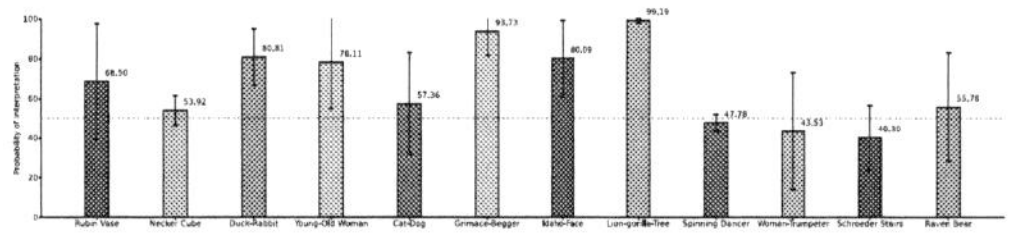

(b) Synonym Labels

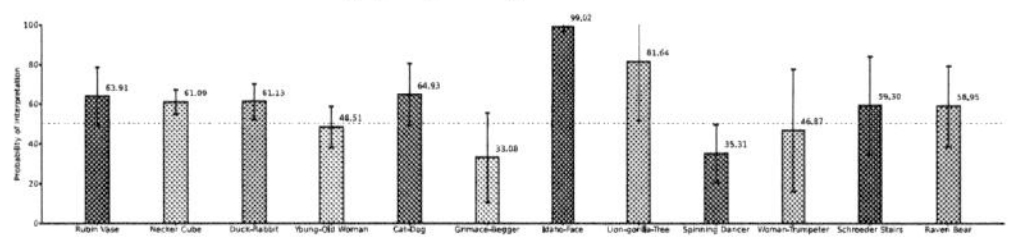

(c) Prompt Variation with Original Labels

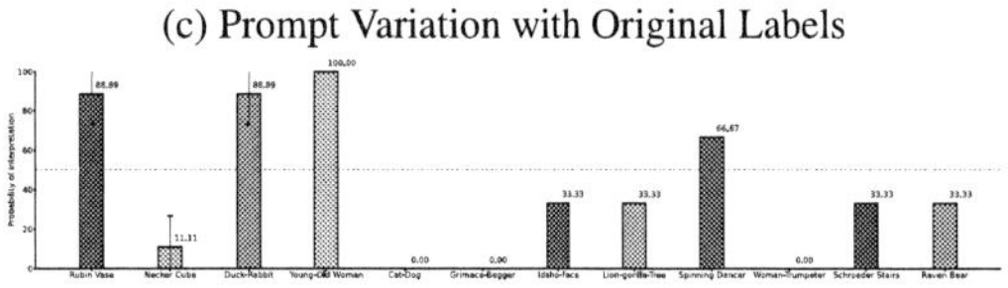

(d) Human Initial Interpretations

Figure 3: Between-model averages of probability of the favored interpretation for each image category.

showed a preference for the two animals over the tree in the 'Lion-Gorilla-Tree' illusion, despite the frequent appearance of all these objects in their training sets. Additionally, there was a consistent preference for the face over the full-body abstract silhouette in the 'Grimace-Begger' illusion across all models, except those based on the Flan T5xl architecture. This further accentuates the significant impact of the underlying LLM on image interpretation in VLMs. Notably, although BLIP2 OPT was trained on the same image-text data as the Flan T5 variants, it exhibited almost opposite preferences in some image categories.

4.2 VLMs on Image Manipulations

We observed minimal effects from image manipulations on interpretation probabilities. When adjusting brightness levels, resolution, color tints, and tint intensities, the probabilities for each model remained largely unchanged. Figures 5a and 5b illustrate the minimal impact of these manipulations on model interpretations. This suggests that VLMs tend to overlook minor, low-level perturbations in favor of holistic image processing. Moreover, this finding highlights a significant divergence between VLM processing and human perception of bistable images, which often relies on bottom-up cues according to certain theories (Ward and

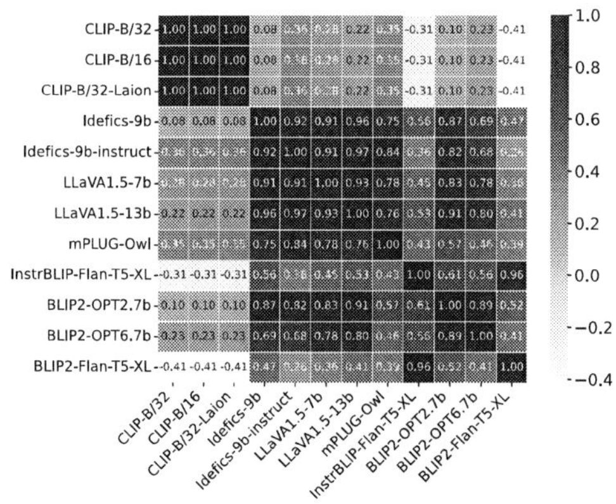

Figure 4: Correlation Among Model Preferences in Original Images

Scholl, 2015). Notably, the models did not shift interpretations based on subtle cues of brightness and color. The primary exception was the CLIP variants, which demonstrated sensitivity to variations in brightness and tint, particularly in the 'Young-Old Woman,' 'Cat-Dog,' 'Grimace-Begger,' and 'Woman-Trumpeter' illusions. We hypothesize that contrastive learning across aggregation of patches in these models enhance their sensitivity to global changes in the image, as each layer encompasses a more substantial portion of the visual input, making any variations more influential to the model's output. This sensitivity was also observed, though to a lesser extent, in BLIP2-OPT6.7, especially regarding brightness changes in the 'Rubin-Vase' and 'Woman-Trumpeter' illusions. These variations were less pronounced in BLIP2-OPT2.7, particularly for the 'Duck-Rabbit' illusion, and were absent in the corresponding FlanT5-xl variant, underscoring the impact of the underlying LLM's priors on generative vision-language models. Interestingly, when transformations were applied at maximum scale, resulting in a monochrome image, most models exhibited similar preferences, reinforcing the role of language priors in their processing.

Figure 5c shows the variation of interpretations across rotated versions of the images. We find that this manipulation causes significantly higher variation to the color-based manipulations. The variations typically follow the same pattern across models for some bistable images, such as 'Rubin-Vase' and 'Duck-Rabbit'. Notably, contrastive based CLIP-variants once again exhibit the most variation despite being trained with 'minor rotations'

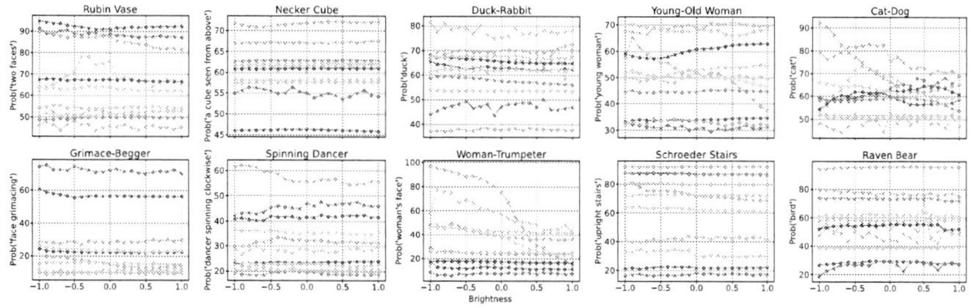

(a) Brightness variation.

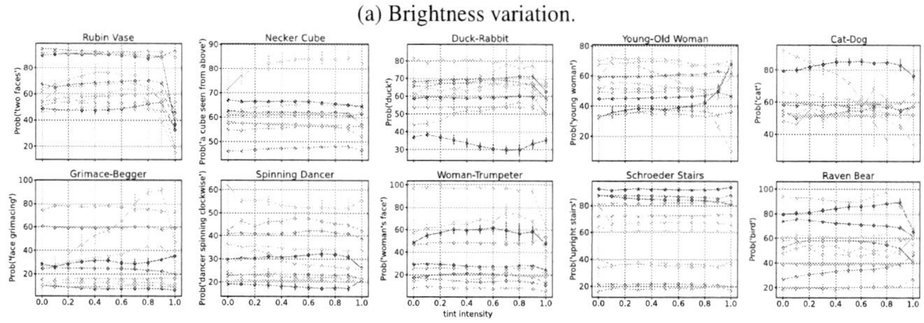

(b) Tint variation. Average across six color tints.

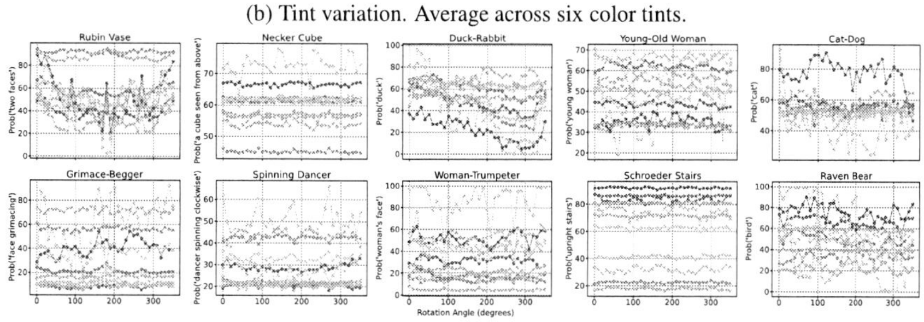

(c) Rotation Variation.

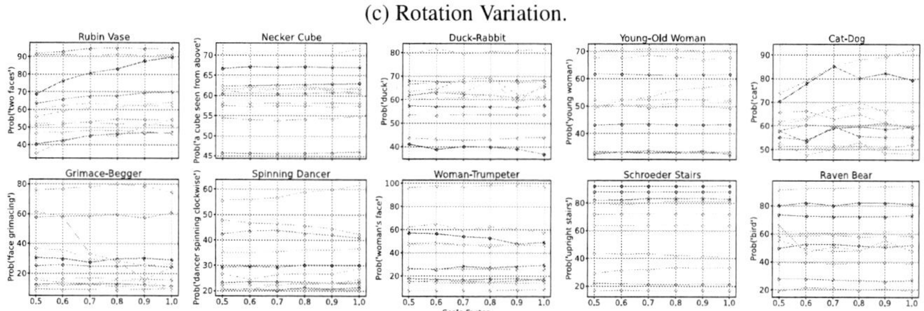

(d) Resolution variation.

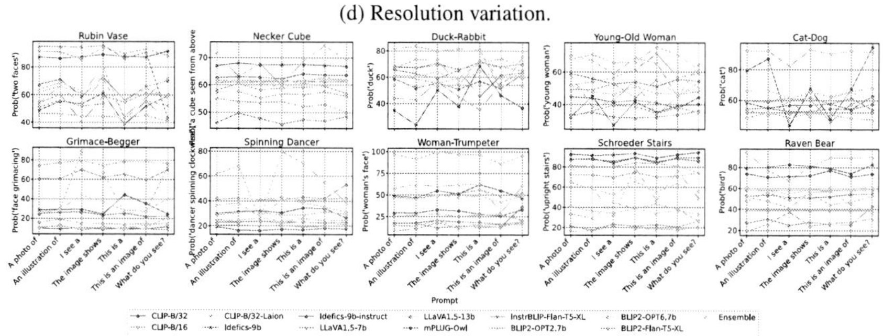

(e) Prompt variation

Figure 5: Bistable image interpretation under brightness (a), tint (b), rotation (c), resolution (d), and prompt (e) manipulations.

data augmentations. From the generative models mPLUG-Owl seems to exhibit the highest sensitivity to rotation despite also employing rotation augmentation in training. We also observe that the larger LLM variants of LLaVA1.5 and BLIP2-OPT exhibit less variation compared to their smaller counterparts, likely due to the stronger language prior.

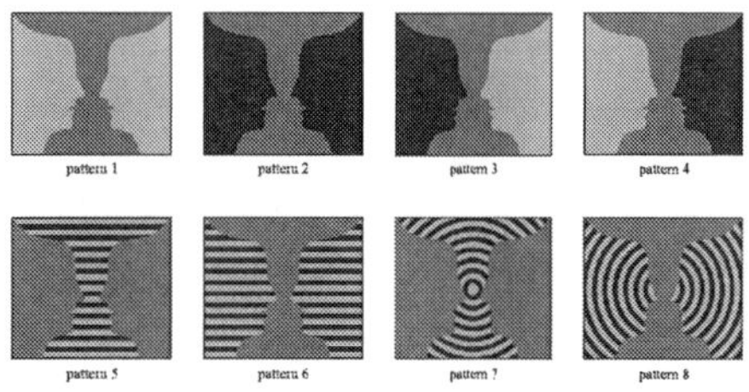

Figure 6: Variations of Rubin Vase images presented to participants in Takashima et al. (2012).

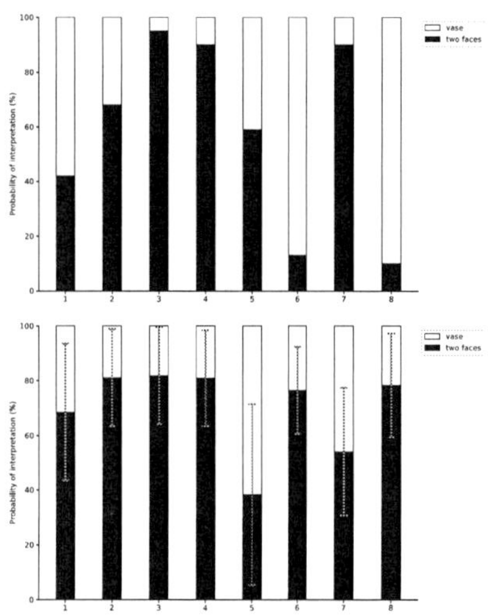

Figure 7: Comparison of between-subject average (top) and between-model average (bottom) probabilities of interpreting each image pattern as two faces in Takashima et al. (2012) and our research, respectively.

4.3 Synonymous Interpretations

To investigate the influence of synonymous interpretation labels on bistable image perception in VLMs, we substituted the original labels with synonyms. Figure 3b displays the effects of these changes on model preferences. The impact is generally mild, but a notable exception occurs with the 'Grimace-Begger' image, where the preference shifts dramatically. In this case, models show a clear preference for interpreting the image as a face rather than a beggar. This shift is likely attributable to the relative unfamiliarity of the synonym 'panhandler' compared to the more commonly recognized term 'face,' making the facial interpretation more likely for the models due to term frequency.

4.4 Prompt Variation

To investigate the effect of prompt variation on VLM bistable image interpretations we examine 7 different prompts. Figure 3c shows little variation on average, however, the individual decomposition of the results in figure 5e shows significant variations within models, especially for CLIP-B/32 and CLIP-B/32-Laion. In fact, while these two models are trained on distinct data of different sizes (400M vs 2B) they exhibit identical behavior across manipulations, indicating the improtance of the architecture in bistable image interpretation. The BLIP family models show higher variation in prompt manipulations compared to LLaVA and Idefics variants. This is likely due to the conditioning of the visual feature extraction module to the instruction prompt.

4.5 Human Interpretations

To compare human initial interpretations with model preferences, we conducted a human evaluation using all original bistable images from our dataset, except for those from Takashima's study (Takashima et al., 2012). We presented these images to three human annotators, asking them to identify "which interpretation they saw first?" They were also given the option to select an alternative interpretation. Figure 3d displays the average results for each interpretation, calculated based on the frequency each interpretation was selected by the annotators across all annotations for that image.

The results reveal a limited correspondence between human and VLM interpretations, contrasting with findings for geometric illusions (Afifi and Brown, 2019; Villa et al., 2019; Gomez-Villa et al., 2020). This discrepancy suggests that the training datasets for VLMs do not trigger the same cognitive biases as those encoded in humans through everyday environmental interactions and conceptual influences. It is important to note that all annotators are students at an American institution, which might influence the results; interpretations could vary significantly based on different socio-cultural experiences and the priors encoded through them.

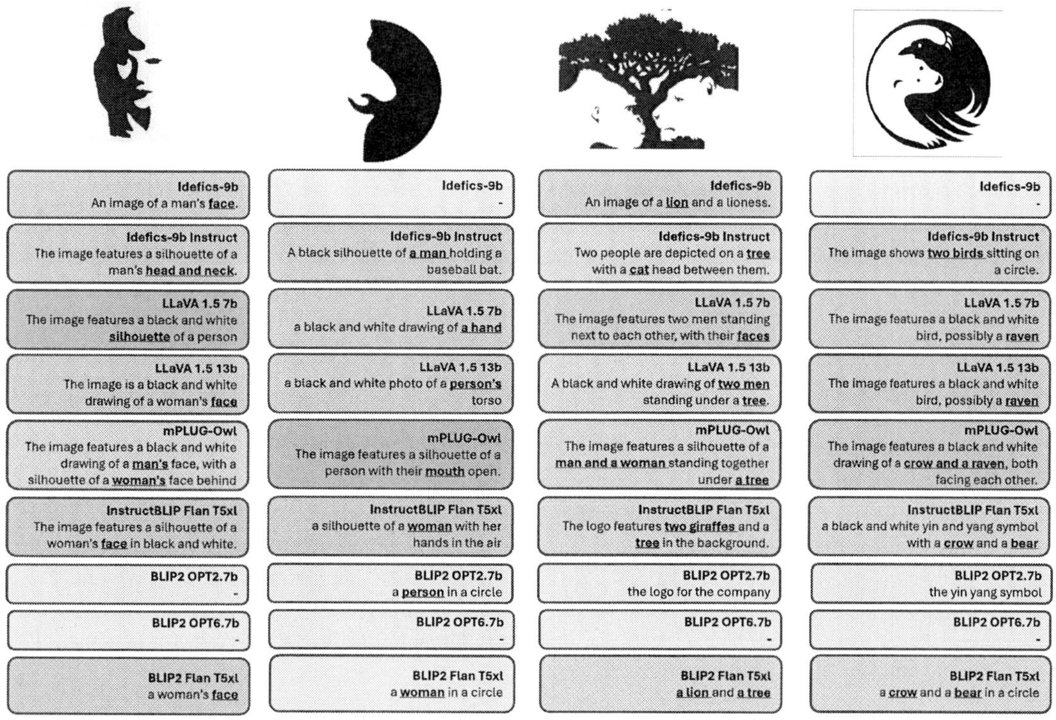

Figure 8: Depiction of generative models' descriptions for various bistable images. Orange and darker blue colors indicate selection of one interpretation, Green of both, and light blue of neither.

4.6 Replicating Takashima et al. (2012)

We sought to evaluate VLM-human alignment on bistable image processing by comparing our results to a human study. Takashima et al. (2012) presented eight versions of the Rubin Vase illusion n=70 participants. The images are shown in Figure 6 and the human results are shown in Figure 7 (top). They highlight two primary findings: human subjects favored the two faces interpretation for patterns where the profiles' homogeneity is broken (patterns 3 and 4) and favored 'vase' interpretation for patterns where the faces form a continuous background by Gestalt principles (Koffka, 1922) (patterns 6 and 8).

VLMs did not replicate these results, as per the bottom plot in Figure 7. While the models exhibited a strong preference for the 'two faces' interpretation on patterns 3 and 4, the same preference is exhibited in patterns 1 and 2 (where profiles are homogeneous). Furthermore, the models did not exhibit any preference for the 'vase' interpretation in patterns 6 and 8. Even when examined individually in Figure 6 no model exhibited similar patterns to humans. Similar to earlier results, LLaVA and Idefics variants showed high consistency across the images in their tamed preferences. The CLIP variants showed identical patterns despite the varying patch size, unlike in the more global interventions of tint and brightness. Finally, BLIP-2 variants trained on the same image-text data with different LLMs show starkly different preferences, reinforcing the importance of language priors.

4.7 Generative Results

In the generative setup, we performed a qualitative analysis of the results. We found that several interpretation preferences discovered in the classification setup were amplified in generation. Across models, the heavily favored interpretations were faces and ducks for Rubin Vase and Duck-Rabbit images. Figure 1 shows the output of each generative model when prompted to describe a Duck-Rabbit image. Each model employs its own explanatory style, but all favor the duck interpretation. Few models commented on the age of the individual in Young-Old Woman images, but the majority of those comments described the woman as a "girl" or "young woman." An overview of the responses of the models on a subset of the images is delineated in figure 8 and all examples are listed in the Appendix Section D. We observe that most models only comment on a single interpretation, if at all, with some notable exceptions highlighted in green. In few cases, models "hallucinate" descriptions, such as InstructBLIP's interpretation of "two giraffes" for the Lion-Gorilla-Tree illusion. Nevertheless, human inspection of the outputs showed that this was a rare occurrence. We find that for the lion-gorilla-tree image, models are able to identify at least one of the animals, and the tree almost consistently. We hypothesize that this is because of the detail expressed in both interpretations of the image, making it easier even for humans to consciously identify both interpretations simultaneously, even if they are unable to visually perceive both at the same time. Indeed, in the human study, the 'Lion-Gorilla-Tree' image received the most balanced responses across the annotators.

5 Discussion and Limitations

This original analysis of VLM behavior on bistable images has yielded some interesting preliminary results. Similar to humans, VLMs have preferred initial interpretations for most classical bistable images. Five out of six models showed a preference for 'two faces' in Rubin Vase images, 'a cube seen from above' in Necker Cube images, and 'a duck' in Duck-Rabbit images. Young-Old Woman images is the only category for which models' preferences were more neutral and mixed.

We have seen minimal alignment between VLMs and humans when replicating Takashima et al. (2012) and conducting human annotations on the rest of the images. This analysis highlights that VLMs are not sensitive to the same variations that heavily impact human preferences. Models vary greatly in their sensitivity to bistablility. CLIP emerged as a model with strong, variable preferences, while LLaVa is more neutral. CLIP's variability could be attributed to the contrastive pretraining, that might sensitize the model to smaller differences. Moreover, the synthetic nature of bistable images renders them out of domain from most pretraining data, especially for VLMs that are predominantly trained on realistic images.

Nevertheless, making comparisons between human and machine perception of bistable images is difficult beyond the initial biases. Human perception of bistable images exhibits the phenomenon of switching interpretations through extended focus on the image. Replicating the phenomenon of switching is difficult because VLMs take static images at a single point in time. We loosely approximated the movement of time by testing the models on dozens of subtle variations of each image, as discussed above. Under the theories that subtle bottom-up cues precipitate switching in human processing, VLMs do not replicate this phenomenon. We saw that all models' preferences remained steady with variations in brightness, resolution, color, and color tint intensity. Nevertheless, this was in contrast to linguistic variations, highlighting the importance of language priors in generative VLMs.

More research is needed to further our understanding of VLM bistable image interpretation. Using VLMs that process videos could be a tractable way of mimicking the passage of time. Furthermore, additional interventions through design manipulations either through the employment of text-to-image models or human artists could reveal additional insight on VLM behavior for bistable image inputs.

6 Conclusion

In this study we explore the behavior of VLMs on bistable images. We construct the largest bistable image dataset and evaluate 12 different models across six model families under various perturbations: pixel-color based perturbations, resolution, rotations, interpretation label synonyms, and prompt variations. We find that prompts have the highest impact on model preferences whereas, pixel-color perturbations have minimal effects. We further conduct human study comparisons, and find that VLMs do not exhibit the same initial biases on bistable images as human subjects.

Acknowledgments

This research was supported by a gift from AWS AI for research in Trustworthy AI.

References

Mahmoud Afifi and Michael S. Brown. 2019. What else can fool deep learning? addressing color constancy errors on deep neural network performance. In *2019 IEEE/CVF International Conference on Computer Vision, ICCV 2019, Seoul, Korea (South), October 27 - November 2, 2019*, pages 243–252. IEEE.

Aishwarya Agrawal, Dhruv Batra, Devi Parikh, and Aniruddha Kembhavi. 2018. Don't just assume; look and answer: Overcoming priors for visual question answering. In *2018 IEEE Conference on Computer*

Vision and Pattern Recognition, CVPR 2018, Salt Lake City, UT, USA, June 18-22, 2018, pages 4971–4980. IEEE Computer Society.

Ari Benjamin, Cheng Qiu, Ling-Qi Zhang, Konrad Kording, and Alan Stocker. 2019. Shared visual illusions between humans and artificial neural networks. In *2019 Conference on Cognitive Computational Neuroscience*, volume 10, pages 2019–1299. Cognitive Computational Neuroscience.

Nicholas Carlini, Matthew Jagielski, Christopher A Choquette-Choo, Daniel Paleka, Will Pearce, Hyrum Anderson, Andreas Terzis, Kurt Thomas, and Florian Tramèr. 2023. Poisoning web-scale training datasets is practical. *ArXiv preprint*, abs/2302.10149.

Soravit Changpinyo, Piyush Sharma, Nan Ding, and Radu Soricut. 2021. Conceptual 12m: Pushing web-scale image-text pre-training to recognize long-tail visual concepts. In *IEEE Conference on Computer Vision and Pattern Recognition, CVPR 2021, virtual, June 19-25, 2021*, pages 3558–3568. Computer Vision Foundation / IEEE.

Xinlei Chen, Hao Fang, Tsung-Yi Lin, Ramakrishna Vedantam, Saurabh Gupta, Piotr Dollár, and C Lawrence Zitnick. 2015. Microsoft coco captions: Data collection and evaluation server. *ArXiv preprint*, abs/1504.00325.

Wei-Lin Chiang, Zhuohan Li, Zi Lin, Ying Sheng, Zhanghao Wu, Hao Zhang, Lianmin Zheng, Siyuan Zhuang, Yonghao Zhuang, Joseph E. Gonzalez, Ion Stoica, and Eric P. Xing. 2023. Vicuna: An open-source chatbot impressing gpt-4 with 90%* chatgpt quality.

Hyung Won Chung, Le Hou, Shayne Longpre, Barret Zoph, Yi Tay, William Fedus, Yunxuan Li, Xuezhi Wang, Mostafa Dehghani, Siddhartha Brahma, et al. 2024. Scaling instruction-finetuned language models. *Journal of Machine Learning Research*, 25(70):1–53.

Wenliang Dai, Junnan Li, Dongxu Li, Anthony Tiong, Junqi Zhao, Weisheng Wang, Boyang Li, Pascale Fung, and Steven Hoi. 2023. InstructBLIP: Towards general-purpose vision-language models with instruction tuning. In *Thirty-seventh Conference on Neural Information Processing Systems*.

Karan Desai, Gaurav Kaul, Zubin Aysola, and Justin Johnson. 2021. Redcaps: web-curated image-text data created by the people, for the people. *Preprint*, arXiv:2111.11431.

Luca Di Blasi. 2014. *Splitting Images: Understanding Irreversible Fractures through Aspect Change*, pages 67–87.

Ning Ding, Yulin Chen, Bokai Xu, Yujia Qin, Shengding Hu, Zhiyuan Liu, Maosong Sun, and Bowen Zhou. 2023. Enhancing chat language models by scaling high-quality instructional conversations. In *The 2023 Conference on Empirical Methods in Natural Language Processing*.

R Fields, Alfonso Araque, Heidi Johansen-Berg, Soo-Siang Lim, Gary Lynch, Klaus-Armin Nave, Maiken Nedergaard, Ray Perez, Terrence Sejnowski, and Hiroaki Wake. 2013. Glial biology in learning and cognition. *The Neuroscientist : a review journal bringing neurobiology, neurology and psychiatry*, 20.

Samir Yitzhak Gadre, Gabriel Ilharco, Alex Fang, Jonathan Hayase, Georgios Smyrnis, Thao Nguyen, Ryan Marten, Mitchell Wortsman, Dhruba Ghosh, Jieyu Zhang, et al. 2024. Datacomp: In search of the next generation of multimodal datasets. *Advances in Neural Information Processing Systems*, 36.

Alexander Gomez-Villa, Adrian Martín, Javier Vazquez-Corral, Marcelo Bertalmío, and Jesús Malo. 2020. Color illusions also deceive cnns for low-level vision tasks: Analysis and implications. *Vision Research*, 176:156–174.

Yash Goyal, Tejas Khot, Douglas Summers-Stay, Dhruv Batra, and Devi Parikh. 2017a. Making the V in VQA matter: Elevating the role of image understanding in visual question answering. In *2017 IEEE Conference on Computer Vision and Pattern Recognition, CVPR 2017, Honolulu, HI, USA, July 21-26, 2017*, pages 6325–6334. IEEE Computer Society.

Yash Goyal, Tejas Khot, Douglas Summers-Stay, Dhruv Batra, and Devi Parikh. 2017b. Making the V in VQA matter: Elevating the role of image understanding in visual question answering. In *2017 IEEE Conference on Computer Vision and Pattern Recognition, CVPR 2017, Honolulu, HI, USA, July 21-26, 2017*, pages 6325–6334. IEEE Computer Society.

Tianrui Guan, Fuxiao Liu, Xiyang Wu, Ruiqi Xian, Zongxia Li, Xiaoyu Liu, Xijun Wang, Lichang Chen, Furong Huang, Yaser Yacoob, et al. 2023. Hallusionbench: An advanced diagnostic suite for entangled language hallucination & visual illusion in large vision-language models. *ArXiv preprint*, abs/2310.14566.

Drew A. Hudson and Christopher D. Manning. 2019. GQA: A new dataset for real-world visual reasoning and compositional question answering. In *IEEE Conference on Computer Vision and Pattern Recognition, CVPR 2019, Long Beach, CA, USA, June 16-20, 2019*, pages 6700–6709. Computer Vision Foundation / IEEE.

Laila Hugrass and David Crewther. 2012. Willpower and conscious percept: volitional switching in binocular rivalry. *PloS one*, 7(4):e35963.

Allan Jabri, Armand Joulin, and Laurens Van Der Maaten. 2016. Revisiting visual question answering baselines. In *European conference on computer vision*, pages 727–739. Springer.

Andrew Jaegle, Felix Gimeno, Andy Brock, Oriol Vinyals, Andrew Zisserman, and João Carreira. 2021. Perceiver: General perception with iterative attention. In *Proceedings of the 38th International Conference on Machine Learning, ICML 2021, 18-24 July 2021,*

Virtual Event, volume 139 of *Proceedings of Machine Learning Research*, pages 4651–4664. PMLR.

Elias L Khalil. 2021. Why does rubin's vase differ radically from optical illusions? framing effects contra cognitive illusions. *Frontiers in Psychology*, 12:597758.

Kurt Koffka. 1922. Perception: an introduction to the gestalt-theorie. *Psychological bulletin*, 19(10):531.

Jürgen Kornmeier and Michael Bach. 2005. The necker cube—an ambiguous figure disambiguated in early visual processing. *Vision Research*, 45(8):955–960.

Ranjay Krishna, Yuke Zhu, Oliver Groth, Justin Johnson, Kenji Hata, Joshua Kravitz, Stephanie Chen, Yannis Kalantidis, Li-Jia Li, David A Shamma, et al. 2017. Visual genome: Connecting language and vision using crowdsourced dense image annotations. *International journal of computer vision*, 123(1):32–73.

Alexander Kuc, Vladimir Maksimenko, Andrey Savosenkov, Nikita Grigorev, Vadim Grubov, Artem Badarin, Victor Kazantsev, Susanna Gordleeva, and Alexander Hramov. 2023. Studying perceptual bias in favor of the from-above necker cube perspective in a goal-directed behavior. *Frontiers in Psychology*, 14:1160605.

Carlo R Laing and Carson C Chow. 2002. A spiking neuron model for binocular rivalry. *Journal of computational neuroscience*, 12:39–53.

Hugo Laurençon, Lucile Saulnier, Léo Tronchon, Stas Bekman, Amanpreet Singh, Anton Lozhkov, Thomas Wang, Siddharth Karamcheti, Alexander Rush, Douwe Kiela, et al. 2024. Obelics: An open web-scale filtered dataset of interleaved image-text documents. *Advances in Neural Information Processing Systems*, 36.

Junnan Li, Dongxu Li, Silvio Savarese, and Steven Hoi. 2023a. Blip-2: Bootstrapping language-image pretraining with frozen image encoders and large language models. In *International conference on machine learning*, pages 19730–19742. PMLR.

Junnan Li, Dongxu Li, Silvio Savarese, and Steven Hoi. 2023b. BLIP-2: Bootstrapping language-image pretraining with frozen image encoders and large language models. In *Proceedings of the 40th International Conference on Machine Learning*, volume 202 of *Proceedings of Machine Learning Research*, pages 19730–19742. PMLR.

Junnan Li, Ramprasaath R. Selvaraju, Akhilesh Gotmare, Shafiq R. Joty, Caiming Xiong, and Steven Chu-Hong Hoi. 2021. Align before fuse: Vision and language representation learning with momentum distillation. In *Advances in Neural Information Processing Systems 34: Annual Conference on Neural Information Processing Systems 2021, NeurIPS 2021, December 6-14, 2021, virtual*, pages 9694–9705.

Lei Li, Yuwei Yin, Shicheng Li, Liang Chen, Peiyi Wang, Shuhuai Ren, Mukai Li, Yazheng Yang, Jingjing Xu, Xu Sun, et al. 2023c. M3it: A large-scale dataset towards multi-modal multilingual instruction tuning. *ArXiv preprint*, abs/2306.04387.

Wing Lian, Guan Wang, Bleys Goodson, Eugene Pentland, Austin Cook, Chanvichet Vong, and "Teknium". 2023. Slimorca: An open dataset of gpt-4 augmented flan reasoning traces, with verification.

Haotian Liu, Chunyuan Li, Yuheng Li, and Yong Jae Lee. 2023a. Improved baselines with visual instruction tuning. In *NeurIPS 2023 Workshop on Instruction Tuning and Instruction Following*.

Haotian Liu, Chunyuan Li, Qingyang Wu, and Yong Jae Lee. 2023b. Visual instruction tuning. In *Thirty-seventh Conference on Neural Information Processing Systems*.

Fuwen Luo, Chi Chen, Zihao Wan, Zhaolu Kang, Qidong Yan, Yingjie Li, Xiaolong Wang, Siyu Wang, Ziyue Wang, Xiaoyue Mi, et al. 2024. Codis: Benchmarking context-dependent visual comprehension for multimodal large language models. *ArXiv preprint*, abs/2402.13607.

Kenneth Marino, Mohammad Rastegari, Ali Farhadi, and Roozbeh Mottaghi. 2019. OK-VQA: A visual question answering benchmark requiring external knowledge. In *IEEE Conference on Computer Vision and Pattern Recognition, CVPR 2019, Long Beach, CA, USA, June 16-20, 2019*, pages 3195–3204. Computer Vision Foundation / IEEE.

Anand Mishra, Shashank Shekhar, Ajeet Kumar Singh, and Anirban Chakraborty. 2019. Ocr-vqa: Visual question answering by reading text in images. In *ICDAR*.

Rubén Moreno-Bote, John Rinzel, and Nava Rubin. 2007. Noise-induced alternations in an attractor network model of perceptual bistability. *Journal of neurophysiology*, 98(3):1125–1139.

Vicente Ordonez, Girish Kulkarni, and Tamara L. Berg. 2011. Im2text: Describing images using 1 million captioned photographs. In *Advances in Neural Information Processing Systems 24: 25th Annual Conference on Neural Information Processing Systems 2011. Proceedings of a meeting held 12-14 December 2011, Granada, Spain*, pages 1143–1151.

Alexander Pastukhov, Philipp Kastrup, Isabel Abs, and Claus-Christian Carbon. 2019. Switch rates for orthogonally oriented kinetic-depth displays are correlated across observers. *Journal of Vision*, 19:1.

Jordi Pont-Tuset, Jasper Uijlings, Soravit Changpinyo, Radu Soricut, and Vittorio Ferrari. 2020. Connecting vision and language with localized narratives. In *ECCV*.

Alec Radford, Jong Wook Kim, Chris Hallacy, Aditya Ramesh, Gabriel Goh, Sandhini Agarwal, Girish Sastry, Amanda Askell, Pamela Mishkin, Jack Clark, Gretchen Krueger, and Ilya Sutskever. 2021. Learning transferable visual models from natural language supervision. In *Proceedings of the 38th International Conference on Machine Learning, ICML 2021, 18-24 July 2021, Virtual Event*, volume 139 of *Proceedings of Machine Learning Research*, pages 8748–8763. PMLR.

Jonathan Schooler. 2015. Bridging the objective/subjective divide towards a meta-perspective of science and experience. *In T. Metzinger J. M. Windt (Eds). Open MIND: 34(T). Frankfurt am Main: MIND Group.*

Christoph Schuhmann, Romain Beaumont, Richard Vencu, Cade Gordon, Ross Wightman, Mehdi Cherti, Theo Coombes, Aarush Katta, Clayton Mullis, Mitchell Wortsman, et al. 2022. Laion-5b: An open large-scale dataset for training next generation image-text models. *Advances in Neural Information Processing Systems*, 35:25278–25294.

Christoph Schuhmann, Richard Vencu, Romain Beaumont, Robert Kaczmarczyk, Clayton Mullis, Aarush Katta, Theo Coombes, Jenia Jitsev, and Aran Komatsuzaki. 2021. Laion-400m: Open dataset of clip-filtered 400 million image-text pairs. *ArXiv preprint*, abs/2111.02114.

Dustin Schwenk, Apoorv Khandelwal, Christopher Clark, Kenneth Marino, and Roozbeh Mottaghi. 2022. A-okvqa: A benchmark for visual question answering using world knowledge. In *European Conference on Computer Vision*, pages 146–162. Springer.

Piyush Sharma, Nan Ding, Sebastian Goodman, and Radu Soricut. 2018. Conceptual captions: A cleaned, hypernymed, image alt-text dataset for automatic image captioning. In *Proceedings of the 56th Annual Meeting of the Association for Computational Linguistics (Volume 1: Long Papers)*, pages 2556–2565, Melbourne, Australia. Association for Computational Linguistics.

Oleksii Sidorov, Ronghang Hu, Marcus Rohrbach, and Amanpreet Singh. 2020. Textcaps: a dataset for image captioning with reading comprehension. In *Computer Vision–ECCV 2020: 16th European Conference, Glasgow, UK, August 23–28, 2020, Proceedings, Part II 16*, pages 742–758. Springer.

Scott D Slotnick and Steven Yantis. 2005. Common neural substrates for the control and effects of visual attention and perceptual bistability. *Cognitive Brain Research*, 24(1):97–108.

Krishna Srinivasan, Karthik Raman, Jiecao Chen, Michael Bendersky, and Marc Najork. 2021. Wit: Wikipedia-based image text dataset for multimodal multilingual machine learning. *ArXiv preprint*, abs/2103.01913.

Eric D Sun and Ron Dekel. 2021. Imagenet-trained deep neural networks exhibit illusion-like response to the scintillating grid. *Journal of Vision*, 21(11):15–15.

Quan Sun, Yuxin Fang, Ledell Wu, Xinlong Wang, and Yue Cao. 2023. Eva-clip: Improved training techniques for clip at scale. *ArXiv preprint*, abs/2303.15389.

Midori Takashima, Teruo Fujii, and Ken Shiina. 2012. Face or vase? areal homogeneity effect. *Perception*, 41(11):1392–1394.

Bart Thomee, David A Shamma, Gerald Friedland, Benjamin Elizalde, Karl Ni, Douglas Poland, Damian Borth, and Li-Jia Li. 2016. Yfcc100m: The new data in multimedia research. *Communications of the ACM*, 59(2):64–73.

Hugo Touvron, Thibaut Lavril, Gautier Izacard, Xavier Martinet, Marie-Anne Lachaux, Timothée Lacroix, Baptiste Rozière, Naman Goyal, Eric Hambro, Faisal Azhar, et al. 2023. Llama: Open and efficient foundation language models. *ArXiv preprint*, abs/2302.13971.

Laura Trautmann. 2021. Emotions evoked by geometric patterns. *J*, 4:376–393.

Alexander Gómez Villa, Adrián Martín, Javier Vazquez-Corral, and Marcelo Bertalmío. 2019. Convolutional neural networks can be deceived by visual illusions. In *IEEE Conference on Computer Vision and Pattern Recognition, CVPR 2019, Long Beach, CA, USA, June 16-20, 2019*, pages 12309–12317. Computer Vision Foundation / IEEE.

Megan Wang, Daniel Arteaga, and Biyu J He. 2013. Brain mechanisms for simple perception and bistable perception. *Proceedings of the National Academy of Sciences*, 110(35):E3350–E3359.

Yiqi Wang, Wentao Chen, Xiaotian Han, Xudong Lin, Haiteng Zhao, Yongfei Liu, Bohan Zhai, Jianbo Yuan, Quanzeng You, and Hongxia Yang. 2024. Exploring the reasoning abilities of multimodal large language models (mllms): A comprehensive survey on emerging trends in multimodal reasoning. *ArXiv preprint*, abs/2401.06805.

Emily J Ward and Brian J Scholl. 2015. Stochastic or systematic? seemingly random perceptual switching in bistable events triggered by transient unconscious cues. *Journal of Experimental Psychology: Human Perception and Performance*, 41(4):929.

Jason Wei, Maarten Bosma, Vincent Y. Zhao, Kelvin Guu, Adams Wei Yu, Brian Lester, Nan Du, Andrew M. Dai, and Quoc V. Le. 2022. Finetuned language models are zero-shot learners. In *The Tenth International Conference on Learning Representations, ICLR 2022, Virtual Event, April 25-29, 2022*. OpenReview.net.

Amanda Wilson. 2012. Multistable perception of art-science imagery. *Leonardo*, 45.

Qinghao Ye, Haiyang Xu, Guohai Xu, Jiabo Ye, Ming Yan, Yiyang Zhou, Junyang Wang, Anwen Hu, Pengcheng Shi, Yaya Shi, et al. 2023. mplug-owl: Modularization empowers large language models with multimodality. *ArXiv preprint*, abs/2304.14178.

Licheng Yu, Patrick Poirson, Shan Yang, Alexander C Berg, and Tamara L Berg. 2016. Modeling context in referring expressions. In *Computer Vision–ECCV 2016: 14th European Conference, Amsterdam, The Netherlands, October 11-14, 2016, Proceedings, Part II 14*, pages 69–85. Springer.

Susan Zhang, Stephen Roller, Naman Goyal, Mikel Artetxe, Moya Chen, Shuohui Chen, Christopher Dewan, Mona Diab, Xian Li, Xi Victoria Lin, et al. 2022. Opt: Open pre-trained transformer language models. *ArXiv preprint*, abs/2205.01068.

Yanzhe Zhang, Ruiyi Zhang, Jiuxiang Gu, Yufan Zhou, Nedim Lipka, Diyi Yang, and Tong Sun. 2023a. Llavar: Enhanced visual instruction tuning for text-rich image understanding. *ArXiv preprint*, abs/2306.17107.

Yichi Zhang, Jiayi Pan, Yuchen Zhou, Rui Pan, and Joyce Chai. 2023b. Grounding visual illusions in language: Do vision-language models perceive illusions like humans? *Preprint*, arXiv:2311.00047.

Bo Zhao, Boya Wu, and Tiejun Huang. 2023. Svit: Scaling up visual instruction tuning. *ArXiv preprint*, abs/2307.04087.

A Model Details

We summarize the architectural differences for the models used in our study in Table 1 and list the various datasets they were trained on both for pre-training and instruction tuning (where applicable) in Table 2.

B Additional Results

B.1 Individual Results: Original Images

Figure 9 we list the individual model results for the original labels.

B.2 Individual Results: Synonymous Interpretations

Figure 10 we list the individual model results for the synononymous labels. We find that there is non-trivial variation that is attributed to the likelihood of the terms used as the labels.

B.3 Individual Results: Takashima et al. (2012)

Figure 11 lists the individual results for each model on the Takashima et al. (2012) image study.

B.4 Tint Variation Individual Plots

Figures 12, 13, 14, 15, 16, 17 show the individual variations of each model for each image category based on tint variations. We find limited effect in preferences with highest variability observed by the CLIP variants. Interestingly, most models seem to show same preferences when full tint is applied, indicating a monochrome image - hence the linguistic priors play a large role in model behavior as indicated by the synonym and prompt variation experiments.

C Bistable Image Collection

We present examples of original images in our dataset, without any visual manipulations in figures 18, 19, 20, 21.

D Generative Examples

We present examples of generations from the models prompted with "describe the image" in figures 22, 23, 24, 25, 26 with the exception of few question based prompts: “What is the orientation of the staircase/cube?" for the Shroeder stairs and Necker Cube illusions, and “What is the dancer’s spinning direction?" for ‘Spinning Dancer’.

Model	#Train Param.	LLM	Res.	ViT	LLM Size	V-L Type	V-L Size	#Tokens	Deep V-L	Frozen LLM	Frozen ViT
Idefics 9b (Laurençon et al., 2024)	9b	LLaMA(Touvron et al., 2023)	224	OpenCLIP-H[9]	7b	Perceiver (Jaegle et al., 2021)	194M	64	✓	✓	✓
Idefics 9b Instruct	9b	LlaMA	224	OpenCLIP	7b	Perceiver	194M	64	✓	✓	✓
LLaVA-1.5 7b (Liu et al., 2023b,a)	20M	Vicuna1.5-7B (Chiang et al., 2023)	336	CLIP ViT-L (Radford et al., 2021)	7b	Linear	20M	577	×	×	✓
LLaVA-1.5 13b	20M	Vicuna1.5-13B	336	CLIP ViT-L	13b	Linear	20M	577	×	×	✓
BLIP-2 OPT2.7b (Li et al., 2023a)	188M	OPT2.7b (Zhang et al., 2022)	224	EVA-CLIP-g	2.7b	Q-Former	188M	32	×	✓	✓
BLIP-2 OPT6.7b	188M	OPT6.7b	224	EVA-CLIP-g	6.7b	Q-Former	188M	32	×	✓	✓
BLIP-2 FlanT5xl	188M	FlanT5xl	224	EVA-CLIP-g	3b	Q-Former	188M	32	×	✓	✓
InstructBLIP FlanT5xl (Dai et al., 2023)	188M	FlanT5xl (Chung et al., 2024)	224	EVA-CLIP-g(Sun et al., 2023)	3b	Q-Former (Li et al., 2023b)	188M	32	×	✓	✓
mPLUG-Owl (Ye et al., 2023)	500M	LLaMA	224	CLIP ViT-L	7b	Visual Abstractor (Ye et al., 2023)		64	×	×	×

Table 1: Overview of Generative VLMs architectures examined on their perception of bistable images.

Model	Pretraining Data	Instruction Tuning Data
CLIP	400M image-caption data (undisclosed)	N/A
Idefics 9b	OBELICS (Laurençon et al., 2024), Wikipedia[10],Conceptual Captions(Sharma et al., 2018), Conceptual Captions 12M (Changpinyo et al., 2021), WIT (Srinivasan et al., 2021), Localized Narratives (Pont-Tuset et al., 2020), RedCaps (Desai et al., 2021), COCO (Chen et al., 2015), SBU Captions (Ordonez et al., 2011), Visual Genome (Krishna et al., 2017), YFCC100M (Thomee et al., 2016)	N/A
Idefics 9b Instruct	OBELICS (Laurençon et al., 2024), Wikipedia[11],CC3M(Sharma et al., 2018), CC12M (Changpinyo et al., 2021), WIT (Srinivasan et al., 2021), Localized Narratives (Pont-Tuset et al., 2020), RedCaps (Desai et al., 2021), COCO (Chen et al., 2015), SBU (Ordonez et al., 2011), Visual Genome (Krishna et al., 2017), YFCC100M (Thomee et al., 2016)	M3IT (Li et al., 2023c), LRV-Instruction (), LLaVA150k (Liu et al., 2023b),LLaVAR-Instruct (Zhang et al., 2023a),SVIT (Zhao et al., 2023), UltraChat (Ding et al., 2023)
LLaVA-1.5	LLaVA (Liu et al., 2023a) [subsets of LAION-400M (Schuhmann et al., 2021), CC3M (Sharma et al., 2018), SBU (Ordonez et al., 2011)]	VQAv2 (Goyal et al., 2017b), GQA (Hudson and Manning, 2019),OKVQA (Marino et al., 2019), A-OKVQA (Schwenk et al., 2022),OCRVQA (Mishra et al., 2019), TextCaps (Sidorov et al., 2020), LLaVA150k (Liu et al., 2023b), ShareGPT[12]
BLIP-2	COCO (Chen et al., 2015), CC3M (Sharma et al., 2018), CC12M (Changpinyo et al., 2021), LAION400M (Schuhmann et al., 2021), Visual Genome (Krishna et al., 2017)	N/A
InstructBLIP	COCO (Chen et al., 2015), CC3M (Sharma et al., 2018), CC12M (Changpinyo et al., 2021), LAION400M (Schuhmann et al., 2021), Visual Genome (Krishna et al., 2017)	COCO (Chen et al., 2015), Web CapFilt (Li et al., 2023a), TextCaps (Sidorov et al., 2020), VQAv2 (Goyal et al., 2017b), OKVQA (Marino et al., 2019), A-OKVQA (Schwenk et al., 2022), LLaVA150k (Liu et al., 2023b), OCRVQA (Mishra et al., 2019)
mPLUG-Owl	LAION-400M (Schuhmann et al., 2021), COYO (Carlini et al., 2023), COCO (Chen et al., 2015), Laion-en (Schuhmann et al., 2022), DataComp (Gadre et al., 2024)	VQAv2 (Goyal et al., 2017b), OKVQA (Marino et al., 2019), OCR-VQA (Mishra et al., 2019), GQA (Hudson and Manning, 2019), A-OKVQA (Schwenk et al., 2022), RefCOCO (Yu et al., 2016), Visual Genome (Krishna et al., 2017), LLaVA150K (Liu et al., 2023b), ShareGPT, SlimOrca (Lian et al., 2023)

Table 2: Overview of Pretraining and Instruction Tuning Datasets (adapted from Wang et al. (2024))

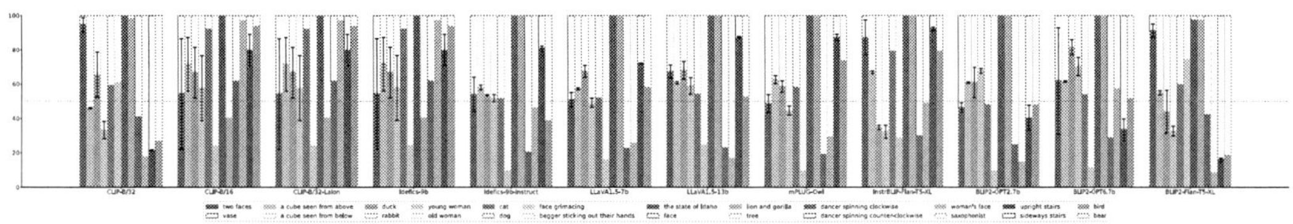

Figure 9: Average probability distributions for each model evaluated on each image category.

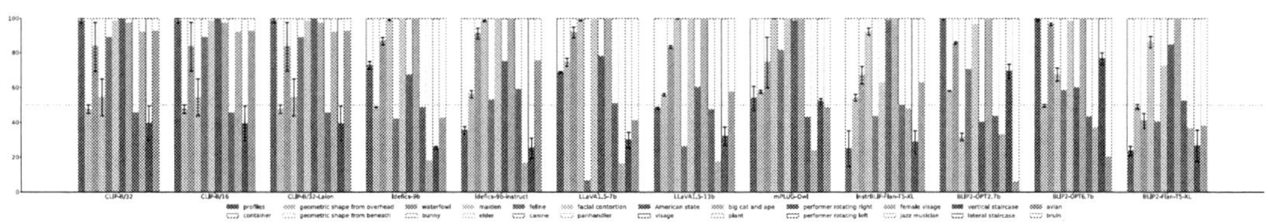

Figure 10: Synonymous Interpretations

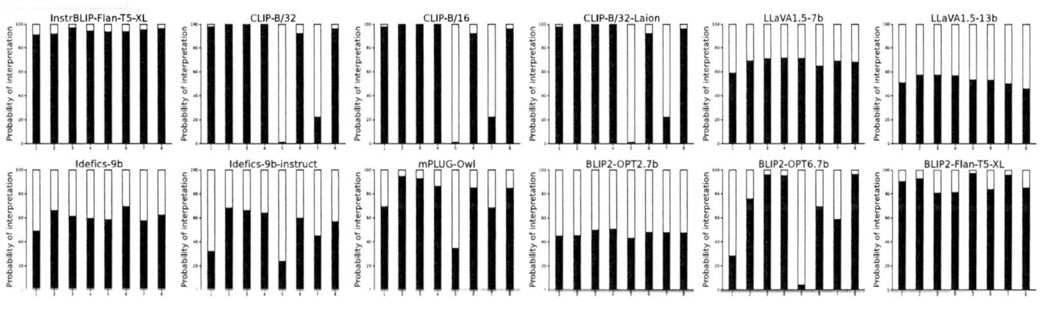

Figure 11: Individual model preferences for Takashima et al. (2012) images.

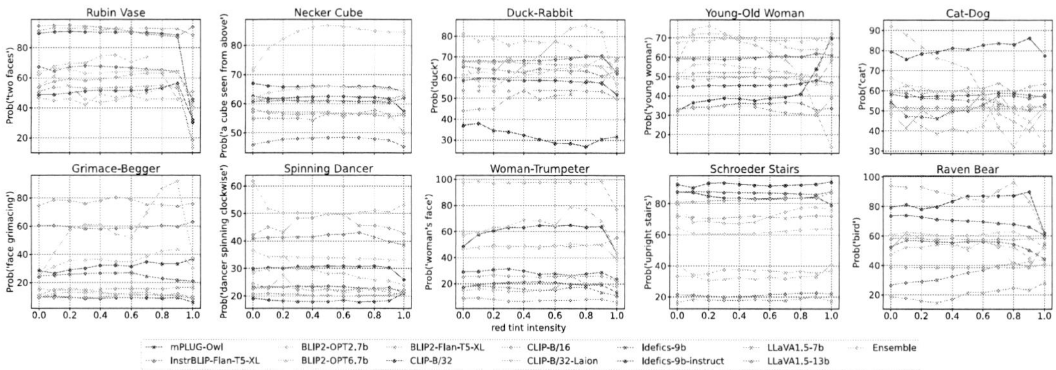

Figure 12: Red Tint Variation

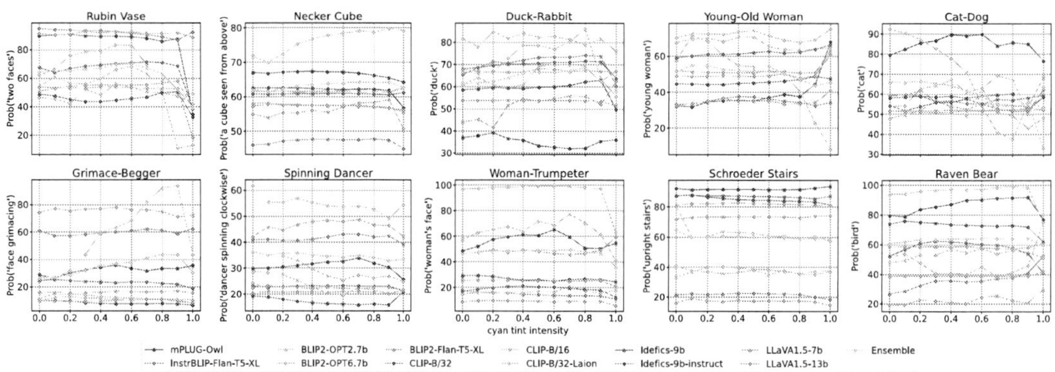

Figure 13: Cyan Tint Variation

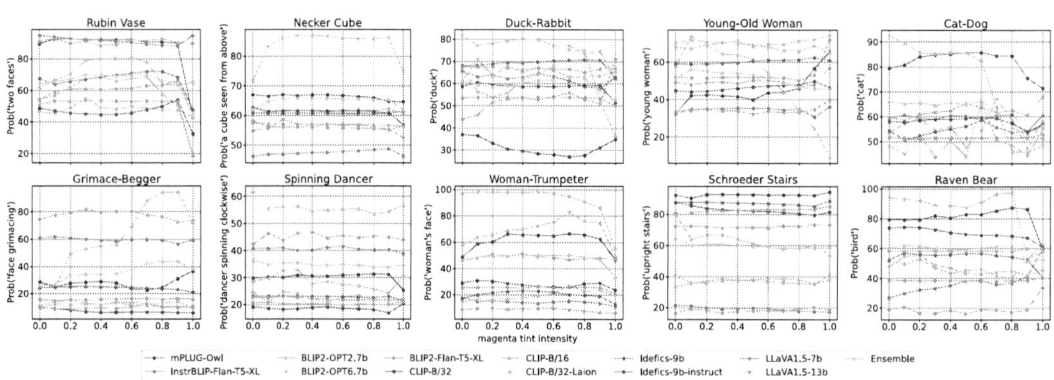

Figure 14: Magenta Tint Variation

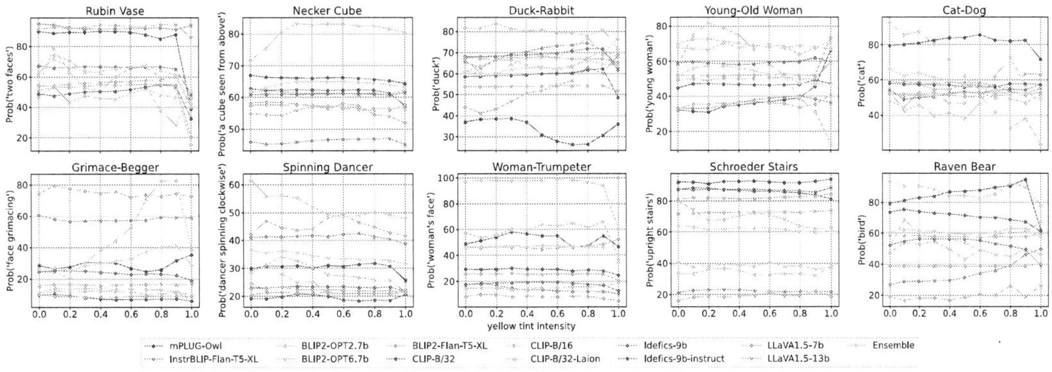

Figure 15: Yellow Tint Variation

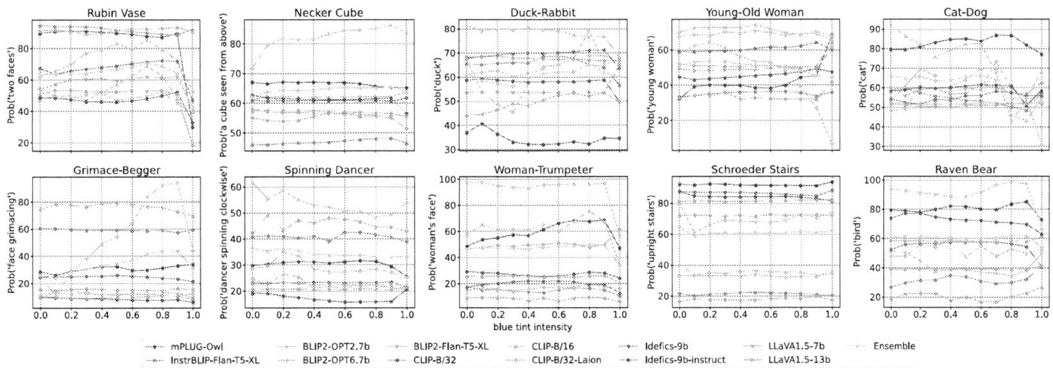

Figure 16: Blue Tint Variation

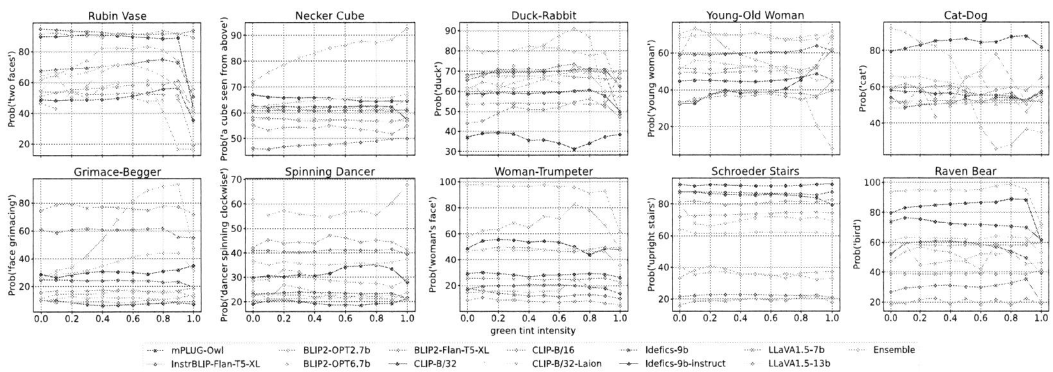

Figure 17: Green Tint Variation

Figure 18: Rubin Vase illusions (interpretations: ["vase", "two faces"]) and Necker Cube illusions (interpretations: ["a cube seen from below", "a cube seen from above"]).

Figure 19: Duck-Rabbit illusion (interpretations: ["duck", "rabbit"]) and Young-Old Woman illusion (interpretations: ["young woman", "old woman"]).

Figure 20: Shroeder Stairs illusion (interpretations: ["upright stairs", "sideways stairs"]), Lion-Gorilla-Tree illusion (interpretations: ["lion and gorilla", "tree"]) and Grimace-Begger illusion (interpretations: ["grimace", "beggar"]).

Figure 21: Various illusions from left to right: Woman-Trumpeter (interpretations: ["woman's face", "saxophonist"], Idaho-Face (interpretations: ["the state of Idaho", "face"]), Spinning Dancer (interpretations: ["dancer spinning clockwise", "dancer spinning counter-clockwise"]), and Raven-Bear (interpretations: ["bird", "bear"]).

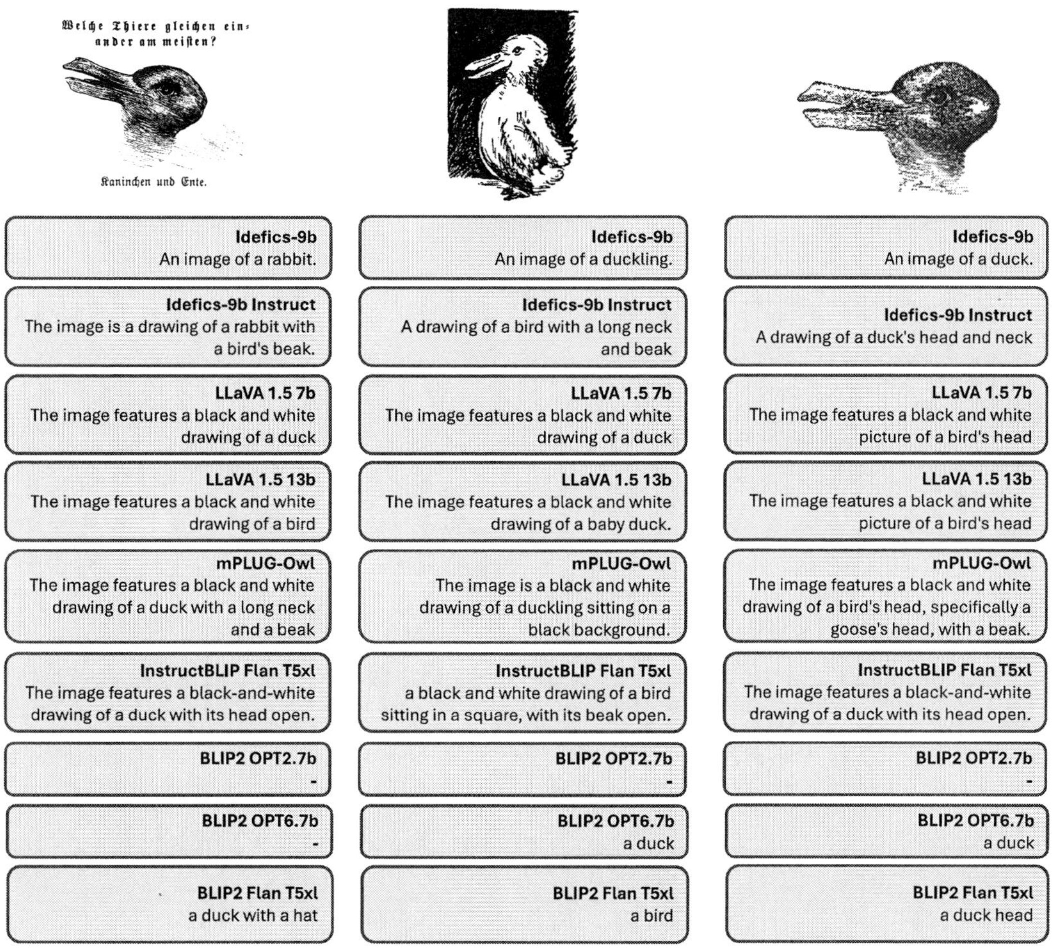

Figure 22: Duck-Rabbit generative examples

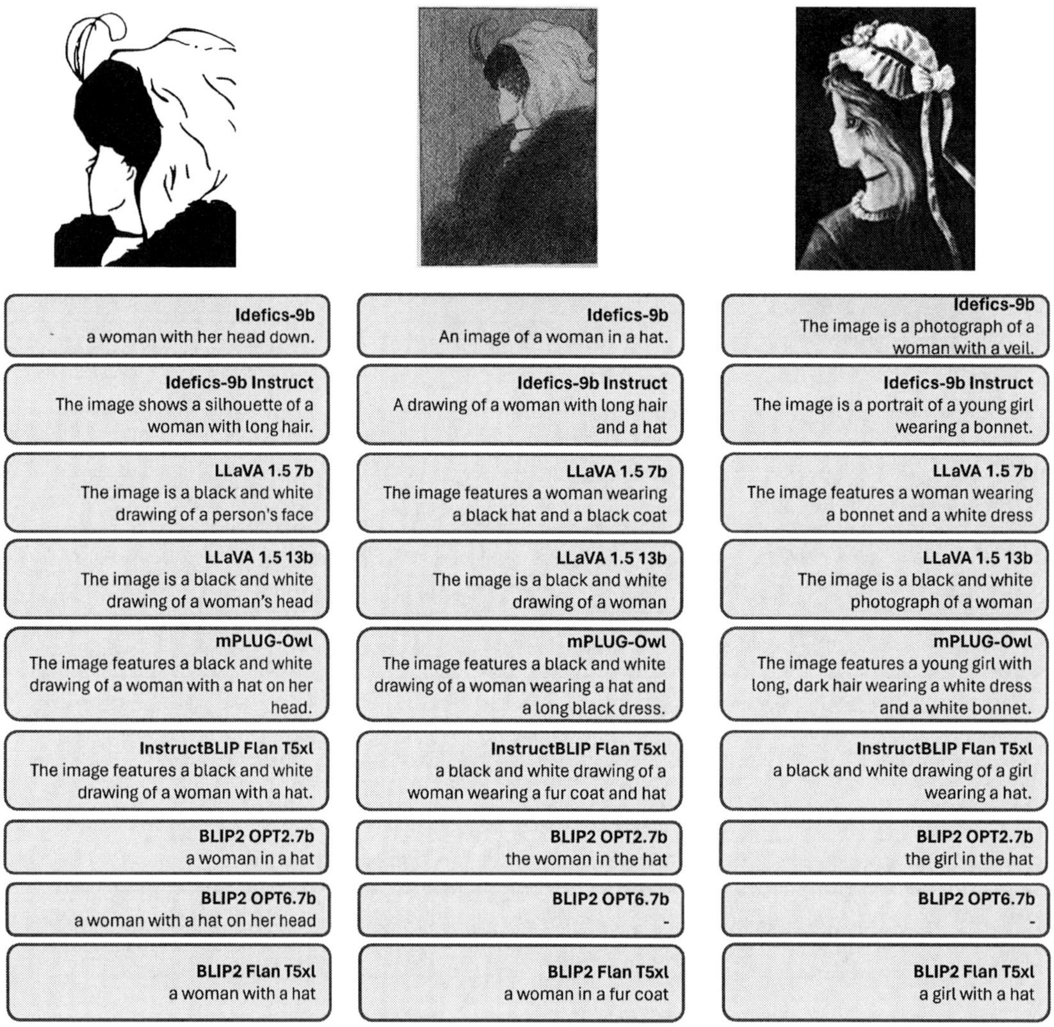

Figure 23: Young Old woman generative examples

Left image	Middle image	Right image
Idefics-9b An image of a person looking in a mirror.	**Idefics-9b** An image of a man's face.	**Idefics-9b** a wrought-iron lattice tower
Idefics-9b Instruct The silhouette of a man and a woman's heads together.	**Idefics-9b Instruct** a silhouette of a man's head and shoulders	**Idefics-9b Instruct** Two faces, one male and one female, are shown on the left side.
LLaVA 1.5 7b The image features a black and white silhouette of a person	**LLaVA 1.5 7b** The image features a black and white drawing of a person's face	**LLaVA 1.5 7b** The image features a black and white drawing of a person's face
LLaVA 1.5 13b The image features a black and white photo of two men's faces	**LLaVA 1.5 13b** The image is a black and white drawing of a person's head	**LLaVA 1.5 13b** The image features a black and white design of two faces,
mPLUG-Owl The image features a black and white silhouette of two people facing each other.	**mPLUG-Owl** The image features a black and white drawing of a man's face,	**mPLUG-Owl** The image features a black and white silhouette of two people's faces.
InstructBLIP Flan T5xl The image features a silhouette of two men facing each other	**InstructBLIP Flan T5xl** The image features a silhouette of a person's head in the shape of a vase.	**InstructBLIP Flan T5xl** two silhouettes of heads facing each other on a black background
BLIP2 OPT2.7b two people in silhouette	**BLIP2 OPT2.7b** -	**BLIP2 OPT2.7b** two people silhouettes
BLIP2 OPT6.7b two people facing each other	**BLIP2 OPT6.7b** -	**BLIP2 OPT6.7b** two people silhouettes
BLIP2 Flan T5xl two heads facing each other	**BLIP2 Flan T5xl** a silhouette of a person	**BLIP2 Flan T5xl** -

Figure 24: Vase-Faces woman generative examples

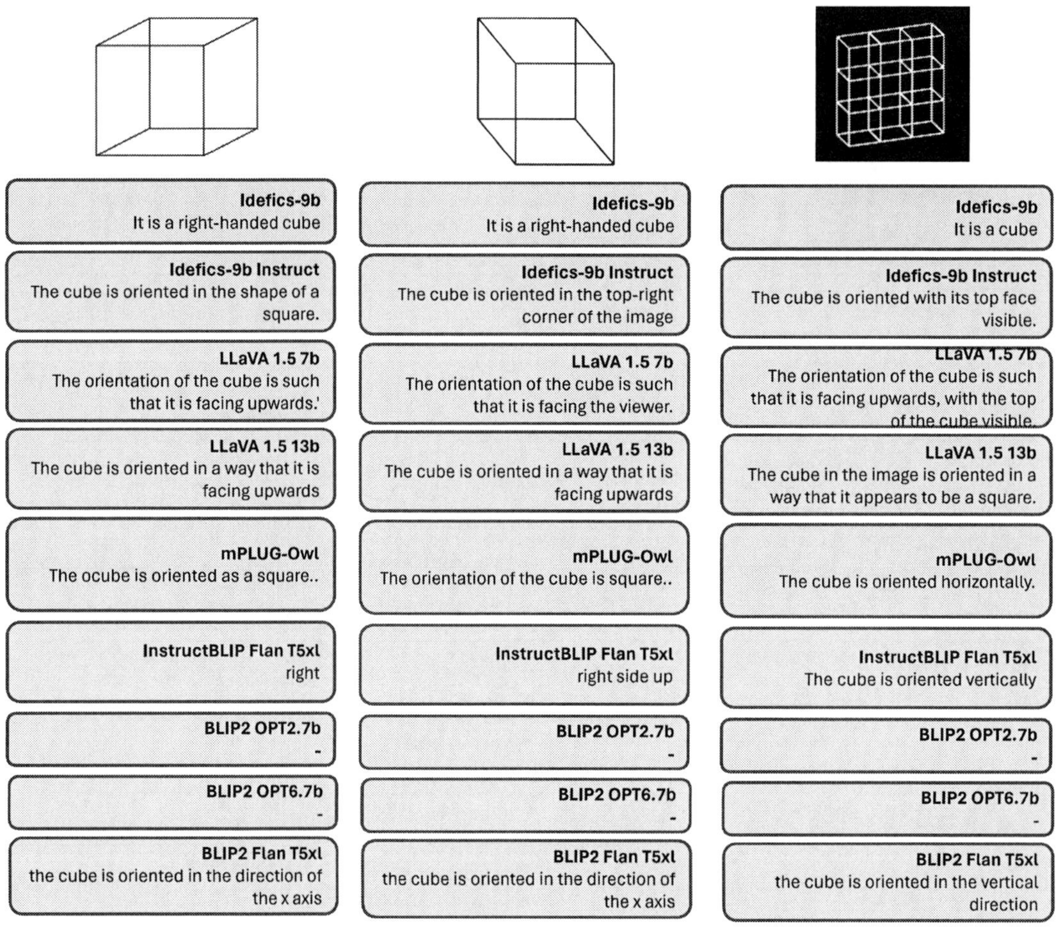

Figure 25: Necker-Cube generative examples on question “What is the orientation of the cube?"

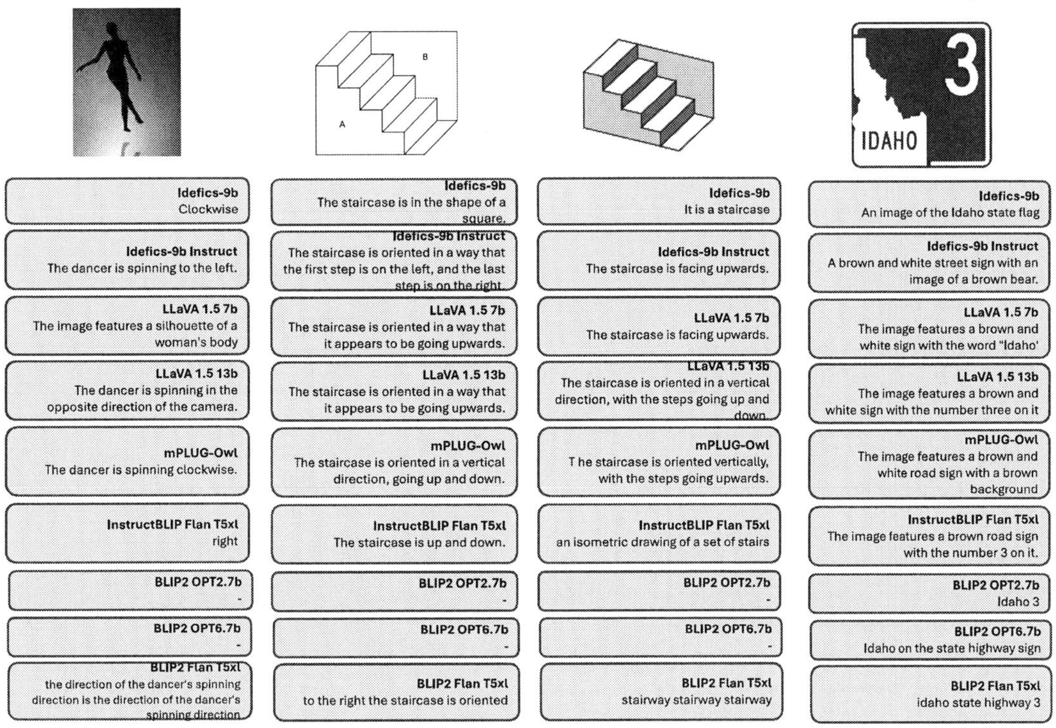

Figure 26: Spinning Dancer results on question “What is the dancer’s spinning direction?", Shroeder Stairs on “What is the orientation of the stairs" and Idaho-Face on "describe the image".

Locally Biased Transformers Better Align with Human Reading Times

Andrea Gregor de Varda
University of Milano – Bicocca
a.devarda@campus.unimib.it

Marco Marelli
University of Milano – Bicocca
marco.marelli@unimib.it

Abstract

Recent psycholinguistic theories emphasize the interdependence between linguistic expectations and memory limitations in human language processing. We modify the self-attention mechanism of a transformer model to simulate a lossy context representation, biasing the model's predictions to give additional weight to the local linguistic context. We show that surprisal estimates from our locally-biased model generally provide a better fit to human psychometric data, underscoring the sensitivity of the human parser to local linguistic information.

1 Introduction

In recent years, transformer models (Vaswani et al., 2017) have gained prominence in psycholinguistics due to their impressive predictive performance in forecasting psychometric measurements such as reading times (Hao et al., 2020; Merkx and Frank, 2021; de Varda et al., 2023; Hoover et al., 2023; Oh and Schuler, 2022, 2023, *inter alia*). These models excel at capturing complex linguistic dependencies, making them valuable tools in analyzing human language-processing behaviors. Much of the work that relates probabilistic estimates from transformer models with human processing has been conducted within the framework of surprisal theory, which posits that the difficulty experienced during processing is proportional to the negative logarithm of the probability of a word given its preceding context. In this context, transformer models, which are able to generate highly accurate probabilistic predictions for sequences of text, have been instrumental in providing empirical support for surprisal theory (Wilcox et al., 2020; Shain et al., 2022; de Varda and Marelli, 2022, 2023). However, despite their substantial predictive power, transformer models exhibit some design features that lack cognitive plausibility. One significant departure from human language processing is their ability to access in parallel the entire linguistic context within their input size. Unlike these models, human language comprehension is inherently incremental (Smith and Levy, 2013). Humans eagerly integrate in their representation of the context each linguistic unit as soon as it is encountered, and they cannot typically store in working memory the whole linguistic context. Thus, the transformer model's *all-at-once* approach to processing information starkly contrasts with the sequential and resource-constrained manner in which humans receive and interpret linguistic input, suggesting a need for models that more closely mirror human cognitive limitations and processing strategies.

To address these limitations, we introduce a modification to the self-attention mechanism of the transformer model, aimed at simulating a lossy memory representation, where linguistic units that are further away from the current word are assigned exponentially decaying attention scores. By doing so, our model aims to replicate the kind of linguistic processing that characterizes the human language parser, where recent information plays a significant role (Goodkind and Bicknell, 2021).

The evaluation of our locally-biased transformer model involves the employment of the surprisal – i.e., negative log probability – it assigns to words in context to predict human psychometric data, considering five large-scale datasets of eye movements and self-paced reading times in English. We show that our locally-biased model provides surprisal estimates that align more closely with human psychometric data than a standard pre-trained model.

2 Related work

Models that can explain the cognitive cost associated with sentence processing can be broadly divided into expectation- and memory-based theories. Expectation-based theories (such as surprisal theory; Levy, 2008; Hale, 2001) emphasize the role of contextual predictability as a core determinant of processing demands. Support for such theo-

Proceedings of the Workshop on Cognitive Modeling and Computational Linguistics, pages 30–36
August 15, 2024 ©2024 Association for Computational Linguistics

ries has come from several studies demonstrating reduced cognitive load in response to predictable words (e.g., Frank and Thompson, 2012; Frank et al., 2015; Wilcox et al., 2020). Memory-based theories, in contrast, are based on the idea that integrating the upcoming words into the context representation depends on the retrieval (Lewis and Vasishth, 2005) and storage (Gibson, 1998, 2000) of previous words in working memory. Support for memory-based theories comes from the difficulty in integrating words that are linearly distant in a sentence (dependency locality effects; Grodner and Gibson, 2005; Fedorenko et al., 2013).

In recent years, there have been proposals to reconcile expectation- and memory-based approaches into unified models. While the first combined theories posited limited (Demberg and Keller, 2008, 2009) or no interaction between memory and predictability (Rasmussen and Schuler, 2018; see Futrell et al., 2020), some recently developed frameworks account for complex interactions between the two (Futrell et al., 2020; Hahn et al., 2022). In particular, *lossy-context surprisal theory* (henceforth LCST; Futrell et al., 2020) holds that the processing difficulty associated with a word is proportional its surprisal, conditioned by a lossy (i.e., noisy) memory representation of the context. Hahn et al. (2022) presented a computationally-specified model of LCST (*resource-rational LCST*) that computes retention probabilities for each word in the context, based on the word's identity and position in the sentence. Similarly, Kuribayashi et al. (2022) have shown that reducing the number of words in input to language models improves the fit of the surprisal estimates to human reading times. Our modelling approach is reminiscent of LCST in that it assumes that the processing cost associated with a word is proportional to its surprisal, conditioned by the previous context where linearly distant words contribute less to its prediction.

In our modelling effort, we modify the attention scores of a transformer model to mimic the human difficulty in retrieving distant linguistic elements. We are not the first in drawing a parallelism between the self-attention mechanism and (cue-based) memory retrieval (Merkx and Frank, 2021; Hyun et al., 2022; Oh and Schuler, 2022; Timkey and Linzen, 2023). Indeed, like the self-attention mechanism scores the weights to assign to the words in input based on the compatibility between keys and queries, cue-based retrieval theories

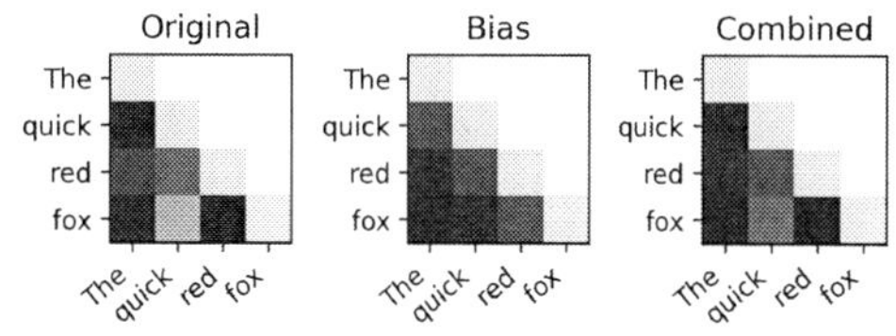

Figure 1: Visual example of our custom modification of the model's attention pattern. The original attention scores (left) and the exponentially decaying bias (center) are summed to derive the combined attention scores (right).

posit that items in working memory are accessed by comparing the retrieval cues of the current word with the features of the items in working memory (Timkey and Linzen, 2023). Our choice to bias the transformer model's retrieval process towards the recent linguistic context is supported by vast evidence in psycholinguistics showing that local information holds a privileged role in human language processing, with a chief example being word frequency. Indeed, it is well-known that the frequency of a word (which is proportional to its unigram probability) influences its reading times above and beyond its contextual predictability (Rayner, 1998; Shain, 2023). Furthermore, other studies have detected an effect of N-gram surprisal beyond the effect of surprisal as calculated from larger sentential contexts (Goodkind and Bicknell, 2021). Note that the idea of assigning reduced weights to distal elements has a long-standing tradition in psychologically-oriented computational models of semantic memory: one of the first distributional semantic models, the Hyperspace Analogue to Language (HAL; Lund and Burgess, 1996), weighs word-by-word co-occurrences as a function of their linear distance. It is noteworthy that the idea that human language processing privileges recent information was explicitly implemented in early work in computational semantics, and lost with later developments in the field.

3 Methods and materials

We modified the pre-trained GPT-2 model (Radford et al., 2019) to increase the attention weights associated to the nearby words. We conducted our analyses on the smallest GPT-2 variant, as it has been proven to be particularly effective at modelling human reading times (Shain et al., 2022).

All the code supporting our analyses is publicly available on GitHub.[1]

[1] https://github.com/Andrea-de-Varda/local_attention_reading_times

3.1 Locally biased attention

Attention weights are initially computed using the standard dot-product attention, involving the multiplication of the query matrix with the transpose of the key matrix ($W = QK^T$). Then, an exponential decay bias matrix B is computed using an exponential decay function based on the absolute differences between positions in the sequence, scaled by a decay rate. Thus, the bias is computed as $B_{i,j} = e^{-\lambda|i-j|}$, where $i, j \in \{0, 1, \ldots, n-1\}$ indicate the position of two tokens in the sequence, n specifies the sequence length, and λ is the decay rate. As a final step, we blend together the original attention weights with the exponential decay bias with a weighted sum to obtain the final attention weights $A = (1-\alpha) \cdot W + \alpha \cdot B$. As a last step, the softmax function is applied to A. A visual summary of this procedure is provided in Figure 1. Note that both α and λ serve as free parameters in our modified attention mechanism. To identify the optimal values for these parameters, we employed hyperparameter tuning techniques as detailed in §3.4.

3.2 Data

The analyses were run on three eye-tracking and three self-paced reading datasets. The eye-tracking resources we considered were the Provo corpus (Luke and Christianson, 2018; $N = 2659$[2]), the English portion of the MECO corpus (Siegelman et al., 2022; $N = 2096$), and the UCL_{ET} corpus (Frank et al., 2013, $N = 1726$). The three self-paced reading datasets were the UCL_{SPR} dataset (Frank et al., 2013, $N = 1726$), the Brown corpus (Smith and Levy, 2013; $N = 5862$), and the Natural Stories reading times corpus (NatStor, Futrell et al., 2021; $N = 8779$). In our analysis of the eye-tracking data, we focused on first-pass gaze duration times, in accordance with previous research in computational psycholinguistics (see for instance Aurnhammer and Frank, 2019; Goodkind and Bicknell, 2018; Smith and Levy, 2013; Wilcox et al., 2020). For words that did not receive any fixation, we assigned a gaze duration time of zero. We excluded words located at the beginning of sentences from our analyses. Beyond this exclusion, we did not implement any further filtering criteria. To obtain word-level gaze duration times, we calculated the average word reading times across all participants. Likewise, for the self-paced reading tasks, we calculated the average reaction times on the target word across participants.

[2] N is the number of datapoints after data aggregation.

3.3 Analyses

In our analyses, the dependent variable of interest (either gaze duration or self-paced reading times) was predicted with a linear model including surprisal, subtitle-based log-frequency (Brysbaert and New, 2009), and orthographic length as regressors.[3] Surprisal values obtained with our locally biased transformer model (s_{loc}) were compared with the estimates produced by the original GPT-2 model (s_{orig}). For each psychometric dataset, we identified the best model with the Akaike Information Criterion (AIC; Akaike, 1998). In particular, we subtracted the AIC_{loc} obtained with s_{loc} to the AIC_{orig} obtained with s_{orig} to obtain a ΔAIC. In interpreting the ΔAIC scores, we refer to the guidelines offered by Burnham and Anderson (2004), which indicate that if two models have a $\Delta\text{AIC} \leq 2$, they both have substantial support; if $4 \leq \Delta\text{AIC} \leq 7$, the best model has considerably more support, and if $\Delta\text{AIC} \geq 10$, the worse model has essentially no support[4].

3.4 Hyperparameter tuning

To identify the best values for the parameters α and λ (see §3.1), we iteratively sampled from the hyperparameter space – restricted to $\lambda \in (0, 100)$ and $\alpha \in (0, 1)$ – using a Tree-structured Parzen Estimator algorithm. For each (λ, α) pair, we specified a locally-biased GPT-2 model with such hyperparameters, and derived surprisal values for the sentences in the Provo corpus. Then, we fit a linear model predicting the reading times in the Provo corpus from the obtained surprisal values, log-frequency, and word length; through hyperparameter tuning we seeked to minimize the negative log likelihood of the model ($N_{trials} = 100$). As a result of this procedure, we identified $\lambda = 82.86$ and $\alpha = 0.37$ as the optimal values for the two parameters. The parameters obtained in the Provo corpus were transferred to the other behavioral datasets without further tuning.

[3] The exact linear model specification was DV $\sim$ LENGTH(w_i) + FREQUENCY(w_i) + SURPRISAL(w_i)

[4] In terms of relative likelihood, if $\Delta\text{AIC} \leq 2$ the worse model is 0.3678 times as probable as the best model to minimize the information loss; with $4 \leq \Delta\text{AIC} \leq 7$, this probability is in the range $(0.0302, 0.1353)$, and with $\Delta\text{AIC} \geq 10$ the probability is lower than 0.0067.

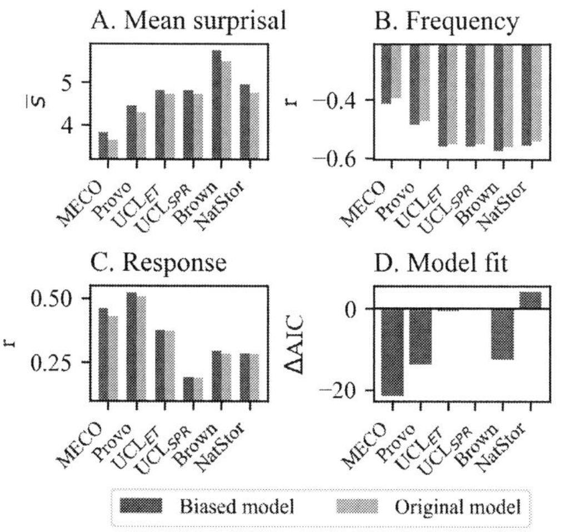

Figure 2: From the top left, clockwise: **A.** Average per-word surprisal as computed with the biased model and the baseline; **B.** Correlation of the obtained surprisal estimates with log frequency; **C.** Correlation of the surprisal estimates with the psychometric measurements; **D.** ΔAIC between the locally biased model and the original model.

4 Results

The results of our analyses are reported in Figure 2. Our locally biased transformer assigned higher average per-word surprisal values to the input texts across all datasets (A), showing a reduced autoregressive accuracy with respect to its unbiased counterpart. The obtained surprisal estimates correlated more strongly with log frequency values (B) and with the behavioral responses considered (C). Furthermore, our comparison between the biased and the original GPT-2 model (D) revealed that our modification of the attention mechanism caused a substantial increase in predictive performance in three behavioral datasets, encompassing both eye-tracking (MECO, ΔAIC $= -21.55$; Provo, ΔAIC $= -13.72$) and self-paced reading (Brown, ΔAIC $= -12.55$). Our manipulation had no effect in the UCL corpus (UCL$_{\mathrm{ET}}$, ΔAIC $= -0.59$; UCL$_{\mathrm{SPR}}$, ΔAIC $= -0.06$) and resulted in a poorer fit in the NatStor dataset (ΔAIC $= 4.31$).

5 Discussion

In this study, we have demonstrated that a modification of the GPT-2 model to emphasize local context via a locally-biased attention mechanism results in surprisal estimates that are more strongly correlated with human reading times, and generally display a better fit to human psychometric data. An exception to this second observation is offered by the NatStor and UCL corpora; in Appendix A, we report tentative evidence that the model improvement seems to be related to the average sentence length in the corpus. In particular, our locally-biased attention seems to be particularly beneficial in cases where the sentences are longer. This finding is compatible with the idea of a lossy representation of the context, where memory constraints become more marked for longer text sequences. Future approaches could consider dynamically manipulating the α parameter as a function of sentence lenght, adjusting the strength of the bias to cases where the human memory is taxed more strongly.

In LCST, the way memory representations degrade typically results in a word's contextual processing cost approaching its context-independent processing cost, as predicted by its standalone probability (Futrell et al., 2020). Essentially, as the fidelity of a listener's memory representations diminishes, their anticipations increasingly align with the prior, context-independent unigram probability. Our findings empirically demonstrate that this is the case, as the surprisal estimates from our locally-biased transformer tend to regress towards word frequency estimates (Figure 2, B). While our intervention on the attention mechanism is directly inspired by LCST, it should be noted that this implementation does not respect all the assumptions of the theory. In particular, LCST posits as an assumption the inaccessibility of the context (Claim 3); here, the context is always available to the model, albeit reduced attention weights are assigned to the elements that are linearly distant from each other.

Importantly, our modification of the attention mechanism resulted in models that were less performant in next-word prediction (see Figure 2, A). This is of course to be expected, as the addition of the exponential decay bias to the attention scores produces final attention weights that deviate from the ones that have been optimized for autoregression. Nonetheless, our results show that a worse NLP model can constitute a better cognitive model in terms of fit to psychometric data. This result challenges the *quality-power hypothesis* (QP; Wilcox et al., 2023), which posits that more accurate language models (i.e., models whose surprisal estimate better approximate the values from the data-generating distribution) should provide surprisal estimates that better fit behavioral data. However, QP does not hold if the probabilistic information that humans deploy in real time is systematically biased with respect to the data-generating distribution. One example of this systematic deviation is offered by the sensitivity of the human parser to local word co-occurrence statistics (Goodkind and Bicknell, 2021), which is exactly what we model in the present paper. Thus, our results show that human-like language processing might inherently involve biases and limitations that deviate from optimal statistical models.

Limitations

This study, while providing insights into the integration of cognitive constraints in transformer models, is not without limitations. The approach assumes a fixed attention decay rate, a simplification that might not fully capture the dynamic nature of human memory in language processing. Furthermore, while we consider more psychometric datasets than most studies in computational psycholinguistics, the fact that we have only five corpora does not allow us to draw conclusive inferences on the impact of average sentence length on the relative performance of our locally biased models.

References

Hirotogu Akaike. 1998. Information theory and an extension of the maximum likelihood principle. *Selected papers of hirotugu akaike*, pages 199–213.

Christoph Aurnhammer and Stefan L Frank. 2019. Comparing gated and simple recurrent neural network architectures as models of human sentence processing.

Marc Brysbaert and Boris New. 2009. Moving beyond kučera and francis: A critical evaluation of current word frequency norms and the introduction of a new and improved word frequency measure for american english. *Behavior research methods*, 41(4):977–990.

Kenneth P Burnham and David R Anderson. 2004. Multimodel inference: understanding aic and bic in model selection. *Sociological methods & research*, 33(2):261–304.

Andrea de Varda and Marco Marelli. 2023. Scaling in cognitive modelling: A multilingual approach to human reading times. In *Proceedings of the 61st Annual Meeting of the Association for Computational Linguistics (Volume 2: Short Papers)*, pages 139–149.

Andrea Gregor de Varda and Marco Marelli. 2022. The effects of surprisal across languages: Results from native and non-native reading. In *Findings of the Association for Computational Linguistics: AACL-IJCNLP 2022*, pages 138–144.

Andrea Gregor de Varda, Marco Marelli, and Simona Amenta. 2023. Cloze probability, predictability ratings, and computational estimates for 205 english sentences, aligned with existing eeg and reading time data. *Behavior Research Methods*, pages 1–24.

Vera Demberg and Frank Keller. 2008. A psycholinguistically motivated version of tag. In *Proceedings of the Ninth International Workshop on Tree Adjoining Grammar and Related Frameworks (TAG+ 9)*, pages 25–32.

Vera Demberg and Frank Keller. 2009. A computational model of prediction in human parsing: Unifying locality and surprisal effects. In *Proceedings of the annual meeting of the cognitive science society*, volume 31.

Evelina Fedorenko, Rebecca Woodbury, and Edward Gibson. 2013. Direct evidence of memory retrieval as a source of difficulty in non-local dependencies in language. *Cognitive science*, 37(2):378–394.

Stefan Frank, Leun J Otten, Giulia Galli, and Gabriella Vigliocco. 2015. The erp response to the amount of information conveyed by words in sentences. *Brain and language*, 140:1–11.

Stefan Frank and Robin Thompson. 2012. Early effects of word surprisal on pupil size during reading. In *Proceedings of the annual meeting of the cognitive science society*, volume 34.

Stefan L Frank, Irene Fernandez Monsalve, Robin L Thompson, and Gabriella Vigliocco. 2013. Reading time data for evaluating broad-coverage models of english sentence processing. *Behavior research methods*, 45(4):1182–1190.

Richard Futrell, Edward Gibson, and Roger P Levy. 2020. Lossy-context surprisal: An information-theoretic model of memory effects in sentence processing. *Cognitive science*, 44(3):e12814.

Richard Futrell, Edward Gibson, Harry J Tily, Idan Blank, Anastasia Vishnevetsky, Steven T Piantadosi, and Evelina Fedorenko. 2021. The natural stories corpus: a reading-time corpus of english texts containing rare syntactic constructions. *Language Resources and Evaluation*, 55:63–77.

Edward Gibson. 1998. Linguistic complexity: Locality of syntactic dependencies. *Cognition*, 68(1):1–76.

Edward Gibson. 2000. The dependency locality theory: A distance-based theory of linguistic complexity. *Image, language, brain*, 2000:95–126.

Adam Goodkind and Klinton Bicknell. 2018. Predictive power of word surprisal for reading times is a linear function of language model quality. In *Proceedings of the 8th workshop on cognitive modeling and computational linguistics (CMCL 2018)*, pages 10–18.

Adam Goodkind and Klinton Bicknell. 2021. Local word statistics affect reading times independently of surprisal. *arXiv preprint arXiv:2103.04469*.

Daniel Grodner and Edward Gibson. 2005. Consequences of the serial nature of linguistic input for sentenial complexity. *Cognitive science*, 29(2):261–290.

Michael Hahn, Richard Futrell, Roger Levy, and Edward Gibson. 2022. A resource-rational model of human processing of recursive linguistic structure. *Proceedings of the National Academy of Sciences*, 119(43):e2122602119.

John Hale. 2001. A probabilistic Earley parser as a psycholinguistic model. In *Second Meeting of the North American Chapter of the Association for Computational Linguistics*.

Yiding Hao, Simon Mendelsohn, Rachel Sterneck, Randi Martinez, and Robert Frank. 2020. Probabilistic predictions of people perusing: Evaluating metrics of language model performance for psycholinguistic modeling. In *Proceedings of the Workshop on Cognitive Modeling and Computational Linguistics*, pages 75–86.

Jacob Louis Hoover, Morgan Sonderegger, Steven T Piantadosi, and Timothy J O'Donnell. 2023. The plausibility of sampling as an algorithmic theory of sentence processing. *Open Mind*, 7:350–391.

Ryu Soo Hyun et al. 2022. Using transformer language model to integrate surprisal, entropy, and working memory retrieval accounts of sentence processing. In *35th Annual Conference on Human Sentence Processing*.

Tatsuki Kuribayashi, Yohei Oseki, Ana Brassard, and Kentaro Inui. 2022. Context limitations make neural language models more human-like. In *Proceedings of the 2022 Conference on Empirical Methods in Natural Language Processing*, pages 10421–10436.

Roger Levy. 2008. Expectation-based syntactic comprehension. *Cognition*, 106(3):1126–1177.

Richard L Lewis and Shravan Vasishth. 2005. An activation-based model of sentence processing as skilled memory retrieval. *Cognitive Science*, 29:375–419.

Steven G Luke and Kiel Christianson. 2018. The provo corpus: A large eye-tracking corpus with predictability norms. *Behavior research methods*, 50:826–833.

Kevin Lund and Curt Burgess. 1996. Producing high-dimensional semantic spaces from lexical co-occurrence. *Behavior research methods, instruments, & computers*, 28(2):203–208.

Danny Merkx and Stefan L Frank. 2021. Human sentence processing: Recurrence or attention? In *Proceedings of the Workshop on Cognitive Modeling and Computational Linguistics*, pages 12–22.

Byung-Doh Oh and William Schuler. 2022. Entropy- and distance-based predictors from gpt-2 attention patterns predict reading times over and above gpt-2 surprisal. In *Proceedings of the 2022 Conference on Empirical Methods in Natural Language Processing*, pages 9324–9334.

Byung-Doh Oh and William Schuler. 2023. Why does surprisal from larger transformer-based language models provide a poorer fit to human reading times? *Transactions of the Association for Computational Linguistics*, 11:336–350.

Alec Radford, Jeffrey Wu, Rewon Child, David Luan, Dario Amodei, and Ilya Sutskever. 2019. Language models are unsupervised multitask learners.

Nathan E Rasmussen and William Schuler. 2018. Left-corner parsing with distributed associative memory produces surprisal and locality effects. *Cognitive science*, 42:1009–1042.

Keith Rayner. 1998. Eye movements in reading and information processing: 20 years of research. *Psychological bulletin*, 124(3):372.

Cory Shain. 2023. Word frequency and predictability dissociate in naturalistic reading.

Cory Shain, Clara Meister, Tiago Pimentel, Ryan Cotterell, and Roger Philip Levy. 2022. Large-scale evidence for logarithmic effects of word predictability on reading time.

Noam Siegelman, Sascha Schroeder, Cengiz Acartürk, Hee-Don Ahn, Svetlana Alexeeva, Simona Amenta, Raymond Bertram, Rolando Bonandrini, Marc Brysbaert, Daria Chernova, et al. 2022. Expanding horizons of cross-linguistic research on reading: The multilingual eye-movement corpus (meco). *Behavior research methods*, pages 1–21.

Nathaniel J Smith and Roger Levy. 2013. The effect of word predictability on reading time is logarithmic. *Cognition*, 128(3):302–319.

William Timkey and Tal Linzen. 2023. A language model with limited memory capacity captures interference in human sentence processing. In *Findings of the Association for Computational Linguistics: EMNLP 2023*, pages 8705–8720.

Ashish Vaswani, Noam Shazeer, Niki Parmar, Jakob Uszkoreit, Llion Jones, Aidan N Gomez, Łukasz Kaiser, and Illia Polosukhin. 2017. Attention is all you need. *Advances in neural information processing systems*, 30.

Ethan Wilcox, Clara Meister, Ryan Cotterell, and Tiago Pimentel. 2023. Language model quality correlates with psychometric predictive power in multiple languages. In *Proceedings of the 2023 Conference on Empirical Methods in Natural Language Processing*, pages 7503–7511.

Ethan Gotlieb Wilcox, Jon Gauthier, Jennifer Hu, Peng Qian, and Roger Levy. 2020. On the predictive power of neural language models for human real-time comprehension behavior. *arXiv preprint arXiv:2006.01912*.

A Sentence length

In our main analysis, we found that the surprisal estimates from our locally biased model were associated with a better fit to human psychometric data in the MECO, Provo, and Brown datasets, while our locally-biased model performed on par with the original GPT-2 model in the UCL datasets, and worse than its counterpart in the NatStor corpus. We noted that the relative performance of the locally biased model was particularly improved in datasets with long average sentence length (MECO, Provo, and Brown). Indeed, the Pearson correlation between mean sentence length (i.e., average number of word per sentence) and ΔAIC is $r = -0.77$ ($p = 0.07$). While the number of observations ($N = 6$) and the absence of statistical significance does not license strong conclusions on this regard, we remark that this trend is compatible with the idea of a lossy representation of the context, where memory constraints are more pronounced in processing longer text sequences.

Do large language models resemble humans in language use?

Zhenguang G. Cai[1,2], Xufeng Duan[1], David A. Haslett[1], Shuqi Wang[1], Martin J. Pickering[3]

1 Department of Linguistics and Modern Languages, The Chinese University of Hong Kong
2 Brain and Mind Institute, The Chinese University of Hong Kong
3 Department of Psychology, University of Edinburgh
zhenguangcai@cuhk.edu.hk, xufeng.duan@link.cuhk.edu.hk, david.a.haslett@link.cuhk.edu.hk, ShuqiWang@link.cuhk.edu.hk, martin.pickering@ed.ac.uk

Abstract

It is unclear whether large language models (LLMs) develop humanlike characteristics in language use. We subjected ChatGPT and Vicuna to 12 pre-registered psycholinguistic experiments ranging from sounds to dialogue. ChatGPT and Vicuna replicated the human pattern of language use in 10 and 7 out of the 12 experiments, respectively. The models associated unfamiliar words with different meanings depending on their forms, continued to access recently encountered meanings of ambiguous words, reused recent sentence structures, attributed causality as a function of verb semantics, and accessed different meanings and retrieved different words depending on an interlocutor's identity. In addition, ChatGPT, but not Vicuna, nonliterally interpreted implausible sentences that were likely to have been corrupted by noise, drew reasonable inferences, and overlooked semantic fallacies in a sentence. Finally, unlike humans, neither model preferred using shorter words to convey less informative content, nor did they use context to resolve syntactic ambiguities. We discuss how these convergences and divergences may result from the transformer architecture. Overall, these experiments demonstrate that LLMs such as ChatGPT (and Vicuna to a lesser extent) are humanlike in many aspects of human language processing.

1 Introduction

The formal linguistic competence apparent in LLMs has led to debates over whether they can serve as cognitive models of human language use (see Mahowald et al., 2023). On the one hand, Chomsky argued that humans are endowed with an innate universal grammar (e.g., Chomsky, 2000), and he and colleagues maintain that this "genetically installed 'operating system'... is completely different from that of a machine learning program" (Chomsky et al., 2023, para. 6) such as ChatGPT, which is simply "a lumbering statistical engine for pattern matching" (para. 5). More optimistic researchers, however, argue that deep neural networks suffice to learn syntactic structure (Piantadosi, 2023), as evidenced by the fact that LLMs abide by complex grammatical rules (e.g., Goldberg, 2019; Linzen & Baroni, 2021; McCoy et al., 2019).

This debate emphasizes grammar, but regularities in language range from phonology to pragmatics. For example, people associate different sounds with different referents (e.g., Köhler, 1929), automatically reinterpret implausible sentences (e.g., Gibson et al., 2013), and expect demographically appropriate content from speakers (e.g., Van Berkum et al., 2008). Do LLMs share these regularities in language use? Piantadosi (2023) pointed out that LLMs integrate syntax and semantics (i.e., all aspects of usage are represented in a single vector space), so other humanlike regularities in language use might emerge along with grammaticality and coherence.

We therefore subjected two LLMs—ChatGPT, from OpenAI (2022), and Vicuna (with 13B parameters), from the Large Model Systems Organization (Chiang et al., 2023)—to a battery of psycholinguistic tests, in 12 preregistered experiments per LLM (with default temperature). These experiments span a range of linguistic levels from sounds to discourse, with two experiments per level. In each experiment, each item was presented to each LLM 1000 times. We used mixed effects modelling to analyse model responses as a function of the experimental manipulations. The

Proceedings of the Workshop on Cognitive Modeling and Computational Linguistics, pages 37–56
August 15, 2024 ©2024 Association for Computational Linguistics

preregistrations, data, and analytical codes are available at osf.io/vu2h3/ (ChatGPT) and osf.io/sygku/ (Vicuna).

2 RESULTS

Sounds: sound-shape association

People tend to associate certain sounds with certain shapes. They assume, for instance, that a novel word such as *takete* or *kiki* refers to a spiky object, whereas a novel word such as *maluma* or *bouba* refers to a round object (Köhler, 1929). We asked ChatGPT and Vicuna to decide if a novel word (10 round-sounding and 10 spiky-sounding, according to Sidhu & Pexman, 2017) refers to a spiky shape or a round shape. Both LLMs assigned round-sounding novel words to round shapes more often than they assigned spiky-sounding novel words to round shapes (ChatGPT: 0.79 vs. 0.49, $\beta = 2.02$, $SE = 0.34$, $z = 5.87$, $p < .001$; Vicuna: 0.38 vs. 0.32, $\beta = 0.27$, $SE = 0.11$, $z = 2.34$, $p = .019$; see Fig 1 top left).

Sounds: sound-gender association

People can guess at above-chance rates whether an unfamiliar name refers to a man or a woman based on how it sounds (Cassidy et al., 1999; Cutler et al., 1990). In English, for example, women's names end in vowels more often than men's names do. We asked ChatGPT and Vicuna to complete 16 preambles containing a consonant-ending or vowel-ending novel name (e.g., *Although Pelcrad / Pelcra was sick...*). Both LLMs were more likely to use a feminine pronoun (*she/her/hers*; e.g., *Although Pelcra was sick,* she *refused to stay in bed and insisted on completing all her tasks for the day*) to refer to vowel-ending names than to consonant-ending names (ChatGPT: 0.71 vs. 0.25, $\beta = 4.33$, $SE = 1.24$, $z = 3.50$, $p < .001$; Vicuna: 0.40 vs. 0.02, $\beta = 5.77$, $SE = 1.23$, $z = 4.70$, $p < .001$; see Fig 1 top right).

Words: word length and predictivity

Corpus evidence suggests that words which carry less information tend to be shorter, making

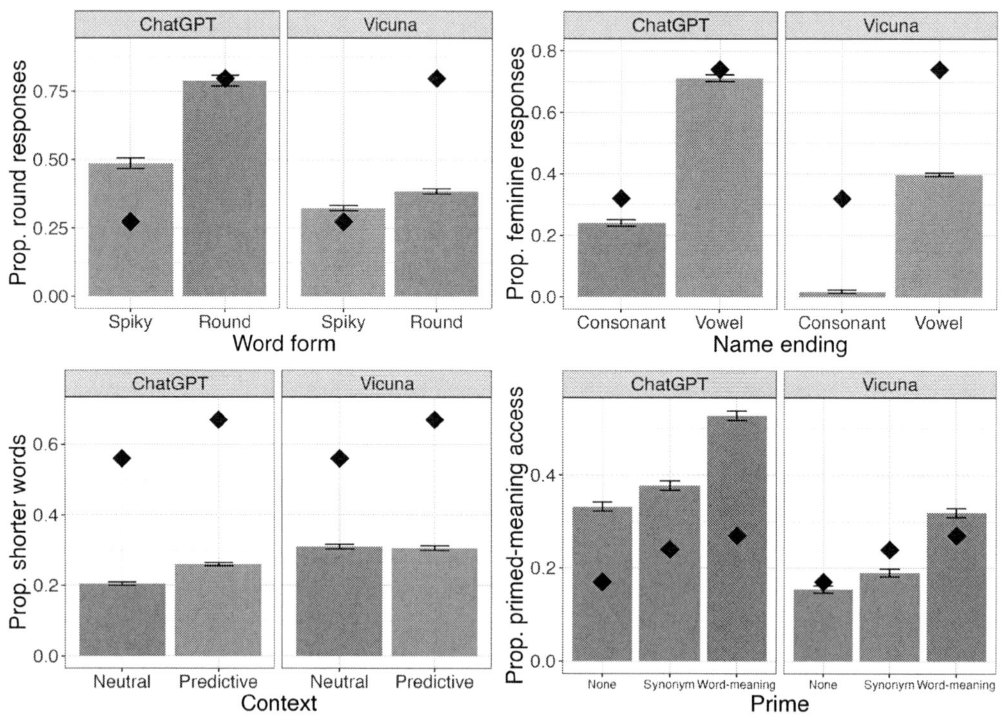

Fig 1. Results of sound-shape associations (top left), sound-gender associations (top right), word length and predictivity (bottom left), and word meaning priming (bottom right). Diamonds stand for human conditional means in existing studies. Error bars stand for 95% confidence intervals.

communication more efficient (e.g., Piantadosi et al., 2011). In support of this hypothesis, Mahowald et al. (2013) showed that, when asked to choose between a shorter and a longer word of nearly identical meanings (e.g., *math* and *mathematics*), participants more often chose the shorter word when the sentence preamble was predictive of the meaning of the target word (i.e., when the word is less informative; e.g., *Susan was very bad at algebra, so she hated...*) than when it was neutral (e.g., *Susan introduced herself to me as someone who loved...*). We replicated Mahowald et al. (2013) on ChatGPT/Vicuna (with 20 items). Neither model was significantly more likely to choose shorter words following predictive than neutral preambles (ChatGPT: 0.26 vs. 0.20, β = 0.35, SE = 0.21, z = 1.64, p = .101; Vicuna: 0.31 vs. 0.31, β = -0.15, SE = 0.20, z = -0.77, p = .444; see Fig 1 bottom left).

Words: word meaning priming

People tend to access the more recently encountered meaning of an ambiguous word (word meaning priming: e.g., Rodd et al., 2013). For example, participants more often supplied an associate related to the job meaning (instead of the mail meaning) of *post* if they had recently read a sentence using that meaning (e.g., *The man accepted the post in the accountancy firm*) than if they had recently read a sentence using a synonym (e.g., *The man accepted the job in the accountancy firm*) or if they had not read such a sentence. We first presented ChatGPT and Vicuna with a set of 44 sentences (adapted from Rodd et al., 2013), including 13 word-meaning primes, 13 synonym primes, and 18 filler sentences; afterwards, we presented them with 39 ambiguous cue words (e.g., *post*) and asked the models to provide an associate, with 13 words per condition, and we measured the proportion of associates related to the primed meaning (e.g., *work*). Neither LLMs produced significantly more associates related to the primed meaning in the synonym condition than the no-prime condition (ChatGPT: 0.38 vs. 0.33, β = 0.36, SE = 0.19, z = 1.90, p = .057; Vicuna: 0.19 vs. 0.15, β = 0.39, SE = 0.28, z = 1.40, p = .162; see Fig 1 bottom right). Crucially, both models produced more associates related to the primed meaning in the word-meaning condition than in the no-prime condition (ChatGPT: 0.53 vs. 0.33, β = 2.47, SE = 0.30, z = 8.20, p < .001; Vicuna: 0.32 vs. 0.15, β = 3.33, SE = 0.50, z = 6.70, p < .001) and also than in the synonym condition (ChatGPT: 0.53 vs. 0.38, β = 2.14, SE = 0.32, z = 6.71, p < .001; Vicuna: 0.32 vs. 0.19, β = 2.86, SE = 0.48, z = 5.91, p < .001). These finding suggest that both LLMs are susceptible to word-meaning priming.

Syntax: structural priming

People tend to repeat a syntactic structure that they have recently encountered (structural priming; e.g., Bock, 1986). For instance, Pickering & Branigan (1998) had participants first complete a prime preamble that was designed to induce a completion of either a double-object (DO) dative structure (e.g., *The racing driver gave/showed the helpful mechanic ...*) or a prepositional-object (PO) dative structure (e.g., *The racing driver gave/showed the torn overall to ...*) and then complete a target preamble that could be continued as either a DO or a PO (e.g., *The patient showed ...*). Participants tended to complete a target preamble using the same structure that they used in completing a prime preamble, and the priming effect was larger when the target had the same than a different verb as the prime (e.g., when the prime preamble had the verb *showed* instead of *gave*). Following Pickering & Branigan (1998), we presented ChatGPT and Vicuna with 32 prime-target pairs consisting of a prime preamble followed by a target preamble. We measured whether ChatGPT completed a target preamble using a PO or DO structure (e.g., *The patient showed his hand to the nurse* vs. *The patient showed the nurse his hand*). We observed structural priming in both LLMs, with a higher proportion of PO completions of a target preamble when the corresponding prime preamble had been completed as a PO than when it had been completed as a DO (ChatGPT: 0.71 vs. 0.58, β = 1.03, SE = 0.12, z = 8.68, p < .001; Vicuna: 0.81 vs. 0.51, β = 2.93, SE = 0.34, z = 8.70, p < .001; see Fig 2 top left). Verb type (different vs. same verbs across prime and target) did not have an effect on completions for either model (ChatGPT: 0.66 vs. 0.63, β = -0.06, SE = 0.09, z = -0.67, p = .504; Vicuna: 0.66 vs. 0.66, β = -0.14, SE = 0.23, z = -0.61, p = .545). But, importantly, verb type interacted with prime structure, indicating a lexical boost, with a stronger priming effect when the prime and the target had the same verb

(ChatGPT: $\beta = 0.40$, $SE = 0.15$, $z = 2.73$, $p = .006$: Vicuna: $\beta = 1.20$, $SE = 0.45$, $z = 2.68$, $p = .007$). These findings suggest that ChatGPT and Vicuna resemble humans in being susceptible to structural priming and the lexical boost.

Syntax: syntactic ambiguity resolution

In what is known as the verb phrase/noun phrase (VP/NP) ambiguity (e.g., *The ranger killed the dangerous poacher with the rifle*), people tend to interpret the syntactically ambiguous prepositional phrase (PP, *with the rifle*) as modifying the VP (*kill the dangerous poacher*; VP attachment) rather than the noun phrase (*the dangerous poacher*; NP attachment) (e.g., Rayner et al., 1983). Critically, humans use contextual information to resolve the ambiguity and were more likely to have NP attachments when the discourse has introduced multiple possible referents than a single referent for the NP (e.g., *There was a hunter and a poacher / two poachers;* Altmann & Steedman, 1988). We tested whether LLMs also use context to disambiguate the VP/NP ambiguity. After reading a discourse sentence (introducing a single referent or multiple possible referents for the critical NP) followed by a sentence containing the VP/NP ambiguity, ChatGPT/Vicuna answered a question regarding the ambiguous sentence (with a total of 32 sets of stimuli). We manipulated whether the question probes the VP attachment (e.g., *Did the hunter use a rifle?*) or the NP attachment (e.g., *Did the dangerous poacher have a rifle?*). Both models attached the ambiguous PP more often to the VP than to the NP (ChatGPT: 0.94 vs. 0.06, $\beta = -9.43$, $SE = 0.72$, $z = -13.04$, $p < .001$; Vicuna: 0.63 vs. 0.37, $\beta = -1.37$, $SE = 0.16$, $z = -8.35$, $p < .001$; see Fig 2 top right). There were similar NP attachments in the multiple-referent context and in the single-referent context (ChatGPT: 0.06 vs. 0.06, $\beta = -0.08$, $SE = 0.43$, $z = -0.18$, $p = .861$; Vicuna: 0.37 vs. 0.36, $\beta = 0.18$, $SE = 0.10$, $z = 1.87$, $p = .061$), but more NP attachments when answering an NP probe than when answering a VP probe (ChatGPT: 0.09 vs. 0.03, $\beta = 3.27$, $SE =$

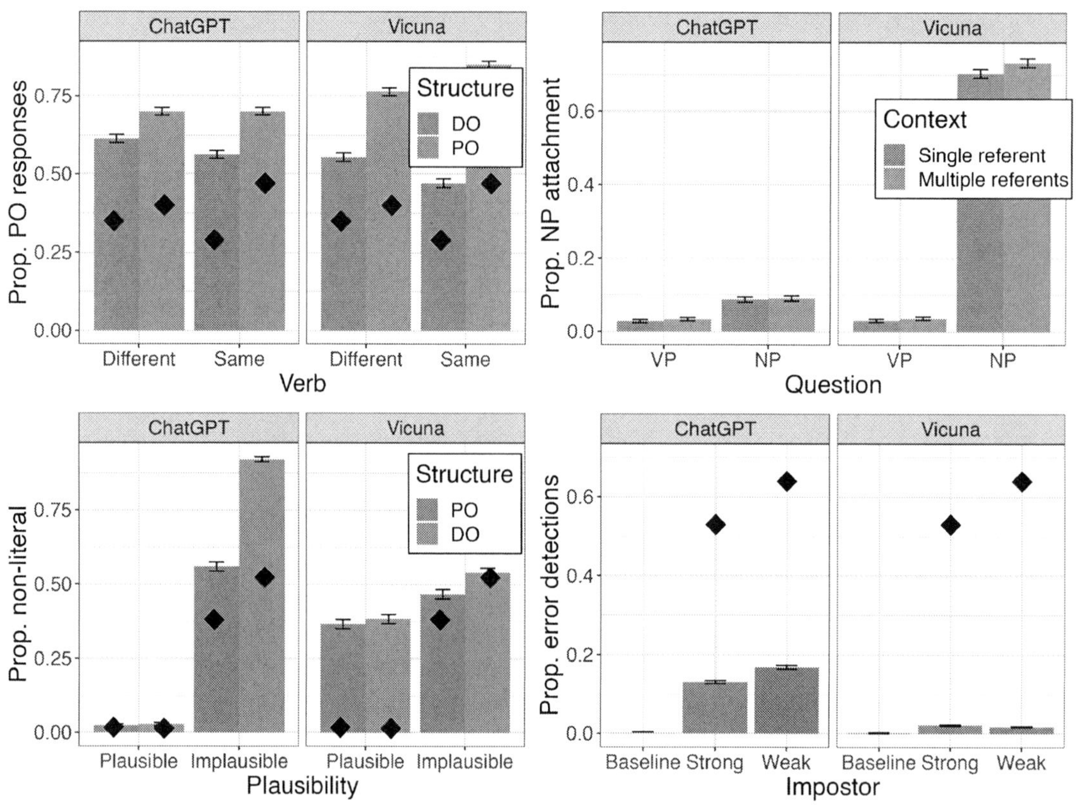

Fig 2. Results of structural priming (top left), syntactic ambiguity resolution (top right), implausible sentence interpretation (bottom left), and semantic illusions (bottom right). Diamonds stand for human conditional means in existing studies. Error bars stand for 95% confidence intervals.

0.97, $z = 3.36$, $p < .001$; Vicuna: 0.72 vs. 0.03, $\beta = 5.63$, $SE = 0.48$, $z = 11.78$, $p < .001$). There was no significant interaction between context and question (ChatGPT: $\beta = 0.13$, $SE = 0.74$, $z = 0.18$, $p = .861$; Vicuna: $\beta = -0.16$, $SE = 0.24$, $z = -0.66$, $p = .511$). These findings suggest, first of all, that neither ChatGPT nor Vicuna used contextual information to resolve syntactic ambiguities (at least the VP/NP ambiguity) as humans do and they might retain multiple representations of the ambiguous sentence (i.e., treating *with the rifle* as potentially modifying both *the poacher* and *kill the poacher*).

Meaning: implausible sentence interpretation

Listeners sometimes have to recover an intended message from noise-corrupted input (Gibson et al., 2013; Levy et al., 2009). For example, an error in production or comprehension may turn a plausible sentence into an implausible one when a word is omitted (e.g., *to* being omitted from a plausible PO such as *The mother gave the candle to the daughter*, resulting in an implausible DO such as *The mother gave the candle the daughter*) or when a word gets inserted (e.g., *to* being inserted into a plausible DO such as *The mother gave the daughter the candle*, resulting in an implausible PO such as *The mother gave the daughter to the candle*). If people believe that an implausible sentence results from a plausible sentence being noise-corrupted, then they can interpret the implausible sentence nonliterally to recover the intended message. Gibson et al. (2013) showed that people nonliterally interpret implausible DO sentences more often than implausible PO sentences, probably because they believe that omissions of *to* are more likely than insertions of *to*. We presented ChatGPT and Vicuna with 20 sentences (plausible or implausible, in a DO or PO structure), each followed by a yes/no question (e.g., *Did the daughter receive something/someone?*) probing whether the sentence is literally or nonliterally interpreted. ChatGPT made more nonliteral interpretations for implausible than plausible sentences (0.74 vs. 0.03, $\beta = 10.85$, $SE = 0.73$, $z = 14.80$, $p < .001$; see Fig 2 bottom left), whereas the difference did not reach significance for Vicuna (0.50 vs. 0.37, $\beta = 2.20$, $SE = 1.24$, $z = 1.77$, $p = .076$). There was an effect of structure on interpretation in ChatGPT, with more nonliteral interpretations for DO than PO sentences (0.47 vs. 0.29, $\beta = 1.15$, $SE = 0.58$, $z = 1.94$, $p = .047$), but not in Vicuna (0.46 vs. 0.42, $\beta = 0.04$, $SE = 0.36$, $z = 0.11$, $p = .910$). The interaction between plausibility and structure was significant such that the increase in nonliteral interpretations for the DO structure compared to the PO structure was larger when a sentence was implausible than when it was plausible in both ChatGPT ($\beta = 4.47$, $SE = 1.17$, $z = 3.81$, $p < .001$) and in Vicuna ($\beta = 1.40$, $SE = 0.69$, $z = 2.02$, $p = .043$). Critically, when we examined the implausible sentences alone, there was humanlike pattern of interpretations in ChatGPT, with more nonliteral interpretations for implausible DO sentences than for implausible PO sentences (0.92 vs. 0.56, $\beta = 3.40$, $SE = 0.74$, $z = 4.59$, $p < .001$) but not in Vicuna (0.54 vs. 0.47, $\beta = 0.77$, $SE = 0.57$, $z = 1.35$, $p = .178$). These findings suggest that ChatGPT (but not Vicuna) was sensitive to syntactic structure, like humans, in the interpretation of implausible sentences.

Meaning: semantic illusions

People often fail to notice what seem to be conspicuous errors in sentences. For example, when asked the question *Snoopy is a black and white cat in what famous Charles Schulz comic strip?*, many people do not notice that Snoopy, from the comic strip *Peanuts*, is a not a cat but a dog. People are more likely to notice an erroneous word when it is semantically less similar to *dog*, such as *mouse* as in *Snoopy is a black and white mouse in what famous Charles Schulz comic strip?* (Erickson & Mattson, 1981). Such semantic illusions suggest that representing word meanings while processing sentences involves partial matches in semantic memory (Reder & Kusbit, 1991). We asked ChatGPT and Vicuna trivia questions that contained a semantically appropriate keyword (baseline), a strong (semantically closely related) impostor, or a weak impostor (e.g., *Snoopy is a black and white dog / cat / mouse in what famous Charles Schulz comic strip?*), with a total of 54 sentences in three conditions, taken from Hannon and Daneman (2001). Following Erickson and Mattson (1981) and Hannon and Daneman (2001), we instructed the models either to answer the question or, if they detected a semantic error (which we illustrated with an example), to say *wrong* (i.e., to report an error). For ChatGPT, compared to the baseline condition, there were more errors reported in the strong impostor condition (0.00 vs. 0,13, $\beta = 0.87$, $SE = 0.00$, $z = 122035$, $p < .001$; see Fig 2 bottom right) and in the weak impostor condition (0.00 vs. 0.17, $\beta = 2.83$, $SE = 0.00$, $z = 677303$, $p < .001$); critically, more errors were reported in the weak than strong imposter condition (0.17 vs. 0.13, $\beta = 1.71$, $SE = 0.82$, $z = 2.10$, $p = .036$). For Vicuna, there similar proportions of errors reported between the baseline and the strong imposter condition (0.002 vs. 0.022, $\beta = -3.01$, $SE = 1.65$, $z = -1.82$, $p = .069$) and between the baseline and the weak imposter condition (0.002 vs. 0.017, $\beta = 0.82$, $SE = 1.27$, $z = 0.65$, $p = .517$); interestingly, we observed significantly more errors reported in the weak than strong imposter condition ($\beta = 3.96$, $SE = 1.31$, $z = 3.02$, $p = .003$), though numerically the mean error report rate was lower in the weak than strong imposter condition (0.017 vs. 0.022). These findings that ChatGPT, but not Vicuna, has the humanlike tendency to gloss over a conspicuous error caused by an expression that is semantically similar to the intended expression.

Discourse: implicit causality

Some verbs lead people to attribute causality to either the subject or the object (Brown & Fish, 1983; Garvey & Caramazza, 1974). For example, a stimulus-experiencer verb such as *scare* often leads people to attribute causality to the subject (e.g., completing *Gary scared Anna because...* with *he was violent*) while an experiencer-stimulus verb such as *fear* often leads people to attribute causality to the object (e.g., completing *Gary feared Anna because...* with *she was violent*). We asked and Vicuna to complete sentences adapted from Fukumura and van Gompel (2010), manipulated to elicit pronouns referring to either subject or objects, with 32 sentences in two conditions. Both LLMs more often completed a sentence with a pronoun referring to the object (e.g., *Gary scared/feared*

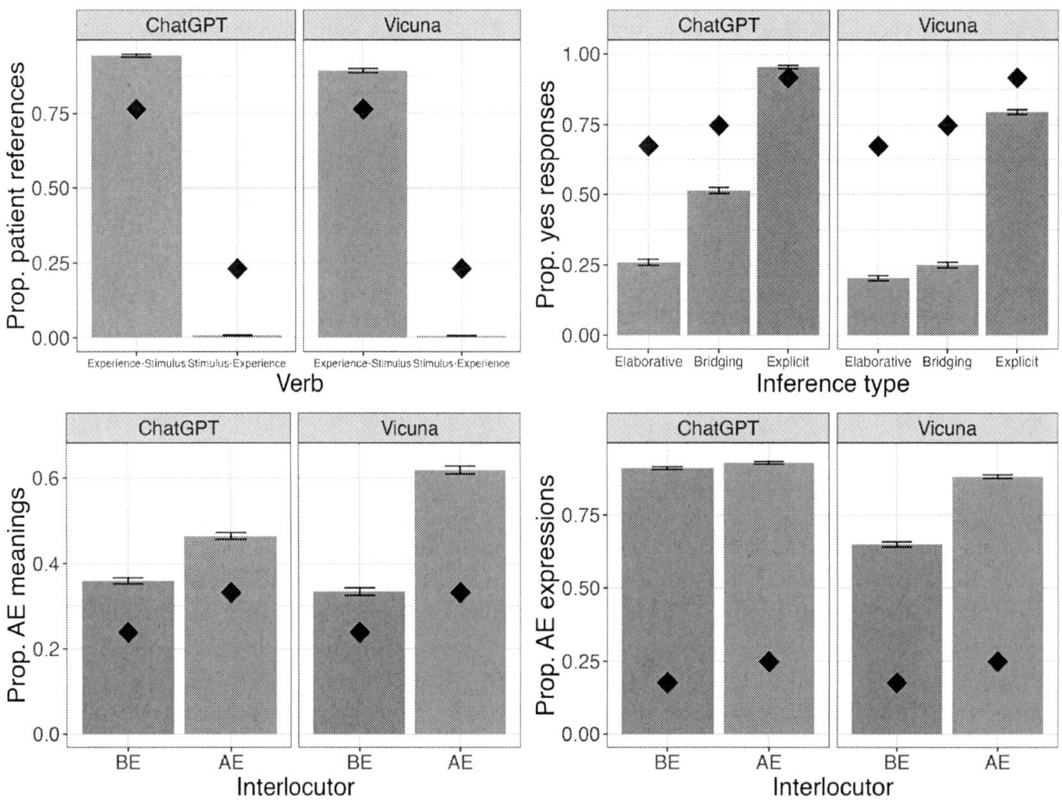

Fig 3. Results of implicit causality (top left), drawing inferences (top right), interlocutor-sensitive word meaning access (bottom left), and interlocutor-sensitive lexical retrieval (bottom right). Diamonds stand for human conditional means in existing studies. Error bars stand for 95% confidence intervals.

Anna because she/he was violent) following an experiencer-stimulus verb such as *fear* than following a stimulus-experiencer verb such as *scare* (ChatGPT: 0.95 vs. 0.00, β = 14.17, *SE* = 0.94, z = 15.11, p < .001; Vicuna: .89 vs. 0.01, β = 14.95, *SE* = 1.57, z = 9.51, p < .001; see Fig 3 top left). These findings suggest that LLMs are sensitive to a verb's semantic biases.

Discourse: drawing inferences

People can make bridging inferences, which connect two pieces of information, more often than they make elaborative inferences, which extrapolate from a single piece of information (Singer & Spear, 2015). For instance, when asking a question like *Did she cut her foot?*, people always (almost) answer "yes" after reading *While swimming in the shallow water near the rocks, Sharon cut her foot on a piece of glass. She had been looking for the watch that she misplaced while sitting on the rocks*, where the message is explicitly stated. They often answer "yes" after reading *While swimming in the shallow water near the rocks, Sharon stepped on a piece of glass. She called desperately for help, but there was no one around to hear her*, as they can make a bridging inference. But they are less likely to answer "yes" after reading *While swimming in the shallow water near the rocks, Sharon stepped on a piece of glass. She had been looking for the watch that she misplaced while sitting on the rocks*, as an elaborative inference is required. We presented ChatGPT and Vicuna with a short passage and a yes/no question, with 24 items based on the design of Singer and Spear (2015) and using materials adapted from McKoon and Ratcliff (1986). A passage either contained explicit information, required a bridging inference, or required an elaborative inference. As all 24 target items were likely to elicit "yes" responses, we also presented the models with 24 fillers designed to elicit "no" responses. Both LLMs produced fewer "yes" responses in the bridging condition than in the explicit condition (ChatGPT: 0.51 vs. 0.95, β = -5.06, *SE* = 0.10, z = - 50.16, p < .001; Vicuna: 0.25 vs. 0.79, β = -4.32, *SE* = 0.50, z = - 8.65, p < .001; see Fig 3 top right) and fewer "yes" responses in the elaborative than explicit condition (ChatGPT: 0.26 vs. 0.95, β = - 7.40, *SE* = 0.12, z = - 62.68, p < .001; Vicuna: 0.20 vs. 0.79, β = -4.41, *SE* = 0.41, z = - 10.73, p < .001). Critically, ChatGPT gave fewer "yes" responses in the elaborative than bridging condition (0.26 vs. 0.51, β = -2.87, *SE* = 0.58, z = -4.93, p < .001), whereas Vicuna gave similar "yes" responses for the bridging and elaborative conditions (0.25 vs. 0.20, β = -0.09, *SE* = 0.42, z = -0.22, p = .830). These findings suggest that ChatGPT, but not Vicuna, is less likely to make elaborative than bridging inferences.

Interlocutor sensitivity: word meaning access

Words and other expressions may mean different things to different people. For example, speakers of British English (BE) typically interpret *bonnet* as referring to a car part, while speakers of American English (AE) typically interpret *bonnet* as referring to a hat, and listeners take such demographic attributes of speakers into account when comprehending language (e.g., Cai et al., 2017; Van Berkum et al., 2008). For instance, Cai et al. (2017) showed that BE-speaking participants were more likely to access AE meanings of cross-dialectally ambiguous words (e.g., *bonnet, gas*) when the words were spoken in an AE than a BE accent. ChatGPT and Vicuna, at the time of testing, did not take spoken input, so we manipulated the interlocutor's dialectal background by explicitly telling ChatGPT and Vicuna that the interlocutor was a BE/AE speaker (*Hi, I am a British / American English speaker. I am from the UK / USA. I am now living in London / New Year and studying for a BA degree at King's College London / the City University of New York*). We then presented, one at a time, 36 cross-dialectally ambiguous words (taken from Cai et al., 2017) and asked ChatGPT and Vicuna to give an associate to each word. We coded whether the models accessed the BE or AE meaning of these words based on the associates it gave (e.g., "hat" as an associate to *bonnet* would suggest that ChatGPT accessed the word's AE meaning). There was more access to the AE meaning of a target word when the interlocutor was introduced as an AE speaker than a BE speaker, in both ChatGPT (0.46 vs. 0.36, β = 1.85, *SE* = 0.26, z = 7.14, p < .001; see Fig 3 bottom left) and Vicuna (0.62 vs. 0.33, β = 2.80, *SE* = 0.54, z = 5.15, p < .001). These findings suggest that both models are sensitive to the user's dialectal background in understanding word meanings.

Interlocutor sensitivity: lexical retrieval

People can take a listener's dialectal background into account when retrieving words during language production (Cai et al., accepted in principle; Cowan et al., 2019). Using a word puzzle game, Cai et al. (accepted in principle) gave participants a definition spoken in either a BE or AE accent and asked them to type the defined word/phrase. Critically, the expected words differed between BE and AE for some of the definitions (e.g., *a housing unit common in big cities that occupies part of a single level in a building block* defines the word *flat* in BE and the word *apartment* in AE). Cai et al. found that participants produced more AE expressions for definitions spoken by an AE speaker than by a BE speaker. In the experiment, we told ChatGPT and Vicuna that the interlocutor was a BE or AE speaker (using the same introductions as in the word meaning access experiment). The interlocutor gave a definition of a word/phrase and the LLM supplied the defined word/phrase. There were more AE expressions supplied when the LLM was told that the definitions came from an AE speaker than from a BE speaker, for both ChatGPT (0.93 vs. 0.91, $\beta = 4.39$, $SE = 1.56$, $z = 2.81$, $p = .005$; see Fig 2 bottom right) and Vicuna (0.88 vs. 0.65, $\beta = 3.54$, $SE = 0.51$, $z = 6.91$, $p < .001$). These findings suggest that both models are sensitive to the user's dialectic background in their lexical choices.

3 Discussion

Our experiments showed that ChatGPT replicated human patterns in language comprehension and production in 10 out of 12 psycholinguistic tasks and Vicuna in 7 out of the same 12 tasks. We further note that the patterns of results mostly held when we removed example words/sentences presented in research papers (see Appendix C), suggesting that these effects are unlikely to be a result of LLMs explicitly learning these effects in training. These findings suggest that both models largely approximate human language processing.

Both ChatGPT and Vicuna are built on transformer architectures (Vaswani et al., 2017), which allow them to vary how much weight they assign to different tokens within recent conversation history when predicting the subsequent token. This context sensitivity can explain LLMs' humanlike tendency to re-use previously-used meaning of ambiguous words, understand and produce words in light of the interlocutor's dialectic background, make inferences, and attribute causality according to verb semantics. In addition, the fact that LLMs change semantic representations of words to fit contexts (Ethayarajh, 2019) may help to account for ChatGPT's humanlike susceptibility to semantic illusions and adjust its interpretation of implausible sentences. The tokenization method might help to capture form-meaning associations available in languages. Finally, the fact that LLMs are not trained on syntactic data but can be structurally primed suggests that they may have developed emergent syntax-like representations (Michaelov et al., 2023; Prasad et al., 2019; Sinclair et al., 2022).

In two of the experiments, neither ChatGPT nor Vicuna replicated the patterns of human participants. It is possible that the tokenization methods lead LLMs to fail to capture the effect of predictivity on word length. For example, GPT-4 segments *roach* into "ro" and "ach" and *cockroach* into "cock" and "roach"; thus, the model may fail to treat the two words as close in meaning as humans would do. In addition, both models failed to take context into account when resolving the VP/NP syntactic ambiguity (e.g., *The hunter killed the dangerous poacher with a rifle*), which is reminiscent of a similar absence of contextual effects in pragmatic understanding observed in ChatGPT (Qiu et al., 2023). This finding is surprising given LLM's superb ability using contextual information. It is also interesting that ChatGPT replicated more humanlike patterns of language use than Vicuna did (10 versus 7 out of the 12 experiments). Given that increasing model size or training data improves performance (e.g., Devlin et al., 2019), we assume that this difference in mimicking the nuances of human language use should be attributed to Vicuna being a smaller model than GPT-3.5.

In conclusion, our results point to the interesting possibility that LLMs such as ChatGPT (and Vicuna to a lesser extent) can be used, by psycholinguists and cognitive psychologists, as models of language users (e.g., Aher et al., 2023; Argyle et al., 2023; Jain et al., 2023). Perhaps researchers can experiment with LLMs to generate hypotheses, assess the replicability of existing psycholinguistic effects, estimate effect sizes, and model language development.

4 Limitations

There are several limitations worth noting. First, the selection of the 12 psycholinguistic tasks might seem arbitrary and lack robust justification, raising concerns about the potential bias towards tasks where LLMs are inherently more successful. Second, there were inherent discrepancies in the experimental designs used for LLMs compared to those for human studies, encompassing differences in materials, procedures, and contexts. Third, many experiments do not include direct comparisons between LLM and human behaviours due to the unavailability of data in corresponding human studies.

References

Altmann, G., & Steedman, M. (1988). Interaction with context during human sentence processing. *Cognition*, *30*(3), 191–238. https://doi.org/10.1016/0010-0277(88)90020-0

Aher, G. V., Arriaga, R. I., & Kalai, A. T. (2023, July). Using large language models to simulate multiple humans and replicate human subject studies. *Proceedings of the 40th International Conference on Machine Learning, PMLR 202:337-371.* https://proceedings.mlr.press/v202/aher23a.html

Argyle, L. P., Busby, E. C., Fulda, N., Gubler, J. R., Rytting, C., & Wingate, D. (2023). Out of one, many: Using language models to simulate human samples. *Political Analysis*, *31*(3), 337-351. https://doi.org/10.1017/pan.2023.2

Bock, J. K. (1986). Syntactic persistence in language production. *Cognitive Psychology*, *18*(3), 355–387. https://doi.org/10.1016/0010-0285(86)90004-6

Brown, R., & Fish, D. (1983). The psychological causality implicit in language. *Cognition*, *14*(3), 237–273. https://doi.org/10.1016/0010-0277(83)90006-9

Cai, Z. G., Dunn, M. S., & Branigan, H. P. (accepted in principle). How do speakers tailor lexical choices according to their interlocutor's accent? *Journal of Experimental Psychology: Learning, Memory, and Cognition*. https://osf.io/b3fcm/

Cai, Z. G., Gilbert, R. A., Davis, M. H., Gaskell, M. G., Farrar, L., Adler, S., & Rodd, J. M. (2017). Accent modulates access to word meaning: Evidence for a speaker-model account of spoken word recognition. *Cognitive Psychology*, *98*, 73–101. https://doi.org/10.1016/j.cogpsych.2017.08.003

Cassani, G., Chuang, Y.-Y., & Baayen, R. H. (2020). On the semantics of nonwords and their lexical category. *Journal of Experimental Psychology: Learning, Memory, and Cognition*, *46*(4), 621. https://doi.org/10.1037/xlm0000747

Cassidy, K. W., Kelly, M. H., & Sharoni, L. J. (1999). Inferring gender from name phonology. *Journal of Experimental Psychology: General*, *128*(3), 362–381. https://doi.org/10.1037/0096-3445.128.3.362

Chiang, W.-L., Li, Z., Lin, Z., Sheng, Y., Wu, Z., Zhang, H., Zheng, L., Zhuang, S., Zhuang, Y., & Gonzalez, J. E. (2023). Vicuna: An open-source chatbot impressing gpt-4 with 90%* chatgpt quality. https://lmsys.org/blog/2023-03-30-vicuna/

Chomsky, N. (2000). *New horizons in the study of language and mind*. Cambridge University Press.

Chomsky, N., Roberts, I., & Watumull, J. (2023, March 8). *Noam Chomsky: The false promise of ChatGPT*. The New York Times. https://archive.is/AgWkn#selection-317.0-317.13

Cowan, B. R., Doyle, P., Edwards, J., Garaialde, D., Hayes-Brady, A., Branigan, H. P., Cabral, J., & Clark, L. (2019). What's in an accent? The impact of accented synthetic speech on lexical choice in human-machine dialogue. *Proceedings of the 1st International Conference on Conversational User Interfaces*, 1–8. https://doi.org/10.1145/3342775.3342786

Cutler, A., McQueen, J., & Robinson, K. (1990). Elizabeth and John: Sound patterns of men's and women's names. *Journal of Linguistics*, *26*(2), 471–482. https://doi.org/doi:10.1017/S0022226700014754

Devlin, J., Chang, M.-W., Lee, K., & Toutanova, K. (2019). *BERT: Pre-training of Deep Bidirectional Transformers for Language Understanding*. arXiv. https://doi.org/10.48550/arXiv.1810.04805

Erickson, T. D., & Mattson, M. E. (1981). From words to meaning: A semantic illusion. *Journal of Verbal Learning and Verbal Behavior*, *20*(5), 540–551. https://doi.org/10.1016/S0022-5371(81)90165-1

Ethayarajh, K. (2019). *How contextual are contextualized word representations? Comparing the geometry of BERT, ELMo, and GPT-2 embeddings*. arXiv. https://doi.org/10.48550/arXiv.1909.00512

Fukumura, K., & van Gompel, R. P. G. (2010). Choosing anaphoric expressions: Do people take into account likelihood of reference? *Journal of Memory and Language*, *62*(1), 52–66. https://doi.org/10.1016/j.jml.2009.09.001

Garvey, C., & Caramazza, A. (1974). Implicit causality in verbs. *Linguistic Inquiry*, *5*(3), 459–464.

Gibson, E., Bergen, L., & Piantadosi, S. T. (2013). Rational integration of noisy evidence and prior semantic expectations in sentence interpretation. *Proceedings of the National Academy of Sciences*, *110*(20), 8051–8056. https://doi.org/10.1073/pnas.1216438110

Goldberg, Y. (2019). *Assessing BERT's syntactic abilities*. https://doi.org/10.48550/arXiv.1901.05287

Hannon, B., & Daneman, M. (2001). Susceptibility to semantic illusions: An individual-differences perspective. *Memory & Cognition, 29*(3), 449–461. https://doi.org/10.3758/BF03196396

Jain, S., Vo, V. A., Wehbe, L., & Huth, A. G. (2023). Computational language modeling and the promise of in silico experimentation. *Neurobiology of Language*, 1-27. https://doi.org/10.1162/nol_a_00101

Köhler, W. (1929). *Gestalt Psychology*. Liveright.

Levy, R., Bicknell, K., Slattery, T., & Rayner, K. (2009). Eye movement evidence that readers maintain and act on uncertainty about past linguistic input. *Proceedings of the National Academy of Sciences, 106*(50), 21086–21090. https://doi.org/10.1073/pnas.0907664106

Linzen, T., & Baroni, M. (2021). Syntactic Structure from Deep Learning. *Annual Review of Linguistics, 7*(1), 195–212. https://doi.org/10.1146/annurev-linguistics-032020-051035

Mahowald, K., Fedorenko, E., Piantadosi, S. T., & Gibson, E. (2013). Info/information theory: Speakers choose shorter words in predictive contexts. *Cognition, 126*(2), 313–318. https://doi.org/10.1016/j.cognition.2012.09.010

Mahowald, K., Ivanova, A. A., Blank, I. A., Kanwisher, N., Tenenbaum, J. B., & Fedorenko, E. (2023). *Dissociating language and thought in large language models: A cognitive perspective*. arXiv. http://arxiv.org/abs/2301.06627

McCoy, R. T., Pavlick, E., & Linzen, T. (2019). *Right for the wrong reasons: Diagnosing syntactic heuristics in natural language inference*. arXiv. https://doi.org/10.48550/arXiv.1902.01007

McKoon, G., & Ratcliff, R. (1986). Inferences about predictable events. Journal of Experimental Psychology: *Learning, Memory, and Cognition*, 12, 82–91. https://doi.org/10.1037/0278-7393.12.1.82

Michaelov, J., Arnett, C., Chang, T., & Bergen, B. (2023). Structural priming demonstrates abstract grammatical representations in multilingual language models. *Proceedings of the 2023 Conference on Empirical Methods in Natural Language Processing*, 3703–3720. https://aclanthology.org/2023.emnlp-main.227/

OpenAI. (2022, November 30). *Introducing ChatGPT*. https://openai.com/blog/chatgpt

Piantadosi, S. (2023). *Modern language models refute Chomsky's approach to language*. Lingbuzz Preprint, 7180. https://lingbuzz.net/lingbuzz/007180/v1.pdf

Piantadosi, S. T., Tily, H., & Gibson, E. (2011). Word lengths are optimized for efficient communication. *Proceedings of the National Academy of Sciences, 108*(9), 3526–3529. https://doi.org/10.1073/pnas.1012551108

Pickering, M. J., & Branigan, H. P. (1998). The representation of verbs: Evidence from syntactic priming in language production. *Journal of Memory and Language, 39*(4), 633–651. https://doi.org/10.1006/jmla.1998.2592

Prasad, G., Van Schijndel, M., & Linzen, T. (2019). *Using priming to uncover the organization of syntactic representations in neural language models*. arXiv. https://doi.org/10.48550/arXiv.1909.10579

Qiu, Z., Duan, X., & Cai, Z. G. (2023). *Pragmatic Implicature Processing in ChatGPT*. PsyArXiv. https://doi.org/10.31234/osf.io/qtbh9.

Rayner, K., Carlson, M., & Frazier, L. (1983). The interaction of syntax and semantics during sentence processing: Eye movements in the analysis of semantically biased sentences. *Journal of Verbal Learning and Verbal Behavior, 22*(3), 358–374. https://doi.org/10.1016/S0022-5371(83)90236-0

Reder, L. M., & Kusbit, G. W. (1991). Locus of the Moses illusion: Imperfect encoding, retrieval, or match? *Journal of Memory and Language, 30*(4), 385–406. https://doi.org/10.1016/0749-596X(91)90013-A

Rodd, J. M., Lopez Cutrin, B., Kirsch, H., Millar, A., & Davis, M. H. (2013). Long-term priming of the meanings of ambiguous words. *Journal of Memory and Language, 68*(2), 180–198. https://doi.org/10.1016/j.jml.2012.08.002

Sidhu, D. M., & Pexman, P. M. (2017). A prime example of the Maluma/Takete effect? Testing for sound symbolic priming. *Cognitive Science, 41*(7), 1958–1987. https://doi.org/10.1111/cogs.12438

Sinclair, A., Jumelet, J., Zuidema, W., & Fernández, R. (2022). Structural persistence in language models: Priming as a window into abstract language representations. *Transactions of the Association for Computational Linguistics, 10*, 1031–1050. https://doi.org/10.1162/tacl_a_00504

Singer, M., & Spear, J. (2015). Phantom recollection of bridging and elaborative inferences. *Discourse Processes, 52*(5–6), 356–375. https://doi.org/10.1080/0163853X.2015.1029858

Van Berkum, J. J. A., van den Brink, D., Tesink, C. M. J. Y., Kos, M., & Hagoort, P. (2008). The neural integration of speaker and message. *Journal of Cognitive Neuroscience, 20*(4), 580–591. https://doi.org/10.1162/jocn.2008.20054

Vaswani, A., Shazeer, N., Parmar, N., Uszkoreit, J., Jones, L., Gomez, A. N., Kaiser, Ł., & Polosukhin, I. (2017). Attention is all you need. *Advances in Neural Information Processing Systems, 30*. https://proceedings.neurips.cc/paper/7181-attention-is-all

A Appendices – Prompts

Sounds: sound-shape association

Hi, I'd like to play a NON-WORD guessing game with you. You need to guess whether the non-word refers to a round or spiky shape, based on its pronunciation. If you don't know the meaning, just guess the shape. Please don't ask any questions. For each non-word, please say only "round" or "spiky". Is that OK?

Sounds: sound-gender association

I'd like to play a sentence completion game with you. I will provide a fragment and I would like you to repeat the fragment and complete it into a full sentence.

Words: word length and predictivity

Hi, I'd like to play a sentence completion game with you. I will provide a sentence preamble and two choices of words to complete the preamble. Please choose a word that you think best completes the sentence. For instance, if you are given the following preamble and choices: The boy went to the park to fly a ... 1. plane 2. kite. You can choose "kite" as a completion. Just give me the one word that you choose. Shall we start?

Words: word meaning priming

(Priming part) I would like to present you with a list of unrelated sentences. Please just read them; you don't have to do anything with them for now. Is that OK?

(Word association part) Next, I am going to present a list of unrelated words one by one; upon reading a word, please provide ONLY ONE word/phrase as an associate. For instance, if I say "milk", you can provide "breakfast" or "cow" as an associate. Is that OK?

Syntax: structural priming

I'd like to play a sentence completion game with you. I will provide a sentence preamble and I would like you to repeat the preamble and continue it into a full sentence.

Syntax: syntactic ambiguity resolution

I will present you a small discourse containing several sentences, followed by a question about the discourse. Please only answer "yes" or "no" to the question according to preceding discourse. For instance, if you read "There was a tiger and a fox. The tiger ate the fox because it was hungry. Did the tiger eat the fox?", you should answer "Yes" to the question. If you read "There was a tiger and a fox. The tiger ate the fox because it was hungry. Did the fox escape from the tiger?", you should answer "No" to the question. Is that OK?

Meaning: implausible sentence interpretation

I'd like to play a sentence comprehension game with you. I will give a sentence and a yes-or-no question regarding the sentence. Please simply answer "Yes" or "No" to the question. Shall we start?

Meaning: semantic illusions

I want you to answer some questions. Usually a one-word answer will be enough. If you don't know the answer, just say "don't know." You will occasionally encounter a question which has something wrong with it. For example, you might see the question: "When was President Gerald Ford forced to resign his office? " The thing that is wrong in this example is that Ford wasn't forced to resign. When you see a question like this, just say "'wrong." OK?

Discourse: implicit causality

I'd like to play a sentence completion game with you. I will provide a sentence preamble and I would like you to repeat the preamble and continue it into a full sentence.

Discourse: drawing inferences

I will present you with sentences and ask a yes or no question about those sentences. Please respond only with "yes", "no", or "don't know". Is that OK?

Interlocutor sensitivity: word meaning access

I'd like to play a word association game with you. I will give you a word, and you are to give ONE word or phrase that you think of at reading the word I gave. For example, if I say "milk", you can say "cow" or "breakfast". I will give you the first word. Shall we start?

Interlocutor sensitivity: lexical retrieval

I'd like to play a word puzzle game with you. I will give you a definition and you are to supply the word/phrase that is defined. For example, if the definition is "an electronic device for storing and processing data, typically in binary form", you can say "computer". I will give you the first definition. Please only give me the defined word/phrase. Shall we start?

B Appendices – Materials and methods

All experiments were preregistered (ChatGPT: osf.io/vu2h3/registrations; Vicuna: osf.io/sygku/registrations), with all materials and analytical plans preregistered prior to data collection and analysis. We ran the ChatGPT experiments with a web interface (https://chat.openai.com/) and the Vicuna experiments with the model's API. For ChatGPT, we adopted a multiple-trial-per-run design, as with a human participant (i.e., there were multiple trials in each session/run with ChatGPT); such a design was adopted because it reduced the number of runs/sessions as at the time of testing it was sometimes difficult to secure a session with ChatGPT. With Vicuna, we used a one-trial-per-run design, where we only presented the experimental instructions and one target trial in each run/session with the model.

Unless otherwise stated, all experiments shared some common procedures, as specified in the preregistrations. First, all ChatGPT experimental materials were assigned to different lists according to the number of within-item conditions (e.g., two lists if there were two within-item conditions) such that different experimental versions of the same item appeared in different lists; all stimuli (targets and fillers) in a list were randomly presented; note that in Vicuna experiments there was only one trial per run so no lists or fillers were needed). Second, we used a Python script to simulate a human interlocutor having a chat with ChatGPT/Vicuna. The simulated interlocutor always began with instructions regarding how the task was to be done. Third, each item in an experiment was run 1000 times with ChatGPT/Vicuna (in ChatGPT, the stimuli in a list); in our pilot, we found that ChatGPT tended to stop responding after a certain number of prompts, so for experiments with more than 70 trials, we split the stimuli into two blocks and ran each block 1000 times. If an experimental run ended prematurely, the run was replaced. The experimental instructions for the experiments can be found in Supplement Information.

Sounds: sound-shape association

There were 20 trials, 10 with a novel word deemed spiky-sounding by human participants (Sidhu & Pexman, 2017) and 10 with a round-sounding novel word (osf.io/6wxp3); in each trial, we presented a novel word (e.g., *tuhkeetee*) and ChatGPT/Vicuna decided whether it referred to a round or spiky shape. We used a Python script to automatically extract "round" and "spiky" from the responses. Responses where automatic text extraction failed to detect a "round" or "spiky" response or where it detected both a "round" and a "spiky" response were coded by a native English speaker (as "round" or "spiky", or, if neither or both apply, as "other") in a condition-blind manner. Sometimes ChatGPT provided a justification or elaboration for its answer; in this case, we used the shape judgement but ignore the elaboration. We excluded "other" responses from the analysis (0.5% and 2.6% of all the data respectively for ChatGPT and Vicuna).

Sounds: sound-gender association

There were 16 target trials and 16 filler trials (osf.io/7yrf8). In a target trial, we presented a preamble that contained a novel name as the subject of the preamble (e.g., *Although Pelcrad was sick ...*) and ChatGPT/Vicuna completed the preamble into a full sentence (e.g., *Although Pelcrad was sick, he got up and went to work*). We determined whether ChatGPT/Vicuna referred to the novel name as feminine or masculine by first automatically extracting pronouns (*she/her/hers* or *he/him/his*) from ChatGPT/Vicuna completions. For responses where no pronoun or multiple pronouns of different genders were detected, we had a native speaker of English determine if the novel name was referred to as feminine or masculine. If a response was judged to refer to the novel name as neither feminine nor masculine, or not to refer to the novel name at all, then it was coded as an "other" response and was excluded from further analyses (24.3% and 7.8% of all the data respectively for ChatGPT and Vicuna).

Words: word length and predictivity

The stimuli were the same as in Mahowald et al. (2013), consisting of 40 target items and 40 fillers (osf.io/n645c), divided into two blocks (10 targets and 10 fillers in each block). In a trial, we presented ChatGPT with a sentence preamble with the last word missing and ChatGPT/Vicuna chose between two words (e.g., *Susan was very bad at algebra, so she hated... 1. math 2. mathematics.*). For ChatGPT, the order of the two choices was counter-balanced across lists (i.e., the order of the long and short candidate words was counterbalanced: On each run, we presented ChatGPT with one of two lists, each containing one order for each item, and 20 short-first and 20 long-first stimuli). We coded whether ChatGPT/Vicuna chose the short or long word in a target trial.

Words: word meaning priming

The experiment consisted of two parts: a priming part and a word association part. In the priming part, we presented a set of 44 sentences in one go to ChatGPT/Vicuna, including 13 word-meaning primes, 13 synonym primes and 18 filler sentences (osf.io/ym7hg); note that when a target word was in the no-prime condition, there was no prime sentence in the priming part. This was immediately followed by the word association part (for ChatGPT, all the 39 ambiguous words were presented one by one in a random order on a run; for Vicuna, only one ambiguous word was presented on a run). For each of 39 target ambiguous words (e.g., *post*), ChatGPT gave an associate (e.g., *mail*). We used the algorithm and database developed by Gilbert and Rodd (2022) to code whether an associate related to the (primed) subordinate meaning of a target word. There were 516 unique target-associate pairs not available in the database (50.2% of all unique pairs), two native speakers of English independently and condition-blindly coded whether an associate related to the subordinate meaning of the target word. Coding disagreements between the two coders (9.7% of manually-coded pairs) were resolved by a third coder, also a native speaker, in a condition-blind manner failed to provide an associate were coded as "other" and removed from further analyses (0.2% and 0% of all the data respectively for ChatGPT and Vicuna).

Syntax: structural priming

This experiment was run concurrently with the ***implicit causality*** experiment for ChatGPT (but not for Vicuna) because they had the same task and their target stimuli could serve as filler stimuli to each other. There were 64 preambles, forming 32 prime-target pairs, together with 64 filler preambles, 32 of which were experimental stimuli for the concurrent experiment (osf.io/k3cfv). For ChatGPT, these stimuli were divided into two blocks. In each pair, the prime (e.g., *The racing driver showed the helpful mechanic ...*) was always presented first for ChatGPT/Vicuna to complete (e.g., *The racing driver showed the helpful mechanic the problem with the car, hoping they would be able to fix it in time for the next race*), followed by the target preamble. For data coding, we made use of a pre-trained language model named "en_core_web_trf" (https://spacy.io/models/en) to generate dependency labels for the arguments of a verb. We specified all the verbs in model responses. The algorithm determined whether a response had a particular structure depending on the labels of the verb's arguments. To test the accuracy of the automatic coding using the algorithm, we did 5 pilot runs of the structural priming experimental items, with a total of 160 responses generated by ChatGPT (i.e., 5 runs of 1 block of 16 items). We first had these responses coded by a native speaker of English as DO, PO, or other sentences. Then we had the algorithm code the same set of model responses. There was a 100% match between the human and automatic coding (see osf.io/wkzr8 for the scripts and the coding test). We then used the algorithm to automatically code both prime and target completions as DO, PO, or "other" responses. Pairs in which either sentence was coded as "other" were removed from further analyses (22.8% and 20.3% of all the data respectively for ChatGPT and Vicuna).

Syntax: syntactic ambiguity resolution

The experiment had 32 target trials and 32 filler trials (osf.io/c28ur). A trial consisted of a context sentence and a target sentence, followed by a probe question (e.g., *There was a hunter and a poacher. The hunter killed the dangerous poacher with a rifle not long after sunset. Did the hunter use a rifle?*). ChatGPT/Vicuna was asked to answer "yes" or "no" to the probe question. We used automatic text extraction of "yes" or "no" from ChatGPT responses. If the method failed to extract "yes" or "no" from a response, a native speaker of English coded it manually and condition-blindly into "yes", "no", or "other". Responses coded as "other" were excluded from the analyses (22.8% and 20.3% of all the data respectively for ChatGPT and Vicuna).

Meaning: implausible sentence interpretation
The stimuli were taken from Experiment 1.4 in Gibson et al. (2013), with 20 target trials and 40 filler trials (osf.io/2pktf). In a target trial, we presented ChatGPT/Vicuna with a sentence (plausible or implausible, in a DO or PO structure) together with a yes/no comprehension question (e.g., *The mother gave the candle the daughter. Did the daughter receive something/someone?*). We used automatic text extraction of "yes" or "no" from model responses; in trials where no "yes" or "no" was extracted, responses were manually inspected by a native speaker of English to determine if the response indicates a "yes" or "no" response; a trial was excluded if ChatGPT/Vicuna gave no clear indication of "yes" or "no" in its response (0.7% and 0.4% respectively for ChatGPT and Vicuna). A "yes"/"no" response was further coded as a literal interpretation of a target sentence (e.g., a "no" response to *The mother gave the candle the daughter. Did the daughter receive something/someone?*) or a nonliteral interpretation (e.g., a "yes" response to the above example).

Meaning: semantic illusions
The experiment contained 72 items, with 54 targets and 18 fillers (osf.io/r67f2); we divided these stimuli into two blocks (for ChatGPT). In a trial, we presented ChatGPT/Vicuna a question (e.g., *Snoopy is a black and white cat in what famous Charles Schulz comic strip?*), which it gave an answer or reported an error if it detected something wrong with the sentence. We coded whether a semantic illusion was detected by ChatGPT/Vicuna (by answering "wrong") or not (by giving any other answer). For Vicuna, 10 responses (out of 20,000) seemed to not relevant to the target question and were removed from the analyses.

Discourse: implicit causality
The experiment was run concurrently with the ***structural priming*** experiment in ChatGPT (but not in Vicuna). The experiment contained 32 target preambles (adapted from Fukumura & van Gompel, 2010) and 96 filler preambles, 64 of which were target stimuli from the structural priming experiment (osf.io/k3cfv); these stimuli were divided into two blocks in ChatGPT (but not in Vicuna). In a target trial, we presented ChatGPT/Vicuna with a sentence preamble in the format of subject-verb-object followed by *because* (e.g., *Gary scared Anna because ...*); the subject and object were personal names that differed in gender (with name gender counter-balanced between the subject and the object across items). ChatGPT/Vicuna repeated and completed the preamble (e.g., *Gary scared Anna because he jumped out from behind a tree and yelled "boo!"*). As in the ***sound-gender association*** experiment, we used automatic text extraction (*he/him/his/* vs *she/her/hers* following *because*) to code the completion as referring to the subject or the object. For responses where automatic text extraction failed to extract the pronouns or extracted multiple pronouns that differed in gender, two native English speakers independently and condition-blindly coded those items, with a third native English speaker resolving any discrepancies between the first two coders. Responses that included no pronouns, pronouns of different genders, or were otherwise ambiguous in terms of subject/object reference were coded as "other" (17% and 5% for ChatGPT and Vicuna respectively) and removed from further analyses.

Discourse: drawing inferences
The experiment contained 48 items (24 targets and 24 fillers; osf.io/e3wxc). A filler item comprised two sentences and a yes/no question (e.g., *While swimming in the shallow water near the rocks, Sharon cut her foot on a piece of glass. She had been looking for the watch that she misplaced while sitting on the rocks. Did she cut her foot?*). For target items, the question should elicit a "yes" response if inferences were made but a "no" response if no inference was made. We used automatic text extraction to extract the "yes" and "no" answers; a native speaker manually inspected a response if no "yes" or "no" response was detected. When a response indicated a "don't

know" response (42% and 44% for ChatGPT and Vicuna respectively), it was excluded from further analyses.

Interlocutor sensitivity: word meaning access
The experiment began with a self-introduction of the simulated interlocutor. For the BE/AE interlocutor, we use the introduction "Hi, I am a British / American English speaker. I am from the UK / USA. I am now living in London / New York and studying for a BA degree at King's College London / the City University of New York"; for the AE interlocutor, we used the introduction "Hi, I am an American English speaker. I am from the USA. I am now living in New York and studying for a BA degree at the City University of New York". The experiment contained 56 trials, with 36 target words that have different meanings between BE and AE (e.g., *bonnet*, see osf.io/k2jgd) and 20 filler words that do not. A trial began with an interlocutor typing a word (e.g., *bonnet*) and ChatGPT/Vicuna gave an associate (e.g., "hat"). We filtered the data for unique responses to each target word and had two native speakers of English, who were provided with definitions of the BE and AE meanings of target words, to independently and condition-blindly code these unique responses as relating the BE meaning of the target word (e.g., "car" as relating to the vehicle meaning of *bonnet*), the AE meaning (e.g., "hat" as relating to the headdress meaning of *bonnet*), or some other meaning. Any disagreement in coding (15.5% of all unique responses) was resolved by a third coder (also a native speaker of English). Trials where the associate related to "other" meanings or the response did not provide an associate (12% and 40% for ChatGPT and Vicuna respectively) were discarded from further analyses.

Interlocutor sensitivity: lexical retrieval
The experiment began with a self-introduction of the simulated interlocutors (BE interlocutor vs. AE interlocutor), using the same wording as in the ***Interlocutor sensitivity: word meaning access*** experiment. It contained 56 definitions, half of which were target definitions for which BE and AE have different lexical expressions (e.g., *potatoes deep-fried in thin strips* defines *chips* in BE but *French fries* in AE; see osf.io/28vt4). A trial began with the interlocutor typing a definition (e.g., *potatoes deep-fried in thin strips*) and ChatGPT/Vicuna giving the defined word/phrase (e.g., *French fries*). We filtered the data for unique responses for each definition and had two coders (native speakers of English) code these responses independently and condition-blindly as a BE expression, an AE expression, or an "other" expression, in reference to the BE/AE expressions associated with each definition. Variants of the reference BE/AE expressions (e.g., "economy class" instead of "economy", "chip" instead of "chips") were accepted as BE or AE expressions. Words/phrases that did not go with the reference expressions were coded as "other". Any disagreement in coding (5.1% of all unique responses) was resolved by a third coder (also a native speaker of English and again in a condition-blind manner). Trials with "other" expressions (5% and 21% for ChatGPT and Vicuna respectively) were discarded from further analyses.

C Appendix - Additional analyses

We provided exploratory analyses (preregistered or non-preregistered) here; preregistered exploratory analyses can also be viewed in the preregistrations (osf.io/vu2h3/registrations).

Sounds: sound-shape association
In a non-preregistered analysis, we tested the possibility that an LLM might have been trained on the papers (or their abstracts) on which our experiments were based and associated a psycholinguistic effect with the exemplar stimuli used in the paper/abstract to illustrate the psycholinguistic effect. If this is the case, we should expect the effect to disappear if we removed the exemplar items from the analyses. Thus, in this experiment, we removed 6 exemplar items (e.g., *maluma*, *takete*), leaving the remaining 14 items for analyses. We observed that excluding the exemplar items did not affect the pattern of results, with round-sounding words still being judged to be round in shape more often than spike-sounding words in both ChatGPT (0.80 vs. 0.58, $\beta = 1.58$, $SE = 0.36$, $z = 4.37$, $p < .001$) and Vicuna (0.39 vs. 0.31, $\beta = 0.35$, $SE = 0.15$, $z = 2.36$, $p = .018$).

In another non-preregistered analysis, we conducted a post-test to see whether ChatGPT identified any of the novel words as English words. It identified *maluma* as an English word almost half the time (8 of 20 trials), so we conducted the same LME analyses as in the main text but while excluding that item. The effect was almost the same as when *maluma* was included: ChatGPT assigned round-sounding novel words to round shapes more often than it assigned spiky-sounding novel words to round shapes (0.79 vs. 0.49, $\beta = 2.03$, $SE = 0.36$, $z = 5.65$, $p < .001$); so did Vicuna (0.39 vs. 0.32, $\beta = 0.28$, $SE = 0.12$, $z = 2.36$, $p = .018$).

Following our preregistered exploratory correlation analysis, we had human means for 10 round-sounding items but only 8 spiky-sounding items because Sidhu and Pexman (2017) did not use one spiky-sounding word (*puhkeetee*) in the corresponding experiment and because another item (*puhtay*) elicited "spiky" judgements from humans only 42% of the time, so we replaced it (with *keepa*). We calculated the proportion of "round" responses for each item and compared that value to the proportion of "round" responses per item by human participants, as reported by Sidhu & Pexman (2017). We found a significant 0.85 correlation between ChatGPT responses and human responses ($t(16) = 6.53$, $p < .001$) and a nonsignificant 0.18 correlation between Vicuna responses and human responses ($t(16) = 0.75$, $p = .463$).

Sounds: sound-gender association

We conducted a non-preregistered analysis by removing 1 exemplar item (i.e., *Corla/Colark*), leaving 15 items in the analysis. The pattern of effects still held, with more use of feminine pronouns to refer to a name ending with a vowel than to one ending with a consonant in both ChatGPT (0.74 vs. 0.23, $\beta = 4.79$, $SE = 1.25$, $z = 3.84$, $p < .001$) and Vicuna (0.39 vs. 0.02, $\beta = 5.40$, $SE = 1.23$, $z = 4.41$, $p < .001$).

Words: word length and predictivity

We conducted a non-preregistered analysis by removing 1 exemplar item (i.e., *math/mathematics*), leaving 39 items in the analysis. The exclusion did not change the pattern of results, with no significant difference between the predictive and neutral contexts in both ChatGPT (0.24 vs. 0.19, $\beta = 0.29$, $SE = 0.22$, $z = 1.32$, $p = .188$) and Vicuna (0.31 vs. 0.31, $\beta = -0.16$, $SE = 0.20$, $z = -0.77$, $p = .439$).

We also conducted a non-preregistered exploratory analysis comparing trial-level data between language models (ChatGPT/Vicuna) and human participants (from Mahowald et al., 2013), treating context and participant group (humans = -0.5, ChatGPT/Vicuna = 0.5) as interacting predictors. We observed a significant difference between ChatGPT/Vicuna and humans, with LLMs being less likely to choose the short word than human participants (ChatGPT vs. humans: $\beta = -3.14$, $SE = 0.22$, $z = -13.98$, $p < .001$; Vicuna vs. humans: $\beta = -1.86$, $SE = 0.24$, $z = -7.61$, $p < .001$; see also Fig 1 bottom left). There was also an effect of context in the ChatGPT-human comparison, with the short word chosen more often in a predictive than neutral context ($\beta = 0.44$, $SE = 0.16$, $z = 2.83$, $p < .005$) but there was no such an effect in the Vicuna-human comparison ($\beta = 0.15$, $SE = 0.12$, $z = 1.24$, $p = .215$). The effect of context was similar between ChatGPT and humans, as indicated by the lack of an interaction between group and context ($\beta = -0.20$, $SE = 0.20$, $z = -0.96$, $p = .336$), but the effect of context was larger in humans than in Vicuna, as indicated by the significant interaction between group and context ($\beta = -0.60$, $SE = 0.22$, $z = -2.76$, $p = .006$).

Words: word meaning priming

We also conducted a non-preregistered analysis by removing 14 exemplar items (e.g., *post*), leaving 25 items in the analysis. In both models, there was no significant difference in meaning access between a synonym prime and no prime (ChatGPT: 0.38 vs. 0.33, $\beta = 0.36$, $SE = 0.19$, $z = 1.90$, $p = .057$; Vicuna: 0.19 vs. 0.15, $\beta = 0.39$, $SE = 0.28$, $z = 1.40$, $p = .162$); there was a significant word-meaning priming effect, with more access to the primed (subordinate) meaning following a word-meaning prime than following no prime (0.53 vs. 0.33, $\beta = 2.47$, $SE = 0.30$, $z = 8.20$, $p < .001$; Vicuna: 0.32 vs. 0.15, $\beta = 3.33$, $SE = 0.50$, $z = 6.70$, $p < .001$) and than following a synonym prime (ChatGPT: 0.53 vs. 0.38, $\beta = 2.65$, $SE = 0.40$, $z = 6.58$, $p < .001$; Vicuna: 0.32 vs. 0.19, $\beta = 2.86$, $SE = 0.48$, $z = 5.91$, $p < .001$).

Rodd et al. (2013, Experiment 3) also performed a secondary analysis where they removed any associate that is a morphological variant of a word in the prime sentence corresponding to an association trial; for example, if a participant gave *firm* or *accountant* as an associate to *post* following the prime sentence *The man accepted the post in the accountancy firm*, that trial was removed from the analysis. We initially preregistered this analysis but later changed to the main analysis in Rodd et al. (2013), as the removal method would lead to a lot of removals in the synonym prime condition, because the synonym could often be given as an associate to the target word (e.g., *job* as an associate of *post*). Nonetheless, we also followed the secondary analysis in Rodd et al. (2013) by excluding associates with the same lemma as any word in the corresponding prime sentence (e.g., we excluded *posting*, *firms*, or *accept* as associates of *post* following the word-meaning prime). Compared to the no-prime condition, the synonym prime led to less subordinate meaning access in ChatGPT (0.33 vs. 0.22, β = -0.79, SE = 0.32, z = -2.47, p = .013) but led to similar access in Vicuna (0.09 vs. 0.11, β = 0.44, SE = 0.30, z = 1.46, p = .146); critically, the word-meaning prime led to more subordinate meaning access than no prime (ChatGPT: 0.47 vs. 0.33, β = 1.88, SE = 0.37, z = 5.10, p < .001; Vicuna: 0.15 vs. 0.09, β = 2.79, SE = 0.51, z = 5.50, p < .001) and than the synonym prime (ChatGPT: 0.47 vs. 0.22, β = 2.65, SE = 0.40, z = 6.58, p < .001; Vicuna: 0.15 vs. 0.11, β = 2.86, SE = 0.50, z = 5.67, p < .001).

Syntax: structural priming

We conducted a non-preregistered analysis by removing 1 exemplar item, leaving 31 items in the analysis. The exclusion did not alter the pattern of results. For ChatGPT, there was a significant main effect of prime structure, with more PO responses following PO and DO primes (ChatGPT: 0.72 vs. 0.59, β = 1.06, SE = 0.11, z = 9.67, p < .001; Vicuna: 0.81 vs. 0.51, β = 2.97, SE = 0.35, z = 8.49, p < .001); there was no significant main effect of verb type, with similar PO responses when the prime and target had different verbs and when they had same verb (ChatGPT: 0.64 vs. 0.67, β = -0.06, SE = 0.09, z = -0.63, p = .528; Vicuna: 0.66 vs. 0.67, β = -0.17, SE = 0.23, z = -0.75, p = .454); there was a significant interaction, with a stronger structural priming effect when the verb was the same between the prime and target than when it was different (ChatGPT: 0.15 vs. 0.10 in priming effects, β = 0.40, SE = 0.15, z = 2.63, p = .009; Vicuna: 0.38 vs. 0.21 in priming effects, β = 1.16, SE = 0.47, z = 2.49, p = .013).

Syntax: syntactic ambiguity resolution

We conducted a non-preregistered analysis by removing 1 exemplar item (Example 5 in the main text), leaving 31 items in the analysis. The exclusion did not alter the pattern of results. There were more VP than NP attachments (ChatGPT: 0.94 vs. 0.06, β = -9.35, SE = 0.74, z = -12.68, p < .001; Vicuna: 0.63 vs. 0.37, β = -1.33, SE = 0.16, z = -8.12, p < .001). There was an effect of context in Vicuna, with more NP attachment interpretations following a multiple-referent context than following a single-referent context (0.38 vs. 0.36, β = 0.20, SE = 0.10, z = 2.10, p = .036) but not in ChatGPT (0.06 vs. 0.06, β = -0.10, SE = 0.43, z = -0.23, p = .820). There was an effect of question, with more NP attachment interpretations for an NP probe than for a VP probe (ChatGPT: 0.09 vs. 0.03, β = 3.37, SE = 0.99, z = 3.42, p < .001; Vicuna: 0.72 vs. 0.03, β = 5.64, SE = 0.48, z = 11.76, p < .001), and no interaction between context and probe (ChatGPT: β = 0.19, SE = 0.70, z = 0.27, p = .785; Vicuna: β = -0.18, SE = 0.25, z = -0.71, p = .480).

Meaning: implausible sentence interpretation

We conducted a non-preregistered analysis by removing 2 exemplar items (*The mother gave the daughter to the candle* and *The girl tossed the apple the boy*), leaving 18 items in the analysis. There was an effect of implausibility in ChatGPT, with more nonliteral interpretations for implausible than plausible sentences (0.75 vs. 0.02, β = 11.59, SE = 0.69, z = 16.90, p < .001) but not in Vicuna (0.49 vs. 0.37, β = 1.99, SE = 1.30, z = 1.53, p = .126). There was an effect of structure in ChatGPT, with more nonliteral interpretations for DO than PO sentences (0.48 vs. 0.29, β = 1.59, SE = 0.45, z = 3.56, p < .001) but not in Vicuna (0.45 vs. 0.41, β = -0.10, SE = 0.38, z = -0.26, p = .794). There was a significant interaction between plausibility and structure in ChatGPT, with the effect of plausibility being stronger in DO sentences than in PO sentences (β = 2.55, SE = 0.76, z = 3.38, p < .001) but not in Vicuna (β = 1.24, SE = 0.66, z = 1.88, p = .060). Analysing implausible sentences alone revealed an effect of structure, with more nonliteral interpretations for implausible DO than PO sentences in ChatGPT (0.92 vs. 0.57, $\beta = 3.13$, SE = 0.68, z = 4.58, p < .001) but not in Vicuna (0.52 vs. 0.46 $\beta = 0.51$, $SE = 0.54$, $z = 0.95$, $p = .342$). In another non-preregistered analysis, we also compared trial-level data between ChatGPT/Vicuna and human participants (from Experiment 1.4 in Gibson et al., 2013) in the interpretation of implausible sentences (excluding plausible sentences). Compared to human participants, ChatGPT had more nonliteral interpretations of implausible sentences (0.45 vs. 0.74, $\beta = 2.08$, $SE = 0.44$, $z = 4.76$, $p < .001$), but Vicuna did not (0.45 vs. 0.50, $\beta = 0.45$, $SE = 0.54$, $z = 0.83$, $p = .410$). There is an effect of structure, with more nonliteral interpretations for implausible DOs than implausible POs in both the ChatGPT/human comparison (0.90 vs. 0.55, $\beta = 2.15$, $SE = 0.43$, $z = 5.03$, $p < .001$) and the Vicuna/human comparison (0.54 vs. 0.46, $\beta = 0.68$, $SE = 0.31$, $z = 2.16$, $p = .031$). The interaction between group and structure was significant in the ChatGPT/human comparison, suggesting that the effect of structure was larger in ChatGPT than in humans ($\beta = 2.75$, $SE = 0.75$, $z = 3.68$, $p < .001$), but the interaction was not significant in the Vicuna/human comparison ($\beta = 0.18$, $SE = 0.55$, $z = 0.33$, $p = .739$).

Meaning: semantic illusions

We conducted a non-preregistered analysis by removing 2 exemplar items ("What board game includes bishops/cardinals/monks, rooks, pawns, knights, kings, and queens?" and "What passenger liner was tragically sunk by an iceberg in the Atlantic/Pacific/Indian Ocean?"), leaving 52 items in the analysis. In ChatGPT, compared to the baseline, there were more error reports in the strong imposter conditions (0.00 vs. 0.14, $\beta = 14.40$, $SE = 1.15$, $z = 12.55$, $p < .001$) and in the weak imposter condition (0.00 vs. 0.17, $\beta = 15.24$, $SE = 1.15$, $z = 13.27$, $p < .001$); there was no statistical difference in error reports between the two imposter conditions ($\beta = 1.33$, $SE = 0.83$, $z = 1.60$, $p = .109$). In Vicuna, there was no statistical difference in error reports between the baseline and the strong imposter condition (0.002 vs. 0.022, $\beta = -2.78$, $SE = 1.62$, $z = -1.72$, $p = .085$) or between the baseline and the weak imposter condition (0.002 vs. 0.018, $\beta = 1.00$, $SE = 1.30$, $z = 0.77$, $p = .445$); the weak imposter condition led to more error reports than the strong imposter condition ($\beta = 3.90$, $SE = 1.16$, $z = 3.36$, $p < .001$), though numerically there was a lower error report rate in the weak than strong imposter condition (0.022 vs. 0.017).

Discourse: implicit causality

We conducted a non-preregistered analysis by removing 3 exemplar items (*Gary scared Anna because he was wearing a mask and making strange noises*, *Toby impressed Susie because he got a perfect score on the math exam*, and *Brian impressed Janet because of his exceptional intelligence and charming personality*), leaving 29 items in the analysis. The exclusion did not alter the pattern of results: more completions with a pronoun referring to the object following an experiencer-stimulus verb than following a stimulus-experiencer verb in ChatGPT (0.95 vs. 0.00, $\beta = 13.82$, $SE = 0.94$, $z = 14.69$, $p < .001$) and also in Vicuna (0.91 vs. 0.01, $\beta = 14.37$, $SE = 1.51$, $z = 9.54$, $p < .001$).

Discourse: drawing inferences

We conducted a non-preregistered analysis by removing 1 exemplar item (the example in (9) in the main text), leaving 23 items in the analysis. The exclusion did not change the results pattern. In both models, compared to the explicit condition, there were fewer "yes" responses in the bridging condition (ChatGPT: 0.49 vs. 0.95, $\beta = -5.05$, $SE = 0.10$, $z = -50.06$, $p < .001$; Vicuna: 0.24 vs. 0.79, $\beta = -4.37$, $SE = 0.52$, $z = -8.33$, $p < .001$) and in the elaborative condition (ChatGPT: 0.23 vs. 0.95, $\beta = -7.40$, $SE = 0.12$, $z = -62.59$, $p < .001$; Vicuna: 0.20 vs. 0.79, $\beta = -4.43$, $SE = 0.43$, $z = -10.22$, $p < .001$). Critically, ChatGPT made fewer "yes" responses in the elaborative than bridging condition (0.23 vs. 0.49, $\beta = -2.94$, $SE = 0.60$, $z = -4.89$, $p < .001$), whereas Vicuna made similar "yes" responses between the bridging and elaborative conditions (0.24 vs. 0.20, $\beta = -0.06$, $SE = 0.44$, $z = -0.13$, $p = .900$).

Interlocutor sensitivity: word meaning access

We conducted a non-preregistered analysis by removing 13 exemplar items (e.g., "*bonnet*"), leaving 23 items in the analysis. The exclusion did not alter the pattern of results. There was more access to the AE meaning with an AE interlocutor than a BE interlocutor in both ChatGPT (0.46 vs. 0.36, β = 1.84, *SE* = 0.25, z = 7.28, $p < .001$) and in Vicuna (0.62 vs. 0.33, β = 2.80, *SE* = 0.54, z = 5.15, $p < .001$).

Following the preregistered exploratory analysis, we also included (log) trial order (i.e., the log order in which a target trial was presented, among both targets and fillers, to ChatGPT in an experimental run) (Note that the Vicuna experiment had one trial per run so there was no trial order). This analysis was to see if the interlocutor sensitivity (if any) varies over time. Thus, the LME model included interlocutor and (log) trial order as interacting predictors. We observed a significant interlocutor effect (β = 2.01, *SE* = 0.25, z = 7.91, $p < .001$), with more access to AE meanings for an AE than BE interlocutor, and a significant effect of trial order (β = -0.49, *SE* = 0.15, z = -3.20, p = .001), with decreasing AE meaning access over time. Importantly, we also observed a significant interaction between interlocutor and (log) trial order (β = -0.54, *SE* = 0.17, z = -3.14, p = .002), showing that the interlocutor effect decreased over time. Such a decrease of interlocutor sensitivity is not observed in human experiments (e.g., Cai et al., 2017) and might be due to the attenuating contextual influence (i.e., the interlocutor dialectal background) over time in ChatGPT.

In a non-preregistered analysis, we also compared trial-level data between ChatGPT/Vicuna and human participants (pooled from Experiment 1 of Cai et al., 2017) and the blocked condition of Experiment 1 of Cai (2022). There was no effect of participant group (ChatGPT: β = 0.53, *SE* = 0.91, z = 0.58, p = .560; Vicuna: β = 0.65, *SE* = 0.68, z = 0.96, p = .338), with a similar proportion of AE meaning access for ChatGPT/Vicuna and human participants (see Fig 3 bottom left). There was an interlocutor effect (ChatGPT: β = 1.13, *SE* = 0.14, z = 8.28, $p < .001$; Vicuna: β = 1.59, *SE* = 0.27, z = 5.97, $p < .001$), with more access to AE meanings for words produced by an AE interlocutor than by a BE interlocutor. There was also an interaction between group and interlocutor (ChatGPT: β = 1.34, *SE* = 0.28, z = 4.70, $p < .001$; Vicuna: β = 2.26, *SE* = 0.58, z = 3.92, $p < .001$), which suggests that ChatGPT/Vicuna was more sensitive to an interlocutor's dialectal background in word meaning access than human participants were (however, it should be noted that ChatGPT/Vicuna was explicitly told about an interlocutor's dialectic background, whereas human participants inferred their dialectal background via their accent).

Interlocutor sensitivity: lexical retrieval

Note that that the human study on which this experiment was based was not published at the time of experiment so we did not conduct any analysis excluding exemplar items.

Following the preregistered exploratory analysis, we also included (log) trial order (i.e., the log order in which a target trial was presented, among both targets and fillers, to ChatGPT in an experimental run). In an LME model with interlocutor and (log) trial order as interacting predictors, we observed an interlocutor effect (β = 4.21, *SE* = 1.76, z = 2.39, p = .017; with more AE meaning access for words from an AE interlocutor than from a BE interlocutor), a trial order effect (β = 1.51, *SE* = 0.60, z = 2.54, p = .011; with increasing AE expressions over time), and an interaction between interlocutor and trial order (β = -0.18, *SE* = 0.09, z = -2.17, p = .030; with a decreasing interlocutor effect over time).

In a non-preregistered analysis, we also compared trial-level data between ChatGPT and human participants (from the pilot experiment of Cai et al., accepted in principle) and between Vicuna and human participants, using participant group and interlocutor to predict whether a BE or AE expression was produced. There was a group effect in both comparisons, with more AE expressions produced by both ChatGPT and Vicuna than by human participants (ChatGPT: β = 12.88, *SE* = 0.00, z = 37044, $p < .001$; Vicuna: β = 5.27, *SE* = 0.64, z = 8.30, $p < .001$; see Fig. 3 bottom right). There was also an interlocutor effect, with more AE expressions when a definition was given by an AE interlocutor than by a BE interlocutor in both ChatGPT and Vicuna compared to in humans (ChatGPT: β = 2.06, *SE* = 0.00, z = 5926, $p < .001$; Vicuna: β = 2.10, *SE* = 0.29, z = 7.24, $p < .001$). The interaction was significant in both ChatGPT-human comparison (β = 2.78, *SE* = 0.00, z = 8006, $p < .001$) and Vicuna-human comparison (β = 2.82, *SE* = 0.52, z = 5.37, $p < .001$), suggesting that both LLMs were more sensitive to an interlocutor's dialectal background than human participants when producing lexical expressions.

The Curious Case of Representational Alignment: Unravelling Visio-Linguistic Tasks in Emergent Communication

Tom Kouwenhoven
LIACS
Leiden University
t.kouwenhoven@liacs.leidenuniv.nl

Max Peeperkorn
School of Computing
University of Kent
m.peeperkorn@kent.ac.uk

Bram van Dijk
LUMC
Leiden University Medical Center
b.m.a.van_dijk@lumc.nl

Tessa Verhoef
LIACS
Leiden University
t.verhoef@liacs.leidenuniv.nl

Abstract

Natural language has the universal properties of being compositional and grounded in reality. The emergence of linguistic properties is often investigated through simulations of emergent communication in referential games. However, these experiments have yielded mixed results compared to similar experiments addressing linguistic properties of human language. Here we address *representational alignment* as a potential contributing factor to these results. Specifically, we assess the representational alignment between agent image representations and between agent representations and input images. Doing so, we confirm that the emergent language does not appear to encode human-like conceptual visual features, since agent image representations drift away from inputs whilst inter-agent alignment increases. We moreover identify a strong relationship between inter-agent alignment and topographic similarity, a common metric for compositionality, and address its consequences. To address these issues, we introduce an alignment penalty that prevents representational drift but interestingly does not improve performance on a compositional discrimination task. Together, our findings emphasise the key role representational alignment plays in simulations of language emergence.

1 Introduction

Human language bears unique properties that make it a powerful tool for communication. A well-known property is compositionality: the ability to combine meaningful words into more complex meanings (Hockett, 1959). The emergence of compositionality is studied extensively in the field of language evolution through human experiments (e.g. Selten and Warglien, 2007; Kirby et al., 2008, 2015; Raviv et al., 2019a). An important finding from this field is that the unique nature of human language can be explained as a consequence of biases for simplicity and expressivity imposed during continuous language learning and use (Smith, 2022). Computational simulations of language emergence have also been used to study the emergence of linguistic properties (e.g. de Boer, 2006; Steels and Loetzsch, 2012), and have seen a rising interest in the field of computational linguistics (Lazaridou and Baroni, 2020). Here, compositionality in the emergent communication protocols is commonly measured through topographic similarity (TOPSIM; Brighton and Kirby, 2006). It measures the topographic relation between meanings and signals, conceptually it gauges whether similar meanings map to similar signals. This metric was first used in recent computational simulations by Lazaridou et al. (2018) and has been used in a large body of work since. Yet, the interpretation of linguistic properties emerging in simulations remains challenging, since language protocols used among artificial agents often show critical mismatches with known properties of human languages (Galke et al., 2022; Lian et al., 2023) such as efficiency, word-order vs. case-marking biases, or compositional generalisation (see §2). Consequently, it is evident that their learning biases and signal-meaning mappings differ from those of humans. This underscores the critical need to obtain deeper insight into referential games in the language learning setting (Rita et al., 2022).

A possible explanation for these mismatches could stem from representational alignment, the degree of agreement between the internal representations of two information processing systems (Sucholutsky et al., 2023). To the best of our knowledge, representational alignment in emergent communication was first reported by (Bouchacourt and Baroni, 2018), who measured the degree to which

Proceedings of the Workshop on Cognitive Modeling and Computational Linguistics, pages 57–71
August 15, 2024 ©2024 Association for Computational Linguistics

agents aligned their internal image interpretations (inter-agent alignment) by performing Representational Similarity Analysis (RSA; Kriegeskorte et al., 2008). Using RSA (§3), they showed that agents establish successful communication artificially by aligning their internal image representations while *losing* any relation to the images presented (image-agent alignment), enabling communication about noise input even though they were trained on real images. As such, their communication protocol captured not conceptual properties of the objects depicted in pictures, but most likely focused on non-human-like spurious image features (e.g., pixel intensities). While inter-agent alignment is not a problem per se, the loss of image-agent alignment is problematic for two reasons. First, for emergent communication simulations to provide meaningful insights into the emergence of natural human language, agent image representations must be grounded in the content of the images. Only then can we deduce *what* the agents communicate about and assess linguistic properties or their ability to generalise to novel concepts. Second, emergent communication setups have been proposed to fine-tune pre-trained (vision-)language models, aiming to enhance machine understanding of natural human language (Lazaridou and Baroni, 2020; Lowe et al., 2020; Steinert-Threlkeld et al., 2022; Zheng et al., 2024). In this context, maintaining substantial alignment between representations and images is crucial for preserving mutual understanding between machines and humans.

Representational alignment, however, did not receive the necessary attention since a host of papers appeared *after* the findings by Bouchacourt and Baroni in which results on referential games were reported without taking RSA into account (e.g. Lazaridou et al., 2018; Guo et al., 2019; Li and Bowling, 2019; Ren et al., 2020; Chaabouni et al., 2020; Dagan et al., 2021; Mu and Goodman, 2021; Chaabouni et al., 2022). Admittedly, some use attribute-value objects instead of real images as input. But importantly, in nearly all cases, neural agents must map inputs—whether attribute-value objects or image representations—onto agent-specific representations. Therefore the problem of inter-agent alignment *can always* occur and is *agnostic* to the input type. Although this warrants further analysis of earlier results, the field is already employing referential games in more complex simulations with real images (e.g. Dessi et al., 2021; Chaabouni et al., 2022; Mahaut et al., 2024).

This work addresses the understudied alignment problem in standard referential game setups used in emergent communication. We train Reinforcement Learning (RL) agents equipped with a recent vision module (DinoV2; Oquab et al., 2024) to communicate about images. In addition to evaluating the agents on MS COCO (Lin et al., 2014) image pairs, we evaluate on noise pairs and image pairs sourced from the Winoground dataset (Thrush et al., 2022). The latter is explicitly created to gauge visio-linguistic compositional reasoning abilities of vision and language models. We first confirm that effective communication in the referential game relies on inter-agent alignment and then move on to our contributions. First, we find a strong correlation between the degree of inter-agent alignment and the TOPSIM metric. Our second contribution consists of a solution to the alignment problem by including an alignment penalty term to the loss, resulting in equivalent communicative success and higher TOPSIM whilst ensuring that the agents communicate about images instead of spurious features (Figure 1). We then argue to start evaluating emergent communication protocols on more strict tasks that directly target the intuition behind popular metrics to obtain a clearer understanding of the protocols. Overall, our results highlight the importance of representational alignment in simulations of language emergence and underscore the need to better understand the divergence in human and artificial language emergence.

2 Background

Most research in simulating emergent communication is modelled after the Lewis signalling game (Lewis, 1969) with a speaker and a listener agent. The speaker observes a state (e.g., an image) and sends a signal to the listener who acts based on this signal. In the case of the referential game, this means selecting a target among distractors. Both agents are rewarded for successful communication, meaning the listener points to the target object. The solution of this game requires the agents to have a shared protocol (i.e., an artificial language) which typically emerges when the agents learn based on trial and error over multiple games. This resembles how for humans, language learning and use impose constraints like pressures for learnability and compression that shape our language design (Kirby et al., 2014, 2015). Importantly, the emer-

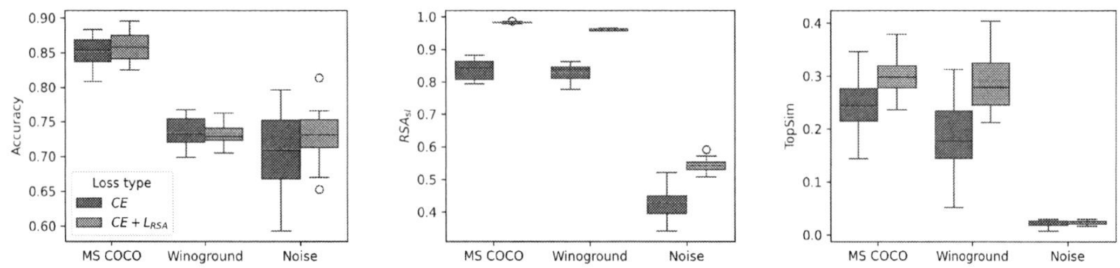

(a) Communicative performance (Accuracy) on discriminating two images.

(b) Inter-agent representational alignment (RSA_{sl}) between agent representations.

(c) Topographic similarity (TOPSIM) between the images and the messages.

Figure 1: Inference results for different datasets after training on MS COCO images. In (a) we see that agents can discriminate MS COCO images but struggle with discriminating Winoground images. In (b) we see the effect of the loss function on the degree of inter-agent representational alignment and (c) implies that according to the TOPSIM metric, messages are more structured if the alignment penalty is used. The presented results are across 15 seeds and use the best-performing parameters resulting from our parameter sweep, dashed green lines indicate averages.

gent language in this setup is also shaped by biases resulting from, for example, the agent architecture, loss function, and learning protocol (Rita et al., 2022). The current work uses the referential game: a variant of the Lewis signalling game extensively used to explore language evolution (e.g. Steels and Loetzsch, 2012; Kirby et al., 2015; Lazaridou et al., 2017; Kottur et al., 2017; Lazaridou et al., 2018; Kharitonov et al., 2020; Chaabouni et al., 2022).

An important challenge in emergent communication is that artificial learners often do not behave the same way as human learners in experimental settings. Some emergent protocols do not follow Zipf's law and thus are anti-efficient unless pressures for brevity are introduced (Chaabouni et al., 2019a), others do not show the word-order vs. case-marking trade-off found in human languages (Chaabouni et al., 2019b; Lian et al., 2021). Additionally, there is an ongoing debate on the degree to which the emergent languages allow for compositional generalisation (Lazaridou and Baroni, 2020; Conklin and Smith, 2023). It has been suggested to introduce communicative (e.g., alternating speaker/listener roles) and cognitive (e.g., memory) constraints (Galke et al., 2022) and use more natural settings to promote more human-like patterns of language emergence with neural agents (Kouwenhoven et al., 2022). Doing so changes the learning pressures to which the agents need to adapt and can recover initially absent linguistic phenomena of natural language in emergent languages (for a review see Galke and Raviv, 2024). An example of such work, investigating the word-order vs. case-marking trade-off, has succeeded in replicating this trade-off for neural learners (Lian et al., 2023). Their setup differs from other work in that agents first learn a miniature language via supervised learning, and then optimise it for communicative success via RL, resulting in emergent languages that share linguistic universals with human language.

To enhance understanding of emergent communication in the Lewis game, Rita et al. (2022) decomposed the standard objective in Lewis games into two key components: a co-adaptation loss and an information loss. In doing so, they shed light on potential sources of overfitting and how they might hinder the emergence of structured communication protocols. They demonstrated that desired linguistic properties (e.g., compositionality and generalisability) emerge when they control the listener's ability to converge to the speaker agent (i.e., control for overfitting on the co-adaptation loss). While the co-adaptation loss has parallels to inter-agent alignment, their work does not address the alignment between the agents' image representation and the input features, which we deem crucial in developing grounded communication protocols.

Another challenge in emergent communication is the disentanglement of the underlying meanings of emergent languages. Earlier studies by Lazaridou et al. (2017) suggested that agents assign symbols to general conceptual properties of objects in images, rather than low-level visual features. However, as previously mentioned, follow-up work from Bouchacourt and Baroni (2018) showed this is not always the case. They found that agents align their agent-specific image representations without developing a language that captures conceptual properties depicted in the images. Moreover, agents lost any sense of meaningful within-category variation where two similar objects in human perception (e.g., two avocados) were observed as maximally dissimilar for the agents. In response to these findings, recent studies have implemented sanity checks, testing whether trained agents can communicate about noise (Dessi et al., 2021; Mahaut et al., 2024). However, to the best of our knowledge, there has been little attention to what we consider to be their main result: the alignment problem.

3 Representational alignment

Representational alignment is the degree of agreement between the internal representations of two information processing systems, whether biological or artificial. Even though widely recognised in cognitive science, neuroscience, and machine learning (Sucholutsky et al., 2023), representational alignment has not seen much interest in the field of emergent communication, except for the work by Bouchacourt and Baroni who analysed the referential game using RSA. This metric measures the alignment between two sets of numerical vectors, for example, image embeddings and agents' representations thereof. In practice, it is calculated by taking the pairwise (cosine) distances between vectors of a set and calculating the Spearman rank correlation between these distances.

In this paper, we also use RSA to operationalise representational alignment. Given the speaker image representations r_s of the DinoV2 input embeddings i and r_l as the same images represented in the listener representation space, we compute the pairwise cosine similarity between the representations for the speaker s_s and for the listener s_l and calculate Spearman's ρ between s_s and s_l. As such, this measures the degree of inter-agent alignment (RSA_{sl}) between image representations s_s and s_l, relative to their input. Additionally, we use it to measure image-agent alignment between the speaker/listener image representations and the DinoV2 embeddings (RSA_{si} and RSA_{li}). Importantly, alignment is *agnostic to the type of input*, being either images or attribute-value objects and can always happen when inputs are projected onto agent-specific representations.

Intuitively, a high inter-agent RSA_{sl} value can be interpreted as agents with *similar* representations for similar images. Importantly, this can have two causes: both agents' image representations either *maintain* a relation to the image input, or *lose* this relation. While the former is desirable, the latter means that the agents are not communicating about the same high-level image features but are likely communicating about non-human-like spurious features. A low RSA_{sl} value entails that the agents have developed *different* interpretations for the same image. While this may well be similar to the question of whether people have different perceptual experiences of colour (Locke, 1847), in the case of emergent communication, the agents should develop a grounded vocabulary with overlapping concept-level properties if we wish machines to have more natural understanding of human language. We use RSA 1) as a metric to reassess findings from Bouchacourt and Baroni and 2) as an auxiliary loss to mitigate the alignment problem and ensure that the agents communicate about image features.

4 Methods

The standard referential game is used as provided by the EGG framework (Kharitonov et al., 2021). Doing so ensures our findings are representative of the widely-used setup, rather than being influenced by specific design decisions. The game is implemented as a multi-agent cooperative RL problem where a speaker and a listener communicate to discriminate a target image from two shuffled distractor images. The speaker receives a target t and generates a message m of at most length L, using vocabulary V. Importantly, the messages and symbols have no a priori meaning but are assumed to obtain meaning and become grounded during the game. Once meaningful, the symbols are ideally combined in a structured manner to create compositional messages that express more complex meanings. Using message m, the listener guesses the target $\hat{t}$. Communicative success is defined as $\hat{t} = t$, meaning that the listener has correctly identified the target image among the candidate images.

4.1 Agents

Agents contain a language and a vision module. The latter consists of a frozen pre-trained visual network (DinoV2) and a learned agent-specific representation layer. While difficult to know what conceptual image features are present in DinoV2 embeddings, they have demonstrated capability in semantic segmentation tasks (Oquab et al., 2024), which is similar to the agents' objective. In contrast to the hybrid structure of the vision module, the language module is entirely trained from scratch.

The speaker agent processes images by applying a linear transformation to the image embeddings, followed by batch normalisation, to create its agent-specific image representation r_s. Its language module embeds this representation and passes it through a single-layer Gated Recurrent Unit (GRU; Cho et al., 2014) that spells out messages to describe the target. *The listener* receives the message and the distractor images. It encodes the message into an embedding using another single-cell GRU layer. Additionally, a listener image representation r_l is obtained for each image by applying a linear transformation and batch normalisation. Subsequently, temperature-weighted (temperature defaults to 0.1) cosine scores construct a multi-modal representation between the image and message representation (Dessi et al., 2021), where a higher probability should be assigned to the target image.

4.2 Optimisation

Communicative success ($\hat{t} = t$) is used to optimise the trainable parameters of both agents. The listener minimises cross-entropy (*ce*) loss using stochastic gradient descent, amounting to supervised learning. The *ce* loss is calculated over the listeners' target distribution, thus providing direct pressure for communicative success. At inference, the candidate image with the highest probability is chosen as the target $\hat{t}$. The gradients required to optimise the speaker are calculated using the REINFORCE (Williams, 1992) update rule as each generated symbol must be assigned a loss. Following common practice (Rita et al., 2024), entropy regularisation (Mnih et al., 2016) is added to the loss to maintain exploration in message generation.

In addition to the conventional *ce* loss, we introduce an alignment loss ($ce + \text{RSA}$) that includes an alignment penalty term to enforce high inter-agent and image-agent alignment. The term

$$L_{\text{RSA}} = (1 - \text{RSA}_{sl}) + (1 - \text{RSA}_{si}) + (1 - \text{RSA}_{li})$$

is added to the *ce* loss with equal importance. We use torchsort (Blondel et al., 2020) to calculate L_{RSA} such that the entire loss term is differentiable. Importantly, L_{RSA} is not influenced by communicative success and does not interact with the *ce* loss (Appendix C). Only adding RSA_{sl} to the *ce* loss is not sufficient as high inter-agent alignment can be achieved while *losing* image-agent alignment (see §3). We therefore also include RSA_{si} and RSA_{li} to ensure that the agents communicate about the content displayed in the images. Including RSA_{sl} entails that representational information is shared between the agents, thus differing from how humans interact. Yet, ranking the speaker and listener representations in calculating RSA_{sl} bears *some* resemblance to projecting beliefs upon the interpretations of the other communicative partner. The current solution should be seen as a step towards more grounded vocabularies prone to refinements such as cognitive plausibility. We train for 30 epochs regardless of the loss used. The hyperparameters (Appendix B) that resulted in the best validation accuracy across 42 different communication channel capacities (Appendix A) were used for our findings.

Figure 2: Exemplar pairs of each dataset used for evaluation. Left: an image pair from MS COCO. Middle: A Winoground example. Right: A Gaussian noise pair. All images are cropped for display purposes.

4.3 Data

Agents are trained to discriminate MS COCO images but tested on three different datasets (Figure 2) to assess out-of-distribution (o.o.d.) performance.

MS COCO – We use a subset of 1200 images from the MS COCO 2017 validation set to train and test the agents using an 80/20 split. To obtain this subset, we first select the categories that contain more than 100 images (12 categories) and subsequently sample 100 images for each supercategory present in the resulting set of images. The distractor images are sampled from the same category to ensure that there is *some* relevance to the target image. Importantly, sampling distractor images is done for each batch, meaning targets have different distractors at each epoch.

Winoground – The Winoground dataset (Thrush et al., 2022) was created to assess the visio-

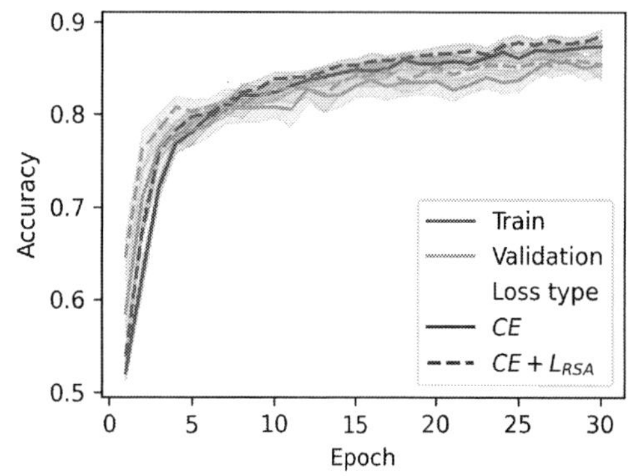

(a) Learning curves for the MS COCO dataset on train and validation data.

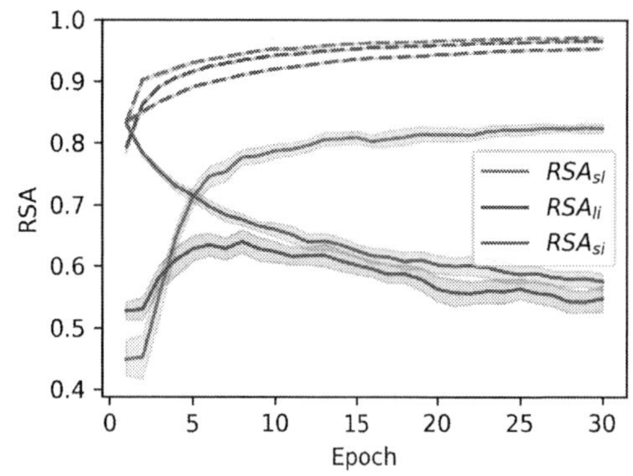

(b) Representational alignment between agent image representations (green) and between the image and the sender/listener representations (purple, red).

Figure 3: In (a) we see that the agents learn to communicate successfully without overfitting on train data. In (b) we see that the alignment problem occurs with the ce but not the ce + RSA loss. Line style indicates the loss type. Data is averaged over 15 seeds, areas indicate the 95% confidence intervals.

linguistic compositional reasoning abilities of vision and language models. Here, we repurpose it as a proxy for the agents' ability to endow in compositional reasoning for image-based settings. The dataset contains 800 images and corresponding captions, comprising 400 Winoground pairs. Image-caption pairs were included when the captions share the same words but are of different *compositions*, implying completely different semantics (e.g., "a tree smashed into a car" versus "a car smashed into a tree" in Figure 2 (middle)). We only use the image pairs, not the captions. Crucially, this task differs from MS COCO since the image pairs are *fixed*, *conceptually similar* and meant to be discriminative if the agents' language allows for compositional reasoning and is grounded in the visual modality.

Noise – Following Bouchacourt and Baroni (2018), we test whether agents can communicate about Gaussian noise ($\mu = 0, \sigma = 1$) pairs when trained on real images. Being able to do so would imply that messages communicate about spurious instead of high-level concept features.

4.4 Metrics

The performance of our agents is assessed by communicative success (accuracy) and RSA (§3) measures alignment. The degree of compositionality in the emergent language is assessed through the TOPSIM metric. Other metrics for compositionality like positional disentanglement, bag-of-symbols disentanglement (Chaabouni et al., 2020) are not straightforward due to the continuous nature of the image embeddings.

5 Results

5.1 Communicative success

Unsurprisingly, results show that agents can successfully disambiguate between image pairs from MS COCO using an emergent language (Figure 3a). Notably, we also confirm previous observations by (Bouchacourt and Baroni, 2018) that agents trained on real images can communicate about Gaussian noise (Figure 1a). Thus again suggesting that the messages convey spurious features rather than concept-level information. Interestingly, their performance on Gaussian noise is comparable to the performance on Winoground pairs, which requires the messages to capture concept-level properties. Thus revealing the difficulty of discriminating between strict pairs of conceptually similar images. The observed decrease in o.o.d. performance aligns with findings from other studies, such as Lazaridou et al. (2018) and Conklin and Smith (2023).

5.2 The alignment problem

The solid lines in Figure 3b clearly show that inter-agent alignment increases while alignment sensitivity to image features decreases for both agents. In principle, it is not a problem that the agents' image representations align. However, it is problematic when the alignment between the image embeddings and the image representations declines. Ablations across different channel capacities (§A) and pre-trained vision modules (§D) showed that these trends appear consistently and are not influenced by the capacity or type of vision model. In addition to the communicative success on Gaussian noise, this re-confirms that the agents do not learn to extract concept-level information from the image embeddings but instead solve this task differently.

5.3 TOPSIM and representational alignment

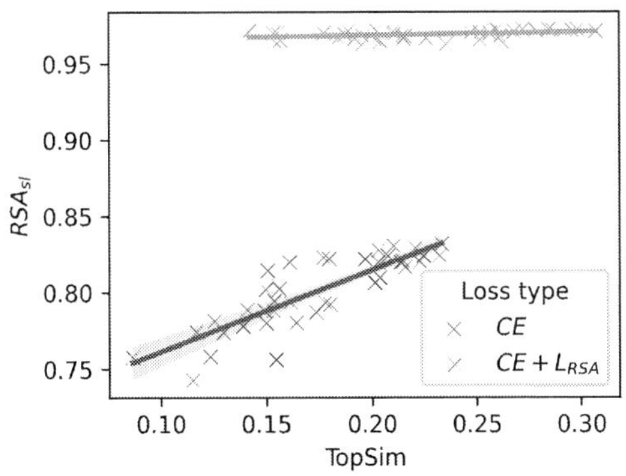

Figure 4: The relationship between TOPSIM and inter-agent alignment (RSA_{sl}) for both loss types.

Earlier findings show mixed results on the relationship between TOPSIM and generalisation in image-based settings, TOPSIM was either related to generalisation (Chaabouni et al., 2022) or not (Rita et al., 2022). Our results indicate that generalisation and TOPSIM are correlated with both *ce* ($r = .856$, $p < .001$) and *ce* + RSA ($r = .767$, $p < .001$) losses. Meaning that more structured languages enable better communication on unseen validation pairs. Moreover, we find a strong positive relationship between RSA_{sl} and TOPSIM ($r = .838, p < .001$) in the *ce* (Figure 4). This relation is also present in the *ce*+RSA setup ($r = .408$, $p = .001$), but is decoupled from TOPSIM given the (very) small spread ($\sigma = .003$) of RSA_{sl}. We do not observe an influence of inter-agent alignment on the number of uniquely produced messages.

5.4 Mitigating the alignment problem

We now focus on the *ce* + RSA setup which was introduced to ensure that the agents maintain alignment with the image embeddings. Figure 3b shows that this is the case: inter-agent alignment *and* agent-image alignment increase during training and remain high at inference. However, there does not seem to be a benefit for communicative success at inference time (Figure 1). This is because the alignment penalty only forces agents to represent images similarly to the image embeddings and is independent of the cross-entropy loss used to assess the success of communication (Appendix C). In the case of noise images, we still observe the above-chance performance, suggesting that communication between the agents still occurs in an artificial manner.

The alignment penalty also leads to increased TOPSIM, indicating a higher level of structure (Figure 1c) and strengthens our finding that TOPSIM and inter-agent alignment are related. Suggesting that the observed variations in TOPSIM, whether higher or lower, as noted in previous studies (e.g. Kottur et al., 2017; Chaabouni et al., 2020), should not be interpreted without considering alignment since they may be attributable to this underlying artefact rather than alterations to the original setup.

When tested on more strict Winoground pairs, communicative success does not improve as a result of using the alignment penalty (Figure 1a). Given the correlation between TOPSIM and generalisation, this is surprising since the higher degree of TOPSIM should imply that the language is more structured. Moreover, both, RSA_{si} and RSA_{li} have not drifted away from the image features. This combination, *in theory*, should be ideal for discriminating image pairs from the Winoground dataset since it was designed to be discriminative with compositional visio-linguistic reasoning. However, in *practice* this is not the case.

6 Discussion

In this work, we revisited the representational alignment problem in a common setup used in emergent communication and proposed a solution to this underrepresented problem. We corroborated earlier findings by showing that agents align their image representations and rely on spurious image features instead of human-like concept-level information (Bouchacourt and Baroni, 2018). We then showed that inter-agent alignment strongly correlates with the commonly used TOPSIM metric. Our solution to the alignment problem involves an alignment penalty that forces the agents to remain aligned with the input features and mitigates the alignment problem without decreasing communicative success. Finally, when agents are tested on more challenging Winoground pairs we observed reasonable but lower performance regardless of whether image representations were similar to the image embeddings or not. With this work, we hope that the alignment problem will receive more attention in the field of emergent communication, as is already the case in adjacent fields (Sucholutsky et al., 2023).

6.1 Importance of representational alignment

It is common practice in simulations of emergent communication to process (visual) inputs into an agent-specific hidden representation and update their weights simultaneously (e.g. Lazaridou et al., 2017; Bouchacourt and Baroni, 2018; Chaabouni et al., 2019a, 2020; Rita et al., 2022). As such, inter-agent alignment, *irrespective of the input form*, likely happens in other simulations too. This phenomenon is therefore potentially widespread and perhaps the cause for findings that are at odds with experimental findings. While it is not always the case that the representation structure we *expect* to help solve a task will do so (e.g. Montero et al., 2021; Xu et al., 2022), such discrepancies may hinder the use of emergent communication models in developing a more natural understanding of human languages and leave them less suitable for directly simulating language evolution phenomena. Especially if we want machine representations of natural language to align with human representations (Sucholutsky et al., 2023). RSA should therefore be used to rule out, or at the bare minimum report about, representational alignment in the future.

6.2 TOPSIM and representational alignment

Measuring representational alignment using RSA is similar to how TOPSIM measures the structure in messages. They differ in their inputs but both calculate the Spearman-ranked correlation between metric-agnostic pairwise distances. Crucially, the input makes all the difference, the inputs for RSA are from both agents and are trained independently, whilst TOPSIM only assesses the relation between the fixed inputs and learned output. Despite the similarities, the metrics thus describe different phenomena and are rarely reported simultaneously.

We hypothesise that the relationship between TOPSIM and inter-agent representational alignment is a by-product of the setup, which in essence implies that the listener has to align its representation r_l to the speaker representation r_s (Rita et al., 2022). It has to do so using only the speakers' messages, being an abstraction of r_s. A solution to this problem is to align representations, which eases the listeners' training objective. If the speaker consistently produces structured messages during training, aligning r_l to r_s is easier, thereby causing higher inter-agent alignment. Essentially, this renders TOPSIM to be an *indirect* metric for the rate of alignment, for which RSA_{sl} is a *direct* metric. In the context of learnability, the relationship between TOPSIM and inter-agent alignment and the fact that alignment always occurs can be seen as reasons for why languages with higher TOPSIM are easier to learn (Li and Bowling, 2019; Cheng et al., 2023). This underscores the need to report inter-agent representational alignment to avoid conclusions drawn about the effect of specific interventions on TOPSIM which may be attributable to inter-agent alignment.

6.3 Targeted o.o.d. evaluations

An important implication of our findings concerns the standard practice of reporting o.o.d. accuracy where the agents are tested on unseen input after training (e.g. Auersperger and Pecina, 2022; Conklin and Smith, 2023). This should inform about the agents' ability to generalise from one dataset (e.g., MS COCO) to another dataset (e.g., the Winoground pairs) much like human language allows us to talk about an infinite number of situations. Crucially, this overlooks the representational alignment problem in that we do not know *what* the agents are precisely generalising about. This problem can be mitigated with the alignment penalty to assess generalisation more directly or at least should be taken into consideration.

We assess o.o.d. performance on the more challenging Winoground pairs as a proxy for the agents' ability to endow in compositional reasoning for image-based settings. Good performance on the Winoground dataset requires a grounded language that can be used to create compositional messages since the objects and their underlying relations need to be described. In general, we suggest to start evaluating simulations of referential games on targeted strict tasks, like probing state-of-the-art vision language models on e.g., visio-compositional (Thrush et al., 2022; Diwan et al., 2022; Hsieh et al., 2023; Ray et al., 2023) or spatial (Kamath et al., 2023) reasoning. Re-purposing such datasets can reveal more directly whether agents develop the attested communicative abilities that are trivial to humans without having to rely on metrics. Our results illustrate this through a shortcoming of the TOPSIM metric. We observed that agents still struggle with distinguishing pairs of *conceptually similar* Winoground images even though TOPSIM is higher with the alignment penalty. If the language protocol were to communicate concept-level information *and* compositional messages were created, we should not observe this struggle, meaning that the emerged protocols do not enable human-like communicative success.

Interestingly, the o.o.d. performance remains substantially above chance in the ce + RSA setting. Given that MS COCO is not a dataset for learning to model compositionality, this delineates the limits of what can be achieved qua performance based on MS COCO image features in the Winoground context. Nevertheless, this leaves open the question of above-chance performance on Gaussian noise with the ce + RSA loss. A tentative explanation is that the higher inter-agent alignment on noise input ($M_{ce} = .428$, $M_{ce+\text{RSA}_{sl}} = .543$, $t = -8.71$, $p < .001$) alleviates part of the problem (Figure 1b). To validate this, future experiments should involve controlling the prior distributions of the agents' image encoders by training their vision modules on different data. Doing so ensures that they have to communicate about novel objects and cannot rely on similar representations.

7 Conclusion

This paper revisits the underrepresented alignment problem present in the referential game often used in simulations of emergent communication. Specifically, we focused on the problem of increasing alignment between agent-image representations in combination with a decreasing alignment between the input and agent representations. We first confirmed that agents align their image representations while losing connection to their input, meaning that the emergent languages do not appear to encode human-like visual features. We then showed that, in the common setup, inter-agent alignment is related to topographic similarity, and argued that this renders TOPSIM an *indirect* metric of the rate of inter-agent alignment. To further investigate the effects of alignment, we introduced an alignment penalty to mitigate the alignment problem and showed that the communicative ability on a strict compositionality benchmark did not improve, leaving the question of inducing compositional generalisation in emergent communication for images unsolved. Our findings underscore the need to better understand the divergence between human and artificial language emergence within the prevalent referential setup and highlight the importance and potential impact of representational alignment. We hope that future work rules out or at least reports about representational alignment.

8 Limitations

Our work has a few notable limitations. First, it only involves the referential game. Another popular variant, the reconstruction game (e.g. Chaabouni et al., 2019a, 2020; Lian et al., 2021; Conklin and Smith, 2023), requires the listener to reconstruct the input object based on the speakers' message. Since this setup has a different objective and presents different learning biases, it may have different results. We still expect the results to be similar as there is no pressure to retain alignment between the image input and agent representation. It would, however, be interesting to investigate whether the language protocol in this scenario is more structured than in the referential game.

Another limitation in our setup is that we only consider the scenario with two agents, which may be a requirement for alignment to be possible. Since experiments with human participants show that larger communities create more systematic languages (Raviv et al., 2019b), simulations on emergent multi-agent communication with populations of agents are also conducted, but these yield mixed results. The emergent communication protocols oftentimes do not evolve to be more structured unless explicit pressures such as population diversity or emulation mechanisms are introduced (Rita et al., 2022; Chaabouni et al., 2022). Michel et al. (2023) however, showed that population setups can result in more compositional languages if agent pairs are trained in a partitioned manner to prevent co-adaptation. Despite the mixed results, we believe that emergent communication with populations of agents is ecologically more valid and could result in different alignment effects. Much like how Tieleman et al. (2019) showed that autoencoders encode better concept category representations when they learn representations in a community-based setting with multiple encoders and decoders collectively.

The final limitation of our study regards its scale. While simulations of emergent communication are typically conducted on relatively small-scale datasets, human language emergence is accompanied by rich and diverse multi-modal experiences. Recent results in the field of computer vision suggest that dataset diversity and scale are the primary drivers of alignment to human representations (Conwell et al., 2023; Muttenthaler et al., 2023). As such, this key difference between the setting of artificial emergent communication and human language emergence can drive the observed differences in representations. Due to the difficulty of interpreting these representations, we see this as another reason to evaluate emergent protocols on more strict datasets with clear pragmatic value for humans.

References

Michal Auersperger and Pavel Pecina. 2022. Defending compositionality in emergent languages. In *Proceedings of the 2022 Conference of the North American Chapter of the Association for Computational Linguistics: Human Language Technologies: Student Research Workshop*, pages 285–291, Hybrid: Seattle, Washington + Online. Association for Computational Linguistics.

Mathieu Blondel, Olivier Teboul, Quentin Berthet, and Josip Djolonga. 2020. Fast differentiable sorting and ranking. In *International Conference on Machine Learning*, pages 950–959. PMLR.

Diane Bouchacourt and Marco Baroni. 2018. How agents see things: On visual representations in an emergent language game. In *Proceedings of the 2018 Conference on Empirical Methods in Natural Language Processing*, pages 981–985, Brussels, Belgium. Association for Computational Linguistics.

Henry Brighton and Simon Kirby. 2006. Understanding linguistic evolution by visualizing the emergence of topographic mappings. *Artificial Life*, 12(2):229–242.

Rahma Chaabouni, Eugene Kharitonov, Diane Bouchacourt, Emmanuel Dupoux, and Marco Baroni. 2020. Compositionality and generalization in emergent languages. In *Proceedings of the 58th Annual Meeting of the Association for Computational Linguistics*, pages 4427–4442, Online. Association for Computational Linguistics.

Rahma Chaabouni, Eugene Kharitonov, Emmanuel Dupoux, and Marco Baroni. 2019a. Anti-efficient encoding in emergent communication. In *Advances in Neural Information Processing Systems*, volume 32. Curran Associates, Inc.

Rahma Chaabouni, Eugene Kharitonov, Alessandro Lazaric, Emmanuel Dupoux, and Marco Baroni. 2019b. Word-order biases in deep-agent emergent communication. In *Proceedings of the 57th Annual Meeting of the Association for Computational Linguistics*, pages 5166–5175, Florence, Italy. Association for Computational Linguistics.

Rahma Chaabouni, Florian Strub, Florent Altché, Eugene Tarassov, Corentin Tallec, Elnaz Davoodi, Kory Wallace Mathewson, Olivier Tieleman, Angeliki Lazaridou, and Bilal Piot. 2022. Emergent communication at scale. In *International Conference on Learning Representations*.

Emily Cheng, Mathieu Rita, and Thierry Poibeau. 2023. On the correspondence between compositionality and imitation in emergent neural communication. In *Findings of the Association for Computational Linguistics: ACL 2023*, pages 12432–12447, Toronto, Canada. Association for Computational Linguistics.

Kyunghyun Cho, Bart van Merriënboer, Caglar Gulcehre, Dzmitry Bahdanau, Fethi Bougares, Holger Schwenk, and Yoshua Bengio. 2014. Learning phrase representations using RNN encoder–decoder for statistical machine translation. In *Proceedings of the 2014 Conference on Empirical Methods in Natural Language Processing (EMNLP)*, pages 1724–1734, Doha, Qatar. Association for Computational Linguistics.

Henry Conklin and Kenny Smith. 2023. Compositionality with variation reliably emerges in neural networks. In *The Eleventh International Conference on Learning Representations*.

Colin Conwell, Jacob S. Prince, Kendrick N. Kay, George A. Alvarez, and Talia Konkle. 2023. What can 1.8 billion regressions tell us about the pressures shaping high-level visual representation in brains and machines? *bioRxiv*.

Gautier Dagan, Dieuwke Hupkes, and Elia Bruni. 2021. Co-evolution of language and agents in referential games. In *Proceedings of the 16th Conference of the European Chapter of the Association for Computational Linguistics: Main Volume*, pages 2993–3004, Online. Association for Computational Linguistics.

Bart de Boer. 2006. Computer modeling as a tool for understanding language evolution. In Nathalie Gontier, Jean Paul Van Bendegem, and Diederik Aerts, editors, *Evolutionary Epistemology, Language and Culture*, pages 381–406. Springer, Dordrecht.

Roberto Dessi, Eugene Kharitonov, and Baroni Marco. 2021. Interpretable agent communication from scratch (with a generic visual processor emerging on the side). In *Advances in Neural Information Processing Systems*, volume 34, pages 26937–26949. Curran Associates, Inc.

Anuj Diwan, Layne Berry, Eunsol Choi, David Harwath, and Kyle Mahowald. 2022. Why is winoground hard? investigating failures in visuolinguistic compositionality. In *Proceedings of the 2022 Conference on Empirical Methods in Natural Language Processing*, pages 2236–2250, Abu Dhabi, United Arab Emirates. Association for Computational Linguistics.

Lukas Galke, Yoav Ram, and Limor Raviv. 2022. Emergent communication for understanding human language evolution: What's missing? In *Emergent Communication Workshop at ICLR 2022*.

Lukas Galke and Limor Raviv. 2024. Emergent communication and learning pressures in language models: a language evolution perspective. *arXiv preprint arXiv:2403.14427*.

Shangmin Guo, Yi Ren, Serhii Havrylov, Stella Frank, Ivan Titov, and Kenny Smith. 2019. The emergence of compositional languages for numeric concepts through iterated learning in neural agents.

Kaiming He, Xiangyu Zhang, Shaoqing Ren, and Jian Sun. 2016. Deep residual learning for image recognition. In *Proceedings of the IEEE Conference on Computer Vision and Pattern Recognition (CVPR)*, pages 770–778.

Charles F Hockett. 1959. Animal" languages" and human language. *Human Biology*, 31(1):32–39.

Cheng-Yu Hsieh, Jieyu Zhang, Zixian Ma, Aniruddha Kembhavi, and Ranjay Krishna. 2023. Sugarcrepe: Fixing hackable benchmarks for vision-language compositionality. In *Advances in Neural Information Processing Systems*, volume 36, pages 31096–31116. Curran Associates, Inc.

Amita Kamath, Jack Hessel, and Kai-Wei Chang. 2023. What's "up" with vision-language models? investigating their struggle with spatial reasoning. In *Proceedings of the 2023 Conference on Empirical Methods in Natural Language Processing*, pages 9161–9175, Singapore. Association for Computational Linguistics.

Eugene Kharitonov, Rahma Chaabouni, Diane Bouchacourt, and Marco Baroni. 2020. Entropy minimization in emergent languages. In *Proceedings of the 37th International Conference on Machine Learning*, volume 119 of *Proceedings of Machine Learning Research*, pages 5220–5230. PMLR.

Eugene Kharitonov, Roberto Dessì, Rahma Chaabouni, Diane Bouchacourt, and Marco Baroni. 2021. EGG: a toolkit for research on Emergence of lanGuage in Games. `https://github.com/facebookresearch/EGG`.

Simon Kirby, Hannah Cornish, and Kenny Smith. 2008. Cumulative cultural evolution in the laboratory: An experimental approach to the origins of structure in human language. *Proceedings of the National Academy of Sciences*, 105(31):10681–10686.

Simon Kirby, Tom Griffiths, and Kenny Smith. 2014. Iterated learning and the evolution of language.

Simon Kirby, Monica Tamariz, Hannah Cornish, and Kenny Smith. 2015. Compression and communication in the cultural evolution of linguistic structure. *Cognition*, 141:87–102.

Satwik Kottur, José Moura, Stefan Lee, and Dhruv Batra. 2017. Natural language does not emerge 'naturally' in multi-agent dialog. In *Proceedings of the 2017 Conference on Empirical Methods in Natural Language Processing*, pages 2962–2967, Copenhagen, Denmark. Association for Computational Linguistics.

Tom Kouwenhoven, Tessa Verhoef, Roy de Kleijn, and Stephan Raaijmakers. 2022. Emerging Grounded Shared Vocabularies Between Human and Machine, Inspired by Human Language Evolution. *Frontiers in Artificial Intelligence*, 5.

Nikolaus Kriegeskorte, Marieke Mur, and Peter A Bandettini. 2008. Representational similarity analysis-connecting the branches of systems neuroscience. *Frontiers in systems neuroscience*, 2:4.

Angeliki Lazaridou and Marco Baroni. 2020. Emergent multi-agent communication in the deep learning era. *arXiv preprint arXiv:2006.02419*.

Angeliki Lazaridou, Karl Moritz Hermann, Karl Tuyls, and Stephen Clark. 2018. Emergence of linguistic communication from referential games with symbolic and pixel input. In *International Conference on Learning Representations*.

Angeliki Lazaridou, Alexander Peysakhovich, and Marco Baroni. 2017. Multi-agent cooperation and the emergence of (natural) language. *5th International Conference on Learning Representations, ICLR 2017 - Conference Track Proceedings*, pages 1–11.

David Lewis. 1969. Convention: A philosophical study. *Cambridge, MA*.

Fushan Li and Michael Bowling. 2019. Ease-of-teaching and language structure from emergent communication. In *Advances in Neural Information Processing Systems*, volume 32. Curran Associates, Inc.

Yuchen Lian, Arianna Bisazza, and Tessa Verhoef. 2021. The effect of efficient messaging and input variability on neural-agent iterated language learning. In *Proceedings of the 2021 Conference on Empirical Methods in Natural Language Processing*, pages 10121–10129, Online and Punta Cana, Dominican Republic. Association for Computational Linguistics.

Yuchen Lian, Arianna Bisazza, and Tessa Verhoef. 2023. Communication Drives the Emergence of Language Universals in Neural Agents: Evidence from the Word-order/Case-marking Trade-off. *Transactions of the Association for Computational Linguistics*, 11:1033–1047.

Tsung-Yi Lin, Michael Maire, Serge Belongie, James Hays, Pietro Perona, Deva Ramanan, Piotr Dollár, and C Lawrence Zitnick. 2014. Microsoft coco: Common objects in context. In *Computer Vision–ECCV 2014: 13th European Conference, Zurich, Switzerland, September 6-12, 2014, Proceedings, Part V 13*, pages 740–755. Springer.

John Locke. 1847. *An essay concerning human understanding*, volume 114. Kay & Troutman.

Ryan Lowe, Abhinav Gupta, Jakob Foerster, Douwe Kiela, and Joelle Pineau. 2020. On the interaction between supervision and self-play in emergent communication. In *International Conference on Learning Representations*.

Matéo Mahaut, Francesca Franzon, Roberto Dessì, and Marco Baroni. 2024. Referential communication in heterogeneous communities of pre-trained visual deep networks.

Paul Michel, Mathieu Rita, Kory Wallace Mathewson, Olivier Tieleman, and Angeliki Lazaridou. 2023. Revisiting populations in multi-agent communication. In *The Eleventh International Conference on Learning Representations*.

Volodymyr Mnih, Adria Puigdomenech Badia, Mehdi Mirza, Alex Graves, Timothy Lillicrap, Tim Harley, David Silver, and Koray Kavukcuoglu. 2016. Asynchronous methods for deep reinforcement learning. In *Proceedings of The 33rd International Conference on Machine Learning*, volume 48 of *Proceedings of Machine Learning Research*, pages 1928–1937, New York, New York, USA. PMLR.

Milton Llera Montero, Casimir JH Ludwig, Rui Ponte Costa, Gaurav Malhotra, and Jeffrey Bowers. 2021. The role of disentanglement in generalisation. In *International Conference on Learning Representations*.

Jesse Mu and Noah Goodman. 2021. Emergent communication of generalizations. In *Advances in Neural Information Processing Systems*, volume 34, pages 17994–18007. Curran Associates, Inc.

Lukas Muttenthaler, Jonas Dippel, Lorenz Linhardt, Robert A. Vandermeulen, and Simon Kornblith. 2023. Human alignment of neural network representations. In *The Eleventh International Conference on Learning Representations*.

Maxime Oquab, Timothée Darcet, Théo Moutakanni, Huy V. Vo, Marc Szafraniec, Vasil Khalidov, Pierre Fernandez, Daniel HAZIZA, Francisco Massa, Alaaeldin El-Nouby, Mido Assran, Nicolas Ballas, Wojciech Galuba, Russell Howes, Po-Yao Huang, Shang-Wen Li, Ishan Misra, Michael Rabbat, Vasu Sharma, Gabriel Synnaeve, Hu Xu, Herve Jegou, Julien Mairal, Patrick Labatut, Armand Joulin, and Piotr Bojanowski. 2024. DINOv2: Learning robust visual features without supervision. *Transactions on Machine Learning Research*.

Alec Radford, Jong Wook Kim, Chris Hallacy, Aditya Ramesh, Gabriel Goh, Sandhini Agarwal, Girish Sastry, Amanda Askell, Pamela Mishkin, Jack Clark, et al. 2021. Learning transferable visual models from natural language supervision. In *International conference on machine learning*, pages 8748–8763. PMLR.

Limor Raviv, Antje Meyer, and Shiri Lev-Ari. 2019a. Compositional structure can emerge without generational transmission. *Cognition*, 182:151–164.

Limor Raviv, Antje Meyer, and Shiri Lev-Ari. 2019b. Larger communities create more systematic languages. *Proceedings of the Royal Society B*, 286(1907):20191262.

Arijit Ray, Filip Radenovic, Abhimanyu Dubey, Bryan Plummer, Ranjay Krishna, and Kate Saenko. 2023. Cola: A benchmark for compositional text-to-image retrieval. In *Advances in Neural Information Processing Systems*, volume 36, pages 46433–46445. Curran Associates, Inc.

Yi Ren, Shangmin Guo, Matthieu Labeau, Shay B. Cohen, and Simon Kirby. 2020. Compositional languages emerge in a neural iterated learning model. In *International Conference on Learning Representations*.

Mathieu Rita, Paul Michel, Rahma Chaabouni, Olivier Pietquin, Emmanuel Dupoux, and Florian Strub. 2024. Language evolution with deep learning. *arXiv preprint arXiv:2403.11958*.

Mathieu Rita, Corentin Tallec, Paul Michel, Jean-Bastien Grill, Olivier Pietquin, Emmanuel Dupoux, and Florian Strub. 2022. Emergent communication: Generalization and overfitting in lewis games. In *Advances in Neural Information Processing Systems*, volume 35, pages 1389–1404. Curran Associates, Inc.

Reinhard Selten and Massimo Warglien. 2007. The emergence of simple languages in an experimental coordination game. *Proceedings of the National Academy of Sciences*, 104(18):7361–7366.

Kenny Smith. 2022. How Language Learning and Language Use Create Linguistic Structure. *Current Directions in Psychological Science*, 31(2):177–186.

Luc Steels and Martin Loetzsch. 2012. The Grounded Naming Game. *Experiments in cultural language evolution*, 3:41–59.

Shane Steinert-Threlkeld, Xuhui Zhou, Zeyu Liu, and C. M. Downey. 2022. Emergent communication fine-tuning (EC-FT) for pretrained language models. In *Emergent Communication Workshop at ICLR 2022*.

Ilia Sucholutsky, Lukas Muttenthaler, Adrian Weller, Andi Peng, Andreea Bobu, Been Kim, Bradley C. Love, Erin Grant, Iris Groen, Jascha Achterberg, Joshua B. Tenenbaum, Katherine M. Collins, Katherine L. Hermann, Kerem Oktar, Klaus Greff, Martin N. Hebart, Nori Jacoby, Qiuyi Zhang, Raja Marjieh, Robert Geirhos, Sherol Chen, Simon Kornblith, Sunayana Rane, Talia Konkle, Thomas P. O'Connell, Thomas Unterthiner, Andrew K. Lampinen, Klaus-Robert Müller, Mariya Toneva, and Thomas L. Griffiths. 2023. Getting aligned on representational alignment.

Tristan Thrush, Ryan Jiang, Max Bartolo, Amanpreet Singh, Adina Williams, Douwe Kiela, and Candace Ross. 2022. Winoground: Probing vision and language models for visio-linguistic compositionality.

In *Proceedings of the IEEE/CVF Conference on Computer Vision and Pattern Recognition (CVPR)*, pages 5238–5248.

Olivier Tieleman, Angeliki Lazaridou, Shibl Mourad, Charles Blundell, and Doina Precup. 2019. Shaping representations through communication: community size effect in artificial learning systems. *arXiv preprint arXiv:1912.06208*.

Ronald J Williams. 1992. Simple statistical gradient-following algorithms for connectionist reinforcement learning. *Machine learning*, 8:229–256.

Zhenlin Xu, Marc Niethammer, and Colin A Raffel. 2022. Compositional generalization in unsupervised compositional representation learning: A study on disentanglement and emergent language. In *Advances in Neural Information Processing Systems*, volume 35, pages 25074–25087. Curran Associates, Inc.

Chenhao Zheng, Jieyu Zhang, Aniruddha Kembhavi, and Ranjay Krishna. 2024. Iterated learning improves compositionality in large vision-language models. In *Proceedings of the IEEE/CVF Conference on Computer Vision and Pattern Recognition (CVPR)*, pages 13785–13795.

A Channel capacity

To test to what degree communicative success, TOPSIM, and representational alignment are confounded with the communication channel capacity, we ran simulations altering the vocabulary size ($V = \{3, 5, 10, 20, 40, 50, 100\}$) and message length ($L = \{2, 3, 5, 10, 50, 100\}$) resulting in 42 parameter settings per loss type.

Overall, performance is relatively independent of the chosen configuration, but vocabulary size influences success more than message length (Figure 5). The hyperparameters that resulted in the best validation accuracy (i.e., generalisation; Chaabouni et al., 2022) for the standard *ce* setup were $V = 40$ and $L = 2$. These parameters are used to produce the results in the main paper. Contra expectations, the vocabulary size also influenced TOPSIM more than message length. It, especially in the case of $ce + L_{\text{RSA}}$, is higher when messages are shorter but have access to a larger vocabulary (Figure 6).

Figure 7 shows that, regardless of capacity, inter-agent alignment (RSA$_{sl}$) increases while image-agent alignment (RSA$_{si}$ and RSA$_{li}$) decreases with the *ce* loss. Interestingly, RSA$_{sl}$ is agnostic to capacity but a larger vocabulary size, not message length, reduces the degree of drifting away from the input. We hypothesise this to result from lower pressure to compress rich continuous embeddings into smaller discrete vocabulary embeddings.

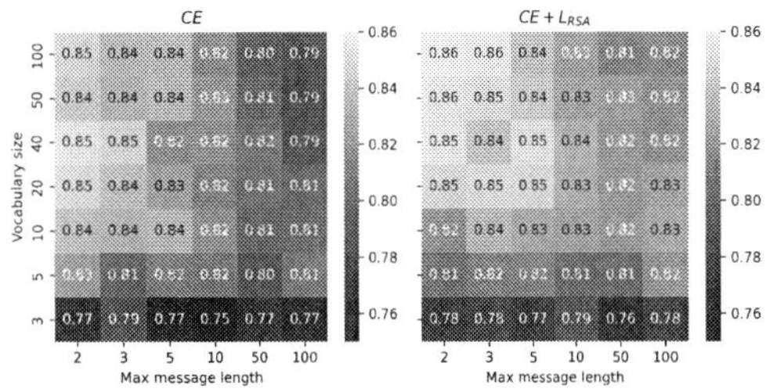

Figure 5: The validation accuracy as a dependent factor of the vocabulary size and maximum message length. Values are averages across 15 seeds.

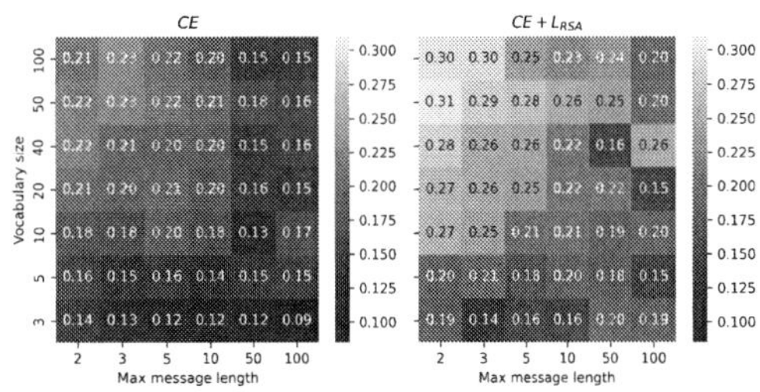

Figure 6: TOPSIM as a dependent factor of the vocabulary size and maximum message length. Values are averages across 15 seeds.

B Best hyperparameters

The parameters used to run the experiments in the main paper were the following:

Parameter	Value
Batch size	32
Optimiser	Adam
Learning Rate (S & L)	0.01 & 0.001
Vocabulary size (V)	40
Message length (L)	2
Hidden size (S & L)	768 & 768
Embedding size	50
Listener cosine temperature	0.1
Seeds	16,22,41,56,67, 77,14,78,99,23, 82,40,51,37,62

Table 1: Best-performing parameters resulting from the parameter sweep.

C Interaction of the alignment term on the cross-entropy loss

To ensure that there is no impact of the alignment penalty on the pressure for communicative success, we ablated the L_{RSA} term of our proposed

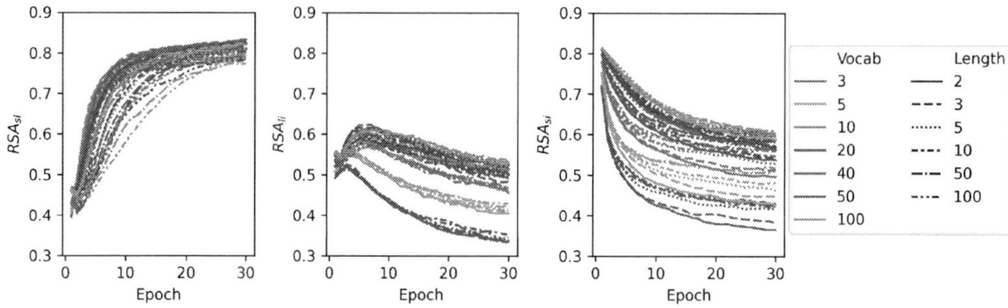

Figure 7: Representational alignment metrics averaged over 15 simulations with the standard ce loss. Regardless of channel capacity, representational alignment always occurs while losing relation to the input.

loss function and found that both, communicative success and ce are not affected by the alignment penalty (Figure 8). Corroborating that only the ce term provides pressure for successful communication (§5.4).

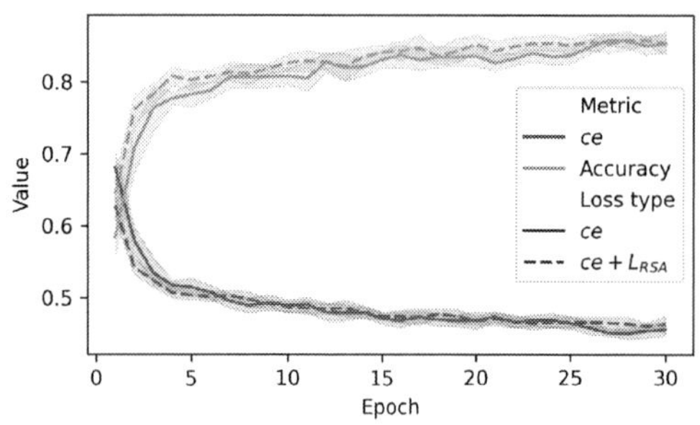

Figure 8: Learning curves (accuracy) and cross-entropy loss (ce) for both loss settings. There is virtually no effect of the auxiliary term L_{RSA} on the cross entropy loss or communicative success.

D Pre-trained vision modules

Although it is in principle possible to train the vision module of the agents from scratch (Dessi et al., 2021), in our work, agents' perception stems from a pre-trained vision-language model. Although there is reason to believe that DinoV2 embeddings capture high-level, conceptual image features useful for discriminating image pairs (Oquab et al., 2024), we assessed the degree to which the alignment problem occurs for different pre-trained models despite encoding the same objects. We ran additional simulations using image features obtained from ResNet (He et al., 2016) and CLIP (Radford et al., 2021) for 6 different parameter settings with the ce loss function. Here we used the parameters that resulted in the best, worst, mean, and quantile validation performance from the parameter sweep in appendix A (see Table 2), and a sensible setup with $V = 10$ and $L = 5$.

Msg. Length (L)	Vocab. Size (V)	Vision
2	40	
3	10	
5	5	DinoV2
5	10	CLIP
10	3	ResNet
50	100	

Table 2: The parameters for running additional simulations with CLIP and ResNet to assess the robustness of our results. Each combination was run for 15 different seeds. Note: results for the DinoV2 simulations are from the sweep.

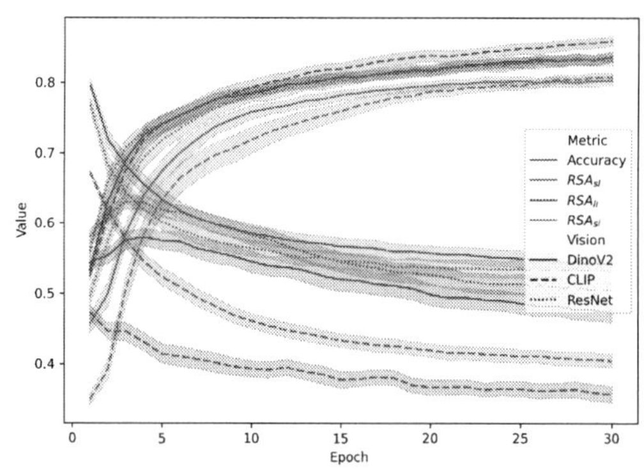

Figure 9: Learning curves (accuracy) and RSA metrics for different vision models averaged over 6 parameter settings with 15 seeds each. The representational alignment problem always occurs. Line style corresponds to the vision module used to obtain image embeddings and colour indicates the metric. Areas indicate the 95% confidence intervals.

Figure 9 shows clearly that inter-agent alignment

increases while agent-image alignment *decreases* for all models. In addition to the similar results reported by Bouchacourt and Baroni (2018) for VGG ConvNet embeddings, both 4096 and 1000 layers, we can confirm that the problem is agnostic to the input embeddings. Interestingly, agent representations drift most for CLIP embeddings. Nevertheless, the agents still develop a successful communication strategy, indicating that out-of-the-box CLIP embeddings are the least useful for agents in finding a (non-grounded) solution. No such differences are seen when the agents are trained with the additional alignment penalty term, inter-agent and image-agent alignment remain high for all models.

Hierarchical syntactic structure in human-like language models

Michael Wolfman
University of Georgia
michael.wolfman@uga.edu

Donald Dunagan
University of Georgia
dgd45125@uga.edu

Jonathan Brennan
University of Michigan
jobrenn@umich.edu

John T. Hale
University of Georgia
jthale@uga.edu

Abstract

Language models (LMs) are a meeting point for cognitive modeling and computational linguistics. How should they be designed to serve as adequate cognitive models? To address this question, this study contrasts two Transformer-based LMs that share the same architecture. Only one of them analyzes sentences in terms of explicit hierarchical structure. Evaluating the two LMs against fMRI time series via the surprisal complexity metric, the results implicate the superior temporal gyrus. and This underlines the need for hierarchical sentence structure in word-by-word models of human language comprehension.

1 Introduction

Interest in language models (LMs) has exploded due to their recent success on language-related tasks (Min et al., 2021), with many commentators speculating about their implications as models of human language processing (see Millière, 2024, §IV.ii, for a review). The methodological utility of natural language processing tools for isolating language-processing functions in the brain is by now well-established (Brennan et al., 2012; Wehbe et al., 2014; Henderson et al., 2016; Shain et al., 2020; Stanojević et al., 2023); however, controversy persists regarding the role of hierarchical structure as useful or not in characterizing human language comprehension (e.g., Frank et al., 2012; Christiansen and Chater, 2015), yielding two related questions.

1. Is hierarchical structure part of the best description of human language comprehension?

2. If so, what brain regions subserve this aspect of processing?

This study investigates these questions by comparing two language models with the same underlying architecture. One is constrained via a special attention mask that captures hierarchical structure in the form of syntactic constituency, while the other lacks this attention mask, capturing only word-level information. The hierarchy-biased model is a Transformer Grammar (TG; Sartran et al., 2022), which differs only from the unconstrained model, Transformer-XL (TXL; Dai et al., 2019), in the presence of this attention mask.

We pair these language models with surprisal, a word-by-word information-theoretic complexity metric (see Hale, 2016, for a review) to derive predictions about neuroimaging data. Surprisal from the hierarchy-biased TG compares against surprisal from the unconstrained TXL in the task of predicting fMRI data (Li et al., 2022). This sets up a clean contrast between hierarchical and non-hierarchical conceptions of language comprehension.

The results, reported in section 6, support the role of hierarchical structure in language comprehension. Surprisal values derived from a Transformer Grammar predict fMRI timecourses in bilateral superior temporal gyrus (STG) better than those from TXL. This supports the view that the STG is sensitive to hierarchical sentence structure (Friederici and Gierhan, 2013; Friederici, 2017).

2 Phrase Structure

The Penn Treebank operationalizes one notion of hierarchical structure (Marcus et al., 1993). The present study uses these trees, exemplified in Figure 1. The syntactic analyses that they express date back to Chomsky's Standard Theory (1965) and can be motivated by considerations such as substitution, compositionality and structure-dependence of transformational rules which are reviewed in introductory linguistics textbooks (e.g. Akmajian et al., 2010). For a broad, comparative discussion of hierarchical structure in language, see Coopmans et al. (2023).

Proceedings of the Workshop on Cognitive Modeling and Computational Linguistics, pages 72–80
August 15, 2024 ©2024 Association for Computational Linguistics

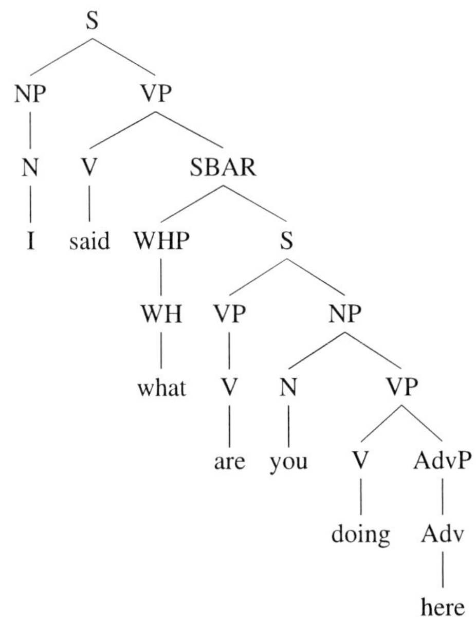

Figure 1: An example sentence attested in the stimulus text (*The Little Prince*) used in the fMRI study, see section 5.3.

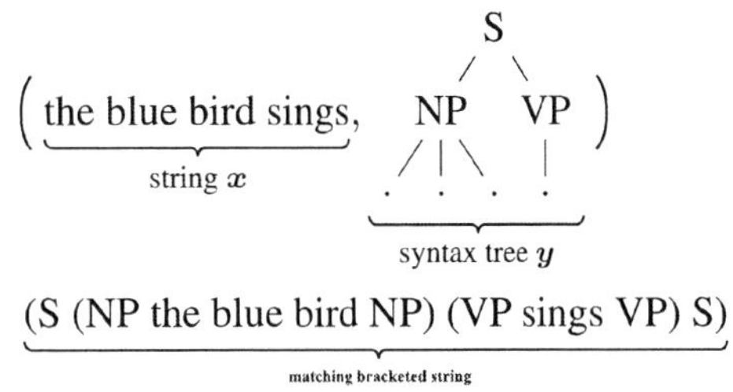

Figure 2: An example of a string x and tree y, which are modeled by a labelled bracketed sequence of (x,y) (Adapted from Sartran et al., 2022, Figure 1).

3 Transformer Grammar

Transformer Grammars (Sartran et al., 2022) model the joint-probability of a surface string x and its corresponding phrase structure tree y, $p(x, y)$. They incorporate an inductive bias toward hierarchical syntax via special attention masks. These attention masks mark the only difference between TG and a general Transformer-XL (Dai et al., 2019).

TGs apply the idea of parsing as language modeling (Vinyals et al., 2015; Dyer et al., 2016; Choe and Charniak, 2016) by assigning probability to labelled, bracketed strings. They innovate on that idea by restricting — via the additional attention mask – the information used in label assignment. This information is restricted to prior composed phrases and the direct subconstituents of the current phrase being composed. These restrictions result in stack representations that correspond to levels of a syntactic derivation (for more details on TG's recursive syntactic composition see Sartran et al., 2022, §2.1).

4 Previous Work Investigating Hierarchy using Computational Modeling and Neuroimaging Data

This work builds on research that compares word-by-word difficulty predictions against neuroimaging data. Previous work of this type has found support for hierarchical structure (Brennan et al., 2012, 2016; Henderson et al., 2016; Li and Hale, 2019; Shain et al., 2020; Reddy and Wehbe, 2021; Stanojević et al., 2023; Sugimoto et al., 2023; Oota et al., 2023). Hale et al. (2022) and Uddén et al. (2020, §2) review this interdisciplinary line of work from computational and neuroscientific perspectives, respectively.

Others, following in the tradition of Elman (e.g., 1990, see also Frank et al., 2012, Christiansen and Chater, 2015), have questioned the need for hierarchical structure. Proponents of this view point to the successes of LMs that rely just on overt word sequences in encoding (or decoding) human brain responses to language (e.g., Caucheteux et al., 2021a; Caucheteux and King, 2022; Toneva et al., 2022; see Karamolegkou et al., 2023 for a review). The most extreme form of this view holds that word-prediction alone suffices to explain human language processing (Schrimpf et al., 2021; Goldstein et al., 2022a).

The present study addresses this debate regarding the role of hierarchy in language comprehension by comparing two language models with the same underlying architecture, the only difference being that hierarchical structure is explicitly present (vis-a-vis the additional attention mask) in one (the TG) and not in the other (the TXL).

5 Methodology

5.1 Language Modeling

A 252M parameter, 16-layer, 8-attention-head TG was used as the hierarchy-biased model.[1] A 252M parameter, 16-layer, 8-attention-head TXL (Dai et al., 2019) was used as the unconstrained lan-

[1] https://github.com/google-deepmind/transformer_grammars

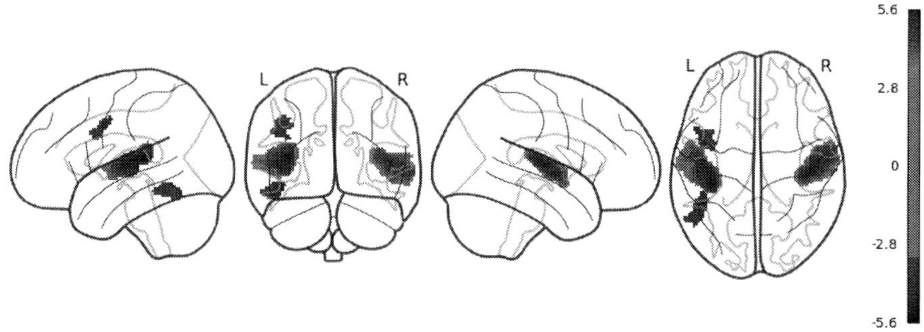

Figure 3: Glass brain z-map showing significant clusters of r^2 increase for hierarchy-biased TG surprisal (red) or unconstrained TXL surprisal (blue), thresholded with an expected false discovery rate (FDR) < 0.05 and a cluster threshold of 50 voxels.

guage model.[2] Both models were trained on the BLLIP-LG dataset (Charniak et al., 2000), as split by Hu et al. (2020). The training set is comprised of 1.8M sentences (≈40M words). Tokenization was performed with SentencePiece (Kudo and Richardson, 2018) using a subword algorithm (Kudo, 2018) with a 32K word-piece vocabulary.

The only difference between the TXL and TG in this study is the additional attention mask. Their number of parameters, layers, attention heads, and training/evaluation data (excluding the annotations used for TG) are identical. Indeed, as reported in Table A.3, the trained models arrive at highly similar test set perplexities.

5.2 Linking assumptions

To link brain data to language models, we use the surprisal complexity metric (Hale, 2001; Levy, 2008). Surprisal is the negative logarithm of the conditional probability of the next token, given previous tokens, on a particular LM (for a review, see Hale, 2016). These per-token numerical values serve as theoretical predictions that may explain time-dependent neural signals from people hearing those words. In this case, the neural signal is the blood oxygen level dependent (BOLD) signal measured with fMRI at each voxel in the brain (see §5.3 below).

Whereas surprisal values from the string-oriented TXL are exact, surprisals from the tree-oriented TG are approximated using the top 300 trees sampled from a Recurrent Neural Network Grammar (Noji and Oseki, 2021).

5.3 fMRI

5.3.1 Data

The fMRI data analyzed was the the English section of the Little Prince Datasets (Li et al., 2022, N = 49). Participants were scanned while they engaged in the naturalistic task of listening to an audiobook recording of David Wilkinson's English translation of *Le Petit Prince* (*The Little Prince*), read by Karen Savage. Data collection protocols and preprocessing steps are reported in the cited paper.

5.3.2 Statistical Analysis

To assess both LMs with respect to human neuroimaging data, we pursue an r^2 analysis, following Crabbé et al. (2019, §5).

Single-Subject Statistics For each subject, we calculate how much the inclusion of the variables of interest—TG surprisal and TXL surprisal—increases cross-validated BOLD r^2 with respect to a base model with only predictors of non-interest. Here, r^2 values indicate the voxel-wise variance explained. Thus, at the first level, two brain maps are calculated for each participant: one indicating the increase in cross-validated brain activity r^2 associated with adding TG surprisal to a baseline model; and one indicating the increase in cross-validated brain activity r^2 associated with adding TXL surprisal to a baseline model. The baseline model included: spoken word rate, word frequency, 5 principal components derived from fastText word vectors (Bojanowski et al., 2016), and the pitch and acoustic intensity of the narrator's voice.

BOLD signal is modeled, at each voxel, for each participant, via generalized linear model.

Region	Cluster size (mm^3)	MNI Coordinates X	Y	Z	Peak Stat (z)
Left Superior Temporal Gyrus (STG)	11208	-38.0	-32.0	10.0	5.57
		-46.0	-14.0	4.0	5.26
Right STG	10680	48.0	-18.0	6.0	5.36
		60.0	-10.0	0.0	5.09
Left Fusiform Gyrus	2224	-46.0	-48.0	-14.0	-4.48
		-52.0	-58.0	-18.0	-4.15
Left Pre-Motor Cortex	1552	-44.0	4.0	38.0	-4.16

Table 1: Results of paired T-test between hierarchy-biased and unconstrained cross-validated r^2 increase, thresholded with an expected false discovery rate < 0.05 and a cluster threshold of 50 voxels.

The word-level metrics are temporally annotated at the offset of each word in the audiobook, while the speech-related metrics are annotated every 10ms. All regressors, described in Table A.1, were convolved with the SPM canonical hemodynamic response function (Poldrack et al., 2011). Regressors of non-interest are included to ensure that any effects found are not due to other facets of linguistic processing (Lund et al., 2006).

Group-Level Statistics The single-subject r^2 increase brain maps (one TG map, one TXL map, per subject) were entered into a paired t-test to compare the impact of the additions of TG surprisal and TXL surprisal to base model of the BOLD signal. The results indicate where the addition of one variable to the base model (either TG surprisal or TXL surprisal) contributes to explaining the BOLD signal significantly better than the other.

6 Results

The addition of surprisal derived from the hierarchy-biased TG model performed above-and-beyond the addition of surprisal derived from the unconstrained TXL model in goodness-of-fit (r^2) to the measured BOLD signal in bilateral STG (Fig. 3; Table 1). The unconstrained model performed above-and-beyond the hierarchy-biased model in the left fusiform gyrus and pre-motor cortex. The significant clusters found were thresholded using an expected false discovery rate < 0.05 and a cluster threshold of 50 voxels.

7 Discussion

The findings support the role of STG in hierarchically-sensitive sentence processing (Friederici and Gierhan, 2013; Friederici, 2017). Notably, the results for surprisal in STG are largely localized to auditory cortex (see also Willems et al., 2016). These results suggest, in line with the sensory hypothesis (Dikker et al., 2009), that hierarchical structure from earlier in the sentence can impact low-level sensory processing. Prior investigation into early (< 150 ms) processing using MEG has found that auditory cortex is sensitive to phrase structure (Herrmann et al., 2009). This early sensitivity to hierarchical structure indicates that previously encountered structure may modulate sensory processing of subsequent words in a top-down manner. Employing a precise regression analysis and holding the architecture of LMs constant, the current study offers novel evidence in support of the sensory hypothesis and the early influence of hierarchical structure in language comprehension.

One region that has been largely implicated in predictive processing such as the type modeled here (e.g., Henderson et al., 2016; Brennan et al., 2020; Shain et al., 2020) is the left inferior frontal gyrus (LIFG). The present study does not implicate LIFG. It is possible that this null result could be due to the fact that the level of prediction and prediction violation here is too modest to invoke the LIFG, which seems more associated with processing particularly complex stimuli.

The success of modern LMs in natural language processing tasks has revived hope (see §4) that hierarchical structure could be left out of an adequate cognitive model. The results reported here suggest contrariwise. This echos Huang et al. (2024), who find that LMs strongly under-predict human reading time on syntactically challenging constructions, Antonello and Huth (2024) who differentiate LM layers that better-predict successor words from layers that better-predict fMRI data, and Yedetore et al. (2023), who find that unbiased LMs fail to generalize structurally-dependent constructions in a human-like way. With Antonello and Huth, we acknowledge that unconstrained LMs learn something about syntax. But it is not enough; in the context of cognitive modeling, additional bias towards hierarchical structure seems to be needed (Coopmans et al., 2022).

8 Conclusion

Hierarchical structure remains a key part of the best characterization of human language comprehension. This conclusion rests upon the increase in BOLD r^2 from the addition of TG-derived surprisal compared to the addition of TXL-derived surprisal. This obtains in a well-known temporal node of the language network and shores up the view of the language-processing brain as a system that performs hierarchical combinatorics. The results here also support recent arguments against unbiased LMs as cognitive models of human language.

Limitations

The TG (Sartran et al., 2022) and TXL (Dai et al., 2019) models used in this study are 16-layer models. A recent study from Mueller and Linzen (2023) found that depth (number of layers) is a more important factor in a language model's generalization performance than width (embedding and hidden dimensions, feed-forward layer size). Applying these findings to the present study by increasing the depth of the TG and TXL models could yield interesting results. It is possible that adding more layers to both models could affect the magnitude and presence of correlations to brain regions by influencing the generalization patterns of both TG and TXL. Given that the procedure here is theoretically motivated and the results align with both these theoretical considerations and previous neuroimaging work (e.g., the large scale brain model of Friederici, 2017), we do not expect the pattern of results to change. Nonetheless, further investigation is warranted.

This study only considers English. Follow-up studies could be performed in additional languages to solidify and expand the conclusions drawn here.

Finally, as previously mentioned, it has been found (e.g., Toneva and Wehbe, 2019; Caucheteux et al., 2021a; Caucheteux and King, 2022) that intermediate layers of LMs are best at encoding neural data. An interesting follow-up to the current study could probe the representations learned by TXL in its earlier layers and compare how well they encode neural data against a TG.

Ethics Statement

Language models pose risks when used outside of their intended scope. The language models used here are available under a CC-BY 4.0 license, allowing free public use. The training data used here (Charniak et al., 2000) is semi-controlled in that it comes from the Wall Street Journal; however, it is generally important to investigate training data for harmful human bias, which could find its way into language models.

References

Adrian Akmajian, Richard A. Demers, Ann K. Farmer, and Robert M. Harnish. 2010. *Linguistics: an introduction to language and communication*. MIT Press.

Richard Antonello and Alexander Huth. 2024. Predictive Coding or Just Feature Discovery? An Alternative Account of Why Language Models Fit Brain Data. *Neurobiology of Language (Cambridge, Mass.)*, 5(1):64–79.

Piotr Bojanowski, Edouard Grave, Armand Joulin, and Tomas Mikolov. 2016. Enriching word vectors with subword information. *arXiv preprint arXiv:1607.04606*.

Jonathan Brennan, Yuval Nir, Uri Hasson, Rafael Malach, David J. Heeger, and Liina Pylkkänen. 2012. Syntactic structure building in the anterior temporal lobe during natural story listening. *Brain and Language*, 120(2):163–173.

Jonathan R. Brennan, Chris Dyer, Adhiguna Kuncoro, and John T. Hale. 2020. Localizing syntactic predictions using recurrent neural network grammars. *Neuropsychologia*, 146:107479.

Jonathan R. Brennan, Edward P. Stabler, Sarah E. Van Wagenen, Wen-Ming Luh, and John T. Hale. 2016. Abstract linguistic structure correlates with temporal activity during naturalistic comprehension. *Brain and Language*, 157-158:81–94.

Charlotte Caucheteux, Alexandre Gramfort, and Jean-Remi King. 2021a. Disentangling syntax and semantics in the brain with deep networks. In *Proceedings of the 38th International Conference on Machine Learning*, volume 139 of *Proceedings of Machine Learning Research*, pages 1336–1348. PMLR.

Charlotte Caucheteux and Jean-Rémi King. 2022. Brains and algorithms partially converge in natural language processing. *Communications Biology*, 5(1):1–10. Publisher: Nature Publishing Group.

Eugene Charniak, Don Blaheta, Niyu Ge, Keith Hall, John Hale, and Mark Johnson. 2000. BLLIP 1987-89 WSJ Corpus Release 1. Artwork Size: 1048576 KB Pages: 1048576 KB.

Do Kook Choe and Eugene Charniak. 2016. Parsing as Language Modeling. In *Proceedings of the 2016 Conference on Empirical Methods in Natural Language Processing*, pages 2331–2336. Association for Computational Linguistics.

Noam Chomsky. 1965. *Aspects of the Theory of Syntax*, 50 edition. The MIT Press.

Morten H. Christiansen and Nick Chater. 2015. The language faculty that wasn't: a usage-based account of natural language recursion. *Frontiers in Psychology*, 6. Publisher: Frontiers.

Cas W. Coopmans, Helen de Hoop, Karthikeya Kaushik, Peter Hagoort, and Andrea E. Martin. 2022. Hierarchy in language interpretation: evidence from behavioural experiments and computational modelling. *Language, Cognition and Neuroscience*, 37(4):420–439. Publisher: Routledge _eprint: https://doi.org/10.1080/23273798.2021.1980595.

Cas W. Coopmans, Karthikeya Kaushik, and Andrea E. Martin. 2023. Hierarchical structure in language and action: A formal comparison. *Psychological Review*, 130(4):935–952.

Benoit Crabbé, Murielle Fabre, and Christophe Pallier. 2019. Variable beam search for generative neural parsing and its relevance for the analysis of neuro-imaging signal. In *Proceedings of the 2019 Conference on Empirical Methods in Natural Language Processing and the 9th International Joint Conference on Natural Language Processing (EMNLP-IJCNLP)*, pages 1150–1160. Association for Computational Linguistics.

Zihang Dai, Zhilin Yang, Yiming Yang, Jaime Carbonell, Quoc V. Le, and Ruslan Salakhutdinov. 2019. Transformer-XL: Attentive Language Models Beyond a Fixed-Length Context.

Suzanne Dikker, Hugh Rabagliati, and Liina Pylkkänen. 2009. Sensitivity to syntax in visual cortex. *Cognition*, 110(3):293–321.

Chris Dyer, Adhiguna Kuncoro, Miguel Ballesteros, and Noah A. Smith. 2016. Recurrent neural network grammars.

Jeffrey L. Elman. 1990. Finding Structure in Time. *Cognitive Science*, 14(2):179–211. Publisher: John Wiley & Sons, Ltd.

Stefan L. Frank, Rens Bod, and Morten H. Christiansen. 2012. How hierarchical is language use? *Proceedings of the Royal Society B: Biological Sciences*, 279(1747):4522–4531.

Angela D. Friederici. 2017. *Language in Our Brain: The Origins of a Uniquely Human Capacity*. The MIT Press.

Angela D. Friederici and Sarah M. E. Gierhan. 2013. The language network. *Current Opinion in Neurobiology*, 23(2):250–254.

Ariel Goldstein, Zaid Zada, Eliav Buchnik, Mariano Schain, Amy Price, Bobbi Aubrey, Samuel A. Nastase, Amir Feder, Dotan Emanuel, Alon Cohen, Aren Jansen, Harshvardhan Gazula, Gina Choe, Aditi Rao, Catherine Kim, Colton Casto, Lora Fanda, Werner Doyle, Daniel Friedman, Patricia Dugan, Lucia Melloni, Roi Reichart, Sasha Devore, Adeen Flinker, Liat Hasenfratz, Omer Levy, Avinatan Hassidim, Michael Brenner, Yossi Matias, Kenneth A. Norman, Orrin Devinsky, and Uri Hasson. 2022a. Shared computational principles for language processing in humans and deep language models. *Nature Neuroscience*, 25(3):369–380. Number: 3 Publisher: Nature Publishing Group.

John Hale. 2001. A probabilistic earley parser as a psycholinguistic model. In *Second meeting of the North American Chapter of the Association for Computational Linguistics on Language technologies 2001 - NAACL '01*, pages 1–8. Association for Computational Linguistics.

John Hale. 2016. Information-theoretical complexity metrics. *Language and Linguistics Compass*, 10(9):397–412.

John T. Hale, Luca Campanelli, Jixing Li, Shohini Bhattasali, Christophe Pallier, and Jonathan R. Brennan. 2022. Neurocomputational models of language processing. *Annual Review of Linguistics*, 8(1):427–446.

John M Henderson, Wonil Choi, Matthew W Lowder, and Fernanda Ferreira. 2016. Language structure in the brain: A fixation-related fMRI study of syntactic surprisal in reading. *NeuroImage*, 132:293–300.

Björn Herrmann, Burkhard Maess, Anna S. Hasting, and Angela D. Friederici. 2009. Localization of the syntactic mismatch negativity in the temporal cortex: An MEG study. *NeuroImage*, 48(3):590–600.

Jennifer Hu, Jon Gauthier, Peng Qian, Ethan Wilcox, and Roger Levy. 2020. A Systematic Assessment of Syntactic Generalization in Neural Language Models. In *Proceedings of the 58th Annual Meeting of the Association for Computational Linguistics*, pages 1725–1744. Association for Computational Linguistics.

Kuan-Jung Huang, Suhas Arehalli, Mari Kugemoto, Christian Muxica, Grusha Prasad, Brian Dillon, and Tal Linzen. 2024. Large-scale benchmark yields no evidence that language model surprisal explains syntactic disambiguation difficulty. *Journal of Memory and Language*, 137:104510.

Antonia Karamolegkou, Mostafa Abdou, and Anders Søgaard. 2023. Mapping brains with language models: A survey. In *Findings of the Association for Computational Linguistics: ACL 2023*, pages 9748–9762, Toronto, Canada. Association for Computational Linguistics.

Taku Kudo. 2018. Subword Regularization: Improving Neural Network Translation Models with Multiple Subword Candidates. In *Proceedings of the 56th Annual Meeting of the Association for Computational Linguistics (Volume 1: Long Papers)*, pages 66–75. Association for Computational Linguistics.

Taku Kudo and John Richardson. 2018. SentencePiece: A simple and language independent subword tokenizer and detokenizer for Neural Text Processing. ArXiv:1808.06226 [cs].

Roger Levy. 2008. Expectation-based syntactic comprehension. *Cognition*, 106(3):1126–1177. Publisher: Elsevier.

Jixing Li, Shohini Bhattasali, Shulin Zhang, Berta Franzluebbers, Wen-Ming Luh, R. Nathan Spreng, Jonathan R. Brennan, Yiming Yang, Christophe Pallier, and John Hale. 2022. Le Petit Prince multilingual naturalistic fMRI corpus. *Scientific Data*, 9(1):530.

Jixing Li and John Hale. 2019. Grammatical predictors for fMRI timecourses. In Robert C. Berwick and Edward P. Stabler, editors, *Minimalist Parsing*. Oxford University Press.

Torben E. Lund, Kristoffer H. Madsen, Karam Sidaros, Wen-Lin Luo, and Thomas E. Nichols. 2006. Non-white noise in fMRI: Does modelling have an impact? *NeuroImage*, 29(1):54–66.

Mitchell P. Marcus, Mary Ann Marcinkiewicz, and Beatrice Santorini. 1993. Building a large annotated corpus of English: the Penn Treebank. *Computational Linguistics*, 19(2):313–330.

Raphael Millière. 2024. Language models as models of language. *Oxford Handbook of the Philosophy of Linguistics*.

Bonan Min, Hayley Ross, Elior Sulem, Amir Pouran Ben Veyseh, Thien Huu Nguyen, Oscar Sainz, Eneko Agirre, Ilana Heintz, and Dan Roth. 2021. Recent advances in natural language processing via large pre-trained language models: A survey. *CoRR*, abs/2111.01243.

Aaron Mueller and Tal Linzen. 2023. How to plant trees in language models: Data and architectural effects on the emergence of syntactic inductive biases. In *Proceedings of the 61st Annual Meeting of the Association for Computational Linguistics (Volume 1: Long Papers)*, pages 11237–11252, Toronto, Canada. Association for Computational Linguistics.

Hiroshi Noji and Yohei Oseki. 2021. Effective Batching for Recurrent Neural Network Grammars. In *Findings of the Association for Computational Linguistics: ACL-IJCNLP 2021*, pages 4340–4352. Association for Computational Linguistics.

Subba Reddy Oota, Mounika Marreddy, Manish Gupta, and Raju Bapi. 2023. How does the brain process syntactic structure while listening? In *Findings of the Association for Computational Linguistics: ACL 2023*, pages 6624–6647, Toronto, Canada. Association for Computational Linguistics.

Russell A. Poldrack, Jeanette A. Mumford, and Thomas E. Nichols. 2011. Statistical modeling: Single subject analysis. In Russell A. Poldrack, Jeanette A. Mumford, and Thomas E. Nichols, editors, *Handbook of Functional MRI Data Analysis*, pages 70–99. Cambridge University Press.

Aniketh Janardhan Reddy and Leila Wehbe. 2021. Can fMRI reveal the representation of syntactic structure in the brain? In *Advances in Neural Information Processing Systems*, volume 34, pages 9843–9856. Curran Associates, Inc.

Laurent Sartran, Samuel Barrett, Adhiguna Kuncoro, Miloš Stanojević, Phil Blunsom, and Chris Dyer. 2022. Transformer Grammars: Augmenting Transformer Language Models with Syntactic Inductive Biases at Scale. *Transactions of the Association for Computational Linguistics*, 10:1423–1439.

Martin Schrimpf, Idan Asher Blank, Greta Tuckute, Carina Kauf, Eghbal A. Hosseini, Nancy Kanwisher, Joshua B. Tenenbaum, and Evelina Fedorenko. 2021. The neural architecture of language: Integrative modeling converges on predictive processing. *Proceedings of the National Academy of Sciences*, 118(45):e2105646118. Publisher: Proceedings of the National Academy of Sciences.

Cory Shain, Idan Asher Blank, Marten van Schijndel, William Schuler, and Evelina Fedorenko. 2020. fMRI reveals language-specific predictive coding during naturalistic sentence comprehension. *Neuropsychologia*, 138:107307.

Miloš Stanojević, Jonathan R. Brennan, Donald Dunagan, Mark Steedman, and John T. Hale. 2023. Modeling Structure-Building in the Brain With CCG Parsing and Large Language Models. *Cognitive Science*, 47(7):e13312.

Yushi Sugimoto, Ryo Yoshida, Hyeonjeong Jeong, Masatoshi Koizumi, Jonathan R. Brennan, and Yohei Oseki. 2023. Localizing Syntactic Composition with Left-Corner Recurrent Neural Network Grammars. *Neurobiology of Language*, pages 1–48.

Mariya Toneva, Tom M. Mitchell, and Leila Wehbe. 2022. Combining computational controls with natural text reveals aspects of meaning composition. *Nature Computational Science*, 2(11):745–757. Number: 11 Publisher: Nature Publishing Group.

Mariya Toneva and Leila Wehbe. 2019. Interpreting and improving natural-language processing (in machines) with natural language-processing (in the brain). *Advances in neural information processing systems*, 32.

Julia Uddén, Mauricio de Jesus Dias Martins, Willem Zuidema, and W. Tecumseh Fitch. 2020. Hierarchical structure in sequence processing: How to measure it and determine its neural implementation. *Topics in Cognitive Science*, 12(3):910–924.

Oriol Vinyals, Łukasz Kaiser, Terry Koo, Slav Petrov, Ilya Sutskever, and Geoffrey Hinton. 2015. Grammar as a foreign language. *Advances in neural information processing systems*, 28.

Leila Wehbe, Brian Murphy, Partha Talukdar, Alona Fyshe, Aaditya Ramdas, and Tom Mitchell. 2014. Simultaneously Uncovering the Patterns of Brain Regions Involved in Different Story Reading Subprocesses. *PLOS ONE*, 9(11):e112575. Publisher: Public Library of Science.

Roel M. Willems, Stefan L. Frank, Annabel D. Nijhof, Peter Hagoort, and Antal van den Bosch. 2016. Prediction During Natural Language Comprehension. *Cerebral Cortex*, 26(6):2506–2516.

Aditya Yedetore, Tal Linzen, Robert Frank, and R. Thomas McCoy. 2023. How poor is the stimulus? evaluating hierarchical generalization in neural networks trained on child-directed speech. In *Proceedings of the 61st Annual Meeting of the Association for Computational Linguistics (Volume 1: Long Papers)*, pages 9370–9393, Toronto, Canada. Association for Computational Linguistics.

A Appendix

Predictor	Description	Model-Inclusion
TG Surprisal	Surprisal derived from TG at a word	hierarchy-biased
TXL Surprisal	Suprisal derived from TXL at a word	unconstrained
Word Rate	Annotation indicating the existence of a spoken word	base, hierarchy-biased, unconstrained
Word Frequency	Log lexical frequency of a word	base, hierarchy-biased, unconstrained
F_0	Pitch (fundamental frequency) of the voice of the narrator	base, hierarchy-biased, unconstrained
RMS Amplitude	Root Mean Square Amplitude of the voice of the narrator (reflecting intensity)	base, hierarchy-biased, unconstrained
Word Vector_5	5 regressors corresponding to values derived from a word's pretrained fastText vector	base, hierarchy-biased, unconstrained

Table A.1: Generalized linear model predictors

Language Model	Perplexity on Test Set
Transformer Grammar (Sartran et al., 2022)	32.82
Transformer-XL (Dai et al., 2019)	34.07

Table A.3: Perplexity values for the TG and TXL language models on the BLLIP-LG test set, as split by (Hu et al., 2020).

Do LLMs Agree with Humans on Emotional Associations to Nonsense Words?

Yui Miyakawa[1], **Chihaya Matsuhira**[1], **Hirotaka Kato**[1], **Takatsugu Hirayama**[2,1], **Takahiro Komamizu**[1], **Ichiro Ide**[1]

[1]Nagoya University, [2]University of Human Environments

Correspondence: miyakaway@cs.is.i.nagoya-u.ac.jp

Abstract

Understanding human perception of nonsense words is helpful to devise product and character names that match their characteristics. Previous studies have suggested the usefulness of Large Language Models (LLMs) for estimating such human perception, but they did not focus on its emotional aspects. Hence, this study aims to elucidate the relationship of emotions evoked by nonsense words between humans and LLMs. Using a representative LLM, GPT-4, we reproduce the procedure of an existing study to analyze evoked emotions of humans for nonsense words. A positive correlation of 0.40 was found between the emotion intensity scores reproduced by GPT-4 and those manually annotated by humans. Although the correlation is not very high, this demonstrates that GPT-4 may agree with humans on emotional associations to nonsense words. Considering that the previous study reported that the correlation among human annotators was about 0.68 on average and that between a regression model trained on the annotations for real words and humans was 0.17, GPT-4's agreement with humans is notably strong.

1 Introduction

Nonsense words (hereinafter called "nonwords") are words that do not exist within the vocabulary of a language. Although these words do not have any meaning, humans often associate specific impressions and feelings to their pronunciation and spelling (Sabbatino et al., 2022). A well-known example is the Bouba/Kiki effect (Köhler, 1929), in which people tend to associate pointy and round shapes with certain sounds. Understanding such human perception of nonwords brings benefits especially in commerce, as it helps to devise new product, character, and brand names that match their characteristics. Also, it can contribute to discovering how humans process words in general (Traxler and Gernsbacher, 2006). However, investigating such human perception requires experiments on humans, which is costly and labor-intensive, making it difficult to obtain large-scale data sufficient for statistical analysis.

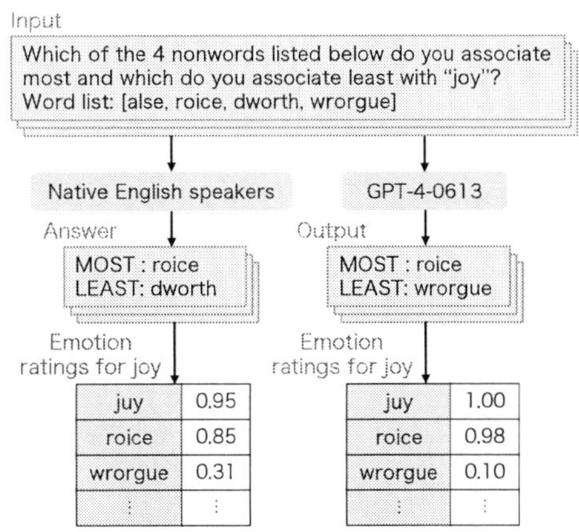

Figure 1: Nonword-emotion annotation procedures by humans and an LLM.

Previous studies have discussed whether Large Language Models (LLMs) can function as cognitive models of natural language (Mahowald et al., 2024), suggesting their usefulness in estimating the evoked impressions of nonwords in humans. Cai et al. (2024) evaluated the association between the sound and form of a nonword and the association between sound and gender in LLMs, namely ChatGPT (OpenAI, 2022) and Vicuna (Chiang et al., 2023). They suggest the usefulness of LLMs for estimating the nonword impressions in humans such as the Bouba/Kiki effect. However, they have not revealed how LLMs work for emotions which is a core component for the meaning of a language vocabulary (Mohammad, 2018).

Mohammad and Turney (2010) constructed a large, high-quality, word–emotion association lexicon to contribute to the study of emotion analysis. Based on their lexicon, Sabbatino et al. (2022) constructed an emotion intensity lexicon targeting 272

Proceedings of the Workshop on Cognitive Modeling and Computational Linguistics, pages 81–85
August 15, 2024 ©2024 Association for Computational Linguistics

Role: System	
Content:	You are a native English speaker. Be sure to answer the question within 200 words.
Role: User	
Content:	Which of the four nonsense words listed below do you associate most and which do you associate least with EMOTION? Word list: [WORD1, WORD2, WORD3, WORD4]. Explain the way you think step by step, and answer with "MOST:" for the choice you associate most and "LEAST:" for the choice you associate least with EMOTION at the end.

Table 1: Input prompt for an LLM. In each prompt, the word list corresponds to a tuple consisting of four nonwords and the EMOTION describes one of the six emotions.

nonwords. For each nonword, six emotion ratings (joy, sadness, anger, disgust, fear, and surprise) were assigned according to Ekman's basic emotions (Ekman, 1972). Crowdsourced best–worst-scaling annotations were used to collect ratings by 120 native English speakers. Sabbatino et al. (2022) constructed a regression model to estimate the emotion ratings of nonwords. In the training phase, the regressor was trained on the emotion ratings of real words, then it was tested on those of nonwords. This regression model showed Pearson's correlation coefficient of 0.17 at best. This indicates the traditional regression approach is insufficient to deal with the emotion rating prediction of nonwords.

Furthermore, since there has been no research focusing on emotion predictions through LLMs, how they can associate nonwords with emotions is elucidated. Hence, the purpose of this study is to elucidate the relationship of the emotions evoked by nonwords between an LLM and humans. Our contributions can be summarized as:

- This paper is the first to evaluate the correlation between an LLM and humans regarding the emotions evoked by nonwords.
- Following the procedure of the annotation by Sabbatino et al. (2022) as in Fig. 1, we found a positive correlation of about 0.40 between an LLM and humans.
- Evaluation demonstrates that an LLM (in particular GPT-4) agrees with humans to some extent on emotional associations to nonwords.

2 Emotion Ratings for Nonwords

To measure the correlation of nonword interpretation between an LLM and humans, this section proposes a method to reproduce Sabbatino et al. (2022)'s best–worst-scaling annotations using an LLM. Following their methodology, we focus on the six basic emotions. The annotation procedures by humans and an LLM are contrasted in Fig. 1.

2.1 Emotion Ratings by Humans

In the best–worst-scaling annotations by Sabbatino et al. (2022), first, they selected a target emotion $e \in \{joy, sadness, anger, disgust, fear, surprise\}$. Then, four words were randomly selected from the 272 nonwords and 68 real words to create a tuple. These nonwords have an orthographically correct spelling, and a monosyllabic pronunciation. The real words were used for comparison to previous studies and for attention checks of the annotators. Each word was selected eight times to create tuples, and for each tuple, three annotators answered the question: "Which of the four words do you associate MOST and which do you associate LEAST with the emotion e?" After 120 annotators had selected the word most and least associated with e, the emotion intensity score $\mathrm{score}_e(w)$ of word w was calculated as follows:

$$\mathrm{score}_e(w) = \frac{\mathrm{most}_e(w) - \mathrm{least}_e(w)}{\mathrm{count}_e(w)}, \quad (1)$$

where $\mathrm{most}_e(w)$ and $\mathrm{least}_e(w)$ are the numbers of times w was selected as MOST and LEAST, respectively, and $\mathrm{count}_e(w)$ is the number of times w was presented. Lastly, they normalized this $\mathrm{score}_e(w)$ to $[0, 1]$. This process was performed for all six emotions.

2.2 Emotion Ratings by LLM

To reproduce this procedure using an LLM, we use the same 272 nonwords. We do not use real words because we are only interested in nonwords, and the relative order of words in an emotion based on the emotion intensity score is not affected to the correlation analysis. Using the 272 nonwords, we randomly created 1,632 tuples consisting of

		Joy	Sadness	Anger	Disgust	Fear	Surprise	Mean
(a)	**GPT-4 & Humans**	0.44*	0.40*	0.41*	0.47*	0.44*	0.26*	0.40*
(b)	**Among humans**	0.72	0.68	0.71	0.72	0.70	0.60	0.69

Table 2: (a) Pearson's correlation coefficients for the six emotions between the LLM's and the humans' ratings (*: p-value is less than 0.05). (b) Split-half reliability for nonword annotation (Sabbatino et al., 2022).

four nonwords. For this, we made sure that each word appeared in 24 different tuples and was not selected more than once within the same tuple to match the number of times each word was rated with the ratings by Sabbatino et al. (2022) (i.e., $\forall w; \mathrm{count}_e(w) = 24$). Then, we create an input prompt for a target emotion e and a tuple of four words.

Table 1 shows the prompt used in our evaluation. The system role indicates the role of the LLM, while the user role asks questions and instructions. In the system role, we instruct the LLM to imitate a native English speaker to make its characteristics closer to the attributes of the annotators in Sabbatino et al. (2022)'s work and to answer the question within 200 words to avoid redundant responses. In the user role, we instruct the LLM to answer the most and least relevant words to the emotion e from the four nonwords in the tuple. In addition, we instruct the LLM to think step by step to answer the question with evidence (Kojima et al., 2022), and to answer with the most relevant word followed by "MOST:" and the least relevant word followed by "LEAST:" to facilitate text processing on it.

Next, we input this prompt into the LLM. This is repeated for all tuples. The nonwords selected as most and least relevant to emotion e are then extracted from the LLM's output sentences, and the emotion intensity scores are calculated by Eqn. (1). This process is performed for all six emotions.

3 Correlation Analysis: An Experiment

We conducted an experiment to investigate the correlation between humans and LLMs regarding the emotions evoked by nonwords.

3.1 Experimental Setup

`GPT-4-0613` from OpenAI API[1] was selected as the target LLM because it was one of the most predominant and powerful LLMs easily available. We set the temperature parameter for output diversity to 0 and the `top_p` parameter to 1 to ensure reproducibility.

[1]https://platform.openai.com/ (Accessed April 28, 2024)

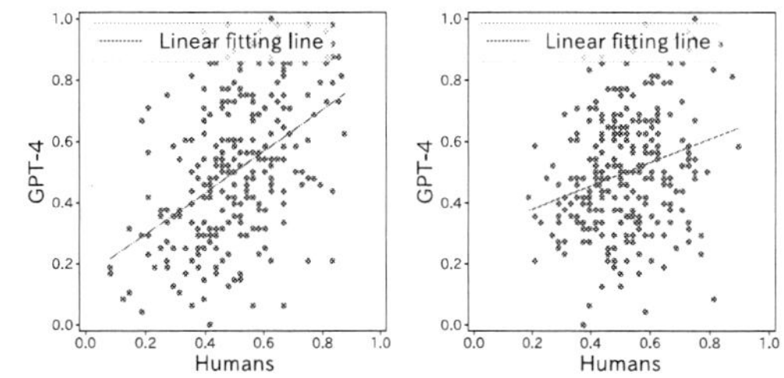

(a) Disgust (b) Surprise

Figure 2: Scatter plots for disgust and surprise. The x-axis represents ratings by humans, while the y-axis represents those reproduced by GPT-4.

To measure the correlation between emotional associations by the LLM and humans, Pearson's correlation coefficient was used. Note that a p-value less than 0.05 indicates a significant correlation between the LLM's and humans' ratings (Sabbatino et al., 2022).

3.2 Results

Table 2(a) shows the correlation coefficients between the LLM's and the humans' ratings with an average correlation of 0.40. The highest correlation was 0.47 for disgust and the lowest was 0.26 for surprise. Notably, p-values were less than 0.05 for all emotions. The scatter plots for disgust and surprise are displayed in Fig. 2. Both plots show an ascending trend to the right which indicates a positive correlation.

Table 3 shows an example of the GPT-4 output including the reason for its best–worst judgements of nonwords. These descriptions indicate a large influence of the meanings of real words with similar spellings on its choice. Examples of the outputs showing such an influence are shown below.

- Part of the evaluation of a tuple containing the nonword "juy" for the emotion "joy":
`MOST: "Juy" - It's phonetically and visually similar to "joy", which makes it the most associated with joy in my opinion.`
"Juy" was highly associated with joy because

```
The association of nonsense words with a concept like "joy" is subjective and depends on
personal interpretation. However, I'll try to explain my thought process. "Alse" sounds
similar to "else" and doesn't evoke any particular emotion. "Dworth" sounds a bit like
"dwarf", which could be associated with fantasy and joy for some, but it also sounds like
"worth" which is neutral. "Wrorgue" sounds harsh and complex, not typically associated with
joy. "Roice" sounds similar to "rejoice", a word strongly associated with joy and happiness.
Therefore, it might be the word most associated with joy due to this phonetic similarity.
So, my choices would be: MOST: Roice - because it sounds similar to "rejoice", a word
that is often used to express joy or happiness. LEAST: Wrorgue - because it sounds harsh
and complex, which are not typically characteristics associated with the feeling of joy.
```

Table 3: GPT-4 output for the tuple of [alse, roice, dworth, wrorgue] targeting the emotion "joy".

its pronunciation resembled "joy".

- Part of the evaluation of "voathe" for the emotion "disgust":
  `MOST: "Voathe" - Because it sounds similar to "loathe", a word that signifies strong dislike or disgust.`
  "Voathe" was highly associated with disgust because it sounded similar to "loathe", which means to intensely dislike.

- Another example for the evaluations of "roice" for joy:
  `MOST: "Roice" - Because it sounds similar to "rejoice", a word that is directly associated with joy. It also has a soft sound due to the "r" and "oi" sounds.`
  As seen in the part "`It also has a soft sound due to the "r" and "oi" sounds`", GPT-4 may not have only associated the nonword with a real word, but also grasped its meaning based on sound symbolism (Hinton et al., 1995; Köhler, 1929; Sapir, 1929) related to the emotion.

3.3 Discussion

In the study of Sabbatino et al. (2022), the average correlation calculated among human annotators was 0.69 (Table 2(b)) This means that the correlation coefficients obtained using an LLM were lower than those among humans. However, the correlation when the regression model trained on real words was applied on nonwords, reported in the study by Sabbatino et al. (2022), was 0.17. Although the number of test data differs between our experiment and theirs, the large gain in correlation suggests that GPT-4 reproduces human evaluation better than the regression model.

The highest correlation for disgust may be due to its larger pool of associated real words (e.g., "loathe" for the nonword "voathe", "filth" for the nonword "fliche", "gross" for the nonword "groose") compared to the other emotions.

In contrast, a possible reason for the lowest correlation for surprise could be that it has a smaller variance in human ratings (See Fig. 2(b)). Since almost no nonword has a human rating of less than 0.2 or more than 0.9, few nonwords obviously evoke or do not evoke surprise in English speakers. This may have made the annotation task difficult and the correlation low.

4 Conclusion and Future Work

Do LLMs agree with humans on emotional associations to nonsense words? —Yes, LLMs somewhat agree with humans. With the aim of elucidating the correlation between an LLM's and humans' understanding of nonwords, our study used GPT-4 to reproduce the emotion ratings of Sabbatino et al. (2022)'s study. We found a positive correlation of approximately 0.40 between GPT-4 and human ratings. This indicates that an LLM can be useful to estimate the emotions evoked by nonwords for humans. GPT-4 suggests that the meaning of real words with similar spellings largely influences its interpretation of nonwords, and that it may utilize knowledge of sound symbolism regarding emotion.

The existing analysis gathered from 120 persons, surely have different personae. In the future, we plan to assign more diverse personae to explore potential variations in ratings based on factors such as gender, age, and nationality. Furthermore, investigating factors affecting the LLM's nonword interpretation will also be promising.

Limitations

Although our results show that GPT-4 can reproduce the nonword emotion ratings by humans, other LLMs, such as PaLM (Chowdhery et al., 2023) and LLaMA (Touvron et al., 2023), may behave differently to nonwords. Additionally, our experiment targeted English speakers' perception of English nonwords. If tested in different settings, e.g., another language speakers' perception, it is still an open question whether LLMs mainly trained on English data can reproduce their ratings.

Acknowledgments

Part of this work was supported by JSPS KAKENHI Grant-in-Aid for Scientific Research (23K24868).

References

Zhenguang G. Cai, Xufeng Duan, David A. Haslett, Shuqi Wang, and Martin J. Pickering. 2024. Do large language models resemble humans in language use? *Computing Research Repository*, arXiv:2303.08014.

Wei-Lin Chiang, Zhuohan Li, Zi Lin, Ying Sheng, Zhanghao Wu, Hao Zhang, Lianmin Zheng, Siyuan Zhuang, Yonghao Zhuang, Joseph E. Gonzalez, Ion Stoica, and Eric P. Xing. 2023. Vicuna: An open-source chatbot impressing GPT-4 with 90%* ChatGPT quality. (Accessed May 16, 2024).

Aakanksha Chowdhery, Sharan Narang, Jacob Devlin, Maarten Bosma, Gaurav Mishra, Adam Roberts, Paul Barham, Hyung Won Chung, Charles Sutton, Sebastian Gehrmann, Parker Schuh, Kensen Shi, Sasha Tsvyashchenko, Joshua Maynez, Abhishek Rao, Parker Barnes, Yi Tay, Noam Shazeer, Vinodkumar Prabhakaran, Emily Reif, Nan Du, Ben Hutchinson, Reiner Pope, James Bradbury, Jacob Austin, Michael Isard, Guy Gur-Ari, Pengcheng Yin, Toju Duke, Anselm Levskaya, Sanjay Ghemawat, Sunipa Dev, Henryk Michalewski, Xavier Garcia, Vedant Misra, Kevin Robinson, Liam Fedus, Denny Zhou, Daphne Ippolito, David Luan, Hyeontaek Lim, Barret Zoph, Alexander Spiridonov, Ryan Sepassi, David Dohan, Shivani Agrawal, Mark Omernick, Andrew M. Dai, Thanumalayan Sankaranarayana Pillai, Marie Pellat, Aitor Lewkowycz, Erica Moreira, Rewon Child, Oleksandr Polozov, Katherine Lee, Zongwei Zhou, Xuezhi Wang, Brennan Saeta, Mark Diaz, Orhan Firat, Michele Catasta, Jason Wei, Kathy Meier-Hellstern, Douglas Eck, Jeff Dean, Slav Petrov, and Noah Fiedel. 2023. PaLM: Scaling language modeling with pathways. *Journal of Machine Learning Research*, 24(240):1–113.

Paul Ekman. 1972. Universal and cultural differences in facial expression of emotions. *Nebraska Symposium on Motivation*, 19:207–283.

Leanne Hinton, Johanna Nichols, and John J. Ohala. 1995. *Sound Symbolism*. Cambridge University Press, Cambridge, England, UK.

W. Köhler. 1929. *Gestalt Psychology*. Liveright, New York, NY, USA.

Takeshi Kojima, Shixiang (Shane) Gu, Machel Reid, Yutaka Matsuo, and Yusuke Iwasawa. 2022. Large language models are zero-shot reasoners. *Advances in Neural Information Processing Systems*, 35:22199–22213.

Kyle Mahowald, Anna A. Ivanova, Idan A. Blank, Nancy Kanwisher, Joshua B. Tenenbaum, and Evelina Fedorenko. 2024. Dissociating language and thought in large language models. *Trends in Cognitive Sciences*, In press.

Saif Mohammad. 2018. Word affect intensities. In *Proceedings of the 11th International Conference on Language Resources and Evaluation (LREC 2018)*, pages 174–183, Miyazaki, Japan.

Saif Mohammad and Peter Turney. 2010. Emotions evoked by common words and phrases: Using Mechanical Turk to create an emotion lexicon. In *Proceedings of the NAACL HLT 2010 Workshop on Computational Approaches to Analysis and Generation of Emotion in Text*, pages 26–34, Los Angeles, CA, USA.

OpenAI. 2022. Introducing ChatGPT. (Accessed May 16, 2024).

Valentino Sabbatino, Enrica Troiano, Antje Schweitzer, and Roman Klinger. 2022. "splink" is happy and "phrouth" is scary: Emotion intensity analysis for nonsense words. In *Proceedings of the 12th Workshop on Computational Approaches to Subjectivity, Sentiment & Social Media Analysis*, pages 37–50, Dublin, Ireland.

Edward Sapir. 1929. A study in phonetic symbolism. *Journal of Experimental Psychology*, 12(3):225–239.

Hugo Touvron, Thibaut Lavril, Gautier Izacard, Xavier Martinet, Marie-Anne Lachaux, Timothée Lacroix, Baptiste Rozière, Naman Goyal, Eric Hambro, Faisal Azhar, Aurelien Rodriguez, Armand Joulin, Edouard Grave, and Guillaume Lample. 2023. LLaMA: Open and efficient foundation language models. *Computing Research Repository*, arXiv:2302.13971.

Matthew J. Traxler and Morton A. Gernsbacher. 2006. *Handbook of Psycholinguistics*. Elsevier, Amsterdam, the Netherlands.

Large language models fail to derive atypicality inferences in a human-like manner

Charlotte Kurch, Margarita Ryzhova and Vera Demberg
Dept. of Language Science and Technology, Saarland University, Germany
chku00001@stud.uni-saarland.de, mryzhova@lst.uni-saarland.de,
vera@lst.uni-saarland.de

Abstract

Recent studies have claimed that large language models (LLMs) are capable of drawing pragmatic inferences (Qiu et al., 2023; Hu et al., 2022; Barattieri di San Pietro et al., 2023). The present paper sets out to test LLM's abilities on atypicality inferences, a type of pragmatic inference that is triggered through informational redundancy. We test several state-of-the-art LLMs in a zero-shot setting and find that LLMs fail to systematically fail to derive atypicality inferences. Our robustness analysis indicates that when inferences are seemingly derived in a few-shot settings, these results can be attributed to shallow pattern matching and not pragmatic inferencing. We also analyse the performance of the LLMs at the different derivation steps required for drawing atypicality inferences – our results show that models have access to script knowledge and can use it to identify redundancies and accommodate the atypicality inference. The failure instead seems to stem from not reacting to the subtle maxim of quantity violations introduced by the informationally redundant utterances.

Keywords: pragmatics; informational redundancy; human-like reasoning; large language models

1 Introduction

Recent studies have shown that large language models (LLMs) can oftentimes provide responses that are consistent with pragmatic interpretations, e.g., Qiu et al. (2023). An analysis of seven different pragmatic phenomena (including humor, coherence and irony) by Hu et al. (2022) found that LLMs to exhibit similar accuracy and error patterns as humans; and research has also reported LLMs performing well on test developed to test the pragmatic ability of humans (Barattieri di San Pietro et al., 2023).

In the present paper, we test whether LLMs are capable of deriving atypicality inferences – the type of pragmatic inferences that arise in the face of mentioning information that is *informationally redundant* (IR). The informational redundancy arises from the fact that the information can be inferred from shared knowledge about typical event sequences (*script knowledge* – knowledge about everyday situations, like dining at a restaurant or shopping; see, Bower et al., 1979). Mentioning easily inferable events violates the quantity maxim which holds that speakers should be informative (Grice, 1975).

For example, eating is the activity that is highly predictable in a restaurant scenario. Thus, the utterance in (1) is informationally redundant:

(1) *Mary went to a restaurant. **She ate there!***

Mentioning the inferable event leads to pragmatic inferences – Kravtchenko and Demberg (2022) showed that subjects lower their beliefs about the highly conventionally habitual activity (e.g., eating). The derivation mechanism assumes that when faced with utterances that are informationally redundant, comprehenders try to 'repair' the utterance informativity by inferring that the mentioned event is atypical for the referent. With relation to (1), it follows that Mary does not usually eat, when going to a restaurant.

The derivation mechanism of atypicality inferences can be summarized in four steps (Ryzhova et al., 2023; Kravtchenko and Demberg, 2022). At first, comprehenders identify redundancy in the message based on script knowledge. Secondly, they realize that redundancy is infelicitous due to violation of the quantity maxim. Thirdly, they infer atypicality (Mary does not usually eat at a restaurant). Finally, they need to accommodate atypicality with their world knowledge (e.g., Mary usually only orders drinks). This decomposition into steps allows us to check what aspect of the pragmatic inference might be particularly challenging for the LLM.

Proceedings of the Workshop on Cognitive Modeling and Computational Linguistics, pages 86–100
August 15, 2024 ©2024 Association for Computational Linguistics

Previous work on the recent generative models suggests that they have a promising understanding of script knowledge – see Huang et al. (2022), where GPT-3 generated plausible script schemata. However, it is not only relevant whether the script knowledge is learned by the model, but also whether the model is able to access it and integrate it into the task solving process. Hong et al. (2024b) tested more than 30 different LLMs on implicit vs. explicit causal relations between two script events. The models, unlike humans, were unable to infer or predict a cause/event from script knowledge, if it was omitted. This might imply either insufficient representation of script knowledge or inability to integrate it.

Recent research on LLMs has explored their ability to understand non-literal language, demonstrating that these models can emulate human-like performance in deriving pragmatic meaning (Hu et al., 2022). For example, Qiu et al. (2023) showed that ChatGPT, to some extent, resembles human behaviour — it consistently derives scalar implicatures by interpreting the quantifier 'some' and disjunctions pragmatically. However, the model exhibited a lack of human-like flexibility when nuanced interpretation required consideration of contextual information.

In the present paper, we investigate pragmatic abilities in the derivation of atypicality inferences of three recent generative models that offered the most promising performance, namely – GPT-3.5-turbo (GPT-3.5-t; t = 1, presence_penalty = 0, top_p = 1), GPT-4 (t = 1, presence_penalty = 0, top_p = 1) and the open-source model LLama 3 8B Instruct (Llama 3; t=0.6, repeat_penalty = 1.2, top_p = 0.9). We present a series of experiments in which we firstly follow a zero-shot approach to replicate the results of Kravtchenko and Demberg (2022) and Ryzhova et al. (2023) with LLMs (Exp. 1). Next, we follow a few-shot prompting approach that has been shown to improve the models' reasoning (Exp. 2) and perform a perturbation analysis with modified few-shot exemplars. Finally, in Exp. 3, we analyse the LLM's ability to perform the different reasoning steps required for atypicality inferences according to Kravtchenko and Demberg (2022) and Ryzhova et al. (2023).

2 Atypicality inferences

We here briefly present the original experiment of Kravtchenko and Demberg (2022) and discuss the derivation steps for atypicality inferences.

The mechanism of atypicality inferences lies in the violation of the quantity maxim where interlocutors are expected to convey the right amount of information to their conversational partners – neither more nor less (Grice, 1975).

Informativity of a message, among other things, is dependent on the mutual knowledge and beliefs of interlocutors about each other. According to the previous literature, humans exhibit a remarkable ability to infer script events, even those left unmentioned in everyday narratives, without causing the discourse to appear odd or inconsistent. This capability is reflected in human communication, too, where individuals don't explicitly mention all script-related events, and yet listeners can seamlessly infer this information from their script knowledge (Bower et al., 1979). Kravtchenko and Demberg (2022) investigated the comprehension of utterances that are overinformative or informationally redundant (IR), and thus violate the maxim of quantity, given comprehender's script knowledge. They examined 24 stories describing common everyday event sequences, such as going to a restaurant or going shopping. In these scenarios, script knowledge consists of specific sequences of events, such as (for a going to a restaurant scenario) reaching the restaurant, taking a table, looking at the menu, ordering food, **eating**, paying, and leaving the place (Bower et al., 1979; Wanzare et al., 2016).

Each story underwent a 2 (ordinary vs. wonky common ground context) x 2 (conventionally habitual vs. non-habitual utterance) manipulation (see an example of an item in all conditions in Table 1). Critically, the conventionally (conv.) habitual utterance "She ate there!" was an event taken from the script schema.

Kravtchenko and Demberg (2022) manipulated the presence of conv. habitual utterance in the story. After reading a story, subjects were asked to express their beliefs about the target activity on a scale ranging from 0 to 100: *How often do you think Mary usually eats, when going to a restaurant?* (Never-Sometimes-Always). Overall, when the context followed script-schema (ordinary condition), subjects assigned high typicality ratings in the baseline condition (where no utterance was present in the story), meaning that subjects believed that Mary usually eats in restaurants, in accordance with script knowledge. However, when the conv. habitual utterance was present in the story, the subjects' ratings about Mary typically eating when going to a restaurant were significantly lower (baseline: 85.79 vs. habitual utterance: 72.37; $p < .001$) – see also Figure 1.

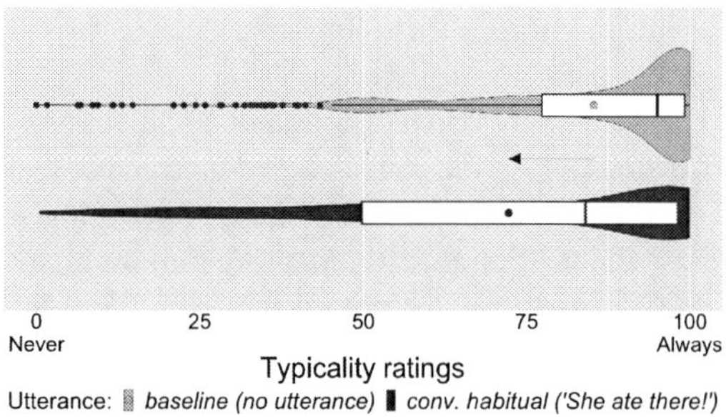

Figure 1: Human ratings of event typicality (e.g., eating when going to a restaurant) taken from Kravtchenko and Demberg (2022). Violin plots, overlaid with box plots, show the distribution of ratings. Circles represent mean values. The arrow indicates a statistically significant difference in ratings between conditions.

This effect crucially depends on informational redundancy – it disappeared (baseline: 48 vs. non-habitual utterance: 45.71) in the context, where the conv. habitual utterance was not informationally redundant (see Table 1, wonky context, where Mary was portrayed as a non-eater). The effect is also not present when the target utterance was not referring to a predictable event "She got to see their kitchen!", see Table 1, non-habitual utterance (ratings for ordinary: 40.80 to 42.47; for wonky: 38.49 to 39.56 – baseline to non-habitual utterance condition, respectively).

2.1 Derivation steps of atypicality inferences

To investigate how subjects accommodated atypicality inferences in the situational context of a story and to better understand the underlying derivation processes of atypicality inferences, Ryzhova et al. (2023) conducted a follow-up study, in which they asked participants to explain a given rating. The ratings were tagged according to whether they provided evidence for an atypicality inference having been drawn. The most important categories from their annotation scheme are shown in Table 2.[1]

In most cases, subjects derived atypicality inference (*atypicality* tag). These responses reflected recognition of informational redundancy and stated the utterance as the reason to assume that Mary does not usually eat in restaurants — this corresponded to low typicality ratings (see mean ratings in column 2 of Table 2). Interestingly, subjects oftentimes effectively augmented the common ground to make the IR utterance informative with respect to the context. In doing so, they provided justification of **why** Mary does not usually eat ("...because she interviews people there"). Sometimes, however, even when subjects arrived at atypicality inference, their answer justified that they did not accept the drawn inference (*atypicality_reject*) – this corresponded to high ratings.

When subjects did not derive atypicality inference, their explanations included various formulations of stating what would be a typical human behaviour (*no_atypicality*). Such answers were associated with high typicality ratings, and comprised a second biggest annotation category.

Results of Ryzhova et al. (2023) thus confirm that informationally redundant utterances lead subjects to infer atypical behaviour, and that they go through an accommodation process: in order to obtain a consistent picture, they come up with a circumstance leading to the activity being worth mentioning (e.g., ordering only drinks or being short of money). These results provide a basis for comparison to reasoning of LLMs.

3 Exp. 1: Zero-Shot Prompting for Eliciting Atypicality Inferences

Our first experiment set out to test the ability of recent LLMs to derive atypicality inferences under conditions similar to the human participants. We used the same 24 stimuli and tested how models rated the typicality of conv. habitual and the non-habitual activity in all conditions used by Kravtchenko and Demberg (2022) (see Table 1). Models were prompted for providing both a typicality rating on a scale from 0% to 100% [2] and a justification for their rating.

We report here the results for conv. habitual activity in the ordinary context – for the wonky context and non-habitual activity the models behaved similarly to humans (for results see appendix B).

Methods The prompt we used underwent iterative prompt engineering to assure consistently sensible and usable output. It includes instructions to use common sense reasoning and speculate based

[1] Ryzhova et al. (2023) report a substantial inter-annotator agreement (Cohen's $\kappa = 0.74$ (p<.0001), 95% CI (0.7, 0.77)).

[2] As previous research has shown that LLMs struggle with tasks involving numbers (Schwartz et al., 2024; Hong et al., 2024a), we have also performed the same experiment using a 7-point Likert scale, and applying the self-calibration method proposed by Tian et al. (2023). These experiments yielded very similar results that can be found in appendix C.

Table 1: An example of a "restaurant" story by context (ordinary vs. wonky) and utterance condition (conv. habitual vs. non-habitual activity is mentioned in the utterance). A baseline for both context conditions does not include an utterance block.

Context	**ordinary** Mary is a journalist **who often goes to restaurants after her interviews**.	**wonky** Mary is a journalist **who often interviews restaurant waiters, but doesn't like eating out**.
	Yesterday, she went to a popular Chinese place. As she was leaving, she ran into her friend David, and they started talking about the restaurant. After they parted, David continued on his way when he suddenly ran into Sally, a mutual friend of him and Mary.	
Utterance	**conventionally habitual activity** David said to Sally: "I ran into Mary leaving that Chinese place. **She ate there!**"	**non-habitual activity** David said to Sally: "I ran into Mary leaving that Chinese place. **She got to see their kitchen!**"
Q habitual	How often do you think Mary usually eats, when going to a restaurant?	
Q non-habit	How often do you think Mary usually gets to see the kitchen, when going to a restaurant?	

Table 2: Annotation scheme from Ryzhova et al. (2023) with examples from human explanations for the restaurant script.

annotation tag (proportion of tag in data)	inference drawn? (mean rating)	example of an answer
atypicality (45.6%)	yes (51.84)	Since David mentioned it, it sounds like she doesn't always eat at restaurants. Maybe she sometimes interviews people in restaurants.
atypicality _reject (6.13%)	unclear (95.46)	After interviews Mary will be tired so she probably eats. She can't just go to a restaurant for a drink after a long day.
no_atypicality (39.46%)	no (93.82)	Usually when you go to a restaurant, it is to eat.
other (8.81%)	unclear (69.33)	He didn't tell Sally which restaurant, he said that restaurant, as though they go there often.

on its knowledge of human behavior to circumvent responses related to an inability to perform the task[3]. The ratings in the different conditions were compared using a paired t-test.

Annotation scheme For evaluating the model reasoning in the habitual utterance condition, we extended the annotation scheme used in Ryzhova et al. (2023) to cover types of answers that were typical in LLMs, but had not been observed in humans. We added the label *reinforced_utterance* as a subtype of *no_atypicality* for explanations where the redundant utterance was considered a reinforcement of the typicality, and the label *hallucination/bad_reasoning* to capture erroneous and nonsensical model generated explanations, see Table 3 for an example[4].

Table 3: Extended annotation scheme for LLMs with examples from the restaurant and the haircut scripts.

annotation tag	inference drawn?	example of an answer
no_atypicality: reinforced utterance	no	The statement "Mary ate there!" suggests that it is a usual occurrence for Mary to eat when she goes to a restaurant after her interviews.
hallucination/ bad_reasoning	unclear	100% because the context states that she usually cuts her hair herself using scissors.

Results In contrast to humans, we found no significant typicality rating changes between the baseline and the habitual utterance condition across the models (see Figure 2). There was non-significant change for GPT-3.5-t (94.40→97.04) and Llama 3 (87.8→94.5) in the opposite direction, i.e. activities are judged to be more frequent, when the utterance is seen. Overall, the models assigned very high typicality ratings to all stimuli, irrespective of condition. Occasionally the models deemed it impossible to answer and gave 50%ratings.

Models' explanations were in accordance with the high ratings – see Table 4. The majority of responses were classified as *no_atypicality*, and especially *reinforced_utterance*, where the models reinforced high typicality based on the utterance. Only a very small number of responses were classified as *atypicality*, but these were still associated with high ratings. Finally, some responses also contained hallucinated facts or incorrect or confused reasoning.

For a sanity check, we also looked into the typicality ratings of the habitual activity when the non-habitual utterance was present in the story. Simi-

[3]See appendix A for details on the prompts.

[4]We annotated a subset of answers (GPT-4, few-shot) with two annotators and found a substantial inter-annotator agreement (Cohen's $\kappa = 0.73$ ($p<.0001$), 95% CI (0.52, 0.93))

larly to human results, the ratings in this condition were high and not significantly different from the baseline for all three models. It shows that presence of the non-habit. utterance does not affect the interpretation of the habitual event typicality. In other words, the fact that Mary got to see the kitchen does not influence the typicality of her eating in the restaurant.

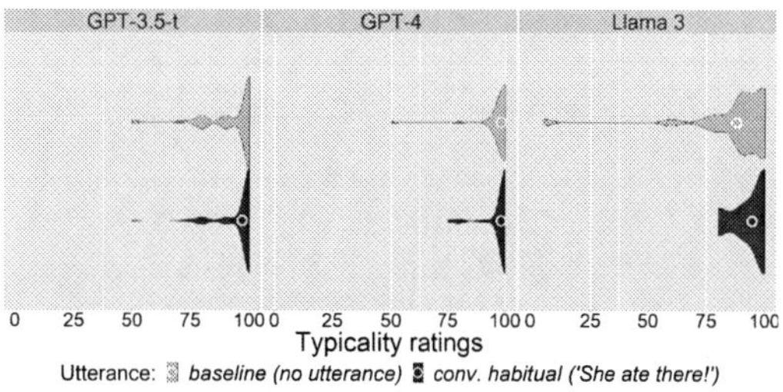

Figure 2: Zero-shot, habitual activity analysis in the ordinary context. Boxplots are omitted, due to high skew in the data.

Discussion In the zero-shot setup, where the models were put in the same settings as humans, we observed no atypicality inferences, contrary to human results. Those few explanations that showed derivation were not associated with lower ratings. So what might cause the observed discrepancy between LLMs and humans?

As the first step of deriving inferences requires identifying the redundancy based on script knowledge, an obvious first consideration is whether models have the relevant script knowledge. However, in the baseline condition (no activity mentioned) typicality ratings are high and the explanations refer to script knowledge. This conclusion is further supported by reduced typicality ratings that were obtained in a wonky context's baseline that we present in appendix B. In this context, the script knowledge is overwritten by stating atypical behaviour, and all models captured this changing lowering their beliefs accordingly.

At that same first step, it is also possible that models may fail to recognize that the observed utterance is informationally redundant. Further, the second step requires assessing that the redundancy violates the conversational norms. A failure to do either of these would be an explanation consistent with the fact that model justifications for high typicality ratings referred to event typicality (*reinforced_utterance*), a type of reasoning that was typically not found in human justifications.

Experiments 2 and 3 below aim to investigate what aspect of the reasoning the models have most difficulty with.

4 Exp. 2: Few-Shot Prompting

Few-Shot prompting (Brown et al., 2020) is a popular technique in which the prompt is enriched with a small number of examples that demonstrate how to do the target task correctly. This has often been found to improve model performance on other NLP tasks (Schick and Schütze, 2020; Zhao et al., 2021).

We selected a total of 4 of the stimuli as exemplars: specifically, the stimuli with conv. activities that were, respectively, rated most and least habitual by the human participants. For each stimulus, responses that follow the output template while mimicking human behavior in the conv. habitual utterance condition were crafted, i.e., the responses showing a lower rating and providing a justification that alluded to an atypicality inference being drawn. The models were prompted twice with two exemplars each (paired according to their ratings) and the instructions prompt was amended to reflect that two examples would be demonstrated.[5] We only collected responses for the conv. habitual activity (Q habitual in Table 1) in the ordinary condition, and present the combined results collapsing across exemplars, using the same analysis as in Exp. 1.

Results In the few-shot setting, we observed a significant difference in typicality ratings between the baseline and habitual utterance conditions for GPT-4 (mean 96.2 $\rightarrow$84.1; t(23) = 5.82, $p < .0001$) and GPT-3.5-t (mean 96.5 $\rightarrow$89.4; t(23) = 2.98, $p < .01$). For Llama 3 there is no change (mean 85.0 $\rightarrow$81.2). The ratings being on average lower for GPT-4 and GPT-3.5-t when the habitual utterance was present is in line with the derivation of an atypicality inference – see Figure 3.

In contrast to Exp. 1, the presence of the non-conv. habitual utterance ("She got to see their kitchen!") did not have an effect on the ratings only for GPT-4 (mean: 96.2 $\rightarrow$95.0). For GPT-3.5-t, however, there was a significant change (mean 96.5 $\rightarrow$84.0; t(23) = 3.50, $p < .01$), meaning that the ratings were on average lower in the presence of any utterance (even the one not related to the activity mentioned in the question), indicating that the model does not actually derive atypicality inferences. Interestingly, we also see a significant

[5]See appendix A for exact prompt formulations.

Table 4: Proportionate distribution in % of the annotations for all responses in habitual utterance condition with ordinary context.

Annotation		Human	Zero-Shot Prompting			Few-Shot Prompting		
			GPT-3.5-t	GPT-4	Llama 3	GPT-3.5-t	GPT-4	Llama 3
atypicality		45.6	4.13	4.17	8.33	11.36	65.9	6.82
no-atypicality	normal	39.46	42.07	58.33	60.41	59.09	13.63	50.0
	reinforced utterance	-	48.62	41.67	29.16	45.45	2.27	40.91
unclear	atypicality_reject	6.13	0.0	2.08	0.0	4.55	18.18	2.27
	hallucination/ bad_reasoning	-	6.88	6.25	0.0	2.27	0.0	9.09
	other	8.81	1.8	0.0	4.16	0.0	0.0	0.0

rating change for Llama 3 (mean 85.0 →73.1; t(23) = 2.61, $p < .05$), further solidifying the model's failure at deriving atypicality inferences.

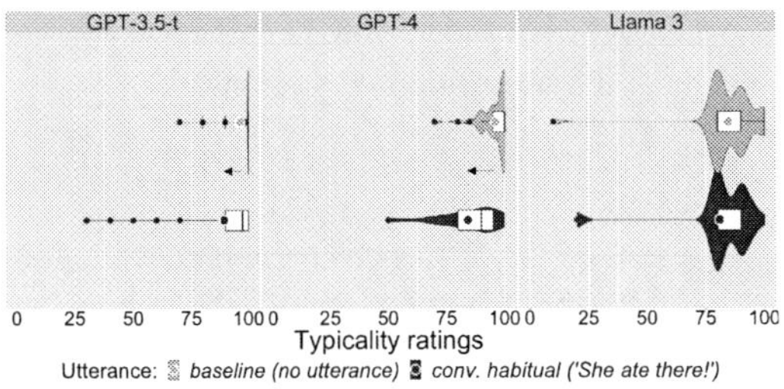

Figure 3: Few-shot, habitual activity analysis

Next, the number of explanations in favor of atypicality inference (*atypicality*) increased strongly in GPT-4, where *atypicality* is the most frequent annotation tag (there's a small increase for GPT-3.5-t and no for Llama 3, Table 4). We note though that the atypicality justifications were sometimes inconsistent with the numerical ratings given by the model: a very cautious explanation stating a slightly decreased typicality would co-occur with a large decrease in the typicality rating. For GPT-3.5-t and Llama 3 the majority of responses are again classified for exhibiting *no_ atypicality*.

Overall, the models now also show more responses that were classified as *atypicality_reject*, where the atypicality is brought up but dismissed in the justification.

Perturbation analysis In addition to the few-shot experiment above, we aimed to test the robustness of the inferencing ability of GPT-4 in the few-shot setting in order to determine whether the model shallowly copies over and adapts the provided exemplars, or whether it uses the exemplars to pick up on the task more deeply.[6]

Perturbation 1 Firstly, we prompted the models using the same items as exemplars, but this time, only one exemplar modeled the conv. habitual utterance condition, while the second one modeled the non-habitual utterance condition. This aimed at the models ability to differentiate between the utterances and apply only the relevant exemplar to the problem it was presented with. This manipulation meant that the results for GPT-4 became less clear: ratings in the conv. habitual utterance condition still vary significantly from the baseline (mean: 96.2 →91.9, t(23) = 2.47, $p < .05$), but the non-habitual utterance condition also varies significantly from the baseline (mean: 94.8, t(23) = 2.49, $p < .05$), and the two utterance conditions no longer vary significantly from each other. This decline in atypicality inferences is supported by the explanations, where we see *no-atypicality* for most stimuli (atypicality is only classified 8 times).

Perturbation 2 We crafted intentionally misleading and incongruent exemplars where 100% ratings paired with reasoning expressing atpicality. We tried two variations of the reasoning: (A) expresses atypicality due to the utterance implying a change from habitual behavior, (B) simply states atypicality without any reference to habitual behavior. Notably, GPT-4 matches the exemplars the majority of the time in setting B, where we do not introduce the concept of habituality due to script knowledge. In setting A, however, it replicates the exemplar less than half the time, and the remaining times rejects the atypicality or assigns no atypicality. For the latter it will frequently assign a different purpose to the utterance, explicitly stating that it does not imply atypicality.

Discussion While the results of the few-shot prompting experiment on GPT-4 seem very promising, we were wondering about whether these responses are given for the "right reasons" (i.e., whether the examples provided in the prompt clari-

[6]Results on the other models are provided in the appendix, as these models failed to show the correct behaviour in the basic few-shot setting.

fied the task to the model) or whether the model is adapting aspects of the answers given in the prompt in a shallow way, e.g., copying down a low rating and adapting the explanation to the new target.

Our first perturbation analysis showed that GPT-4 cannot consistently differentiate between redundant and non-redundant utterances, or apply the conversational norm leading to atypicality. With the second analysis we observed two behaviors: (1) matching both reasoning and rating to the exemplar even if they are incongruent, and (2) copying of the rating and adjusting the reasoning. While (1) mostly implies some degree of blind copying, the occurrence of (2) shows the model applying some level of reasoning or knowledge. Interestingly, this behavior is prevalent when the exemplars provide the script knowledge and resulting habituality, and how it is voided by the utterance, leading the model to explicitly disagree with this modeled reasoning. This leads us to hypothesize that model does not see a problem with redundancies and hence does not apply the conversational norm that leads to the derivation of atypicality inferences, even to the point of rejecting it.

In order to better understand the performance of GPT-4 and to obtain better insights on the performance of all models on the reasoning steps that were previously hypothesized to be part of human reasoning for this task, we tested the performance of all models on the component steps of atypicality reasoning in Exp. 3.

5 Exp 3: Analysing the steps of reasoning process

In Exp. 3, we decomposed the atypicality inference reasoning task into its sub-components as outlined in Kravtchenko and Demberg (2022) and Ryzhova et al. (2023): 1) identify the redundancy based on script knowledge; 2) realize that redundancy is infelicitous, as it violates conversational norms; 3) infer activity atypicality; 4) explicitly accommodate atypicality in situational context. Our goal was to clarify how well the models perform on each of these steps. The models were prompted with adjusted instructions, telling them that they were experts on human behavior and had the task of answering a question based on a provided context. As context, they were given each stimulus in the conv. habitual utterance condition, and then one question at a time.

Notably, this method of prompting the model with questions that are aimed specifically at performing each of the steps does not reliably show whether or not a given model is actually able to perform this step unprompted, or in a different context. We do however believe in the merits of assessing the models' abilities and behaviors in this controlled setting for providing initial insights into potential points of failure.

Experimental results on the variations of the prompts are presented in appendix E. Below, we only report on the question formulations that most successfully elicited what we were looking for across models.

Step 1: Identifying Redundancy For identifying the informational redundancy, we report the results of the following two prompts:

- Q1: Does the direct speech contain any redundancies?
- Q2: The direct speech contains redundant information. Can you identify the redundancy and elaborate why it is one?

For Q1, where the presence of redundancy is open-ended, GPT-4 and Llama 3 succeeded at explicitly identifying the informational redundancies (18 and 14 times, respectively), while GPT-3.5-t did not.

For Q2, where the presence of a redundancy was presupposed, GPT-4 identified it for all 24 stimuli and the performance of GPT-3.5-t was also generally improved: it correctly reported the redundancy in 13 stories. For Llama 3 there is no positive effect as it reported the expected redundancy 13 times for this prompt. Overall, we take this finding as evidence that the model successfully draws on script knowledge and can in principle identify the informational redundancy.

Step 2: Realizing that redundancy is infelicitous The drawing of an atypicality inference is an accommodation process in which the comprehender 'repairs' an utterance that otherwise may be viewed as infelicitous due to the redundancy. We consequently wondered whether the conversational norm under which redundancies should be avoided (Maxim of Quantity) is known and accessible to the model. However, this aspect proved to be very difficult to assess via prompting, due to its subtlety (explicit reasoning about them would also be hard to elicit from humans, as pragmatic implicatures can always be denied – see e.g., Garmendia, 2023).

When asking the model whether the utterance including informationally redundant information was a good / acceptable way of communicating, GPT-3.5-t and GPT-4 tended to respond that redundancies could be a problem, but provided non-specific albeit reasonable examples of why redundancies can be ok. Llama 3's outputs most of the time said that redundancy was problematic and unacceptable, while exhibiting an improved ability for correctly identifying the informational redundancy.

Step 3: Inferring Atypicality Next, we tested whether the model can infer atypicality based on the mentioning of redundant information, using prompt Q3:

- Q3: The direct speech contains seemingly redundant information. Can you identify what I mean and explain why the speaker made the effort of conveying this information?

This wording improved the models' ability to identify the informational redundancy. GPT-4 correctly identified the redundancy for all stimuli, and provided lists of generic potential reasons (most commonly including emphasis, occasionally some level of atypicality, i.e. forgetting, but also mentioning humor or the wish to establish a connection). GPT-3.5-t pointed towards undefined noteworthiness and attributed it to a desire to emphasize this information. Despite Llama 3 labelling redundancies as problematic, the model provides reasonable and specific reasons for the redundancy. For the most part, the proposed reasons related to the conversational situation instead of the discussed activity.

We additionally experimented with further prompt formulations in order to elicit more specific explanations from the models. Best results were obtained when adjusting the question for each stimulus and detailing the specific redundancy, as shown in Q4:

- Q4: The second sentence in the direct speech conveys seemingly redundant information, because eating is a usual part of going to a restaurant. However, since it was mentioned explicitly, it can be assumed that it is new or relevant information. Why could Mary eating be new or relevant information?

For this prompt, atypicality was more often provided as the reason, or was listed among the possible reasons. GPT-4 mentioned atypicality 20 times, though often generically in form of the person potentially forgetting sometimes. Answers from GPT-3.5-t were consistent with atypicality inferences 11 times and mentioned information's noteworthiness as the reason, without elaborating any further. Llama 3 gave very specific and logical explanations of the noteworthiness for 22 stimuli, but only two of those could be classified as atypicality.

Step 4: Explicitly Accommodating Atypicality Finally, we were interested whether the model is in theory capable of 'completing' the picture that is caused by an atypicality by coming up with an alternative behavior or an explanation, i.e., whether the atypicality of the action can be accommodated if it is presupposed. The model was given the following prompt (again adjusted for each stimulus):

- Q5: The second sentence in the direct speech conveys seemingly redundant information, because eating is a usual part of going to a restaurant. However, since it was mentioned explicitly, it can be assumed that it is new or relevant information. That probably means that Mary doesn't typically eat. What does she do instead?

Here, GPT-4 provided sensible alternative behaviors for 13 stimuli while GPT-3.5-t managed to provide an alternative behavior for 14 stimuli (7 of these answers only weakly specified the alternative, i.e., 'uses alternative method'). In other cases, the models either rejected the premise for atypicality, provided alternatives that were not valid in the given context, or stated that the alternative could not be inferred from the text. Llama 3 again commited to specific and reasonable alternative behavior for most stimuli, only twice offering a weakly specified alternative and once an illogical one.

6 Conclusions

Exp. 1 demonstrated that the tested models are unable to draw atypicality inferences when prompted in a way that is similar to the instructions that humans receive. On the other hand, Exp. 2 showed that GPT-4 (but not the other two models) could draw atypicality inferences sometimes when prompted with examples, doing so in 65% of our stimuli. However, we also saw that typicality ratings were not always consistent with the generated justifications and that GPT-4's ability to draw these inferences is inconsistent and not robust. We conclude that performance improvements may stem from successful template matching rather than emulating the process correctly.

Our experiments into decomposing the atypicality inference task into different reasoning steps revealed that all models have the relevant script knowledge and can use this knowledge to identify the informationally redundant utterance. However, the models needed to be specifically prompted to identify these utterances, supporting the idea that the models' failure may relate to inability to apply conversational norms. Further evidence comes from the observation that Llama 3 fails to translate its excellent performance in accommodating explicit atypicality inferences and its claims about redundancies never being acceptable into good performance on Exp. 1 or Exp. 2.

Finally, we'd like to note that humans also do not uniformly draw atypicality inferences – variability exists at the level of items (some items exhibit a larger rate of atypicality inferences than others) and at the level of participants: Ryzhova et al. (2023) showed that in humans, the ability to draw atypicality inferences is correlated with reasoning ability. These two factors provide interesting leads for future research.

7 Limitations

One limitation from the NLP perspective of our study is that the size of the dataset is small (only 24 stories) and only in English. This is a common limitation of psycholinguistic studies due to the costs of human experiments.

This work only tests Zero-, and Few-Shot prompting and does not make use of any additional prompting methods designed for reasoning tasks. While we showed that the inferences are not derived in a human like manner without further input, it is therefore possible that the models could perform this task when prompted in a way that guides their reasoning more directly (i.e Fei et al. (2023) proposed a method called Three-hop Reasoning that breaks a task down into distinct reasoning steps that build on each other and increase in difficulty, and we see potential for applying such a method to our task in the future).

Another limitation lies in the selection of models, as it is does not cover the full range of different available architectures, due to not only the number of different models, but also the frequency at which they are released. For that reason we also do not include the newest OpenAI model GPT-4o.

A major limitation stems from only analysing the generated tokens and not their probabilities, as this is not supported by the OpenAI API. Furthermore, our efforts at testing a Likert scale in addition to 0% to 100% scale and requesting self-calibration (see appendix C) from the model through considering multiple answers cannot fully mitigate the potential problems of having the models output concrete values, and within our limited data we were unable to satisfyingly assess how consistently the model can actually adhere to any given scale. In that same vein, the faithfulness of externalized model reasoning has been previously questioned, and we can again not reliably assess the degree of faithfulness exhibited in our experiments. While this opens up avenues for further research, we believe that the combination of concrete values and explanations obtained, paired with our qualitative analysis of the performance on different steps provide a solid initial picture of the models abilities in terms of deriving atypicality inferences.

Finally, we have treated each model as a black box, only assessing their abilities through prompting, and only with a limited number of manually engineered prompts. Further research aimed more at the models' internal mechanisms, i.e. by probing and investigating the layer-wise capabilities, would be recommendable.

8 Acknowledgments

This work was supported by the Deutsche Forschungsgemeinschaft (DFG), Funder Id: http://dx.doi.org/10.13039/501100001659, Project-ID 232722074 – SFB1102: Information Density and Linguistic Encoding.

We would like to thank the anonymous reviewers for their helpful comments. We thank Mayank Jobanputra for his help with the Llama model.

References

Chiara Barattieri di San Pietro, Federico Frau, Veronica Mangiaterra, and Valentina Bambini. 2023. The pragmatic profile of chatgpt: Assessing the communicative skills of a conversational agent. *Sistemi intelligenti*, 35(2):379–400.

Gordon H. Bower, John B. Black, and Terrence J. Turner. 1979. Scripts in memory for text. *Cognitive Psychology*, 11:177–220.

Tom B. Brown, Benjamin Mann, Nick Ryder, Melanie Subbiah, Jared Kaplan, Prafulla Dhariwal, Arvind Neelakantan, Pranav Shyam, Girish Sastry, Amanda Askell, Sandhini Agarwal, Ariel Herbert-Voss, Gretchen Krueger, Tom Henighan, Rewon Child, Aditya Ramesh, Daniel M Ziegler, Jeffrey Wu,

Clemens Winter, Christopher Hesse, Mark Chen, Eric Sigler, Mateusz Litwin, Scott Gray, Benjamin Chess, Jack Clark, Christopher Berner, Sam Mccandlish, Alec Radford, Ilya Sutskever, and Dario Amodei. 2020. Language models are few-shot learners. *Advances in Neural Information Processing Systems*, 33:1877–1901.

Hao Fei, Bobo Li, Qian Liu, Lidong Bing, Fei Li, and Tat Seng Chua. 2023. Reasoning implicit sentiment with chain-of-thought prompting. *Proceedings of the Annual Meeting of the Association for Computational Linguistics*, 2:1171–1182.

Joana Garmendia. 2023. Lies we don't say: Figurative language, commitment, and deniability. *Journal of Pragmatics*, 218:183–194.

Herbert P Grice. 1975. Logic and conversation. In *Speech acts*, pages 41–58. Brill.

Simon Jerome Han, Keith J. Ransom, Andrew Perfors, and Charles Kemp. 2024. Inductive reasoning in humans and large language models. *Cognitive Systems Research*, 83:101155.

Pengfei Hong, Deepanway Ghosal, Navonil Majumder, Somak Aditya, Rada Mihalcea, and Soujanya Poria. 2024a. Stuck in the quicksand of numeracy, far from agi summit: Evaluating llms' mathematical competency through ontology-guided perturbations. *arXiv preprint arXiv:2401.09395*.

Xudong Hong, Margarita Ryzhova, Daniel Adrian Biondi, and Vera Demberg. 2024b. Do large language models and humans have similar behaviors in causal inference with script knowledge? In *Proceedings of the 13th Joint Conference on Lexical and Computational Semantics (* SEM 2024)*.

Jennifer Hu, Sammy Floyd, Olessia Jouravlev, Evelina Fedorenko, and Edward Gibson. 2022. A fine-grained comparison of pragmatic language understanding in humans and language models. *arXiv preprint arXiv:2212.06801*.

Wenlong Huang, Pieter Abbeel, Deepak Pathak, and Igor Mordatch. 2022. Language models as zero-shot planners: Extracting actionable knowledge for embodied agents. pages 9118–9147.

Ekaterina Kravtchenko and Vera Demberg. 2022. Informationally redundant utterances elicit pragmatic inferences. *Cognition*, 225:105159.

Zhuang Qiu, Xufeng Duan, and Zhenguang Garry Cai. 2023. Pragmatic implicature processing in chatgpt. *PsyArXiv*.

Margarita Ryzhova, Alexandra Mayn, and Vera Demberg. 2023. What inferences do people actually make upon encountering informationally redundant utterances? an individual differences study. *Proceedings of the Annual Meeting of the Cognitive Science Society*, 45.

Timo Schick and Hinrich Schütze. 2020. It's not just size that matters: Small language models are also few-shot learners. *arXiv preprint arXiv:2009.07118*.

Eli Schwartz, Leshem Choshen, Joseph Shtok, Sivan Doveh, Leonid Karlinsky, and Assaf Arbelle. 2024. Numerologic: Number encoding for enhanced llms' numerical reasoning. *arXiv preprint arXiv:2404.00459*.

Katherine Tian, Eric Mitchell, Allan Zhou, Archit Sharma, Rafael Rafailov, Huaxiu Yao, Chelsea Finn, and Christopher Manning. 2023. Just ask for calibration: Strategies for eliciting calibrated confidence scores from language models fine-tuned with human feedback. In *Proceedings of the 2023 Conference on Empirical Methods in Natural Language Processing*, pages 5433–5442, Singapore. Association for Computational Linguistics.

Lilian D. A. Wanzare, Alessandra Zarcone, Stefan Thater, and Manfred Pinkal. 2016. A crowdsourced database of event sequence descriptions for the acquisition of high-quality script knowledge. In *Proceedings of the Tenth International Conference on Language Resources and Evaluation (LREC'16)*, pages 3494–3501, Portorož, Slovenia. European Language Resources Association (ELRA).

Zihao Zhao, Eric Wallace, Shi Feng, Dan Klein, and Sameer Singh. 2021. Calibrate before use: Improving few-shot performance of language models. In *International Conference on Machine Learning*, pages 12697–12706. PMLR.

A Prompts: Exp. 1 & Exp. 2

For Exp. 1 and Exp. 2 each model was given a system prompt that describes the task and provides an output template, and then each stimulus was appended in each setting individually. The system prompt for Exp. 1 was engineered iteratively with a small subset of stimuli using GPT-3.5-t, until arriving at prompt (1). The three main components we tweaked were the scale, the output format, and the behavioral directions. After optimizing the prompt for the GPT-3.5-t, it worked equally well for GPT-4 and Llama 3, hence the same prompt was used across all models.

> (1) You will receive a context (C) and two questions (Q1, Q2). Answer the questions by rating the frequency on a scale from 0% of the time to 100% of the time. Explain your answer in no more than two sentences. Always give a definitive answer, even if that means making assumptions and speculating based on common knowledge of human behavior. Additionally, tell me how a person that

knows the people mentioned in the context would answer the below questions, using the same scale and explaining their answer in no more than two sentences.

Use the following template for your output, where '<>' is a placeholder for content:

X: <Responder: AI or Human>

Q: <Question>

A: <Answer>

R: <Reasoning>

For the scale, the experiments by Kravtchenko Demberg (2022) used a continuous sliding scale from Never to Always, mapping to values of 0 and 100 respectively. Attempts at similar scale failed to elicit consistent response categories, and ultimately we needed the model to output its ratings directly in values. Hence a scale of 0% o 100% of the time was established, which closely corresponds to the initial scale, but appeared more consistent and accessible to the model.

The model output needed to be constrained to a format from which the ratings and reasonings could easily be retrieved. We experimented with different instructions as well as template designs (i.e. different placeholders, separators etc.) and found the simple and concise variant presented in (1) to be most consistently adhered to. While GPT-3.5-t and Llama 3 somewhat frequently generated output that did not fully adhere to this format, we also found that this template constrained the output enough that the majority of output could be parsed automatically, hence minimizing the ratings that needed to be extracted manually. GPT-4 generated output that very closely adhered to the template.

For the behavioral instructions, we found that the models needed to be explicitly told to speculate and make assumptions, as they would else refuse a response on the grounds of a lack of necessary context or information. Telling the models that a definitive answer was required further facilitated their ability to commit to a response, though occasionally a definitive answer was still not given. We initially encountered frequent problems with the model refusing to answer because it was "just a language model", which led us to additionally request a second response, where the model pretends to be a human who knows the characters in the stimulus. Ultimately, the other tweaks to the prompt improved this behavior to the point where the model also consistently provided answers as "itself". Since a paired t-test revealed no significant difference between the two types of responses (i.e. responses as the model and responses pretending to be a human), we did not uphold a distinction between those data points in the further analysis.[7]

For Exp. 2 we used the same system prompt, only adding the information that the model would be provided with two examples (2). The two examples were appended prior to the stimulus, and were crafted manually to mirror the atypicality response we expected in the habitual utterance condition. Notably, providing examples in the correct output format increased GPT-3.5-t's and Llama 3's ability to adhere to the template.

(2) You will receive a context (C) and two questions (Q1, Q2).

Answer the questions by rating the frequency on a scale from 0% of the time to 100% of the time. Explain your answer in no more than two sentences. Always give a definitive answer, even if that means making assumptions and speculating based on common knowledge of human behavior.

Additionally, tell me how a person that knows the people mentioned in the context would answer the below questions, using the same scale and explaining their answer in no more than two sentences.You will be provided with 2 examples (Ex1, Ex2).

Use the following template for your output, where '<>' is a placeholder for content:

X: < Responder: AI or Human >

Q: <Q1 or Q2>

A: <Answer>

R: <Reasoning>

B Exp. 1: Additional Results

As noted, we obtained results from the Zero-Shot prompting in a total of 6 conditions. The manipulation of the context to state atypical behavior

[7]The data for the recently released Llama 3 was collected after we had already deemed this distinction unecessary, hence the relevant sentence was removed from the prompt when prompting Llama 3 and we only collected one data point for each stimulus.

(wonky context) reduced the baseline typicality ratings in all models. The rating change after encountering redundancies was minimal for GPT-3.5-t, only somewhat higher for GPT-4 and almost double for Llama 3 (cf. Table 5). Encountering only a minor rating change is in line with the human results obtained by KD. As indicated by a very high standard deviation the effect of voiding script knowledge did vary greatly across stimuli, i.e. not all activities were equally strongly influenced by the manipulated background.

Additionally, we also looked at the typicality ratings in the non-conv. habitual utterance condition. At baseline the activity was indeed rated to be very atypical, with a high standard deviation again showing differences across the stimuli, and there was a relatively high rating change in the utterance condition (cf. Table 6). While the low baseline rating is in line with the observations in Kravtchenko and Demberg (2022), the effect size is larger in the models than in humans. While we did not annotate the provided explanations for these conditions, the observation that the typicality is higher in the utterance condition appears to be in line with the reinforced utterance reasoning that we observed for habitual activity, i.e. something being rated as typical because it was mentioned.

C Zero-Shot: Likert Scale and Calibration

To increase our confidence in the validity of concrete values the model has been outputting, we also collected ratings on the below 7-point Likert scale:

1. Never
2. Rarely, less than 10% of the time
3. Occasionally, 30% of the time
4. Sometimes, about 50% of the time
5. Frequently, about 70% of the time
6. Usually, about 90% of the time
7. Every time

Using this scale did once again not yield significant rating change for GPT-3.5-t. For Llama 3 and GPT-4 the rating change is significant and occurs, as previously seen, in the opposite direction, i.e the conv. habitual activity is judged to be more frequent when the utterance is seen (GPT-4 6.58 →6.75; t(23) = -2.14, $p < .05$; Llama 3 5.62 →6.32; t(23) = -3.39, $p < .005$)

The same sanity check as performed above did show that for all three models there is no significant rating change for the conv. habitual utterance when the non-habitual utterance is present. Furthermore the results of using a wonky context, i.e. voiding the script knowledge, and the typicality rating of the non-habitual activity are in line with results reported in appendix B.

Additionally, we tried an approach for asking the model to self-calibrate its responses that was introduced by Tian et al. (2023). They have taken inspiration from human psychology showing that considering multiple possible answers can mitigate over-confidence, and consequently ask the models to provide multiple responses that they had to assign likelihood to. We applied their strongest approach of considering 4 responses and assigning a probability p = (0.0, 1.0).

We were not able to adjust the proposed calibration method to our task in such a way that Llama 3 could consistently generate multiple responses, despite the Tian et al. (2023) using Llama-2-70b-chat for their experiments. We attribute this to our more complex task and output format, and consequently cannot report results for Llama 3. For GPT-3.5-t and GPT-4 the results were indiscernible from the regular zero-shot prompting presented in 3, i.e for the conv. habitual activity the non-significant rating change for GPT-3.5-t is in the opposite direction (88.5 →94.0), and for GPT-4 we see very high typicality ratings and no rating change in the presence of the conv. habitual utterance.

D Perturbation Analysis: Further Results

Here we provide the results of the first and second perturbation analysis for GPT-3.5-t and Llama 3, as well as the results of an additional prompt perturbation experiment for all three models.

D.1 Perturbation 1

Both GPT-3.5-t and Llama 3 stopped drawing atypicality inferences both in ratings and reasonings, with a more drastic effect in Llama 3, which reverted back to assigning very high ratings in the conv. utterance condition (mean: 84.5 →93.9) and did not have atypicality represented in that ratings at all. In the non-habitual utterance condition, the ratings did not increase or decrease (mean: 83.2). GPT-3.5-t did keep with the previous trend of lower

	Wonky baseline		Wonky habitual utterance	
model	mean	sd	mean	sd
GPT-3.5-t	52.71	37.34	50.20	41.84
GPT-4	35.89	39.19	41.46	40.29
Llama 3	16.2	24.8	31.9	38.9

Table 5: Typicality ratings for the habitual activity in the wonky context conditions

	Baseline		Non-conventional utterance	
model	mean	sd	mean	sd
GPT-3.5-t	21.19	24.27	27.25	31.54
GPT-4	33.96	25.19	44.39	25.15
Llama 3	36.2	36.2	23.3	23.8

Table 6: Typicality ratings for the non-conventional activity in the normal context condition

ratings that were not statistically significant, and exhibited atypicality twice in the provided reasonings.

D.2 Perturbation 2

For GPT-3.5-t the difference between A and B is not as pronounced, and *atypicality_reject* is observed much less frequently than in GPT-4. Both the modeled rating with the modeled atyp reasoning (i.e. copying down), and the modeled rating with an adjusted matching *no_atypicality* reasoning appear approximately equally frequently. For (B) there is notably an increased number of the modeled atypicality reasoning being paired with an adjusted rating. Llama 3, on the other hand, rarely emulated both the modeled reasoning and rating. For (B) it matches the rating of 100% with an appropriate reasoning more than half the time, and for (A) this happens the majority of the time. When the model does replicate the modeled atypicality reasoning, it is most of the time paired with a typicality rating of 0%. Notably, Llama 3 does actually generate a few nonsensical or incongruent responses in this setting.

D.3 Additional perturbation experiments

We also crafted a second set of intentionally misleading and incongruent exemplars, modeling the reverse behavior, i.e. pairing a low rating that implies atypicality with a reasoning that models no atypicality. We tried both providing a low rating (<40%) and a rating of 0% . In these experiments, all three models very consistently reproduce the reasoning but ignore the modeled rating and assign a high matching rating instead.

E Prompts: Exp. 3

Below we provide the alternative questions/wordings for the steps and discuss briefly why they were less efficient than their counterparts. Additionally, we adjusted the system prompt to reflect the new instruction, telling them that they were experts on human behavior and had the task of answering a question based on a provided context (3)[8]. The models were then given each stimulus in the critical condition, and one question aimed at identifying the redundancy at a time.

> (3) You are an expert on human behavior and communication who will be answering a question based on short contexts (C). There is no right or wrong answer to the questions you'll see, and you are willing to use your best judgement and commit to a concrete, specific response, even in cases where you can't be sure that you are correct.
>
> Please keep your answer as short and concise as possible. Use the following template for your output, where '<>' is a placeholder for content:
>
> Q: <Question>
>
> A: <Answer>

E.1 Step 1:

For this step, the following alternative questions were tested:

[8]This system prompt is adapted from Han et al. (2024). It was also tested as a system prompt for Exp. 1 during the prompt engineering process but unlike here, it did not lead to a more consistent performance.

- A_Q1: Is any part of the direct speech superfluous or unnecessary?
- A_Q2: Does the context (C) contain any redundancies?

With A_Q1 we replaced the word redundancy, as we thought it might be too specialized, i.e. not be the word a laymen would chose to describe the phenomenon. For the most part this did however perform on par with Q1 reported in the paper, ultimately showing that this distinction did not matter to the models. With A_Q2 we opted for an even more open-ended approach by not restricting the potential redundancies to the direct speech. This did however, unsurprisingly yield even fewer identifications of the desired redundancy.

E.2 Step 2:

As explained before, identifying the models' ability to perform this step was challenging through a set of questions was challenging due to its subtlety, and since humans might also not verbalize their implicit understanding of the conversational norm that is violated by redundancies (Maxim of Quantity). Ultimately, we used the following questions to gauge a more general understanding of the models' awareness of conversational norms:

- A_Q3: The second sentence in the direct speech provides redundant information, since the action it talks about is already implied in the first sentence. Do you think this was an acceptable utterance?
- A_Q4: The direct speech contains redundant information. Is providing redundant information a good and efficient way of communication?
- A_Q5: The direct speech contains redundant information. Do you see any issue with that?

For A_Q3 the utterance was mostly deemed acceptable by GPT-3.5-t and GPT-4, and when reasoning was provided in the model response, it would be very general, usually suggesting that the redundancy served the purpose of emphasizing or expressed general noteworthiness. Llama 3 on the other hand found the utterance mostly not acceptable, sometimes reasoning that it may serve as emphasis or to provide nuance, but mostly classifying them as unnecessary or even awkward. For A_Q4 GPT-3.5-t answered no 24 times without elaborating further. GPT-4 and Llama 3 also agreed that it is not acceptable and elaborated why (i.e. confusing, waste of time), but the majority of time it was then also stated that there still might be good reasons (i.e. emphasizing, clarification). For A_Q5, GPT-3.5-t saw no issue for most items, and the remaining times it said there was an issue with redundancy, though usually not the informational redundancy we were investigating but one from the broader context (i.e. "Don mentions that he took a train with Jane, which is already implied by the fact that he saw Jane at the subway station and they took the train together", which is arguably not a redundancy because the character he tells this to does not know that he saw her and that they took a train). GPT-4 generally saw no issue, occasionally stating the (correct informational) redundancy and for each item elaborating reasons the redundancy occurred. These reasons are however mostly very general and broad (i.e. emphasis, enthusiasm, creating a relaxed atmosphere, establishing a connection). Similarly, saw either no issue, or no major issue with the redundancy, and when elaborating on the informational redundancy it provided a reasonable purpose for expressing it. Finally, with A_Q5 Llama 3 did actually identify the informational redundancy we were looking for for the majority of the stimuli, and did proclaim that it was an issue.

E.3 Step 3:

Find below additional questions we tested for this step:

- A_Q6: The second sentence in the direct speech conveys seemingly redundant information. Providing redundant information can be unnecessary and inefficient for communication. Why was the redundant utterance made?
- A_Q7: The second sentence in the direct speech conveys seemingly redundant information. Providing redundant information can be unnecessary and inefficient for communication. Consider only what you can tell about the people from the provided context (C) and tell me definitively: Why did the speaker still choose to express the redundant information in this specific situation?
- A_Q8: The second sentence in the direct speech conveys seemingly redundant information. Providing redundant information can

be unnecessary and inefficient for communication. However, the speaker made the effort of conveying this information. Since they have no reason to be inefficient, this information must actually be new or important. What new or relevant information can you infer from the second sentence?

A_Q6 and A_Q7 resulted in very general responses from GPT-3.5-t and GPT-4 that covered the same potential reasons for redundancy that have been stated in previous steps. Llama 3 also provided similar reason but once again did a better job of applying them to the specific scenario rather than keeping them general. Notably, atypicality was not among the reasons that Llama 3 came up with. For A_Q8, GPT-3.5-t defaulted to just stating the exact contents of the sentence, while GPT-4 performed slightly worse than with the for each item adjusted Q4 reported in the paper (i.e. it gave appropriate reasons, but not as specific to the item content, and fewer explanations pointing towards atypicality). Llama 3 unsurprisingly showed a similar performance to the other questions as the model has less of a tendency to generalize.

E.4 Step 4:

For step 4 we did not experiment further, and instead just directly adapted the best performing question from step 3 by inserting the desired atypicality answer and then adding a simple question to elicit alternative behavior.

Predict but Also Integrate: an Analysis of Sentence Processing Models for English and Hindi

Nina Delcaro
Eindhoven University of Technology,
The Netherlands
n.delcaro@student.tue.nl

Luca Onnis
Linguistics and Scandinavian Studies,
University of Oslo, Norway
lucao@uio.no

Raquel G. Alhama
Institute for Logic, Language and Computation
University of Amsterdam,
The Netherlands
rgalhama@uva.nl

Abstract

Fluent speakers make implicit predictions about forthcoming linguistic items while processing sentences, possibly to increase efficiency in real-time comprehension. However, the extent to which prediction is the primary mode of processing human language is widely debated. The human language processor may also gain efficiency by integrating new linguistic information with prior knowledge and the preceding context, without actively predicting. At present, the role of probabilistic integration, as well as its computational foundation, remains relatively understudied. Here, we explored whether a Delayed Recurrent Neural Network (d-RNN, Turek et al., 2020), as an implementation of both prediction and integration, can explain patterns of human language processing over and above the contribution of a purely predictive RNN model. We found that incorporating integration contributes to explaining variability in eye-tracking data for English and Hindi.

1 Introduction

Languages are acquired and processed in real time. The transient quality of spoken language is evident, as it vanishes the moment it is spoken. And while written words appear fixed on a page, skilled readers assimilate them in sequence rapidly, seldom needing to double-back and review past words, and even skipping words entirely. This transitory aspect of language, coupled with the remarkable efficiency and speed at which humans use it, suggests that our brains harness specialized processes for managing information that fluidly unfolds in a sequence.

One proposed cognitive mechanism is prediction, the process by which a listener or reader anticipates upcoming linguistic information during language comprehension. This anticipation is based on internalized knowledge of language, previous local context information, and accumulated world-knowledge from semantic and episodic long-term memory. Psycholinguistic research suggests that individuals often implicitly predict elements such as the next word or grammatical structure while engaging with language, which allows for more efficient processing and understanding (Hale, 2016; Pimentel et al., 2023; Wilcox et al., 2023a). Prediction can occur at multiple levels, from anticipating the completion of a familiar phrase to forecasting the thematic content of a conversation or narrative. Probabilistic word prediction has been explicitly implemented in a class of cognitive recurrent models since the inception of the Recurrent Neural Network (Elman, 1990).

However, an unresolved debate in psycholinguistics centers around the extent to which the human language processor anticipates upcoming information (prediction) and how it assimilates incoming linguistic information with existing knowledge (integration, Ferreira and Chantavarin, 2018; Kuperberg and Jaeger, 2016; Nieuwland et al., 2020). A mechanism of probabilistic integration would not necessarily try to predict upcoming material, but instead increase efficiency by evaluating the probability of the preceding context given each heard/read linguistic item (e.g., the current word). In recent work (Onnis and Huettig, 2021; Onnis et al., 2022) this mechanism has been modeled successfully using n-gram language models as the backward transitional probability, *P(prior context | word)* as a proxy for integration, as opposed to prediction in the form of forward transitional probability, *P(word | current word).*

Here, we conducted an exploratory analysis to determine whether a recurrent language model implementing integration can explain patterns of human language processing (online reading times revealed by eye movements from existing psycholinguistic datasets) over and above the contribution of a purely predictive language model. We did so by comparing two types of Recurrent Neural Networks (RNNs), namely the classic RNN, and the Delayed

Proceedings of the Workshop on Cognitive Modeling and Computational Linguistics, pages 101–108

RNN (d-RNN) as proposed by Turek et al. (2020). The classic RNN can be considered an implementation of prediction, while the d-RNN implements both prediction and integration (see details below). To test the robustness of our method, we applied it to reading data from two languages, English and Hindi, that differ typologically in several ways, reflecting their distinct linguistic origins, families, and structures. Our work has value in attempting to model probabilistic integration explicitly, as an additional important cognitive mechanism underlying language processing that is currently underappreciated in psycholinguistic modeling.

2 Model Architectures

We evaluate two Recurrent Neural Network architectures: a vanilla Recurrent Neural Network (RNN, Elman, 1990), and a variant that introduces a processing delay (d-RNN, Turek et al., 2020). The former has a long tradition in cognitive modeling (Elman, 1990; Rohde and Plaut, 1997; Christiansen and Chater, 1999; Cartling, 2008), as it is naturally suited to implement forward prediction over sequential inputs. The latter was first proposed in the context of NLP, to incorporate sensitivity to backward dependencies (i.e., approximating bidirectional RNNs); however, it has also been used to model language acquisition (Alhama et al., 2021).

RNNs are forward models by design because they are trained to predict the upcoming word in a sentence (x_{t+1}) based on two sources of information: the current word x_t and the hidden state of the network, computed in the previous step (h_{t-1}). The d-RNN implements next-word prediction in the same way, but its key feature is the addition of a processing delay d such that, for an input word x_t, its output is produced at time $t + d$ (i.e. the predicted word is $\hat{y}_{t+d}$). Thus, the weights of the d-RNN are only updated after d extra words, delaying learning. Turek et al. (2020) showed that a large enough delay approximates bidirectional processing, suggesting that the delay allows the network to capture backward dependencies. Importantly, while bidirectional models do exploit context to the left and right of a target word to be predicted, they appear unsuited as cognitive models of real-time incremental language processing, as they require entire sentences or paragraphs to compute their predictions. Instead, and crucially, the d-RNN combines classic forward prediction for incremental input with sensitivity to backward dependencies, making it a suitable cognitive model of prediction *and* integration.

3 Data

Sources. The choice of English and Hindi is based on three criteria. First, we required languages with different word order, to ensure enough variability in forward and backward dependencies. While English is strictly SVO, Hindi favours SOV order. Second, we chose languages that differ in terms of morphological typology. Our statistical analysis is done at the word level, so we use this criterion to ensure the languages are comprised of words that cannot easily be separated into multiple morphemes, as in agglutinative languages. English is an analytic language that uses specific words rather than inflection to express syntactic relations. Generally, this entails having one morpheme per word. Hindi is a fusional language: it 'fuses' morphemes together in a word where it is not easy to distinguish the individual morphemes (Ramoo, 2021).

Thirdly, for model training and validation against human reading patterns (specifically, eye fixations on words), we sourced publicly accessible datasets for each language, containing texts of a uniform style. We utilized the Potsdam-Allahabad Hindi Eye-tracking Corpus (PAC, Husain et al., 2015; Vasishth, 2021) comprising word-level eye-tracking data from 30 individuals reading 83 sentences sourced from newspapers. For English, our source was the Multilingual Eye-tracking Corpus (MECO, Siegelman et al., 2022), which includes eye-tracking data captured from 46 participants reading 112 encyclopedic sentences. Both human reading datasets align with expository writing, prompting us to select Wikipedia articles for training our language models. These articles provide a congruent encyclopedic text style and are widely available across languages from Wikimedia Foundation dumps.

Pre-processing. We pre-process the Wikipedia articles and the PAC and MECO sentences using the Stanza library (Qi et al., 2020) for tokenization, Part-of-Speech annotation and lemmatization. We use lowercased text and remove all punctuation (but we process sentences separately). In the case of Wikipedia texts, we remove article titles using regular expressions, and randomly sample 200,000 sentences for each language. The chosen corpora appear comparable in their mean sentence lengths: 18.73 and 21.07 words-per-sentence (wps) for the English training set and MECO sentences, respectively, and 18.94 and 16.2 wps for the Hindi training set and PAC sentences, respectively.

We introduce an unknown token to handle out-of-vocabulary (OOV) and rare words. When setting low frequency words in the corpus to the unknown token, we are reducing the vocabulary size the RNNs need to train on. This simplifies the task, reducing training time (Chen et al., 2019), but it also reduces the amount of text in MECO and PAC sentences. We find that a cut-off word frequency of 24 leaves us with almost 90% of the data within MECO and PAC, while the vocabulary of the training set in English and Hindi is reduced to some 11 thousand words.

The type-token ratio (TTR) calculated after the vocabulary size reduction shows MECO and PAC have a higher degree of lexical variety than the RNN training sets[1]. This is as expected since these datasets contain fewer sentences compared to the amount sampled from Wikipedia. Moreover, the similarity of the training sets' TTRs indicates that the RNNs' task difficulty is similar across languages.

Finally, MECO and PAC require minor preprocessing. In both human reading datasets, we remove skipped words, as they do not help us quantify the predictability of a word and the processing effort required to read it. The code used for preprocessing and the rest of our research is available at `https://github.com/ninadelcaro/predict-integrate-cmcl`.

4 Experimental Setup

Language Models. We use the code for the RNN and d-RNN by Alhama et al. (2021), with a delay of 1 for the d-RNN. Both networks have three layers: an embedding layer, a recurrent one, and a fully connected layer with softmax activation. We feed the networks with the tokenized sentences described above, and we use cross-entropy loss on next-word prediction objective. We update the weights with Stochastic Gradient Descent. We train until the loss becomes stable (around 45 epochs) in the classic RNN and use the same number of epochs to train the d-RNN (41 epochs for English and 45 for Hindi).

Hyperparameter optimization is done using random search (Bergstra and Bengio, 2012). We train on 80% of the Wikipedia articles, using 10% as the validation set and the other 10% as the testing set. The hyperparameters we optimize are the word embedding and hidden state dimensions as well as the learning rate. We select the RNN model with the lowest loss on the validation set and make sure there is no overfitting by comparing the validation loss to the training loss. Our final model has a hidden state size of 682, an embedding size of 426, and a learning rate of 0.001. We use these same hyperparameters across all models (i.e., for both RNN variants and languages).

Predictor Variables from Language Models. Following established computational psycholinguistics literature, we use per-word information-theoretic measures of entropy and surprisal (Hale, 2016). Word surprisal is the negative log-probability of said word, and it intuitively quantifies its unexpectedness. This measure has been linked to human sentence processing difficulty and is predictive of eye movements (Levy, 2008; Wilcox et al., 2023b; Aurnhammer and Frank, 2018; Boston et al., 2008; Ehrlich and Rayner, 1981; Merkx and Frank, 2021; Oh and Schuler, 2023; Demberg and Keller, 2008; Smith and Levy, 2013; Shain et al., 2020). Entropy, on the other hand, quantifies the degree of uncertainty over possible outcomes (Shannon, 1948), and it has also been shown to correlate with human sentence processing effort (Keller, 2004; Linzen and Jaeger, 2014; Wilcox et al., 2023b; Hale, 2003; Linzen and Jaeger, 2016; Roark et al., 2009). We compute these metrics for each word in the MECO and PAC datasets, using the probability distributions predicted by our language models.

Outcome Variables: Eye gazes while reading. Metrics of reading processing difficulty available from MECO and PAC include: first fixation duration, first-pass reading time, and total fixation time. Because no consensus exists on whether these measures underlie separate cognitive processes, these reading times (RTs) were used as dependent variables in separate regression models (Agrawal et al., 2017; Boston et al., 2008; Keller, 2004; Merkx and Frank, 2021). RTs were log-transformed for normalization, variance stabilization, and outlier influence reduction (Aurnhammer and Frank, 2018).

Statistical Inference Model. As in previous research (Agrawal et al., 2017; Aurnhammer and

[1]MECO: $TTR = .34$; PAC: $TTR = .25$; English training set: $TTR = .0023$; Hindi training set: $TTR = .0022$

Frank, 2018; Boston et al., 2008; Merkx and Frank, 2021), we analyze the relationship between the per-word information-theoretic metrics of entropy and suprisal from our language models as predictors, and human reading times as outcomes, using Generalised Linear Mixed Effects Regression models (GLMER) that incorporate both fixed and random effects. The hierarchical structure of MECO and PAC reading data makes the word-level observations non-independent, because the sentences contain words that are embedded in sentences that are read by specific participants. Therefore, we require random intercepts for the participant and the word read to be part of the linear regression models.

We use nested modelling to compare GLMER models with additional independent variables to a baseline GLMER model. Besides random effects, the baseline regresses the eye-tracking data on these control fixed effects covariates known to affect reading times: word length, and order of appearance of each word within the sentence presented to the reader. Model comparison is performed with a log-likelihood ratio test, allowing us to test whether a single predictor added at each step explains any more variance in the outcome variable by improving the model fit.

Entropy and surprisal are not correlated (Pearson's $r(119306) = 0.36, p < 0.001$) in the RNN regression, but they are in the d-RNN regression (Pearson's $r(119306) = 0.99$, $p < 0.001$). Therefore, we choose to separate these two metrics in two sets of stepwise GLMER models, one using entropy and another using surprisal as predictor variables. Each set consists of a) the baseline model, b) a model adding the RNN's metric, and c) a model adding the d-RNN's metric to the previous model. We can thus rigorously evaluate our key theoretical conjecture: does the d-RNN architecture, which incorporates a form of language integration, contribute incremental variance over and above an RNN that operates solely on a predictive mechanism?

5 Results

Table 1 presents the core outcomes of our GLMER analysis, with detailed model comparisons, log-likelihood ratio tests, and α significance levels provided in Appendix A.

English. For the English reading dataset, word entropy of the RNN did not improve the baseline model for any of the three dependent variables,

		English		**Hindi**	
Metric	**Model**	**Ent.**	**Surp.**	**Ent.**	**Surp.**
FFD	RNN	.39	.002	.02	.11
	d-RNN	.01	.13	.1	.19
TFD	RNN	.22	<.001	<.001	<.001
	d-RNN	<.001	.07	.02	.3
FPRT	RNN	.8	.002	.02	.08
	d-RNN	.08	.56	.02	.05

Table 1: Nested model comparison results for human reading time outcomes. Each model comprises various predictors—RNN Model with baseline predictors plus RNN metric, and d-RNN Model with added d-RNN metric. The table shows *p-values* from log-likelihood ratio tests for model comparisons. FFD: First Fixation Duration; TFD: Total Fixation Duration; FPRT: First Pass Reading Time; Ent.: Entropy; Surp.: Surprisal.

whereas the d-RNN's entropy did so when considering first fixation and total fixation duration as dependent variables. Conversely, adding the surprisal of the RNN improved model fit for all three dependent variables, while adding the surprisal of the d-RNN did not improve model fit further.

Hindi. In the Hindi reading dataset, adding the RNN's word entropy to the baseline model improved the model, and so did adding the d-RNN's entropy when predicting total fixation duration and first pass reading time. On the other hand, model comparison revealed no model fit improvement when entering word surprisal, with a notable exception: the addition of the RNN's surprisal to the model regressing total fixation duration.

6 Discussion

The ephemeral nature of language is evident, as it rapidly vanishes from our sensory experience upon its completion – being spoken or read. While current psycholinguistics research primarily emphasizes probabilistic prediction as a mechanism that facilitates efficient language learning and real-time processing, the computational modeling of integration and its interplay with prediction in human sentence processing remain less understood. Addressing this, we used an RNN to model pure prediction and a d-RNN for the combined processes of prediction and integration, and assessed the relationship between language model-derived entropy and surprisal measures and eye-tracking data.

The d-RNN's entropy contribution across languages suggests that language models incorporating integration explain variability in eye-tracking data beyond prediction alone, although surprisal did not yield similar results. A tentative interpretation is that the time course of integration is better reflected in a metric like entropy, which measures uncertainty based on the current state of knowledge of the model, rather than in an a-posteriori and word-specific metric like surprisal. This may be a consequence of the specific operationalization of integration provided by the d-RNN, which delays learning until subsequent words have been processed. Such operationalization is in fact reminiscent of the *lookahead* mechanism used in the parsing literature, which peeks at a number of upcoming tokens in a sentence in order to decide between alternative syntactic analyses (Marcus, 1980; Stabler, 1983; Nozohoor-Farshi, 1986).

The different outcomes in English and Hindi data could suggest that integration and prediction may be employed differently in various languages, possibly influenced by the distinct word orders of the languages we examined—English being SVO and Hindi SOV— and how they interact with RNN model metrics and eye-tracking measures. These observations call for additional investigations into a broader spectrum of languages to discern how language structure might tip sentence processing toward either integration or prediction.

Note that in modeling reading processes, we strived for cognitive plausibility. While more recent and powerful architectures such as bidirectional recurrent networks and encoder-decoder transformers could potentially implement integration, they also do it using text from the future, i.e. they require entire sentences or passages to predict a masked word and train its algorithm. Since relying on future words is not cognitively plausible when processing language word-by-word incrementally, we opted for classic RNN implementations. Other models like Long-Short Term Memory Networks (Hochreiter and Schmidhuber, 1997) and decoder-only transformers trained unidirectionally (Radford et al., 2019) meet our requirements, and we leave the investigation of their suitability to future work.

Acknowledgments

We thank Samar Husain and Shravan Vasishth for additional information on the PAC dataset and appreciate Tilburg University's GPU4EDU project for the GPU resources provided.

References

Arpit Agrawal, Sumeet Agarwal, and Samar Husain. 2017. Role of expectation and working memory constraints in hindi comprehension: An eye-tracking corpus analysis. *Journal of Eye Movement Research*, 10.

Raquel G. Alhama, Francesca Zermiani, and Atiqah Khaliq. 2021. Retrodiction as delayed recurrence: the case of adjectives in Italian and English. *Proceedings of the 19th Workshop of the Australasian Language Technology Association*, pages 163–168.

Christoph Aurnhammer and Stefan Frank. 2018. Comparing gated and simple recurrent neural network architectures as models of human sentence processing. In *Proceedings of the 41st Annual Conference of the Cognitive Science Society*.

James Bergstra and Y. Bengio. 2012. Random search for hyper-parameter optimization. *The Journal of Machine Learning Research*, 13:281–305.

Marisa Ferrara Boston, John Tracy Hale, Reinhold Kliegl, Umesh Patil, and Shravan Vasishth. 2008. Parsing costs as predictors of reading difficulty: An evaluation using the potsdam sentence corpus. *Journal of Eye Movement Research*, 2.

Bo Cartling. 2008. On the implicit acquisition of a context-free grammar by a simple recurrent neural network. *Neurocomputing*, 71(7):1527–1537.

Wenhu Chen, Yu Su, Yilin Shen, Zhiyu Chen, Xifeng Yan, and William Yang Wang. 2019. How large a vocabulary does text classification need? a variational approach to vocabulary selection. In *Proceedings of the 2019 Conference of the North American Chapter of the Association for Computational Linguistics: Human Language Technologies, Volume 1 (Long and Short Papers)*, pages 3487–3497, Minneapolis, Minnesota. Association for Computational Linguistics.

Morten H Christiansen and Nick Chater. 1999. Toward a connectionist model of recursion in human linguistic performance. *Cognitive Science*, 23(2):157–205.

Vera Demberg and Frank Keller. 2008. Data from eye-tracking corpora as evidence for theories of syntactic processing complexity. *Cognition*, 109(2):193–210.

Susan F. Ehrlich and Keith Rayner. 1981. Contextual effects on word perception and eye movements during reading. *Journal of Verbal Learning and Verbal Behavior*, 20(6):641–655.

Jeffrey L. Elman. 1990. Finding structure in time. *Cognitive Science*, 14(2):179–211.

Fernanda Ferreira and Suphasiree Chantavarin. 2018. Integration and prediction in language processing: A synthesis of old and new. *Current Directions in Psychological Science*, 27:096372141879449.

Wikimedia Foundation. Wikimedia Downloads.

John Hale. 2016. Information-theoretical complexity metrics. *Language and Linguistics Compass*, 10(9):397–412.

John Tracy Hale. 2003. The information conveyed by words in sentences. *Journal of Psycholinguistic Research*, 32:101–123.

Sepp Hochreiter and Jürgen Schmidhuber. 1997. Long short-term memory. *Neural Computation*, 9(8):1735–1780.

Samar Husain, Shravan Vasishth, and Narayanan Srinivasan. 2015. Integration and prediction difficulty in Hindi sentence comprehension: Evidence from an eye-tracking corpus. *Journal of Eye Movement Research*, 8:1–12.

Frank Keller. 2004. The entropy rate principle as a predictor of processing effort: An evaluation against eye-tracking data. In *Proceedings of the 2004 Conference on Empirical Methods in Natural Language Processing*, pages 317–324, Barcelona, Spain. Association for Computational Linguistics.

Gina R Kuperberg and T Florian Jaeger. 2016. What do we mean by prediction in language comprehension? *Language, cognition and neuroscience*, 31(1):32–59.

Roger Levy. 2008. Expectation-based syntactic comprehension. *Cognition*, 106(3):1126–1177.

Tal Linzen and Florian Jaeger. 2014. Investigating the role of entropy in sentence processing. In *Proceedings of the Fifth Workshop on Cognitive Modeling and Computational Linguistics*, pages 10–18, Baltimore, Maryland, USA. Association for Computational Linguistics.

Tal Linzen and T. Florian Jaeger. 2016. Uncertainty and expectation in sentence processing: Evidence from subcategorization distributions. *Cognitive Science*, 40(6):1382–1411.

Mitchell P. Marcus. 1980. *Theory of Syntactic Recognition for Natural Languages*. MIT Press, Cambridge, MA, USA.

Danny Merkx and Stefan L. Frank. 2021. Human sentence processing: Recurrence or attention? In *Proceedings of the Workshop on Cognitive Modeling and Computational Linguistics*, pages 12–22, Online. Association for Computational Linguistics.

Mante S Nieuwland, Dale J Barr, Federica Bartolozzi, Simon Busch-Moreno, Emily Darley, David I Donaldson, Heather J Ferguson, Xiao Fu, Evelien Heyselaar, Falk Huettig, et al. 2020. Dissociable effects of prediction and integration during language comprehension: Evidence from a large-scale study using brain potentials. *Philosophical Transactions of the Royal Society B*, 375(1791):20180522.

R. Nozohoor-Farshi. 1986. On formalizations of Marcus' parser. In *Coling 1986 Volume 1: The 11th International Conference on Computational Linguistics*, pages 533–535.

Byung-Doh Oh and William Schuler. 2023. Why does surprisal from larger transformer-based language models provide a poorer fit to human reading times? *Transactions of the Association for Computational Linguistics*, 11:336–350.

Luca Onnis and Falk Huettig. 2021. Can prediction and retrodiction explain whether frequent multi-word phrases are accessed 'precompiled' from memory or compositionally constructed on the fly? *Brain Research*, 1772:147674.

Luca Onnis, Alfred Lim, Shirley Cheung, and Falk Huettig. 2022. Is the mind inherently predicting? exploring forward and backward looking in language processing. *Cognitive Science*, 46(10):e13201.

Tiago Pimentel, Clara Meister, Ethan Wilcox, Kyle Mahowald, and Ryan Cotterell. 2023. Revisiting the optimality of word lengths. In *Proceedings of the 2023 Conference on Empirical Methods in Natural Language Processing*, pages 2240–2255, Singapore. Association for Computational Linguistics.

Peng Qi, Yuhao Zhang, Yuhui Zhang, Jason Bolton, and Christopher D. Manning. 2020. Stanza: A Python natural language processing toolkit for many human languages. In *Proceedings of the 58th Annual Meeting of the Association for Computational Linguistics: System Demonstrations*.

Alec Radford, Jeffrey Wu, Rewon Child, David Luan, Dario Amodei, Ilya Sutskever, et al. 2019. Language models are unsupervised multitask learners. *OpenAI blog*, 1(8):9.

Dinesh Ramoo. 2021. Morphology of different languages. In *Psychology of Language*. BCcampus.

Brian Roark, Asaf Bachrach, Carlos Cardenas, and Christophe Pallier. 2009. Deriving lexical and syntactic expectation-based measures for psycholinguistic modeling via incremental top-down parsing. In *Proceedings of the 2009 Conference on Empirical Methods in Natural Language Processing*, pages 324–333, Singapore. Association for Computational Linguistics.

Douglas L. T. Rohde and David C. Plaut. 1997. Simple recurrent networks and natural language: How important is starting small?

Cory Shain, Idan Asher Blank, Marten van Schijndel, William Schuler, and Evelina Fedorenko. 2020. fmri reveals language-specific predictive coding during naturalistic sentence comprehension. *Neuropsychologia*, 138:107307.

C. E. Shannon. 1948. A mathematical theory of communication. *Bell System Technical Journal*, 27(3):379–423.

Noam Siegelman, Sascha Schroeder, Cengiz Acarturk, Hee-Don Ahn, Svetlana Alexeeva, Simona Amenta, Raymond Bertram, Rolando Bonandrini, Marc Brysbaert, Daria Chernova, Sara Fonseca, Nicolas Dirix,

Wouter Duyck, Argyro Fella, Ram Frost, Carolina Gattei, Areti Kalaitzi, Nayoung Kwon, Kaidi Lõo, and Victor Kuperman. 2022. Expanding horizons of cross-linguistic research on reading: The multilingual eye-movement corpus (meco). *Behavior Research Methods*, 54:1–21.

Nathaniel J. Smith and R. Levy. 2013. The effect of word predictability on reading time is logarithmic. *Cognition*, 128:302–319.

Edward P. Stabler. 1983. Deterministic and bottom-up parsing in Prolog. In *Proceedings of the Third AAAI Conference on Artificial Intelligence*, AAAI'83, page 383–386. AAAI Press.

Javier Turek, Shailee Jain, Vy Vo, Mihai Capotă, Alexander Huth, and Theodore Willke. 2020. Approximating stacked and bidirectional recurrent architectures with the delayed recurrent neural network. In *Proceedings of the 37th International Conference on Machine Learning*, volume 119 of *Proceedings of Machine Learning Research*, pages 9648–9658. PMLR.

Shravan Vasishth. 2021. vasishth/lingpsych: Data and Functions used in the Book "Linear Mixed Models in Linguistics and Psychology: A Comprehensive Introduction". *rdrr.io*.

Ethan Wilcox, Clara Meister, Ryan Cotterell, and Tiago Pimentel. 2023a. Language model quality correlates with psychometric predictive power in multiple languages. In *Proceedings of the 2023 Conference on Empirical Methods in Natural Language Processing*, pages 7503–7511, Singapore. Association for Computational Linguistics.

Ethan G Wilcox, Tiago Pimentel, Clara Meister, Ryan Cotterell, and Roger P Levy. 2023b. Testing the predictions of surprisal theory in 11 languages. *Transactions of the Association for Computational Linguistics*, 11:1451–1470.

A Appendix

Outcome	Predictors	English AIC	English χ^2	English p-value	Hindi AIC	Hindi χ^2	Hindi p-value
	Baseline	55443			23932		
First fixation duration	RNN entropy	55444	0.74	.39	23928	5.8	.02
	d-RNN entropy	55440	6.36	.01	23927	2.75	.1
	Baseline	94736			37375		
Total fixation duration	RNN entropy	94737	1.52	.22	37366	11.16	<.001
	d-RNN entropy	94727	12.08	<.001	37363	5.23	.02
	Baseline	72201			32505		
First pass reading time	RNN entropy	72203	0.06	.8	32502	5.84	.02
	d-RNN entropy	72202	2.97	.08	32499	5.06	.02

Table 2: Results of stepwise nested model comparisons predicting human reading time outcomes. Each inference model includes different predictors: Baseline Model (word length, sentence position, and subject and word random intercepts), RNN Entropy Model (Baseline predictors plus RNN word entropy), and d-RNN Entropy Model (RNN Model predictors plus d-RNN word entropy). Models are assessed using log-likelihood ratio tests.

Outcome	Predictors	English AIC	English χ^2	English p-value	Hindi AIC	Hindi χ^2	Hindi p-value
	Baseline	55443			23932		
First fixation duration	RNN surprisal	55436	9.22	.002	23931	2.54	.11
	d-RNN surprisal	55436	2.27	.13	23932	1.74	.19
	Baseline	94736			37375		
Total fixation duration	RNN surprisal	94709	28.96	<.001	37360	17.7	<.001
	d-RNN surprisal	94708	3.23	.07	37360	1.08	.3
	Baseline	72201			32505		
First pass reading time	RNN surprisal	722194	9.84	.002	32504	3.1	.08
	d-RNN surprisal	722195	0.34	.56	32503	3.72	.05

Table 3: Results of stepwise nested model comparisons predicting human reading time outcomes. Each inference model includes different predictors: Baseline Model (word length, sentence position, and subject and word random intercepts), RNN surprisal Model (Baseline predictors plus RNN word surprisal), and d-RNN surprisal Model (RNN Model predictors plus d-RNN word surprisal). Models are assessed using log-likelihood ratio tests.

Transformer Attention vs Human Attention in Anaphora Resolution

Anastasia Kozlova[1], Albina Akhmetgareeva[1], Aigul Khanova[2], Semen Kudriavtsev[2], Alena Fenogenova[1]
[1]SaluteDevices, [2]HSE University
Correspondence: anastasi2510@gmail.com

Abstract

Motivated by human cognitive processes, attention mechanism within transformer architecture has been developed to assist neural networks in allocating focus to specific aspects within input data. Despite claims regarding the interpretability achieved by attention mechanisms, the extent of correlation and similarity between machine and human attention remains a subject requiring further investigation. In this paper, we conduct a quantitative analysis of human attention compared to neural attention mechanisms in the context of the anaphora resolution task. We collect an eye-tracking dataset based on the Winograd schema challenge task for the Russian language. Leveraging this dataset, we conduct an extensive analysis of the correlations between human and machine attention maps across various transformer architectures, network layers of pre-trained and fine-tuned models. Our aim is to investigate whether insights from human attention mechanisms can be used to enhance the performance of neural networks in tasks such as anaphora resolution. The results reveal distinctions in anaphora resolution processing, offering promising prospects for improving the performance of neural networks and understanding the cognitive nuances of human perception.

1 Introduction

The term *attention* describes both human cognitive processes, crucial for tasks like reading and comprehension, and the attention mechanism in neural networks (Bahdanau et al., 2016), which dynamically adjusts focus to specific input data. Despite their apparent differences, this paper aims to analyze the correlations between transformer attention and human attention during anaphora resolution task.

Successful language comprehension requires understanding the discursive connections in the sentences and the logical relationships between discourse structures in the text. Coreference resolution, a standard NLP task, determines which mentions in a text refer to the same entity. Two mentions (i.e., textual phrases) are called coreferent if they refer to the same real-world objects or events. Anaphora, one of the types of coreference resolution, highlights this challenge by requiring the matching of an anaphor (typically a pronoun) in a sentence with its antecedent (noun) in the preceding sentence. The Winograd Schema (Levesque et al., 2012) is a well-established method for evaluating language model performance in anaphora resolution tasks, assessing the model's logical reasoning and real-world knowledge in resolving coreference ambiguities. It is an evaluation dataset within the SuperGLUE (Wang et al., 2019) suite across various languages.

Video oculography, known as eye-tracking, is a prevalent psycholinguistic method for studying reading processes. It involves recording the reader's eye movements via video and subsequent interpolation of their gaze onto a display screen. This method breaks down the reading process into fixations (periods of steady gaze) and saccades (rapid eye movements) between them with precision up to milliseconds. This approach enables a detailed examination of reading acquisition. We used eye-tracking techniques to gather information on human fixations and focuses during the anaphora resolution and create the eye-tracking Winograd schema dataset.

Leveraging the dataset, we investigate the correlation between machine and human attention across various transformer architectures and network layers. The research aims to confirm whether integrating insights from human attention patterns can significantly improve the language model's ability to resolve anaphoras effectively.

The contributions of the current study are the following:

Proceedings of the Workshop on Cognitive Modeling and Computational Linguistics, pages 109–122
August 15, 2024 ©2024 Association for Computational Linguistics

- we collect and propose the new dataset [1] based on the data from human eye-tracking for anaphora resolution;
- we conduct a set of experiments on different models fine-tuned on the data to explore the attention mechanisms;
- we provide a detailed comparative analysis of human and neural attention mechanisms;
- we integrate the human gaze into the transformer's attention mechanisms.

2 Related Work

In the subsequent sections, we outline related works encompassing attention mechanisms in transformers, human attention datasets of eye-tracking data, methods of correlation analysis between human and machine attention, and the incorporation of eye-gaze data into models during training.

2.1 Attention Mechanisms in Transformers

The machine attention determines the degree of attention allocated to other segments of the input sentence during the encoding process of a word at a particular position. The attention mechanism in transformers is initially described in Vaswani et al. (2017) as a process of mapping input vectors – a query and a set of key-value pairs, to yield an output. The attention function for each word of the input sentence against a single word is computed as follows:

$$\text{Attention}(Q, K, V) = \text{softmax}(\frac{QK^T}{\sqrt{d_k}})V \quad (1)$$

The input consists of the query and the key vectors, each with a dimension of d_k, and the values vectors of dimension d_v. The output is computed as a weighted sum of the values, where the weights (attention score) are calculated as a softmax of dot products of the query with the corresponding keys, scaled by $\frac{1}{\sqrt{d_k}}$. The attention function is computed over a set of input vectors, enabling their aggregation into a matrix structure for queries Q, keys K, and values V.

In performing multi-head attention, the singular attention function is computed h times (a number of attention layers, or heads) in parallel with different linear projections of the queries, keys, and values.

$$\text{head}_\text{i} = \text{Attention}(QW_i^Q, KW_i^K, VW_i^V) \quad (2)$$

where the projections are parameter matrices $W_i^Q \in R^{d_{model} \times d_k}$, $W_i^K \in R^{d_{model} \times d_k}$, $W_i^V \in R^{d_{model} \times d_v}$. Subsequently, the concatenated outputs, each possessing a dimension of d_v, undergo further projection with parameter matrices $W^O \in R^{hd_v \times d_{model}}$.

This mechanism enables the model to jointly attend to information across various representation subspaces at different positions. The transformer uses multi-head attention in three ways based on its architectural design. In the first configuration, denoted as the "encoder-decoder" layers, the queries come from the previous decoder layer, and the memory keys and values come from the output of the encoder. In the second configuration, referred to as the encoder self-attention layer, all of the keys, values, and queries come from the output of the previous layer in the encoder. Analogously, self-attention layers in the decoder enable each position to attend to all positions in the decoder, encompassing those up to and including the respective position.

2.2 Human Attention

Eye-tracking datasets have emerged as invaluable resources for investigating various aspects of human cognition and behavior. These datasets provide researchers with fine-grained information about eye movements. The PROVO corpus (Luke and Christianson, 2017) includes eye-tracking data of passages taken from online news articles, magazines, and works of fiction. This dataset offers detailed information on participants' eye movements, fixations, and regressions, allowing researchers to explore phenomena such as syntactic ambiguity resolution and semantic processing during reading. Another widely utilized monolingual dataset is the ZuCo corpus (Hollenstein et al., 2018), which contains eye-tracking data of full sentences from movie reviews and Wikipedia articles in English. It includes features like a total number of gaze fixations and different fixation duration data collected from native English speakers during the execution of reading tasks. As for the Russian monolingual dataset, the Russian Sentence Corpus (Laurinavichyute et al., 2019) introduces a corpus of eye movements of silent reading by skilled Russian readers.

In addition to these established datasets, recent efforts have focused on collecting eye-tracking data from diverse populations and linguistic backgrounds to facilitate cross-cultural and multilingual

[1] https://huggingface.co/datasets/RussianNLP/EyeWino

research, for example, the corpus GECO (Cop et al., 2016). In particular, it includes five word-level reading time measures from English and Dutch monolinguals reading an entire novel. Furthermore, the MECO corpora (Siegelman et al., 2022; Kuperman et al., 2022) provides comparable cross-linguistic eye-tracking data and includes 13 different languages. Furthermore, numerous studies have utilized eye-tracking to investigate anaphora resolution across various languages and populations during reading (Wolna et al., 2024; Naido and Jaafar, 2022; Costa et al., 2011; Duffy and Rayner, 1990).

Additionally, datasets are utilized to enhance model performance by incorporating eye-gaze information to solve NLP tasks. For example, the eye-tracking dataset MQA-RC (Sood et al., 2020a), in which participants read movie plots taken from the MovieQA (Tapaswi et al., 2015) and answered predefined questions. In addition, the eye-gaze dataset from Mishra et al. (2016), where eye-movement parameters enhance the quality of models to solve a sarcasm detection task.

2.3 Eye-Tracking and Transformers

Recent research has focused on the correlation between attention mechanisms in transformer models and human eye-gaze patterns. The notable stream of the studies is to investigate the correlation between eye-gaze features and attention layers during reading tasks (Bensemann et al., 2022; Morger et al., 2022; Toneva and Wehbe, 2019). The results show a high correlation, primarily in the first attention layer. The paper (Sood et al., 2020b) evaluated correlations on the reading comprehension task for fine-tuned XLNet. They compared attention from the last encoder layer with eye-gaze features and reported a non-significant correlation. Moreover, the studies conduct experiments to explore whether task-specific fine-tuning influences the correlation with human reading attention (Eberle et al., 2022).

Another notable stream of research is a cross-lingual comparison of correlations. For example, due to results from Brandl and Hollenstein (2022), the correlation analysis across languages shows that considerable differences between languages, individual reading behavior, and vocabulary knowledge (LexTALE) influence the alignment between humans and models. In addition, the papers (Sen et al., 2020; Morger et al., 2022) provide methods to analyze word importance correlations between machines and humans. The paper (Morger et al., 2022) compares human and model relative word importance to investigate whether models focus on the same words as humans cross-lingually.

Furthermore, a promising area of research has explored the integration of eye-gaze data into the models to enhance task performance (i.e., sarcasm detection, question answering) and to deepen the understanding of language processing and human cognition (Sood et al., 2020b; Mishra et al., 2016; Zhang and Hollenstein, 2024).

3 Eye-tracking Data

Objective The anaphora resolution task was chosen to investigate the distinction between attention mechanisms in neural networks and humans. This study explores the potential benefits of integrating human-inspired attention mechanisms into transformer architectures. The research question seeks to confirm whether the language model's incorporation of information regarding human attention distribution during text reading improves its performance in the anaphora resolution task.

Experimental Setup For the experiment, we employed eye-tracking via video oculography, utilizing the EyeLink 1000 Plus device. Participants' gaze was calibrated until validation error values reached less than 1 (maximum) and 0.5 (average). The indication 0.5 is the maximum average deviation. When calibrating at 9 points, the error of each point is calculated. If the average is not more than 0.5 and the total error is not more than 1, then the calibration is considered successful, and incentives are presented to the participants. The EyeLink 1000 Plus device is one of the most accurate systems, with a validation error of about 0.2-0.5, within the standard protocol according to the system manual (Holmqvist et al., 2011).

The Russian Winograd Schema Challenge dataset from TAPE (Taktasheva et al., 2022) was utilized for the anaphora resolution task to gather information on participants' eye movements. The experiment comprised 150 complex or compound-complex sentences extracted from the Winograd schema challenge dataset, each containing an anaphoric pronoun and its antecedent.

Each participant was shown a sentence with an anaphoric pronoun highlighted in red on the screen, followed by a question about the presumed antecedent of the anaphora. The question was the following: "Does the highlighted pronoun refer to <antecedent> ?". An example of the participants' screen is presented in App. A. For each sentence, two presumed antecedents (one correct, one incorrect) were identified for each sentence. Thus, each screen was read by fifty participants. The sentences were randomized for each participant to ensure balanced conditions.

One hundred people (81 women, average age – 22.68, standard deviation – 4.27) who are native speakers of Russian participated in the experiment. They were instructed to read the provided sentences carefully and answer the question using the keyboard (key 1 for agreement, key 0 for disagreement). Participants completed three training sentences to ensure task comprehension before proceeding to three blocks of 50 sentences each, with breaks provided between blocks. To enhance recording quality, each trial began with a calibration check, requiring participants to focus precisely on the point where the first word of the text would appear. Upon successful calibration, the text was displayed; otherwise, recalibration commenced. After responding to each question, participants automatically advanced to the next trial. The experiment duration averaged 45 minutes.

Dataset statistics Observations with missing values and parsing errors were excluded from the dataset. The final dataset consists of 296 sentence-question pairs, which contain 9319 words and 148 unique sentences. The average number of participants per word is 48. The total number of observations for each variable is 448047. The resulting fields of the dataset are presented in the App. B.

4 Comparative analysis of attention mechanisms

In order to investigate the potential advantages of incorporating attention mechanisms similar to human processes into transformer architecture, we first need to examine and compare different attention mechanisms. We carried out a set of experiments on various architectures, fine-tuned using the data, and compared them with data on human attention. Our aim was to provide a detailed comparative analysis of human and neural attention mechanisms on the Winograd schema challenge.

4.1 Human Attention

We use the three word-level gaze measures extracted from the eye-tracking dataset (see Sec. 3) to quantify human attention:

- **Total reading time, TRT**, the sum of all fixation durations on the current word, ms;
- **Gaze duration, GD**, the sum of all fixation durations on the current word in the first-pass reading, ms;
- **Fixations, F**, the number of all fixations on the current word.

We use TRT because it highly correlates with model attention in similar works (Eberle et al., 2022; Bensemann et al., 2022; Morger et al., 2022). GD and F reflect which words attracted the most attention. We use these measures to determine the relative importance of words in a sentence. Each word is assigned a value between 0 and 1, which is normalized for each participant. The sum of the values of all words in a sentence is 1. These values are averaged across all participants to obtain the human relative importance of the word in a sentence (w_i):

$$w_i = \frac{1}{N}\sum_{j=1}^{N}\frac{m_{ij}}{\sum_{i=1}^{T} m_{ij}} \tag{3}$$

where m_{ij} is the gaze observation of the j-th participant for the i-th word, N – a number of participants, T – a number of words in a sentence.

For each example, we aggregate participants' responses using majority voting. The percentage of correct answers is 97.97%.

4.2 Transformer Attention

We use attention scores from the encoder layers of pre-trained and fine-tuned models across various transformer architectures to describe model attention.

4.2.1 Models

Multilingual models represent multiple languages within a shared space, aiming for a more universal understanding of language. The Russian language is well-represented in the pre-training corpus of various multilingual language models. To evaluate the impact of multilingual data in the training set on the model's attention distribution, we compare the performance of monolingual and multilingual models that have the same architecture and similar size. We use six publicly available language models from 3 model families:

BERT-based models include ruBERT-base (Zmitrovich et al., 2023) and mBERT-base (Devlin et al., 2019)

RoBERTa-based models include ruRoberta-large (Zmitrovich et al., 2023) and XLM-R-large (Conneau et al., 2020).

T5-based models include ruT5-base (Zmitrovich et al., 2023) and mT5-base (Xue et al., 2021).

Refer to Tab. 1 for the statistical details.

4.2.2 Datasets

Fine-tuning datasets The fine-tuning data represents a collection of Winograd schemas from various data sources.

For the Russian-language models, we used data from the RWSD task from the MERA benchmark (Fenogenova et al., 2024) and the Winograd task from the TAPE benchmark (Taktasheva et al., 2022). From the TAPE dataset, we exclude duplicates that were included in the eye-tracking dataset.

For the multilingual models, we combined Russian-language data and the XWINO dataset (Tikhonov and Ryabinin, 2021) without Russian to avoid duplication. Japanese and Chinese languages were excluded due to the special preprocessing required for this task.

For the comparative experiments of models on the anaphora task, we use the eye-tracking dataset for evaluation and the RWSD test set from the MERA benchmark.

Preprocessing Since we conducted an evaluation process for both the model and humans under the same conditions, all datasets were preprocessed to replicate the human experiment. For each sentence, an antecedent and an anaphoric pronoun were identified. The corresponding pronoun was highlighted in the text using uppercase. We formulated the question about the presumed antecedent of the anaphora using the human experiment design described in Sec. 3 and the answer for this question ("Yes" or "No"). The question and the answer were formulated in the language of the **text**. Each example also contains information about whether the question is about the correct or incorrect antecedent, with labels equal to 1 and 0, respectively.

- **text:** *"Bob collapsed on the sidewalk. Soon he saw Carl coming to help. HE was very concerned."*
- **question:** *"Does the highlighted pronoun refer to Carl ?"*
- **antecedent:** *"Carl"*
- **reference:** *"He"*
- **answer:** *"Yes"*
- **label:** *1*

The datasets were filtered so that the reference attribute was a pronoun and contained no more than one word. For example, "there" and "he does/did" were excluded from the dataset.

Finally, the training dataset was balanced with respect to the labels and filtered from duplicates. Tab. 2 provides the number of examples by language in the final datasets.

4.2.3 Fine-tuning

We fine-tune pre-trained models using train sets presented in Sec. 4.2.2. The original case of the input text is preserved during tokenization.

The encoder-only models are fine-tuned using a sequence classification head on top. We add a [SEP] token between the text and the question to get the input text for the models during the training process.

The encoder-decoder models are fine-tuned using a language modeling head on top. The text was concatenated with the question about antecedent to get the input text for the models.

Implementation The models are fine-tuned using AdamW optimizer (Loshchilov and Hutter, 2017) and a linear learning rate scheduler.

For the encoder-only models, we use a context window of 256, learning rate of $1e^{-5}$, batch size of 8, and 12 epochs.

For the encoder-decoder-based models, we use a context window of 200 and a batch size of 8. We also use a learning rate of $1e^{-5}$ and 35 epochs for ruT5-base, a learning rate of $1e^{-4}$ and 25 epochs for mT5-base. We use the generation hyperparameters: $max\_length = 20$, $temperature = 1$, $top\_k = 50$, $top\_p = 1$.

Metrics Models' performance is evaluated using the Accuracy score. Accuracy measures the percentage of correct predictions. This metric was chosen due to the balance of classes.

Results We take the checkpoints with the best performance on the validation set to evaluate them on the eye data test, and RWSD test set from Sec. 4.2.2. The results are presented in Tab. 3. The models demonstrate higher accuracy after fine-tuning, especially ruBERT-base, ruRoberta-large, ruT5-base and mT5-base. The encoder-decoder model mT5-base appears to outperform other models in solving the question-answering task.

Model	Architecture	Language	Parameters	Layers	Heads	Hugging Face Hub
ruBERT-base	Encoder-only	Russian	178M	12	12	ai-forever/ruBert-base
mBERT-base	Encoder-only	Multi	178M	12	12	google-bert/bert-base-multilingual-cased
ruRoberta-large	Encoder-only	Russian	355M	24	16	ai-forever/ruRoberta-large
XLM-R-large	Encoder-only	Multi	560M	24	16	FacebookAI/xlm-roberta-large
ruT5-base	Encoder-decoder	Russian	222M	12	12	ai-forever/ruT5-base
mT5-base	Encoder-decoder	Multi	580M	12	12	google/mt5-base

Table 1: Summary of the model architecture configurations.

Language	Train	Val	Test
English	2846	1216	-
French	108	56	-
Portuguese	358	116	-
Russian	872	326	260*
Total	4184	1714	260

Table 2: The sets statistics. The sizes of the set in the number of examples. * – the RWSD test set.

Model	Checkpoint	Eye data	RWSD
ruBERT-base	pre-trained	49.7	51.2
	fine-tuned	<u>63.2</u>	**58.5**
mBERT-base	pre-trained	49.0	52.3
	fine-tuned	50.0	50.0
ruRoberta-large	pre-trained	50.3	49.6
	fine-tuned	61.5	51.5
XLM-R-large	pre-trained	50.0	50.0
	fine-tuned	50.0	50.0
ruT5-base	pre-trained	50.0	50.0
	fine-tuned	57.4	55.8
mT5-base	pre-trained	50.0	50.0
	fine-tuned	**71.3**	<u>56.2</u>

Table 3: The models' performance (Accuracy) on the Winograd schema challenge task for the Russian language. The best score is in bold, and the second score is underlined.

4.2.4 Word-level attention

We use attention weights from the encoder layers to obtain the importance of a word in a sentence for the model. The decoder attention layers are only allowed to process earlier positions in the sequence, so we exclude them from the analysis.

We convert the texts into the format presented in Sec. 4.2.3 and tokenize them, preserving the original case of the words. The tokenized data is fed into the model. We extract the attention weights for each layer and average them across all attention heads.

$$\begin{aligned} \mathrm{A}' &= \mathrm{Average}(\mathrm{A}_1, \ldots, \mathrm{A}_\mathrm{h}) \\ \mathrm{A}_\mathrm{i} &= \mathrm{softmax}(\frac{QK^T}{\sqrt{d_k}}) \end{aligned} \tag{4}$$

where A_i is an attention score of the i-th head with a dimension of $n \times n$, n – a length of the input sequence, h – a number of attention heads.

Each row $a^{(t)}$ of matrix A' is an attention vector for token t. We use the following matrix aggregations to obtain a vector of token importance:

- *mean* – the average of all the rows in each column.
- *row* – the average of pronoun tokens in each column: we extract only the rows corresponding to pronoun tokens from matrix A' and average these rows.

The special tokens are used for the attention calculations but are excluded from the final vector. During tokenization, some words are encoded as multiple tokens. The weights of the tokens that make up each word are summed to obtain word-level attention weights. The final vector is interpreted as a relative word importance for the model.

4.3 Correlation Analysis

We matched human and model attention scores so that each word had a normalized attention score from both sources.

Since we assume a monotonic relationship between variables but do not assume that the variables are normally distributed, we calculate the Spearman's rank correlation coefficient ρ (Hollander et al., 2013) to analyze the correlation between human attention and model attention. The correlation coefficient quantifies the strength and direction of the relationship between two variables. It ranges from -1 to $+1$, where 0 indicates no correlation.

The p-value is used to determine the statistical significance of the correlation coefficient. It indicates the probability of observing the calculated correlation coefficient under the assumption that the variables are actually uncorrelated in the population. If the p-value is less than the significance level, the hypothesis of no correlation is rejected. This suggests that there is a statistically significant correlation between the variables. We use a significance level of 0.05.

5 Results

Correlations of human attention with model attention are reported in Tab. 4. We found significant correlations ($p > 0.05$) for all experiments. There are moderate correlations for T5-based and RoBERTa-based models and strong correlations for BERT-based models on the first layer.

The comparison of different aggregation setups for T5-based architectures underscores the prevalence of the *mean* aggregation with high correlations. Conversely, for other architectures, we noted a contrasting trend where *row* aggregation predominates.

The first layers have high correlations in comparison to the last layer in most setups. For example, there are extremely small correlations for ruRoberta-large on the last layer; meanwhile, the maximum correlation is almost even with other values. For several models, the highest correlation is noted on a particular layer. Moreover, the layer demonstrating the highest correlation varies notably across different architectures.

For most of the models, there is no difference between pre-trained and fine-tuned versions, except for a slight correlation decrease for multilingual mT5-base after tuning on the Winograd schemas. Furthermore, we can compare the outcomes across different eye-gaze metrics and observe minimal discrepancies among them in terms of correlation analyses. Finally, we highlight the model mBERT-base, which demonstrates the highest correlation with human attention. We conclude that task-specific fine-tuning did not enhance the correlation between human attention and machine attention.

The analysis suggests that encoder-only models provide more significant insights for evaluating attention correlation. A detailed visualization of the correlation between human attention and models' attention on different layers is presented in App. C. Additionally, App. D provides a visualization of the important words for the human and the models for one example from the eye-tracking dataset.

6 Integrating Human Gaze into Transformers

Based on the results obtained in Sec. 5, there are significant correlations between human attention and the models' attention during the task of anaphora resolution. It can be assumed that using eye movement data when training models for this task will increase their performance. We conducted experiments to integrate eye movement data into the model training process by using an additional term in the loss function to bring the model's attention closer to human attention.

6.1 Experimental setup

Data for human gaze integration For the experiments with human gaze integration during model training, we use the eye-tracking dataset as a training set. We use the Russian language sets from Sec. 4.2.2 as validation and test sets.

Method We use the procedure proposed by Bensemann et al. (2022) to investigate the effect of injecting human eye-gaze bias during training as the baseline. We introduce an additional loss function to align the distribution of model attention on a given layer with the distribution of human attention. The final loss function is calculated according to the following formula:

$$L = H(y, \hat{y}) + \alpha H(p, \hat{p}) \quad (5)$$

Where $H(y, \hat{y})$ is the cross-entropy loss that measures the model's performance on the anaphora resolution task. $H(p, \hat{p})$ is the cross-entropy loss that measures the difference between two probability distributions: the distribution of the model's attention values on a particular layer (p) and the distribution of the human relative word importance ($\hat{p}$). The hyperparameter α controls the weight of the second term in the loss function. We use the hyperparameter α of 0.05. The remaining hyperparameters for fine-tuning models are contained in Sec. 4.2.3.

We use the average of all the rows in each column (*mean*) and the average of all pronoun tokens in each column (*row*) to obtain the models' attention values. We conduct experiments with different layers: the first, the last, and the layers where the highest correlation values between model attention and human attention are observed.

6.2 Results

The findings on incorporating human gaze data into models are presented in Tab. 5. Based on the results, we can conclude that using an additional loss does not usually improve the model's performance. However, a significant increase in Accuracy is observed for the tuned mT5-base and tuned ruRoberta-large models with row aggregation when using human attention on layers 1 and 14, respectively. It can be concluded that, in most

Model	Agg.	Checkpoint	Layer	Fixations			Gaze duration			Total reading time		
			(max)	first	max	last	first	max	last	first	max	last
ruBERT-base	mean	pre-trained	1	0.601	←	0.382	0.606	←	0.394	0.592	←	0.376
		tuned	1	0.603	←	0.364	0.608	←	0.373	0.595	←	0.355
	row	pre-trained	1	0.722	←	0.578	0.71	←	0.568	0.719	←	0.581
		tuned	1	**0.723**	←	0.487	0.711	←	0.472	0.719	←	0.485
mBERT-base	mean	pre-trained	1	0.684	←	0.581	0.683	←	0.585	0.674	←	0.575
		tuned	1	0.684	←	0.59	0.683	←	0.592	0.673	←	0.582
	row	pre-trained	1	**0.771**	←	0.54	0.758	←	0.536	0.764	←	0.54
		tuned	1	**0.771**	←	0.601	0.758	←	0.597	0.765	←	0.598
ruRoberta-large	mean	pre-trained	16	0.485	0.543	0.076	0.495	0.551	0.088	0.475	0.538	0.067
		tuned	16	0.487	0.542	0.154	0.496	0.555	0.166	0.477	0.542	0.146
	row	pre-trained	16	0.452	**0.653**	0.064	0.453	0.641	0.067	0.445	0.652	0.058
		tuned	14	0.453	0.608	0.115	0.454	0.602	0.116	0.446	0.611	0.11
XLM-R-large	mean	pre-trained	14	0.498	0.592	0.394	0.506	0.605	0.404	0.491	0.593	0.385
		tuned	17	0.497	0.588	0.427	0.505	0.595	0.44	0.489	0.582	0.421
	row	pre-trained	11	0.556	0.703	0.424	0.554	0.688	0.414	0.551	0.701	0.418
		tuned	11	0.553	**0.717**	0.45	0.551	0.706	0.449	0.548	0.713	0.446
ruT5-base	mean	pre-trained	1	0.593	←	0.31	0.605	←	0.32	0.587	←	0.308
		tuned	1	0.594	←	0.323	**0.606**	←	0.333	0.588	←	0.321
	row	pre-trained	8	0.552	0.562	0.407	0.544	0.548	0.4	0.549	0.56	0.411
		tuned	8	0.552	0.577	0.442	0.544	0.563	0.434	0.549	0.576	0.445
mT5-base	mean	pre-trained	9	0.575	0.619	0.522	0.583	**0.63**	0.538	0.563	0.611	0.516
		tuned	1	0.573	←	0.471	0.58	←	0.484	0.561	←	0.468
	row	pre-trained	8	0.543	0.621	0.5	0.527	0.615	0.491	0.534	0.619	0.495
		tuned	7	0.535	0.569	0.437	0.518	0.561	0.436	0.526	0.569	0.436

Table 4: Spearman's rank correlations between human attention and models' attention on the first, last, and the layer with the highest correlation values. *Model* – the model's architecture. *Agg.* – the attention scores aggregation: the average of all the rows in each column (*mean*) and the average of all pronoun tokens in each column (*row*). *Checkpoint* – the configuration of the *Model* before (pre-trained) and after (tuned) tuning on the Winograd schema task. *Layer (max)* – the model's layer with the highest correlation value. *Fixations*, *Gaze duration*, *Total reading time* – the human attention characteristics. *first*, *max*, *last* – the model's layers. ← means that the first layer has the highest correlation value (see column *first*). The highest correlation values for each architecture are in bold.

cases, the Accuracy of the pre-trained model is lower than that of fine-tuned models. There are several exceptions for ruRoberta-large, ruT5-base, and XLM-R-large models with incorporated total reading time. The findings from comparing Accuracy between various eye-gaze measurements (*Fixations*, *Gaze duration*, *Reading time*) do not reveal a consistent trend, making it challenging to identify the optimal human signal for incorporating into loss functions.

7 Conclusion

In summary, this paper examines the transformer and human attention mechanisms in the anaphora resolution task. We collected a dataset for the anaphora resolution task using video oculography and released it under the MIT license [2]. We used this dataset to analyze the correlation between machine and human attention across various transformer architectures and network layers. The results show a strong correlation between human and machine attention, but fine-tuning did not enhance this correlation. Therefore, we conducted experiments integrating eye movement data into the model training process. This was done by adding an extra term to the loss function to align the model's attention more closely with human attention. However, the results did not show a consistent trend in the proposed setup, indicating that further research is needed for incorporation approaches.

Limitations

Data Specificity The study relies on an eye-tracking dataset limited to one specific coreference type with a relatively small number of instances. We investigate the results based on data specifically tailored to the Russian language. Therefore, the findings may not be generalizable to other languages or datasets with different linguistic structures and nuances.

We take the privacy and confidentiality of participants seriously when collecting eye-tracking data. All participants provided informed consent, fully understanding the nature of the study and how their data would be utilized. However, we acknowledge that such data may introduce linguistic biases that

[2]https://huggingface.co/datasets/RussianNLP/EyeWino

Model	Agg.	Checkpoint	Layer (max)	Without integration	Fixations			Gaze duration			Total reading time		
					first	max	last	first	max	last	first	max	last
ruBERT-base	mean	pre-trained	1	55.77	55.77	←	**59.23**	56.15	←	58.08	55.77	←	58.46
		tuned	1	58.08	58.08	←	58.08	58.08	←	58.08	58.08	←	58.08
	row	pre-trained	1	55.77	55.77	←	57.69	55.77	←	55.77	55.77	←	56.92
		tuned	1	58.08	58.08	←	58.08	58.08	←	58.46	58.08	←	58.08
mBERT-base	mean	pre-trained	1	54.62	56.15	←	56.92	53.08	←	50.00	56.15	←	53.08
		tuned	1	56.15	56.92	←	55.38	55.38	←	56.54	55.00	←	56.54
	row	pre-trained	1	54.62	53.85	←	53.85	55.00	←	54.62	54.62	←	52.69
		tuned	1	56.15	55.38	←	**57.31**	55.38	←	56.92	55.38	←	55.77
ruRoberta-large	mean	pre-trained	16	56.92	58.08	59.23	55.38	53.85	57.31	57.69	56.92	59.23	58.46
		tuned	16	55.38	55.38	54.23	53.85	55.38	58.08	54.23	55.77	56.92	**60.77**
	row	pre-trained	16	56.92	58.08	59.62	59.62	55.00	59.23	59.23	56.54	60.0	56.54
		tuned	14	55.38	53.08	59.62	56.54	58.46	59.23	55.77	54.23	56.54	56.54
XLM-R-large	mean	pre-trained	14	55.00	55.38	48.85	55.00	50.38	52.69	50.00	54.23	56.92	54.23
		tuned	17	54.62	52.31	55.77	56.54	53.46	56.54	55.00	56.92	51.54	56.92
	row	pre-trained	11	55.00	51.15	55.38	54.23	51.15	56.15	54.62	54.23	54.23	51.15
		tuned	11	54.62	53.46	56.54	56.15	54.23	**59.62**	58.85	55.00	55.0	56.92
ruT5-base	mean	pre-trained	1	52.69	**61.15**	←	53.46	56.54	←	58.46	57.31	←	63.46
		tuned	1	55.77	54.62	←	57.31	54.62	←	51.92	52.31	←	50.77
	row	pre-trained	8	52.69	57.69	58.46	51.92	56.54	60.0	53.08	58.08	56.15	49.23
		tuned	8	55.77	53.08	48.08	54.23	53.46	53.46	53.85	51.92	53.85	48.08
mT5-base	mean	pre-trained	9	53.08	53.08	54.23	54.62	54.23	51.54	54.62	54.62	52.69	54.62
		tuned	1	58.46	58.85	←	59.62	58.08	←	57.31	59.23	←	58.46
	row	pre-trained	8	53.08	54.62	54.62	52.69	57.31	51.15	53.46	55.38	52.69	53.08
		tuned	7	58.46	**64.23**	56.54	58.85	59.23	60.0	58.08	62.31	62.31	61.54

Table 5: Accuracy of the experiments with human gaze integration during model training on the first, last, and the layer with the highest correlation values. *Model* – the model's architecture. *Agg.* – the attention scores aggregation: the average of all the rows in each column (*mean*) and the average of all pronoun tokens in each column (*row*). *Checkpoint* – the configuration of the *Model* before (pre-trained) and after (tuned) tuning on the Winograd schema task. *Layer (max)* – the model's layer with the highest correlation value. *Without integration* - the Accuracy of the experiments without human gaze integration. *Fixations*, *Gaze duration*, *Total reading time* – the human attention characteristics. *first*, *max*, *last* – the model's layers. ← means that the first layer has the highest correlation value (see column *first*). The best scores for each architecture are in bold.

can be further transmitted to the neural model by incorporating the attention mechanisms.

Experimental setup The analysis was based on various transformer architectures, but it is important to note that we could not cover all possible attention mechanisms and neural approaches. We focused on the encoder attention layers in the paper, as these layers capture context from the entire input sequence. In contrast, the decoder attention layers can only process earlier positions in the sequence. Investigating the decoder's attention is an issue for future research. Additionally, the quantitative comparison between human and machine attention may be influenced by the intrinsic limitations of the experimental setups, such as the weaknesses of eye-tracking technology, the design of the Winograd schema tasks and the collected dataset, and the interpretability techniques applied to the neural models.

Human attention complexity is a multifaceted phenomenon influenced by numerous cognitive, cultural, and situational factors that have not been investigated. Thus, the current machine attention mechanisms are artificial approximations that are hard to compare. Our study, while comprehensive, only captures a subset of these factors, particularly those that are quantifiable through eye-tracking.

Acknowledgments

We would like to express our heartfelt gratitude to Olga Dragoy and Nina Zdorova from HSE University, as well as Tatiana Shavrina, for their invaluable support in preparing the datasets for our experiments.

References

Dzmitry Bahdanau, Kyunghyun Cho, and Yoshua Bengio. 2016. Neural machine translation by jointly learning to align and translate. *Preprint*, arXiv:1409.0473.

Joshua Bensemann, Alex Peng, Diana Benavides-Prado, Yang Chen, Neset Tan, Paul Michael Corballis, Patricia Riddle, and Michael Witbrock. 2022. Eye gaze and self-attention: How humans and transformers attend words in sentences. In *Proceedings of the*

Workshop on Cognitive Modeling and Computational Linguistics, pages 75–87, Dublin, Ireland. Association for Computational Linguistics.

Stephanie Brandl and Nora Hollenstein. 2022. Every word counts: A multilingual analysis of individual human alignment with model attention. In *Proceedings of the 2nd Conference of the Asia-Pacific Chapter of the Association for Computational Linguistics and the 12th International Joint Conference on Natural Language Processing (Volume 2: Short Papers)*, pages 72–77, Online only. Association for Computational Linguistics.

Alexis Conneau, Kartikay Khandelwal, Naman Goyal, Vishrav Chaudhary, Guillaume Wenzek, Francisco Guzmán, Edouard Grave, Myle Ott, Luke Zettlemoyer, and Veselin Stoyanov. 2020. Unsupervised cross-lingual representation learning at scale. In *Proceedings of the 58th Annual Meeting of the Association for Computational Linguistics*, pages 8440–8451, Online. Association for Computational Linguistics.

Uschi Cop, Nicolas Dirix, Denis Drieghe, and Wouter Duyck. 2016. Presenting geco: An eyetracking corpus of monolingual and bilingual sentence reading. *Behavior Research Methods*, 49.

Armanda Costa, Gabriela Matos, and Paula Luegi. 2011. Using eye-tracking to study anaphoric relations processing in european portuguese.

Jacob Devlin, Ming-Wei Chang, Kenton Lee, and Kristina Toutanova. 2019. BERT: Pre-training of deep bidirectional transformers for language understanding. In *Proceedings of the 2019 Conference of the North American Chapter of the Association for Computational Linguistics: Human Language Technologies, Volume 1 (Long and Short Papers)*, pages 4171–4186, Minneapolis, Minnesota. Association for Computational Linguistics.

Susan A Duffy and Keith Rayner. 1990. Eye movements and anaphor resolution: Effects of antecedent typicality and distance.

Oliver Eberle, Stephanie Brandl, Jonas Pilot, and Anders Søgaard. 2022. Do transformer models show similar attention patterns to task-specific human gaze? pages 4295–4309.

Alena Fenogenova, Artem Chervyakov, Nikita Martynov, Anastasia Kozlova, Maria Tikhonova, Albina Akhmetgareeva, Anton Emelyanov, Denis Shevelev, Pavel Lebedev, Leonid Sinev, et al. 2024. Mera: A comprehensive llm evaluation in russian. *arXiv preprint arXiv:2401.04531*.

Myles Hollander, Douglas A Wolfe, and Eric Chicken. 2013. *Nonparametric statistical methods*. John Wiley & Sons.

Nora Hollenstein, Jonathan Rotsztejn, Marius Tröndle, Andreas Pedroni, Ce Zhang, and Nicolas Langer. 2018. Zuco, a simultaneous eeg and eye-tracking resource for natural sentence reading. *Scientific Data*, 5:180291.

K. Holmqvist, M. Nyström, R. Andersson, R. Dewhurst, H. Jarodzka, and J. van de Weijer. 2011. *Eye Tracking: A comprehensive guide to methods and measures*. OUP Oxford.

Victor Kuperman, Noam Siegelman, Sascha Schroeder, Cengiz Acarturk, Svetlana Alexeeva, Simona Amenta, Raymond Bertram, Rolando Bonandrini, Marc Brysbaert, Daria Chernova, Sara Fonseca, Nicolas Dirix, Wouter Duyck, Argyro Fella, Ram Frost, Carolina Gattei, Areti Kalaitzi, Kaidi Lõo, Marco Marelli, and Kerem Usal. 2022. Text reading in english as a second language: Evidence from the multilingual eye-movements corpus. *Studies in Second Language Acquisition*, 45:1–35.

Anna Laurinavichyute, Irina Sekerina, Svetlana Alexeeva, Kristina Bagdasaryan, and Reinhold Kliegl. 2019. (2019). article russian sentence corpus: Benchmark measures of eye movements in reading in russian. *Behavior Research Methods*, 51:1161–1178.

Hector J. Levesque, Ernest Davis, and Leora Morgenstern. 2012. The winograd schema challenge. In *Proceedings of the Thirteenth International Conference on Principles of Knowledge Representation and Reasoning*, KR'12, page 552–561. AAAI Press.

Ilya Loshchilov and Frank Hutter. 2017. Decoupled weight decay regularization. *arXiv preprint arXiv:1711.05101*.

Steven Luke and Kiel Christianson. 2017. The provo corpus: A large eye-tracking corpus with predictability norms. *Behavior research methods*, 50.

Abhijit Mishra, Diptesh Kanojia, and Pushpak Bhattacharyya. 2016. Predicting readers' sarcasm understandability by modeling gaze behavior. In *Proceedings of the AAAI Conference on Artificial Intelligence*, volume 30.

Felix Morger, Stephanie Brandl, Lisa Beinborn, and Nora Hollenstein. 2022. A cross-lingual comparison of human and model relative word importance. In *Proceedings of the 2022 CLASP Conference on (Dis)embodiment*, pages 11–23, Gothenburg, Sweden. Association for Computational Linguistics.

Shamita Chantherasarathy Naido and Nurjanah Mohd Jaafar. 2022. Anaphora resolution in reading among malaysian l2 english speakers: An eye-tracking investigation. *Jurnal Wacana Sarjana*, 6(4):1–13.

Cansu Sen, Thomas Hartvigsen, Biao Yin, Xiangnan Kong, and Elke Rundensteiner. 2020. Human attention maps for text classification: Do humans and neural networks focus on the same words? pages 4596–4608.

Noam Siegelman, Sascha Schroeder, Cengiz Acarturk, Hee-Don Ahn, Svetlana Alexeeva, Simona Amenta, Raymond Bertram, Rolando Bonandrini, Marc Brysbaert, Daria Chernova, Sara Fonseca, Nicolas Dirix, Wouter Duyck, Argyro Fella, Ram Frost, Carolina Gattei, Areti Kalaitzi, Nayoung Kwon, Kaidi Lõo, and Victor Kuperman. 2022. Expanding horizons of cross-linguistic research on reading: The multilingual eye-movement corpus (meco). *Behavior Research Methods*, 54:1–21.

Ekta Sood, Simon Tannert, Diego Frassinelli, Andreas Bulling, and Ngoc Thang Vu. 2020a. Interpreting attention models with human visual attention in machine reading comprehension. In *Proceedings of the 24th Conference on Computational Natural Language Learning*, pages 12–25, Online. Association for Computational Linguistics.

Ekta Sood, Simon Tannert, Philipp Müller, and Andreas Bulling. 2020b. Improving natural language processing tasks with human gaze-guided neural attention.

Ekaterina Taktasheva, Tatiana Shavrina, Alena Fenogenova, Denis Shevelev, Nadezhda Katricheva, Maria Tikhonova, Albina Akhmetgareeva, Oleg Zinkevich, Anastasiia Bashmakova, Svetlana Iordanskaia, Alena Spiridonova, Valentina Kurenshchikova, Ekaterina Artemova, and Vladislav Mikhailov. 2022. TAPE: Assessing few-shot Russian language understanding. In *Findings of the Association for Computational Linguistics: EMNLP 2022*, pages 2472–2497, Abu Dhabi, United Arab Emirates. Association for Computational Linguistics.

Makarand Tapaswi, Yukun Zhu, Rainer Stiefelhagen, Antonio Torralba, Raquel Urtasun, and Sanja Fidler. 2015. Movieqa: Understanding stories in movies through question-answering. *2016 IEEE Conference on Computer Vision and Pattern Recognition (CVPR)*, pages 4631–4640.

Alexey Tikhonov and Max Ryabinin. 2021. It's All in the Heads: Using Attention Heads as a Baseline for Cross-Lingual Transfer in Commonsense Reasoning. In *Findings of the Association for Computational Linguistics: ACL-IJCNLP 2021*, pages 3534–3546, Online. Association for Computational Linguistics.

Mariya Toneva and Leila Wehbe. 2019. Interpreting and improving natural-language processing (in machines) with natural language-processing (in the brain).

Ashish Vaswani, Noam Shazeer, Niki Parmar, Jakob Uszkoreit, Llion Jones, Aidan N Gomez, Ł ukasz Kaiser, and Illia Polosukhin. 2017. Attention is all you need. In *Advances in Neural Information Processing Systems*, volume 30. Curran Associates, Inc.

Alex Wang, Yada Pruksachatkun, Nikita Nangia, Amanpreet Singh, Julian Michael, Felix Hill, Omer Levy, and Samuel Bowman. 2019. Superglue: A stickier benchmark for general-purpose language understanding systems. *Advances in neural information processing systems*, 32.

Agata Wolna, Joanna Durlik, and Zofia Wodniecka. 2024. Correction: Pronominal anaphora resolution in polish: Investigating online sentence interpretation using eye-tracking.

Linting Xue, Noah Constant, Adam Roberts, Mihir Kale, Rami Al-Rfou, Aditya Siddhant, Aditya Barua, and Colin Raffel. 2021. mT5: A massively multilingual pre-trained text-to-text transformer. In *Proceedings of the 2021 Conference of the North American Chapter of the Association for Computational Linguistics: Human Language Technologies*, pages 483–498, Online. Association for Computational Linguistics.

Leran Zhang and Nora Hollenstein. 2024. Eye-tracking features masking transformer attention in question-answering tasks. In *Proceedings of the 2024 Joint International Conference on Computational Linguistics, Language Resources and Evaluation (LREC-COLING 2024)*, pages 7057–7070, Torino, Italia. ELRA and ICCL.

Dmitry Zmitrovich, Alexander Abramov, Andrey Kalmykov, Maria Tikhonova, Ekaterina Taktasheva, Danil Astafurov, Mark Baushenko, Artem Snegirev, Tatiana Shavrina, Sergey Markov, et al. 2023. A family of pretrained transformer language models for russian. *arXiv preprint arXiv:2309.10931*.

Appendix

A Participant Instructions

Fig. 1 contains an example format of a task for participants, consisting of the following parts: a text, a question about the text, and an instruction for the task.

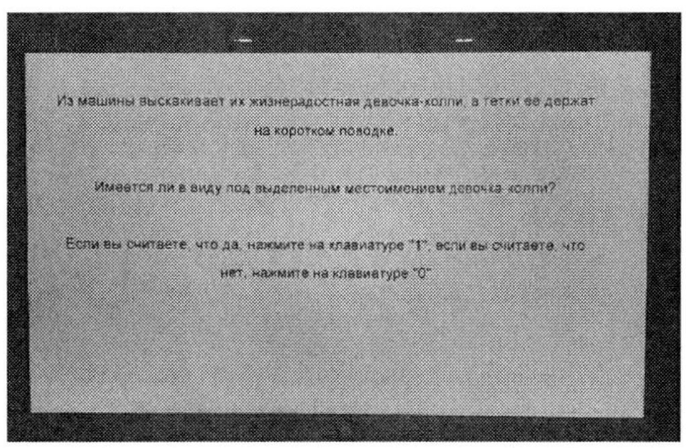

Figure 1: The example of a task shown to participants on the screen.

B Eye-movement Measures

The eye-tracking dataset contains the following fields:

- **word**, a word in a sentence;
- **example_id**, id of the example in the dataset;

- **text_id**, id of the unique text in the dataset;
- **position_id**, position of the word in the sentence;
- **annotator_id**, experiment participant id;
- **is_answer_correct**, the correctness of the experiment participant's answer;
- **reading_time**, the sum of all fixation durations on the current word, ms;
- **gaze_duration**, the sum of all fixation durations on the current word in the first-pass reading, ms;
- **fixations**, the number of all fixations on the current word;
- **first_fixation_duration**, the duration of the first fixation on the word, ms;
- **x_coordinate_first_fixation**, the coordinate of the first fixation on the word along the x axis, where the screen is the coordinate plane;
- **y_coordinate_first_fixation**, the coordinate of the first fixation on the word along the y axis, where the screen is the coordinate plane;
- **amplitude_first_saccade**, the amplitude of the first saccade, deg;
- **correct_antecedent**, the correct antecedent for example_id;
- **incorrect_antecedent**, the incorrect antecedent for example_id;
- **pronoun**, an anaphoric pronoun for example_id;
- **is_pronoun**, an indicator of whether the word is the anaphoric pronoun;
- **label**, an indicator of whether the question is about the correct antecedent.

C Visualization of Correlations

Fig. 2 provides the correlations between the attention of different model architectures, aggregated using the *mean* approach, and eye-tracking data.

D Visualization of Attention Maps

Fig. 3 provides a visualization of the important words for the human and the models.

Human attention is characterized by the relative importance of words based on *Fixations*. Checkpoints, layers, and aggregations with the highest correlations with the relative importance of words for humans are used to describe the relative importance of words for the models.

The original examples and relative importance of words are in Russian. Below the Russian texts are the English translations of these texts and an adapted visualization of the relative importance of words.

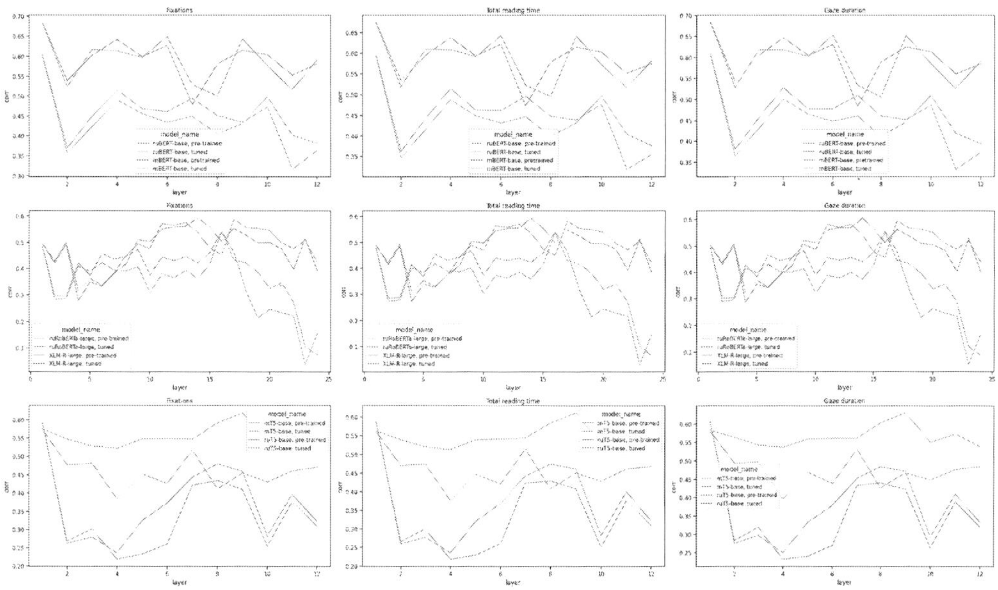

Figure 2: The correlations between models' attention on different layers and eye-tracking data.

answer: Да (Yes)

human:

Надо заметить, что Зубр владел высшим искусством экспериментатора — ОН умел задавать природе вопросы, на которые она должна была ответить да или нет. Имеется ли в виду под выделенным местоимением Зубр ?

It should be noted that Zubr mastered the supreme art of experimentation - HE knew how to ask nature questions to which it had to answer yes or no. Does the highlighted pronoun refer to Zubr ?

ruBERT-base, tuned, L1, row

Надо заметить, что Зубр владел высшим искусством экспериментатора — ОН умел задавать природе вопросы, на которые она должна была ответить да или нет. Имеется ли в виду под выделенным местоимением Зубр ?

It should be noted that Zubr mastered the supreme art of experimentation - HE knew how to ask nature questions to which it had to answer yes or no. Does the highlighted pronoun refer to Zubr ?

mBERT-base, tuned, L1, row

Надо заметить, что Зубр владел высшим искусством экспериментатора — ОН умел задавать природе вопросы, на которые она должна была ответить да или нет. Имеется ли в виду под выделенным местоимением Зубр ?

It should be noted that Zubr mastered the supreme art of experimentation - HE knew how to ask nature questions to which it had to answer yes or no. Does the highlighted pronoun refer to Zubr ?

ruRoberta-large, pretrain, L16, row

Надо заметить, что Зубр владел высшим искусством экспериментатора — ОН умел задавать природе вопросы, на которые она должна была ответить да или нет. Имеется ли в виду под выделенным местоимением Зубр ?

It should be noted that Zubr mastered the supreme art of experimentation - HE knew how to ask nature questions to which it had to answer yes or no. Does the highlighted pronoun refer to Zubr ?

XLM-R-large, tuned, L11, row

Надо заметить, что Зубр владел высшим искусством экспериментатора — ОН умел задавать природе вопросы, на которые она должна была ответить да или нет. Имеется ли в виду под выделенным местоимением Зубр ?

It should be noted that Zubr mastered the supreme art of experimentation - HE knew how to ask nature questions to which it had to answer yes or no. Does the highlighted pronoun refer to Zubr ?

ruT5-base, tuned, L1, mean

Надо заметить, что Зубр владел высшим искусством экспериментатора — ОН умел задавать природе вопросы, на которые она должна была ответить да или нет. Имеется ли в виду под выделенным местоимением Зубр ?

It should be noted that Zubr mastered the supreme art of experimentation - HE knew how to ask nature questions to which it had to answer yes or no. Does the highlighted pronoun refer to Zubr ?

mT5-base, pretrain, L8, row

Надо заметить, что Зубр владел высшим искусством экспериментатора — ОН умел задавать природе вопросы, на которые она должна была ответить да или нет. Имеется ли в виду под выделенным местоимением Зубр ?

It should be noted that Zubr mastered the supreme art of experimentation - HE knew how to ask nature questions to which it had to answer yes or no. Does the highlighted pronoun refer to Zubr ?

Figure 3: Visualizations of human and models' attentions. The words with high relative importance for Russian texts are highlighted in green. The third quartile is used to determine a word's importance.

Evaluating Lexical Aspect with Large Language Models

Bolei Ma
LMU Munich & Munich Center for Machine Learning
bolei.ma@lmu.de

Abstract

In this study, we explore the proficiency of large language models (LLMs) in understanding two key lexical aspects: duration (durative/stative) and telicity (telic/atelic). Through experiments on datasets featuring sentences, verbs, and verb positions, we prompt the LLMs to identify aspectual features of verbs in sentences. Our findings reveal that certain LLMs, particularly those closed-source ones, are able to capture information on duration and telicity, albeit with some performance variations and weaker results compared to the baseline. By employing prompts at three levels (sentence-only, sentence with verb, and sentence with verb and its position), we demonstrate that integrating verb information generally enhances performance in aspectual feature recognition, though it introduces instability. We call for future research to look deeper into methods aimed at optimizing LLMs for aspectual feature comprehension.

1 Introduction

Aspect is a verbal category that is closely linked to concepts such as tense, temporality, verbal semantics, and quantification. In linguistics, aspect refers to different perspectives on the internal temporal constitution of a situation (Comrie, 1976; Leiss, 1992; Klein, 1994; Xiao and McEnery, 2004). There is two main sub groups of aspect, the grammatical aspect which refers to the verbal flexion in languages such as Slavic Languages, and the lexical aspect which contains the semantics of the event or state of a verb phrase situated in time.

In this paper, we focus on the lexical aspect with two important aspect features: duration and telicity. Duration (durative/stative) is the property of a verb or verb phrase that presents a state or an action, regardless of their endpoints. Durative aspect denotes the reading of an action, while stative aspect denotes the reading of a state. Telicity (telic/atelic) distinguishes between verbs that describe an action or event as having a specific endpoint. Telic aspect denotes the reading of the endpoint of an action or event, while atelic aspect denotes the reading of no endpoint. Table 1 shows examples for each feature in English.

Label	Sentence
durative	The boxer **is hitting** his opponent.
stative	Bread **consists** of flour, water and yeast.
telic	I **ate** a fish for lunch.
atelic	Cork **floats** on water.

Table 1: Examples of the two aspect features: duration (durative/stative) and telicity (telic/atelic) (Metheniti et al., 2022).

The identification of the aspectual features of the verbs in the sentence could be difficult as other verb categories or sentence elements such as tense, temporal adverbials, and context could affect the reading of the aspect (Zhang, 1995). Using computational models to identify the aspectual features could be therefore more challenging. There are various existing works on building datasets for lexical aspect and training models to classify the sentences in terms of their aspectual features (Friedrich and Palmer, 2014; Friedrich and Pinkal, 2015; Friedrich et al., 2016; Friedrich and Gateva, 2017; Kober et al., 2020; Metheniti et al., 2022). Nowadays, the vast expanse of LLMs has also opened the chance to study linguistics using LLMs (Opitz et al., 2024). Therefore, it is interesting to probe the proficiency of LLMs on aspectual features.

In this paper, based on a dataset on duration and telicity (Metheniti et al., 2022), we evaluate the ability of 6 different LLMs to identify the two aspectual features of sentences by zero-shot prompting the LLMs in three different levels: sentence-only, sentence with verb, and sentence with verb and its position. Our experimental results show that some LLMs are capable of capturing aspectual information, while there are some variations and

Proceedings of the Workshop on Cognitive Modeling and Computational Linguistics, pages 123–131
August 15, 2024 ©2024 Association for Computational Linguistics

weaker performance compared to the fine-tuning baseline. In addition, adding verb information generally improves the prediction performance of LLMs. Overall, our study provides valuable insights into the challenges and opportunities in leveraging LLMs for evaluating lexical aspect.

2 Related Work

The evaluation and classification of aspectual features of verbs using NLP have been explored extensively in previous research. Siegel and McKeown (2000) are the first to employ supervised machine learning methods for aspectual classification.

Friedrich and Palmer (2014) introduced a semi-supervised approach that combined linguistic and distributional features to predict a verb's stativity/duration, also providing two annotated datasets for stativity. Furthermore, Friedrich and Pinkal (2015) focused on classifying clauses based on their aspectual properties, and expanded the scope to include situation entity types in Friedrich et al. (2016). Friedrich and Gateva (2017) contributed two English datasets with gold and silver annotations of telicity and duration, utilizing an L1-regularized multi-class logistic regression model.

Hermes et al. (2015) computationally modeled Vendler classes (Vendler, 1957) for 95 German verbs, combining distributional vectors with supervised classification. Additionally, Ramm et al. (2017) developed the first open-source tool for annotating morphosyntactic tense, mood, and voice for verbal complexes in multiple languages. Kober et al. (2020) introduced a dataset for tense and aspect concepts using natural language inference and proposed modeling aspect of English verbs in context using compositional distributional models.

In a more recent study by using a bunch of transformer-based models, Metheniti et al. (2022) conducted experiments on transformer models to identify aspectual features, revealing biases towards verb tense and word order. However, in the current era of the advances of LLMs, it is still unexplored whether the LLMs are able to capture the aspectual features.

A more detailed introduction to aspect concepts and their computational approaches can be found in this survey (Friedrich et al., 2023).

3 Experiments

Dataset. We use the dataset with telicity and duration-annotated sentences created by Metheniti et al. (2022). The dataset was built upon two previous datasets from Friedrich and Gateva (2017) and Alikhani and Stone (2019). It has two main subsets, one for duration and the other for telicity. Each subset contains sentences with the main verbs and their positions in sentences, as well as binary labels for durative ('1') or stative aspect ('0') in the duration subset, and telic ('1') or atelic ('0') aspect in the telicity subset. The label distribution in the test sets is presented in §A.1.

Prompt. Each question consists of a general instruction with a choice of answers (e.g. durative or stative) and the example sentence. We include the sentence, verb and verb information into the prompt. In addition, to test the robustness of the models as well as the ability of the models to comprehend the aspectual features both in the sentence level (without explicitly mentioning the verb) and the verb level (with explicitly mentioning the verb), we conduct the experiments in three different levels with different prompt formats. Table 2 shows the prompt formats of the three levels in the examples of duration subset with durative and stative aspects. In level 1, we only provide the sentence and ask for the aspect features. In level 2, we include the verb into the prompt. In level 3, we include the verb along with its position in the sentence into the prompt. The prompts are outlined in Table 2.

Models. We evaluate the aspect tasks with the following close- and open-source instruction-tuned LLMs: `GPT-3.5` (Brown et al., 2020) and `GPT-4` (OpenAI et al., 2024), `Llama-2-13b-chat-hf` and `Meta-Llama-3-8B-Instruct` (Touvron et al., 2023), `Gemma-7b-it` (Team et al., 2024), and `Mixtral-8x7B-Instruct-v0.1` (Jiang et al., 2024).

Baseline. We compare our zero-shot prompting of LLMs with the baselines of fine-tuning BERT-based models (Devlin et al., 2019) on the training data with and without adding information on the verb position as in Metheniti et al. (2022). We select the best performing model `bert-large-cased` in their work for fine-tuning as baseline.

LLM Output Extraction. Although we prompt the LLMs to give answers with single tokens of telic/atelic and durative/stative, in most cases, the LLMs respond with more tokens in different formats, and sometimes with explanation of their choices. We use a string matching method using `RegEx` to map the responses to the categories,

Level	Prompt
Level 1	`Does this sentence have durative aspect or stative aspect? Answer with durative or stative.\n Sentence:\n {sentence}`
Level 2	`Does the verb {verb} in this sentence have durative aspect or stative aspect? Answer with durative or stative.\n Sentence:\n {sentence}`
Level 3	`Does the verb {verb} in position {position} of this sentence have durative aspect or stative aspect? Answer with durative or stative.\n Sentence:\n {sentence}`

Table 2: Instruction prompt in three different constraint levels for the durative and stative aspects. Level 1 only shows the sentence, level 2 shows the sentence and the main verb of the sentence, level 3 shows the sentence, the main verb and its position of the sentence.

which is commonly used in extracting LLM outputs (Argyle et al., 2023). Afterwards, we manually evaluate the coded outputs and in case of uncertain responses, we note them accordingly.

4 Results

4.1 Main Results

We summarize the main results of the six LLMs in Table 3 on the duration test set and the Telicity test set, as well as the performance of the fine-tuned model `bert-large-cased` as the baseline for comparison.

On the duration test set, GPT-4 achieves the highest performance among the LLMs with an accuracy of 0.74 and an F1 score of 0.76. This is followed by GPT-3.5 and Llama-2, which both show comparable results in the 0.67 to 0.69 range for both metrics. The Llama-3 and Mixtral models also perform similarly with slightly lower scores. The Gemma model demonstrates the lowest performance among the LLMs with an accuracy of 0.54 and an F1 score of 0.42. Notably, the baseline large bert model significantly outperforms all LLMs, achieving an accuracy and F1 score of 0.96.

On the telicity test set, GPT-4 again leads among the LLMs with an accuracy of 0.71 and an F1 score of 0.72. GPT-3.5 and Llama-3 also show strong performances with scores around the 0.65 to 0.67 range for both metrics. The Mixtral model has slightly lower scores, and Llama-2 and Gemma exhibit the lowest performance. The fine-tuning bert-large-cased baseline still outperforms all LLMs.

We show that prompting LLMs to recognize the two aspectual features in verbs results in lower performance compared to the fine-tuning baseline, which exhibits high performance. This suggests that LLMs might lack the capability to probe the deep linguistic features of given words and may require adaptation (i.e., fine-tuning) to effectively perform the task. When comparing the two aspectual features, we observe that the performance of most models is slightly lower on the telicity test set than on the duration test set, indicating that recognizing a/telic aspects is more challenging. Additionally, among the LLMs, the closed-source models (GPT-3.5 and GPT-4) demonstrate better performance than the open-source models.

Model	Duration		Telicity	
	Acc	F1	Acc	F1
Gemma	0.54	0.42	0.52	0.41
GPT-3.5	0.68	0.69	0.67	0.65
GPT-4	0.74	0.76	0.71	0.72
Llama-2	0.67	0.67	0.53	0.42
Llama-3	0.64	0.63	0.65	0.65
Mixtral	0.62	0.63	0.59	0.60
`bert-large-cased`	0.96	0.96	0.88	0.87

Table 3: Accuracy and F1 scores for various zero-shot prompted LLMs vs. the fine-tuned baseline model `bert-large-cased` on duration and telicity test sets.

4.2 Verb and Verb Position Can Influence the Evaluation

In this section, we analyze the impact of including the verb and its position in the sentence on the evaluation of aspectual features by LLMs in the duration and telicity test sets. we present F1 scores across three levels of prompting (sentence-only, sentence with verb, and sentence with verb and its position) in the bar plots in Figure 1 and they reveal significant insights partially.

In the duration set, Gemma's performance remains consistent across different levels of context, while GPT-3.5 and GPT-4 show substantial improvements with additional contextual information, although GPT-3.5 experiences a slight drop at the

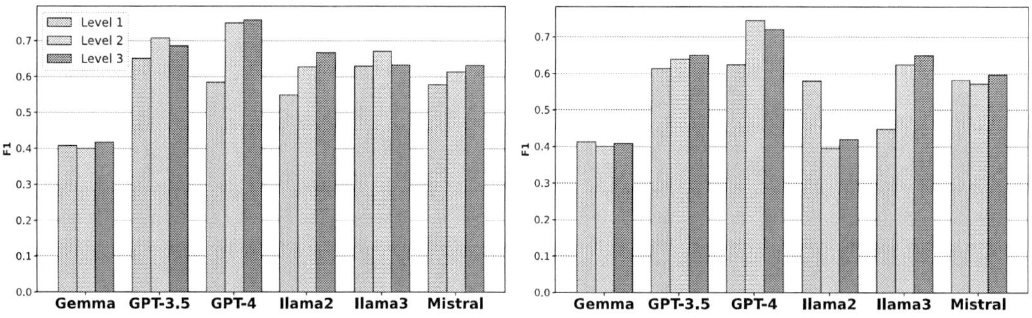

(a) Duration (b) Telicity

Figure 1: F1 results of models in three different levels

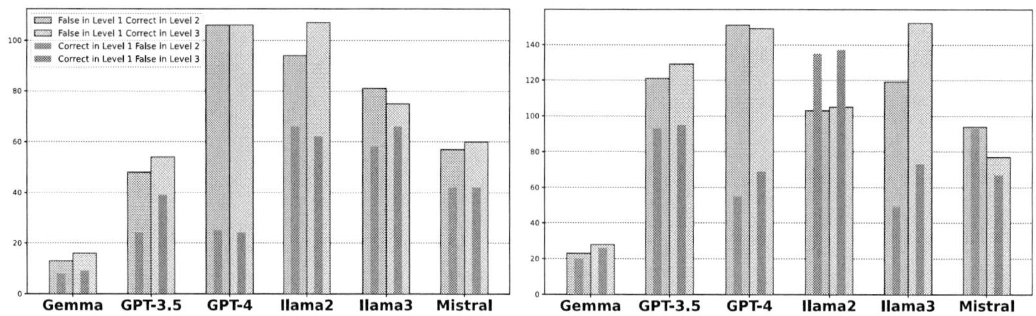

(a) Duration (b) Telicity

Figure 2: Count of prediction differences in three different levels. The dark bars represent the count of correct predictions in level 1 which are falsely predicted in level 2&3. The light bars represent the count of false predictions in level 1 which are correctly predicted in level 2&3.

highest level. Llama-2 and Llama-3 generally benefit from more context, but Llama-3's performance slightly decreases at the highest level. Mistral demonstrates modest but consistent improvements. In the telicity set, Gemma again shows minimal variation, and GPT-3.5 and GPT-4 improve with more context, although GPT-4 has a slight decline at the highest level. Llama-2 struggles with additional context, while Llama-3 shows significant improvement. Mistral exhibits stable performance with slight gains.

We further examine the count of prediction differences across the three levels for both the duration and telicity sets in Figure 2. For the duration set, models like GPT-4 and GPT-3.5 showed substantial improvements with more corrections than regressions when additional context was provided, indicating a positive impact from including the verb and its position. For instance, GPT-4 had 106 corrections at both Levels 2 and 3, compared to 25 and 24 regressions. Llama-2 and Llama-3 also benefited from the additional context, though to a lesser extent., with Llama-2 showing 94 and 107 corrections versus 66 and 62 regressions. Mistral saw steady but modest improvements, while Gemma displayed minimal changes, suggesting limited sensitivity to the added information. On the telicity set, GPT-4 and GPT-3.5 again demonstrated significant improvements with more corrections (151 and 129) than regressions (55 and 95). However, Llama-2 struggled with additional context, showing more regressions than corrections, indicating potential confusion. Llama-3 and Mistral exhibited notable but smaller benefits from the detailed prompts.

Overall, our analysis underscores that while additional context including the verbs and verb positions generally enhances performance, the degree of improvement varies across models.

4.3 Error Analysis

In this section, we conduct a brief analysis of certain specific error predictions we observed during inference, which are outlined in Table 4.

Case 1 illustrates instances at prompt level 1,

Case, Input, Output
Case 1, Mistral on duration set, in level1 **Sentence:** Should be alright then . **Label:** durative **Output:** This sentence is stative in nature. It expresses a state of being or a condition, rather than an ongoing action. The word ""then"" suggests a conclusion or a result, which is also indicative of a stative aspect.
Case 2, Llama-2 on duration set, in level3 **Sentence:** Bake at 180 degrees of 40 - 50 minutes . Do n't think highly too that cheese was n't overroasted . **Label:** durative **Output:** The verb "think" in position 12 of the sentence does not have a durative or stative aspect. It is a stative aspect.
Case 3, Gemma on telicity set **Sentence:** I was born here , and I was lucky enough not to get attached to any particular river . **Label:** telic **Output (level1):** The sentence is telic because the verb ""was born"" is telic and the verb ""get attached"" is also telic. **Output (level2):** The verb ""attach"" in this sentence has telic aspect because the verb is completed with a specific object, which is ""river"". **Output (level3):** The verb attached in position 13 is ""attach"". The answer is atelic.
Case 4, GPT-4 on telicity set, level3 **Sentence:** A TV mounted above a fireplace in a nicely furnished living room . **Label:** telic **Output:** The verb ""mounted"" in position 2 in the sentence ""A TV mounted above a fireplace in a nicely furnished living room"" does not by itself convey a clear aspect because the sentence is a noun phrase, not a complete sentence with a tense that would allow us to determine aspect.

Table 4: Example error cases.

where the absence of verb ("be alright") or verb position information leads the model to predict the aspect for the entire sentence, resulting in inaccurate predictions.

Case 2 highlights instances of model hallucinations, where initially, the model denies the presence of probed aspects in the verb but subsequently provides an aspect in the following sentence.

Case 3 demonstrates the prediction disparity across the three prompt levels. While the predictions are accurate and nuanced in the first two levels, they become nonsensical and incorrect in level 3, underscoring the model's tendency towards hallucinations and instability.

Case 4 presents a scenario where the model fails to provide an aspectual feature, incorrectly concluding that the verb lacks an aspect.

These error cases underscore that employing LLMs may introduce unexpected errors due to model complexity and hallucinations. Additionally, the inconsistency of model output remains a pertinent question for further investigation.

5 Discussion & Conclusion

This preliminary study evaluates the performance of various LLMs in recognizing lexical aspects, specifically duration and telicity, in zero-shot scenarios. We notice while LLMs, especially the closed-source ones (GPT-3.5 and GPT-4), are capable of recognizing the lexical aspects of verbs in sentences, they lie behind the fine-tuned baselines, indicating the potential need for further adaptation to effectively probe deep linguistic features. We conduct experiments across three levels of prompting to assess the impact of including the verb and its position in the sentence. Our results reveal that LLMs, particularly the closed-source ones, benefit from the additional context of verbs. However, this added complexity sometimes introduced regressions, indicating that while context aids comprehension, it can also pose challenges. The case analysis also introduces concerns about the complexity of hallucinations within the models.

Future research could explore methods to optimize LLMs for aspectual feature recognition, such as fine-tuning LLMs or incorporating additional linguistic knowledge into model training. Currently, we only conduct the prompt in zero-shot settings, i.e. without context information. Previous work showed that prompt-based methods may underestimate the linguistic knowledge of LLMs (Hu and Levy, 2023). Therefore, we call for future exploration in different settings, such as few-shot prompting and Chain-of-Thought (CoT, Wei et al., 2023) prompting.

Overall, our study offers valuable insights into the challenges and opportunities of utilizing LLMs for linguistic feature recognition.

Limitations

The primary limitation of our preliminary work lies in the complexity and instability of LLMs, as detailed in §4.3. The models exhibit sensitivity to prompts and parameter settings. Our study tested only three curated prompts with varying information levels and observed significant variations across these conditions. Future research should delve deeper into these variations to provide explanations for these changes.

Additionally, as noted in previous work (e.g., Zhang, 1995), aspectual readings are sensitive to the context surrounding the verb. Our current study tested aspectual features using a single curated dataset with individual sentences and labels. Future research should explore data with longer texts containing more verbs and possibly provide sequential predictions on verbs within context. This would help to better understand the deeper linguistic comprehension capabilities of LLMs.

Acknowledgements

The research is supported by Munich Center for Machine Learning.

References

Malihe Alikhani and Matthew Stone. 2019. "caption" as a coherence relation: Evidence and implications. In *Proceedings of the Second Workshop on Shortcomings in Vision and Language*, pages 58–67, Minneapolis, Minnesota. Association for Computational Linguistics.

Lisa P. Argyle, Ethan C. Busby, Nancy Fulda, Joshua R. Gubler, Christopher Rytting, and David Wingate. 2023. Out of one, many: Using language models to simulate human samples. *Political Analysis*, 31(3):337–351.

Tom B. Brown, Benjamin Mann, Nick Ryder, Melanie Subbiah, Jared Kaplan, Prafulla Dhariwal, Arvind Neelakantan, Pranav Shyam, Girish Sastry, Amanda Askell, Sandhini Agarwal, Ariel Herbert-Voss, Gretchen Krueger, Tom Henighan, Rewon Child, Aditya Ramesh, Daniel M. Ziegler, Jeffrey Wu, Clemens Winter, Christopher Hesse, Mark Chen, Eric Sigler, Mateusz Litwin, Scott Gray, Benjamin Chess, Jack Clark, Christopher Berner, Sam McCandlish, Alec Radford, Ilya Sutskever, and Dario Amodei. 2020. Language models are few-shot learners. *Preprint*, arXiv:2005.14165.

Bernard Comrie. 1976. *Aspect*. Cambridge Textbooks in Linguistics. Cambridge University Press, Cambridge.

Jacob Devlin, Ming-Wei Chang, Kenton Lee, and Kristina Toutanova. 2019. BERT: Pre-training of deep bidirectional transformers for language understanding. In *Proceedings of the 2019 Conference of the North American Chapter of the Association for Computational Linguistics: Human Language Technologies, Volume 1 (Long and Short Papers)*, pages 4171–4186, Minneapolis, Minnesota. Association for Computational Linguistics.

Annemarie Friedrich and Damyana Gateva. 2017. Classification of telicity using cross-linguistic annotation projection. In *Proceedings of the 2017 Conference on Empirical Methods in Natural Language Processing*, pages 2559–2565, Copenhagen, Denmark. Association for Computational Linguistics.

Annemarie Friedrich and Alexis Palmer. 2014. Automatic prediction of aspectual class of verbs in context. In *Proceedings of the 52nd Annual Meeting of the Association for Computational Linguistics (Volume 2: Short Papers)*, pages 517–523, Baltimore, Maryland. Association for Computational Linguistics.

Annemarie Friedrich, Alexis Palmer, and Manfred Pinkal. 2016. Situation entity types: automatic classification of clause-level aspect. In *Proceedings of the 54th Annual Meeting of the Association for Computational Linguistics (Volume 1: Long Papers)*, pages 1757–1768, Berlin, Germany. Association for Computational Linguistics.

Annemarie Friedrich and Manfred Pinkal. 2015. Automatic recognition of habituals: a three-way classification of clausal aspect. In *Proceedings of the 2015 Conference on Empirical Methods in Natural Language Processing*, pages 2471–2481, Lisbon, Portugal. Association for Computational Linguistics.

Annemarie Friedrich, Nianwen Xue, and Alexis Palmer. 2023. A kind introduction to lexical and grammatical aspect, with a survey of computational approaches. In *Proceedings of the 17th Conference of the European Chapter of the Association for Computational Linguistics*, pages 599–622, Dubrovnik, Croatia. Association for Computational Linguistics.

Jürgen Hermes, Michael Richter, and Claes Neuefind. 2015. Automatic induction of german aspectual verb classes in a distributional framework. In *Proceedings of the International Conference of the German Society for Computational Linguistics and Language Technology (GSCL)*.

Jennifer Hu and Roger Levy. 2023. Prompting is not a substitute for probability measurements in large language models. In *Proceedings of the 2023 Conference on Empirical Methods in Natural Language Processing*, pages 5040–5060, Singapore. Association for Computational Linguistics.

Albert Q. Jiang, Alexandre Sablayrolles, Antoine Roux, Arthur Mensch, Blanche Savary, Chris Bamford, Devendra Singh Chaplot, Diego de las

Casas, Emma Bou Hanna, Florian Bressand, Gianna Lengyel, Guillaume Bour, Guillaume Lample, Lélio Renard Lavaud, Lucile Saulnier, Marie-Anne Lachaux, Pierre Stock, Sandeep Subramanian, Sophia Yang, Szymon Antoniak, Teven Le Scao, Théophile Gervet, Thibaut Lavril, Thomas Wang, Timothée Lacroix, and William El Sayed. 2024. Mixtral of experts. *Preprint*, arXiv:2401.04088.

Wolfgang Klein. 1994. *Time in Language*. Routledge, London.

Thomas Kober, Malihe Alikhani, Matthew Stone, and Mark Steedman. 2020. Aspectuality across genre: A distributional semantics approach. In *Proceedings of the 28th International Conference on Computational Linguistics*, pages 4546–4562, Barcelona, Spain (Online). International Committee on Computational Linguistics.

Elisabeth Leiss. 1992. *Die Verbalkategorien des Deutschen*. De Gruyter, Berlin, Boston.

Eleni Metheniti, Tim Van De Cruys, and Nabil Hathout. 2022. About time: Do transformers learn temporal verbal aspect? In *Proceedings of the Workshop on Cognitive Modeling and Computational Linguistics*, pages 88–101, Dublin, Ireland. Association for Computational Linguistics.

OpenAI, Josh Achiam, Steven Adler, Sandhini Agarwal, Lama Ahmad, Ilge Akkaya, Florencia Leoni Aleman, Diogo Almeida, Janko Altenschmidt, Sam Altman, Shyamal Anadkat, Red Avila, Igor Babuschkin, Suchir Balaji, Valerie Balcom, Paul Baltescu, Haiming Bao, Mohammad Bavarian, Jeff Belgum, Irwan Bello, Jake Berdine, Gabriel Bernadett-Shapiro, Christopher Berner, Lenny Bogdonoff, Oleg Boiko, Madelaine Boyd, Anna-Luisa Brakman, Greg Brockman, Tim Brooks, Miles Brundage, Kevin Button, Trevor Cai, Rosie Campbell, Andrew Cann, Brittany Carey, Chelsea Carlson, Rory Carmichael, Brooke Chan, Che Chang, Fotis Chantzis, Derek Chen, Sully Chen, Ruby Chen, Jason Chen, Mark Chen, Ben Chess, Chester Cho, Casey Chu, Hyung Won Chung, Dave Cummings, Jeremiah Currier, Yunxing Dai, Cory Decareaux, Thomas Degry, Noah Deutsch, Damien Deville, Arka Dhar, David Dohan, Steve Dowling, Sheila Dunning, Adrien Ecoffet, Atty Eleti, Tyna Eloundou, David Farhi, Liam Fedus, Niko Felix, Simón Posada Fishman, Juston Forte, Isabella Fulford, Leo Gao, Elie Georges, Christian Gibson, Vik Goel, Tarun Gogineni, Gabriel Goh, Rapha Gontijo-Lopes, Jonathan Gordon, Morgan Grafstein, Scott Gray, Ryan Greene, Joshua Gross, Shixiang Shane Gu, Yufei Guo, Chris Hallacy, Jesse Han, Jeff Harris, Yuchen He, Mike Heaton, Johannes Heidecke, Chris Hesse, Alan Hickey, Wade Hickey, Peter Hoeschele, Brandon Houghton, Kenny Hsu, Shengli Hu, Xin Hu, Joost Huizinga, Shantanu Jain, Shawn Jain, Joanne Jang, Angela Jiang, Roger Jiang, Haozhun Jin, Denny Jin, Shino Jomoto, Billie Jonn, Heewoo Jun, Tomer Kaftan, Łukasz Kaiser, Ali Kamali, Ingmar Kanitscheider, Nitish Shirish Keskar, Tabarak Khan, Logan Kilpatrick, Jong Wook Kim, Christina Kim, Yongjik Kim, Jan Hendrik Kirchner, Jamie Kiros, Matt Knight, Daniel Kokotajlo, Łukasz Kondraciuk, Andrew Kondrich, Aris Konstantinidis, Kyle Kosic, Gretchen Krueger, Vishal Kuo, Michael Lampe, Ikai Lan, Teddy Lee, Jan Leike, Jade Leung, Daniel Levy, Chak Ming Li, Rachel Lim, Molly Lin, Stephanie Lin, Mateusz Litwin, Theresa Lopez, Ryan Lowe, Patricia Lue, Anna Makanju, Kim Malfacini, Sam Manning, Todor Markov, Yaniv Markovski, Bianca Martin, Katie Mayer, Andrew Mayne, Bob McGrew, Scott Mayer McKinney, Christine McLeavey, Paul McMillan, Jake McNeil, David Medina, Aalok Mehta, Jacob Menick, Luke Metz, Andrey Mishchenko, Pamela Mishkin, Vinnie Monaco, Evan Morikawa, Daniel Mossing, Tong Mu, Mira Murati, Oleg Murk, David Mély, Ashvin Nair, Reiichiro Nakano, Rajeev Nayak, Arvind Neelakantan, Richard Ngo, Hyeonwoo Noh, Long Ouyang, Cullen O'Keefe, Jakub Pachocki, Alex Paino, Joe Palermo, Ashley Pantuliano, Giambattista Parascandolo, Joel Parish, Emy Parparita, Alex Passos, Mikhail Pavlov, Andrew Peng, Adam Perelman, Filipe de Avila Belbute Peres, Michael Petrov, Henrique Ponde de Oliveira Pinto, Michael, Pokorny, Michelle Pokrass, Vitchyr H. Pong, Tolly Powell, Alethea Power, Boris Power, Elizabeth Proehl, Raul Puri, Alec Radford, Jack Rae, Aditya Ramesh, Cameron Raymond, Francis Real, Kendra Rimbach, Carl Ross, Bob Rotsted, Henri Roussez, Nick Ryder, Mario Saltarelli, Ted Sanders, Shibani Santurkar, Girish Sastry, Heather Schmidt, David Schnurr, John Schulman, Daniel Selsam, Kyla Sheppard, Toki Sherbakov, Jessica Shieh, Sarah Shoker, Pranav Shyam, Szymon Sidor, Eric Sigler, Maddie Simens, Jordan Sitkin, Katarina Slama, Ian Sohl, Benjamin Sokolowsky, Yang Song, Natalie Staudacher, Felipe Petroski Such, Natalie Summers, Ilya Sutskever, Jie Tang, Nikolas Tezak, Madeleine B. Thompson, Phil Tillet, Amin Tootoonchian, Elizabeth Tseng, Preston Tuggle, Nick Turley, Jerry Tworek, Juan Felipe Cerón Uribe, Andrea Vallone, Arun Vijayvergiya, Chelsea Voss, Carroll Wainwright, Justin Jay Wang, Alvin Wang, Ben Wang, Jonathan Ward, Jason Wei, CJ Weinmann, Akila Welihinda, Peter Welinder, Jiayi Weng, Lilian Weng, Matt Wiethoff, Dave Willner, Clemens Winter, Samuel Wolrich, Hannah Wong, Lauren Workman, Sherwin Wu, Jeff Wu, Michael Wu, Kai Xiao, Tao Xu, Sarah Yoo, Kevin Yu, Qiming Yuan, Wojciech Zaremba, Rowan Zellers, Chong Zhang, Marvin Zhang, Shengjia Zhao, Tianhao Zheng, Juntang Zhuang, William Zhuk, and Barret Zoph. 2024. Gpt-4 technical report. *Preprint*, arXiv:2303.08774.

Juri Opitz, Shira Wein, and Nathan Schneider. 2024. Natural language processing relies on linguistics. *Preprint*, arXiv:2405.05966.

Anita Ramm, Sharid Loáiciga, Annemarie Friedrich, and Alexander Fraser. 2017. Annotating tense, mood and voice for English, French and German. In *Proceedings of ACL 2017, System Demonstrations*, pages 1–6, Vancouver, Canada. Association for Computational Linguistics.

Eric V. Siegel and Kathleen R. McKeown. 2000. Learning methods to combine linguistic indicators:improving aspectual classification and revealing linguistic insights. *Computational Linguistics*, 26(4):595–627.

Gemma Team, Thomas Mesnard, Cassidy Hardin, Robert Dadashi, Surya Bhupatiraju, Shreya Pathak, Laurent Sifre, Morgane Rivière, Mihir Sanjay Kale, Juliette Love, Pouya Tafti, Léonard Hussenot, Pier Giuseppe Sessa, Aakanksha Chowdhery, Adam Roberts, Aditya Barua, Alex Botev, Alex Castro-Ros, Ambrose Slone, Amélie Héliou, Andrea Tacchetti, Anna Bulanova, Antonia Paterson, Beth Tsai, Bobak Shahriari, Charline Le Lan, Christopher A. Choquette-Choo, Clément Crepy, Daniel Cer, Daphne Ippolito, David Reid, Elena Buchatskaya, Eric Ni, Eric Noland, Geng Yan, George Tucker, George-Christian Muraru, Grigory Rozhdestvenskiy, Henryk Michalewski, Ian Tenney, Ivan Grishchenko, Jacob Austin, James Keeling, Jane Labanowski, Jean-Baptiste Lespiau, Jeff Stanway, Jenny Brennan, Jeremy Chen, Johan Ferret, Justin Chiu, Justin Mao-Jones, Katherine Lee, Kathy Yu, Katie Millican, Lars Lowe Sjoesund, Lisa Lee, Lucas Dixon, Machel Reid, Maciej Mikuła, Mateo Wirth, Michael Sharman, Nikolai Chinaev, Nithum Thain, Olivier Bachem, Oscar Chang, Oscar Wahltinez, Paige Bailey, Paul Michel, Petko Yotov, Rahma Chaabouni, Ramona Comanescu, Reena Jana, Rohan Anil, Ross McIlroy, Ruibo Liu, Ryan Mullins, Samuel L Smith, Sebastian Borgeaud, Sertan Girgin, Sholto Douglas, Shree Pandya, Siamak Shakeri, Soham De, Ted Klimenko, Tom Hennigan, Vlad Feinberg, Wojciech Stokowiec, Yu hui Chen, Zafarali Ahmed, Zhitao Gong, Tris Warkentin, Ludovic Peran, Minh Giang, Clément Farabet, Oriol Vinyals, Jeff Dean, Koray Kavukcuoglu, Demis Hassabis, Zoubin Ghahramani, Douglas Eck, Joelle Barral, Fernando Pereira, Eli Collins, Armand Joulin, Noah Fiedel, Evan Senter, Alek Andreev, and Kathleen Kenealy. 2024. Gemma: Open models based on gemini research and technology. *Preprint*, arXiv:2403.08295.

Hugo Touvron, Louis Martin, Kevin Stone, Peter Albert, Amjad Almahairi, Yasmine Babaei, Nikolay Bashlykov, Soumya Batra, Prajjwal Bhargava, Shruti Bhosale, Dan Bikel, Lukas Blecher, Cristian Canton Ferrer, Moya Chen, Guillem Cucurull, David Esiobu, Jude Fernandes, Jeremy Fu, Wenyin Fu, Brian Fuller, Cynthia Gao, Vedanuj Goswami, Naman Goyal, Anthony Hartshorn, Saghar Hosseini, Rui Hou, Hakan Inan, Marcin Kardas, Viktor Kerkez, Madian Khabsa, Isabel Kloumann, Artem Korenev, Punit Singh Koura, Marie-Anne Lachaux, Thibaut Lavril, Jenya Lee, Diana Liskovich, Yinghai Lu, Yuning Mao, Xavier Martinet, Todor Mihaylov, Pushkar Mishra, Igor Molybog, Yixin Nie, Andrew Poulton, Jeremy Reizenstein, Rashi Rungta, Kalyan Saladi, Alan Schelten, Ruan Silva, Eric Michael Smith, Ranjan Subramanian, Xiaoqing Ellen Tan, Binh Tang, Ross Taylor, Adina Williams, Jian Xiang Kuan, Puxin Xu, Zheng Yan, Iliyan Zarov, Yuchen Zhang, Angela Fan, Melanie Kambadur, Sharan Narang, Aurelien Rodriguez, Robert Stojnic, Sergey Edunov, and Thomas Scialom. 2023. Llama 2: Open foundation and fine-tuned chat models. *Preprint*, arXiv:2307.09288.

Zeno Vendler. 1957. Verbs and times. *The Philosophical Review*, 66(2):143–160.

Jason Wei, Xuezhi Wang, Dale Schuurmans, Maarten Bosma, Brian Ichter, Fei Xia, Ed Chi, Quoc Le, and Denny Zhou. 2023. Chain-of-thought prompting elicits reasoning in large language models. *Preprint*, arXiv:2201.11903.

Richard Xiao and Tony McEnery. 2004. *Aspect in Mandarin Chinese: A corpus-based study*. John Benjamins.

Lihua Zhang. 1995. *A Contrastive Study of Aspectuality in German, English and Chinese*. Peter Lang, New York.

A Appendix

A.1 Label Distribution in Test Sets

We present the label distributions from the original test sets (Metheniti et al., 2022) in Table 5.

Test Set	Label '0'	Label '1'	Total
Duration	186	223	409
Telicity	315	292	607

Table 5: Test set statistics for duration and telicity. In the duration subset, '0' and '1' stand for stative and durative aspects, respectively. In the telicity subset, '0' and '1' stand for atelic and telic aspects, respectively.

A.2 Label Distribution in Predictions

Table 6 shows the label distribution from the model predictions. We notice some imbalanced label distribution especially in model Gemma on both duration and telicity sets across three prompt levels. This great imbalance also results in low prediction accuracies, as shown in §4.1. This indicates that the Gemma model might not be adequate to probe the aspectual features. The same imbalance can be found in Llama-2 in level3 on the telicity set.

Model	Level	'0'	'1'	'2'	'3'	'-99'
Gemma	level1	27	382	0	0	0
	level2	14	395	0	0	0
	level3	20	389	0	0	0
GPT-3.5	level1	211	195	1	0	2
	level2	194	214	0	0	1
	level3	193	215	0	0	1
GPT-4	level1	150	196	36	21	6
	level2	208	189	11	0	1
	level3	213	177	18	0	1
Llama2	level1	265	144	0	0	0
	level2	176	230	0	3	0
	level3	180	229	0	0	0
Llama3	level1	202	190	13	4	0
	level2	238	171	0	0	0
	level3	259	149	1	0	0
Mistral	level1	141	252	10	4	2
	level2	122	267	17	2	1
	level3	150	237	15	1	6

(a) Duration

Model	Level	'0'	'1'	'2'	'3'	'-99'
Gemma	level1	558	49	0	0	0
	level2	575	32	0	0	0
	level3	566	40	0	1	0
GPT-3.5	level1	252	348	0	0	7
	level2	454	147	0	0	6
	level3	450	153	0	0	4
GPT-4	level1	213	295	71	16	12
	level2	344	243	14	0	6
	level3	353	227	22	1	4
Llama2	level1	350	255	0	2	0
	level2	586	19	0	2	0
	level3	565	41	0	0	1
Llama3	level1	73	523	8	3	0
	level2	194	412	1	0	0
	level3	260	346	1	0	0
Mistral	level1	280	314	4	8	1
	level2	401	193	3	5	5
	level3	334	263	1	4	5

(b) Telicity

Table 6: Label distribution from the model predictions on duration and telicity set. '0' and '1' are the original binary labels of the dataset. '2' means model cannot find an aspect or thinks the verb doesn't have an aspect. '3' means nonsense output. '-99' means model refusal.

Daily auditory environments in French-speaking infants: A longitudinal dataset

Estelle Hervé
CNRS & Aix Marseille Univ
Laboratoire Parole et Langage
Aix-en-Provence, France
estelle.herve@univ-amu.fr

Clément François
CNRS & Aix Marseille Univ
Laboratoire Parole et Langage
Aix-en-Provence, France
clement.francois@cnrs.fr

Laurent Prévot
CNRS & MEAE
CEFC
Taipei, Taiwan
laurent.prevot@cnrs.fr

Abstract

Babies' daily auditory environment plays a crucial role in language development. Most previous research estimating the quantitative and qualitative aspects of early speech inputs has predominantly focused on English- and Spanish-speaking families. In addition, validation studies for daylong recordings' analysis tools are scarce on French data sets. In this paper, we present a French corpus of daylong audio recordings longitudinally collected with the LENA (Language ENvironment Analysis) system from infants aged 3 to 24 months. We conduct a thorough exploration of this data set, which serves as a quality check for both the data and the analysis tools. We evaluate the reliability of LENA metrics by systematically comparing them with those obtained from the Child-Project set of tools and checking the known dynamics of the metrics with age. These metrics are also used to replicate, on our data set, findings from Warlaumont et al. (2014) about the increase of infants' speech vocalizations and temporal contingencies between infants and caregivers with age.

1 Introduction

Infants rely on their daily auditory environment to develop language and other cognitive skills. Pioneering studies interested in these early auditory inputs used observatory experiments in laboratory settings or short recordings that were manually annotated (Hart and Risley, 1992; Keller et al., 2004). In the last decades, technological advances brought new tools that allowed the collection and analysis of more considerable and ecological datasets. Daylong recordings are now increasingly used in developmental studies (Ganek and Eriks-Brophy, 2018; Bergelson et al., 2023), especially since the release of the Language Environment Analysis (LENA) system in 2004.

Daily auditory environments have been described in a variety of populations (Christakis et al., 2009; Aragon and Yoshinaga-Itano, 2012; Caskey et al., 2014; Warren et al., 2010), highlighting the positive effects of early caregiver-infant interactions on language development (Warlaumont et al., 2014; Gilkerson and Richards, 2008; Bergelson and Aslin, 2017). Nonetheless, only two datasets were collected in French-speaking households (Canault et al., 2016; Orena et al., 2019). Here, we expand the literature by describing an original dataset of infants' daylong audio recordings gathered in twenty French-speaking families.

We focused on 3-to-24-month-old babies for several reasons: (1) it allows a direct comparison with Canault et al. (2016)'s and Warlaumont et al. (2014) results ; (2) it includes crucial steps for language development, including the emergence of phonemic categories between 6 and 10 months (Werker and Tees, 1984; Cheour et al., 1998), and the vocabulary spurt between 18 and 24 months (Benedict, 1979; Goldfield and Reznick, 1990; Nazzi and Bertoncini, 2003) ; (3) the two first years of life constitute a critical period where caregiver-infant interactions are early precursors of later language outcomes and cognitive skills (Warlaumont et al., 2022; Gilkerson and Richards, 2009; Weisleder and Fernald, 2013; Bergelson and Aslin, 2017).

LENA's output correlation with human annotations has been assessed in several languages, suggesting good reliability (Xu et al., 2008b; Weisleder and Fernald, 2013; Gilkerson et al., 2015; Busch et al., 2018; Pae et al., 2016; Ganek and Eriks-Brophy, 2017). However, only one study provided evidence for LENA system reliability in European French, yielding relatively good results (Canault et al., 2016). Moreover, LENA validation studies implied listening to the continuous raw audio recordings. In addition to being highly time-consuming, this approach raises critical ethical issues associated with data privacy (Casillas and Cristia, 2019; Cychosz et al., 2020). Here, we override these difficulties by comparing the LENA metrics outputs with other

Proceedings of the Workshop on Cognitive Modeling and Computational Linguistics, pages 132–151
August 15, 2024 ©2024 Association for Computational Linguistics

annotation systems.
The paper has the following contributions: (i) describe a new French corpus of auditory LENA-recorded data, (ii) compare different automatic annotation tools, (iii) provide a picture of the daily auditory environment in French-speaking families in 3-to-24-months infants, (iv) show the potential of the data set by replicating daylong recordings-based results on developmental trajectories.

2 Related Work

This section is a brief overview of the existing literature regarding daylong recording studies in developmental populations. We identified two main types of studies: (i) experimental studies that used daylong recordings as a tool to answer a specific research question and (ii) validation studies that focused on assessing the reliability of the recording and analysis tools themselves.

2.1 Experimental studies

Daylong recording studies in infants often involved the LENA system. Four years after its release, the first LENA normative study, the "Natural Language Study (NLS)" was conducted by the LENA Research Foundation (Gilkerson and Richards, 2008). This report relied on the three main LENA metrics (Adult Word Count: AWC; Child Vocalization Count: CVC; Conversational Turn Counts: CTC) to describe daily auditory environments in 329 English-speaking infants aged 2 to 48 months. Then, more experimental works involving daylong recordings in infants began to emerge (see Ganek and Eriks-Brophy (2018) for a review).
Studies that focused on the characteristics of the daily auditory environment in typically developing infants revealed that children's vocalizations and child-caregiver interactions increased with age within the first two years of life (Gilkerson and Richards, 2008; Pae et al., 2016). Warlaumont et al. (2014) proposed a "social feedback loop" in which contingencies between adult-child and child-adult speech-like vocalizations contribute to increasing interactions between infants and adults through age. Additionally, a higher proportion of adult-child interactions has been associated with larger vocabulary size (Weisleder and Fernald, 2013). The impact of various factors like multilingualism (Oller et al., 2010; Orena et al., 2019; Ramírez and Hippe, 2024), socio-economic status (Bergelson et al., 2023), exposure to TV Christakis et al. (2009); Zimmerman et al. (2009), musical inputs (Mendoza and Fausey, 2021), activity during the day (Soderstrom and Wittebolle, 2013) and temporal dynamics of the surrounding sounds (Warlaumont et al., 2022) have been investigated as well. Daylong recording studies in clinical populations showed the importance of understanding infants' daily soundscape for early language intervention (Caskey et al., 2011; Warren et al., 2010; Warlaumont et al., 2014; Aragon and Yoshinaga-Itano, 2012).

Overall, age ranges, sample sizes, and recording spans varied across studies. Some infants were included as early as 2 months of age (Aragon and Yoshinaga-Itano, 2012; Bergelson and Aslin, 2017; Zimmerman et al., 2009), while others started after 12 months of age (Oller et al., 2010; Warren et al., 2010; Weisleder and Fernald, 2013). Children could be followed longitudinally within various periods (Gilkerson et al., 2018; Sy et al., 2023) but not systematically (Weisleder and Fernald, 2013; Bergelson and Aslin, 2017).
Although most studies relied on the LENA system, methodological choices regarding data collection and analysis were various. For example, some authors chose to rely on preexisting datasets that already fitted their research questions (Christakis et al., 2009; Aragon and Yoshinaga-Itano, 2012; Warren et al., 2010). For data analysis, the LENA metrics were mostly used although some preferred to develop their own tools (MacWhinney, 2000; Al Futaisi et al., 2019; Lavechin et al., 2020; Räsänen et al., 2021).

2.2 Validation studies

The first LENA validation study was led in 2008 on American English, as part of the NLS (Xu et al., 2008b). Human annotations were compared with automatic outputs provided by the LENA software to determine agreement scores, measured with Pearson's correlations. LENA's AWC and CVC reached $r = 0.82$ and $r = 0.76$ respectively, indicating reliable LENA annotations for subsequent English-speaking environment studies (Christakis et al., 2009; Warren et al., 2010; Xu et al., 2008a; Zimmerman et al., 2009; Gilkerson et al., 2017).
Later, the same validation procedure was applied to other languages, focusing on the three main LENA metrics (AWC, CVC, and CTC). Overall, the AWC metric was the most reliable, although several authors reported that, on average,

the LENA's estimations were lower than the human counts (Xu et al., 2009; Canault et al., 2016). Agreement scores for AWC were reported in Spanish ($r = 0.80$, Weisleder and Fernald (2013)), Mandarin ($r = 0.72$, Gilkerson et al. (2015)), Korean ($r = 0.72$, Pae et al. (2016)), and Dutch ($r = 0.87$, Busch et al. (2018)). CVC and CTC's reliability were not systematically assessed and yielded variable results, ranging from $r = 0.52$ (Busch et al., 2018) to $r = 0.84$ (Gilkerson and Richards, 2008) (see Table 3 in Appendices). In French, we found Canault et al. (2016)'s report as the only existing validation study so far. They manually annotated and transcribed 324 ten-minute samples recorded in 3-to-48-month-olds: Pearson's correlation scores were $r = 0.64$ for AWC and $r = 0.71$ for CVC. These results suggest good reliability for LENA metrics in French, although slightly below the abovementioned languages.

Cristia et al. (2021)'s comprehensive validation study in three different linguistic and socio-cultural environments calls for more validation studies with more detailed and systematic methods. However, the concurrent emergence of annotation tools (MacWhinney, 2000; Al Futaisi et al., 2019; Lavechin et al., 2020; Räsänen et al., 2021) tends to increase methodological variability. To converge toward a standardized pipeline for daylong data management, Gautheron et al. (2023) developed the ChildProject package. It is compatible with many existing annotation formats and allows annotation systems comparisons. Here, we relied on these tools to compare LENA's metrics with measures extracted from the `Voice Type Classifier (VTC)` from Lavechin et al. (2020) and the `VoCalisation Maturity analysis (VCM)` from Al Futaisi et al. (2019).

3 Rationale

3.1 Participants

Infants were recruited between 3 and 18 months of age in three daycare centers in south-east France. An official collaboration between our team and the daycare centers was established to facilitate both participants' recruitment and data collection. We met parents in person to communicate the project and obtain their informed consent. The French Ethics Committee Review Board approved the study (Agreement 2022-A02281-42) which was conducted according to the guidelines of the Declaration of Helsinki (World Health Organisation, 2008). Parents filled out a questionnaire to ensure that infants did not have any hearing, cognitive, or developmental disorders and that they were raised in a dominant French-speaking environment. Other metadata were gathered through this questionnaire: number of caregivers, musical practice of the caregiver(s), linguistic environment (which language(s) spoken around the child), and socio-economic status (SES) assessed via profession.

Independently of their age at the inclusion date, we followed infants until 24 months of age when possible, or as long as possible otherwise. Twenty infants were involved, with a mean age at inclusion of 12 months (m = 360 days, sd = 132.5). Six additional babies were recruited but excluded from the analysis because parents did not provide enough recordings (<5).

3.2 Procedure

As mentioned above, we collaborated with three daycare centers that became a hub for data collection. Once parents had given their informed consent, they were provided with the LENA materials: a recorder and a t-shirt with a frontal pocket. Each infant had one unique recorder that they kept until the end of data collection. Clothing size was adapted to infants and changed throughout the months when needed. To help parents get used to the LENA system, we gave them some oral instructions when possible so they could ask questions and we could make sure they understood everything. Additionally, all families were given an instruction sheet that was taken from LENA's support materials and adapted to our study. Instructions comprised information about when and how often to record, how to use the device, various recommendations, and the procedure for device deposit and pickup at daycare. Parents also had our contact information and could reach us whenever they needed.

Parents were asked to have their child wear the recorder once a week for a full day, preferentially at home or during the weekends. To limit attrition, we accepted recordings at daycare occasionally, when they could not record another day or if they forgot. The frequency of the recordings was hard to maintain for some families, so we had to send them kind reminders sometimes. But overall, all families were very involved and consistent. We recommended that during a recording day, they never turn the recorder off, limit noisy environments, and let the recorder nearby while showering and during bedtimes. Once the recording was completed, they were asked to bring the LENA recorders back to the daycare center once a week. Then, the investigator could transfer the data to the database the same day, so parents could get the recorder back and start over for a new week. At the end of data collection (when the child reached 24 months or when families decided to stop), infants were given a "baby researcher" diploma and a customized t-shirt as a reward.

4 Tools and Methods

Daylong recordings present a set of challenges in terms of processing. The first constraint is the data set size: we gathered 10^4 hours of highly heterogeneous recordings (both across and within recordings) that need to be sampled. Existing literature has used the notion of *hot spots* (areas in the recordings with a high density of speech events) as well as a method consisting of human labeling of extremely short sound events (Semenzin et al., 2021). Due to the required infrastructure, the latter approach was not considered for our work. Instead, we applied state-of-the-art computational techniques and packages to perform step-by-step reliability tests and calculate agreement scores between them. The automatic tools we used for our analyses are the LENA suite (Gilkerson and Richards, 2008) and a set of tools developed or adapted whithin the framework of ChildProject (Lavechin et al., 2020).

4.1 LENA

We used the LENA system for both data collection and analysis. For data collection, LENA provides a small digital language processor (DLP) that is easily held in a child's hand and can be directly inserted into child-adapted clothing equipped with a specific pocket on the front. The DLP can save up to 16 hours of auditory input. Recordings are then processed with the LENA software, which provides automatic annotations and quantification reports.
The annotation process starts by segmenting the continuous audio recordings based on acoustic features such as intensity and pitch. The segments are then compared to general models of eight categories (Christakis et al., 2009) to be labeled as target child (CHN), adult male (MAN), adult female (FAN), other child (CXN), TV/electronic sounds (TVN), noise (NOI), silence (SIL), or overlapping sounds (OVL). Next, the four categories CHN, MAN, FAN, and CXN are further analyzed to differentiate speech-related from non-speech vocalizations (see Figure 17). The LENA software provides estimations of the number of words produced by adults (AWC) and infants' speech-related vocalizations (CVC). In this study, we only used the raw sound event segmentation (timestamps) and labeling.

4.2 VTC and VCM

The ChildProject suite starts processing recordings with the *voice-type-classifier (VTC)* (Lavechin et al., 2020), which relies on the state-of-the-art speech diarization tool, *pyannote* (Bredin et al., 2020). *VTC* identifies sound activity segments that can be mapped to some of LENA's categories: target key child (KCHI), other children (CHI), female (FEM), and male (MAL). Another tool, *VoCalisation Maturity analysis (VCM)* (Al Futaisi et al., 2019), refines the output of *VTC*. *VCM* is grounded on the state-of-the-art signal processing and emotion recognition tool, *SMILE* (Eyben et al., 2010), and more precisely on the Geneva Minimal Acoustic Parameter Set (GeMAPS) (Eyben et al., 2015). It adds information to the labeled categories (e.g., speech from the target child) by determining whether the targeted speech is Canonical (CNS), Non-canonical (NCS), cries (CRY), or other sounds (noise, laughter). Such classification has been used in (Casillas et al., 2017), for example.

5 Data set

The corpus currently consists of 8286 hours of LENA daylong recordings. Table 1 indicates the mean, minimum, and maximum values for the recording period (age span), number of recording sessions, and length of the recordings.

	Avg	Min	Max	Sum
Age span (months)	9.85	3	18	-
# sessions	27.0	6	66	540
Duration (hours)	414	87	1022	8286

Table 1: The data set. N = 20 children. Age span: number of months between the first and the last recording.

Table 1 reflects a high variability in parents' use of the LENA device. As mentioned earlier, we asked them to turn the DLP on in the morning and leave it until it automatically turns off after 16 hours of recording. However, some families turned the device on and off multiple times during the day or stopped the recording before reaching 16 hours. Thus, we observed variability across participants in recording length and number. Additionally, there was variability in the recording span: not all children started the recordings at the same age, and not all were followed until 24 months of age. Given these observations, we selected a sample of children that 1) had at least 9 months of recording span and 2) provided at least 10 recordings. These thresholds allowed us to focus on more representative datasets while maintaining a sufficient number of data points to observe developmental trajectories. A sample of 10 children met these two criteria and were selected for complementary analyses (see Table 2).

	Avg	Min	Max	Sum
Age span (months)	14.2	10	18	-
# sessions	40.9	12	66	409
Duration (hours)	637	192	1022	6366

Table 2: Selected children for individual longitudinal metrics and plots. N = 10 children (age recording span $\geq$ 9 months; number of recordings $\geq$ 10).

6 Investigating the data set

6.1 Testing age

Our first goal was to test the reliability of the metrics extracted with the three targeted tools (LENA, VTC, VCM) on our data. A crucial check for our dataset consisted of testing whether children's production evolved with age. We expected an increase in children's speech-related metrics (such as speaking time and ratio, vocalization counts, etc.), while adults' metrics would remain stable. Finally, the voices of other children present in the recordings were expected to increase as the siblings of the target child followed their own development. We began by examining the production time ratio (the percentage of the recording time occupied by a given category), for example, for the target child as shown in Figure 1 (See Appendix D for other categories).

More precisely, we examined the production ratio calculated from LENA (sum of the duration of intervals labeled with *CHN* as the speaker, divided by recording duration), VTC (using the same approach with the label *KCHI*), as well as the correlation between the two measures. Importantly, the ratios obtained for the different voices from these two tools were highly correlated. More generally, all the metrics extracted with both approaches were highly correlated for all comparable categories.

We tested whether age remained a dominant factor when controlling for the available metadata. In Figure 2, we plot the production ratio alongside gender, socio-economic status (high vs. low), and linguistic context (monolingual vs. plurilingual). From these figures, a general observation is that children's speaking ratio increased with age. This was tested by conducting a linear mixed model analysis using pymer4 (Jolly, 2018). We treated *'target child speaking ratio'* as the dependent variable and *'age'* as the fixed effect, with *'child ID'* as the random effect. Only *'age'* had a significant effect on the target child production ratio ($\beta = 0.261$, $SE = 0.028$, and $p < 0.001$), controlling for *'gender'*, *'linguistic environment'*, and *'socio-economic status'* (all not significant).

VCM metrics allowed us to refine our evaluation of child production with age. We applied it to our set of selected children and found (Figure 3) that the increase in speaking ratio was due to an increase in real child speech (both canonical and non-canonical) rather than to a variation in the proportion of cries, laughter, or noise. In addition, we replicated findings from Warlaumont et al. (2014), who tested the evolution of speech-related vocalization ratio (versus non-speech-related) produced by the target child. Using our own pipeline and analysis, we also found a significant increase in this ratio with age while controlling for all metadata ($\beta = 0.219$, $SE = 0.022$, $p < 0.001$) (See Appendix C.1).

6.2 Interactional metrics

Conversations arguably constitute the most important aspect of the linguistic environment. First, we approached this by examining temporal contingencies (Bloom et al., 1987; Warlaumont et al., 2014) between the child and the other voices in the recordings. Specifically, we analyzed instances of target child productions followed by another participant, as well as target child productions preceded by other participants. Working with manually transcribed data, Nikolaus et al. (2022) explored the effect of time-contingent responses on children's intelligibility. These studies found that (1) caregivers provided more time-contingent responses to intelligible utterances from the child and (2) children

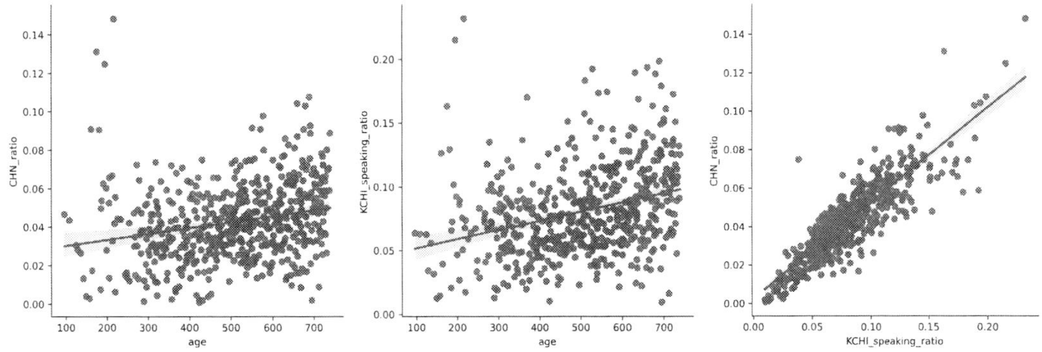

(a) LENA (b) VTC (c) Correlation ($r = 0.862$)

Figure 1: Target Child Speaking Time Ratio for (a) LENA (controlled for child id, $\beta = 0.159$; SE = 0.027; p < 0.001); (b) VTC ($\beta = 0.242$; SE = 0.029; p < 0.001) and (c) correlation plot between LENA and VTC. All children included (n=20). Age in days.

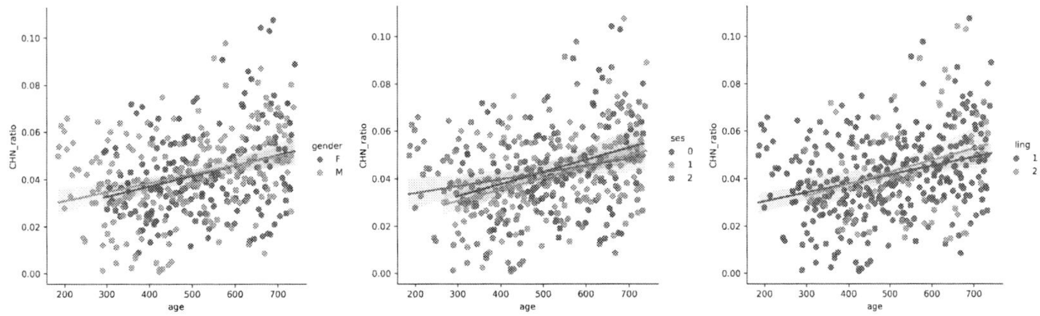

(a) Gender (b) Socio Economic Status (c) Linguistic Context

Figure 2: Target child Production Time (from LENA) differentiating for (a) gender ; (b) socio-economic status ; (c) linguistic background. Only age is significant. The three other variables are not. See Appendix D for details. Selected children. Age in days.

produced more intelligible utterances if their caregivers were responsive. Then, we investigated the "social feedback loop" as proposed by Warlaumont et al. (2014).

We employed a similar approach for both tools at our disposal. For *CHILD>ADULT* contingencies, we selected all target child productions and checked whether there was a production from an adult (MAL + FEM) participant **1 second after**. While LENA metrics extract similar information, we aimed to use the same method for both tools to enable a direct comparison. Figure 4 depicts the comparison for *CHILD>ADULT* contingencies. We also looked at ANY>CHILD contingencies by considering any activity occurring **2 seconds before**[1] before a child production. Figure 5 provides the VTC extraction for *ANY>CHILD* contingencies (additional combinations are included in Appendix E). We tested, for VTC data, the relationship between *age* and temporal contingencies for *CHILD>ADULT* ($\beta = 0.326$, $SE = 0.026$, $p < 0.001$) and *ANY>CHILD* ($\beta = 0.158$, $SE = 0.030$, $p < 0.001$), while controlling for gender, linguistic environment, and socio-economic status. This result was further refined by replicating the second finding from Warlaumont et al. (2014) on our dataset (and with LENA metrics this time). Specifically, we confirmed that children's speech-related productions tend to elicit more feedback from adults (See Appendix C.2).

Finally, we also replicated Warlaumont's result about the social loop on our data. We tested whether initial speech-related CHILD productions

[1]We considered allowing for a longer gap for children's follow-up to be appropriate. To count "turns", LENA metrics use a 5-second threshold.

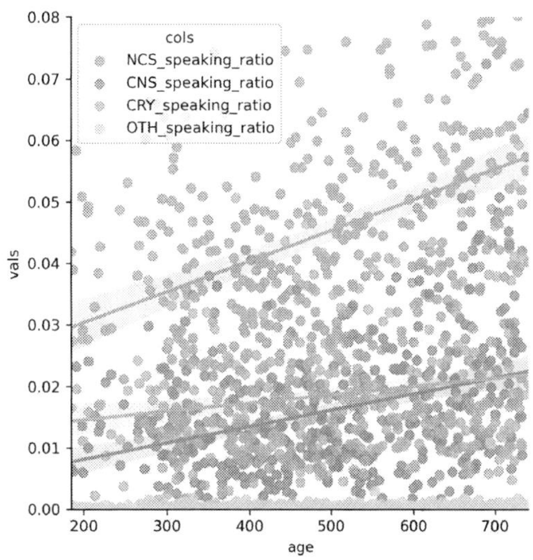

Figure 3: Speech vs. Non-speech VCM extraction for the selected children.

that were followed by an ADULT production 1 second after[2] were more likely to be followed by a speech-related CHILD production than a non-speech CHILD production within 3.5 seconds, compared to initial speech-related CHILD productions that did not receive an adult response.[3] This is illustrated in Figure 6, which shows the difference in speech-related / non-speech related ratio in child's production after an adult's response versus no response. This difference is positive, indicating that adult responses to children's speech-related productions tend to increase the proportion of child speech-related follow-ups.

7 Discussion

The collection and investigation of our original corpus in French households facilitated the comparison of different analysis tools and the replication of previous results within the same age ranges.

First, we identified a robust relationship between target child production metrics and age. As expected, we did not observe a similar significant change for adult voices. However, the evolution was also positive and significant for other children's voices ($\beta = 0.179$, $SE = 0.027$, $p < 0.001$). This can be attributed to the behavioral path of siblings as well as other children in kindergartens. All these results were obtained using both LENA and VTC pipelines. Finally, we found coherent results in line with existing literature and across the tools we used. These results strengthen our confidence in both our recording protocol and in the metrics extraction and analysis.

These comments hold for interactional metrics as well: the increases in temporal contingencies involving the children were consistent with findings from previous studies (Warlaumont et al., 2014; Nikolaus et al., 2022). We calculated temporal contingencies in a way that ensured these increases were not influenced by the overall amount of child productions.

Furthermore, our more detailed analysis (depicted in Figure 3) and the replication of Warlaumont's first results, showed that the increase in child's productions with age was due to speech-related productions and not to vegetative sounds or noise. In summary, our data show that children do produce more speech while growing up in their first two years of life. These increased productions are temporally contingent on other speakers, regardless of the initiator of the interaction (target child or other speaker).

This is further elaborated by the replication of Warlaumont's third result about the social loop that showed the benefit of follow-up productions of adult feedback on children's speech. Contrary to Warlaumont et al. (2014) (but in line with Bergelson et al. (2023) we did not find any effect of parental SES, gender, or linguistic environment on children's productions. This was the same for temporal contingencies used as a proxy for measuring linguistic interaction with the child.

Other studies have attempted to dive further into linguistic metrics from large child-caregiver datasets. Some refined the speech contingencies to distinguish corrective feedback or to approach the grammaticality evaluation of the productions in these datasets (Nikolaus et al., 2023). However, those datasets have been manually transcribed, while ours did not (and will not) receive such a transcription. A second major difference is the age range of the children. Most of the existing studies involved children from 12-24 months up to

[2]Following Warlaumont et al. (2014) and Nikolaus et al. (2022), who followed Oller et al. (2010), which used a 1-second window to extract relevant vocal activity to investigate the "social feedback loop" for children between 8 to 48 months.

[3]This 3.5 second is between the end of initial CHILD production and the start of the following one. The delay is to allow for a potential ADULT response to occur in between. It is not possible to use the ADULT production for proposing a simpler time threshold for the following utterance since there is not always an ADULT production in-between.

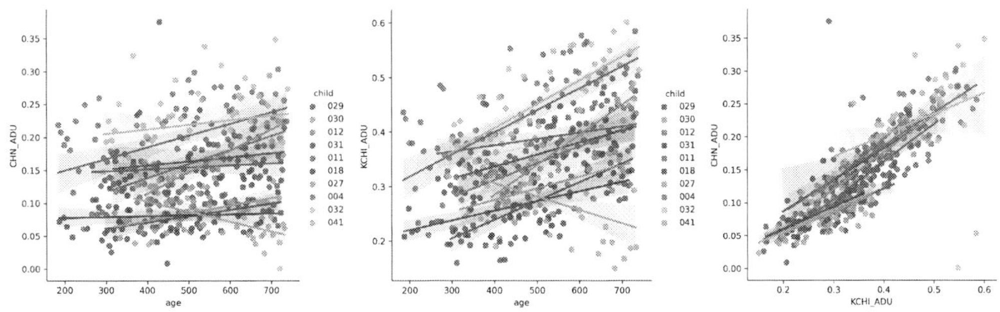

(a) LENA (b) VTC (c) Correlation ($r = 0.831$

Figure 4: CHILD>ADULT contingencies for (a) LENA ($\beta = 0.131$; SE = 0.024; p < 0.001), (b) VTC ($\beta = 0.130$, $SE = 0.024$, $p < 0.001$) and (c) correlation plot. Selected children. Age in days.

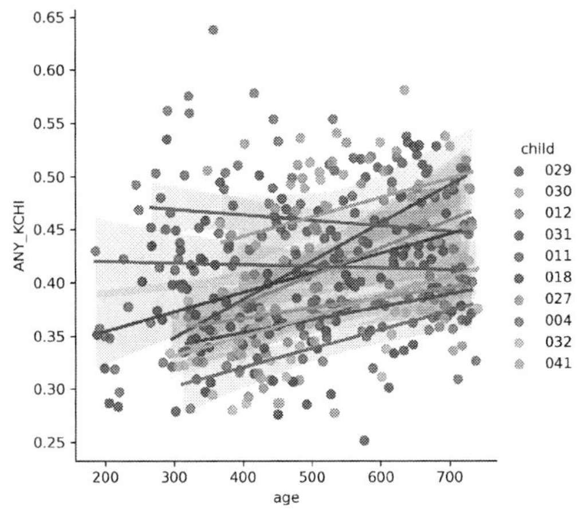

Figure 5: ANY>CHILD contingencies from VTC speech extraction. ($\beta = 0.158$, $SE = 0.030$, $p < 0.001$)

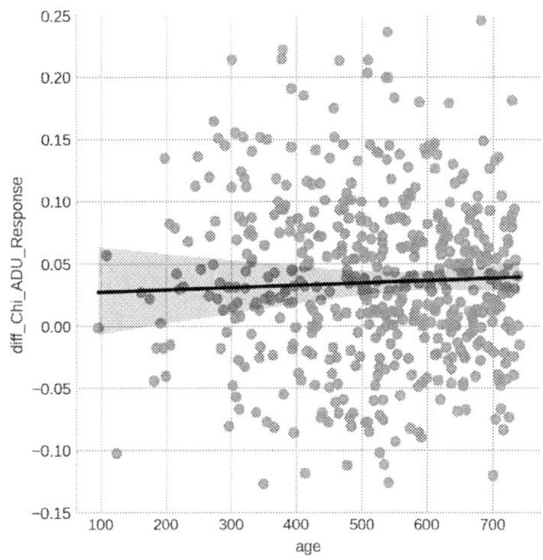

Figure 6: Child ratio difference between Child speech and non-speech productions depending on whether or not an initial child speech-related utterance was responded by an adult or not (positive mean : indicating a tendency for more speech-related responses), replication of Warlaumont et al. (2014).

later ages. This inevitably changes the nature and characteristics of the metrics that can be extracted. Another trend of work focuses on phonetic learning based on daylong recordings, such as Lavechin et al. (2024) on perceptual attunement. Finally, in a more cultural and typological direction, Bergelson et al. (2023) studied a global sample of 1,001 child-centered audio capturing 2- to 48-months-olds from many countries and various cultural backgrounds.

8 Conclusion

This work first constitutes a replication of earlier results on daylong recordings, on a completely new and independent data set, using two different tools. This contributes to answer Cruz Blandón et al. (2023)'s call for more and better meta-studies on long recordings. Indeed, despite their creation cost, daylong recordings' significance is growing in cognitive science. Showing that these data sets, despite their noisy nature, do present enough reliability to gain insights about the children's language and communicative skills development is crucial.

The second contribution consists of the characterization of our data set itself. It is a large data set (>8000 hours of recordings) that is still growing at the time of writing. It is unique by being truly longitudinal with some children's environments being recorded over a two-year span. Finally, other experimental data were collected longitudinally in the same sample of infants. These are beyond the scope of this paper but open up the possibilities of cross-analyses between the characterization of the linguistic environment and other experimental results regarding language development. The present study, therefore, constitutes a crucial first step in this direction through the thorough exploration of the data set, and by considering individual variability.

From here, we now plan to refine the analyses by entering into more linguistic characterizations of these productions in terms of richness. We will consider tools that allow for more phonological measures such as Räsänen et al. (2021) and more content-based metrics (Nikolaus et al., 2023, 2024) that have been used so far only on transcript-based corpora from CHILDES (MacWhinney, 2000) and that can be now explored on daylong recordings thanks to the improvement of automatic speech recognition engines.

9 Limitations

One major limitation of this work is the absence of manual annotation. For legal and ethical reasons, we are not in position to perform extensive manual annotations of raw audio data, as well as sharing raw audio. We needed to find other ways to check the reliability of our dataset. By replicating previous results from the literature and comparing different computational tools, we reinforced our trust in our dataset and overcame this constraint. All metrics derived from the corpus related to this paper as well as for future work will be made available in the `LLDC` public repository on Ortolang institutional platform `https://www.ortolang.fr/`. Moreover the code for producing the analyses presented in this paper is available at : `https://github.com/prevotlaurent/LENA_CMCL`.

Acknowledgments

We thank all the babies and their families for participating in the study. We also thank the directors and the staff of the Babilou daycare centers where the babies were evaluated. We thank Mathilde Gaujard for her help in the recruitment and data collection. This research has been supported by an ANR grant ("BabyLang project", ANR-20-CE28-0017) to CF and a CNRS 80PRIME grant to CF and LP ("LangDev project"). This work, carried out within the Institut Convergence ILCB (ANR-16-CONV-0002), has benefited from support from the French government, managed by the French National Agency for Research (ANR) and the Excellence Initiative of Aix-Marseille University (A*MIDEX).

References

Najla Al Futaisi, Zixing Zhang, Alejandrina Cristia, Anne Warlaumont, and Bjorn Schuller. 2019. Vcm-net: Weakly supervised learning for automatic infant vocalisation maturity analysis. In *2019 International Conference on Multimodal Interaction*, pages 205–209.

Miranda Aragon and Christine Yoshinaga-Itano. 2012. Using language environment analysis to improve outcomes for children who are deaf or hard of hearing. In *Seminars in Speech and Language*, volume 33, pages 340–353. Thieme Medical Publishers.

Helen Benedict. 1979. Early lexical development: Comprehension and production. *Journal of child language*, 6(2):183–200.

Elika Bergelson and Richard N Aslin. 2017. Nature and origins of the lexicon in 6-mo-olds. *Proceedings of the National Academy of Sciences*, 114(49):12916–12921.

Elika Bergelson, Melanie Soderstrom, Iris-Corinna Schwarz, Caroline F Rowland, Nairán Ramírez-Esparza, Lisa R. Hamrick, Ellen Marklund, Marina Kalashnikova, Ava Guez, Marisa Casillas, et al. 2023. Everyday language input and production in 1,001 children from six continents. *Proceedings of the National Academy of Sciences*, 120(52):e2300671120.

Kathleen Bloom, Ann Russell, and Karen Wassenberg. 1987. Turn taking affects the quality of infant vocalizations. *Journal of child language*, 14(2):211–227.

Hervé Bredin, Ruiqing Yin, Juan Manuel Coria, Gregory Gelly, Pavel Korshunov, Marvin Lavechin, Diego Fustes, Hadrien Titeux, Wassim Bouaziz, and Marie-Philippe Gill. 2020. Pyannote. audio: neural building blocks for speaker diarization. In *ICASSP 2020-2020 IEEE International Conference on Acoustics, Speech and Signal Processing (ICASSP)*, pages 7124–7128. IEEE.

Tobias Busch, Anouk Sangen, Filiep Vanpoucke, and Astrid van Wieringen. 2018. Correlation and agreement between language environment analysis (lena™) and manual transcription for dutch natural language recordings. *Behavior research methods*, 50:1921–1932.

Mélanie Canault, Marie-Thérèse Le Normand, Samy Foudil, Natalie Loundon, and Hung Thai-Van. 2016. Reliability of the language environment analysis system (lena™) in european french. *Behavior research methods*, 48:1109–1124.

Marisa Casillas, John Bunce, Melanie Soderstrom, Celia Rosemberg, Maia Migdalek, Florencia Alam, Alejandra Stein, and Hallie Garrison. 2017. Introduction: the aclew das template. `https://osf.io/aknjv`.

Marisa Casillas and Alejandrina Cristia. 2019. A step-by-step guide to collecting and analyzing long-format speech environment (lfse) recordings. *Collabra: Psychology*, 5(1):24.

Melinda Caskey, Bonnie Stephens, Richard Tucker, and Betty Vohr. 2011. Importance of parent talk on the development of preterm infant vocalizations. *Pediatrics*, 128(5):910–916.

Melinda Caskey, Bonnie Stephens, Richard Tucker, and Betty Vohr. 2014. Adult talk in the nicu with preterm infants and developmental outcomes. *Pediatrics*, 133(3):e578–e584.

Marie Cheour, Rita Ceponiene, Anne Lehtokoski, Aavo Luuk, Jüri Allik, Kimmo Alho, and Risto Näätänen. 1998. Development of language-specific phoneme representations in the infant brain. *Nature neuroscience*, 1(5):351–353.

Dimitri A Christakis, Jill Gilkerson, Jeffrey A Richards, Frederick J Zimmerman, Michelle M Garrison, Dongxin Xu, Sharmistha Gray, and Umit Yapanel. 2009. Audible television and decreased adult words, infant vocalizations, and conversational turns: a population-based study. *Archives of pediatrics & adolescent medicine*, 163(6):554–558.

Alejandrina Cristia, Marvin Lavechin, Camila Scaff, Melanie Soderstrom, Caroline Rowland, Okko Räsänen, John Bunce, and Elika Bergelson. 2021. A thorough evaluation of the language environment analysis (lena) system. *Behavior research methods*, 53:467–486.

María Andrea Cruz Blandón, Alejandrina Cristia, and Okko Räsänen. 2023. Introducing meta-analysis in the evaluation of computational models of infant language development. *Cognitive Science*, 47(7):e13307.

Margaret Cychosz, Rachel Romeo, Melanie Soderstrom, Camila Scaff, Hillary Ganek, Alejandrina Cristia, Marisa Casillas, Kaya De Barbaro, Janet Y Bang, and Adriana Weisleder. 2020. Longform recordings of everyday life: Ethics for best practices. *Behavior research methods*, 52:1951–1969.

Florian Eyben, Klaus R Scherer, Björn W Schuller, Johan Sundberg, Elisabeth André, Carlos Busso, Laurence Y Devillers, Julien Epps, Petri Laukka, Shrikanth S Narayanan, et al. 2015. The geneva minimalistic acoustic parameter set (gemaps) for voice research and affective computing. *IEEE transactions on affective computing*, 7(2):190–202.

Florian Eyben, Martin Wöllmer, and Björn Schuller. 2010. Opensmile: the munich versatile and fast open-source audio feature extractor. In *Proceedings of the 18th ACM international conference on Multimedia*, pages 1459–1462.

Hillary Ganek and Alice Eriks-Brophy. 2018. Language environment analysis (lena) system investigation of day long recordings in children: A literature review. *Journal of Communication Disorders*, 72:77–85.

Hillary V Ganek and Alice Eriks-Brophy. 2017. A concise protocol for the validation of language environment analysis (lena) conversational turn counts in vietnamese. *Communication Disorders Quarterly*, 39(2):371–380.

Lucas Gautheron, Nicolas Rochat, and Alejandrina Cristia. 2023. Managing, storing, and sharing long-form recordings and their annotations. *Language Resources and Evaluation*, 57(1):343–375.

Jill Gilkerson and Jeffrey A Richards. 2008. The lena natural language study. *Boulder, CO: LENA Foundation. Retrieved March*, 3(2009):15–17.

Jill Gilkerson and Jeffrey A Richards. 2009. The power of talk. *Impact of adult talk, conversational turns and TV during the critical 0-4 years of child development: Boulder, CO: LENA Foundation.*

Jill Gilkerson, Jeffrey A Richards, Steven F Warren, Judith K Montgomery, Charles R Greenwood, D Kimbrough Oller, John HL Hansen, and Terrance D Paul. 2017. Mapping the early language environment using all-day recordings and automated analysis. *American journal of speech-language pathology*, 26(2):248–265.

Jill Gilkerson, Jeffrey A Richards, Steven F Warren, D Kimbrough Oller, Rosemary Russo, and Betty Vohr. 2018. Language experience in the second year of life and language outcomes in late childhood. *Pediatrics*, 142(4).

Jill Gilkerson, Yiwen Zhang, Dongxin Xu, Jeffrey A Richards, Xiaojuan Xu, Fan Jiang, James Harnsberger, and Keith Topping. 2015. Evaluating language environment analysis system performance for chinese: A pilot study in shanghai. *Journal of Speech, Language, and Hearing Research*, 58(2):445–452.

Beverly A Goldfield and J Steven Reznick. 1990. Early lexical acquisition: Rate, content, and the vocabulary spurt. *Journal of child language*, 17(1):171–183.

Betty Hart and Todd R Risley. 1992. American parenting of language-learning children: Persisting differences in family-child interactions observed in natural home environments. *Developmental psychology*, 28(6):1096.

Eshin Jolly. 2018. Pymer4: Connecting r and python for linear mixed modeling. *Journal of Open Source Software*, 3(31):862.

Heidi Keller, Elke Hentschel, Relindis Dzeaye Yovsi, Bettina Lamm, Monika Abels, and Verena Haas. 2004. The psycho-linguistic embodiment of parental ethnotheories: A new avenue to understanding cultural processes in parental reasoning. *Culture & Psychology*, 10(3):293–330.

Marvin Lavechin, Ruben Bousbib, Hervé Bredin, Emmanuel Dupoux, and Alejandrina Cristia. 2020. An open-source voice type classifier for child-centered daylong recordings. In *Interspeech 2020 - Conference of the International Speech Communication Association*, Shanghai / Virtual, China.

Marvin Lavechin, Maureen de Seyssel, Marianne Métais, Florian Metze, Abdelrahman Mohamed, Hervé Bredin, Emmanuel Dupoux, and Alejandrina Cristia. 2024. Modeling early phonetic acquisition from child-centered audio data. *Cognition*, 245:105734.

Brian MacWhinney. 2000. The childes project. *Computational Linguistics*, 26(4):657–657.

Jennifer K Mendoza and Caitlin M Fausey. 2021. Everyday music in infancy. *Developmental Science*, 24(6):e13122.

Thierry Nazzi and Josiane Bertoncini. 2003. Before and after the vocabulary spurt: Two modes of word acquisition? *Developmental Science*, 6(2):136–142.

Mitja Nikolaus, Abhishek Agrawal, Petros Kaklamanis, Alex Warstadt, and Abdellah Fourtassi. 2024. Automatic annotation of grammaticality in child-caregiver conversations.

Mitja Nikolaus, Laurent Prévot, and Abdellah Fourtassi. 2022. Communicative feedback as a mechanism supporting the production of intelligible speech in early childhood. In *Proceedings of the Annual Meeting of the Cognitive Science Society*, volume 44.

Mitja Nikolaus, Laurent Prévot, and Abdellah Fourtassi. 2023. Communicative feedback in response to children's grammatical errors. In *Proceedings of the Annual Meeting of the Cognitive Science Society*, volume 45.

D Kimbrough Oller, Partha Niyogi, Sharmistha Gray, Jeffrey A Richards, Jill Gilkerson, Dongxin Xu, Umit Yapanel, and Steven F Warren. 2010. Automated vocal analysis of naturalistic recordings from children with autism, language delay, and typical development. *Proceedings of the National Academy of Sciences*, 107(30):13354–13359.

Adriel John Orena, Krista Byers-Heinlein, and Linda Polka. 2019. Reliability of the language environment analysis recording system in analyzing french–english bilingual speech. *Journal of Speech, Language, and Hearing Research*, 62(7):2491–2500.

Soyeong Pae, Hyojin Yoon, Ahyoung Seol, Jill Gilkerson, Jeffrey A Richards, Lin Ma, and Keith Topping. 2016. Effects of feedback on parent–child language with infants and toddlers in korea. *First Language*, 36(6):549–569.

Naja Ferjan Ramírez and Daniel S Hippe. 2024. Estimating infants' language exposure: A comparison of random and volume sampling from daylong recordings collected in a bilingual community. *Infant Behavior and Development*, 75:101943.

Okko Räsänen, Shreyas Seshadri, Marvin Lavechin, Alejandrina Cristia, and Marisa Casillas. 2021. Alice: An open-source tool for automatic measurement of phoneme, syllable, and word counts from child-centered daylong recordings. *Behavior Research Methods*, 53:818–835.

Chiara Semenzin, Lisa Hamrick, Amanda Seidl, Bridgette Kelleher, and Alejandrina Cristia. 2021. Towards large-scale data annotation of audio from wearables: validating zooniverse annotations of infant vocalization types. In *2021 IEEE Spoken Language Technology Workshop (SLT)*, pages 1079–1085. IEEE.

Melanie Soderstrom and Kelsey Wittebolle. 2013. When do caregivers talk? the influences of activity and time of day on caregiver speech and child vocalizations in two childcare environments. *PloS one*, 8(11):e80646.

Yaya Sy, William Havard, Marvin Lavechin, Emmanuel Dupoux, and Alejandrina Cristia. 2023. Measuring language development from child-centered recordings. In *Interspeech 2023*, pages 4618–4622. ISCA.

Anne S Warlaumont, Kunmi Sobowale, and Caitlin M Fausey. 2022. Daylong mobile audio recordings reveal multitimescale dynamics in infants' vocal productions and auditory experiences. *Current directions in psychological science*, 31(1):12–19.

Anne S. Warlaumont, Anne S. Warlaumont, Jeffrey A. Richards, Jeffrey A. Richards, Jill Gilkerson, Jill Gilkerson, D. Kimbrough Oller, and D. Kimbrough Oller. 2014. A social feedback loop for speech development and its reduction in autism. *Psychological Science*.

Steven F Warren, Jill Gilkerson, Jeffrey A Richards, D Kimbrough Oller, Dongxin Xu, Umit Yapanel, and Sharmistha Gray. 2010. What automated vocal analysis reveals about the vocal production and language learning environment of young children with autism. *Journal of autism and developmental disorders*, 40:555–569.

Adriana Weisleder and Anne Fernald. 2013. Talking to children matters: Early language experience strengthens processing and builds vocabulary. *Psychological science*, 24(11):2143–2152.

Janet F Werker and Richard C Tees. 1984. Cross-language speech perception: Evidence for perceptual reorganization during the first year of life. *Infant behavior and development*, 7(1):49–63.

Dongxin Xu, Umit Yapanel, and Sharmi Gray. 2009. Reliability of the lena language environment analysis system in young children's natural home environment. *Boulder, CO: Lena Foundation*, pages 1–16.

Dongxin Xu, Umit Yapanel, Sharmi Gray, and Charles T Baer. 2008a. The lena language environment analysis system: The interpreted time segments (its) file. *Boulder, CO: Lena Foundation*, pages 1–7.

Dongxin Xu, Umit Yapanel, Sharmi Gray, Jill Gilkerson, Jeff Richards, and John Hansen. 2008b. Signal processing for young child speech language development. In *First Workshop on Child, Computer and Interaction*.

Frederick J Zimmerman, Jill Gilkerson, Jeffrey A Richards, Dimitri A Christakis, Dongxin Xu, Sharmistha Gray, and Umit Yapanel. 2009. Teaching by listening: The importance of adult-child conversations to language development. *Pediatrics*, 124(1):342–349.

A Validation studies

Reference	Language(s)	r(AWC)	r(CVC)	r(CTC)
Busch et al. (2018)	Dutch	0.87	0.77	0.52
Canault et al. (2016)	European French	0.64	0.71	NI
Caskey et al. (2014)	American English and Spanish	0.93	NI	NI
Cristia et al. (2021)	American English	0.76	0.76	0.57
Ganek and Eriks-Brophy (2017)	Vietnamese	NI	NI	0.70*
Gilkerson et al. (2015)	Mandarin	0.72	0.84; 0.70**	0.72
Pae et al. (2016)	Korean	0.72	NI	0.67
Weisleder and Fernald (2013)	Spanish	0.80	NI	NI
Xu et al. (2008b)	American English	0.82	0.76	NI

Table 3: Pearson's r correlation scores between human and LENA automatic annotations for AWC, CVC and CTC in various languages. NI = No Information.*agreement score assessed via a Spearman rank correlation test. **0.84 for speech-like vocalizations, 0.70 for non-speech-like vocalizations.

B Meta-data

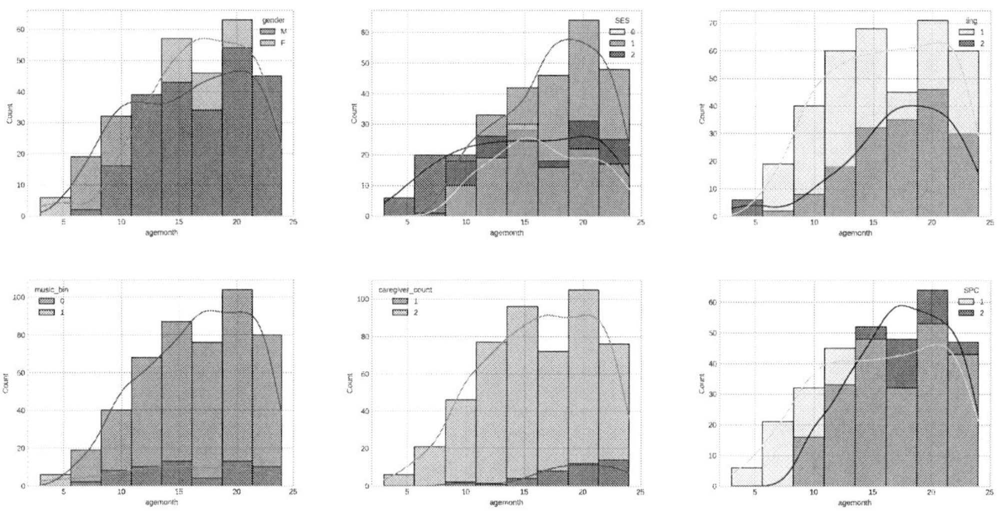

Figure 7: Distribution of session through age, depending on various demographic information: from left to right, top to bottom : gender, socio-economic status (SES: low,mid,high), linguistic environment (1:monolingual, 2: plurilingual), music practice at home(yes/no), number of cargiver, socio-professional category of the parents.

C Replication (Warlaumont et al., 2014)

C.1 Ratio of Speech Related Vocalisations

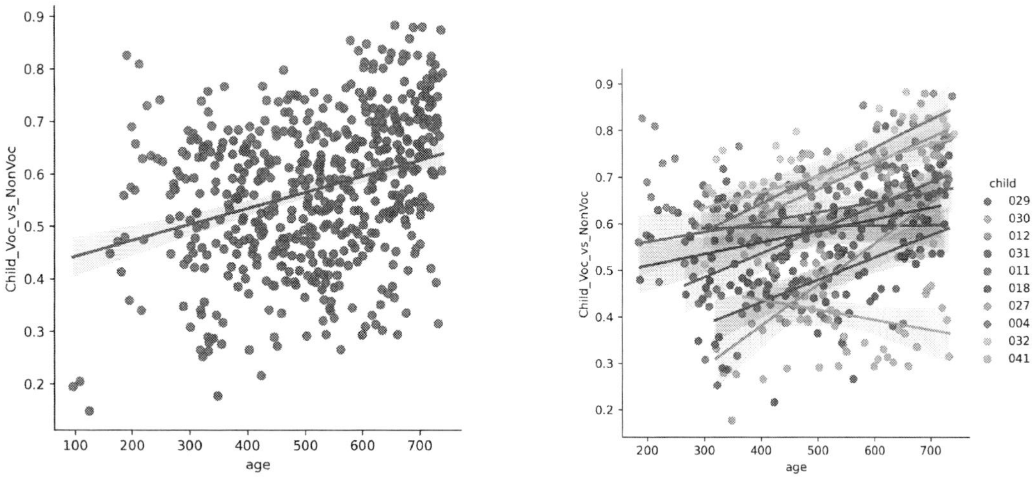

(a) All children

(b) Selected Children

Figure 8: Ratio between the child total amount of speech related productions (`ChildVocDuration`) and all production (including Non speech related) (`ChildNonVocDuration`)(age significant $\beta = 0.219$, $p < 0.001$; `child_id` and all metadata variables not significant). Age in days.

The Figure 8 presents the first result of (Warlaumont et al., 2014), which is that the speech related percentage productions of children increase with age. See the figure caption and below for statistics.

```
Formula:
Child_Voc_vs_NonVoc~age_rs+gender+ses_bin+ling_bin+gender*ses_bin
                       +gender*ling_bin+ling_bin*ses_bin+(1|child)}

Number of observations: 540  Groups: {'child': 20.0}
```

Random effects:

	Name	Var	Std
child	(Intercept)	0.008	0.090
Residual		0.010	0.098

Fixed effects:

	Estimate	2.5_ci	97.5_ci	SE	DF	T-stat	P-val	Sig
(Intercept)	0.443	0.356	0.530	0.044	17.986	9.964	0.000	***
age_rs	0.219	0.175	0.262	0.022	532.437	9.910	0.000	***
genderM	0.001	-0.114	0.117	0.059	13.872	0.021	0.984	
ses_binL	0.028	-0.113	0.169	0.072	14.613	0.385	0.706	
ling_binP	-0.111	-0.245	0.024	0.069	14.548	-1.611	0.129	
genderM:ses_binL	0.104	-0.143	0.351	0.126	14.711	0.824	0.423	
genderM:ling_binP	0.096	-0.109	0.301	0.104	14.535	0.917	0.374	

C.2 Adult response to Child speech vs. non-speech productions

Figure 9 illustrates that children's speech-related productions tend to elicit more feedback from adults.

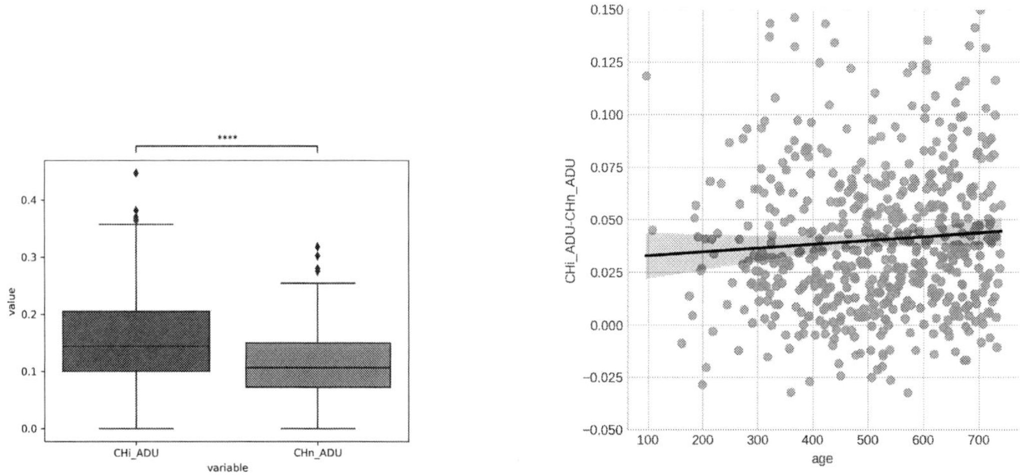

(a) Adult response to Child speech vs. non-speech productions (Mann-Whitney-Wilcoxon test two-sided, ****: p <= 1.00e-04)

(b) Adult responses ratio difference between Child speech and non-speech productions (positive mean indicating a tendency for more responses to speech-related productions.

Figure 9: Adult response to Child speech vs. non-speech productions, replication of the second result of (Warlaumont et al., 2014)

C.3 Social Loop

The Figure 6 present the replication of the result on the social loop from (Warlaumont et al., 2014). More precisely it shows that given a children speech-related utterance, adult providing a response increase the proportion of speech-related (instead of non-speech related) follow-up utterance from the child.

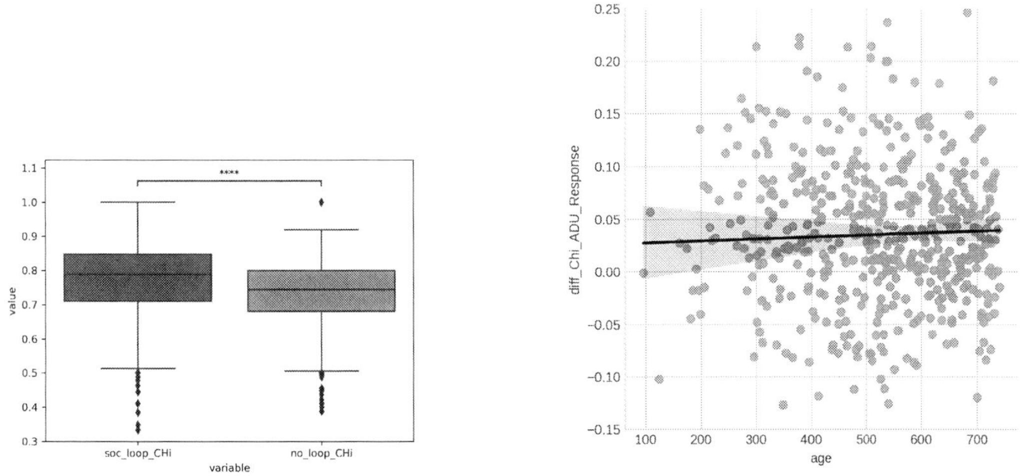

(a) Child speech ratio (vs. non-speech) follow-up depending on whether or not an initial child speech-related utterance was responded by an adult or not (Mann-Whitney-Wilcoxon test two-sided, ****: p <= 1.00e-04)

(b) Child ratio difference between Child speech and non-speech productions depending on whether or not an initial child speech-related utterance was responded by an adult or not (positive mean : indicating a tendency for more speech-related responses)

Figure 10: Adult response to Child speech vs. non-speech productions, replication of the second result of (Warlaumont et al., 2014) (left repeated from 6 in main text)

D Producing time ratios

The Figures 11-13 are showing the ration of the time occupied by a category when available for both LENA and VTC as well as the correlation metrics. The Figure 14 focuses on individual children recordings from the selected data set.

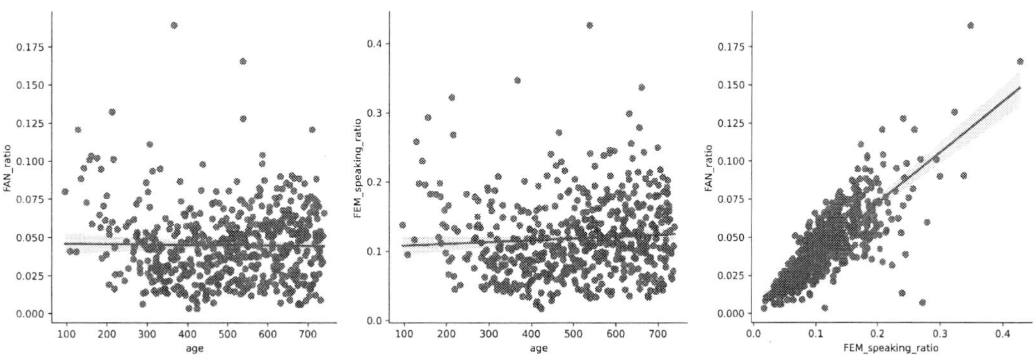

(a) LENA

(b) VTC

(c) Correlation ($r = 0.773$)

Figure 11: Female Speaking Time Ratio for LENA (a), VTC (b) and correlation plot between LENA and VTC (c). All children included (n = 20). Age in days.

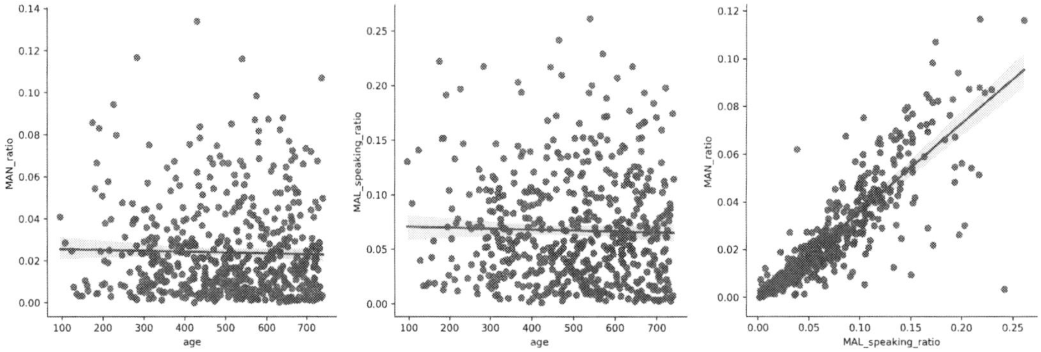

(a) LENA (b) VTC (c) Correlation ($r = 0.871$)

Figure 12: Male Speaking Time Ratio for LENA (a), VTC (b) and correlation plot between LENA and VTC (c). All children included (n = 20). Age in days.

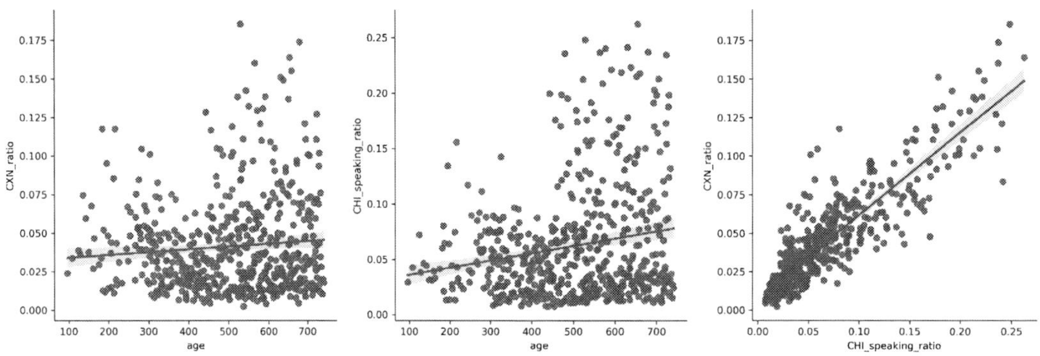

(a) LENA (b) VTC (c) Correlation ($r = 0.917$)

Figure 13: Other child (than target child) Speaking Time Ratio for LENA (a), VTC (b) and correlation plot between LENA and VTC (c). All children included (n = 20). Age in days.

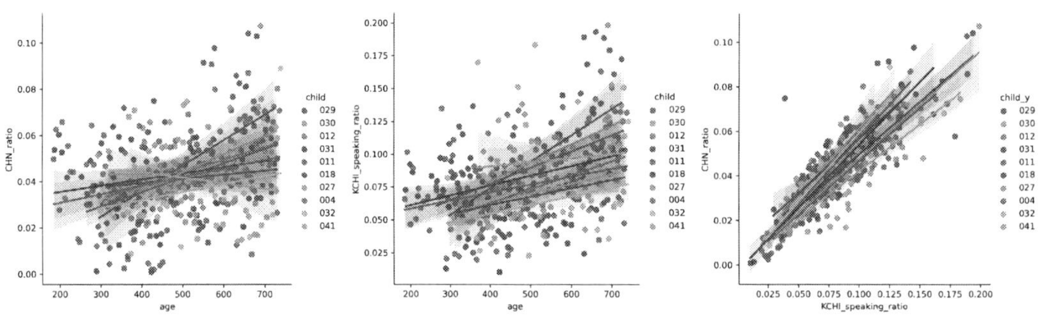

(a) LENA (b) VTC (c) Corelation

Figure 14: Target Child Speaking Time Ratio for LENA (a), VTC (b) and correlation plot (c). Selected children (n = 10, age span $\geq$ 9 months). Age in days.

```
Formula: chn_rs~age_rs+gender+ses_bin+ling_bin+gender*ses_bin
         +gender*ling_bin+ling_bin*ses_bin+(1|child)

Number of observations: 540  Groups: {'child': 20.0}
```

Random effects:

	Name	Var	Std
child	(Intercept)	0.012	0.109
Residual		0.014	0.119

Fixed effects:

	Estimate	2.5_ci	97.5_ci	SE	DF	T-stat	P-val	Sig
(Intercept)	0.218	0.113	0.323	0.054	15.968	4.059	0.001	***
age_rs	0.163	0.110	0.215	0.027	532.415	6.063	0.000	***
genderM	-0.024	-0.163	0.115	0.071	12.270	-0.336	0.742	
ses_binL	-0.104	-0.275	0.066	0.087	12.936	-1.201	0.251	
ling_binP	0.046	-0.117	0.208	0.083	12.878	0.549	0.593	
genderM:ses_binL	0.104	-0.194	0.402	0.152	13.024	0.684	0.506	
genderM:ling_binP	-0.040	-0.288	0.207	0.126	12.866	-0.319	0.755	

E Temporal Contingencies Plots

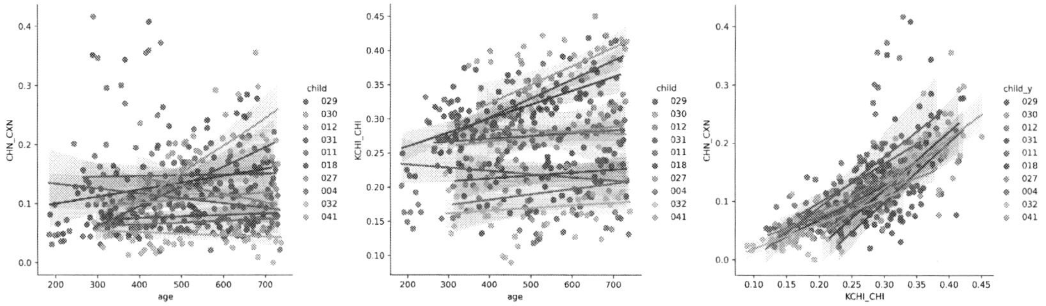

(a) LENA (b) VTC (c) Correlation

Figure 15: CHILD>OTHER CHILD contingencies for LENA (a), VTC (b) and correlation plot (c). Selected children. Age in days.

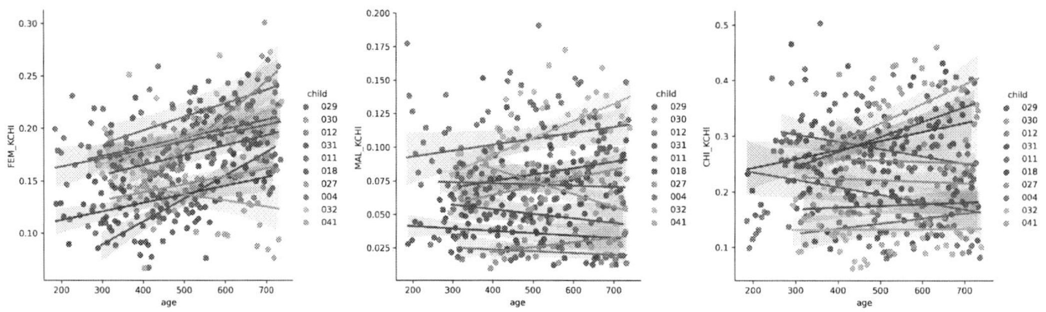

(a) Female>Child (b) Male>Child (c) Other Child > Child

Figure 16: FEM>CHILD, MAL>CHILD, and OTHER CHILD > CHILD contingencies with VTC. Selected children. Age in days.

F Lena Annotation Process

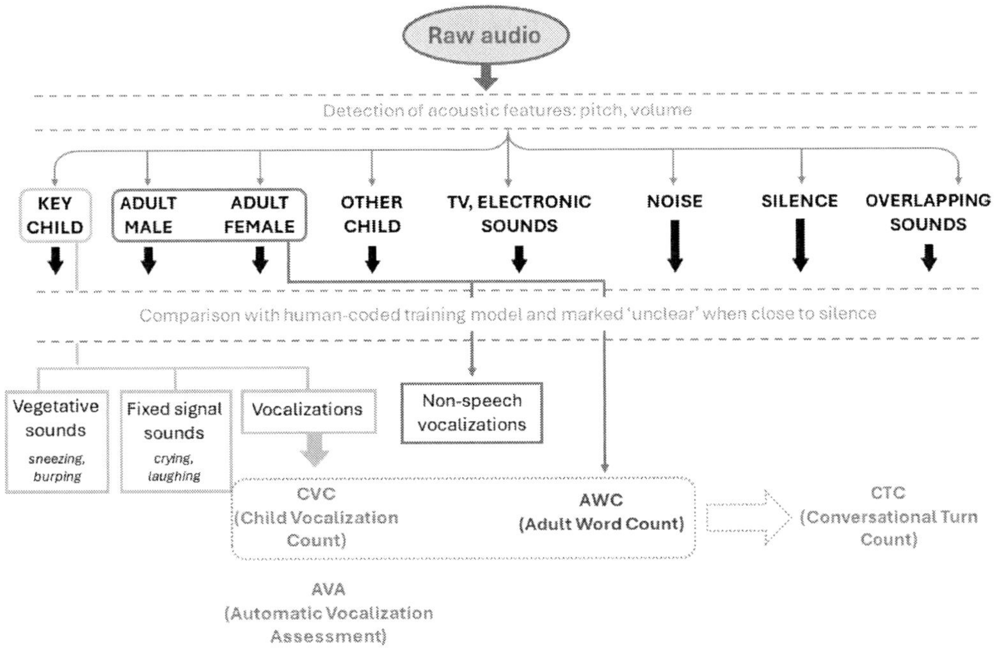

Figure 17: LENA annotation process.

G Instructions given to the families to use LENA

The instructions that were given to families were the following:

1. *When to record: once a week for a full day, until the child is 24 months old. Please prefer a day when you spend some time with your child (on the weekends for example). If you have no other choice, you can activate the device at daycare occasionally. We recommend that you record always on the same day of the week, to create a routine. Keep in mind that any day is a good day to record!*
2. *How to record: the instructions were kept identical to those provided by the LENA team. 1) Switch it on by pressing POWER; the screen should display "Paused". 2) Press RECORD for about 4 seconds; the screen should display "Recording". 3) Put the device in your child's shirt, the screen facing out, and close the pocket. 4) Leave it until the device turns off on its own at the end of the day.*
3. *Some various recommendations: never put the device out of the shirt; don't cover it with too many clothing layers; avoid noisy places as much as possible; remove the shirt (but leave the recorder inside) and keep it nearby during bath or nap times.*
4. *What to do after recording: bring the device back to the daycare center before a specific day of the week. The recorder will be ready for another week at the end of this day.*

Analysing and Validating Language Complexity Metrics Across South American Indigenous Languages

Felipe Ribas Serras
Miguel de Mello Carpi
Matheus Castello Branco
Marcelo Finger
Institute of Mathematics and Statistics, University of São Paulo
R. do Matão, 1010 - Butantã, São Paulo - SP, Brazil, 05508-090
{frserras, miguel, matheus.castello, mfinger}@ime.usp.br

Abstract

Language complexity is an emerging concept critical for NLP and for quantitative and cognitive approaches to linguistics. In this work, we evaluate the behavior of a set of compression-based language complexity metrics when applied to a large set of native South American languages. Our goal is to validate the desirable properties of such metrics against a more diverse set of languages, guaranteeing the universality of the techniques developed on the basis of this type of theoretical artifact. Our analysis confirmed with statistical confidence most propositions about the metrics studied, affirming their robustness, despite showing less stability than when the same metrics were applied to Indo-European languages. We also observed that the trade-off between morphological and syntactic complexities is strongly related to language phylogeny.

1 Introduction

The development of means for quantifying linguistic properties is essential for cognitive approaches to computational linguistics, becoming simultaneously more challenging and useful as the property of interest is transversal to different languages and, therefore, an important clue for accessing cognitive processes behind human language. This is the case of language complexity.

The concept of language complexity, whether of an utterance or of a language as a whole, is instinctive for us. People know how to recognize when a text is written in a difficult or elaborate way and they usually recognize that certain languages are less or more complicated to learn depending on their linguistic background.

Informally, we can say that: (i) the *complexity of an utterance* encompasses the quantity and sophistication of linguistic constructs necessary to form and understand the utterance and (ii) *the complexity of a language as a whole* refers to the quantity and sophistication of communicative strategies available for the formation of such utterances in that language.

Despite a relative consensus around these intuitions, we lack established formal and quantifiable definitions of language complexity. It is difficult to find a definition that encompasses the heterogeneous range of human language manifestations, both in terms of different languages and of different levels in which meaning can be conveyed within a language.

Even in light of these challenges, it is crucial to establish rigorous, theoretically and experimentally validated definitions of language complexity. Both cognitive and non-cognitive approaches to Linguistics can significantly enhance their expressive capacity and theoretical framework. In NLP, complexity measures can be used in automatic text simplifiers, translators, domain-sensitive correctors and completers (Leal et al., 2023), but can also be integrated into the of training machine learning models, to increase performance (Sarti et al., 2021).

Another challenge for the construction of a robust theory for language complexity is that of inclusion: historically, the construction of tools and theories of human language has included Indo-European languages, to the detriment of other linguistic manifestations, e.g. American native languages. For a concept that aims to be transversal to different languages and provide universal insights into them and their underlying cognitive processes, as is the case with language complexity, it is necessary to include the broadest possible range of languages in its development and validation.

This inclusion is the focus of our work. Here, we examine a set of language complexity metrics derived from Information Theory, proposed in Juola (1998, 2005, 2008), and Ehret and Szmrecsanyi (2016). The authors ran several experiments with the proposed metrics, drawing on data from a sub-

Proceedings of the Workshop on Cognitive Modeling and Computational Linguistics, pages 152–165
August 15, 2024 ©2024 Association for Computational Linguistics

stantial set of languages, with a predominant focus on those belonging to the Indo-European language family.

Here, we repeat these experiments with data from South American indigenous languages, attempting to ascertain whether the desirable properties of these metrics remain solid when incorporating frequently excluded languages. We seek to verify the robustness of the proposed metrics and include a more diverse set of linguistic manifestations in the construction of a quantifiable theory of human language complexity.

Our text is structured as follows: In section 2, we present our theoretical background and related works; section 3 outlines our methodology, complexity metrics and its properties, the data used and the experimental pipeline employed; in section 4 we exhibit our results and, in section 5, we present our conclusions.

2 Related Works

Nichols (1998) was a pioneer in proposing a quantifiable language complexity metric. She defines the morphological complexity of a language as the number of inflection points in its typical sentence. She computed it for more than 200 languages. In this, work we evaluate the consistency of our targeted metrics with hers.

In contrast to the computational challenges of Nichols (1998)'s metric, Juola (1998, 2005, 2008) proposes a set of compression-based complexity metrics based on information theory. The author compares these metrics to alternatives, extend them to different linguistic tiers, and evaluate them on different parallel *corpora*. This family of metrics is the main object of study in this paper, with a focus on their behavior when applied to indigenous South American languages, not explored in the original works. Ehret and Szmrecsanyi (2016) suggests modifications to them, proposing improvements for eliminating potential spurious correlations, and experiment on semi-parallel and non-parallel data.

Several subsequent works draw directly or indirectly from the notion of compression-based complexity metrics (Juvonen, 2008; Sadeniemi et al., 2008; Fenk-Oczlon and Fenk, 2008; Ehret et al., 2021; Szmrecsanyi, 2021; Pellegrino et al., 2011; Ackerman and Malouf, 2013; Kettunen, 2014; Housen et al., 2019), in particular, to quantify the difficulty of acquiring a second language (Bulté and Housen, 2014; Clercq and Housen, 2019).

An alternative approach, which characterizes complexity as a function of linguistic features, was explored in Graesser et al. (2004, 2011); Graesser and McNamara (2011) for English and in Leal et al. (2023) for the Portuguese language. Similar works study language complexity from the perspective of readability, instead of the typological approach adopted here, focusing on text simplification or elaboration (McNamara et al., 2014; Carroll et al., 1998; Max, 2006; Shardlow, 2014; Siddharthan, 2006; DuBay, 2007; Leal and Aluísio, 2024).

Regarding the study of indigenous languages of South America, several classic works studied and documented the languages explored here, e.g. Callow (1962); Derbyshire and Pullum (1986–1991); Dixon and Aikhenvald (2006) *inter alia*. The investigation into the computational complexity of indigenous languages remains much less explored and our work is completely original, to the best of our knowledge. Bentz et al. (2017), Gutierrez-Vasques et al. (2023), Oh and Pellegrino (2023), Bentz et al. (2016), Nichols and Bentz (2018) and Bentz et al. (2023) are the works that closely resemble the work we present here, assessing various complexity metrics or associated measures on language sets that incorporate South American languages. Nevertheless, these studies diverge from ours in terms of goals, methodology, and/or the quantity of included indigenous languages, typically covering a significantly smaller number compared to our assessment.

3 Methodology

This paper aims to evaluate a collection of compression-based language complexity metrics $\mathcal{M}$ introduced in previous works (Juola, 1998, 2005, 2008; Ehret and Szmrecsanyi, 2016). The evaluation is conducted on a dataset $\mathcal{D}$ encoded in a broad range of South American indigenous languages $\mathcal{L}$. The objective is to determine the validity of the theoretical and experimental propositions $\mathcal{P}$ regarding $\mathcal{M}$, as observed in the aforementioned studies, when $\mathcal{M}$ is applied to the languages in $\mathcal{L}$.

In this section, we present the methodology adopted to achieve this goal. In subsection 3.1, we define the set $\mathcal{M}$ of language complexity metrics evaluated; in subsection 3.2, we present the set $\mathcal{L}$ of South American languages tested and the data $\mathcal{D}$ used to represent them; in subsection 3.4 we present the propositions $\mathcal{P}$ about $\mathcal{M}$, whose validity we wish to verify when $\mathcal{M}$ are applied to $\mathcal{L}$ through $\mathcal{D}$; in subsection 3.5, we outline the experimental processing pipeline employed for conducting this verification. Subsection 3.3 presents a brief interlude on the writing systems used to encode the languages in $\mathcal{L}$.

3.1 Complexity Metrics

The language complexity metrics $\mathcal{M}$ evaluated in this work (Juola, 1998, 2005, 2008; Ehret and Szmrecsanyi, 2016) are based on a teleological approach to human language, that can be traced back to (Zipf, 1949) . This view reduces natural language to its primary functionality - the transmission of meaning or information - in line with Shannon's Information Theory (MacKay, 2003).

In this approach, each textual excerpt is seen as a message encoding a certain amount of information. The complexity of the message is the amount of information encoded. For a sufficiently long message, the amount of information can be approximated by the size of the message when compressed by an efficient compression algorithm.

However, experimental results show that natural languages tend to maintain a relatively uniform information density during communication (Manin, 2006; Aylett and Turk, 2004; Jaeger, 2006; Jaeger and Levy, 2006; Jaeger, 2010). Some works model this through the hypothesis that natural languages try to maximize information transmission without overloading the cognitive systems of senders and receivers (Piantadosi et al., 2011), but with limited results (Pimentel et al., 2023). Regardless of the exact mechanisms behind this uniformity, one consequence is that longer texts contain more information, resulting in larger compressed versions.

This correlation between a text's length and its compressed size must be considered by any complexity metric using compressed text size to estimate overall text complexity. To address this issue, Ehret and Szmrecsanyi (2016) proposes that the overall language complexity should be computed as a measure of how much the size of the compressed message deviates from the expected correlation with the size of the uncompressed version. This can be computed from the residuals (res) of the linear regression between the compressed message size and its original size. This definition of overall complexity $\mu^{\mathbb{A}}$ is shown in Equation 1 (For details about the mathematical notation, see InfoBox 1).

$$\mu^{\mathbb{A}}(\mathscr{T}) = res(|C(\mathscr{T})|, |\mathscr{T}|) \qquad (1)$$

Mathematical Notation Key

Throughout this text we will use the following notation conventions:

- $\mathscr{T}$ represents a textual excerpt or message encoded in a natural language;
- Degraded texts are represented with subscripts and superscripts. The subscript symbol represents the type of degradation ($\circ$ for replacement, $\times$ for deletion). The superscript represents the target tier of the degradation process.
- Language complexity metrics are functions represented by $\mu_{\_}^{\mathbb{Y}}(\cdot)$, where, the subscript symbol indicates the type of degradation associated with the metric and the superscript symbol indicates the target language tier accessed by the metric;
- $C(\mathscr{T})$ represents the text $\mathscr{T}$ after compression ;
- $|\cdot|$ represents the size of an object in bytes.

InfoBox 1: Mathematical notation adopted throughout this text.

Nevertheless, the complexity of a text cannot be determined solely by the overall information transmitted ($\mathbb{A}$). Natural languages have different mechanisms of encoding information and adopt different strategies to distribute the information transmitted through these mechanisms. Finnish, for example, has a rich morphological case system, in which a noun such as "talo" (house) becomes "talolta" to express the concept "from the house". This same concept is expressed syntactically in English through the association with a preposition, external to the word "house".

In information theory terms, each message encoded in a natural language consists of different tiers through which one can distribute the information conveyed by the message, and therefore its complexity. A text would then have a different level of complexity for each tier.

In an effort to grasp these subtleties, Juola (2008)

introduce a set of metrics designed to capture the relative complexities across three distinct linguistic tiers: morphological ($\mathbb{M}$), syntactic ($\mathbb{S}$), and pragmatic ($\mathbb{P}$). The principle underlying these three metrics is the same: to degenerate[1] the information conveyed only by the targeted linguistic tier and to compute the ratio between the size of the degenerated compressed text to that of the original compressed text. In this way it is possible to access how much of the overall information is being transmitted by the targeted tier.

The more dependent a language is on a particular tier for conveying information, the more the degradation of that tier leads to information loss in the text. This intensified information loss hinders pattern recognition for compression algorithms, resulting in reduced compressibility and higher complexity metric values for that tier.

Juola (2008) achieves degeneration through a deletion process, wherein 10% of the units in the text are randomly erased. The choice of textual unit to be erased depends on the targeted linguistic tier: characters for morphology, words[2] for syntax, and verses for pragmatics[3].

Ehret and Szmrecsanyi (2016) argue that an expected exception to this general template is morphological complexity: languages with rich morphology use systems to convey information within words that other languages express through external elements. As a result, a single word in this languages can have several allowed forms. Thus, in languages with high morphological complexity, deleting a character still often yields a valid word form, minimizing disruption in text compressibility. To address this, a negative sign is incorporated in the definition of morphological complexity. Ehret and Szmrecsanyi (2016) also experimentally confirms the need for this sign correction.

These complexity metrics, as described, are represented by equations 2, 3, and 4. In all cases, we follow the mathematical notation conventions outlined in InfoBox 1.

$$\mu_{\times}^{\mathbb{M}}(\mathscr{T}) = -\frac{|C(\mathscr{T}_{\times}^{\mathbb{M}})|}{|C(\mathscr{T})|} \tag{2}$$

$$\mu_{\times}^{\mathbb{S}}(\mathscr{T}) = \frac{|C(\mathscr{T}_{\times}^{\mathbb{S}})|}{|C(\mathscr{T})|} \tag{3}$$

$$\mu_{\times}^{\mathbb{P}}(\mathscr{T}) = \frac{|C(\mathscr{T}_{\times}^{\mathbb{P}})|}{|C(\mathscr{T})|} \tag{4}$$

Juola (2008) proposes an alternative technique to morphological degeneration using substitution instead of deletion. He replaces all tokens of the same type in the original text with an integer, removing information about the internal structure of words without affecting information about their relative positioning within the sentences. This is represented in Equation 5. Here the numerator and denominator are inverted compared to the previous metrics. This inversion is an attempt to address the same problem related to the morphological complexity that led to the proposition of sign inversion in equation 2, but with a different mathematical strategy.

$$\mu_{\circ}^{\mathbb{M}}(\mathscr{T}) = \frac{|C(\mathscr{T})|}{|C(\mathscr{T}_{\circ}^{\mathbb{M}})|} \tag{5}$$

The process of calculating a complexity metric value from a text $\mathcal{T}$, as previously described, is illustrated in Figure 1. This example employs the metric $\mu_{\times}^{\mathbb{M}}$, defined in Equation 2.

Juola (2008) provides a cognitive argument to why compression-based metrics would work for measuring language complexity. Any measure of the complexity of an object is computed as the number of primitive operations necessary for its functioning. We can reduce the compression process to storage and querying operations over a lexicon of frequent textual patterns. These operations, he argues, align with how human mind uses language, storing frequent linguistic patterns and querying them. Compression-based metrics should thus work well, as they are an approximation, albeit simple, of human cognitive linguistic procedures.

3.2 Data

In order to access the properties of complexity metrics across different languages, Juola (2008) opts to eliminate other potential factors of complexity variation, conducting experiments with a parallel corpus comprising the same text translated into different languages. The Christian Bible was his main

[1] In this text, the terms "degeneration" and "degradation" are used interchangeably.

[2] As in Juola (2008), we adopt here the work definition of words as maximal non-blank sequences.

[3] In Juola (2008), as well as here, the main text used in the experiments is a subset of the Christian Bible, given the high availability of translations into different languages. As the Bible is divided into verses and verses correspond roughly to sentences, this is used as the pragmatic unit for computing pragmatic complexity metrics.

Figure 1: Diagram exemplifying the pipeline for computing complexity metrics. This example refers to the metric of morphological complexity through deletion $\mu_{\times}^{\mathbb{M}}$ defined in equation 2.

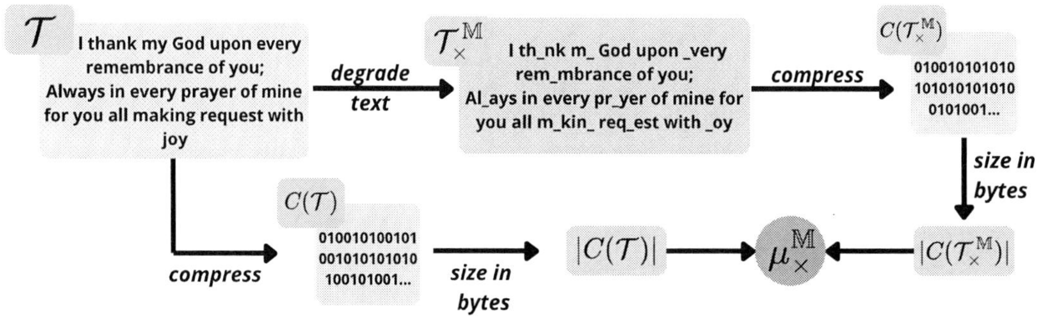

selected text, chosen for its extensive range of translations and convenient accessibility. In an effort to maintain maximum fidelity to his experiments and isolate potential factors of variation that could undermine the validity of our results, we also have opted to use texts from the Christian Bible.

Another reason for using these texts in our case is the unfortunate scarcity of translations simultaneously available in a wide range of indigenous South American languages. Notably, even the Brazilian constitution lacks versions in the various indigenous languages spoken within its territory. The Bible stands out as one of the rare texts extensively translated into these languages, primarily due to its central role in the colonization process of these communities. A further contributing factor to the limited data availability is the lack of written tradition in the languages studied here. Historically, many of them were primarily oral and only recently adopted a writing system, often developed specifically for the translation and dissemination of christian texts, such as the Bible.

Acknowledging the problematic context in which these translations were produced, we refrain from disclosing the data or deploying any models based on it. Our sole purpose is to leverage these translations to explore aspects of these languages that might otherwise be challenging to investigate. Our aim is to emphasize the importance of considering these languages in the examination of properties that are said to be universal, encompassing human diverse cultural manifestations in our view of natural languages.

We are also aware that these translations were probably produced with very little care for the languages and its cultural meanings and nuances, and that the distribution of language in the Bible may be not representative of these languages as a whole and can be skewed. These may be confounding factors reflected in the obtained values of the aforementioned complexity metrics.

Our dataset, kindly provided by IBM Research Brazil, was originally assembled to explore language classification and machine translation between indigenous languages. It consists of the texts of the Catholic Bible's New Testament, translated into a diverse set of South American indigenous languages and is separated by books, chapters and verses.

The dataset includes 51 South American indigenous languages: Apalaí (*apl*), Apinayé (*api*), Apurinã (*apu*), Asheninka (*cax*), Bakairi (*bki*), Borôro (*brr*), Canela (*cnl*), Culina (*cul*), Desano (*des*), Guajajara (*gjj*), Guarani Eastern Bolivian (*crg*), Guarani Mbya (*[gun]*), Guarani Paraguay (*gua*), Guarani Western Bolivian (*[gnw]*), Hixkaryána (*hix*), Jamamadi (*jmm*), Kaapor (*urk*), Kadiwéu (*kdw*), Kaigang (*kng*), Kaiwá (*kaw*), Karajá (*jva*), Kashinawa (*csh*), Kayabí (*kyz*), Kayapó (*kyp*), Kubeo (*cub*), Macushi (*mac*), Makuna (*mcn*), Matsés (*myr*), Maxakali (*max*), Mundurukú (*muu*), Nadeb (*nad*), Nambikuára (*nmb*), Nheengatu (*[yrl]*), Palikúr (*plk*), Parecís (*pex*), Paumarí (*pau*), Piratapúya (*prt*), Rikbaktsa (*rik*), Sanumá (*snm*), Sateré-Mawé (*[mav]*), Siriano (*sri*), Tenharim (*[pah]*), Terêna (*trn*), Ticuna (*tic*), Tucano (*tuc*), Tuyúca (*tuy*), Wanana (*gno*), Wapishana (*wps*), Xavante (*xav*), Yamináswa (*yam*), and Yanomami (*[guu]*). The geographical distribution of these languages is represented in Figure 2. Additional information about them can be found in Appendix B.

Figure 2: Geographical distribution by family for the languages explored in our experiments. Latitude, Longitude and Phylogenetic data were obtained from the Glottolog Database (Hammarström et al., 2024).

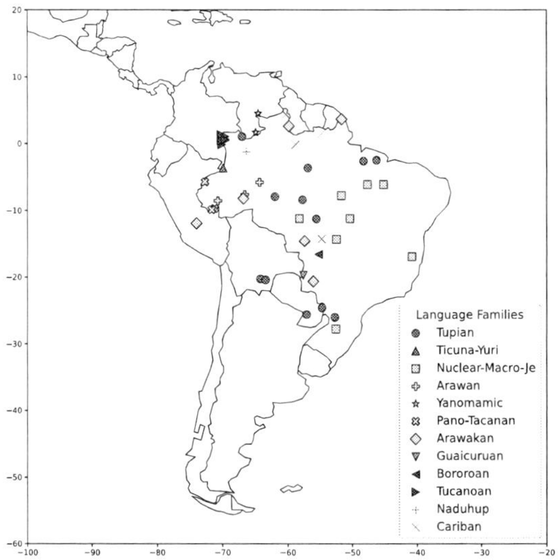

Furthermore it also includes 5 Indo-European languages: English (*eng*), French (*fre*), German (*ger*), Portuguese (*por*), and Spanish (*spa*), which we use for comparison purposes.

We also collected the New Testament in Ancient Greek (*[grc]*) [4] for verifying the proposition that overall complexity of a text is always smaller in its original language (see Section 3.4).

3.3 Writing Systems

The metrics defined in previous sections assess language complexity through the degradation of orthographic elements and sequences such characters and words, thus linking these metrics to the writing systems employed by the targeted languages under evaluation. Both Juola (2008)'s and our experiments focus on languages with alphabetic and low-logographic writing systems derived from the Latin alphabet (Sproat, 2000). Consequently, our conclusions are constrained to this region of the orthographic space. Further research is needed to validate these complexity metrics across diverse regions of the orthographic space that are beyond the scope of this paper. Figure 5 in Appendix A provides a visual representation of the types of writing systems not addressed in our experiments.

[4]https://www.greekbible.com/

3.4 Propositions

We used the data described above to assess whether the desirable properties of the proposed complexity metrics remain consistent when evaluated over our broad set of native South American languages.

These expected properties can be formulated as propositions falling into two broad groups: *prior hypotheses* about how a language complexity metric should behave, and *a posteriori observations*, found in Juola (2008)'s experiments.

The prior hypotheses evaluated in this work are:

- $\mathcal{H}_1$: the overall complexity ($\mu^{\mathbb{A}}$) of a text in its original language is lower than in other languages, as a result of the introduction of cultural clarifications in the translation process;

- $\mathcal{H}_2$ (equi-complexity hypothesis): all languages have (approximately) the same overall complexity ($\mu^{\mathbb{A}}$)[5];

- $\mathcal{H}_3$ (trade-off hypothesis): there is a trade-off between the syntactic ($\mu_{\times}^{\mathbb{S}}$) and morphological ($\mu_{\times}^{\mathbb{M}}$) complexities of a language.

The *a posteriori* observations of Juola (2008), accessed in this work are:

- $\mathcal{O}_1$: there is a positive correlation between morphological complexity by replacement ($\mu_{\circ}^{\mathbb{M}}$) and the number of types in the sample and a negative correlation with the number of tokens;

- $\mathcal{O}_2$: all languages are approximately equal in terms of their pragmatic complexity ($\mu_{\times}^{\mathbb{P}}$); in other words, the variance of pragmatic complexity is significantly lower than that of morphological and syntactic equivalents;

- $\mathcal{O}_3$: the morphological complexity metric $\mu_{\circ}^{\mathbb{M}}$ is consistent with Nichols (1998) morphological complexity metric (see Section 2);

- $\mathcal{O}_4$: the results were equivalent when varying the compression algorithm between *gzip* and *bz2*.

[5]Contact languages are possible exceptions to this, but without a representative dataset of contact languages, we cannot verify this hypothesis.

Figure 3: Trade-off between syntactic and morphological complexities by deletion, computed with *gzip* for both $D90$ and $DAll$ sets. The legend is the same for both plots. Phylogenetic data was obtained from Glottolog (Hammarström et al., 2024).

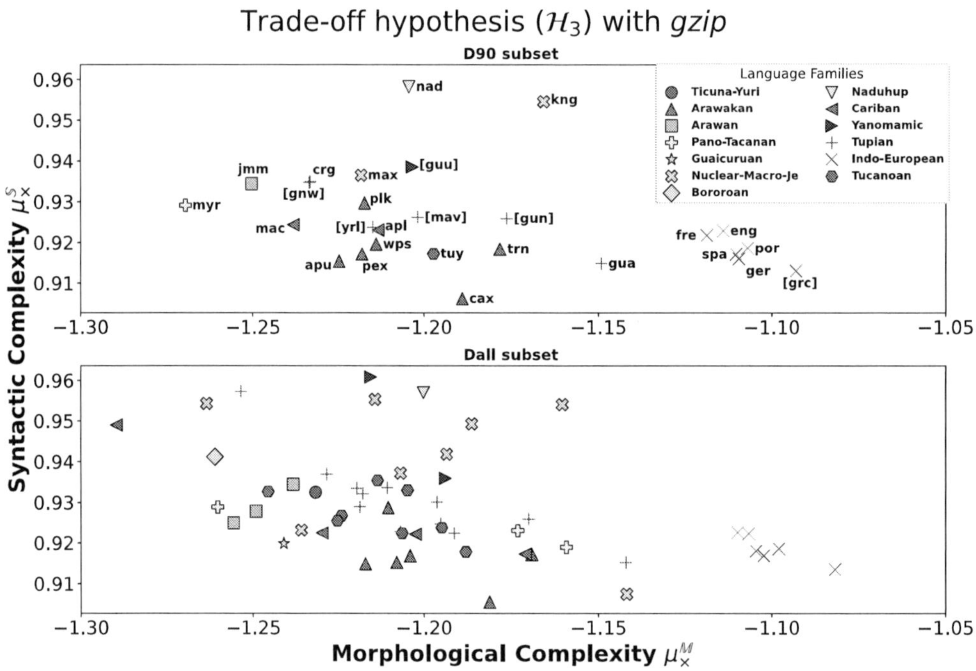

3.5 Experimental Pipeline

Our experimental pipeline consists of five steps:

1. Data normalization: this step ensures that characters that appear identical are indeed encoded identically in UTF-8 representation;

2. Data processing: here, we create two datasets Dall and D90. Dall contains only verses that appear in all languages (2585 verses across 27 languages), while D90 contains verses from languages where the intersection of verses makes up at least 90% of the total (7159 verses across 27 languages).

3. Outlier detection and removal: we analyzed the dataset, detecting the Nambikuára data as a potential anomaly. Nambikuára is a language family spoke in *Mato Grosso*, Brazil. These are tonal languages, i.e. languages in which the pitches produced are grammatically or lexically distinctive, with tones marked orthographically by special characters "¹," "²," and "³" in all syllables of our sample (Lowe, 1999). Orthographic tone marking varies widely across languages, but even where pervasive, it typically evolves organically with compensatory mechanisms to ensure easy written communication. Nambikuára, like many of the languages studied here, does not have a long written tradition, and the development of its writing system is connected the contact between native speakers and peoples of European descent. It is likely that our sample's ubiquitous tonal marking reflects the needs of people unfamiliar with tonality rather than those of it's native speakers. Consequently, this marking likely increases information redundancy without appropriate compensation, affecting the comparability of complexity metrics [6]. We thus removed Nambikuára from our analysis.

4. Encoding choice: since UTF-8 is a variable-size encoding, we encoded our data in UTF-16, to ensure all characters use exactly the same amount of storage;

[6]A similar argument can be found in Sproat (2000, pp. 21–23), using as an example the differences between the standard Hebrew writing system and the Masoretic Hebrew system. The later includes annotations designed to help people who don't speak Hebrew to read the Bible with the correct pronunciation.

5. Compression: we employed Gzip (*gzip*) and Bzip2 (*bz2*) from Python's 3.11.8 standard library. In both cases, we used the maximum compression level available (level 9).

With this pipeline, we have a total of four experimental settings for each metric *(gzip, D90)*, *(bz2, D90)*, *(gzip, Dall)*, *(bz2, Dall)*.

The programs developed for this work are available in an online repository[7].

4 Results and Discussion

Using the complexity metrics computed from the described experimental pipeline, we conducted analyses to empirically validate each proposition outlined in section 3.4, obtaining the following results:

- $\mathcal{H}_1$: we ordered the languages of each dataset by overall complexity $\mu^{\mathbb{A}}$ in ascending order. For instance, the ranking obtained for the setting *(gzip, D90)* was *Nheengatu, Jamamadi, Eastern Bolivian Guarani, Western Bolivian Guarani, Matsés, Maxakali, Guarani Mbya, Parecís, Nadeb, Asheninka, Paraguay Guarani, Tuyúca, Apurinã, Apalaí, English, Kaigang, Macushi, Portuguese, French, Palikúr, Wapishana, Yanomami, German, Spanish, Terêna, Ancient Greek.* It's clear that this ranking does not follow the expectation posed by $\mathcal{H}_1$ that Ancient Greek would be the least complex language, however we have no information on the translation history that connects the different versions of the Bible and which could influence our ranking. Another confounding factor is that Juola (2008) uses the Old Testament as experimental data, originally written in Hebrew. Hebrew, being a Semitic language, lacks orthographic representation of vowels, thus reducing character count. Ancient Greek, our approximate basis for the New Testament original language, features a highly intricate orthographic system with numerous diacritics, significantly increasing character count. Analyzing the correlation between overall complexity and number of distinct characters per language reveals a non-negligible correlation ($\rho = 0.45$, p-value$= 0.019$), suggesting orthographic complexity as a confounding variable that warrants consideration for a more precise assessment of this hypothesis. The fact that *Nheengatu* is in all settings one of the languages of least complexity may be related to its role as a *lingua franca*, or to the possibility that it was used as a basis for the other translations. The evaluation of $\mathcal{H}_1$ is therefore inconclusive, and is subject to a more in-depth study of the translation history of the different versions of the text and orthographic complexity;

- $\mathcal{H}_2$: we observed that the variance of the compressed text sizes is two orders of magnitude smaller than the variance of the original text sizes while the variance of the overall complexity metric $\mu^{\mathbb{A}}$ is three orders of magnitude smaller, in all scenarios, confirming the hypothesis within our experimental limitations. This is illustrated in Figure 4.

- $\mathcal{H}_3$: we computed the correlation between syntactic and morphological complexity, obtaining negative values in all scenarios and confirming the trade-off hypothesis. In particular, for the set containing all languages, we obtained $\rho = -0.45$, p-value$= 0.0004$ with *gzip* and $\rho = -0.47$, p-value$= 0.0002$ with *bz2*. Analysing the relationship between these complexities, as illustrated in Figure 3, we noted (i) a significant cohesion in complexity space between languages that belong to the same family. This is clearly observable, for example, for the Indo-European, Tupian, Nuclear-Macro-Je, and Arawakan families; (ii) a significant separation between the cluster of Indo-European languages and the clusters of South American languages, indicating that the distance in complexity space can be a meaningful metric of language dissimilarity; (iii) that South American languages have a much greater dispersion in complexities between them than Indo-European languages, reinforcing the need to validate the desired properties of this metrics in a more diverse set of languages, instead of generalizing the results obtained for Indo-European languages. We consider these results as evidence that the trade-off between syntactic and morphological complexities may be dependent on the phylogeny of languages, and usable as feature or tool in language differentiation.

- $\mathcal{O}_1$: as expected, we observed significant positive correlations between morphological com-

[7]Our source code is available in this repository

Figure 4: Compared distributions of original text size $|\mathcal{T}|$, compressed text size $|C(\mathcal{T})|$ and overall complexity $\mu^{\mathbb{A}}$ for the *Dall* subset. The differences in the dispersion of the distributions corroborate $\mathcal{H}_2$.

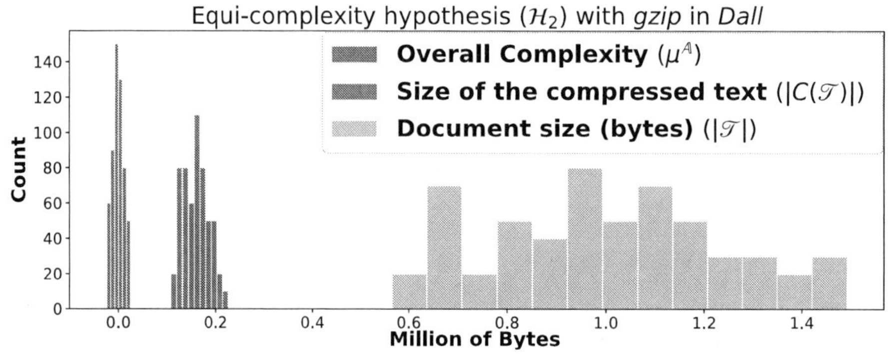

plexity and the number of types and negative correlations with the number of tokens for all settings. In particular, for *(gzip, D90)* we obtained $\rho_{types} = 0.92$ and $\rho_{tokens} = -0.77$, both with p-value $< 10^{-6}$. This hypothesis was therefore validated;

- $\mathcal{O}_2$: in all scenarios, we observed that the variance of the pragmatic complexity metric is one to three orders of magnitude smaller than the variance of the morphological and syntactic complexities, confirming this hypothesis within our experimental limitations. This corroborates Juola (2008)'s hypothesis that the amount of information transmitted at the inter-sentential level is language universal, perhaps related to the general cognitive processes of sequential reasoning.

- $\mathcal{O}_3$: we collected the available values of Nichols (1998) morphological complexity metric for the languages in our dataset. Unfortunately, this came down to a small set of six languages. This number of points was too small to obtain a statistically reliable measure of correlation. The evaluation of this hypothesis is therefore inconclusive;

- $\mathcal{O}_4$: the assessment of all previously validated propositions yielded equivalent results for both *gzip* and *bz2*. The hypothesis of their equivalence as base for language complexity measurements is therefore validated within our experimental limitations. Despite this, it's evident that *bz2* typically achieves superior compression compared to *gzip*. However, this isn't always advantageous, as *bz2*'s compression capacity may flatten complexities distributions, complicating the assessment of the trade-off hypothesis $\mathcal{H}_3$.

5 Conclusions and Future Steps

The majority of propositions about the studied complexity metrics ($\mathcal{H}_2$, $\mathcal{H}_3$, $\mathcal{O}_1$, $\mathcal{O}_2$, and $\mathcal{O}_4$) were successfully validated in our vast dataset of South American indigenous languages. These results confirm the robustness of such metrics and indicate the universality of the techniques proposed by (Juola, 2008) to compute the different forms of linguistic complexity. As we used a greater variety of languages, we were also able to document that the trade-off between morphological and syntactic complexities strongly relates with language phylogeny.

Although we confirmed most of our propositions, we obtained inconclusive results for $\mathcal{H}_1$ and $\mathcal{O}_3$, and even for the confirmed hypothesis, we found them to be weaker in South American languages compared to the sets of predominantly Indo-European languages used in the original experiments. This highlights the need to validate and adjust these metrics for a wider range of human languages, a task we have initiated here.

In future research, we aim to investigate the inconclusive propositions, particularly focusing on the impact of orthographic complexity on overall linguistic complexity, extending our results to a greater set of writing systems.

Our findings add to those of (Juola, 2008) and (Ehret and Szmrecsanyi, 2016), expanding the set of languages on which these family of language complexity metrics have been validated.

Limitations

Authors

We, the authors, speak Portuguese, English, and Spanish, with Brazilian Portuguese as our native language. Consequently, we cannot provide insights requiring in-depth knowledge of other languages studied in this work.

Nomenclature of Complexity Metrics

We adhered here to Juola (2008)'s classification of complexity metrics as morphological, syntactic, and pragmatic. However, we believe these names might be misleading.

Regarding syntactic and morphological complexity metrics, it is known that polysynthetic languages like Central Siberian Yupik (not studied here) embed almost all sentence information within words. Many researchers view these process as syntactic rather than morphological, constituting an internal syntax within words (de Reuse, 2006). The metrics studied here would categorize this as morphological complexity instead of syntactic, therefore a more appropriate terminology might be "word complexity" and "sentential complexity."

Regarding pragmatic complexity, the metric used here measures relationships between text parts rather than between the text and external context, typically studied by pragmatics. Thus, a term like "intersentential complexity" might be more suitable.

Data

We used data from the New Testament of the Christian Bible for our experiments. The language in these texts has its own bias, not reflecting the cultural reality of the studied languages. Many translations of this text were made to facilitate colonization, with little regard for cultural and linguistic nuances of each language and people. This could affect our results. We also lacked access to a clear history of translation relationships between versions in different languages, which could have provided a more comprehensive interpretation of $\mathcal{H}_1$. We aim to obtain this data in future work.

Writing Systems

As noted in Section 3.3, the metrics studied here are strongly dependent on the writing systems used to represent target languages. Their applicability is therefore currently limited to alphabetic and low-logographic writing systems. Extensions are needed to apply them to other writing systems.

Acknowledgments

This work was partly supported by Coordenação de Aperfeiçoamento de Pessoal de Nível Superior - Brasil (CAPES) - Finance Code 001; and partly supported by the Ministry of Science, Technology and Innovation, with resources of Law N. 8.248, of October 23, 1991, within the scope of PPI-SOFTEX, coordinated by Softex and published as Residence in TIC 13, DOU 01245.010222/2022-44. This work was carried out at the Center for Artificial Intelligence (C4AI-USP), supported by FAPESP grant 2019/07665-4 and by the IBM Corporation. Marcelo Finger was partly supported by CNPq grant PQ 302963/2022-7 and Fapesp grant 2023/00488-5. Felipe R. Serras was supported by the IBM Corporation in a grant managed by FUSP under number 3541 and in a PPI-SOFTEX grant managed by FUSP under number 3970. We would like to thank IBM Research Brazil for providing the data that made our experiments possible. We thank Sandro Preto for helping us better understand the Bible's internal structure.

References

Farrell Ackerman and Robert Malouf. 2013. Morphological organization: The low conditional entropy conjecture. *Language*, 89:429–464.

Matthew Aylett and Alice Turk. 2004. The smooth signal redundancy hypothesis: A functional explanation for relationships between redundancy, prosodic prominence, and duration in spontaneous speech. *Language and speech*, 47(1):31–56.

Christian Bentz, Dimitrios Alikaniotis, Michael Cysouw, and Ramon Ferrer i Cancho. 2017. The entropy of words—learnability and expressivity across more than 1000 languages. *Entropy*, 19:275.

Christian Bentz, Ximena Gutierrez-Vasques, Olga Sozinova, and Tanja Samardžić. 2023. Complexity tradeoffs and equi-complexity in natural languages: a meta-analysis. *Linguistics Vanguard*, 9(s1):9–25.

Christian Bentz, Tatyana Ruzsics, Alexander Koplenig, and Tanja Samardžić. 2016. A comparison between morphological complexity measures: Typological data vs. language corpora. In *Proceedings of the Workshop on Computational Linguistics for Linguistic Complexity (CL4LC)*, pages 142–153, Osaka, Japan. The COLING 2016 Organizing Committee.

Bram Bulté and Alex Housen. 2014. Conceptualizing and measuring short-term changes in l2 writing complexity. *Journal of Second Language Writing*, 26:42–65.

John Campbell Callow. 1962. The apinaye language: Phonology and grammar.

John Carroll, Guido Minnen, Yvonne Canning, Siobhan Devlin, and John Tait. 1998. Practical simplification of english newspaper text to assist aphasic readers. In *Proceedings of the AAAI-98 workshop on integrating artificial intelligence and assistive technology*, pages 7–10. Association for the Advancement of Artificial Intelligence.

Paulo Cavalin, Pedro Domingues, Julio Nogima, and Claudio Pinhanez. 2023. Understanding native language identification for brazilian indigenous languages. pages 12–18. Association for Computational Linguistics.

Bastien De Clercq and Alex Housen. 2019. The development of morphological complexity: A cross-linguistic study of l2 french and english. *Second Language Research*, 35:71–97.

W.J. de Reuse. 2006. Polysynthetic language: Central siberian yupik. In Keith Brown, editor, *Encyclopedia of language & linguistics (second edition)*, second edition edition, pages 745–748. Elsevier, Oxford.

Desmond C. Derbyshire and Geoffrey K. Pullum. 1986–1991. *Handbook of Amazonian Languages: Volumes 1–4*. De Gruyter Mounton, Berlin, New York. 4 volumes.

R.M.W. Dixon and A.Y. Aikhenvald. 2006. *The Amazonian Languages*. Cambridge Language Surveys. Cambridge University Press.

William H DuBay. 2007. *Smart Language: Readers, Readability, and the Grading of Text*. ERIC.

Katharina Ehret, Alice Blumenthal-Dramé, Christian Bentz, and Aleksandrs Berdicevskis. 2021. Meaning and measures: Interpreting and evaluating complexity metrics. *Frontiers in Communication*, 6.

Katharina Ehret and Benedikt Szmrecsanyi. 2016. *An information-theoretic approach to assess linguistic complexity*, pages 71–94.

Gertraud Fenk-Oczlon and August Fenk. 2008. *Complexity trade-offs between the subsystems of language*, pages 43–65.

Arthur C. Graesser and Danielle S. McNamara. 2011. Computational analyses of multilevel discourse comprehension. *Topics in Cognitive Science*, 3:371–398.

Arthur C. Graesser, Danielle S. McNamara, and Jonna M. Kulikowich. 2011. Coh-metrix. *Educational Researcher*, 40:223–234.

Arthur C. Graesser, Danielle S. McNamara, Max M. Louwerse, and Zhiqiang Cai. 2004. Coh-metrix: Analysis of text on cohesion and language. *Behavior Research Methods, Instruments, & Computers*, 36:193–202.

Ximena Gutierrez-Vasques, Christian Bentz, and Tanja Samardžić. 2023. Languages Through the Looking Glass of BPE Compression. *Computational Linguistics*, 49(4):943–1001.

Harald Hammarström, Robert Forkel, Martin Haspelmath, and Sebastian Bank. 2024. Glottolog 5.0. Available online at `http://glottolog.org`, Accessed on 2024-07-03.

Alex Housen, Bastien De Clercq, Folkert Kuiken, and Ineke Vedder. 2019. Multiple approaches to complexity in second language research. *Second Language Research*, 35:3–21.

T Jaeger and Roger Levy. 2006. Speakers optimize information density through syntactic reduction. *Advances in neural information processing systems*, 19.

T Florian Jaeger. 2010. Redundancy and reduction: Speakers manage syntactic information density. *Cognitive psychology*, 61(1):23–62.

Tim Florian Jaeger. 2006. *Redundancy and syntactic reduction in spontaneous speech*. Ph.D. thesis, Stanford University Stanford, CA.

Patrick Juola. 1998. Measuring linguistic complexity: The morphological tier. *Journal of Quantitative Lin-Druckguistics*, 5(3):206–213.

Patrick Juola. 2005. Compression-based analysis of language complexity. *Approaches to Complexity in Language*.

Patrick Juola. 2008. Assessing linguistic complexity. *Language Complexity: Typology, Contact, Change. John Benjamins Press, Amsterdam, Netherlands*.

Päivi Juvonen. 2008. *Complexity and simplicity in minimal lexica: The lexicon of Chinook Jargon*, pages 321–340.

Kimmo Kettunen. 2014. Can type-token ratio be used to show morphological complexity of languages? *Journal of Quantitative Linguistics*, 21:223–245.

Sidney Evaldo Leal and Sandra Maria Aluísio. 2024. Complexidade textual e suas tarefas relacionadas. In H. M. Caseli and M. G. V. Nunes, editors, *Processamento de Linguagem Natural: Conceitos, Técnicas e Aplicações em Português*, 2 edition, book chapter 23. BPLN.

Sidney Evaldo Leal, Magali Sanches Duran, Carolina Evaristo Scarton, Nathan Siegle Hartmann, and Sandra Maria Aluísio. 2023. Nilc-metrix: assessing the complexity of written and spoken language in brazilian portuguese. *Language Resources and Evaluation*.

Ivan Lowe. 1999. Nambiquara. In R. M. W. Dixon and Alexandra Y. Aikhenvald, editors, *The Amazonian Languages*, pages 269–91. Cambridge University Press, Cambridge.

D.J.C. MacKay. 2003. *Information Theory, Inference and Learning Algorithms*. Cambridge University Press.

Dmitrii Manin. 2006. Experiments on predictability of word in context and information rate in natural language. *Journal of Information Processes*, 6(3):229–236.

Aurélien Max. 2006. Writing for language-impaired readers. In *International Conference on Intelligent Text Processing and Computational Linguistics*, pages 567–570. Springer.

Danielle S McNamara, Arthur C Graesser, Philip M McCarthy, and Zhiqiang Cai. 2014. *Automated evaluation of text and discourse with Coh-Metrix*. Cambridge University Press.

Johanna Nichols. 1998. *Linguistic diversity in space and time*. University of Chicago Press.

Johanna Nichols and Christian Bentz. 2018. Morphological complexity of languages reflects the settlement history of the americas. *New Perspectives on the Peopling of the Americas*, pages 13–26.

Yoon Mi Oh and François Pellegrino. 2023. Towards robust complexity indices in linguistic typology: A corpus-based assessment. *Studies in Language*, 47(4):789–829.

François Pellegrino, Christophe Coupé, and Egidio Marsico. 2011. Across-language perspective on speech information rate. *Language*, 87:539–558.

Steven T Piantadosi, Harry Tily, and Edward Gibson. 2011. Word lengths are optimized for efficient communication. *Proceedings of the National Academy of Sciences*, 108(9):3526–3529.

Tiago Pimentel, Clara Meister, Ethan Wilcox, Kyle Mahowald, and Ryan Cotterell. 2023. Revisiting the optimality of word lengths. In *Proceedings of the 2023 Conference on Empirical Methods in Natural Language Processing*, pages 2240–2255, Singapore. Association for Computational Linguistics.

Markus Sadeniemi, Kimmo Kettunen, Tiina Lindh-Knuutila, and Timo Honkela. 2008. Complexity of european union languages: A comparative approach. *Journal of Quantitative Linguistics*, 15:185–211.

Gabriele Sarti, Dominique Brunato, and Felice Dell'Orletta. 2021. That looks hard: Characterizing linguistic complexity in humans and language models. pages 48–60. Association for Computational Linguistics.

Matthew Shardlow. 2014. A survey of automated text simplification. *International Journal of Advanced Computer Science and Applications*, 4(1):58–70.

Advaith Siddharthan. 2006. Syntactic simplification and text cohesion. *Research on Language and Computation*, 4:77–109.

Richard William Sproat. 2000. *A computational theory of writing systems*. Cambridge University Press.

Benedikt Szmrecsanyi. 2021. *Uncovering the Big Picture: Measuring the Typological Relatedness of Varieties of English*, pages 184–208. Cambridge University Press.

G K Zipf. 1949. *Human Behavior and the Principle of Least Effort*. Addison-Wesley Press.

A A contextualization within a planar taxonomy of writing systems

Figure 5: Sproat (2000)[p. 142]'s planar taxonomy of writing systems, organizing them by the *Ammount of Logography*, i.e. the degree to which a system uses single symbols to represent entire words, and the *Type of Phonography*, i.e. which sound units are represented by the symbols in the system. The region of the plane colored in pink (alphabetic and low-logographic systems) corresponds to the types of writing systems where the explored metrics were validated.

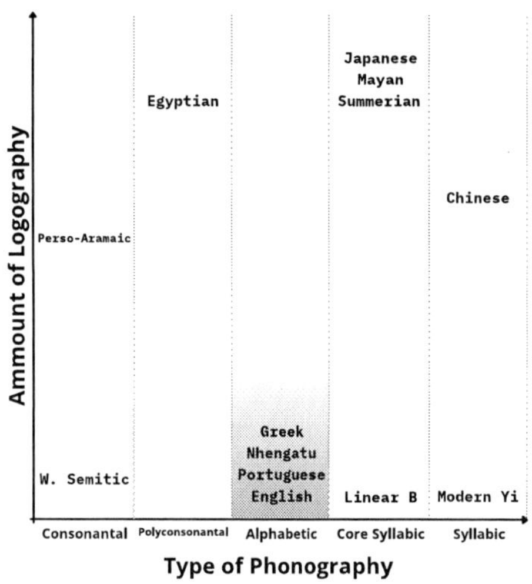

B Reference Information for the South American languages studied in this work

Table 1: Reference information about the native South American languages used in this work (Apalaí - Kayapó), partially based on Cavalin et al. (2023)

Language	Code	Family	Countries
Apalaí	apl	Cariban	Brazil
Apinayé	api	Nuclear-Macro-Je	Brazil
Apurinã	apu	Arawakan	Brazil
Asheninka	cax	Arawakan	Peru
Bakairí	bki	Cariban	Brazil
Bororo	brr	Bororoan	Brazil
Canela	cnl	Nuclear-Macro-Je	Brazil
Culina	cul	Arawan	Brazil Peru
Desano	des	Tucanoan	Colombia Brazil
Guajajara	gjj	Tupian	Brazil
Guarani Eastern Bolivia	crg	Tupian	Argentina Bolivia Paraguay
Guarani Mbya	[gun]	Tupian	Argentina Brazil Paraguay
Guarani Paraguay	gua	Tupian	Paraguay
Guarani Western Bolivia	[gnw]	Tupian	Argentina Bolivia Paraguay
Hixkaryána	hix	Cariban	Brazil
Jamamadi	jmm	Arawan	Brazil
Kaapor	urk	Tupian	Brazil
Kadiwéu	kdw	Guaicuruan	Brazil
Kaigang	kng	Nuclear-Macro-Je	Brazil
Kaiwá	kaw	Tupian	Brazil Paraguay
Karajá	jva	Nuclear-Macro-Je	Brazil
Kashinawa	csh	Pano-Tacanan	Brazil Peru
Kayabí	kyz	Tupian	Brazil
Kayapó	kyp	Nuclear-Macro-Je	Brazil

Table 2: Reference information about the native South American languages used in this work (Kubeo - Yanomami).

Language	Code	Family	Countries
Kubeo	cub	Tucanoan	Colombia
Macushi	mac	Cariban	Brazil Guyana Venezuela
Makuna	mcn	Tucanoan	Brazil Colombia
Matsés	myr	Pano-Tacanan	Brazil Peru
Maxakali	max	Nuclear-Macro-Je	Brazil
Mundurukú	muu	Tupian	Brazil
Nadeb	nad	Naduhup	Brazil
Nambikuára	nmb	Nambikwára	Brazil
Nheengatu	[yrl]	Tupian	Brazil Colombia Venezuela
Palikúr	plk	Arawakan	Brazil
Parecís	pex	Arawakan	Brazil
Paumarí	pau	Arawan	Brazil
Piratapúya	prt	Tucanoan	Brazil Colombia
Rikbaktsa	rik	Nuclear-Macro-Je	Brazil
Sanumá	snm	Yanomamic	Brazil Venezuela
Sateré-Mawé	[mav]	Tupian	Brazil
Siriano	sri	Tucanoan	Brazil Colombia
Tenharim	[pah]	Tupian	Brazil
Terêna	trn	Arawakan	Brazil
Ticuna	tic	Ticuna-Yuri	Brazil Peru
Tucano	tuc	Tucanoan	Brazil Colombia
Tuyúca	tuy	Tucanoan	Brazil Colombia
Wanana	gno	Tucanoan	Brazil Colombia
Wapishana	wps	Arawakan	Brazil Guyana
Xavante	xav	Nuclear-Macro-Je	Brazil
Yamináwa	yam	Pano-Tacanan	Brazil Peru
Yanomami	[guu]	Yanomamic	Brazil

How can large language models become more human?

Daphne Wang
University College London
Quandela

Mehrnoosh Sadrzadeh
University College London

Miloš Stanojević
University College London

Wing-Yee Chow
University College London

Richard Breheny
University College London

Abstract

Psycholinguistic experiments reveal that efficiency of human language use is founded on predictions at both syntactic and lexical levels. Previous models of human prediction exploiting LLMs have used an information theoretic measure called *surprisal*, with success on naturalistic text in a wide variety of languages, but under-performance on challenging text such as garden path sentences. This paper introduces a novel framework that combines the lexical predictions of an LLM with the syntactic structures provided by a dependency parser. The framework gives rise to an *Incompatibility Fraction*. When tested on two garden path datasets, it correlated well with human reading times, distinguished between easy and hard garden path, and outperformed surprisal.

1 Introduction

Psycholinguistic research develops models of human language understanding using experimental techniques such as self-paced reading and eye-tracking. Natural Language Processing research develops algorithms that enable machines solve human language tasks. Novel lines of research bringing these two fields together have emerged, where a question of interest has been whether machines are able to process language in ways similar to humans. The goal of this paper is to show that the answer can be yes, but only when they are equipped with human capabilities that enable them to predict with a combination of both syntactic structure and lexical statistics.

In order to model these characteristics, one needs a computational framework with at least two levels (more if we take pragmatics and other language features into account). We work with *presheaves* and specific instances of them, which consist of (1) a base that models linear structure, and (2) data that encode the statistics of different interpretations of the base. The data can be manifold recording outcomes of events, which can themselves be binary or many-valued, and their probabilities. For these reasons, presheaves provide a good candidate framework for modelling features of human language understanding.

We use a simple topological space as the base of our presheaf: that of a pre-ordered set. The elements of this set are sub-phrases of a sentence. The pre-order relation over the elements is the prefix relation between the sub-phrases. This relation will be used to the represent the incrementality of the parsing process. Our data is the probabilities of syntactic structures of sub-phrases. First, we obtained completions and their statistical information from the predictions of the large language model `GPT-2`. Then, to get the syntactic structures of the sub-phrases, we use the dependency parser `spaCy`. Our sheaf theoretic framework gives rise to a schematic fraction that measures how incompatible is the syntactic probability of a phrase from its completions. We refer to this fraction as the *incompatibility fraction* (**IF**). Well known distance measures between probability distributions exist and can be used when instantiating **IF**; we worked with `Kullback-Leibler divergence` (KL), `Jensen-Shannon divergence` (JS), and a measure similar to `Earth Movers` (EM).

Deep learning algorithms, especially attention-based ones, have made impressive advances in predicting the next words of a sentence. A statistical quantity known as "surprisal" has been found to correlate with human reading times (Levy, 2008; Hale, 2003, 2006). This, however, has only been the case for naturalistic text such as news paper articles. The jury is still out regarding a class of challenging sentences known as garden path (GP) sentences (Bever, 1970; Frazier, 1987; Frazier and Rayner, 1982). Psycholinguistic research has shown that humans experience processing difficulty and show longer reading times when processing GP sentences. Further, different types of

Proceedings of the Workshop on Cognitive Modeling and Computational Linguistics, pages 166–176

syntactic ambiguities have been shown to result in different levels of processing difficulty (Sturt et al., 1999). So far, surprisal has not been able to accurately predict the human reading times of GP sentences and more importantly has not been able to distinguish between easy versus hard sentences (Schijndel and Linzen, 2018; van Schijndel and Linzen, 2021; Huang et al., 2023).

In order to test the applicability of our framework, we tested it on two GP datasets (Pickering and Traxler, 1998), with hard (i.e., subordinate clause) and easy (i.e., complement clause) ambiguities. Both datasets had a disambiguated control for each of their GP sentences. They also had variants of them which were either semantically plausible or implausible. **IF** was measured for all these sentences and its predictions compared with with human reading times and surprisal. All of the instances we worked with, i.e. KL, JS, and EM, correlated well with human reading times and had very low errors, predicted the differences between GP sentences and their disambiguated controls well, could distinguish between easy and hard garden path, and outperformed surprisal. On the semantic front, all the measures including surprisal validated one of the hypotheses, that a semantically implausible sub-phrase take longer to read. The other hypothesis was about shorter GP effects in implausible sentences, which could not be detected by any of the measures. Dealing with these needs an explicit encoding of the semantic structure of sentences and we believe presheaves can also help. Working out the details is left to future work.

2 Related Work

Inspired by applications of information theory to Psycholinguistics (Attneave, 1959), Hale argued that *suprisal* is a good measure for the cognitive load faced by humans during sentence processing (Hale, 2001, 2003, 2006). Surprisal measures the degree of unpredictability of a word w given its prefix context $w_1 \cdots w_n$ and is computed via the following formula:

$$SP(w_n|w_1...w_{n-1}) = -\log(P(w_n|w_1...w_{n-1}))$$

Hale argued in favour of the use of surprisal in incremental parsing procedures. Building on this, Levy (2008) and later Smith and Levy (2013) showed that surprisal can also model the cognitive load modelled by constraint-based theories. The focus of Hale's work was on GP sentences, but he only provided experimental data for a couple of examples. Large scale validations on large datasets (Levy, 2008; Smith and Levy, 2013) and eleven different languages from five different language families followed suit (Wilcox et al., 2023). These only considered naturalistic text such as Wikipedia and news articles. Large scale data for GP sentences were not taken into account until more recent times (Schijndel and Linzen, 2018; van Schijndel and Linzen, 2021; Huang et al., 2023), where it was found out that surprisal does not provide good correlation. This has been the case for the surprisal computed over either syntactic predictions of a probabilistic parser or the lexical predictions of a statistical language model. In either case, the predictions largely underestimated human reading times. Weighted combinations of the syntactic and lexical surprisal were also computed but still underestimated (Arehalli et al., 2022). Another drawback of surprisal is that it has been unable to distinguish between easy and hard GP sentences.

Much of the original work on GP sentences focused on structural ambiguities. Here we have the original work, insights and examples of Bever (Bever, 1970), which was followed by the indepth analysis of Frazier (Frazier, 1979, 1987; Frazier and Rayner, 1990). Later work brought the role of semantics into the forefront. Since humans process language incrementally, it was expected that the existence of relevant semantic information would increase the speed of recovery from a local ambiguity. In this regard, Altmann et al. (1992); Altmann and Steedman (1988) studied the role of referential information, Trueswell et al. (1994) worked on the tenses of the verbs, and Pickering and Traxler (1998) on the lexical information encoded in sentential sub-phrases such as subject-verb and verb-object. Most of this work has only been verified by Psycholinguistic experiments on human subjects, but some of it was also verified using statistical machine learning methods such as clustering (Padó et al., 2009).

Presheaves and sheaves are general mathematical models introduced to formalise and reason about abstract notions of global consistency. They originate from the work of Jean Leray (Leray, 1959), whose aim was to study partial differential equations from a purely topological perspective. Subsequent work then extended the use of sheaf theory to other areas of mathematics, such as algebraic geometry (Cartan, 1950; Serre, 1955; Grothendieck, 1957) and logic (Lawvere,

1970; Tierney, 2011). More recently, sheaves and presheaves have been applied to formalise the consistency of different forms of concrete data. Here we have examples of data coming from quantum mechanics (Abramsky and Brandenburger, 2011), signal processing (Robinson, 2017), graph neural networks (Bodnar et al., 2022), and natural language (Wang et al., 2021a,b; Lo et al., 2022; Huntsman et al., 2024; Philips, 2019; Bradley et al., 2022). Notably, measures similar to **IF** were developed for physical experiments to compute the amount of unsharpness of experimental data (Vallée et al., 2024). These were preliminarily also tested on linguistic data, e.g. for the interpretations of phrases with semantic and anaphoric ambiguities (Wang et al., 2021a; Lo et al., 2022, 2023). A recent paper explores their applicability to ambiguities arising in garden path sentences but does not consider the general case nor the range of instantiations we offer here, works with the masked feature of BERT and has not been tested on semantic plausibility (Wang and Sadrzadeh, 2024).

3 Methodology

We use topological spaces and their associated data to model the sub-phrases of a sentence and their interpretations. The topological spaces model the relation between the sub-phrases as they are read by a human subject from a piece of text, i.e. incrementally and according to the linear flow of time. This order is also known as the *prefix order* or the *information order*. The data associated to each sub-phrase models the possible different interpretations of each sub-phrase and their probabilities. Here, we work with the completions of sub-phrases into a sentence and the probability of their syntactic structures. This is obtained via a combination of `GPT-2` and `spaCy` (with transformers). In what follows, we first go over the abstract model, then instantiate it to the concrete data of natural language, finally develop a set of measure that compute the differences between the different interpretations, giving rise to the notion of an **Incompatibility Fraction**.

3.1 Abstract Model

A topological space $\mathcal{X}$ is a tuple (X, τ) where X is a set of *points* and $\tau \subset \mathcal{P}(X)$ is the set of *open sets* which contains the empty set and is closed under arbitrary unions and finite intersections.

The open sets of a topological space can also have data associated to them. These are formalised through the notion of a *presheaf*, which is a map P that sends each subset U of X to the set PU of its data. The elements of the set PU are called *sections* over U, and can be seen as the possible data points on U. Here, we are interested in *events* and the *event presheaf* defined as follows. Given a set O of outputs (e.g. syntactic or semantic structures), an event is a map of the type $s\colon U \to O$. Whenever V is a subset of U, i.e. $V \subseteq U$, the presheaf *restricts* PU, i.e. the data points on U, to PV, i.e. the data points on V. For each element of $s \in PU$, the restriction is denoted by $s|_V$. This procedure is depicted in Fig. 1.

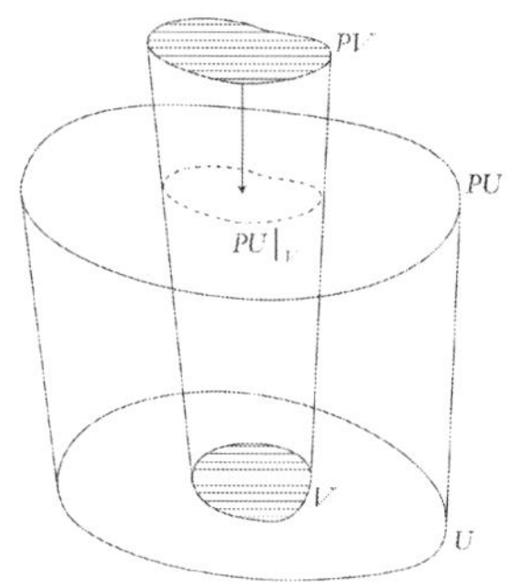

Figure 1: The restriction map of a presheaf.

Presheaves define a notion of *consistency* within sets via restriction maps. Consistency can also be defined across different sets. Given a presheaf P over a topological space $\mathcal{X}$, we say that there is *a gluing* between two sections $s_U \in PU$ and $s_V \in PV$ iff s_U and s_V are *locally consistent* or *compatible*, i.e. $s_U|_{U\cap V} = s_V|_{U\cap V}$. This definition leads to the fact that if there exists a gluing between two sections in PU and PV, then there will be an intersection between their restrictions $PU|_{U\cap V}$ and $PV|_{U\cap V}$, see Fig.2.

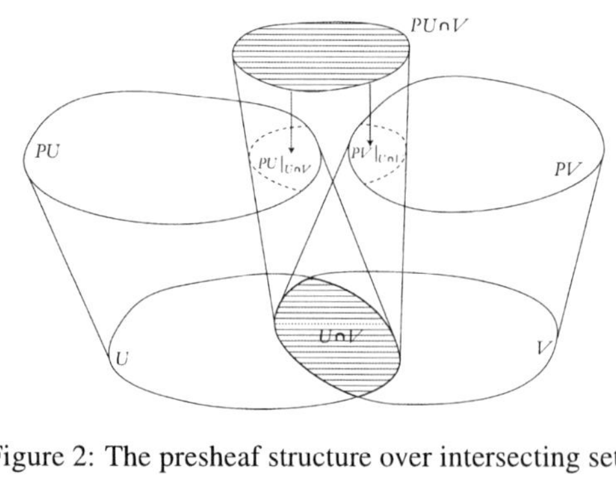

Figure 2: The presheaf structure over intersecting sets.

In order to model probabilistic events, an event

presheaf P is post-composed with a distribution map $\mathcal{D}$ giving rise to a probabilistic event presheaf $\mathcal{D}P$. To a subset U of $\mathcal{X}$ the probabilistic presheaf assigns a set of probability distributions $\{d \mid d : U \to \mathbf{R}^+\}$. Whenever $V \subseteq U$, it computes the marginals of the probabilities of elements of U when restricted to V. Formally, this is as follows:

$$d_V(v) = \sum_{u \in V} d_U(u)$$

These probabilities are measured over our original set of outcomes O, via the principles events of the framework, i.e. $s\colon U \to O$.

3.2 Concrete Model

In the context of human sentence processing, our topological space $\mathcal{X}$ is the set of all incremental sub-phrases of the sentence under consideration. The order of the topology is the prefix relation over the sub-phrases of this sentence. Formally speaking, given the vocabulary σ of the sentences and σ^* the set of phrases over it, for $a, b, c, \cdots \in \sigma^*$, we have

$$a \leq ab \leq abc \leq \cdots$$

As an example consider the sentence "The employees understood the contract", where we have the following instances of the prefix ordering:

The employees $\leq$ *The employees understood* $\leq$ *The employees understood the contract* $\leq$ *The employees understood the contract would change.*

In this sentence, however, there is no order relation between sub-phrases such as "The employees" and "employees understood". Despite the fact that they share "employees", none of them is a prefix of the other.

For the purposes of the current paper, we focus on a *syntactic* event presheaf, which assigns syntactic structures to completions of the sub-phrases into a full sentence. A section of the probabilistic event presheaf $\mathcal{D}P$ will then consist of a probability distribution over the syntactic structures of these completions. The syntactic structures are obtained using the transformer version of the dependency parser spaCy (Choi et al., 2015; Robinson, 1970). This parser returns a single parse for a full sentence. For example, the dependency parse for the sentence "The employees understood the contract would change" is as follows:

The completions of the sub-phrases and their statistics are obtained using the GPT-2 model. See

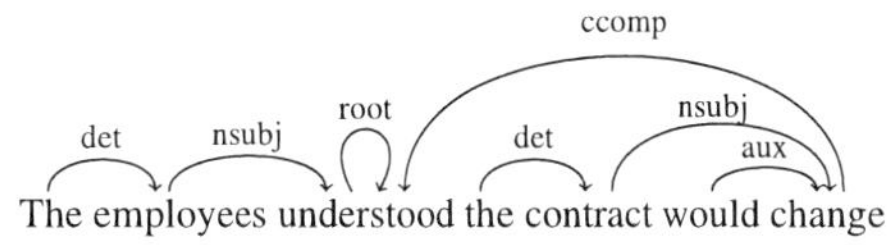

Figure 3: Dependency relations in the sentence *The employees understood the contract would change..*

below for three different completions of the sub-phrase of "The employee understood" and their dependency structures.

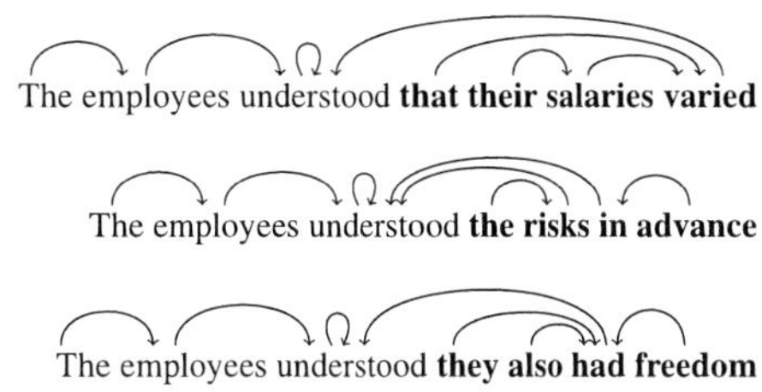

All of these lead to the same partial parse when restricted to the context "The employees understood", namely:

To obtain a syntactic structure for a sub-phrase, we use the restriction operations from the the presheaf, where we only keep the dependency information of each sub-phrase and ignore the rest of the sentence. For instance, the structure of the sub-phrase "The employees understood" restricted to "The employees" is obtained as follows:

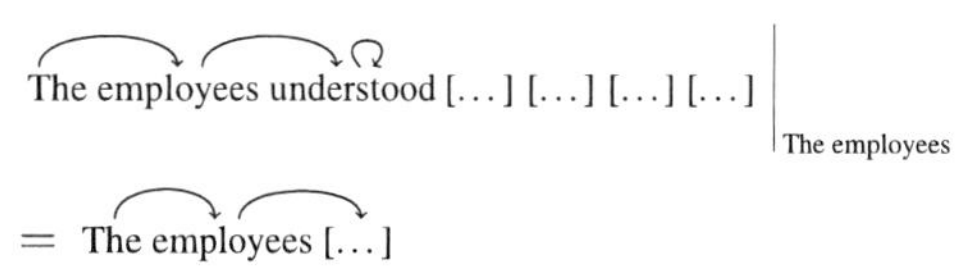

The probability distributions associated to each parse are obtained from the predictions of GPT-2 after sampling from 1000 instances and normalising the results. An example distribution is as follows:

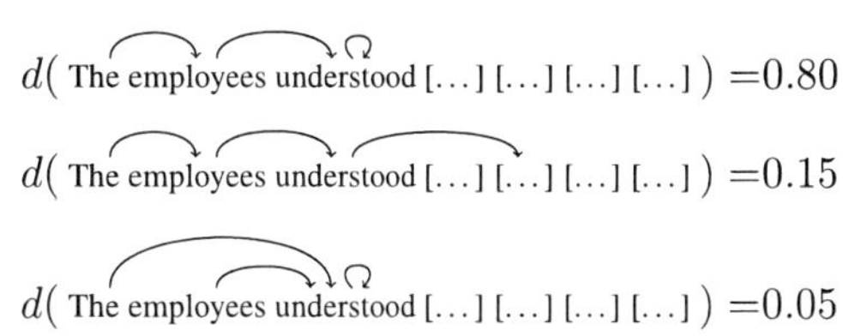

Given two sub-phrases m_1 and m_1m_2 of $\mathcal{X}$ with $m_1 \leq m_1m_2$, suppose $d_{m_1m_2}$ is the probability distribution of the syntactic structures of m_1m_2. Then the restriction of $d_{m_1m_2}$ to m_1 for any syntactic structure $o \in O$ of m_1 is computed as follows:

$$d_{m_1m_2}|_{m_1}(o) = \Sigma_{o' \in O}\, d_{m_1m_2}(oo')$$

This restriction sums the probabilities of all completions of m_1 into m_1m_2, where m_1 retained the same syntactic structure after being completed by m_2. Note that, in general:

$$d_{m_1m_2}|_{m_1} \neq d_{m_1}$$

This is because the reader may have to do some reanalysis when going from m_1 to m_1m_2.

3.3 Measures

Each stage of the human reading process is modelled by a pair of succeeding sub-phrases of a sentence, e.g. (m_1, m_1m_2). The overall process of reading a sentence is modelled by a sequence of these pairs, i.e. $\{(m_i, m_{i+1})_j\}_{a\leq j\leq n-1}$ where n is the number of words or regions in a sentence. As an example, here is the first two pairs of a sequence that models the employee sentence:

$(\textit{The}, \textit{The employees})$
$(\textit{The employees}, \textit{The employees understood})$

As humans read an incoming sub-phrase m_1 of a sentence, they construct interpretations for it and assign probabilities to their interpretations. When the next region m_2 is read, a new set of interpretations and probabilities are constructed, this time for the sub-phrase m_1m_2. The reader expects that the interpretations and probabilities of m_1m_2 to be consistent with those of m_1. If this is the case, the sub-phrase m_1m_2 is comprehended and sentence processing can carry on linearly. For critical regions of GP sentences, however, this is not the case and as a result sentence processing is halted. This leads to a pause and possibly a reversal of the order of reading thus higher reading times are observed. Take our employee sentence and the pair of sub-phrases therein ("The employees understood the contract, The employees understood the contract would change"). This pair sits at the critical region of the garden path effect of the sentence. The shared prefix "The employees understood the contract" has a subject-verb-object structure in the first sub-phrase, which is not consistent with the subject-verb-subject structure after seeing "would change" in the second sub-phrase.

In order to check whether the structure and probabilities of the two succeeding sub-phrases m_1 and m_1m_2 of a sentence match, the larger sub-phrase m_1m_2 is restricted to the smaller one m_1 and the degree of their divergence is estimated. This divergence is what we refer to as the *Incompatibility Fraction* **IF**.

A common choice for measuring divergence is the Kullback–Leibler or KL-divergence. In our case, we measure the KL-divergence between a distribution d_{m_1} to $d_{m_1m_2|m_1}$, given below:

$$KL(d_{m_1}||d_{m_1m_2|m_1}) = \sum_o d_{m_1}(o)\log\frac{d_{m_1}(o)}{d_{m_1m_2|m_1}(o)}$$

KL is not always defined, in which case its symmetric variant Jensen-Shannon divergence is used. In the interest of space will not provide the formula.

Another choice is a metric similar to what is known as Earth-Mover's and measures the overlap between two distributions by taking their min, i.e. $\sum_o \min(d_{m_1m_2}|_{m_1}(o), d_{m_1}(o))$. The divergence between the two distributions is then computed by subtracting the overlap from 1. This leaves us with the following formula:

$$1 - \sum_o \min(d_{m_1m_2}|_{m_1}(o), d_{m_1}(o))$$

All three of these instantiations can be used, giving rise to the following three measures:

$$\begin{array}{rc} \textbf{IF-min}: & 1 - \Sigma_o \min(d_{m_1}(o), d_{m_1m_2}|_{m_1}(o)) \\ \textbf{IF-KL}: & \mathrm{KL}(d_{m_1}||d_{m_1m_2}|_{m_1}) \\ \textbf{IF-JS}: & \mathrm{JS}(d_{m_1}||d_{m_1m_2}|_{m_1}) \end{array}$$

4 Experiments

We worked with two datasets put forwards by Pickering and Traxler in Pickering and Traxler (1998). Dataset 1 has GP sentences with complement clause ambiguities. An example is the following:

> Dataset 1. (i) GP. The dog catcher worried the terrier which fell wouldn't fit into the box.

Dataset 2 has GP sentences with subordinate-clause ambiguities. An example is the following:

	Equation	ρ	p-value
IF-min First Pass	$0.0018 \times \mathbf{IF}_{\min} - 0.0776$	**0.595**	0.00032
IF-min Total	$0.0006 \times \mathbf{IF}_{\min} + 0.14387$	0.448	0.00999
IF-JS First Pass	$0.0016 \times \mathbf{IF}_{JS} - 0.1333$	0.568	0.00068
IF-JS Total	$0.00053 \times \mathbf{IF}_{JS} + 0.0633$	0.4231	0.01580
IF-KL First Pass	$0.0066 \times \mathbf{IF}_{KL} - 0.4238$	0.445	0.0106
IF-KLTotal	$0.0021 \times \mathbf{IF}_{KL} + 0.4022$	0.326	0.06773
SP First Pass	$0.7361 \times \mathbf{SP} + 268.8467$	0.356	0.045
SP Total	$2.1326 \times \mathbf{SP} + 441.9445$	**0.459**	0.008

Table 1: Regression Equations with ρ's and their p-values.

Dataset 2. (i) GP. After the judge decided the verdict of the trial caught the old man's attention.

Each dataset has 24 sets of four sentences: (i) a plausible main sentence with a GP effect, and (ii) its disambiguated control, (iii) an implausible variant of the main sentence, and (iv) its disambiguated control. See below for examples of the disambiguated controls of Dataset 1. (i) GP and Dataset 2. (i) GP:

Dataset 1. (ii) DisAmb. The dog catcher worried that the terrier which fell wouldn't fit into the box.
Dataset 2. (ii) DisAmb. After the judge decided, the verdict of the trial caught the old man's attention.

The disambiguated controls of dataset 1 are obtained by adding a complementiser, such as 'that' to the garden path sentences. The disambiguated controls of dataset 2 are obtained by adding a comma. Sentences of dataset 1 are also known are as NP/S. They are an example of **easy** GP. Sentences of dataset 2 are known as NP/Z and are an example of **hard** GP.

The GP effect should occur after the second verb is encountered which we will refer to as the *critical region*, for example in "wouldn't fit in the box" in Dataset 1. (i) GP and in "caught the old man's attention" in Dataset 2. (i) GP.

Our hypothesis is that in either dataset, the reading times (both first-pass reading times and total reading times) of (i) sentences are longer than (ii) sentences. This is since the (ii) sentences are the disambiguated controls with no GP whereas the (i) sentences each contain a GP. A GP effect is computed by subtracting the reading time of (ii) sentences from the reading time of (i) sentences over the critical region. We expect that this effect is higher in Dataset 2 (which has hard GP sentences) than in Dataset 1 (which has easy GP sentences).

Items (iii) and (iv) differ from (i) and (ii) according to the plausibility of the sub-phrases preceding their critical regions. Here are examples of the implausible variants of the sentences from both datasets with their disambiguated controls:

Dataset 1. (iii) GP. The dog catcher worried the book which fell wouldn't fit into the box.
Dataset 1. (iv) DisAmb. The dog catcher worried that the book which fell wouldn't fit into the box.

Dataset 2. (iii) GP. After the judge packed the verdict of the trial caught the old man's attention.
Dataset 2. (iv) DisAmb. After the judge packed, the verdict of the trial caught the old man's attention.

The difference in plausibility has an impact on the magnitude of the GP effect. Here, we have two hypotheses: first that the garden path effects of the these, e.g. (iii), in either Dataset 1 or 2, are shorter than the ones without them, e.g. (i), and second that, the total reading times of implausible sentences are longer when the implausibility occurs, e.g. in "the book which fell" in Dataset 1. (iii). GP or "the verdict of the trial" in Dataset 2. (iii) GP; we will refer to this region as the *plausibility region*. The reason for hypothesis 1 is that the implausibility is designed to diminish the misanalysis and lead to a smaller GP effects. Indeed, it was shown in Pickering and Traxler (1998) that GP sentence with implausible prefixes exhibit a smaller effect as compared to plausible ones, since the reader will be less inclined to "take the garden path". The

Method	All GPE	All SE	**Hard** (NP/Z) **GP** GPE	**Hard** (NP/Z) **GP** SE	**Easy** (NP/S) **GP** GPE	**Easy** (NP/S) **GP** SE
IF-min First Pass	**39.47**	**0.17**	53.94	2.72	24.99	2.74
IF-min Total	66.17	10.92	90.44	11.18	41.90	10.65
IF-JS First Pass	39.69	0.43	**52.22**	**2.40**	**27.16**	**2.31**
IF-JS Total	65.73	10.94	86.49	11.35	44.97	10.51
IF-KL First Pass	52.81	3.64	62.20	4	43.42	3.30
IF-KL Total	86.28	9.96	**101.62**	**10.67**	**70.94**	**9.19**
Surprisal First Pass	0.35	0.16	0.72	0.32	-0.02	0.05
Surprisal Total	1.01	0.47	2.10	0.92	-0.07	0.16
Human First Pass	39.5		46.5		32.5	
Human Total	185.5		215.5		155.5	

Table 2: Garden Path Effects (GPE) and their Standard Errors (SE). All numbers are in milliseconds.

reason for hypothesis 2 is simply that implausible sentences are harder to comprehend than plausible ones, hence producing a slowdown in reading times when the implausibility is encountered. However, it was shown in Pickering and Traxler (1998) that this slowdown is more marked in the total reading times, and less effect is found in the first-pass.

5 Results and Analysis

We trained a regression model between human first pass and total reading times for all of the regions in all sentences and each of our distance measures. The individual regression equations, their resulting degrees of correlations and corresponding p-values are presented in in Table 1. All of our **IF** measures achieved a high correlation with both human reading times. In most cases these correlations were statistically significant. **IF**-min provided the highest and most significant correlations for first-pass reading, closely followed first by **IF**-JS, **IF**-KL and then surprisal. On the other hand, surprisal appears to correlate better with total reading time, although both the correlation coefficient and p-values are comparable with the ones obtained for **IF**-min. This means that **IF**-min is a good predictor of human reading times, and more specifically that they are better predictors of first-pass reading-times.

The individual regression models were used to predict reading times for sentences of types (i)-(iv). Given that our **IF** measures are all well correlated with human reading times, we expect to observe a significant difference between the ambiguous and unambiguous sentences, i.e. a high garden path effect (GPE). This is presented in column "All" of Table 2. **IF**-min achieves the best results with a high GPE of 39.47 millisecond and the lowest standard errors (SE) of 0.17. Although surprisal correlated well with reading times in general, it predicted very low GPE's, and sometimes does not even predict the existence of a garden path-effect (notably for NP/S sentences). This shows that our measures indeed perform better than surprisal in predicting the garden path effects.

The GPE of hard versus easy sentences are presented in columns "NP/Z" and "NP/S" of Table 2, respectively. We expect to see a higher GPE for hard sentences. This is indeed the case for all models. The GPE's of NP/Z column are higher than the GPE's of NP/S columns. Our best measure for this distinction were **IF**-JS for first pass reading times and IF-KL for total reading times. They both predicted their GPE's with the lowest error. All of the **IF** measures outperformed surprisal, which had the highest errors with the overall GPE. This was also individually the case for each of our tests: (1) our NP/Z test had an SE of 6.79 for first pass and an SE of 14.54 for total reading times, (2) our NP/S test had an SE of 5.68 for first pass and an SE of 12.39 for total reading times. Overall, all the models predicted the first pass reading times better than the total ones.

So far we have only considered syntactic effects. In order to evaluate whether our model is able to detect some semantic effects, we study the predictions for plausible and implausible sentences. The reading times for plausible and implausible sentences are in Tables 3 and 4. The results in Table 3 show that none of the measures could predict that GPE's diminish with implausible cues. In fact, all of the measures showed the opposite. As we can see, the GPE's of implausible sentences are all higher than for plausible ones.

	Plausible	Implausible
Method	GPE	GPE
IF-min First Pass	28.66	50.28
IF-min Total	48.05	84.29
IF-JS First Pass	26.55	52.83
IF-JS Total	43.98	87.48
IF-KL First Pass	39.58	66.05
IF-KL Total	64.66	107.90
Surprisal First Pass	-0.11	0.81
Surprisal Total	-0.33	2.35
Human First Pass	50.5	28.5
Human Total	265	106

Table 3: Garden Path Effects (GPE) for plausible and implausible sentences. All numbers are in milliseconds.

	Plausible	Implausible
Method	RT	RT
IF-min First Pass	565.03	597.69
IF-min Total	988.30	1043.06
IF-JS First Pass	562.63	589.18
IF-JS Total	984.75	1028.75
IF-KL First Pass	560.50	578.13
IF-KL Total	981.79	1010.60
Surprisal First Pass	616.43	616.53
Surprisal Total	1112.01	1112.30
Human First Pass	673.5	686.25
Human Total	1222.5	1275.75

Table 4: Reading Time (RT) for plausible and implausible sentences (over the plausiblity region). All numbers are in milliseconds.

Table 4 shows that all of the **IF** measures could however verify our second hypothesis. As we can see, all the measures, including surprisal, predicted a longer reading time for implausible sub-phrases, although the differences where much more marked in the case of the **IF** measures. Indeed, although the absolute values of the surprisal predictions are closer to the human baseline, the differences in predicted reading times of plausible and implausible sentences were closer to the observed human one for using the **IF** measures. For the first pass reading times, this difference in the human time was 12.75 ms. All the **IF** measures predicted a similar distance; the lowest predicted difference was KL with a difference of 17.63 ms and the higher used **IF**-min with a difference of 32.66 ms. Surprisal, on the other hand, predicted a very low difference of 0.10 ms. Regarding the total reading times: the difference in human times was 53.25 ms; **IF**-min was our best measure, which predicted a difference of 54.76 ms, followed by KL with a prediction of 44 ms and finally JS with 28.81 ms. Surprisal came last, with a very low difference of 0.29 ms.

6 Conclusions and Future Work

Our work highlights the importance of combining syntactic structure and lexical statistics when modelling human language understanding. For syntactic structure we worked with the linear prefix ordering between sub-phrases of a sentence and their dependency structures. For lexical statistics, we worked with sub-phrase completions and their probabilities provided by an LLM. An incompatibility fraction was developed to measure the distance between probability distributions of sub-phrases and their completions. We experimented with known relative entropy distances (KL and JS) and Earth Movers, all of which showed a strong correlation with human behaviour in syntactic GP sentences and outperformed surprisal. None of the measures however, neither any of ours nor surprisal, were successful when it came to GP sentences with semantic implausibilities. We believe these sentences are too complex and in order to deal with them, one needs to explicitly model semantic structure. As it is, the predictions of the parser are over shadowed by the probabilities provided by the LLM, which predicts very high incompatibility and surprisal for implausible phrases.

Kullback–Leibler has a long history of applications in natural language tasks, e.g. in measuring the semantic content of words (Herbelot and Ganesalingam, 2013) and deriving objective functions for language models(Labeau and Cohen, 2019). Notably, Levy showed that under certain assumptions it equates surprisal (Levy, 2008). `Earth Movers` has also been applied in Natural Language Processing, e.g. to compute the relationship between a document and its words (Kusner et al., 2015) and the distance between bilingual lexicons (Huang et al., 2016; Zhang et al., 2016). The main difference between the modelling part of these works and ours is the measurement events. We work with sub-phrases and their syntactic structures, whereas the other measures only consider word co-occurrence. Despite these, we believe there should be a relationship between the incompatibility of two phrases and their degree of surprisal. Formalising this relation is work in progress.

There are four other directions that we aim to pursue in future work. These are as follows: (I) The focus of the paper was on garden path sentences. More work is required to test the performance of our measures on a wider range of naturally occurring sentences. (II) The plausibility element of the dataset used in this work may not be representative of the garden-path effect as a whole. We therefore also plan to replicate our results using different datasets, notably the ones of (Huang et al., 2023; Prasad and Linzen, 2021) (III) As structure, we only considered syntax. Modelling semantic structure of sub-phrases and sentences, e.g. as agent-patient relations or event structures and/or the thematic information associated with verbs needs to be done. (IV) Our framework is by default only forward looking; experimenting with regression and back tracking to model repair and recovery is left to future work.

References

Samson Abramsky and Adam Brandenburger. 2011. The sheaf-theoretic structure of non-locality and contextuality. *New J. Phys.*, 13:113036.

Gerry Altmann and Mark Steedman. 1988. Interaction with context during human sentence processing. *Cognition*, 30(3):191–238.

Gerry T.M Altmann, Alan Garnham, and Yvette Dennis. 1992. Avoiding the garden path: Eye movements in context. *Journal of Memory and Language*, 31(5):685–712.

Suhas Arehalli, Brian Dillon, and Tal Linzen. 2022. Syntactic surprisal from neural models predicts, but underestimates, human processing difficulty from syntactic ambiguities. In *Proceedings of the 26th Conference on Computational Natural Language Learning (CoNLL)*, pages 301–313, Abu Dhabi, United Arab Emirates (Hybrid). Association for Computational Linguistics.

Fred Attneave. 1959. *Applications of Information Theory to Psychology: A summary of basic concepts, methods and results*. Holt, Rinehart and Winston.

Thomas Bever. 1970. The cognitive basis for linguistic structures. *Cognition and the Development of Language*, pages 279–362.

Cristian Bodnar, Francesco Di Giovanni, Benjamin Chamberlain, Pietro Lio, and Michael Bronstein. 2022. Neural sheaf diffusion: a topological perspective on heterophily and oversmoothing in GNNs. In *Proceedings of the Thirty-Sixth Conference on Neural Information Processing Systems*, volume 35.

Tai-Danae Bradley, John Terilla, and Yiannis Vlassopoulos. 2022. An enriched category theory of language: From syntax to semantics. *La Matematica*, 1:551—-580.

Henri Cartan. 1950. Idéaux et modules de fonctions analytiques de variables complexes. *Bulletin de la Société mathématique de France*, 78:29–64.

Jinho D Choi, Joel Tetreault, and Amanda Stent. 2015. It depends: Dependency parser comparison using a web-based evaluation tool. In *Proceedings of the 53rd Annual Meeting of the Association for Computational Linguistics and the 7th International Joint Conference on Natural Language Processing (Volume 1: Long Papers)*, pages 387–396.

Lyn Frazier. 1979. *On comprehending sentences: Syntactic parsing strategies*. Ph.D. thesis, Doctoral dissertation, University of Connecticut.

Lyn Frazier. 1987. *Sentence processing: A tutorial review.*, pages 559–586. Attention and performance 12: The psychology of reading. Lawrence Erlbaum Associates, Inc, Hillsdale, NJ, US.

Lyn Frazier and Keith Rayner. 1982. Making and correcting errors during sentence comprehension: Eye movements in the analysis of structurally ambiguous sentences. *Cognitive Psychology*, 14(2):178–210.

Lyn Frazier and Keith Rayner. 1990. Taking on semantic commitments: Processing multiple meanings vs. multiple senses. *Journal of Memory and Language*, 29.

Alexander Grothendieck. 1957. Sur quelques points d'algèbre homologique, I. *Tohoku Mathematical Journal*, 9(2):119 – 221.

John Hale. 2001. A Probabilistic Earley Parser as a Psycholinguistic Model. In *Proceedings of the Second Meeting of the North American Chapter of the Association for Computational Linguistics on Language Technologies*, NAACL '01, page 1–8, USA. Association for Computational Linguistics.

John Hale. 2003. The information conveyed by words in sentences. *Journal of Psycholinguistic Research*, 32(2):101–123.

John Hale. 2006. Uncertainty about the rest of the sentence. *Cognitive Science*, 30(4):643–672.

Aurélie Herbelot and Mohan Ganesalingam. 2013. Measuring semantic content in distributional vectors. In *Proceedings of the 51st Annual Meeting of the Association for Computational Linguistics (Volume 2: Short Papers)*, pages 440–445, Sofia, Bulgaria. Association for Computational Linguistics.

Gao Huang, Chuan Guo, Matt J Kusner, Yu Sun, Fei Sha, and Kilian Q Weinberger. 2016. Supervised word mover's distance. In *Advances in Neural Information Processing Systems (NIPS)*.

Kuan-Jung Huang, Suhas Arehalli, Mari Kugemoto, Christian Muxica, Grusha Prasad, Brian Dillon, and Tal Linzen. 2023. Surprisal does not explain syntactic disambiguation difficulty: evidence from a large-scale benchmark.

Steve Huntsman, Michael Robinson, and Ludmilla Huntsman. 2024. Prospects for inconsistency detection using large language models and sheaves.

Matt Kusner, Yu Sun, Nicholas Kolkin, and Kilian Weinberger. 2015. From word embeddings to document distances. In *Proceedings of the 32nd International Conference on Machine Learning*, volume 37 of *Proceedings of Machine Learning Research*, pages 957–966. PMLR.

Matthieu Labeau and Shay B. Cohen. 2019. Experimenting with power divergences for language modeling. In *Proceedings of the 2019 Conference on Empirical Methods in Natural Language Processing and the 9th International Joint Conference on Natural Language Processing (EMNLP-IJCNLP)*, pages 4104–4114, Hong Kong, China. Association for Computational Linguistics.

F William Lawvere. 1970. Quantifiers and sheaves. In *Actes du congres international des mathematiciens, Nice*, volume 1, pages 329–334.

Jean Leray. 1959. Théorie des points fixes : indice total et nombre de lefschetz. *Bulletin de la Société Mathématique de France*, 87:221–233.

Roger Levy. 2008. Expectation-based syntactic comprehension. *Cognition*, 106(3):1126–1177.

Kin Ian Lo, Mehrnoosh Sadrzadeh, and Shane Mansfield. 2022. A model of anaphoric ambiguities using sheaf theoretic quantum-like contextuality and bert. In *Proceedings End-to-End Compositional Models of Vector-Based Semantics,* NUI Galway, 15-16 August 2022, volume 366 of *Electronic Proceedings in Theoretical Computer Science*, pages 23–34. Open Publishing Association.

Kin Ian Lo, Mehrnoosh Sadrzadeh, and Shane Mansfield. 2023. Generalised winograd schema and its contextuality. In *Proceedings of 20th International Conference on Quantum Physics and Logic*, Institut Henri Poincare, Paris, France.

Ulrike Padó, Matthew W. Crocker, and Frank Keller. 2009. A probabilistic model of semantic plausibility in sentence processing. *Cognitive Science*, 33(5):794–838.

Steven Philips. 2019. A universal construction for semantic compositionality. *Phil. Trans. R. Soc.*, B375.

Martin J Pickering and Matthew J Traxler. 1998. Plausibility and recovery from garden paths: An eye-tracking study. *Journal of Experimental Psychology: Learning, Memory, and Cognition*, 24(4):940.

Grusha Prasad and Tal Linzen. 2021. Rapid syntactic adaptation in self-paced reading: Detectable, but only with many participants. *Journal of Experimental Psychology: Learning, Memory, and Cognition*, 47(7):1156.

Jane J. Robinson. 1970. Dependency structures and transformational rules. *Language*, 46(2):259–285.

Michael Robinson. 2017. Sheaves are the canonical data structure for sensor integration. *Information Fusion*, 36:208–224.

M. Van Schijndel and T. Linzen. 2018. Modeling garden path effects without explicit hierarchical syntax. In *CogSci*.

Jean-Pierre Serre. 1955. Faisceaux algébriques cohérents. *Annals of Mathematics*, pages 197–278.

Nathaniel J Smith and Roger Levy. 2013. The effect of word predictability on reading time is logarithmic. *Cognition*, 128(3):302–319.

Patrick Sturt, Martin J Pickering, and Matthew W Crocker. 1999. Structural change and reanalysis difficulty in language comprehension. *Journal of Memory and Language*, 40(1):136–150.

M. Tierney. 2011. *Axiomatic Sheaf Theory : Some Constructions and Applications*, pages 249–326. Springer Berlin Heidelberg, Berlin, Heidelberg.

John C. Trueswell, Michael K. Tanenhaus, and Susan M. Garnsey. 1994. Semantic influences on parsing: Use of thematic role information in syntactic ambiguity resolution. *Journal of Memory and Language*, 33(3):285–318.

Kim Vallée, Pierre-Emmanuel Emeriau, Boris Bourdoncle, Adel Sohbi, Shane Mansfield, and Damian Markham. 2024. Corrected bell and non-contextuality inequalities for realistic experiments. *Philosophical Transactions of the Royal Society A: Mathematical, Physical and Engineering Sciences*, 382(2268):20230011.

Marten van Schijndel and Tal Linzen. 2021. Single-stage prediction models do not explain the magnitude of syntactic disambiguation difficulty. *Cognitive Science*, 45(6):e12988.

D. Wang, M. Sadrzadeh, S. Abramsky, and V. Cervantes. 2021a. Analysing Ambiguous Nouns and Verbs with Quantum Contextuality Tools. *Journal of Cognitive Science*, 22(3):391–420.

D. Wang, M. Sadrzadeh, S. Abramsky, and V. Cervantes. 2021b. On the Quantum-like Contextuality of Ambiguous Phrases. In *Proceedings of the 2021 Workshop on Semantic Spaces at the Intersection of NLP, Physics, and Cognitive Science*, page 42–52. Association for Computational Linguistics.

Daphne Wang and Mehrnoosh Sadrzadeh. 2024. Causality and signalling of garden-path sentences. *Philosophical Transactions of the Royal Society A: Mathematical, Physical and Engineering Sciences*, 382(2268):20230013.

Ethan G. Wilcox, Tiago Pimentel, Clara Meister, Ryan Cotterell, and Roger P. Levy. 2023. Testing the Predictions of Surprisal Theory in 11 Languages. *Transactions of the Association for Computational Linguistics*, 11:1451–1470.

Meng Zhang, Yang Liu, Huanbo Luan, Maosong Sun, Tatsuya Izuha, and Jie Hao. 2016. Building earth mover's distance on bilingual word embeddings for machine translation. In *Proceedings of the AAAI Conference on Artificial Intelligence (AAAI)*.

Morphology Matters: Probing the Cross-linguistic Morphological Generalization Abilities of Large Language Models through a Wug Test

Anh Dang
LEADS group, Max Planck Institute for Psycholinguistics, Nijmegen, NL
CLS, Radboud University, NL
Utrecht University, NL
thithaoanh.dangthithaoanh@ru.nl

Limor Raviv
LEADS group, Max Planck Institute for Psycholinguistics, Nijmegen, NL
cSCAN, University of Glasgow, UK
limor.raviv@mpi.nl

Lukas Galke
LEADS group, Max Planck Institute for Psycholinguistics, Nijmegen, NL
lukas.galke@mpi.nl

Abstract

We develop a multilingual version of the Wug Test, an artificial word completion experiment that is typically used to test the morphological knowledge of children, and apply it to the GPT family of large language models (LLMs). LLMs' performance on this test was evaluated by native speakers of six different languages, who judged whether the inflected and derived forms generated by the models conform to the morphological rules of their language. Our results show that LLMs can generalize their morphological knowledge to new, unfamiliar words, but that their success in generating the "correct" generalization (as judged by native human speakers) is predicted by a language's morphological complexity (specifically, integrative complexity). We further find that the amount of training data has surprisingly little on LLMs' morphological generalization abilities within the scope of the analyzed languages. These findings highlight that "morphology matters", and have important implications for improving low-resource language modeling.

1 Introduction

Large language models (LLMs) have been very successful in learning and generating grammatically-correct language as humans do (Brown et al., 2020; OpenAI, 2023). This poses the question of whether they actually have linguistic capability that would allow them to generalize beyond the training distribution (Hupkes et al., 2023). In addition, does this capability manifest differently in different languages that LLMs were trained on? Here, we investigate whether LLMs' linguistic knowledge with respect to morphology differs between languages. Specifically, we test the ability of multilingual LLMs to generalize their morphological knowledge to nonce words in six languages.

Testing cross-linguistic differences in the morphosyntactic abilities of LLMs trained on large amounts of human-generated text is particularly interesting given recent findings on the behavioral similarity between humans and language models in a variety of language learning and processing tasks (Galke et al., 2023; Webb et al., 2023; Srikant et al., 2022) and syntactic structure in the models' learned attention patterns (Manning et al., 2020; Chen et al., 2023). One of the key concerns of contemporary efforts in language modeling is to improve the ability to generalize well across the variety of human languages, especially regarding low-resource languages (e.g., Schäfer et al., 2024; Zheng et al., 2022; Hedderich et al., 2021; Lauscher et al., 2020; Conneau et al., 2020).

Given the importance of the training data to LLM's abilities (Kandpal et al., 2023), conventional wisdom would suggest that the amount of exposure to a given language would be the dominant factor in determining the models' ability to learn the language's morphological patterns. Here, we argue that factors beyond the amount of training data play an important role for LLMs' generalization abilities, and in particular suggest that languages' morphological complexity needs to be taken into account. Notably, languages vary in their degree of morphological complexity (Dryer and Haspelmath, 2013; Evans and Levinson, 2009; Hengeveld and Leufkens, 2018; Ackerman and Malouf, 2013), for

Proceedings of the Workshop on Cognitive Modeling and Computational Linguistics, pages 177–188
August 15, 2024

For each of six languages, Vietnamese, French, Spanish, Romanian, Portuguese, German:

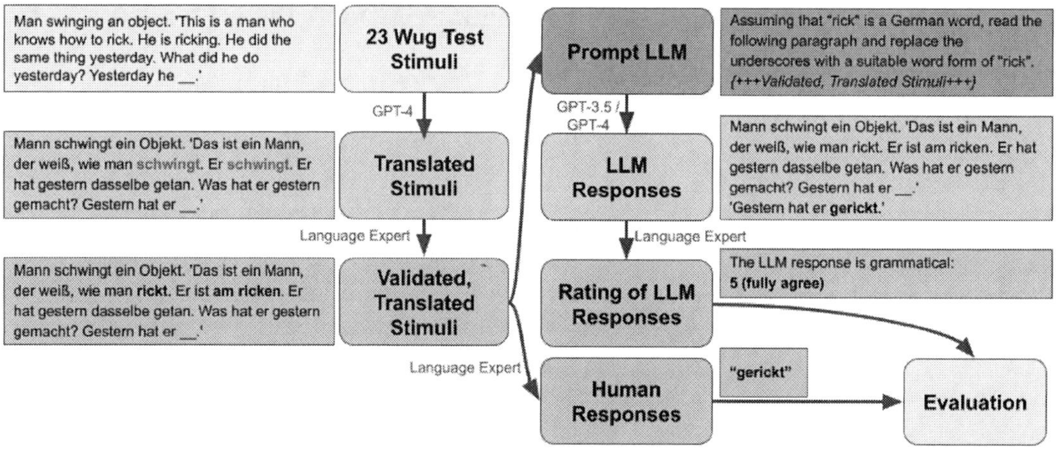

Figure 1: Overview of our experimental procedure with exemplary data and the employed prompt pattern

example in the number of morphological inflection paradigms and their degree of irregularity.

A recent study has shown that LLMs, like humans, are particularly sensitive to the degree of compositional linguistic structure in their input when generating novel forms to new meanings in a matched experiment using a miniature artificial language, with higher degrees of compositionality leading to more systematic generalizations and to a higher agreement with humans (Galke et al., 2023). This finding implies that the morphological learning ability of LLMs across different human languages should similarly be affected by languages' degree of systematic morphological structure, as quantified by measures from typological linguistics (Bentz et al., 2016; Baerman et al., 2015). In the current paper, we test to what extent languages with more systematic structures are indeed learned better by LLMs using an established morphological knowledge test used in the field of child language acquisition: the Wug-test (Berko, 1958).

Even though morphology is heavily studied in the field of computational linguistics (e.g. Batsuren et al., 2022; Wu et al., 2019; Wilson and Li, 2021; Liu and Mao, 2016), and despite its importance to human language learning (Kempe and Brooks, 2008; DeKeyser, 2005; Dressler, 2003, 2010; Slobin, 1985; Raviv et al., 2021), there is little work on the cross-linguistic morphological knowledge of LLMs, especially with respect to the potential effect of languages' morpho-syntactic structure (Weissweiler et al., 2023). Rather, it has been found that LLMs often fail to generate the correct inflected forms of words that were not a part of their training data, regardless of the size of the training set (Liu and Hulden, 2022). Given that only one study to date has probed LLMs' morphological generalization abilities with a multilingual variant of the Wug test (Weissweiler et al., 2023), it is currently unclear to what extent can LLMs generalize their morphological knowledge to new contexts, and to what extent their generalization capabilities are affected by the morphological complexity of language compared to its representation in the training data. Here, we take one step further in this line of work and test the relationship between languages' morphological structure and the generalization ability of multilingual LLMs.

Specifically, as shown in Figure 1, we develop a multilingual version of the Wug Test, an artificial word completion test that is typically used to probe the morphological knowledge of children with respect to inflectional and derivational morphology (Berko, 1958), and apply it to the GPT family of large language models (Brown et al., 2020; Ouyang et al., 2022). We consider six different languages, namely German, Vietnamese, Portuguese, Spanish, French, and Romanian, which vary in their degree of morphological complexity based on several established measures (Lupyan and Dale, 2010; Bentz et al., 2015). For each language, we first employed GPT-4 to translate 23 questions with nonce words from the original Wug Test. The translations were then evaluated and corrected by linguistically-trained native speakers, and the nonce words were adapted to fit each language's phonotactic rules. LLMs were then provided with the translations as prompts (e.g., "This is a Wug.

Now there are two of them. There are two __"), and were prompted to generate the missing inflected form (e.g,. "wugs").

Since the nonce words are new, unfamiliar words, the models need to generalize their morphological knowledge beyond their training data. The model responses were then evaluated by native speakers, who judged whether the inflected and derived forms generated by the LLMs conform to their native language's morphological rules. We then tested LLMs' generalization success across languages against two measures of morphological complexity, namely, the richness of the morphological system and how irregular it is.

In sum, our contributions are

- A multilingual version of the Wug Test for 6 languages
- A human evaluation of GPT-3.5 and GPT-4 responses on this multilingual Wug Test
- A cross-linguistic analysis linking LLM performance to morphological complexity
- An error analysis revealing new patterns of failure modes in morphological generalization

2 Related Work

Morphological capabilities of LLMs Probing machine learning models for linguistic information is a long-standing endeavour (e.g., Conneau et al., 2018; Jawahar et al., 2019; Manning et al., 2020; Warstadt et al., 2020; Rogers et al., 2021; Zhang et al., 2022; Irwin et al., 2023). In terms of morphological capabilities, Liu and Hulden (2022) conducted a Wug-like test with Transformer models (Vaswani et al., 2017), such as the ones underlying LLMs (but trained from scratch), using the SIGMORPHON 2018 shared task (Cotterell et al., 2018a), and found that models struggled to generalize morphological knowledge to new words.

However, to date, there is only one study that assessed the morphological generalization of LLMs to nonce words: Weissweiler et al. (2023), who also took inspiration from the Wug test (Berko, 1958) and prompted ChatGPT with morphological tasks in 4 different languages. The authors created a new dataset by modifying and re-annotating UniMorph 4.0 (Batsuren et al., 2022), and LLMs were prompted to fill in the blank in example sentences. While instructing LLMs to only emit the inflected form, the first word of the generated response was then compared against human responses and supervised morphology models: the affix rule learner (Liu and Mao, 2016) and the minimal generalization learner (Wilson and Li, 2021). Their results showed that GPT-3.5 is not yet on par with humans regarding its generalization performance on nonce words and also underperforms supervised morphology models.

Our work complements this endeavour in several aspects: First, we opt to manually evaluate every response from the LLMs instead of an automated evaluation strategy (which took on the first word of the model response). Second, we analyze a different set of languages, with only German overlapping across studies. And third, we test the impact of other important factors such as languages' morphological complexity scores.

The effect of morphological complexity on language modeling Some studies have explored the relationship between morphological complexity and the learnability of languages by LLMs, but show mixed results. Cotterell et al. (2018b) estimated the predictability of text in a parallel corpora of 21 languages, and found that text in languages with rich inflectional morphology (and thus higher word entropy) was more difficult to predict by n-gram language models and LSTM-based language models. However, when Mielke et al. (2019) use a similar approach with three times more languages and more diverse language families, they did not find a correlation between prediction difficulty and the number of inflectional distinctions that languages have.

Gerz et al. (2018) further showed a positive correlation between multilingual language models' perplexity (how well a language model is able to predict the next work) and type/token ratios (i.e., the ratio between the number of word types and the total number of tokens in the text). More recently, Park et al. (2021) used an even larger parallel corpus of 92 languages, and incorporated more measures of morphological complexity – including corpus-based measures and features from the World Atlas of Languages Structure (WALS) (Dryer and Haspelmath, 2013). Using surprisal as an estimate for difficulty, they found that models' performance was correlated with several complexity measures, and that this correlation was stronger for language models whose tokenizer relied on byte-pair-encoding (Sennrich et al., 2015).

Together, these studies imply that language learnability by LLMs is potentially affected by at least some of the specific morphological features of languages, though which features (and which metrics can capture them) is largely unknown – a question on which we aim to shed new light here.

3 Background on measuring morphological complexity

Languages vary in the degree of morphological complexity, which can be measured using a variety of tools (Dryer and Haspelmath, 2013) and dimensions (Ackerman and Malouf, 2013). Morphological complexity measures can be categorized into integrative complexity (I-complexity) and enumerative complexity (E-complexity) (Ackerman and Malouf, 2013). E-complexity refers to the number of cases and inflectional paradigms that exist in a language's grammar. The more inflected forms a language can have (e.g., for gender, number, tense, case, mood etc.), the higher its E-complexity score is. I-complexity refers to the predictability of inflected form from its context. The more irregular a morphological paradigm is (e.g., many verbs in English show an irregular past tense inflection), i. e. how often irregular forms are used, the higher the I-complexity score.

A well-known example of an E-complexity measure is Lupyan and Dale (2010)'s measure for morphological complexity, which was based on 28 morphological features extracted from the World Atlas of Language Structure (WALS, Dryer and Haspelmath, 2013), such as the number of inflectional distinctions. For I-complexity, Wu et al. (2019) introduced an information-theoretic measure to quantify the frequency of irregular forms, and Bentz et al. (2015) proposed three measures to capture the the variety of word types used to encode identical information ("lexical diversity"). These measures include type-token ratio and Shannon entropy (H), which measures the degree of uncertainty of words. The last measure is the Zipf-Mandelbrot parameter (α), based on the Zipf's law of word distribution. Languages with higher TTR and Shannon entropy are more lexically diverse, and languages with a higher Zipf parameter are less lexically diverse.

For our study, we chose one representative measure for E-complexity and one for I-complexity, relying on previous comparative work that showed that different measures are highly correlated (Çöltekin and Rama, 2023; Bentz et al., 2016). For E-complexity, we use Lupyan and Dale (2010)'s complexity measure based on WALS features (Dryer and Haspelmath, 2013). For I-complexity, we use Bentz et al. (2015)'s entropy-based measure H.

4 Methodology

4.1 Input Languages

Bloomfield (1933) distinguished between four types of languages with respect to morphological structure. In our study, we consider two of them: inflected languages and isolating languages. While Spanish, German, French, Romanian, and Portuguese are highly inflected languages, Vietnamese is an isolating language which does not have explicit grammatical markers within word boundaries. We briefly describe the considered languages below.

Vietnamese is an *isolating language* and thus there are no bound morphemes in the form of suffixes and affixes. As such, there are no inflectional or derivational processes. Instead, semantic and grammatical information is expressed using free morphemes (i.e., standalone words). For instance, Vietnamese does not have plural word forms, but instead expresses plurality by adding a number word before the noun.

French is an *inflected* language in the Romance branch. Verbal inflection is used to indicate tense, person, number, mood, and aspect. Verbs are inflected such that they agree with the subject in terms of person and number. For example, the past tense formation process in French includes combining the correct conjugated form of the auxiliary verbs and the participle form of the main verb, which is formed by adding the correct ending morpheme to it. Nouns carry number and grammatical gender, with number being governed by the endings of the nous.

Spanish is also *inflected* language belonging to the Romance language family, which also includes French, Portuguese and Romanian. The choice of morphemes is governed by grammatical gender when inflecting nouns, pronouns, and adjectives. Verbs are conjugated differently depending on whether the endings of the infinitive forms are *-ar*, *-er*, or *-ir*. They also include inflectional agreement with the person and number of the subject. Another characteristic of Spanish and other Romance languages is that it has fusional morphology, such that a single word form can expresses various grammatical features.

Romanian, as another member of the Romance family, is also highly inflected language with both nominal and verbal inflection, indicating a wide range of grammatical features. The inflected forms of nouns and adjectives are determined by the grammatical gender of the nouns as well as their endings. For verbss, there are 4 conjugation classes, depending on the endings of the infinitive forms.

Portuguese is an Indo-European language in the Romance branch, Portuguese is also an inflectional language that bears similarity to Spanish, although the exact number of possible distinctions/inflections and the degree of irregularity is different. For certain word endings (e.g., *-s* or *-z*), plural and singular Portuguese forms are the same.

German is an *inflected and fusional language* where affixes are added to the stem to convey grammatical information. such as number, case, aspect, and gender. There can be several affixes that encode the same grammatical information. The choice of affixes usually depends on the gender of the noun. If it is masculine, plurality is often expressed by adding *-e*. Feminine nouns often end with *-en*. However, there are many additional rules in German, often involving changing the vowel to an umlaut (e.g., plural of "Zug" is "Züge").

4.2 The Wug Test in Different Languages

The Wug test (Berko, 1958) was originally designed to test the morphological knowledge of children. It tests knowledge of both inflectional morphology and derivational morphology in English. In 23 out of 28 questions, children hear a nonce word embedded in the context of an utterance, and need to complete the utterance with the nonce word's inflected form. The questions test knowledge of a wide range of morphological features, including numbers, tenses, diminutive, possessive, and derivation inflections.

We first used GPT-4 to translate the original Wug-test questions from English into the considered 6 different languages (see Figure 1). Then, to ensure the translation is correct, we had language experts (linguistically-trained native speakers) evaluate the machine-translated questions and correct the translation if necessary. In addition, we adjusted the nonce words to fit the phonotactic rules of the language, according to feedback from the language experts. That is, in many languages word have certain rules regarding the combination of different sounds. For example, French verbs must end with *-er* or *-ir*, while a consonant cluster like *zmrzl* would be unacceptable in English but fine in Czech. Thus, we also asked native speakers to modify the original nonce words so that they become phonotactically valid in the corresponding language. If there were any words that already existed in the language, we also removed those from the test.

After checking all translations, we prompted the LLMs to complete the Wug test in each of the 6 languages. Specifically, we consider GPT-4 (OpenAI, 2023) (version: `gpt4-0613` and GPT-3.5 (Ouyang et al., 2022) (version: `gpt-3.5-turbo-0613`). Since these models are fine-tuned on instruction-following, they can deal with prompts that are phrased as an instruction (Ouyang et al., 2022), we opted to prompt the language models in a zero-shot way, i. e., without supplying similar examples. We did not provide an explicit instruction about which word form that should be generated (e.g., past or plural) such that the LLMs have to infer that information from the context, yet instruct the model to assume that the nonce word is a word of the respective language.

Specifically, we employed the following English-language prompt prefix "Assuming that "{word}" is a {language} word, read the following paragraph and replace the underscores with a suitable word form of "{word}"" to each question (see Figure 1). We repeat this procedure to have the two LLMs complete the Wug Test across the six languages. Below we show an example for one question of the Vietnamese Wug test.

Vietnamese Wug Test: Assuming that "bing" is a Vietnamese word, read the paragraph and replace the underscores with a suitable form of "bing". *Người đàn ông đứng trên trần nhà. "Đây là một người biết cách bing. Anh ta đang* ***bing****. Anh ta đã làm điều tương tự ngày hôm qua. Anh ta đã làm gì hôm qua? Hôm qua anh ta __. (bing/đã bing)"*

In this example, a word should be filled in to indicate past tense of the nonce word "bing". Past tense in Vietnamese does not require changing the word form. The correct form should be the same nonce word. The word "đã" can be optionally added to further clarify that the action is in the past.

Notably, the original Wug test had a pre-defined ground truth response for each question, which were not available for our newly translated languages. Therefore, we asked the language experts to judge whether the model's responses conform to the morphological rules of their language, evaluating the correctness of each answer on a scale of 1 (fully disagree) to 5 (fully agree). Finally, we asked these speakers to provide their own preferred completion of the task.

5 Results

5.1 Accuracy

To calculate accuracy, we binarized the ratings from native speakers into correct and wrong. We consider responses with human ratings of score 4 and 5 to be correct, and those responses rated as 1 and 2 to be wrong. For responses rated with 3, we assign "correct" if the human response matches exactly with the model's response, and "wrong" otherwise.

Language	T	E	I	Model	Acc.
Vietnamese	0.03%	-16	-1.2099	GPT-3.5	87%
				GPT-4	91%
French	1.78%	-11	0.0469	GPT-3.5	52%
				GPT-4	87%
Spanish	0.79%	-11	0.0470	GPT-3.5	78%
				GPT-4	70%
Romanian	0.17%	-8	0.1106	GPT-3.5	56%
				GPT-4	65%
Portuguese	0.54%	-6	0.2948	GPT-3.5	56%
				GPT-4	74%
German	1.68%	-12	0.4648	GPT-3.5	66%
				GPT-4	62%

Table 1: Results from the Human Evaluation of LLM's completions on the Multilingual Wug Test. Column *T* lists the representation of each language GPT-3's training data. E-complexity (column *E*) is the Lupyan and Dale (2010)'s morphological complexity score. I-complexity (*I*) is Bentz et al. (2015)'s entropy-based measure for lexical diversity.

Table 1 shows the results for the six tested languages, as judged by native speakers. Descriptive statistics reveals that both GPT-4 and GPT-3.5 are generally able to generate correct morphemes for the nonce words. The mean accuracy is 0.69 (SD = .46). GPT-4 scores slightly higher than GPT-3.5 (M = .74, SD = .44 versus M = .64, SD = .48), but this difference is not significant under a *t*-test, $t(2{,}274) = -1.69$, $p = .09$. We cannot conclude that GPT-4 is more capable than GPT-3.5.

5.2 Effect of Morphological Complexity

To connect our results per with the languages' morphological complexity, we quantify to what extent accuracy is affected by a language's E-complexity using a measure from Lupyan and Dale (2010) and I-complexity using a measure from Bentz et al. (2015), as well as the percentage of GPT-3's training data per language, for which we take the dataset statistics from GPT-3[1] as estimates.

To test whether morphological complexity scores predict LLMs' performance on the Wug test, we fitted mixed-effect logistic regression models to predict accuracy from morphological complexity values, potentially modulated by the amount of training data. The analysis is conducted in R using the `lme4` package. All variables were centered and scaled before the analysis. We consider the question number as a random effect because it is expected that the difficulty varies per question. We have experience with adding more random effects (e.g., type of GPT model, evaluator, language), yet those did not yield a better fit as tested via ANOVA. Due to high co-linearity (VIF>10 for I-complexity and VIF>5 for E-complexity), we split the model into Model 1 with I-complexity and Model 2 with E-complexity – with the language's representation in the training data being present in both.

The results of Model 1 (see Table 2) show that I-complexity scores have a significant weak negative effect on accuracy scores ($\beta = -.67$, $p = .0187$). The results of Model 2 (see Table 3) show that E-complexity scores do not predict LLMs' performance on the Wug test ($\beta = .10$, $p = .7463$). The amount of training data was found not predictive of Wug test performance in both models ($\beta = .10$, $p = .5853$ and $\beta = -.02$, $p = .9137$, respectively). Further, there is no interaction effect between I and the amount of training data. The interaction effect between E-complexity and training data is, however, nearly significant. These results suggest that it is the irregularity of the morphological system rather than the number of inflectional categories that predicts the morphological capabilities of the investigated LLMs. Notably, the amount of training data does not seem to affect the morphological knowledge learned by LLMs. Figure 2 visualizes the relationship between binary accuracy and each of the predictors (E-complexity, I-complexity, and training data percentage).

5.3 Error Analysis

We also analyzed the models' incorrect responses (rated 2 or lower, or 3 with mismatching responses)

[1] `https://github.com/openai/gpt-3/blob/master/dataset_statistics/languages_by_character_count.csv`

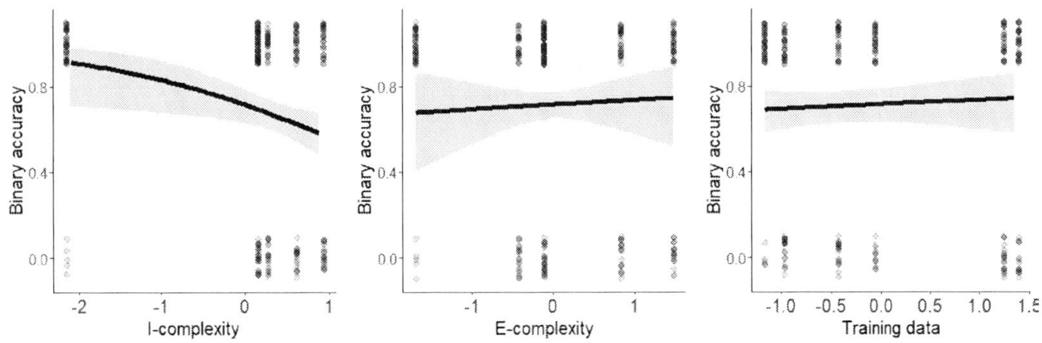

Figure 2: Binary accuracy based on human ratings of LLM responses (y-axis, added jitter) with respect to I-complexity *(Left)* and E-complexity *(Center)*, with higher being more complex, as well as training data percentage *(Right)*. Regression lines are logistic regression with the factor of the (scaled) x-axis as sole predictor and question number as random effect. Results show a trend that LLM responses to the Wug Test in languages that are more complex under these measures receive lower ratings from native speakers.

Var	Estimate	SE	z value	*p*-value
T	0.1036	0.1898	0.546	0.5853
I	-0.6744	0.2869	-2.351	***0.0187**
T:I	-0.0461	0.2389	-0.193	0.8468

Table 2: Results of mixed effect logistic regression with binary accuracy as dependent variable and question number as random effect. Fixed effects are training data (T) and I-complexity (I) and their interaction (T:I).

Var	Estimate	SE	z value	*p*-value
T	-0.0207	0.1914	-0.108	0.9137
E	0.1049	0.3243	0.324	0.7463
T:E	0.7331	0.3857	1.901	0.0574

Table 3: Results of mixed effect logistic regression with binary accuracy as dependent variable and question number as random effect. Fixed effects are training data (T) and E-complexity (E) and their interaction (T:E).

with the goal of detecting any systematic patterns in LLMs' morphological knowledge (or lack thereof). When zooming in on the incorrect responses only, we detected four types of errors:

One type of error is that the models do not inflect the nonce word at all, when it should be inflected, e.g., using an affix (*inflection ignorance*). For example, the correct plural form for the nonce word "tass" in Spanish would be "tasses". However, GPT-3.5 did not add the suffix *-es*, and simply produced the uninflected singular form.

A second type of error was that models occasionally failed to choose the correct affixes (*inflection mismatch*). For example, in German the model generated accusative plural "Lunen", instead of nominative plural "Lune" for the word "Lun".

A third type of error was that the models sometimes applies English morphological rules to nonce words in other languages (*English fall-back*). For example, in Vietnamese, "đã" should be added before the verb to create the past form. In the case of the nonce verb "bing", the models should have responded with "đã bing". However, the model's response was "binged" – which wrongfully follows the grammatical rule of English. We attribute this kind of error to the dominance of English and possibly due to the English Wug test being present in the models' training data. Although "bing" is a phonotactically valid in Vietnamese, the models mistakenly considered it as an English nonce word, as in the original Wug test, and thus completed the sentence with the English past form.

As a fourth type of error, we also observe the *real-word bias*, as reported by Weissweiler et al. (2023), whereby the models sometimes treated the nonce word as if it was a similar existing word in the language, and provide an inflected form for that word. For example, the nonce word "tass" was wrongly pluralized to "Tassen", which is the plural of the very similar existing German word "Tasse".

6 Discussion

Our goal was to investigate how well multilingual LLMs learn the underlying morphosyntactic structure of different languages and how this is influenced by languages' degree of morphosyntactic complexity. We did this by applying a Wug test in 6 different languages, and evaluating the models' responses as a function of two measures of complexity, as well as the representation of the language in the training data.

Morphology matters We found that integrative morphological complexity (I-complexity) is more predictive of LLMs' out-of-distribution performance than the language's representation in the pre-training data – a surprising finding given that the amount of training data is usually considered the main driving factor for language modeling performance. For example, despite having the least amount of training data (0.03%), the models' performance was much better on Vietnamese compared to other languages (average accuracy of 85%), which has the lowest E- and I-complexity scores. Notably, all of the observed failures on the Vietnamese Wug test belong to the first error category: the misuse of English morphological rules.

Our results also show that different dimensions of morphological complexity affect LLMs' performance to different degrees. Specifically, we found that only I-complexity (which corresponds to predictability of word forms from context) predicts Wug test accuracy, but not E-complexity. Thus, while languages with a lot of word forms are more challenging for LLMs to learn, the predictability of these word forms given appears to have a greater impact on LLM performance.

Lastly, our results show that the amount of training data seems to be less important than morphological complexity. Specifically, we did not find that the language's representation in the model's training data is not predictive of its morphological capabilities. With this finding, we further support Liu and Hulden (2022), who found that Transformer-based models fail to inflect unknown words despite them being trained on a large amount of data.

Error types Our error analysis shows that LLM's occasionally make mistakes in inflecting the nonce words. Besides the real word bias revealed by Weissweiler et al. (2023), our error analysis revealed three more types of errors beyond real-world bias: inflection ignorance, inflection mismatch, and English fall-back. We attribute the English fall-back to the high prominence of English in the model's training data (90%+).

Comparison with previous studies Previous studies found the effect of E-complexity on LLMs' performance (Cotterell et al., 2018b; Park et al., 2021; Gerz et al., 2018). However, we do not find any effect of E-complexity on LLMs' Wug test accuracy. Rather, we found that I-complexity predicts morphological capability of LLMs. It should be noted that these studies measure the relationship between morphological complexity and different metrics of LLMs. While we attempt to use behavioral probing to measure morphological knowledge of LLMs, other work uses modeling difficulty (Cotterell et al., 2018b), perplexity (Gerz et al., 2018), and surprisal (Park et al., 2021; Mielke et al., 2019). Furthermore, the high correlation between the analyzed morphological complexity measures confirms the findings of Cöltekin and Rama (2023).

Comparing our results with Weissweiler et al. (2023), we can confirm that LLM's accuracy on the morphological completion of nonce words is not perfect. A particularly interesting case is German: Among the languages studied here, German has a relatively low E-complexity score, but the highest I-complexity score. Weissweiler et al. (2023) found German to be the best-performing language, with 86.49% accuracy, taking into account the five most probable completions for each stimulus $k = 5$. However, comparing German on a $k = 1$ setup with long prompts (most similar to ours), the other study reports 62.18% accuracy, which is indeed comparable with our results for German: 62% (GPT-4) and 66% (GPT-3.5). Therefore, we assume that this drastic drop in accuracy (86% to 62%) can be attributed to the number of possible generation attempts that are taken into account ($k = 5$ vs. $k = 1$). For future studies, it is therefore important to take into account the number of generation attempts.

In the context of comparing large language models to humans, our results suggest that what is more complex for us is also more complex for LLMs. Specifically, work on first and second language acquisition suggests that languages with more complex morphosyntactic structures are harder to learn (Kempe and Brooks, 2008; DeKeyser, 2005; Dressler, 2003, 2010; Slobin, 1985). Our study is in line with this conclusion, and extend it to LLMs. It also confirms recent insights from artificial language learning experiments, which found that artificial miniature languages with more systematic structures are easier to learn and generalize across adult humans, small recurrent neural networks trained from scratch, and large language models (Galke et al., 2023; Raviv et al., 2021).

Implications Our findings have important implications for low-resource language processing.

Specifically, it is worth paying attention to languages' morphological complexity. When aiming for equal capabilities across languages in multilingual LLMs, the classic approach would be to counterbalance the representation of low-resource languages in the training data. However, our results suggest that this is not sufficient: we found no significant effect of training data representation on Wug test accuracy (within the frame of the analyzed data). Potentially, other tokenization strategies, such as single-byte tokenization (Xue et al., 2022) or morphology-guided tokenization (Creutz and Lagus, 2007) could help improve LLM's performance on low-resource language processing.

7 Conclusion

We tested whether languages' morphological complexity affected the performance of multilingual large language models on a classic language task. We ran the Wug test in 6 languages and analyzed how task performance was affected by the degree of morphological complexity in each language. Our results show that languages' morphological complexity (specifically, integrative complexity), is more important than its relative representation in the training data of large language models – a finding that challenges conventional wisdom and comes with important implications for low-resource language modeling. We have further identified additional error types beyond real-world bias such as English fall-back and inflection ignorance, whose cause we will explore in future work by investigating the role of tokenization.

Data Availability

The translations of the Wug test into the six considered languages, the script for querying the language models, and the script for our statistical analysis is available under `https://github.com/dangthithaoanh/multilingual-wug-test-on-LLMs`.

Limitations

We have limited ourselves to comparing only two large language models because we prioritized having an expert judgement for each individual model response. The share of each language in the LLM's pre-training data is taken from the original GPT-3 repository as estimates for GPT-3.5 and GPT-4. Another limitation is that the nonce words could appear more irregular in some languages than in others. Moreover, for most languages, we only had one language expert providing the ratings of grammatical correctness. However, we have qualitatively checked the interrater agreement on Vietnamese and found high agreement. Lastly, we have only considered one language (Vietnamese) for the category of isolating morphology.

Ethical Considerations

We emphasize that morphological complexity of languages bears no implication on their quality – having more complexity does not make one language better than another (see Raviv et al., 2022).

Acknowledgements

We are extremely grateful for the effort that the language experts have put into evaluating the responses of the large language models: Mathilde Josserand, Oxana Grosseck, Sergio Miguel Pereira Soares, Lucia de Hoyos, Tin Le, and Lois Dona. We further appreciate the helpful comments and feedback that we received from the audience of the Evolang conference in Madison, WI, USA, 2024.

References

Farrell Ackerman and Robert Malouf. 2013. Morphological organization: The low conditional entropy conjecture. *Language*, 89(3):429–464.

Matthew Baerman, Dunstan Brown, and Greville G Corbett. 2015. *Understanding and measuring morphological complexity*. Oxford University Press, USA.

Khuyagbaatar Batsuren, Omer Goldman, Salam Khalifa, Nizar Habash, Witold Kieraś, Gábor Bella, Brian Leonard, Garrett Nicolai, Kyle Gorman, Yustinus Ghanggo Ate, Maria Ryskina, Sabrina Mielke, Elena Budianskaya, Charbel El-Khaissi, Tiago Pimentel, Michael Gasser, William Abbott Lane, Mohit Raj, Matt Coler, Jaime Rafael Montoya Samame, Delio Siticonatzi Camaiteri, Esaú Zumaeta Rojas, Didier López Francis, Arturo Oncevay, Juan López Bautista, Gema Celeste Silva Villegas, Lucas Torroba Hennigen, Adam Ek, David Guriel, Peter Dirix, Jean-Philippe Bernardy, Andrey Scherbakov, Aziyana Bayyr-ool, Antonios Anastasopoulos, Roberto Zariquiey, Karina Sheifer, Sofya Ganieva, Hilaria Cruz, Ritván Karahóğa, Stella Markantonatou, George Pavlidis, Matvey Plugaryov, Elena Klyachko, Ali Salehi, Candy Angulo, Jatayu Baxi, Andrew Krizhanovsky, Natalia Krizhanovskaya, Elizabeth Salesky, Clara Vania, Sardana Ivanova, Jennifer White, Rowan Hall Maudslay, Josef Valvoda, Ran Zmigrod, Paula Czarnowska, Irene Nikkarinen, Aelita Salchak, Brijesh Bhatt, Christopher Straughn, Zoey Liu, Jonathan North

Washington, Yuval Pinter, Duygu Ataman, Marcin Wolinski, Totok Suhardijanto, Anna Yablonskaya, Niklas Stoehr, Hossep Dolatian, Zahroh Nuriah, Shyam Ratan, Francis M. Tyers, Edoardo M. Ponti, Grant Aiton, Aryaman Arora, Richard J. Hatcher, Ritesh Kumar, Jeremiah Young, Daria Rodionova, Anastasia Yemelina, Taras Andrushko, Igor Marchenko, Polina Mashkovtseva, Alexandra Serova, Emily Prud'hommeaux, Maria Nepomniashchaya, Fausto Giunchiglia, Eleanor Chodroff, Mans Hulden, Miikka Silfverberg, Arya D. McCarthy, David Yarowsky, Ryan Cotterell, Reut Tsarfaty, and Ekaterina Vylomova. 2022. UniMorph 4.0: Universal Morphology. In *Proceedings of the Thirteenth Language Resources and Evaluation Conference*, pages 840–855, Marseille, France. European Language Resources Association.

Christian Bentz, Tatyana Ruzsics, Alexander Koplenig, and Tanja Samardžić. 2016. A comparison between morphological complexity measures: Typological data vs. language corpora. In *Proceedings of the Workshop on Computational Linguistics for Linguistic Complexity (CL4LC)*, pages 142–153, Osaka, Japan. The COLING 2016 Organizing Committee.

Christian Bentz, Annemarie Verkerk, Douwe Kiela, Felix Hill, and Paula Buttery. 2015. Adaptive Communication: Languages with More Non-Native Speakers Tend to Have Fewer Word Forms. *PLOS ONE*, 10(6):e0128254.

Jean Berko. 1958. The child's learning of english morphology. *Word*, 14(2-3):150–177.

Leonard Bloomfield. 1933. *Language*. H. Holt.

Tom Brown, Benjamin Mann, Nick Ryder, Melanie Subbiah, Jared D Kaplan, Prafulla Dhariwal, Arvind Neelakantan, Pranav Shyam, Girish Sastry, Amanda Askell, Sandhini Agarwal, Ariel Herbert-Voss, Gretchen Krueger, Tom Henighan, Rewon Child, Aditya Ramesh, Daniel Ziegler, Jeffrey Wu, Clemens Winter, Chris Hesse, Mark Chen, Eric Sigler, Mateusz Litwin, Scott Gray, Benjamin Chess, Jack Clark, Christopher Berner, Sam McCandlish, Alec Radford, Ilya Sutskever, and Dario Amodei. 2020. Language models are few-shot learners. In *Advances in Neural Information Processing Systems*, volume 33, pages 1877–1901. Curran Associates, Inc.

Angelica Chen, Ravid Schwartz-Ziv, Kyunghyun Cho, Matthew L. Leavitt, and Naomi Saphra. 2023. Sudden Drops in the Loss: Syntax Acquisition, Phase Transitions, and Simplicity Bias in MLMs.

Cagri Cöltekin and Taraka Rama. 2023. What do complexity measures measure? Correlating and validating corpus-based measures of morphological complexity. *Linguistics Vanguard*, 9(s1):27–43.

Alexis Conneau, Kartikay Khandelwal, Naman Goyal, Vishrav Chaudhary, Guillaume Wenzek, Francisco Guzmán, Edouard Grave, Myle Ott, Luke Zettlemoyer, and Veselin Stoyanov. 2020. Unsupervised Cross-lingual Representation Learning at Scale. In *Proceedings of the 58th Annual Meeting of the Association for Computational Linguistics*, pages 8440–8451, Online. Association for Computational Linguistics.

Alexis Conneau, German Kruszewski, Guillaume Lample, Loïc Barrault, and Marco Baroni. 2018. What you can cram into a single $&!#* vector: Probing sentence embeddings for linguistic properties. In *Proceedings of the 56th Annual Meeting of the Association for Computational Linguistics (Volume 1: Long Papers)*, pages 2126–2136, Melbourne, Australia. Association for Computational Linguistics.

Ryan Cotterell, Christo Kirov, John Sylak-Glassman, Géraldine Walther, Ekaterina Vylomova, Arya D. McCarthy, Katharina Kann, Sabrina J. Mielke, Garrett Nicolai, Miikka Silfverberg, David Yarowsky, Jason Eisner, and Mans Hulden. 2018a. The CoNLL–SIGMORPHON 2018 shared task: Universal morphological reinflection. In *Proceedings of the CoNLL–SIGMORPHON 2018 Shared Task: Universal Morphological Reinflection*, pages 1–27, Brussels. Association for Computational Linguistics.

Ryan Cotterell, Sabrina J. Mielke, Jason Eisner, and Brian Roark. 2018b. Are all languages equally hard to language-model? In *Proceedings of the 2018 Conference of the North American Chapter of the Association for Computational Linguistics: Human Language Technologies, Volume 2 (Short Papers)*, pages 536–541, New Orleans, Louisiana. Association for Computational Linguistics.

Mathias Creutz and Krista Lagus. 2007. Unsupervised models for morpheme segmentation and morphology learning. *ACM Transactions on Speech and Language Processing (TSLP)*, 4(1):1–34.

Robert M DeKeyser. 2005. What makes learning second-language grammar difficult? a review of issues. *Language learning*, 55.

Wolfgang U Dressler. 2003. Degrees of grammatical productivity in inflectional morphology. *Italian Journal of Linguistics*, 15:31–62.

Wolfgang U Dressler. 2010. A typological approach to first language acquisition. *Language acquisition across linguistic and cognitive systems*, 52:109–124.

Matthew S Dryer and Martin Haspelmath. 2013. Wals online (v2020. 3). *Zenodo https://doi.org/10.5281/zenodo*, 7385533.

Nicholas Evans and Stephen C Levinson. 2009. The myth of language universals: Language diversity and its importance for cognitive science. *Behavioral and brain sciences*, 32(5):429–448.

Lukas Galke, Yoav Ram, and Limor Raviv. 2023. What makes a language easy to deep-learn?

Daniela Gerz, Ivan Vulić, Edoardo Maria Ponti, Roi Reichart, and Anna Korhonen. 2018. On the relation between linguistic typology and (limitations of) multilingual language modeling. In *Proceedings of the 2018 Conference on Empirical Methods in Natural Language Processing*, pages 316–327, Brussels, Belgium. Association for Computational Linguistics.

Michael A. Hedderich, Lukas Lange, Heike Adel, Jannik Strötgen, and Dietrich Klakow. 2021. A survey on recent approaches for natural language processing in low-resource scenarios. In *Proceedings of the 2021 Conference of the North American Chapter of the Association for Computational Linguistics: Human Language Technologies*, pages 2545–2568, Online. Association for Computational Linguistics.

Kees Hengeveld and Sterre Leufkens. 2018. Transparent and non-transparent languages. *Folia Linguistica*, 52(1):139–175.

Dieuwke Hupkes, Mario Giulianelli, Verna Dankers, Mikel Artetxe, Yanai Elazar, Tiago Pimentel, Christos Christodoulopoulos, Karim Lasri, Naomi Saphra, Arabella Sinclair, Dennis Ulmer, Florian Schottmann, Khuyagbaatar Batsuren, Kaiser Sun, Koustuv Sinha, Leila Khalatbari, Maria Ryskina, Rita Frieske, Ryan Cotterell, and Zhijing Jin. 2023. A taxonomy and review of generalization research in NLP. *Nature Machine Intelligence*, 5(10):1161–1174.

Tovah Irwin, Kyra Wilson, and Alec Marantz. 2023. BERT Shows Garden Path Effects. In *Proceedings of the 17th Conference of the European Chapter of the Association for Computational Linguistics*, pages 3220–3232, Dubrovnik, Croatia. Association for Computational Linguistics.

Ganesh Jawahar, Benoît Sagot, and Djamé Seddah. 2019. What does BERT learn about the structure of language? In *Proceedings of the 57th Annual Meeting of the Association for Computational Linguistics*, pages 3651–3657, Florence, Italy. Association for Computational Linguistics.

Nikhil Kandpal, Haikang Deng, Adam Roberts, Eric Wallace, and Colin Raffel. 2023. Large language models struggle to learn long-tail knowledge. In *Proceedings of the 40th International Conference on Machine Learning*, volume 202 of *Proceedings of Machine Learning Research*, pages 15696–15707. PMLR.

Vera Kempe and Patricia J Brooks. 2008. Second language learning of complex inflectional systems. *Language Learning*, 58(4):703–746.

Anne Lauscher, Vinit Ravishankar, Ivan Vulić, and Goran Glavaš. 2020. From Zero to Hero: On the Limitations of Zero-Shot Language Transfer with Multilingual Transformers. In *Proceedings of the 2020 Conference on Empirical Methods in Natural Language Processing (EMNLP)*, pages 4483–4499, Online. Association for Computational Linguistics.

Ling Liu and Mans Hulden. 2022. Can a Transformer Pass the Wug Test? Tuning Copying Bias in Neural Morphological Inflection Models. In *Proceedings of the 60th Annual Meeting of the Association for Computational Linguistics (Volume 2: Short Papers)*, pages 739–749, Dublin, Ireland. Association for Computational Linguistics.

Ling Liu and Lingshuang Jack Mao. 2016. Morphological reinflection with conditional random fields and unsupervised features. In *Proceedings of the 14th SIGMORPHON Workshop on Computational Research in Phonetics, Phonology, and Morphology*, pages 36–40, Berlin, Germany. Association for Computational Linguistics.

Gary Lupyan and Rick Dale. 2010. Language structure is partly determined by social structure. *PLoS ONE*, 5(1):e8559.

Christopher D. Manning, Kevin Clark, John Hewitt, Urvashi Khandelwal, and Omer Levy. 2020. Emergent linguistic structure in artificial neural networks trained by self-supervision. *Proceedings of the National Academy of Sciences*, 117(48):30046–30054.

Sabrina J. Mielke, Ryan Cotterell, Kyle Gorman, Brian Roark, and Jason Eisner. 2019. What kind of language is hard to language-model? In *Proceedings of the 57th Annual Meeting of the Association for Computational Linguistics*, pages 4975–4989, Florence, Italy. Association for Computational Linguistics.

OpenAI. 2023. GPT-4 Technical Report.

Long Ouyang, Jeffrey Wu, Xu Jiang, Diogo Almeida, Carroll Wainwright, Pamela Mishkin, Chong Zhang, Sandhini Agarwal, Katarina Slama, Alex Ray, John Schulman, Jacob Hilton, Fraser Kelton, Luke Miller, Maddie Simens, Amanda Askell, Peter Welinder, Paul F. Christiano, Jan Leike, and Ryan Lowe. 2022. Training language models to follow instructions with human feedback. *Advances in Neural Information Processing Systems*, 35:27730–27744.

Hyunji Hayley Park, Katherine J. Zhang, Coleman Haley, Kenneth Steimel, Han Liu, and Lane Schwartz. 2021. Morphology matters: A multilingual language modeling analysis. *Transactions of the Association for Computational Linguistics*, 9:261–276.

Limor Raviv, Marianne de Heer Kloots, and Antje Meyer. 2021. What makes a language easy to learn? a preregistered study on how systematic structure and community size affect language learnability. *Cognition*, 210:104620.

Limor Raviv, Louise R Peckre, and Cedric Boeckx. 2022. What is simple is actually quite complex: A critical note on terminology in the domain of language and communication. *Journal of Comparative Psychology*, 136(4):215.

Anna Rogers, Olga Kovaleva, and Anna Rumshisky. 2021. A Primer in BERTology: What We Know About How BERT Works. *Transactions of the Association for Computational Linguistics*, 8:842–866.

Anton Schäfer, Shauli Ravfogel, Thomas Hofmann, Tiago Pimentel, and Imanol Schlag. 2024. Language imbalance can boost cross-lingual generalisation. *arXiv preprint arXiv:2404.07982*.

Rico Sennrich, Barry Haddow, and Alexandra Birch. 2015. Neural machine translation of rare words with subword units. *arXiv preprint arXiv:1508.07909*.

Dan I Slobin. 1985. The child as a linguistic icon-maker. *Iconicity in syntax*, pages 221–248.

Shashank Srikant, Ben Lipkin, Anna A. Ivanova, Evelina Fedorenko, and Una-May O'Reilly. 2022. Convergent Representations of Computer Programs in Human and Artificial Neural Networks. In *Advances in Neural Information Processing Systems*.

Ashish Vaswani, Noam Shazeer, Niki Parmar, Jakob Uszkoreit, Llion Jones, Aidan N Gomez, Łukasz Kaiser, and Illia Polosukhin. 2017. Attention is all you need. *Advances in neural information processing systems*, 30.

Alex Warstadt, Alicia Parrish, Haokun Liu, Anhad Mohananey, Wei Peng, Sheng-Fu Wang, and Samuel R. Bowman. 2020. BLiMP: The benchmark of linguistic minimal pairs for english. *Transactions of the Association for Computational Linguistics*, 8:377–392.

Taylor Webb, Keith J. Holyoak, and Hongjing Lu. 2023. Emergent analogical reasoning in large language models. *Nature Human Behaviour*, pages 1–16.

Leonie Weissweiler, Valentin Hofmann, Anjali Kantharuban, Anna Cai, Ritam Dutt, Amey Hengle, Anubha Kabra, Atharva Kulkarni, Abhishek Vijayakumar, Haofei Yu, et al. 2023. Counting the bugs in chatgpt's wugs: A multilingual investigation into the morphological capabilities of a large language model. In *Proceedings of the 2023 Conference on Empirical Methods in Natural Language Processing*, pages 6508–6524.

Colin Wilson and Jane S.Y. Li. 2021. Were we there already? Applying minimal generalization to the SIGMORPHON-UniMorph shared task on cognitively plausible morphological inflection. In *Proceedings of the 18th SIGMORPHON Workshop on Computational Research in Phonetics, Phonology, and Morphology*, pages 283–291, Online. Association for Computational Linguistics.

Shijie Wu, Ryan Cotterell, and Timothy O'Donnell. 2019. Morphological Irregularity Correlates with Frequency. In *Proceedings of the 57th Annual Meeting of the Association for Computational Linguistics*, pages 5117–5126, Florence, Italy. Association for Computational Linguistics.

Linting Xue, Aditya Barua, Noah Constant, Rami Al-Rfou, Sharan Narang, Mihir Kale, Adam Roberts, and Colin Raffel. 2022. Byt5: Towards a token-free future with pre-trained byte-to-byte models. *Transactions of the Association for Computational Linguistics*, 10:291–306.

Lining Zhang, Mengchen Wang, Liben Chen, and Wenxin Zhang. 2022. Probing GPT-3's linguistic knowledge on semantic tasks. In *Proceedings of the Fifth BlackboxNLP Workshop on Analyzing and Interpreting Neural Networks for NLP*, pages 297–304, Abu Dhabi, United Arab Emirates (Hybrid). Association for Computational Linguistics.

Yanan Zheng, Jing Zhou, Yujie Qian, Ming Ding, Chonghua Liao, Li Jian, Ruslan Salakhutdinov, Jie Tang, Sebastian Ruder, and Zhilin Yang. 2022. FewNLU: Benchmarking state-of-the-art methods for few-shot natural language understanding. In *Proceedings of the 60th Annual Meeting of the Association for Computational Linguistics (Volume 1: Long Papers)*, pages 501–516, Dublin, Ireland. Association for Computational Linguistics.

Evaluating Grammatical Well-Formedness in Large Language Models: A Comparative Study with Human Judgments

Zhuang Qiu, Xufeng Duan, Zhenguang G. Cai
Department of Linguistics and Modern Languages
The Chinese University of Hong Kong
Hong Kong SAR
zhuangharveyqiu@gmail.com, xufeng.duan@link.cuhk.edu.hk
zhenguangcai@cuhk.edu.hk

Abstract

Research in artificial intelligence has witnessed the surge of large language models (LLMs) demonstrating improved performance in various natural language processing tasks. This has sparked significant discussions about the extent to which large language models emulate human linguistic cognition and usage. This study delves into the representation of grammatical well-formedness in LLMs, which is a critical aspect of linguistic knowledge. In three preregistered experiments, we collected grammaticality judgment data for over 2400 English sentences with varying structures from ChatGPT and Vicuna, comparing them with human judgment data. The results reveal substantial alignment in the assessment of grammatical correctness between LLMs and human judgments, albeit with LLMs often showing more conservative judgments for grammatical correctness or incorrectness.

1 Introduction

The rise of LLMs has been extraordinary, demonstrating proficiency across numerous linguistic tasks such as resolving ambiguities (Ortega-Martín et al., 2023), addressing queries (Brown et al., 2020), and facilitating multilingual translation (Jiao et al., 2023). Despite not being initially programmed with a human-like hierarchical syntax structure, these models have managed to identify complex syntactic patterns and generate sophisticated syntactic interpretations (Wilcox et al., 2022; Van Schijndel and Linzen, 2018; Futrell et al., 2019). However, the critical question remains: Do LLMs truly mirror human linguistic cognition? Prominent figures such as Chomsky et al. (2023) argue that LLMs and humans process and understand language differently, while others like Piantadosi (2023) suggest that LLMs might indeed reflect genuine human linguistic processes.

Recent empirical research has become key to this debate. Innovative experiments by Binz and Schulz (2023) subjected GPT-3 to a battery of psychological tests originally crafted to understand facets of human thought processes, ranging from decision-making matrices to reasoning pathways. The outcomes were intriguing, with GPT-3 not just mirroring but at times outperforming human benchmarks in specific scenarios. Similarly, Kosinski (2023) assessed the capacity of LLMs to understand and respond to false-belief scenarios, which are utilized to gauge human empathy and comprehension. Here, the responses from ChatGPT echoed the patterns seen in school-going children, though subsequent research from Brunet-Gouet et al. (2023) voiced concerns about the consistency of such responses. Further, Cai et al. (2023) subjected ChatGPT to a range of psycholinguistic tests, revealing significant alignment in language use between the model and humans, although differences such as in word length preference were observed (e.g., Mahowald et al. (2013)). Qiu et al. (2023) assessed ChatGPT's ability to compute pragmatic implicatures and found that ChatGPT did not demonstrate human-like flexibility in switching between pragmatic and semantic processing. Additionally, ChatGPT did not exhibit the effect of communicative context on the rates of computing scalar implicatures, which is a well-established effect for human participants.

When examining LLM-human similarities, it's crucial to assess the extent to which LLMs' representations of linguistic knowledge align with those of humans. Contemporary linguistic theories often distinguish between the inherent mental systems that enable language comprehension and production and the actual use of language–illustrated by distinctions like "Langue vs. Parole" from Saussure (1916) and "Competence vs Performance" by Chomsky (1965). Grammaticality judgement is a central method to assess linguistic representation competence. Chomsky (1986) highlighted that evidence for linguistic theorizing largely depends on

Proceedings of the Workshop on Cognitive Modeling and Computational Linguistics, pages 189–198
August 15, 2024 ©2024 Association for Computational Linguistics

"the judgements of native speakers". While there are other sources of evidence like speech corpus or acquisition sequences (Devitt, 2006), formal linguists typically favor native speakers' grammaticality intuitions. The prevailing assumption is that our language knowledge comprises abstract rules and principles forming intuitions about sentence well-formedness (Graves et al., 1973; Chomsky, 1980; Fodor, 1981).

Our study focuses on the representation of grammatical well-formedness in LLMs. Recent research on the grammatical capabilities of language models has primarily focused on binary grammaticality judgments using minimally different sentence pairs. Marvin and Linzen (2018) evaluated various language models on syntactic phenomena and found that while models handle local dependencies well, they struggle with non-local dependencies. Similarly, Warstadt et al. (2019) introduced the Corpus of Linguistic Acceptability (CoLA) to test neural network models on binary acceptability judgments, revealing that these models still fall short of human performance on complex syntactic structures. Dentella and et al. (2023) further examined GPT-3's performance on less frequent grammatical constructions, highlighting its limitations in understanding underlying meanings. While these studies have provided valuable insights into the grammatical abilities of language models, they primarily relied on binary judgment tasks and focused on specific syntactic phenomena. In contrast, our preregistered study (`https://osf.io/75dtk`) adopts a more comprehensive approach by incorporating both binary and graded naturalness judgments, allowing for a finer-grained analysis of language model performance. We collected grammaticality judgment data for over 2400 English sentences from ChatGPT and Vicuna, comparing them with human judgment data. Our findings indicate substantial agreement between ChatGPT and humans regarding grammatical intuition, although noticeable differences were also observed.

2 Experiment 1

In this experiment, we presented ChatGPT and Vicuna with English sentences of varying grammaticality and asked them to judge the sentences as either natural or unnatural. We compared the LLMs' judgement data with human judgement data, examining the similarities and differences in their knowledge of sentence grammaticality.

2.1 Method

We did not recruit human participants ourselves; instead, in all experiments reported in this paper, we utilized datasets from Lau et al. (2017) which were made publicly available. In their study, human participants recruited from Amazon Mechanical Turk performed a series of judgement tasks, including the grammaticality judgement of English sentences. We adopted their data from three judgement tasks as a proxy for humans' grammatical knowledge and later compared the human data with the LLM data that we gathered.

The stimuli used for the judgement tasks were adopted from the experimental materials in Lau et al., which consisted of English sentences of graded grammaticality. These sentences were created following an automated procedure in which texts from the British National Corpus were selected and translated into four different languages: Norwegian, Spanish, Chinese, and Japanese. The sentences were then translated back to English, resulting in 2500 English sentences of various degrees of grammaticality. According to Lau and colleagues, this automated procedure created a ranked distribution of relative grammatical well-formedness in English, with Norwegian texts yielding the best results and Japanese texts yielding the most distorted versions (Lau et al., 2014). Table 1 provides a breakdown of the languages from which experimental sentences were derived.

Language	Counts
English	500
Spanish	491
Japanese	500
Norwegian	480
Chinese	498

Table 1: The number of stimuli derived from each language in Exp 1&2.

A set of five related sentences used in the experiment is shown in Table 2. Note that there were 31 duplicated stimuli in Lau et al. due to some translated sentences being identical across languages. Consequently, we only included the 2469 distinct sentences as our experimental items.

Our data collection followed a "one trial per run" procedure where each interaction with the LLMs contained only a singular experimental trial. Unlike the procedure in Lau et al., where each participant

Language	Text
English	This essential motion cannot take place except in a liquid medium.
Norwegian	This required movement cannot take place except in a liquid medium.
Spanish	This fundamental movement cannot take place except in a liquid medium.
Chinese	The necessary motion in addition to the liquid medium does not occur.
Japanese	This exercise is essential cannot take place except for the liquid medium.

Table 2: A set of related stimuli adopted from Lau et al. (2014). The original English sentence was translated into four languages specified in the "Language" column, and then the translated version was translated back to English, resulting in corresponding sentences in the "Text" column.

was given a multi-item survey, our "one trial per run" method minimized potential biases stemming from preceding trials on the current judgment. This approach also circumvented an issue observed in prior projects where LLMs would occasionally lose track of the instructions midway through. Additionally, the shorter sessions characteristic of the "one trial per run" design were less vulnerable to potential server or connectivity problems.

Judgement data from ChatGPT (gpt-3.5-turbo-0613) and Vicuna (vicuna 13b 1.1) were collected separately using the R package MacBehaviour (Duan et al., 2024). In each trial, we presented ChatGPT or Vicuna with an English sentence from our inventory of stimuli and prompted the model to judge whether the sentence was natural or unnatural. The sentences to be judged were the 2469 distinct experimental items from Lau et al. (2014, 2017). Each sentence was randomly selected following the one trial per run procedure, and we conducted 50 runs for each experimental item. A detailed description of the data collection pipeline is available in the project's preregistration report on the OSF website (`https://osf.io/75dtk`). Following Lau et al. (2014, 2017), LLMs' responses were coded as integer scores, with "1" standing for "unnatural" and "4" for "natural". We combined human judgement data with ChatGPT and Vicuna data and performed two sets of analyses to examine the degree of similarity between human and LLMs' judgements. First, we conducted correlational analyses to examine whether sentences judged as grammatical by humans are more likely to be judged as grammatical by LLMs and vice versa. To do this, we calculated the mean rating score of each sentence stimulus for humans, ChatGPT, and Vicuna, and then computed the correlation coefficients between ChatGPT and humans as well as between Vicuna and humans.

To examine how human and LLMs' ratings were influenced by the grammaticality of the stimuli, we recoded the "natural" and "unnatural" response as "1" and "0" respectively and constructed a Bayesian mixed-effects logistic regression model using the R package `brm` (Bürkner, 2017) with default priors. We treated the logit of the "natural" response as a function of participant type (human vs. ChatGPT vs. Vicuna) and the language from which the stimuli sentences were derived (English vs. Norwegian vs. Spanish vs. Chinese vs. Japanese). The predictors were dummy-coded, with the human data in the English condition being the reference level. Random effects structures were constructed, including item intercepts and slopes:

$$\text{Logit of "natural" response} \sim 1 + \text{participant} \times \text{language} + (1 + \text{participant} \times \text{language} \mid \text{item})$$

2.2 Results

The correlation between human and LLM judgements of sentence naturalness is shown in Figure 1. There was a significant correlation between human and ChatGPT judgement ($r = 0.83$, 95% CI = [0.82, 0.84], $p < 0.01$), indicating that sentences judged as natural by humans tended to be judged as natural by ChatGPT as well and vice versa. A significant correlation was also found between human and Vicuna judgement ($r = 0.66$, 95% CI = [0.63, 0.68], $p < 0.01$). According to Cohen (2013), a correlation coefficient of 0.5 or larger represents a strong correlation. A strong and significant correlation between humans and LLMs in their naturalness judgement suggested a considerable extent of shared grammatical knowledge. We also noticed that the ChatGPT-human correlation was stronger than the Vicuna-human correlation, as evidenced by their respective 95% confidence intervals (95% CI = [0.82, 0.84] vs. 95% CI = [0.63, 0.68]).

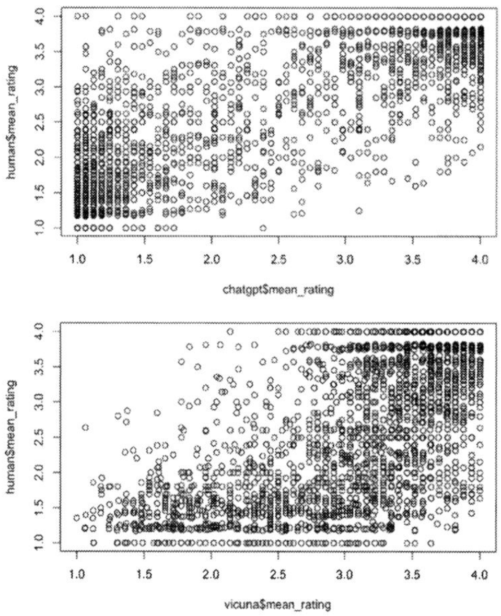

Figure 1: Correlation of naturalness judgement between humans and LLMs in Exp.1. Each point represents the mean rating score of a sentence. Top panel: human vs. ChatGPT. Bottom panel: human vs. Vicuna.

The mixed-effects model, on the other hand, revealed noticeable variations in the naturalness judgement across participant types and the languages from which the stimuli sentences were derived. The baseline for comparison was the human participants' judgement of the original English sentences. Compared with human participants, ChatGPT was more likely to judge the original English sentences as natural ($\beta = 0.39$, 95% CI = [0.19, 0.58]), while Vicuna was less likely to judge the original English sentences as natural ($\beta = -0.32$, 95% CI = [-0.47, -0.18]). For human participants, the probability of a "natural" response decreased for sentences derived from languages other than English, as seen from the negative slopes in the language conditions other than English ($\beta = -1.81$ for Spanish; $\beta = -3.69$ for Japanese; $\beta = -1.55$ for Norwegian; $\beta = -3.06$ for Chinese). Noticeably, this decrease was more dramatic for ChatGPT but reversed for Vicuna. As shown in Figure 2, sentences derived from other languages were rated higher by Vicuna than by human participants.

2.3 Discussion

In this experiment, we investigated the extent to which LLMs share grammatical knowledge with human beings by replicating the binary judgement

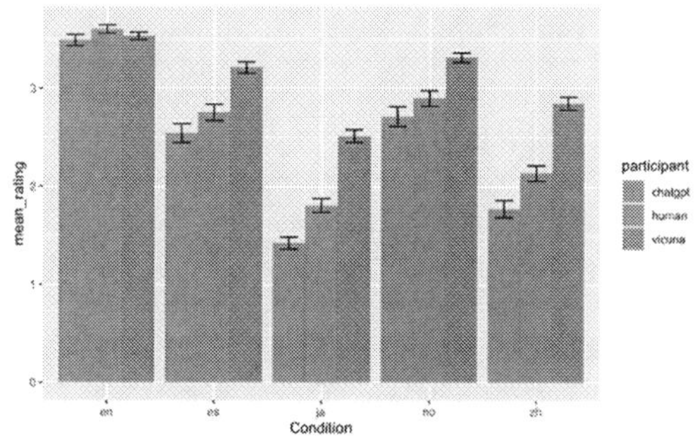

Figure 2: Comparison of mean rating scores across participant types and language conditions in Exp1. An error bar represents the 95% confidence interval of the mean calculated using bootstrapping methods.

task from Lau et al. (2014, 2017), using ChatGPT and Vicuna as participants. We found strong correlations between human and LLM naturalness judgements, with sentences judged to be more natural by human participants generally being judged more natural by LLMs, and vice versa. Adopting the perspective that naturalness judgement is a proxy grammatical knowledge (Lau et al., 2014, 2017), we interpreted this strong correlation as evidence of LLMs and humans sharing a considerable range of knowledge in sentence grammaticality. Though both LLMs' judgements correlated highly with human judgements, the correlation between ChatGPT and humans was stronger than that between Vicuna and humans.

The major difference between human and LLMs lies in their tolerance towards ungrammatical sentences. Compared with human participants, ChatGPT was less tolerant of ungrammaticality, as it gave much lower ratings to sentences auto-translated from languages other than English. On the other hand, Vicuna offered a much higher ratings to those less grammatical sentences than human participants did. This suggests a degree of heterogeneity among current LLMs in that a general label of large language model does not provide detailed information on an individual model's performance in language tasks.

One limitation for this current research design is the response type. The stimuli were created following the procedure that aimed towards a graded profile of sentence grammaticality; however, participants were required to provide binary judgements on the naturalness of the sentences. It is possible that the binary nature of the response type may not be optimal for judging graded grammaticality. We address this limitation in the second experiment by changing the response type from binary to a ranked measure.

3 Experiment 2

Our second experiment replicated the four-category grammaticality judgement in Lau et al. (2014, 2017) with ChatGPT and Vicuna as the participants. We then compared human performance with that of the LLMs.

3.1 Method

We used the same experimental stimuli as in the first experiment but followed a similar procedure with an important modification: instead of asking LLMs to judge whether a given sentence is natural or unnatural, we instructed them to judge if the sentence is extremely unnatural, somewhat unnatural, somewhat natural, or extremely natural. By employing a four-point Likert scale as the response type, we believe that participants' judgement should be more sensitive to the graded nature of the stimuli. A detailed description of the experimental procedure is available from the project's preregistration report on the OSF website (`https://osf.io/75dtk`).

We combined LLMs' and human participants' judgements for statistical analysis in which the four-point responses were numerically represented using numbers from one to four. Following the same rationale as the first experiment, we conducted two sets of analyses to compare the grammatical knowledge between humans and LLMs. First, we conducted correlational analyses following the same steps as in Experiment 1. Second, we constructed a Bayesian mixed-effects model that treated the naturalness ratings as a function of participant type (human vs. ChatGPT vs. Vicuna) and the language from which the stimuli sentences were derived (English vs. Norwegian vs. Spanish vs. Chinese vs. Japanese). The predictors were dummy coded with the human data in the English condition serving as the reference level. Random effects structures were constructed, including item intercepts and slopes:

$$\text{judgment} \sim 1 + \text{participant} \times \text{language} \\ + (1 + \text{participant} \times \text{language} \mid \text{item})$$

3.2 Results

There is a significant correlation between human and ChatGPT's judgement ($r = 0.84$, 95% CI = [0.83, 0.85], $p < 0.01$) as well as between human and Vicuna's judgement ($r = 0.49$, 95% CI = [0.45, 0.52], $p < 0.01$). The ChatGPT-human correlation was stronger than the Vicuna-human correlation (Figure 3).

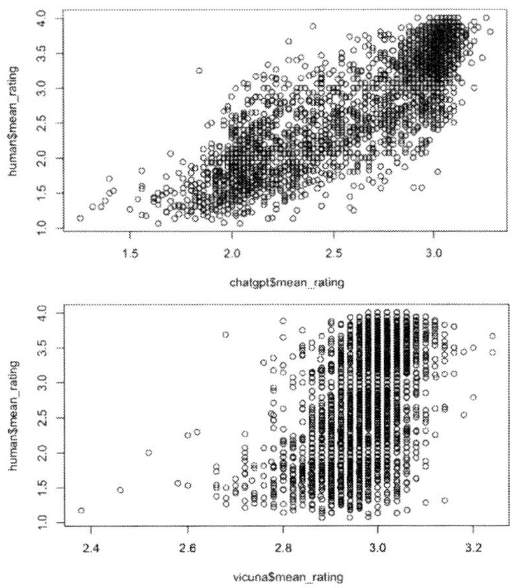

Figure 3: Correlation of naturalness ratings between humans and LLMs in Exp.2. Each point represents the mean rating score of a sentence. Top panel: human vs ChatGPT. Bottom panel: human vs Vicuna.

The mixed-effects model showed that human participants on average judged the original English stimuli (baseline) as between "somewhat natural" and "extremely natural" ($\beta = 3.4$, 95% CI = [3.35, 3.45]). On the other hand, stimuli derived from languages other than English were rated lower than the baseline ($\beta = -0.56$ for Spanish; $\beta = -1.35$ for Japanese; $\beta = -0.42$ for Norwegian; $\beta = -1.06$ for Chinese). Furthermore, for the original English stimuli, human participants' ratings were significantly higher than ChatGPT's ratings ($\beta = -0.44$, 95% CI = [-0.48, -0.40]) and Vicuna's ratings ($\beta = -0.39$, 95% CI = [-0.44, -0.34]).

Additionally, the variation in Vicuna's responses was minimal within a specific language condition and across different language conditions. This is evident in Figure 4 from the small 95% confidence intervals of the mean and from the similar rating scores Vicuna provided across language conditions. Roughly speaking, stimuli sentences were judged as "somewhat natural" (a score of 3) by Vicuna regardless of the actual grammaticality of the sen-

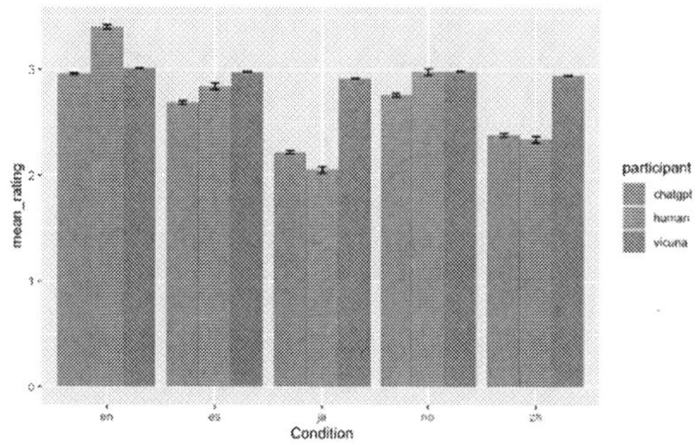

Figure 4: Comparison of mean rating scores across participant types and language conditions in Exp2. An error bar represents the 95% confidence interval of the mean calculated using bootstrapping methods.

tences. This behavior contrasted greatly with ChatGPT, which exhibited a noticeable variation in its naturalness judgement across sentence types. Mimicking the pattern observed among human participants, ChatGPT provided higher naturalness ratings for the original English sentences while provided lower ratings for sentences derived from languages that are typologically further than English such as Japanese and Chinese.

3.3 Discussion

In this study, we replicated Experiment 1 using the same stimuli while modifying the response type to a four-point Likert scale. Major findings of Experiment 1 were successfully replicated. First, we observed strong correlations between LLMs and human participants regarding their ratings of sentences of varying grammaticality. Secondly, significant differences were observed between human participants and LLMs in the ratings of sentences in specific language conditions. These findings suggest that although there is a general agreement between humans and LLMs regarding the relative grammaticality of various sentence structures, the grammatical knowledge of LLMs and human participants differs in terms of the degree of endorsement to specific sentence structures. For sentences deemed very natural by human participants, the naturalness judgements from LLMs were more conservative. Conversely, for sentences judged as "unnatural" by human participants, Vicuna placed them on the "natural" side of the scale. This revealed the heterogeneity among current LLMs previously discussed in Experiment 1. Though both Vicuna and ChatGPT are representative of current LLMs, they nevertheless differed in their performance of naturalness judgement. While ChatGPT closely mimicked human participants in the naturalness rankings of different stimuli categories (en > no/es > zh/ja), Vicuna showed minimal variation in its judgments across stimuli derived from different languages.

4 Experiment 3

This experiment aimed to further our understanding of human and LLMs' knowledge of grammaticality by replicating the previous two experiments using a sliding scale judgement task that was adopted from Lau et al. (2014, 2017).

4.1 Method

Following the design of Lau and colleagues, we instructed our participants, ChatGPT and Vicuna, to rate the naturalness of stimuli sentences with integer scores from 1 (extremely unnatural) to 100 (extremely natural), after which we compared LLMs' judgement data with that of human participants following the same data analysis procedure as the previous two experiments.

The original study of Lau et al. (2017) sampled 250 items from the same inventory of the previous two experiments as the stimuli of the sliding scale judgement task. Two out of the 250 items were duplicated and thus we included 248 unique sentences as the experimental items. Since the experimental items were a subset of the previous experimental items, they were derived from the same automatic procedure as the previous experiments. A breakdown of the languages they were derived from is shown in Table 3.

Language	Counts
English	50
Spanish	44
Japanese	59
Norwegian	45
Chinese	50

Table 3: The number of stimuli derived from each language in Exp 3.

4.2 Results

Consistent with the findings of the previous experiments, we again observed a strong and significant correlation between human and ChatGPT's rating (r = 0.81, 95% CI = [0.77, 0.85], $p < 0.01$)

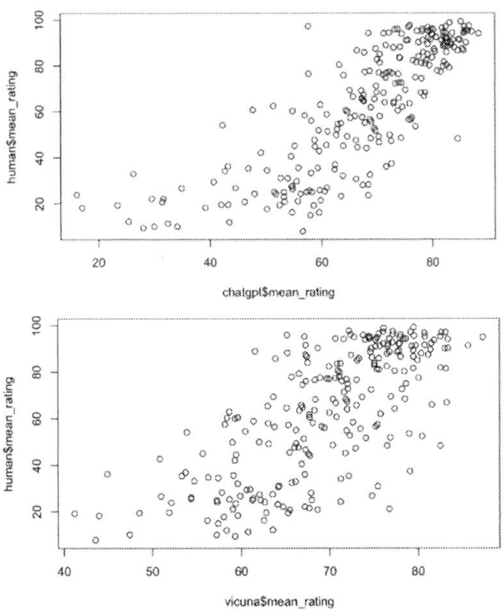

Figure 5: Correlation of naturalness ratings between humans and LLMs in Exp.3. Each point represents the mean rating score of a sentence. Top panel: human vs ChatGPT. Bottom panel: human vs Vicuna.

as well as between human and Vicuna's rating ($r = 0.72$, 95% CI = [0.65, 0.77], $p < 0.01$) in the sliding scale judgement task.

The output of the mixed-effects model was consistent with what we found in Experiment 2. The original English stimuli received a naturalness rating of 86.96 out of 100 from human participants (95% CI = [81.98, 91.85]). Compared with this baseline, the stimuli derived from languages other than English received a lower naturalness rating ($\beta = -15.58$ for Spanish; $\beta = -47.13$ for Japanese; $\beta = -16.76$ for Norwegian; $\beta = -39.33$ for Chinese). Moreover, for the original English stimuli, human participants' ratings were significantly higher than ChatGPT's ratings ($\beta = -9.86$, 95% CI = [-13.6, -6.25]) and Vicuna's ratings ($\beta = -11.46$, 95% CI = [-15.68, -7.14]).

Due to a much smaller number of stimuli adopted in this experiment, the estimates from the mixed-effects model had a larger error term associated with them as compared with the previous experiments. The variation in rating score across different language conditions was specifically noticeable for human participants, as shown from the bootstrapped confidence intervals in Figure 6.

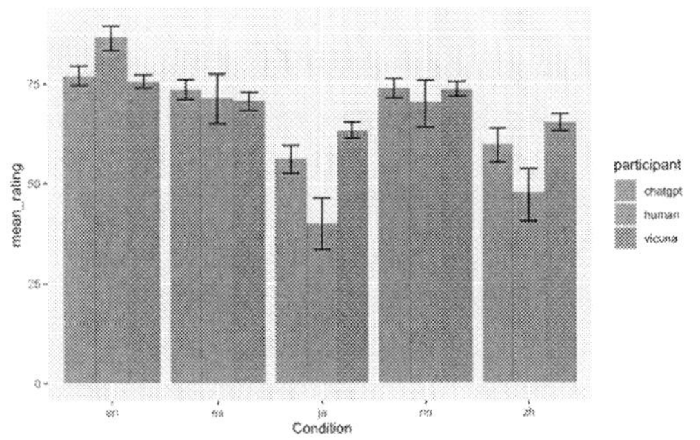

Figure 6: Figure 6 Comparison of mean rating scores across participant types and language conditions in Exp3. An error bar represents the 95% confidence interval of the mean calculated using bootstrapping methods.

4.3 Discussion

In this experiment, we adopted a sliding scale judgement task to elicit finer-grained responses regarding sentence grammaticality. Compared with Experiment 2, the response type of this experiment allowed for more nuanced patterns to occur; nevertheless, major findings of Experiment 2 were replicated. First, human and LLMs shared a considerable amount of grammatical knowledge as evident from the strong correlation in the naturalness rating score. This shared knowledge determines the relative soundness of various sentence structures. For example, the sentence "This essential motion cannot take place except in a liquid medium" is viewed by human and LLMs as more grammatical than the sentence "This exercise is essential cannot take place except for the liquid medium". Second, original sentences from the British National Corpus were rated higher by human participants than by LLMs, while translated sentences, especially those derived from Chinese and Japanese, were rated lower in naturalness by humans than by LLMs. It seems that LLMs are more "conservative" in naturalness judgement compared with human participants. This revealed the differences between human and LLMs in terms of the "distributional knowledge" of sentence grammaticality, which will be further elaborated in the general discussion section.

Compared with Experiment 2, the rating scores in this experiment exhibited larger variations within and across experimental manipulations. For instance, in Experiment 2, Vicuna ratings were largely stable across language conditions; however, in this experiment, we clearly observed a ranked distribution of Vicuna's judgement. The original English stimuli received the highest ratings, and the Japanese-oriented sentences received the lowest ratings, while the stimuli derived from Norwegian and Spanish received intermediate naturalness ratings. We attributed the increased variation to the reduced size of the stimuli in this experiment, which is only one-tenth of the number of stimuli in the previous experiments.

5 General Discussion

Expanding upon Lau et al. (2014, 2017), our study introduced ChatGPT and Vicuna as LLM counterparts for grammaticality judgment, seeking to determine the extent to which LLMs align with humans in their linguistic knowledge. In general, we observed a strong correlation between human and LLM judgments on the naturalness of sentences, which according to Lau et al. (2014, 2017) suggests a significant overlap in their grammatical knowledge. However, this overlap does not imply equivalence, as our data revealed consistent statistical differences in ratings between humans and LLMs across all three experiments. In the binary judgment task, human participants were more conservative than ChatGPT. Conversely, in the four-point and sliding scale tasks, human participants displayed greater variability in their judgments towards both grammatical and less grammatical sentences compared to ChatGPT. Vicuna's ratings, while generally aligning with those of ChatGPT and humans, exhibited less variation across tasks, suggesting a different processing model.

We posit that a fundamental distinction between human and LLM representations of language lies in the 'distributional knowledge' of sentence grammaticality. Humans acquire an understanding of grammaticality through diverse daily language experiences, enriched by a dynamic array of cognitive and contextual cues. In contrast, LLMs rely predominantly on statistical patterns derived from their training data. This difference in linguistic input is crucial, with human language input being inherently more diverse and dynamic, incorporating a wide array of linguistic registers, dialects, and styles shaped by social interactions and cultural contexts. This exposure enables humans to develop a nuanced and contextually adaptive understanding of language, an aspect of linguistic competence that LLMs with their data-driven learning processes cannot fully replicate (Qiu et al., 2023).

Moreover, human language processing is inherently multi-modal, incorporating auditory, visual, and contextual cues that enhance comprehension and interpretation. This multi-modal integration includes body language, tone, facial expressions, and environmental context, all of which contribute to a rich, intuitive grasp of language nuances and grammaticality. In contrast, LLMs such as ChatGPT and Vicuna process language purely as text tokens, which are sequences abstracted from their communicative contexts. The tokenization process specific to each model's architecture often strips away nuanced information that humans naturally use to infer meaning, leading to potential discrepancies in understanding subtle linguistic cues or complex semantic structures.

Additionally, the cognitive processes in humans, including memory, attention, and inference, dynamically interact during language processing, allowing for a rich contextual interpretation of language that adapts in real-time. This level of cognitive engagement in language processing is not mirrored in current LLM architectures, which primarily rely on recognizing patterns and statistical generalizations from extensive datasets. These fundamental differences imply that the grammaticality of a sentence is judged against different distributions of possible sentence structures by humans and LLMs. Understanding these variations is crucial for recognizing the limitations and potential biases of LLM-generated language assessments. It also underscores the importance of incorporating diverse real-world language data and sophisticated cognitive models into LLM training protocols to improve their linguistic adaptability and judgment accuracy.

6 Conclusion

Our investigation into the alignment of LLMs with human grammaticality judgments has revealed both promising correlations and significant nuances in their linguistic capabilities. While LLMs like ChatGPT and Vicuna can effectively mirror human judgments in broad strokes, discrepancies in sensitivity and the conservativeness of their ratings underscore the importance of careful model selection and calibration for specific linguistic tasks.

7 Limitations

While our study provides valuable insights into the grammatical capabilities of LLMs, it is worth noting that the experiments were conducted using prompting methods. As Hu and Levy (2023) argued, LLMs may be better judges of grammaticality when evaluated using sentence probabilities rather than prompts. A reviewer suggested that this approach aligns more closely with the langue versus parole (competence vs. performance) distinction. Their findings suggest that using probability measures can yield more accurate grammaticality judgments by LLMs. Future work should replicate our study using probability measures to provide a more comprehensive understanding of LLMs' linguistic capabilities.

References

M. Binz and E. Schulz. 2023. Using cognitive psychology to understand gpt 3. *Proceedings of the National Academy of Sciences*, 120(6):e2218523120.

T. Brown, B. Mann, N. Ryder, M. Subbiah, J. D. Kaplan, P. Dhariwal, and D. Amodei. 2020. Language models are few-shot learners. *Advances in neural information processing systems*, 33:1877–1901.

E. Brunet-Gouet, N. Vidal, and P. Roux. 2023. Do conversational agents have a theory of mind? a single case study of chatgpt with the hinting false beliefs and false photographs and strange stories paradigms. *HAL Open Science*.

P. C. Bürkner. 2017. brms: An r package for bayesian multilevel models using stan. *Journal of statistical software*, 80:1–28.

Z. G. Cai, D. A. Haslett, X. Duan, S. Wang, and M. J. Pickering. 2023. Does chatgpt resemble humans in language use? *arXiv preprint arXiv:2303.08014*.

N. Chomsky. 1965. *Aspects of the Theory of Syntax*. MIT Press Cambridge MA.

N. Chomsky. 1986. *Knowledge of Language: Its Nature, Origin, and Use*. Praeger Publishers, New York.

N. Chomsky, I. Roberts, and J. Watumull. 2023. Noam chomsky: The false promise of chatgpt. *The New York Times*.

Noam Chomsky. 1980. Rules and representations. *Behavioral and brain sciences*, 3(1):1–15.

Jacob Cohen. 2013. *Statistical power analysis for the behavioral sciences*. Routledge.

Laura Dentella and et al. 2023. Testing ai performance on less frequent aspects of language reveals insensitivity to underlying meaning. *arXiv preprint arXiv:2302.12313*.

M. Devitt. 2006. Intuitions in linguistics. *British Journal for the Philosophy of Science*, 57:481–513.

Xufeng Duan, Shixuan Li, and Zhenguang G Cai. 2024. Macbehaviour: An r package for behavioural experimentation on large language models. *arXiv preprint arXiv:2405.07495*.

J. Fodor. 1981. Introduction: Some notes on what linguistics is about. *In The Language and Thought Series*, pages 197–207.

R. Futrell, E. Wilcox, T. Morita, P. Qian, M. Ballesteros, and R. Levy. 2019. Neural language models as psycholinguistic subjects: Representations of syntactic state. *arXiv preprint arXiv:1903.03260*.

C. Graves, J. J. Katz, Y. Nishiyama, S. Soames, R. Stecker, and P. Tovey. 1973. Tacit knowledge. *The Journal of Philosophy*, 70(11):318–330.

Jennifer Hu and Roger Levy. 2023. Prompting is not a substitute for probability measurements in large language models. In *Proceedings of the 2023 Conference on Empirical Methods in Natural Language Processing*, pages 5040–5060, Singapore. Association for Computational Linguistics.

W. Jiao, W. Wang, J. T. Huang, X. Wang, and Z. Tu. 2023. Is chatgpt a good translator? a preliminary study. *arXiv preprint arXiv:2301.08745*.

M. Kosinski. 2023. Theory of mind may have spontaneously emerged in large language models. *arXiv preprint arXiv:2302.02083*.

J. H. Lau, A. Clark, and S. Lappin. 2014. Measuring gradience in speakers' grammaticality judgements. *In Proceedings of the annual meeting of the cognitive science society*, 36(36).

J. H. Lau, A. Clark, and S. Lappin. 2017. Grammaticality, acceptability, and probability: A probabilistic view of linguistic knowledge. *Cognitive science*, 41(5):1202–1241.

K. Mahowald, E. Fedorenko, S. T. Piantadosi, and E. Gibson. 2013. Info/information theory: Speakers choose shorter words in predictive contexts. *Cognition*, 126(2):313–318.

Rebecca Marvin and Tal Linzen. 2018. Targeted syntactic evaluation of language models. In *Proceedings of the 2018 Conference on Empirical Methods in Natural Language Processing*, pages 1192–1202.

M. Ortega-Martín, Ó. García-Sierra, A. Ardoiz, J. Álvarez, J. C. Armenteros, and A. Alonso. 2023. Linguistic ambiguity analysis in chatgpt. *arXiv preprint arXiv:2302.06426*.

S. T. Piantadosi. 2023. Modern language models refute chomsky's approach to language. *Lingbuzz Preprint lingbuzz/007180*.

Z. Qiu, X. Duan, and Z. Cai. 2023. Does chatgpt resemble humans in processing implicatures? *Proceedings of the 4th Natural Logic Meets Machine Learning Workshop*.

F. Saussure. 1916. Cours de linguistique générale. *Paris: Payot.*

M. Van Schijndel and T. Linzen. 2018. Modeling garden path effects without explicit hierarchical syntax. *Proceedings of the 40th Annual Meeting of the Cognitive Science Society.*

Alex Warstadt, Amanpreet Singh, and Samuel R Bowman. 2019. Neural network acceptability judgments. *Transactions of the Association for Computational Linguistics*, 7:625–641.

E. G. Wilcox, R. Futrell, and R. Levy. 2022. Using computational models to test syntactic learnability. *Linguistic Inquiry*, pages 1–88.

What does Kiki look like? Cross-modal associations between speech sounds and visual shapes in vision-and-language models

Tessa Verhoef*, **Kiana Shahrasbi**, **Tom Kouwenhoven***
Leiden Institute of Advanced Computer Science
Leiden University, The Netherlands
t.verhoef@liacs.leidenuniv.nl, k.shahrasbi@umail.leidenuniv.nl,
t.kouwenhoven@liacs.leidenuniv.nl

Abstract

Humans have clear cross-modal preferences when matching certain novel words to visual shapes. Evidence suggests that these preferences play a prominent role in our linguistic processing, language learning, and the origins of signal-meaning mappings. With the rise of multimodal models in AI, such as vision-and-language (VLM) models, it becomes increasingly important to uncover the kinds of visio-linguistic associations these models encode and whether they align with human representations. Informed by experiments with humans, we probe and compare four VLMs for a well-known human cross-modal preference, the bouba-kiki effect. We do not find conclusive evidence for this effect but suggest that results may depend on features of the models, such as architecture design, model size, and training details. Our findings inform discussions on the origins of the bouba-kiki effect in human cognition and future developments of VLMs that align well with human cross-modal associations.

1 Introduction

The development of machine understanding and generation of natural language has benefited immensely from the introduction of transformer-based architectures (Vaswani et al., 2017). These architectures have since then been adapted and extended to handle multimodal data, leading to the creation of various types of multimodal models, including vision-and-language models. These models can potentially revolutionize how AI systems understand the world and interact with humans. However, we lack direct access to the exact representations and associations they encode. How VLMs integrate representations in the two modalities and whether associations between modalities are made in a human-like way is still being actively investigated (Alper et al., 2023; Kamath et al., 2023; Zhang et al., 2024b; Karamcheti et al., 2024).

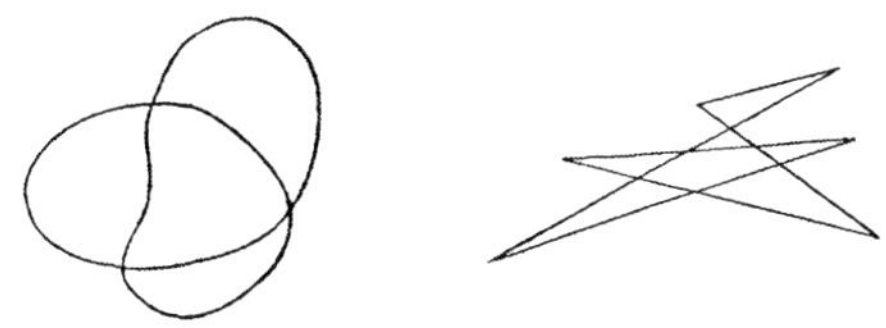

Figure 1: Which of these two shapes is Kiki? Images from Köhler (1929, 1947)

Here, we use a well-known paradigm from the field of cognitive science to probe into a specific cross-modal association between speech sounds and visual shapes: the bouba-kiki effect. When humans see two figures, one with jagged and one with smooth edges, and are told one is a Kiki and the other a Bouba, 95% will name the jagged figure Kiki (Ramachandran and Hubbard, 2001). This effect was initially discovered and described anecdotally by Wolfgang Köhler (Köhler, 1929, 1947), using the two images shown in Figure 1 with the labels *maluma* and *takete*. Since then it has been widely studied (as reviewed in Section 2), and expanded with many other cross-modal preferences in human processing of (speech) sounds and visual imagery. Moreover, a wealth of evidence suggests that such preferences widely influence patterns we see in human languages (e.g., Ramachandran and Hubbard, 2001; Cuskley and Kirby, 2013; Imai and Kita, 2014; Verhoef et al., 2015, 2016; Tamariz et al., 2018). Even though non-arbitrariness in language is often still regarded as an exception in some disciplines, in fields such as language evolution, and sign language linguistics, iconic form-meaning mappings are considered omnipresent (Perniss et al., 2010). Given the central role cross-modal preferences play in human visio-linguistic representations and their effects on language, it is pertinent to investigate whether VLMs associate non-words and visual stimuli in a human-like way.

*Equal contribution

Proceedings of the Workshop on Cognitive Modeling and Computational Linguistics, pages 199–213
August 15, 2024

Examining universal human cross-modal preferences in VLMs can help us gain key insights across disciplines. First, it may reveal whether VLMs process multimodal information in a human-like way and whether similar biases drive their understanding of visual-auditory form-meaning mappings. Overlap in cognitive biases can potentially increase mutual understanding and improve interactions between humans and machines (Kouwenhoven et al., 2022). Second, it may help pinpoint what is missing to make VLMs more suitable for realistic simulations of human language emergence. Increasingly, VLMs are used in emergent communication settings, where agents communicate with each other and develop a novel language (Bouchacourt and Baroni, 2018; Mahaut et al., 2023; Kouwenhoven et al., 2024). These models are used to improve machine understanding of human language (Lazaridou and Baroni, 2020; Lowe et al., 2020; Steinert-Threlkeld et al., 2022; Zheng et al., 2024), but also to simulate and study human language evolution processes (Galke et al., 2022; Lian et al., 2023). While the influence of cross-modal associations on the emergence of language has been studied extensively in language evolution experiments with humans (Verhoef et al., 2015, 2016; Tamariz et al., 2018; Little et al., 2017), the phenomenon is still absent from current emergent communication paradigms. Evidently, cognitively plausible VLMs are more suitable for simulating aspects of the evolution of meaning in language. Finally, the actual origin of the bouba-kiki effect is still being debated within cognitive science and linguistics, with proposed explanations ranging from attributing it to similarities between shape features and features of either orthography (Cuskley et al., 2017), acoustics and articulation (Ramachandran and Hubbard, 2001; Maurer et al., 2006; Westbury, 2005), affective–semantic properties of human and non-human vocal communication (Nielsen and Rendall, 2011), or physical properties relating to audiovisual regularities in the environment (Fort and Schwartz, 2022). If the bouba-kiki effect can be reproduced in a VLM, it can help reveal the crucial ingredients for this effect, potentially leading to models better aligned with human representations.

To the best of our knowledge, only one previous paper discussed the bouba-kiki effect in VLMs. Alper and Averbuch-Elor (2023) tested two models, CLIP (Radford et al., 2021) and Stable Diffusion (Rombach et al., 2022), and reported to find strong evidence for the effect in these models. This is somewhat surprising given the way these models are trained and the absence of relevant data sources such as auditory information and experience with physical object properties. Therefore, we introduce nuance in this discussion and show, contrary to this previous finding, that the bouba-kiki effect does not occur consistently in VLMs, and the presence of this cross-modal preference may depend on the way it is tested and properties like model architecture, attention mechanism, and training details.

2 Background

2.1 Sound-symbolism and cross-modal associations in language and cognition

When Hockett (1960) listed a set of design features deemed essential to natural human language, "arbitrariness" was included. This feature refers to the arbitrary/unmotivated mapping between words and their meanings. However, when exploring beyond Indo-European languages, non-arbitrary form-meaning mappings appear to play a significant role in many languages (Imai et al., 2008; Perniss et al., 2010; Dingemanse, 2012). Most obviously, perhaps, sign languages are rich in non-arbitrary "iconic" mappings, with articulators that lend themselves particularly well to representing meanings by mimicking, for example, shapes or actions. However, some spoken languages also have specific classes of words where characteristics of the meaning are mimicked or iconically represented in the word. Examples have been identified as "ideophones," "mimetics", or "expressives," and this phenomenon is often called sound-symbolism (Imai et al., 2008; Imai and Kita, 2014; Dingemanse, 2012). Even in languages not typically considered rich in sound symbolism, such as English and Spanish, vocabulary items from specific lexical categories, like adjectives, are rated high in iconicity as well (Perry et al., 2015). Perhaps the most overwhelming evidence for the widespread importance of sound-symbolism in human languages comes from a study by Blasi et al. (2016), who analyzed vocabularies of two-thirds of the world's languages and found evidence for strong associations between speech sounds and particular meanings across geographical locations and linguistic lineages. Consequently, non-arbitrariness is an important property of all languages.

In addition, human language learning, processing, and evolution are affected by cross-modal associations. Sound-symbolic mappings help young children acquire new words (Imai et al., 2008), and iconic words are learned earlier in child language development (Perry et al., 2015). Furthermore, parents use sound-symbolic words in their infant-directed speech more often than in adult-to-adult conversations (Imai et al., 2008). In a novel word learning task, participants trained on a mapping congruent with a known cross-modal association performed better than participants in an incongruent condition (Nielsen and Rendall, 2012). Sound-symbolic mappings in language have been connected to cross-modal mappings in the human brain (Simner et al., 2010; Ramachandran and Hubbard, 2001; Lockwood and Dingemanse, 2015) and processing of sound-symbolic words is less affected by aphasia (language-affecting brain damage after left-hemisphere stroke), than arbitrary words (Meteyard et al., 2015). It is also argued that universally shared cross-modal biases play an essential role in the evolution of language by bridging the gap between sensory input and meaning by providing a basis for linguistic conventions (Ramachandran and Hubbard, 2001; Cuskley and Kirby, 2013; Imai and Kita, 2014). Shared biases can help to create mutual understanding because communicative partners will automatically understand what is meant when a word like "kiki" is used for the first time in a context like the one shown in Figure 1.

While the bouba-kiki effect may be the most famous example of a universal cross-modal association, many other cognitive biases in cross-modal perception have been reported. For example, non-arbitrary associations exist in human processing between high pitch sounds and light shades (Marks, 1974; Melara, 1989; Ward et al., 2006), light shades with rising intonation (Hubbard, 1996), graphemes and colours (Cuskley et al., 2019), vowel height and lightness (Cuskley et al., 2019), small size and high pitch (Evans and Treisman, 2010; Parise and Spence, 2009) and vowel openness and visual size (Schmidtke et al., 2014). Therefore, the findings presented in this paper only scratch the surface of what is possible in this domain.

2.2 Testing the bouba-kiki effect in humans

After its initial discovery, the bouba-kiki effect has been studied increasingly rigorously, extending the initial pair of two images with more possible pairs (Maurer et al., 2006; Westbury, 2005), and even randomly generated ones to control for biases related to deliberate selection by the researchers (Nielsen and Rendall, 2011, 2013). In addition, various sets of labels and pseudowords have been contrasted and compared to study the relative importance of vowels versus consonants in the labels (Westbury, 2005; Nielsen and Rendall, 2011, 2013). The role of orthography, in addition to auditory properties of speech sounds, has also been studied (Cuskley et al., 2017; Bottini et al., 2019). Across set-ups, non-arbitrary preferences are found robustly across varying cultures and writing systems (Ćwiek et al., 2022). Remarkably, to some extent this can even be found in blind individuals who undergo a haptic version of the bouba-kiki task (Bottini et al., 2019).

Most experiments in this domain are conducted using a two-alternative forced choice design, where two contrasting images are shown side by side (one jagged and the other curved), and two possible labels are offered, asking participants to make the "correct" mapping. However, it has been argued that this is an anti-conservative method in the sense that the concurrent presentation of two images that differ along one dimension and two labels that also differ along one dimension strongly primes participants to match the two, noticing their similarities. Nielsen and Rendall (2013) therefore introduced a different method, in which images are presented independently, and participants are asked to generate novel pseudowords to match the images. Here, we adopt their approach as a stringent method for probing VLMs for the bouba-kiki effect.

2.3 Vision-and-language models

Despite recent advances in multi-modal models (Zhang et al., 2024a) using transformer architectures, they remain poorly understood and often show unwanted behaviors such as poor visio-compositional reasoning (Thrush et al., 2022; Diwan et al., 2022) or spatial reasoning skills (Kamath et al., 2023). In addition, in the visual question-answering domain it is a well-known problem that models often lack visual grounding and have trouble integrating textual and visual data (Goyal et al., 2017; Jabri et al., 2016; Agrawal et al., 2018). This makes it perhaps even more puzzling that Alper and Averbuch-Elor (2023) found strong evidence for a bouba-kiki effect in CLIP and Stable Diffusion: even if these models are able to extract sound-symbolic information in the absence of auditory data, they will likely struggle to actually associate that information with visual properties.

Their approach involved generating two large sets of pseudowords, where one set was more likely associated with round shapes (examples: *bodubo,*

Model	Train objective	Architecture	Attention	#Params	#imgs,caps (M)
CLIP	CON	Dual-Stream	Modality-specific	151.3M	400, 400
ViLT	ITM&MLM	single-stream	Merged	87.4M	4.10, 9.85
BLIP2	CON&IGTG&ITM	Dual-stream	Q-Former	~3.8B	129, 258
GPT-4o	Unknown	Unknown	Unknown	Unknown	Unknown

Table 1: Overview of the models. Objectives are Image Text Matching(ITM), Masked Language Modelling(MLM), Image-grounded Text Generation(IGTG), or Contrastive Learning(CON). Numbers are millions(M) or billions(B).

gunogu, momomo) and the other set would evoke associations with jagged shapes (examples: *kitaki, hipehi, texete*). The CLIP embedding vector space was used to define a visual semantic dimension that best separates two sets of pre-selected adjectives (various synonyms of round and jagged). Within this space, pseudoword properties could reliably predict adjective type (round or jagged), and geometric properties associated with those adjectives could predict the category of pseudowords. With Stable Diffusion, novel images were generated based on pseudowords and analyzed by embedding them using CLIP and through human evaluation. Both methods revealed evidence for the presence of sound symbolic mappings in these models (Alper and Averbuch-Elor, 2023).

While their methods mainly involved text-to-image generation (with Stable Diffusion) or text-to-text mapping (with CLIP embeddings), we focus on image-to-text classification. We use images previously used in experiments with humans, as well as novel images generated following a procedure previously used to generate items for human experimentation. This approach provides an additional way of testing for cross-modal associations in VLMs and yields data that can be more directly compared to human data from studies into the bouba-kiki effect. Moreover, Alper and Averbuch-Elor (2023) did not explicitly compare different VLMs (Stable Diffusion also uses CLIP). However, it would not be surprising if properties relating to the architecture, for example, affect the presence of this effect since these properties directly determine how the modality gap is bridged. Previous findings suggest that dataset diversity and scale are the primary drivers of alignment to human representations (Conwell et al., 2023; Muttenthaler et al., 2023). We compare four models here, with different architectures, attention mechanisms, and training objectives.

While many different architectures exist, they typically use single or dual-stream architectures. Either combining the inputs from two modalities and encoding them jointly (single-stream) or encoding them by two separate modality-specific encoders (dual-stream). Single-stream architectures typically use merged attention, where the language and visual input attend to both themselves and the other modality. Dual-stream architectures often use some form of cross-model attention, like co-attention and modality-specific attention, in addition to merged attention. Recently, Li et al. (2023) introduced a lightweight Querying Transformer (Q-Former) to bridge the modality gap between any arbitrary pre-trained frozen vision model and a language model, resulting in BLIP2. Frequently, image text matching and masked language modeling are used as learning objectives (e.g., ViLT; Kim et al., 2021), but some methods use a contrastive learning objective (e.g., CLIP) or use image-grounded text generation loss (e.g., BLIP, BLIP2). The models used in this paper are shown in Table 1. They are different in the above aspects, allowing investigation into the effect of their designs and input data on the bouba-kiki effect. In addition, we include GPT-4o; even though no information is available for this model, its generative performance is unprecedented.

3 Methods

To test for the presence of a bouba-kiki effect in VLMs we employ previously used as well as newly generated images (§3.1) and use a method for constructing pseudowords (3.2) that is directly borrowed from Nielsen and Rendall (2013). Probing (§3.3) was used to obtain image-text scores and responses were analyzed in two ways (§3.4).

3.1 Image selection and generation

The original set of images used by Köhler (1929, 1947), as shown in figure 1, has been expanded in subsequent experiments. Maurer et al. (2006) for example introduced additional line drawings and Westbury (2005) used images with white shapes on a black background. Here we use the original pair and the two sets of four image pairs by Maurer et al. (2006); Westbury (2005). In addition, we generated new random curved and jagged images using a method inspired by Nielsen and Rendall (2013). We generated 10 uniformly distributed points within a circle with a radius of 1. These points were connected with either smooth curves or straight lines. For curved images, we generated curves that pass through the given points such that they form a closed path. Jagged images were generated by connecting the ordered points with straight lines, also forming a closed path. All images are displayed in Appendix A.

3.2 Pseudoword generation

Following the experiment conducted by Nielsen and Rendall (2013) with human participants, we present the VLMs with a constrained set of syllables that can be used to construct novel pseudowords. Based on previously established cross-modal association patterns, Nielsen and Rendall (2013) selected sets of vowels and consonants that were expected to evoke a sense of correspondence with either jagged or curved visual shapes. We adopt exactly their set here, consisting of sonorant consonants M, N and L and rounded vowels OO, OH and AH, expected to match to curved shapes, and plosive consonants T, K and P and non-rounded vowels EE, AY and UH, expected to match to jagged shapes. Syllables were created by making consonant-vowel combinations. In total 36 different syllables (e.g., loo, nah, kee, puh) can be constructed in this way, with nine different versions of each syllable type: sonorant-rounded (S-R), plosive-rounded (P-R), sonorant-non-rounded (S-NR) and plosive-non-rounded (P-NR).

In addition to single syllables, we generated pseudowords by concatenating two syllables, as this was exactly the task human participants were asked to complete in the experiment (Nielsen and Rendall, 2013). However, since we are not primarily interested here in distinguishing the separate roles played by consonants versus vowels in the bouba-kiki effect, and Nielsen and Rendall (2013) demonstrated that both have an effect, we limit the set of possible syllables in two-syllable probing to combinations of S-R syllables and P-NR syllables.

An important difference between the human setup and our work, is that their participants also listened to a spoken version of the pseudowords, while our models are only exposed to the written form. Since the bouba-kiki effect is most often assumed to integrate vision and sound, this may influence the result. However, the relation between orthographic shapes and the sounds they represent is not arbitrary either and has presumably been shaped by human iconic strategies in their development and evolution (Turoman and Styles, 2017). This perhaps also explains why a role for English orthography has been demonstrated in the bouba-kiki effect for humans (Cuskley et al., 2017), while at the same time it is robust across different writing systems (Ćwiek et al., 2022).

3.3 VLM probing

To assess the preferences of BLIP2, CLIP, and ViLT, in each trial, we extract probabilities for all possible labels (i.e., syllables and pseudowords) conditioned on an image. Instead of only embedding the label, each label is fed in a sentence ('The label for this image is {label}') such that embedding the textual input is closer to the models' natural objective[1]. Importantly, only the labels differ between inferences such that variance in the probability given an image is caused by the label only. Where Alper and Averbuch-Elor (2023) use an *indirect* metric by embedding the inputs in CLIP space, our method uses the model probabilities as a more *direct* measure of how well a given syllable or pseudoword matches a novel image. For GPT-4o, we prompt the model to generate a label and use its probability directly (Appendix B).

3.4 Analysis

All findings were analyzed for statistical significance using Bayesian models with the *brms* package (Bürkner, 2021) in R (R Core Team, 2023). To analyze VLM probability scores, we fitted Bayesian multilevel linear models (4 chains of 4000 iterations and a warmup of 2000, family = *gaussian*) to predict probability with image shape (Jagged versus Curved), consonant (plosive or sonorant) and vowel (rounded or non-rounded) categories ($Probability \sim shape * (consonant + vowel)$). For all models of this type, the random effects structure consists of varying intercepts for image and label with by-label random slopes for shape. When comparing proportions of vowels, consonants, or selected pseudoword types, we fitted Bayesian logistic models (4 chains of 1000 iterations and a warmup of 500, family = *binomial*) to

[1] Additional analysis revealed that the overall results remain consistent even when only the label is provided.

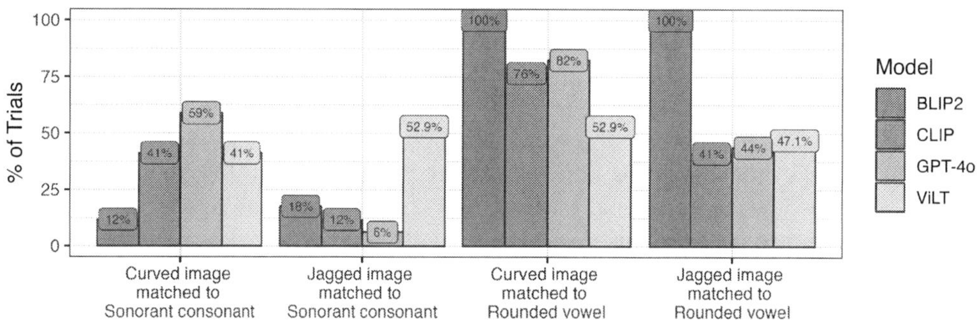

Figure 2: Percentages of trials in which selected syllables contain sonorant consonants or rounded vowels, separated by image shape (Jagged or Curved) for all four VLMs

test whether shape predicts the occurrence of particular vowels, consonants or pseudoword types $(Occurrence|trials(SampleSize) \sim Shape)$. Effects are considered significant when the computed 95% Credible Interval does not include 0, i.e. the lower and the upper bounds of the CI have to be either both positive or both negative. All plots were created in ggplot2 (Wickham, 2016).

4 Results

The findings are analyzed in two ways. First, we compare the results of VLM probing to the performance of human participants (Nielsen and Rendall, 2013). For BLIP2, CLIP and ViLT this means we first only consider the syllable or pseudoword with the highest probability for each image. These are then analyzed similarly to those selected by humans or generated by GPT-4o. Second, we examine the probabilities for *each* possible syllable or pseudoword from BLIP2, CLIP and ViLT, to obtain a more comprehensive measure of cross-modal associations. For the GPT-4o results reported below, one image in the Jagged shape condition is consistently missing since it (top right image in Figure 7 in Appendix A) was flagged as 'content that is not allowed by our safety system'.

4.1 Single syllable selection

VLMs were first probed using single syllables, here we are interested to see if the models predominantly pair Jagged images with P-NR and Curved images with S-R syllables, as was found with humans. Figure 2 shows these results as the percentage of trials (where each individual image of the set of 17 pairs forms a trial) in which model probabilities where highest for sonorant consonants or rounded vowels with either Curved or Jagged shapes. A result that fits the expected human pattern would show higher bars for the Curved than for the Jagged shapes in both sets. The only models where this seems to go in the right direction are CLIP and GPT-4o. BLIP2 mostly displays a general preference for P-R syllables, without considering the shape and ViLT does not display any clear preference. To test whether the differences in percentages for CLIP and GPT-4o are significant, we use Bayesian logistic models (as described in 3.4). For both models, Jagged images are paired with sonorant consonants significantly less often than Curved images (CLIP: b = -1.79, Bayesian 95 % Credible Interval $[-3.86, -0.05]$, GPT-4o: b = -3.51, 95 % CI $[-6.69, -1.37]$) and Jagged images are paired with rounded vowels significantly less often than Curved images (CLIP: b = -1.62, 95 % CI $[-3.06, -0.19]$, GPT-4o: b = -1.97, 95 % CI $[-3.66, -0.36]$).

4.2 Probability scores for novel syllables

While GPT-4o only selects the best fitting syllable out of all options for each image, CLIP, BLIP2 and ViLT provide probability scores for each possible syllable, yielding more comprehensive data. Here we therefore also analyze the probability scores for these three models, to investigate whether higher scores occur when pairing S-R syllables with Curved images than with Jagged images and vice versa for P-NR syllables. Figure 3 shows the probabilities for the pseudoword pairs that were used in the classic experiments with humans (bouba & kiki, takete & maluma) and the four different syllable types (S-R, S-NR, P-R, P-NR).

Looking at the original pseudowords, none of the models display a clear bouba-kiki or takete-maluma effect. Probabilities for the different words

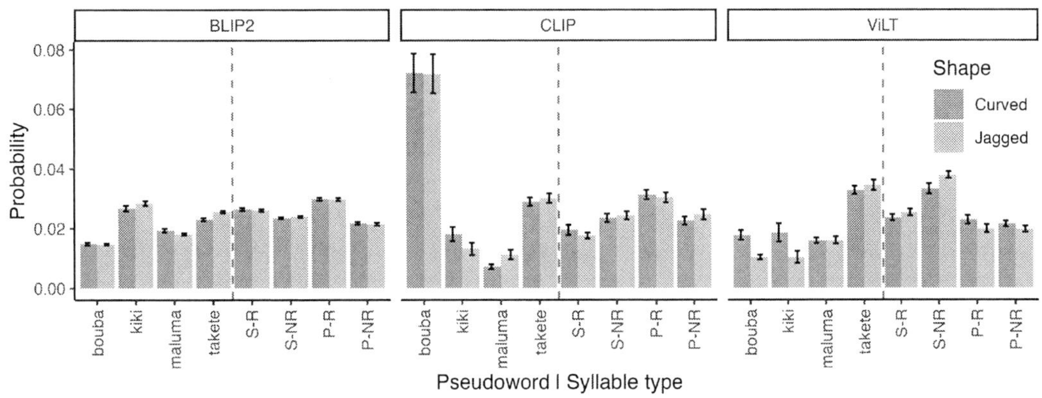

Figure 3: Probability scores for the original pseudowords (bouba, kiki, takete and maluma), as well as for the four different generated syllable types: Sonorant-Rounded (S-R), Sonorant-Non-Rounded (S-NR), Plosive-Rounded (P-R) and Plosive-Non-Rounded (P-NR), paired with two types of shapes (Jagged or Curved) for three VLMs

differ overall (with a curiously high probability for "bouba" in CLIP), but this does not seem modulated by the visual shape. For the syllables, BLIP2 shows no shape-modulated variation at all, and ViLT displays contradictory patterns (e.g. higher probability scores for S-NR than S-R syllables with Curved shapes and higher scores for S-NR with Jagged than with both P-R and P-NR). Only CLIP gets close to the expected pattern, with equal scores for the ambiguous syllable types (S-NR and P-R) but slightly higher scores for P-NR with Jagged and S-R with Curved. Yet, no significant effects are found when testing whether CLIP shows a pattern of preferring the expected consonants and vowels with their associated shapes using a Bayesian multilevel linear model (as described in 3.4). For ViLT, we find one (tiny) interaction between shape and consonants in the opposite direction of what is expected, where scores for Jagged shapes are significantly higher when paired with sonorant versus plosive consonants ($b = .0056$, 95 % CI [.0001, .0112]). For BLIP2, we find a significant overall preference for rounded vowels (b = 0.0055, 95 % CI [.0019, .0091]), but no other effects.

4.3 Two-syllable pseudoword selection

Although the results in Nielsen and Rendall (2013) were analyzed by looking at single syllables, the actual task human participants performed involved creating novel pseudowords consisting of two syllables. We therefore also used our VLMs to generate (GPT-4o) or provide probability scores (CLIP, BLIP2 and ViLT) for two-syllable pseudowords that were created by concatenating two of the possible syllables from the set of S-R (most Curved) and P-NR (most Jagged) syllables resulting in 324 words. For CLIP, BLIP2 and ViLT we first look at the "preferred" pseudowords, by only considering the option with the highest probability score for each image. Figure 4 shows the percentages of trials in which S-R syllables were matched to either Curved or Jagged images, counting each one of the two syllables in a word separately. BLIP2 never used S-R syllables and only selected pseudowords that contained two P-NR syllables, independently from which image was shown. Both CLIP and GPT-4o show a higher percentage of Curved matched to S-R compared to Jagged, but GPT-4o seems to mostly just prefer S-R syllables overall. A manual inspection of GPT-4o's generated pseudowords revealed that in 25 out of 33 trials the word "nohmoh" was used, 12 times for Jagged and 13 times for Curved images. For ViLT, if a preference is present, it is in the wrong direction. In the case of CLIP, we find that Jagged images are indeed paired with S-R syllables significantly less often than Curved images (b = -1.00, 95 % CI [-2.04, -0.04]).

4.4 Probability scores for novel two-syllable pseudowords

We obtained probability scores for all possible two-syllable pseudowords when paired with each image for CLIP, BLIP2 and ViLT. Figure 5 shows these results by plotting probabilities for four different pseudoword types. The pseudoword on the left combines two P-NR syllables and is therefore expected to result in higher probabilities for Jagged shapes. Conversely, the most right pseudoword

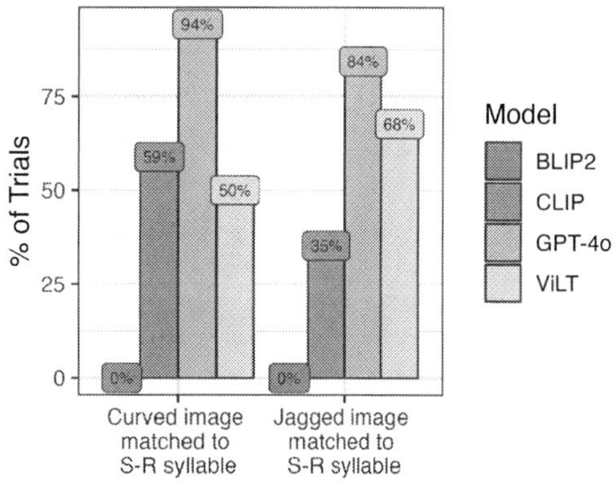

Figure 4: Percentages of trials in which Jagged or Curved visual shapes were matched to Sonorant-Rounded (S-R) syllables embedded in two-syllable pseudowords for all VLMs. Here 0% for S-R syllables implies a 100% preference for P-NR syllables.

combines two S-R syllables and should evoke higher probabilities for Curved shapes. A pattern in which pink (Curved) bars rise while green (Jagged) bars fall would therefore reflect evidence for the bouba-kiki effect. None of the tested VLMs fit this pattern. Since GPT-4o generated "nohmoh" (and similar variants like "moomoh") almost exclusively when given the freedom to select two syllables from the full set of Jagged-associated and Curved-associated syllables, we also independently obtained probabilities for both syllable types. For this, we asked GPT-4o to generate a pseudoword for each image twice, once when given only the set of Jagged-associated syllable options, and once with only the Curved-associated syllables as options. Yet, again no significant effect of shape on probability scores for different syllable types was found. Figure 9 in Appendix C shows this result.

4.5 Summary

In summary, the bouba-kiki effect appeared absent for BLIP2 and ViLT, while for CLIP and GPT-4o, the results varied depending on how the effect was tested, and results were analyzed. When asking the model to select one best-fitting syllable, CLIP and GPT-4o both display the effect in the expected direction. However, this pattern disappears when looking at a richer dataset of probability scores (from CLIP, BLIP2, and ViLT) for each possible syllable. In the case of two-syllable words, GPT-4o results no longer display significant evidence for a bouba-kiki effect.

5 Discussion

Our findings partly contradict previous work, which found that sound-symbolic associations are present in CLIP and Stable Diffusion (Alper and Averbuch-Elor, 2023). We use a different method, focusing on image-to-text probabilities, which is more similar to how the effect has been tested with humans. We show that it is too early to conclude that VLMs understand sound-symbolism or map visio-linguistic representations in a human-like way since the results depend heavily on which specific model is tested and how the task is formulated. This is unsurprising given that CNN-based models often classify based on superficial textural rather than shape features (Baker et al., 2018; Geirhos et al., 2019; Hermann et al., 2020) and, albeit less so, this texture bias is also present in vision transformers (Geirhos et al., 2021). Moreover, Darcet et al. (2024) identified that, during inference, ViT networks create artifacts at low-informative background areas of images that are used for computations rather than describing visual information. Both findings are in stark contrast with what, at its core, is required for sound symbolism. However, the fact that some evidence for a bouba-kiki effect could be found in two of the four models tentatively suggests that real-world physical experience with different object properties may not be needed to develop this cross-modal preference but that it can, to some extent, be learned from statistical regularities in data containing text and images.

Human language on its own already contains many non-arbitrary regularities between speech sounds and meaning (Blasi et al., 2016), and these regularities, like phonesthemes (Bergen, 2004), can be detected and interpreted by models such as word embeddings (Abramova and Fernández, 2016) and LSTM based language models (Pimentel et al., 2019). No visual input is needed for this, and perhaps this is also what caused the appearance of the bouba-kiki effect in the work by Alper and Averbuch-Elor (2023). In our work, we gave more prominence to the visual input and found much less convincing evidence for the effect.

Regarding the design features of the models we tested, we see that the model with the best bouba-kiki alignment to human preferences, CLIP, is also trained on the largest amount of data (comparing the three models we have information on, not including GPT-4o). This finding aligns with previous work showing that dataset properties affect

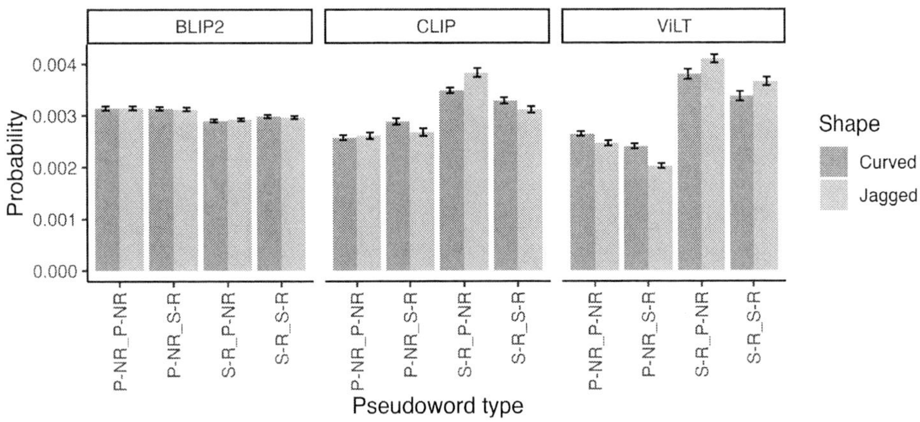

Figure 5: Probability scores for four pseudoword types, combining Sonorant-Rounded (S-R) and Plosive-Non-Rounded (P-NR) syllables, paired with two types of shapes (Jagged or Curved) for three VLMs

alignment with human representations (Conwell et al., 2023; Muttenthaler et al., 2023). However, despite having much more parameters than CLIP, BLIP2 does not show the effect. In addition, while both BLIP2 and CLIP use dual-stream architectures, only CLIP, which uses modality-specific attention mechanisms, displays some evidence of a bouba-kiki effect. Despite impressive performance on vision-language tasks, the Q-Former in BLIP2 apparently does not promote sound-symbolic associations. This is important knowledge for developing models with vision-language representations that align with those of humans. More aligned models show more robust few-shot learning (Sucholutsky and Griffiths, 2023) and promote more natural interactions between humans and machines (Kouwenhoven et al., 2022). Although we find modest evidence for a bouba-kiki effect in GPT-4o, we cannot know the origin of this effect as model details are unknown.

6 Conclusion

Given the pervasive role cross-modal associations play in human linguistic processing, learning and evolution, we tested for the presence of a bouba-kiki effect in four VLMs that differ along various dimensions such as architecture design, training objective, number of parameters, and input data. Evidence for this effect is limited, but not entirely absent, in the tested VLMs and these findings inform discussions on the origins of the bouba-kiki effect in human cognition and future developments of VLMs that align well with human cross-modal associations.

7 Limitations

Our work has a few notable limitations. First, we used synthetic images that were previously used in experiments with humans. Even though this makes our results easily comparable to those of human studies, there is a potential risk that these images are out-of-domain for models that are predominantly trained on realistic images. In future extensions of this work we therefore plan to include more naturalistic images.

A second limitation manifests itself in the tokenization of the textual input. While humans in the experiment evaluate pseudowords as a whole, the tokenization process in language models may split our syllables or pseudowords into tokens that would not necessarily evoke the expected cross-modal associations in humans either (e.g., a separate evaluation of H in OH may invite a jagged association instead of curved). Despite being a fundamental difference, the primary goal of this work was to assess the preferences of VLMs in their most basic form. Further work should investigate whether tokenization affects results and identify whether there may be model-specific cross-modal associations on a token instead of word level.

Third, the pseudowords we used were based on an experiment with humans but were different from those used by Alper and Averbuch-Elor (2023), who did find a strong bouba-kiki effect in CLIP embeddings. To allow for a better comparison with their findings, future work should also test our image-to-text approach with their set of pseudowords.

Finally, our experiments included a relatively

small number of trials, limited by available experimental stimuli from human studies. By combining images from several previous studies and augmenting this set with additional newly generated images, we used more trials than most studies conducted with humans, though. The set of generated images can easily be expanded in future work. However, given the current pattern of results, this is not expected to lead to a more robust bouba-kiki effect in most models.

References

Ekaterina Abramova and Raquel Fernández. 2016. Questioning arbitrariness in language: a data-driven study of conventional iconicity. In *Proceedings of the 2016 Conference of the North American Chapter of the Association for Computational Linguistics: Human Language Technologies*, pages 343–352, San Diego, California. Association for Computational Linguistics.

Aishwarya Agrawal, Dhruv Batra, Devi Parikh, and Aniruddha Kembhavi. 2018. Don't just assume; look and answer: Overcoming priors for visual question answering. In *Proceedings of the IEEE conference on computer vision and pattern recognition*, pages 4971–4980.

Morris Alper and Hadar Averbuch-Elor. 2023. Kiki or bouba? sound symbolism in vision-and-language models. In *Advances in Neural Information Processing Systems*, volume 36, pages 78347–78359. Curran Associates, Inc.

Morris Alper, Michael Fiman, and Hadar Averbuch-Elor. 2023. Is bert blind? exploring the effect of vision-and-language pretraining on visual language understanding. In *Proceedings of the IEEE/CVF Conference on Computer Vision and Pattern Recognition*, pages 6778–6788.

Nicholas Baker, Hongjing Lu, Gennady Erlikhman, and Philip J. Kellman. 2018. Deep convolutional networks do not classify based on global object shape. *PLOS Computational Biology*, 14(12):1–43.

Benjamin K. Bergen. 2004. The psychological reality of phonaesthemes. *Language*, 80(2):290–311.

Damián E Blasi, Søren Wichmann, Harald Hammarström, Peter F Stadler, and Morten H Christiansen. 2016. Sound–meaning association biases evidenced across thousands of languages. *Proceedings of the National Academy of Sciences*, 113(39):10818–10823.

Roberto Bottini, Marco Barilari, and Olivier Collignon. 2019. Sound symbolism in sighted and blind. the role of vision and orthography in sound-shape correspondences. *Cognition*, 185:62–70.

Diane Bouchacourt and Marco Baroni. 2018. How agents see things: On visual representations in an emergent language game. In *Proceedings of the 2018 Conference on Empirical Methods in Natural Language Processing*, pages 981–985, Brussels, Belgium. Association for Computational Linguistics.

Paul-Christian Bürkner. 2021. Bayesian item response modeling in R with brms and Stan. *Journal of Statistical Software*, 100(5):1–54.

Colin Conwell, Jacob S. Prince, Kendrick N. Kay, George A. Alvarez, and Talia Konkle. 2023. What can 1.8 billion regressions tell us about the pressures shaping high-level visual representation in brains and machines? *bioRxiv*.

Christine Cuskley, Mark Dingemanse, Simon Kirby, and Tessa M Van Leeuwen. 2019. Cross-modal associations and synesthesia: Categorical perception and structure in vowel–color mappings in a large online sample. *Behavior research methods*, 51:1651–1675.

Christine Cuskley and Simon Kirby. 2013. 869Synesthesia, Cross-Modality, and Language Evolution. In *Oxford Handbook of Synesthesia*. Oxford University Press.

Christine Cuskley, Julia Simner, and Simon Kirby. 2017. Phonological and orthographic influences in the bouba–kiki effect. *Psychological research*, 81:119–130.

Aleksandra Ćwiek, Susanne Fuchs, Christoph Draxler, Eva Liina Asu, Dan Dediu, Katri Hiovain, Shigeto Kawahara, Sofia Koutalidis, Manfred Krifka, Pärtel Lippus, Gary Lupyan, Grace E. Oh, Jing Paul, Caterina Petrone, Rachid Ridouane, Sabine Reiter, Nathalie Schümchen, Ádám Szalontai, Özlem Ünal-Logacev, Jochen Zeller, Marcus Perlman, and Bodo Winter. 2022. The bouba/kiki effect is robust across cultures and writing systems. *Philosophical Transactions of the Royal Society B*, 377(1841):20200390.

Timothée Darcet, Maxime Oquab, Julien Mairal, and Piotr Bojanowski. 2024. Vision transformers need registers. In *The Twelfth International Conference on Learning Representations*.

Mark Dingemanse. 2012. Advances in the cross-linguistic study of ideophones. *Language and Linguistics Compass*, 6(10):654–672.

Anuj Diwan, Layne Berry, Eunsol Choi, David Harwath, and Kyle Mahowald. 2022. Why is winoground hard? investigating failures in visuolinguistic compositionality. In *Proceedings of the 2022 Conference on Empirical Methods in Natural Language Processing*, pages 2236–2250, Abu Dhabi, United Arab Emirates. Association for Computational Linguistics.

Karla K Evans and Anne Treisman. 2010. Natural cross-modal mappings between visual and auditory features. *Journal of vision*, 10(1):6–6.

Mathilde Fort and Jean-Luc Schwartz. 2022. Resolving the bouba-kiki effect enigma by rooting iconic sound symbolism in physical properties of round and spiky objects. *Scientific reports*, 12(1):19172.

Lukas Galke, Yoav Ram, and Limor Raviv. 2022. Emergent communication for understanding human language evolution: What's missing? In *Emergent Communication Workshop at ICLR 2022*.

Robert Geirhos, Kantharaju Narayanappa, Benjamin Mitzkus, Tizian Thieringer, Matthias Bethge, Felix A. Wichmann, and Wieland Brendel. 2021. Partial success in closing the gap between human and machine vision. In *Advances in Neural Information Processing Systems*, volume 34, pages 23885–23899. Curran Associates, Inc.

Robert Geirhos, Patricia Rubisch, Claudio Michaelis, Matthias Bethge, Felix A. Wichmann, and Wieland Brendel. 2019. Imagenet-trained CNNs are biased towards texture; increasing shape bias improves accuracy and robustness. In *International Conference on Learning Representations*.

Yash Goyal, Tejas Khot, Douglas Summers-Stay, Dhruv Batra, and Devi Parikh. 2017. Making the v in vqa matter: Elevating the role of image understanding in visual question answering. In *Proceedings of the IEEE conference on computer vision and pattern recognition*, pages 6904–6913.

Katherine Hermann, Ting Chen, and Simon Kornblith. 2020. The origins and prevalence of texture bias in convolutional neural networks. In *Advances in Neural Information Processing Systems*, volume 33, pages 19000–19015. Curran Associates, Inc.

Charles F. Hockett. 1960. The origin of speech. *Scientific American*, 203:88–96.

Timothy L Hubbard. 1996. Synesthesia-like mappings of lightness, pitch, and melodic interval. *The American journal of psychology*, pages 219–238.

Matsumi Imai, Sotaro Kita, Miho Nagumo, and Hiroyuki Okada. 2008. Sound symbolism facilitates early verb learning. *Cognition*, 109(1):54–65.

Mutsumi Imai and Sotaro Kita. 2014. The sound symbolism bootstrapping hypothesis for language acquisition and language evolution. *Philosophical transactions of the Royal Society B: Biological sciences*, 369(1651):20130298.

Allan Jabri, Armand Joulin, and Laurens Van Der Maaten. 2016. Revisiting visual question answering baselines. In *European conference on computer vision*, pages 727–739. Springer.

Amita Kamath, Jack Hessel, and Kai-Wei Chang. 2023. What's "up" with vision-language models? investigating their struggle with spatial reasoning. In *Proceedings of the 2023 Conference on Empirical Methods in Natural Language Processing*, pages 9161–9175, Singapore. Association for Computational Linguistics.

Siddharth Karamcheti, Suraj Nair, Ashwin Balakrishna, Percy Liang, Thomas Kollar, and Dorsa Sadigh. 2024. Prismatic VLMs: Investigating the design space of visually-conditioned language models. In *Forty-first International Conference on Machine Learning*.

Wonjae Kim, Bokyung Son, and Ildoo Kim. 2021. Vilt: Vision-and-language transformer without convolution or region supervision. In *Proceedings of the 38th International Conference on Machine Learning*, volume 139 of *Proceedings of Machine Learning Research*, pages 5583–5594. PMLR.

Wolfgang Köhler. 1929. *Gestalt Psychology*. New York: Horace Liveright.

Wolfgang Köhler. 1947. *Gestalt Psychology*. (2nd ed.) New York: Horace Liveright.

Tom Kouwenhoven, Max Peeperkorn, Bram van Dijk, and Tessa Verhoef. 2024. The curious case of representational alignment: Unravelling visio-linguistic tasks in emergent communication. In *Proceedings of the Workshop on Cognitive Modeling and Computational Linguistics*, Bangkok, Thailand. Association for Computational Linguistics.

Tom Kouwenhoven, Tessa Verhoef, Roy De Kleijn, and Stephan Raaijmakers. 2022. Emerging grounded shared vocabularies between human and machine, inspired by human language evolution. *Frontiers in Artificial Intelligence*, 5:886349.

Angeliki Lazaridou and Marco Baroni. 2020. Emergent multi-agent communication in the deep learning era. *arXiv preprint arXiv:2006.02419*.

Junnan Li, Dongxu Li, Silvio Savarese, and Steven Hoi. 2023. BLIP-2: Bootstrapping language-image pretraining with frozen image encoders and large language models. In *Proceedings of the 40th International Conference on Machine Learning*, volume 202 of *Proceedings of Machine Learning Research*, pages 19730–19742. PMLR.

Yuchen Lian, Arianna Bisazza, and Tessa Verhoef. 2023. Communication drives the emergence of language universals in neural agents: Evidence from the word-order/case-marking trade-off. *Transactions of the Association for Computational Linguistics*, 11:1033–1047.

Hannah Little, Kerem Eryılmaz, and Bart De Boer. 2017. Signal dimensionality and the emergence of combinatorial structure. *Cognition*, 168:1–15.

Gwilym Lockwood and Mark Dingemanse. 2015. Iconicity in the lab: A review of behavioral, developmental, and neuroimaging research into sound-symbolism. *Frontiers in psychology*, 6:145602.

Ryan Lowe, Abhinav Gupta, Jakob Foerster, Douwe Kiela, and Joelle Pineau. 2020. On the interaction between supervision and self-play in emergent communication. In *International Conference on Learning Representations*.

Matéo Mahaut, Francesca Franzon, Roberto Dessì, and Marco Baroni. 2023. Referential communication in heterogeneous communities of pre-trained visual deep networks. *arXiv preprint arXiv:2302.08913*.

Lawrence E. Marks. 1974. On associations of light and sound: The mediation of brightness, pitch, and loudness. *The American journal of psychology*, pages 173–188.

Daphne Maurer, Thanujeni Pathman, and Catherine J Mondloch. 2006. The shape of boubas: Sound–shape correspondences in toddlers and adults. *Developmental science*, 9(3):316–322.

Robert D Melara. 1989. Dimensional interaction between color and pitch. *Journal of Experimental Psychology: Human Perception and Performance*, 15(1):69.

Lotte Meteyard, Emily Stoppard, Dee Snudden, Stefano F Cappa, and Gabriella Vigliocco. 2015. When semantics aids phonology: A processing advantage for iconic word forms in aphasia. *Neuropsychologia*, 76:264–275.

Lukas Muttenthaler, Jonas Dippel, Lorenz Linhardt, Robert A. Vandermeulen, and Simon Kornblith. 2023. Human alignment of neural network representations. In *The Eleventh International Conference on Learning Representations*.

Alan Nielsen and Drew Rendall. 2011. The sound of round: evaluating the sound-symbolic role of consonants in the classic takete-maluma phenomenon. *Canadian Journal of Experimental Psychology/Revue canadienne de psychologie expérimentale*, 65(2):115.

Alan Nielsen and Drew Rendall. 2012. The source and magnitude of sound-symbolic biases in processing artificial word material and their implications for language learning and transmission. *Language and cognition*, 4(2):115–125.

Alan Nielsen and Drew Rendall. 2013. Parsing the role of consonants versus vowels in the classic taketemaluma phenomenon. *Canadian Journal of Experimental Psychology/Revue canadienne de psychologie expérimentale*, 67(2):153.

Cesare Valerio Parise and Charles Spence. 2009. 'when birds of a feather flock together': Synesthetic correspondences modulate audiovisual integration in nonsynesthetes. *PloS one*, 4(5):e5664.

Pamela Perniss, Robin Thompson, and Gabriella Vigliocco. 2010. Iconicity as a general property of language: evidence from spoken and signed languages. *Frontiers in Psychology*, 1(227).

Lynn K Perry, Marcus Perlman, and Gary Lupyan. 2015. Iconicity in english and spanish and its relation to lexical category and age of acquisition. *PloS one*, 10(9):e0137147.

Tiago Pimentel, Arya D. McCarthy, Damian Blasi, Brian Roark, and Ryan Cotterell. 2019. Meaning to form: Measuring systematicity as information. In *Proceedings of the 57th Annual Meeting of the Association for Computational Linguistics*, pages 1751–1764, Florence, Italy. Association for Computational Linguistics.

R Core Team. 2023. *R: A Language and Environment for Statistical Computing*. R Foundation for Statistical Computing, Vienna, Austria.

Alec Radford, Jong Wook Kim, Chris Hallacy, Aditya Ramesh, Gabriel Goh, Sandhini Agarwal, Girish Sastry, Amanda Askell, Pamela Mishkin, Jack Clark, et al. 2021. Learning transferable visual models from natural language supervision. In *International conference on machine learning*, pages 8748–8763. PMLR.

Vilayanur S. Ramachandran and Edward M. Hubbard. 2001. Synaesthesia–a window into perception, thought and language. *Journal of Consciousness Studies*, 8(12):3–34.

Robin Rombach, Andreas Blattmann, Dominik Lorenz, Patrick Esser, and Björn Ommer. 2022. High-resolution image synthesis with latent diffusion models. In *Proceedings of the IEEE/CVF conference on computer vision and pattern recognition*, pages 10684–10695.

David S Schmidtke, Markus Conrad, and Arthur M Jacobs. 2014. Phonological iconicity. *Frontiers in psychology*, 5:80.

Julia Simner, Christine Cuskley, and Simon Kirby. 2010. What sound does that taste? cross-modal mappings across gustation and audition. *Perception*, 39(4):553.

Shane Steinert-Threlkeld, Xuhui Zhou, Zeyu Liu, and C. M. Downey. 2022. Emergent communication finetuning (EC-FT) for pretrained language models. In *Emergent Communication Workshop at ICLR 2022*.

Ilia Sucholutsky and Tom Griffiths. 2023. Alignment with human representations supports robust few-shot learning. In *Advances in Neural Information Processing Systems*, volume 36, pages 73464–73479. Curran Associates, Inc.

Mónica Tamariz, Seán G Roberts, J Isidro Martínez, and Julio Santiago. 2018. The interactive origin of iconicity. *Cognitive Science*, 42(1):334–349.

Tristan Thrush, Ryan Jiang, Max Bartolo, Amanpreet Singh, Adina Williams, Douwe Kiela, and Candace Ross. 2022. Winoground: Probing vision and language models for visio-linguistic compositionality. In *Proceedings of the IEEE/CVF Conference on Computer Vision and Pattern Recognition (CVPR)*, pages 5238–5248.

Nora Turoman and Suzy J Styles. 2017. Glyph guessing for 'oo'and 'ee': Spatial frequency information in sound symbolic matching for ancient and unfamiliar scripts. *Royal Society open science*, 4(9):170882.

Ashish Vaswani, Noam Shazeer, Niki Parmar, Jakob Uszkoreit, Llion Jones, Aidan N Gomez, Ł ukasz Kaiser, and Illia Polosukhin. 2017. Attention is all you need. In *Advances in Neural Information Processing Systems*, volume 30. Curran Associates, Inc.

Tessa Verhoef, Simon Kirby, and Bart De Boer. 2016. Iconicity and the emergence of combinatorial structure in language. *Cognitive science*, 40(8):1969–1994.

Tessa Verhoef, Seán G Roberts, and Mark Dingemanse. 2015. Emergence of systematic iconicity: Transmission, interaction and analogy. In *37th Annual Meeting of the Cognitive Science Society (CogSci 2015)*, pages 2481–2486. Cognitive Science Society.

Jamie Ward, Brett Huckstep, and Elias Tsakanikos. 2006. Sound-colour synaesthesia: To what extent does it use cross-modal mechanisms common to us all? *Cortex*, 42(2):264–280.

Chris Westbury. 2005. Implicit sound symbolism in lexical access: Evidence from an interference task. *Brain and language*, 93(1):10–19.

Hadley Wickham. 2016. *ggplot2: Elegant Graphics for Data Analysis*. Springer-Verlag New York.

Jingyi Zhang, Jiaxing Huang, Sheng Jin, and Shijian Lu. 2024a. Vision-language models for vision tasks: A survey. *IEEE Transactions on Pattern Analysis and Machine Intelligence*, pages 1–20.

Yi Zhang, Ce Zhang, Yushun Tang, and Zhihai He. 2024b. Cross-modal concept learning and inference for vision-language models. *Neurocomputing*, 583:127530.

Chenhao Zheng, Jieyu Zhang, Aniruddha Kembhavi, and Ranjay Krishna. 2024. Iterated learning improves compositionality in large vision-language models. In *Proceedings of the IEEE/CVF Conference on Computer Vision and Pattern Recognition (CVPR)*, pages 13785–13795.

A Full set of images

This appendix presents the full set of images with visual shapes that were used in the experiments. Besides the original image pair from Köhler (1929, 1947) which was shown in Figure 1, we used four image pairs from Maurer et al. (2006), displayed in figure 6, four from Westbury (2005), displayed in figure 7, and 8 additional pairs we newly generated using a method inspired by the one described by Nielsen and Rendall (2013), displayed in Figure 8. For each image pair, the Curved version is displayed on the left and the Jagged version on the right.

Figure 6: Images from (Maurer et al., 2006)

B GPT-4o prompting

Image-label matching is not directly possible for GPT-4o since the probabilities of the input tokens cannot be accessed. We therefore prompt (B.1) this model, with the temperature being 0.0, to generate a syllable or pseudoword given an image and use the log probabilities of the generated tokens to calculate the probability for a label conditioned on an image. Just like in the sentence setup used in the other models, our interest lies not primarily in the variability that may arise from using different prompts but rather focuses on the influence of the image on the predictions by using a simple and effective prompt that is identical for each image. Doing so allows us to use the resulting probabilities as a gauge for the models' preference of a label for a given image.

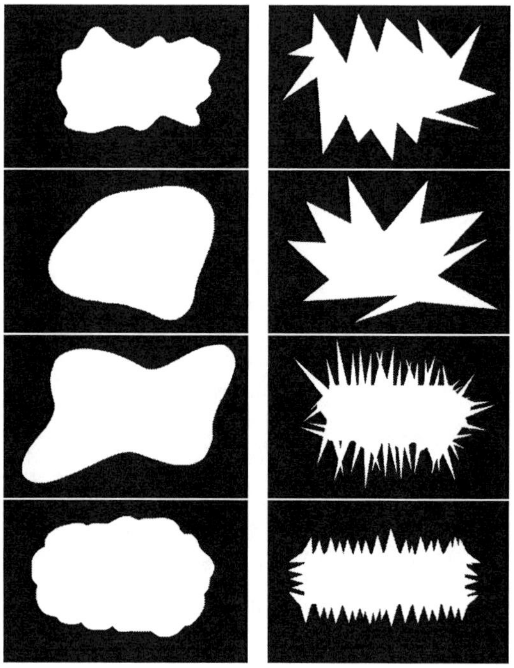

Figure 7: Images from (Westbury, 2005)

```
You are given an image for which you
need to assign a label. Use {one/two} of
 the following labels: {possible_labels
}. Only respond with the label.
```

Prompt B.1: The exact prompt used to obtain GPT-4o probabilities. *possible_labels* corresponds to the syllables of interest.

C GPT-4o pseudoword probabilities

In section 4.4 we describe results for an experiment in which we asked GPT-4o to generate a pseudoword for each image twice, once when given only the set of Jagged-associated syllable options, and once with only the Curved-associated syllables as options. Figure 9 shows the probabilities associated with these generated pseudowords. As concluded in the main text, no evidence for a preference to match P-NR syllables with Jagged shapes and S-R syllables with Curved shapes was found.

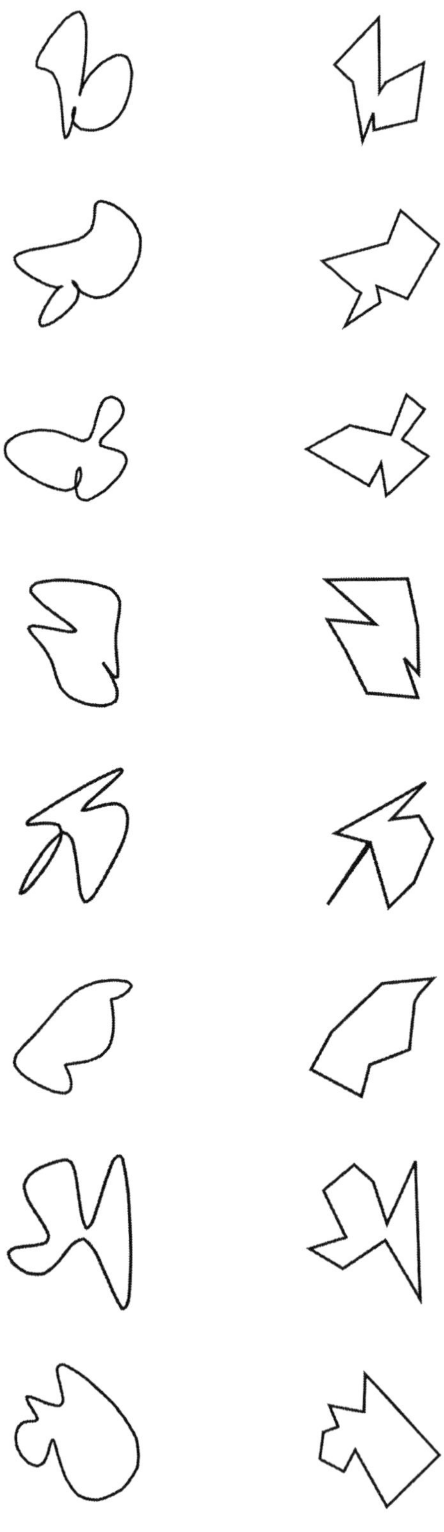

Figure 8: Newly generated images

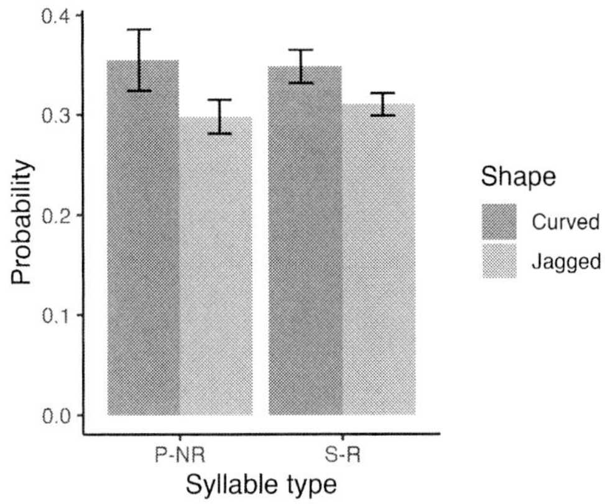

Figure 9: Probability scores for GPT-4o when forced to generate a pseudoword for each image twice, once by combining two Jagged-associated syllables, and once with only the Curved-associated syllables as options.

Evaluating Semantic Relations in Predicting Textual Labels for Images of Abstract and Concrete Concepts

Tarun Tater[1], **Sabine Schulte im Walde**[1], **Diego Frassinelli**[2,3]
[1]Institute for Natural Language Processing, University of Stuttgart, Germany
[2]Department of Linguistics, University of Konstanz, Germany
[3]Center for Information and Language Processing, LMU Munich, Germany
{tarun.tater, schulte}@ims.uni-stuttgart.de
frassinelli@cis.lmu.de

Abstract

This study investigates the performance of SigLIP, a state-of-the-art Vision-Language Model (VLM), in predicting labels for images depicting 1,278 concepts. Our analysis across 300 images per concept shows that the model frequently predicts the exact user-tagged labels, but similarly, it often predicts labels that are semantically related to the exact labels in various ways: synonyms, hypernyms, co-hyponyms, and associated words, particularly for abstract concepts. We then zoom into the diversity of the user tags of images and word associations for abstract versus concrete concepts. Surprisingly, not only abstract but also concrete concepts exhibit significant variability, thus challenging the traditional view that representations of concrete concepts are less diverse.

1 Introduction

Concrete concepts, such as *apple* and *dog*, are easily perceivable through our senses, whereas abstract concepts such as *happiness* and *justice* lack physical referents and are not directly linked to our sensory experiences (Paivio et al., 1968; Brysbaert et al., 2014). These differences have played a crucial role in various applications involving both textual and multi-modal inputs (Turney et al., 2011; Tsvetkov et al., 2013; Köper and Schulte im Walde, 2016; Köper and Schulte im Walde, 2017; Cangelosi and Stramandinoli, 2018; Su et al., 2021; Ahn et al., 2022). Recent advances in multi-modal learning with Vision-Language Models (VLMs) like CLIP (Radford et al., 2021), ALIGN (Jia et al., 2021), and SigLIP (Zhai et al., 2023), have improved the alignment of textual and visual data to generate context-aware representations. However, the ability of VLMs to capture semantic relationships between concepts and their visual representations remains underexplored. For example, the concept *idea* is semantically related to the synonym *thought* and the hyponym *belief*, and associated with *invention*. This example highlights the range of possible labels for the visual representation of a concept and the importance of including not only human-assigned labels but also their semantically related counterparts to enhance applications like image retrieval and visual question answering. Inspired by this, we evaluate how well SigLIP, a state-of-the-art VL model, predicts image labels that are generated by users, as well as their synonyms, hypernyms, co-hyponyms, and associative words. Assessing the impact on model performance, we aim to determine if integrating these relations into VLM training can potentially improve the representation of abstract and concrete concepts.

People use a variety of cues, including visual and linguistic, to perceive and understand concepts (Lynott et al., 2020). Traditionally, concrete concepts, which are directly related to sensory experiences, are considered less diverse in their visual representations compared to abstract concepts (Hessel et al., 2018; Kastner et al., 2019), and are expected to have more consistent tags and associations. In contrast, abstract concepts, being inherently diverse, are expected to have varied word associations and user tags, reflecting the complexity of understanding these concepts across modalities. To evaluate these differences, we pose the following questions:

RQ1: How do different semantic relations of user tags affect the prediction of image labels for abstract and concrete concepts?

RQ2 How do user tags given a visual cue (image), and word associations given a linguistic cue, differ in characterizing abstract versus concrete concepts?

Our findings show that SigLIP often predicts semantically related labels (such as hypernyms) instead of the original user tags. Our analysis of association data and user tags reveals that concrete concepts, like abstract ones, invoke a diverse range of descriptors, challenging the traditional view of less diversity.

Proceedings of the Workshop on Cognitive Modeling and Computational Linguistics, pages 214–220
August 15, 2024

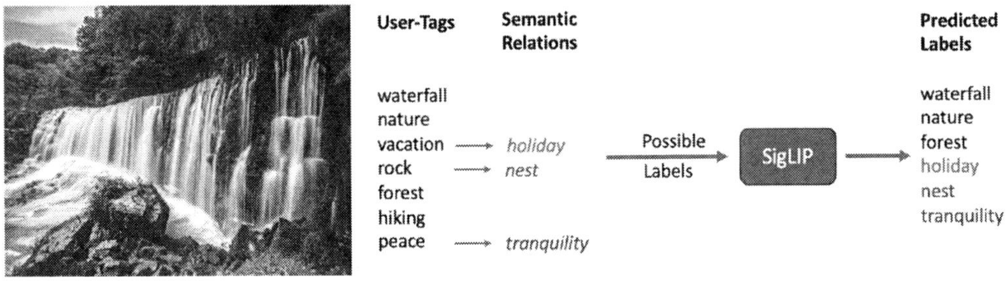

Figure 1: Example of an image and the corresponding user tags. Here, *holiday* is a synonym of *vacation*, *nest* is a co-hyponym of *rock*, and *tranquility* is a hypernym of *peace*. For this image, the SigLIP model might predict *waterfall, nature, forest, holiday, nest, tranquility*.

2 Experimental Design

2.1 Materials

Target Concepts & Concreteness Norms: We selected concrete and abstract nouns using the concreteness ratings from Brysbaert et al. (2014). The ratings range from 1 (abstract) to 5 (concrete) and were collected via crowdsourcing. We utilized the filtered dataset of $5,438$ nouns from Schulte im Walde and Frassinelli (2022) to reduce ambiguity through frequency thresholds and POS tagging. To better understand the differences between the two extremes of the concreteness spectrum, we focused on the most concrete and most abstract nouns. At the same time, we wanted to ensure a sufficient number of nouns from both extremes with at least 300 images available for each concept. However, acquiring a sufficient number of images (300) was challenging for many abstract nouns. Therefore, we selected concrete nouns rated from $4.5 - 5$, and used a broader range for abstract nouns from $1 - 2.5$. From these, we excluded all nouns which occur in the $1,000$ classes of the ILSVRC-2012 ImageNet dataset (Russakovsky et al., 2015), since many vision models are trained or evaluated on these classes. We also filtered out nouns that could lead to images depicting explicit content, as well as the nouns *camera*, *picture* and *photo* which were very common user tags because of the nature of the dataset.

Image Dataset and user tags: We used images from the YFCC100M Multimedia Commons Dataset (*YFCC*; Thomee et al. (2016)), the largest publicly available user-tagged dataset containing ≈ 100 million media objects from Flickr. Each image has tags provided by users (user tags) when uploading the image. For example, Figure 1 is an image with the corresponding possible user tags: *waterfall, nature, vacation, rock, forest, hiking, peace*. We only retained user tags that consisted solely of English characters. We randomly selected 300 images where the target concept appeared among the user tags and consider them as relevant images of that concept. This resulted in $1,278$ nouns (371 abstract and 907 concrete) with 300 images each.

Semantic Relations and Associations: We used WordNet (Miller, 1995) to extract synonyms, hypernyms and co-hyponyms for each user tag, and utilized association norms from De Deyne et al. (2019), which were gathered by prompting annotators to provide three words that came to mind for a given word. For example, the concept *idea* might have associations like *thought*, *bulb*, and *invention*. We restricted our analysis to nouns that were assessed by at least 100 annotators to ensure enough annotations, filtering our set to 682 nouns (527 concrete and 155 abstract) for RQ2.

2.2 Models and Evaluation

In this study, we perform multi-label classification, where each image can have multiple relevant labels. For instance, for Figure 1, the SigLIP model might predict *waterfall*, *nature* and *forest* as labels of the image[1]. Our goal is to evaluate how well the SigLIP model predicts either these user tags or their semantically related words as labels. We utilize the SigLIP model (Zhai et al., 2023), the only publicly available pre-trained multi-label classification VLM specifically trained with a contrastive sigmoid loss designed to align text and images. For each image, we evaluate various semantic relations as labels, including synonyms, hypernyms, co-hyponyms and association words in separate experiments. SigLIP assigns a score to each label,

[1]Please note this is only a walk-through example and the actual results may vary.

Concept class	Avg. number of user tags	Avg. number of noun user tags	Avg. % of tags pred. as labels	Avg. % images where no label was pred.	Avg. % of images where target concept not pred.
Abstract	8.69	5.40	54.41	8.06	48.87
Concrete	6.85	4.58	62.17	4.11	26.93

Table 1: User-tag prediction (pred.) results for SigLIP model with 300 images of 1,278 concepts.

Semantic Relation	Concept class	Avg. number of user tags with semantic relations	Avg. % of labels pred.	Avg. % images where ≥ 1 tag not pred. but their relation pred.	Avg. % user tag not pred. but their semantic relation pred.	Avg. % of images where no label was pred.
Hypernym	Abstract	80.67	27.96	76.40	40.06	3.39
	Concrete	71.48	28.66	66.94	32.02	1.39
Co-hyponym	Abstract	684.04	26.51	70.25	33.23	1.56
	Concrete	608.55	27.44	55.28	22.97	1.00
Synonym	Abstract	41.15	38.00	53.24	18.60	7.14
	Concrete	33.73	44.26	38.61	12.00	4.26

Table 2: SigLIP prediction (pred.) results when considering semantic relations of user tags as labels.

and those with a score ≥ 0.0001, we consider as predicted labels. This threshold is chosen to ensure that only the most relevant tags are considered. In our experiments, we compare synonyms, hypernyms, and co-hyponyms for the subset of noun tags. The primary evaluation metrics include the average percentage of labels predicted, the average percentage of images where no label was predicted, the average percentage of images where at least one user tag was not predicted but its semantic relation was, and the percentage of user tags not predicted as labels, but whose semantically related tags were predicted as labels.

3 RQ1 - Impact of Semantic Relations on Model Predictions

We first analyze the number of user tags associated with each image and the model's performance in predicting these tags as labels. Then, we evaluate whether the model also predicts synonyms, hypernyms, and co-hyponyms of user tags as possible labels. We hypothesize that synonyms will provide alternative labels that capture variations in naming, potentially improving prediction accuracy for both abstract and concrete concepts. Hypernyms are expected to offer more general category labels. Co-hyponyms will highlight sibling relationships between concepts, improving label prediction by capturing related yet distinct categories.

Table 1 presents the results of user-tag predictions comparing abstract and concrete concepts, when using 300 images.[2] We found that images associated with abstract concepts tend to have more user tags on average (8.69, with 5.40 being nouns) compared to those associated with concrete (6.85, with 4.58 being nouns). The model successfully identified a higher percentage of labels for images associated with concrete concepts (62.17%) than for abstract concepts (54.41%). There was a low ratio of images where no user tag was predicted as a label: 8.06% for abstract and 4.11% for concrete concepts. Notably, a high percentage of images did not have the target concept predicted (which we associated the image with): 48.87% for abstract and 26.93% for concrete concepts. These findings suggest that SigLIP struggles to consistently label images with the same tags used by humans. This is especially true for images of abstract concepts, highlighting the difficulty in aligning model predictions with human annotations for these concepts. The findings also point out the diversity involved in tagging abstract concepts, thus emphasizing the importance of accepting a wider selection of relevant labels for multimodal representations.

[2]We also analyzed concepts with 400 available images to check for sampling bias. We did not use them in the main study as it resulted in losing many abstract nouns and causing class imbalance. Overall, we find similar results for 400 images and include them in the Appendix.

Class	Avg. number of unique user tags	Avg. number of unique associations	Association not in user tags	Association predicted	Association predicted for at least one image
Abstract	751	36.00	64.96%	27.89%	99.67%
Concrete	747	33.75	46.79%	38.68%	99.66%

Table 3: Overlap between user tags and word associations.

Table 2 presents the model's performance in predicting synonyms, hypernyms and co-hyponyms of user tags as potential labels. The number of possible labels increases considerably when considering semantically related words of user tags, especially regarding co-hyponyms (684.04 for abstract and 608.55 for concrete concepts). Synonyms had the highest percentage of labels predicted, especially for concrete concepts (44.26%), indicating that the model better captures meaning variations for concrete nouns. For abstract concepts, a majority of images had at least one user tag not predicted, but their hypernym was (76.40%). Abstract concepts also had a higher percentage of labels (40.06%) where hypernyms were predicted but original user tags were not. Similarly, co-hyponyms also showed that abstract concepts (70.25%) had a higher percentage of images where at least one user tag was not predicted but a co-hyponym was, compared to concrete concepts (55.28%). This suggests that concepts, especially abstract, could benefit considerably from broader categorical information provided by hypernyms and co-hyponyms. There are very few images where no label was found, ranging from 1.00% to 7.14% when considering different semantically related words. Overall, our results highlight the importance of considering semantic relations as a possible means to improve the robustness and accuracy of multi-modal models for both abstract and concrete concepts.

4 RQ2 - Relationship between Association Norms and User Tags

We analyzed the overlap between user tags for images and word associations. We expected abstract concepts to show higher diversity in both visual associations (user tags of images) and word associations due to their inherently diverse nature, while we expected concrete concepts to show a larger overlap between user tags and word associations. We analyzed 682 concepts (527 concrete and 155 abstract) for which we had 300 images and 100 annotators. From De Deyne et al. (2019), we selected association words with a frequency of ≥ 2. For each image where the target concept was one of the user tags, we evaluated how well SigLIP predicts the associated words of the target concept as possible labels.

Table 3 presents the number of unique associations and user tags, and the performance of SigLIP for multi-label classification of images considering association words as possible labels. Contrary to our hypothesis, the average number of unique user tags for both abstract (751) and concrete (747) concepts across 300 images is similar. This indicates that people associate diverse words with both abstract and concrete concepts when tagging images, suggesting high diversity in visual interpretation even for concrete concepts, which are traditionally considered less vague and less diverse. However, abstract concepts have a slightly higher average number of unique associations (36.00) compared to concrete concepts (33.75), indicating a slightly greater associative diversity for abstract concepts. This shows that when users are presented with images of a concept, they produce a greater variety of descriptive tags than when producing associations, highlighting the impact of visual context on the descriptive process. It is important to note that this comparison is a bit skewed because our dataset averages 7 tags per image for 300 images of a concept, while word associations are gathered from 100 annotators with 3 associations each per concept. Another surprising finding is the proportion of associations not present as user tags: 64.96% for abstract concepts and 46.79% for concrete concepts. This discrepancy highlights that, despite the directly perceivable nature of concrete concepts, they evoke different personal or contextual mental associations that may not directly translate into visual depictions and vice-versa, similar to abstract concepts. This suggests that concrete concepts possess more semantic diversity than what is visually observable. The SigLIP model on average predicted 27.89% associations as labels for images associated with abstract concepts vs. 38.68% for concrete concepts. However, almost all the associations (99.67% for abstract and 99.66% for concrete) were predicted for at least one of the 300 images associated with each concept, indicating that the model could recognize the majority of associations as labels across different images.

These findings point towards the need to further explore whether and how current models trained on user-generated tags might fail to capture the full range of human conceptual associations. Models might benefit from integrating these broader associative data to enhance their understanding and representation of concepts.

5 Conclusion

Our study highlights the potential of integrating diverse semantic relationships in improving the representations in Vision-Language Models (VLMs), particularly SigLIP, for abstract and concrete concepts. The results demonstrate that for images associated with both abstract and concrete concepts, SigLIP often predicts semantically related words such as synonyms, hypernyms, and co-hyponyms of a user tag even when the user tag itself is not predicted as a label. Furthermore, the distinction between visual and linguistic associations revealed differences in how these concepts are perceived and described. Our findings suggest that leveraging semantic relationships and associations should be further explored to enhance representations of abstract and concrete concepts in VLMs, aligning them more closely with human cognitive variation.

Limitations

Our findings are based on the SigLIP model, other VLMs may yield different results. Additionally, we have considered all labels from SigLIP with probability scores ≥ 0.0001, and the results may vary if a different threshold is considered. Also, another selection of images may introduce some variability into the results.

Ethics Statement

We anticipate no ethical concerns with this work. All modeling experiments utilized open-source libraries, which have been appropriately cited.

Acknowledgements

This research is supported by the DFG Research Grant SCHU 2580/4-1 *Multimodal Dimensions and Computational Applications of Abstractness*.

References

Michael Ahn, Anthony Brohan, Noah Brown, Yevgen Chebotar, Omar Cortes, Byron David, Chelsea Finn, Chuyuan Fu, Keerthana Gopalakrishnan, Karol Hausman, Alex Herzog, Daniel Ho, Jasmine Hsu, Julian Ibarz, Brian Ichter, Alex Irpan, Eric Jang, Rosario Jauregui Ruano, Kyle Jeffrey, Sally Jesmonth, Nikhil J Joshi, Ryan Julian, Dmitry Kalashnikov, Yuheng Kuang, Kuang-Huei Lee, Sergey Levine, Yao Lu, Linda Luu, Carolina Parada, Peter Pastor, Jornell Quiambao, Kanishka Rao, Jarek Rettinghouse, Diego Reyes, Pierre Sermanet, Nicolas Sievers, Clayton Tan, Alexander Toshev, Vincent Vanhoucke, Fei Xia, Ted Xiao, Peng Xu, Sichun Xu, Mengyuan Yan, and Andy Zeng. 2022. Do as I can, not as I say: Grounding language in robotic affordances. arXiv:2204.01691v2.

Marc Brysbaert, Amy Beth Warriner, and Victor Kuperman. 2014. Concreteness ratings for 40 thousand generally known English word lemmas. *Behavior Research Methods*, 64:904–911.

Angelo Cangelosi and Francesca Stramandinoli. 2018. A review of abstract concept learning in embodied agents and robots. *Philosophical Transactions of the Royal Society B: Biological Sciences*, 373(1752):20170131.

Simon De Deyne, Danielle J Navarro, Amy Perfors, Marc Brysbaert, and Gert Storms. 2019. The "small world of words" English word association norms for over 12,000 cue words. *Behavior Research Methods*, 51:987–1006.

Jack Hessel, David Mimno, and Lillian Lee. 2018. Quantifying the visual concreteness of words and topics in multimodal datasets. In *Proceedings of the 2018 Conference of the North American Chapter of the Association for Computational Linguistics: Human Language Technologies, Volume 1 (Long Papers)*, pages 2194–2205, New Orleans, Louisiana. Association for Computational Linguistics.

Chao Jia, Yinfei Yang, Ye Xia, Yi-Ting Chen, Zarana Parekh, Hieu Pham, Quoc Le, Yun-Hsuan Sung, Zhen Li, and Tom Duerig. 2021. Scaling up visual and vision-language representation learning with noisy text supervision. In *International Conference on Machine Learning*, pages 4904–4916.

Marc A Kastner, Ichiro Ide, Yasutomo Kawanishi, Takatsugu Hirayama, Daisuke Deguchi, and Hiroshi Murase. 2019. Estimating the visual variety of concepts by referring to web popularity. *Multimedia Tools and Applications*, 78:9463–9488.

Maximilian Köper and Sabine Schulte im Walde. 2016. Distinguishing literal and non-literal usage of German particle verbs. In *Proceedings of the Conference of the North American Chapter of the Association for Computational Linguistics: Human Language Technologies*, pages 353–362, San Diego, CA, USA.

Maximilian Köper and Sabine Schulte im Walde. 2017. Complex verbs are different: Exploring the visual modality in multi-modal models to predict compositionality. In *Proceedings of the 13th Workshop on Multiword Expressions*, pages 200–206, Valencia, Spain.

Dermot Lynott, Louise Connell, Marc Brysbaert, James Brand, and James Carney. 2020. The Lancaster sensorimotor norms: Multidimensional measures of perceptual and action strength for 40,000 English words. *Behavior Research Methods*, 52:1–21.

George A Miller. 1995. WordNet: A lexical database for English. *Communications of the ACM*, 38(11):39–41.

Allan Paivio, John C. Yuille, and Stephen A. Madigan. 1968. Concreteness, imagery, and meaningfulness values for 925 nouns. *Journal of Experimental Psychology (Monograph Supplement)*, 76(1/2):1–25.

Alec Radford, Jong Wook Kim, Chris Hallacy, Aditya Ramesh, Gabriel Goh, Sandhini Agarwal, Girish Sastry, Amanda Askell, Pamela Mishkin, Jack Clark, et al. 2021. Learning transferable visual models from natural language supervision. In *International conference on machine learning*, pages 8748–8763. PMLR.

Olga Russakovsky, Jia Deng, Hao Su, Jonathan Krause, Sanjeev Satheesh, Sean Ma, Zhiheng Huang, Andrej Karpathy, Aditya Khosla, Michael Bernstein, Alexander C. Berg, and Li Fei-Fei. 2015. ImageNet Large Scale Visual Recognition Challenge. *International Journal of Computer Vision*, 115(3):211–252.

Sabine Schulte im Walde and Diego Frassinelli. 2022. Distributional measures of abstraction. *Frontiers in Artificial Intelligence: Language and Computation 4:796756. Alessandro Lenci and Sebastian Padó (topic editors): "Perspectives for Natural Language Processing between AI, Linguistics and Cognitive Science".*

Chang Su, Weijie Chen, Ze Fu, and Yijiang Chen. 2021. Multimodal metaphor detection based on distinguishing concreteness. *Neurocomputing*, 429:166–173.

Bart Thomee, Benjamin Elizalde, David Shamma, Karl Ni, Gerald Friedland, Douglas Poland, Damian Borth, and Li-Jia Li. 2016. YFCC100M: The new data in multimedia research. *Communications of the ACM*, 59:64–73.

Yulia Tsvetkov, Elena Mukomel, and Anatole Gershman. 2013. Cross-lingual metaphor detection using common semantic features. In *Proceedings of the First Workshop on Metaphor in NLP*, pages 45–51, Atlanta, Georgia.

Peter D. Turney, Yair Neuman, Dan Assaf, and Yohai Cohen. 2011. Literal and metaphorical sense identification through concrete and abstract context. In *Proceedings of the Conference on Empirical Methods in Natural Language Processing*, pages 680–690, Edinburgh, UK.

Xiaohua Zhai, Basil Mustafa, Alexander Kolesnikov, and Lucas Beyer. 2023. Sigmoid loss for language image pre-training. In *Proceedings of the IEEE/CVF International Conference on Computer Vision*, pages 11975–11986.

6 Appendix

6.1 Extending association norms analysis

In our main study, we consider association words for a noun if they have a frequency of ≥ 2, meaning the association is provided by at least 2 annotators. Here, we validate our findings by incorporating all possible association words, without a frequency threshold. The results, presented in Table 4, are similar to those in Table 3. The number of unique associations for abstract concepts (130) remains higher than for concrete concepts (105), and are also high for concrete concepts. A majority of association words (80% for abstract and 69% for concrete concepts) do not appear among the user tags associated with the target concepts, thus demonstrating the gap between associations given a linguistic cue and user tags given an image (visual cue). Similar to Table 3, almost all associations were predicted for at least one image, out of the 400 images associated with the target concept.

Class	Avg. unique assoc.	Assoc. not in user tags	Assoc. pred.	Assoc. pred. for any image
Abstract	130	80%	25%	99.28%
Concrete	105	69%	31%	98.94%

Table 4: Overlap between user tags and word associations.

6.2 Multi-label prediction with 400 images

To ensure that our findings were not influenced by sampling bias, we also experimented with the subset of concepts where 400 images were available. These are $1,191$ concepts with 400 images (864 concrete and 327 abstract). We present the results in Table 5. The results are similar to when considering 300 images for each concept.

Semantic Relation	Concept class	Avg. number of user tags with semantic relations	Avg. % of labels pred.	Avg. % of images where no label was pred.	Avg. % images where ≥ 1 tag not pred. but their relation pred.	Avg. % user tag not pred. but their semantic relation pred.
Hypernym	Abstract	80.98	27.68	3.40	76.35	39.97
	Concrete	71.50	28.59	1.39	67.00	32.04
Co-hyponym	Abstract	692.67	26.41	1.62	70.23	33.23
	Concrete	606.32	27.40	0.98	55.22	22.97
Synonym	Abstract	41.57	37.81	7.26	52.97	18.47
	Concrete	33.79	44.21	4.30	38.68	12.03

Table 5: SigLIP prediction (pred.) results when considering semantic relations of user tags as labels for 400 images per concept.

Diachronic change in verb usage statistics predicts differences in sentence processing across the lifespan

Ellis Cain
University of California, Merced
ecain@ucmerced.edu

Rachel Ryskin
University of California, Merced
rryskin@ucmerced.edu

Abstract

Diachronic corpus analyses reveal that syntactic usage patterns change over time. Are these changes reflected in differences in language processing across the human lifespan? We use the attachment of *with*- prepositional phrases (PPs) as a case study for investigating this question: a *with*-PP can attach to a verb, describing an *instrument* with which to perform the action (e.g., Slice the cake [with a knife]), or to a direct object (DO), *modifying* the noun (e.g., Slice the cake [with the pink frosting]). The relative frequencies of the instrument and modifier constructions differ depending on the verb in the sentence — the 'verb bias'. Using two diachronic corpora, Syntgram and CCOHA, we analyzed the co-occurrence statistics of 27 verbs and instrument vs. modifier *with*-PPs. Between the 1940s and the 2000s, some verbs were more instrument-biased (i.e., more likely to co-occur with *with*-PPs that attach to the verb than the DO) than others and co-occurrence patterns were more similar for temporally close decades, suggesting subtle diachronic changes in usage patterns. We collected sentence interpretation data probing *with*-PP attachment preferences in participants ranging in age from 25 to 75. Interpretations of globally ambiguous sentences (e.g., Pet the rabbit with the towel) differed depending on the verb (i.e., some verbs elicit more instrument than modifier interpretations of the PP than others and vice versa) and on the age of the participant. In particular, verbs which became less instrument-biased over time elicited more instrument interpretations among older adults than young adults, suggesting that variation in language comprehension can be in part predicted from the corpus statistics of the time periods that an individual experienced.

1 Introduction

Language is constantly changing and evolving over time (Beckner et al., 2009; Chater and Christiansen, 2010). Each generation inherits the form-meaning mappings that previous generations have developed. New words and usages may arise due to colexification or word-sense extension as new generations need to fill a communicative gap (Brochhagen et al., 2023; Srinivasan and Rabagliati, 2015). Similarly, some syntactic forms can proliferate while others disappear (i.e., Josserand et al., 2021; Thompson et al., 2016). Given that the language changes, the usage patterns that are experienced by an individual over their lifetime differ across generations. Here, we investigate whether syntactic change over time, at the level of the language, is reflected in different patterns of online language processing across generations within the same time period.

1.1 Syntactic Change

Corpus studies have demonstrated shifts over time in the usage patterns of certain grammatical structure. Using the Google books corpus, Michel et al. (2011) showed that many verbs became more regular over the course of two centuries (i.e., from chide/chode to chided; from burnt to burned) while a few verbs reverted to being irregular in more recent decades (light/lit, wake/woke). Additionally, the rate of change varies by geographical region, with the US having a much faster rate of regularization than the UK, for example.

Wolk et al. (2013) conducted a corpus analysis comparing the diachronic trends in genitive and dative alternations. The genitive alternation consists of the *Of-genitive* (e.g., "the fall of Rome") and *S-genitive* (e.g., "Rome's fall") constructions. The dative alternation consists of *PP-dative* (e.g., "Flann gave the book to Max") and *NP-dative* (e.g., "Flann gave Max the book"). Replicating previous studies, they found stable factors (i.e., word length of the constituents, animacy) that predicted usage of particular constructions (e.g., as the length of the constituents increases, the proportion of *PP-datives* decreases). Critically, both the usage proportions of each alternation and those factors

Proceedings of the Workshop on Cognitive Modeling and Computational Linguistics, pages 221–230
August 15, 2024 ©2024 Association for Computational Linguistics

exhibited diachronic changes. For instance, the frequency of the *Of-genitive* construction peaked around the 1800s, but declined afterwards, with the *S-genitive* construction increasing in frequency after the 1800s. Likewise, the influence of word length on construction choice increased over time, whereas the effect of animacy on choice decreased in weight over time for both constructions (likely corresponding to increased frequency of reference to inanimate or collective entities).

Syntactic change is reflected in real-time language processing measures as well. Bornkessel-Schlesewsky et al. (2020) explored whether changes in language processing or production drive language change using the case of Icelandic, which is currently in a transitional period that parallels the evolution of English. It has fixed subject position (like modern English) and morphological case marking (similar to earlier stages of English). In present-day Icelandic, use of linear order is becoming more frequent while case marking is decreasing in frequency. Bornkessel-Schlesewsky et al. (2020) found that, in explicit judgments of acceptability, Icelandic speakers preferred the standard case-marked forms, but event-related potentials (ERP) revealed that the emerging non-case-marked forms elicited less real-time processing difficulty. It is noteworthy that the participants were young adults. Whether older adults would have less difficulty processing the standard case-marked form (and perhaps more difficulty processing the linear order form) is an open question.

1.2 Language Change and Aging

Older and younger adults differ systematically in the structure of their lexical-semantic networks (Cosgrove et al., 2023; Wulff et al., 2021). Using word association data, Dubossarsky et al. (2017) constructed semantic networks for different age groups. They found that networks were sparse during early language acquisition, peaked in density during middle adulthood, and were largest but somewhat less dense during late adulthood due to continued language acquisition and increased vocabulary size (Baayen et al., 2017; Ramscar et al., 2014).

However, it remains unknown whether these age-related differences are related to different experiences with a language that is changing. Cain and Ryskin (2023) collected relatedness judgments from young and older adults for word pairs that have and have not changed in meaning over time (between 1950 and 2000). They found that these word relatedness judgments were quite similar between the age groups, in that the ratings from both age groups most closely matched the similarities derived from the most recent decade of historical word embeddings (Hamilton et al., 2016). In contrast, Li and Siew (2022) used response time data from a semantic decision task to show that words that had undergone meaning change elicited greater processing difficulty in middle-aged adults compared to younger adults, perhaps because the middle-aged adults were familiar with a greater number of competitors (i.e., meanings that were no longer prevalent). In sum, lexico-semantic change over time, at the level of the language, may result in differences in online processing across generations within the same time period.

1.3 Current Study

In the current work, we investigate syntactic change and its consequences for online processing across different age groups who may have experienced distinct usage patterns over their lifetime. We use the attachment of *with*- prepositional phrases (PPs) as a case study for investigating this question: a *with*-PP can attach to a verb, describing an *instrument* with which to perform an action (e.g., Slice the cake [with a knife]), or to a direct object (DO), *modifying* the noun (e.g., Slice the cake [with the pink frosting]). The relative frequencies of the instrument and modifier constructions differ depending on the verb in the sentence — the 'verb bias' (Gahl et al., 2004; Ryskin et al., 2017; Snedeker and Trueswell, 2004). For example, "strike" is biased to appear in instrument structures, whereas "pet" is biased toward modifier structures.

Previous psycholinguistic work indicates that these verb biases guide online processing. For instance, when the *with*-PP attachment is globally ambiguous (e.g., "Pet the rabbit [with the towel]" when there is both a rabbit wrapped in a towel and a separate towel available as an instrument in the visual environment), listeners rely on verb bias to guide their interpretation. They are more likely to look at and reach for (or click on) the instrument towel for instrument-biased verbs than for modifier-biased verbs (Ryskin et al., 2017; Snedeker and Trueswell, 2004). Further, these biases are shaped by language experience. Participants were more likely to interpret ambiguous sentences with an (initially) equi-biased verb like "spot' as having a modifier structure when they were repeatedly exposed to "spot" in unambiguous modifier constructions relative to when they were repeatedly exposed to "spot" in unambiguous instrument constructions (Ryskin et al., 2017).

In the present work, we first tested whether verb biases change over time. Using two diachronic corpora, Syntgram (Goldberg and Orwant, 2013), a corpus of verb-specific syntactic annotations based on the Google N-grams corpus, and the (cleaned) Corpus of Historical American English (CCOHA; Alatrash et al., 2020; Davies, 2012), we analyzed the co-occurrence statistics of 27 verbs (from Ryskin et al., 2017) and instrument vs. modifier *with*-PPs.

Second, we probed differences in verb biases between individuals of different ages. Participants (25–75 years old) clicked on images in a 4-picture display in response to sentences with ambiguous *with*-PP attachment (e.g., Pet the rabbit with the towel). The locations of their clicks indicated which interpretation they had chosen (e.g., instrument vs. modifier).

Third, we used a Bayesian multilevel logistic regression model to examine the relationship between diachronic changes in verb bias and age-related differences in interpretation.

Instrument	equi-biased	Modifier
Strike	Feed	Pet
Whack	Scuff	Look at
Hit	Pinch	Squeeze
Rub	Knock on	Pick out
Poke	Pat	Cuddle
Bop	Locate	Find
Smack	Feel	Hug
Clean	Spot	Select
Tease	Point to	Choose

Table 1: Verbs from Ryskin et al., 2017 grouped according to sentence completion norming data.

2 Quantifying Diachronic Changes in Verb Biases

Our first aim was to quantify how much the verb-specific usage of the instrument and modifier constructions changes over time. We specifically focused on the 27 verbs (see Table 1) from Ryskin et al. (2017) and on the construction frequencies from the 1940s to the 2000s, since the participants from our behavioral experiment would have potentially experienced those decades (Section 3).

2.1 Methods and Data

In Syntgram, we identified relevant instances of verb appearances as ones where the target verb was the root of the dependency tree fragment, and the word "with" appeared in the fragment. Next, using the dependency tree fragments, we categorized these instances as instrument if the *with*-PP attaches to the verb, modifier if it attaches to the DO of the verb, or neither. We were able to find relevant instances for 24 of the original 27 verbs, three verbs were not found in any relevant constructions in the corpus ("bop", "scuff", "pet"). Overall, there were 1,761,679 total instances, with an average of 67,757 instances per verb, and an average of 251,668 instances per decade. For each of the 24 verbs included in the analysis, we computed the average instrument bias, for each decade, to get stable estimates of how often they participate in instrument constructions.

In CCOHA, we first filtered the corpus to instances where the target verbs were used with "with," and then used the spaCy dependency parser to annotate the sentences (Honnibal and Montani, 2017). Using this dependency tree structure, we then identified whether the construction was instrument, modifier, or neither based on the attachment of the *with*-PP. We then filtered the verbs to those where every decade had at least one instrument and one modifier construction, which resulted in eleven verbs. Overall, there were 5,691 total instances, with an average of 517 instances per verb, and an average of 813 instance per decade.

In both of these corpora, the majority of relevant instances are unambiguous in terms of which construction is being used. Most of the *instrument* constructions do not have a direct object (i.e., "He was hit with the bat."), and most of the *with*-PPs in *modifier* instances describe the noun phrase (i.e., "...pick out the gym bag with black plastic handles..."). Therefore, we expect the dependency parser to accurately identify which construction is being used.

2.2 Results

As seen in Figure 1, analysis of the Syntgram corpus reveals a variety of diachronic trends in the verb biases: some had a consistent, strong instrument bias (e.g., "cuddle" or "pick"), others had weak instrument bias (e.g., "hit" or "point"), and some did indeed change over time (e.g.,, "clean", "poke"). To identify patterns of change over time,

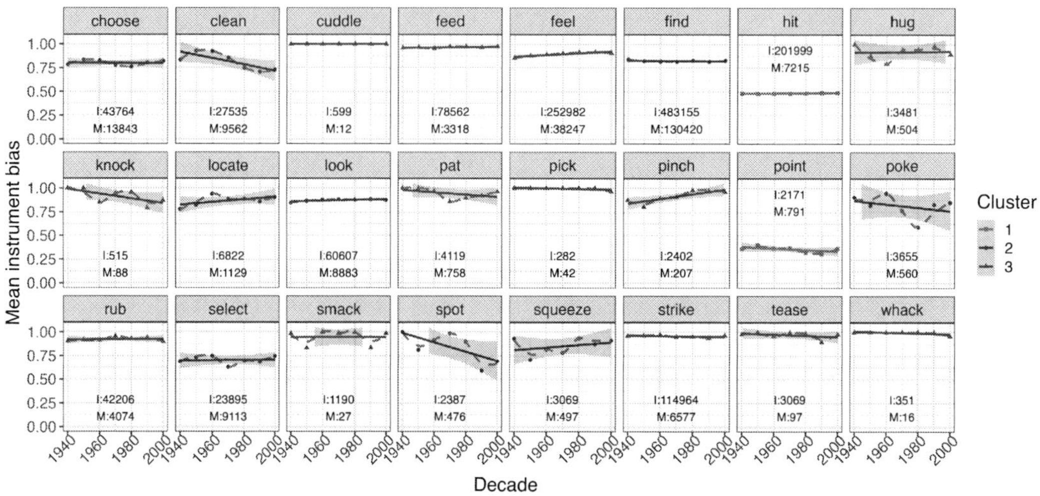

Figure 1: Average instrument bias per decade, as derived from the Google Syntgram corpus. Cluster is indicated by the color (k = 3). The frequency of each construction type is included.

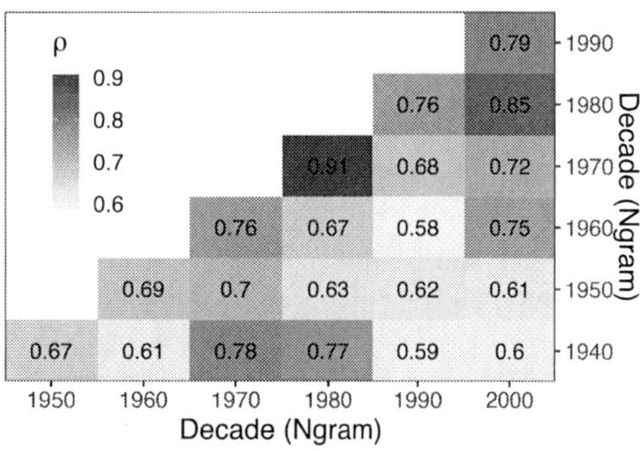

Figure 2: Spearman rank correlation of average instrument biases between different decades in the Google Syntgram corpus. The diagonal has been excluded since it would be a perfect correlation.

we used K-means clustering. The clustering was performed on verb-specific instrument biases for each decade. Three clusters were identified (we set $k = 3$) and can be seen in Figure. 1). The clustering results suggest that there are three types of patterns: low instrument bias (i.e., "hit" and "point"), high instrument bias (i.e., "feed" and "pick"), and a moderate-decreasing instrument bias (i.e., "clean" and "spot").

In order to quantify the amount of change over time across all verbs, we calculated the pairwise Spearman rank correlations between the verb-specific instrument biases of each decade (Figure 2). While there were changes in instrument biases for some verbs, overall, the decade-level instrument biases had relatively high correlations ($0.58 \leq \rho \leq 0.91$). Yet, as the temporal distance between the decades increases, the correlation tends to decrease (with the exception of $\rho_{1940,1970}$ and $\rho_{1940,1980}$).

Figure 3 shows the average instrument bias for the CCOHA subset. Relative to the previous analysis (Fig. 1), these diachronic trends seem to have more variation, likely due to the decreased corpus size. Due to the lower number of verbs (11) that were available for analysis from the CCOHA dataset, we did not perform clustering. The verb biases across decades were moderately correlated (Fig. 4), though not as highly as the verb biases derived from Syntgram ($0.05 \leq \rho_{ccoha} \leq 0.79$ vs $0.58 \leq \rho_{Syntgram} \leq 0.91$). The exception seem to be the 1940s, which had low correlations with several of the other decades.

Comparing the instrument bias proportions between the two corpora, the correlation between the decade-level average instrument biases of the two corpora are widely varied ($-0.42 \leq \rho \leq 0.53$), with the 1980_{CCOHA} having the highest correlation with every decade from Syntgram, and 1940_{CCOHA} having the lowest. This variability may reflect the smaller size of the CCOHA dataset or differences in composition (e.g., genre balance) between the two corpora.

Across the two datasets, these analyses demonstrates that verb biases do appear to change over time, even within a limited time frame (60 years). There does not appear to be a unitary trend across this set of verbs, as some remain quite consistent,

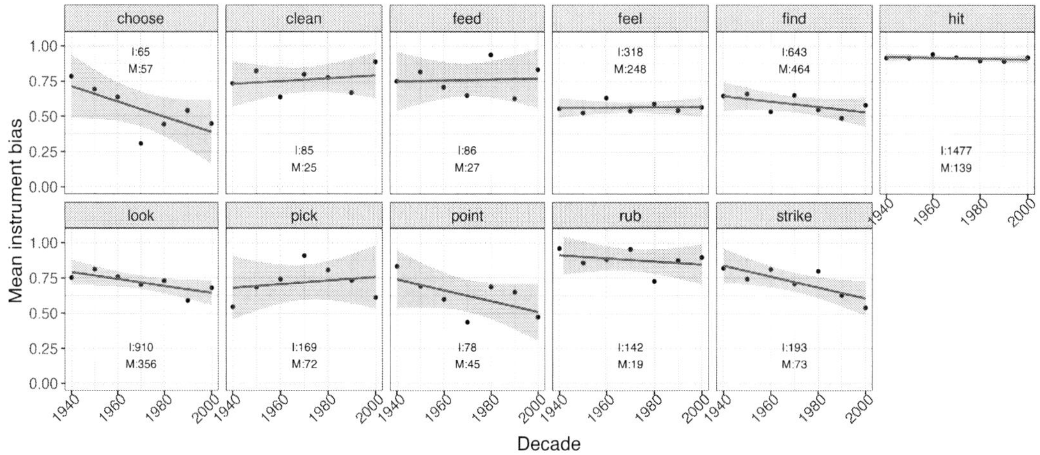

Figure 3: Average instrument bias per decade, as derived from CCOHA. The frequency of each construction type is included.

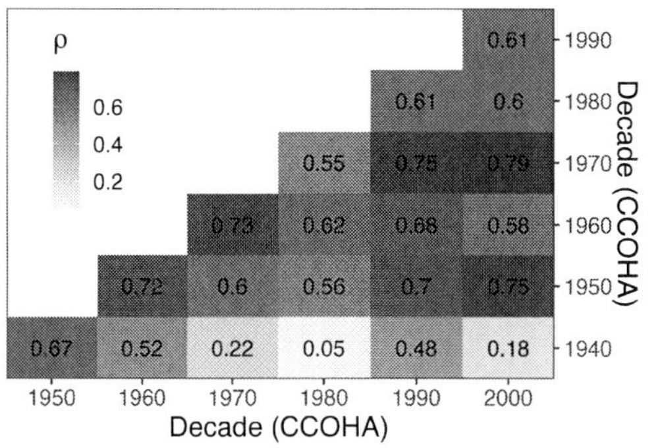

Figure 4: Spearman rank correlation of average instrument biases between different decades in CCOHA. The diagonal has been excluded since it would be a perfect correlation.

while others change in bias across the time frame.

3 Verb Biases across the Lifespan

Next, we conducted a web-based replication of Experiment 1 from Ryskin et al. (2017), but intentionally collected data from participants across the lifespan (ages 25–75).

3.1 Methods and Data

209 participants were recruited through Amazon Mechanical Turk. Participants heard instructions while looking at a computer display with four pictures (e.g., a feather, a frog holding a feather, a dolphin, and a sponge). The location of their first click was recorded. Participants heard instructions containing each of the 27 critical verbs, each time paired with different pictures. There were 81 trials total, consisting of three practice trials at the start, 24 filler trials, and 54 critical trials (each verb appeared twice). On the critical trials, the instructions ended with an ambiguous *with*-PP (e.g., "Pet the frog with the feather"). On the filler trials, the instructions did not have an ambiguous *with*-PP and was not related to the instrument or modifier constructions (e.g., "Make the animals wrestle."). The critical and filler trials were intermixed and the order was randomized for each participant.

Interpretations were coded as *instrument* if participants clicked on the 'instrument' and used that to carry out the action (e.g., clicked on the feather), or as *modifier* if they clicked on the animal that had the instrument with it (e.g., clicked on the frog holding the feather). Figure 5 shows the age distribution grouped by decade. There were not enough participants in the 70 y.o. cohort to be a separate group ($n = 8$), so they were included in the 60 y.o. cohort.

3.2 Results

Figure 6 shows the proportion of instrument interpretations across the lifespan. Each verb is colored according to the norm-based verb bias categories from Ryskin et al. (2017). We used a Bayesian multilevel logistic regression model to test the relationship between interpretations and age, based on the verb bias categories[1] (fitted using the brms package in R, Bürkner, 2017). The equi-biased verbs coded as the reference for the norm-based

[1]Formula: $instrument = bias\ norm * age + (1 \mid verb + (1 \mid participant)$

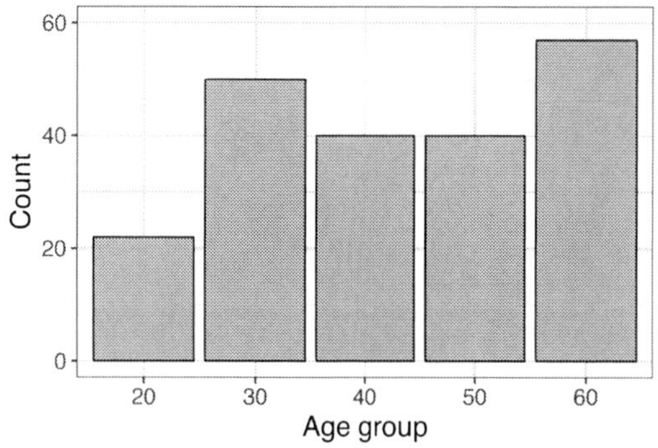

Figure 5: Participant age distribution, grouped by age decade.

verb bias category, and age was scaled and centered. Replicating Ryskin et al. (2017), overall, participants were more likely to first click on the target instrument in response to verbs that have an instrument bias relative to equi-biased verbs ($\beta_{Instr.\ norm} = 0.85$, $95\%CrI = [0.20, 1.49]$), and modifier biased verbs were the least likely to elicit instrument interpretations ($\beta_{Mod.\ norm} = -0.91$, $95\%CrI = [-1.55, -0.26]$).

Additionally, the interpretations of older adults appear to become more equi-biased relative to the youngest age group: the equi-biased verbs seem to be consistent over the lifespan ($\beta_{Age} = -0.07$, $95\%CrI = [-0.24, 0.11]$), while the difference between the verb bias categories becomes smaller ($\beta_{Instr.\ norm * Age} = -0.07$, $95\%CrI = [-0.17, 0.04]$, $\beta_{Mod.\ norm * Age} = 0.13$, $95\%CrI = [0.02, 0.25]$).

In sum, this analysis indicates that verb biases do differ subtly between age groups. One possibility is that younger adults may have stronger biases (toward instrument or modifier), whereas older adults appear to be more equi-biased in general. Alternatively, it may be that the norms used to categorize the verbs, which were collected from young adults, may reflect the biases of young adults better than older adults. Older adults may have systematically different verb biases as a result of different language experience over their lifetime.

4 Predicting Differences in Interpretations from Diachronic Change

The results from Section 2 indicate that, based on corpus frequencies, verb biases change over time (Fig. 1). The results from Section 3 indicate that, verb biases appear to change across the lifespan

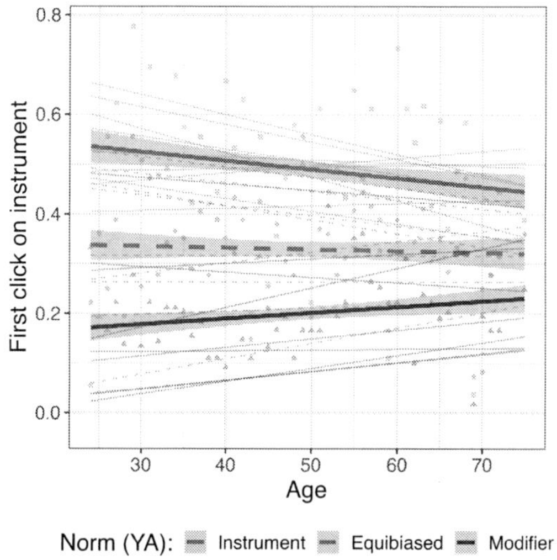

Figure 6: Proportion of instrument interpretations across the lifespan, colored by by verb bias category as determined by norms from young adults (Ryskin et al., 2017). Opaque lines indicate lines of best-fit across all verbs in a verb bias category. The transparent points represent individual participants' average interpretations for each verb, and the transparent lines indicate the per-verb lines of best-fit.

(Fig. 6). In this section, we aimed to test whether age-related differences in interpretation are related to diachronic changes in verb biases.

4.1 Analysis & Results

Instead of using the young adult norms from previous research to separate verbs into bias categories, we used the corpus-based clusters from Syntgram to categorize the verbs. Based on this new grouping (Figure 7), for the two out of the three clusters that changed minimally over time (stable low and high instrument biases), older participants appear to become slightly less likely to use an instrument interpretation. For the cluster that does change over time (decreasing instrument bias cluster), this age trend reverses, such that older participants are more likely to give an instrument interpretation than the younger participants.

We used a Bayesian multilevel logistic regression model to predict whether participants clicked on the instrument (i.e., used an instrument interpretation). We used the Syntgram-based verb bias clusters as a predictor along with age and their interaction. We included random intercepts for verb and participant, along with random slopes for age

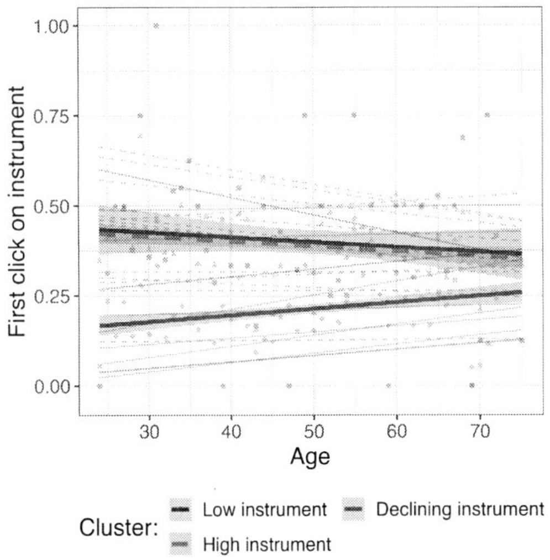

Figure 7: Proportion of instrument interpretations across the lifespan, grouped by the corpus-based clusters, as indicated by the three opaque lines. The transparent points represent individual participants' average interpretations for each verb, and the transparent lines indicate the per-verb averages. Note that the low instrument cluster only contains 2 verbs.

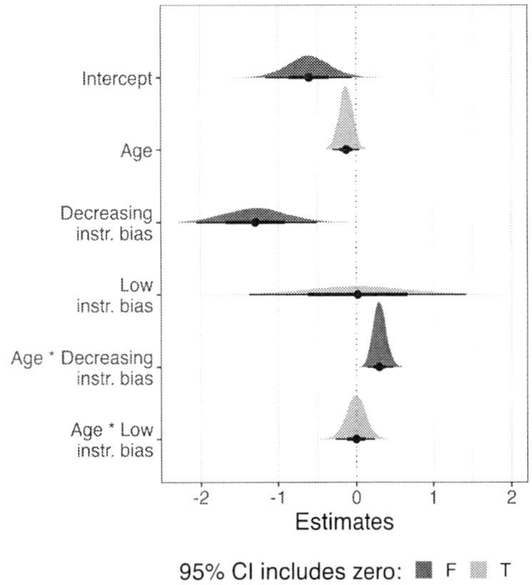

Figure 8: Model estimates for the Syntgram model. Color indicates whether the 95% CI includes zero.

by verb, and cluster by participant[2]. The high instrument bias cluster was coded as the reference level for cluster, and age was scaled and centered.

The model estimates can be seen in Figure 8. Based on the credible intervals, there were three significant effects. First, participants on average were less likely to click on the instrument than on one of the other pictures ($\beta_{Intercept} = -0.61, 95\%CI = [-1.15, -0.05]$). Second, relative to the high instrument bias cluster, the decreasing instrument bias cluster verbs were less likely to be interpreted with an instrument construction on average ($\beta_{Decreasing\ cluster} = -1.31$, $95\%CI = [-2.16, -0.51]$; Estimated marginal means: $Est_{Decreasing\ cluster} = 0.129$, 95% CI = [0.07, 0.21] vs $Est_{High\ cluster} = 0.353$, 95% CI = [0.24, 0.21]). Lastly, the decreasing bias cluster interacted with age such that older adults were more likely to give an instrument response for the verbs in that cluster ($\beta_{Age*Decreasing\ cluster} = 0.31, 95\%CI = [0.15, 0.49]$).

While there are a variety of different ways that experience and language learning may accumulate over the lifespan, this pattern matches the direction of change in the corpora, going from a strong instrument bias early on to a lower instrument bias more recently. In other words, older adults would have experienced a stronger instrument bias early on, while younger adults would have experienced the decades with a lower bias.

We then performed an analogous analysis with diachronic verb bias data from the CCOHA corpus. Since there were not enough relevant verbs in the CCOHA corpus to use K-means clustering, we directly compared the decade-level biases to the behavioral data.

We used another Bayesian binomial model to explore the relationship between the individual verbs and instrument interpretations[3]. "Hit" was coded as the reference verb, since it had a consistent high instrument bias over time (see Fig. 3, top right), and age was scaled and centered.

Figure 9 shows the posterior estimates for age and the interactions across the eleven verbs (simple effects of each verb are not included for clarity). For the verb 'hit,' participants appear to be less likely to use an instrument interpretation as age increases ($\beta_{Age} = -0.34, 95\%CrI = [-0.60, -0.09]$).

For the six verbs that interact with age (the 95% CrI of the interaction effect doesn't include zero), the direction of the estimate indicates that older adults are more likely to use an instrument interpretation, relative to 'hit.' This matches the direction

[2]Formula: $instrument = age_{scaled} * cluster_{ngram} + (1 + age_{scaled} \mid verb) + (1 + cluster_{ngram} \mid participant)$

[3]Formula: $instrument = age_{scaled} * verb + (1 + verb \mid participant)$

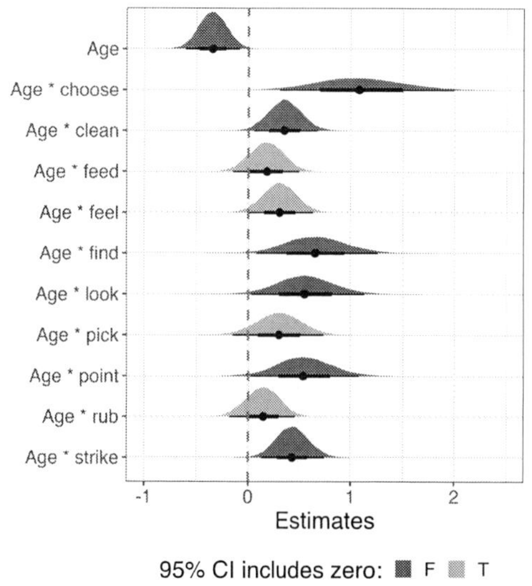

Figure 9: Model posteriors for age and the interactions between verb and age for CCOHA. Color indicates whether the 95% CrI includes zero.

of verb bias change in CCOHA, as those verbs have a decreasing instrument bias (see Figure 3). One exception was the verb 'clean' which did not have a decreasing instrument bias according to the analysis of CCOHA in Section 2, yet it also appears to elicit more instrument interpretations among older adults relative to 'hit.' However, this interaction effect ($\beta_{age*clean} = 0.36$, $95\%CrI = [0.05, 0.68]$) was smaller than for the other verbs ($\beta_{age*choose} = 1.10$, $95\%CrI = [0.31, 2.03]$; $\beta_{age*find} = 0.66$, $95\%CrI = [0.08, 1.26]$;$\beta_{age*look} = 0.56$, $95\%CrI = [0.03, 1.13]$; $\beta_{age*point} = 0.55$, $95\%CrI = [0.02, 1.08]$; $\beta_{age*strike} = 0.44$, $95\%CrI = [0.12, 0.75]$).

In summary, this last analysis demonstrated that verbs that underwent syntactic change over time predicted differences in interpretations across the lifespan.

5 Discussion

Through two corpus analyses (Section 2), we found that verb biases (whether a verb co-occurs more frequently with instrument or modifier constructions) often change over time. While many verbs have largely stable biases, the most frequent type of diachronic change between 1940 and 2000 is a decrease in instrument bias.

Our behavioral experiment (Section 3) replicated prior findings that the interpretations of sentences with globally ambiguous *with*-PP attachment were predicted by a verb's bias. These verb bias effects appeared stronger for younger adults than older adults. This may be in part due to the fact that verbs' biases were categorized using norms from a previous study, which were collected from a sample of young adults.

Finally, we used two Bayesian models to test the relationship between the corpus-based verb bias trends over time and the lifespan data (Section 4). While there were some discrepancies in the verb-specific trends between the two corpora, the model results were consistent. When the instrument bias of a verb decreased between 1940 and 2000, the verb was more likely to elicit instrument interpretations among older adults than young adults. This suggests that the experience with verb biases of past decades (greater instrument bias for some verbs in the past), unique to the older adults, impacted their in-the-moment sentence processing.

Our results extend previous findings that language users update their syntactic representations based on experience with the statistics of the environment (Ryskin et al., 2017) and indicate that, at least for the alternation studied here, this updating unfolds over many decades (perhaps due to infrequent encounters of some verbs in the key constructions).

5.1 Limitations and future studies

In the present work, we only used one syntactic alternation as a case study for the relationship between diachronic syntactic change and lifespan differences in language processing. Other syntactic alternations are known to have undergone syntactic change (e.g, genitive and dative, Wolk et al., 2013). Future studies could investigate the relationship between diachronic change and processing across the lifespan for these syntactic alternations .

Additionally, while the diachronic changes in verb biases found in the analysis of CCOHA were more pronounced than in Syntgram, the reduced corpus size should still be taken into account: the amount of relevant instances for each verb was greatly reduced ($range_{ccoha} = 110 - 1,616$ vs $range_{Syntgram} = 324 - 613,575$), and the number of valid verbs was also lower in CCOHA ($n_{ccoha} = 11/27$ vs $n_{Syntgram} = 24/27$). Future studies could examine syntactic structures that occur more frequently in diachronic corpora.

Moreover, the dependency parsers used in the corpora analyses may not be sensitive to the contextual, fine-grained semantics of the constituents, such as the plausibility of using the *with*-PP prepositional object to carry out the action. Certain objects may be viewed as canonical instruments and therefore strongly favor instrument constructions for certain verbs, but are incompatible with other verbs. A 'sponge' may be used to 'rub' or 'clean' but is very unlikely to be used with 'feed' or 'hug.' Therefore, future studies could use context-sensitive models, such as BERT, to augment or replace the dependency parsers. For example, Manning et al. (2020) used the self-attention heads in BERT to parse different types of syntactic relationships.

Lastly, future studies should take age-related differences into account when comparing behavioral data to norms generated by one age group. Therefore we plan to collect production data from across the lifespan.

6 Conclusion

Language is continually changing over time, due to a variety of factors. Previous studies have highlighted the relationship between online sentence processing and recent linguistic experience. Our findings additionally suggest that previous linguistic experience continues to influence online sentence processing on the timescale of decades.

References

Reem Alatrash, Dominik Schlechtweg, Jonas Kuhn, and Sabine Schulte Im Walde. 2020. Ccoha: Clean corpus of historical american english. In *Proceedings of the Twelfth Language Resources and Evaluation Conference*, pages 6958–6966.

Harald Baayen, Fabian Tomaschek, Susanne Gahl, and Michael Ramscar. 2017. The Ecclesiastes Principle in Language Change. In Marianne Hundt, Sandra Mollin, and Simone E. Pfenninger, editors, *The Changing English Language*, 1 edition, pages 21–48. Cambridge University Press.

Clay Beckner, Richard Blythe, Joan Bybee, Morten H. Christiansen, William Croft, Nick C. Ellis, John Holland, Jinyun Ke, Diane Larsen-Freeman, and Tom Schoenemann. 2009. Language Is a Complex Adaptive System: Position Paper. *Language Learning*, 59:1–26.

Ina Bornkessel-Schlesewsky, Dietmar Roehm, Robert Mailhammer, and Matthias Schlesewsky. 2020. Language processing as a precursor to language change: Evidence from icelandic. *Frontiers in Psychology*, 10:466901.

Thomas Brochhagen, Gemma Boleda, Eleonora Gualdoni, and Yang Xu. 2023. From language development to language evolution: A unified view of human lexical creativity. *Science*, 381(6656):431–436.

Paul-Christian Bürkner. 2017. brms: An r package for bayesian multilevel models using stan. *Journal of statistical software*, 80:1–28.

Ellis Cain and Rachel Ryskin. 2023. Diachronic language change and its influence on lexico-semantic representations across the lifespan. In *Proceedings of the Annual Meeting of the Cognitive Science Society*, volume 45.

Nick Chater and Morten H. Christiansen. 2010. Language Acquisition Meets Language Evolution. *Cognitive Science*, 34(7):1131–1157.

Abigail L Cosgrove, Roger E Beaty, Michele T Diaz, and Yoed N Kenett. 2023. Age differences in semantic network structure: Acquiring knowledge shapes semantic memory. *Psychology and aging*, 38(2):87.

Mark Davies. 2012. Expanding horizons in historical linguistics with the 400-million word Corpus of Historical American English. *Corpora*, 7(2):121–157.

Haim Dubossarsky, Simon De Deyne, and Thomas T. Hills. 2017. Quantifying the structure of free association networks across the life span. *Developmental Psychology*, 53(8):1560–1570.

Susanne Gahl, Dan Jurafsky, and Douglas Roland. 2004. Verb subcategorization frequencies: American english corpus data, methodological studies, and cross-corpus comparisons. *Behavior Research Methods, Instruments, & Computers*, 36(3):432–443.

Yoav Goldberg and Jon Orwant. 2013. A dataset of syntactic-ngrams over time from a very large corpus of english books. In *Second Joint Conference on Lexical and Computational Semantics (* SEM), Volume 1: Proceedings of the Main Conference and the Shared Task: Semantic Textual Similarity*, pages 241–247.

William L. Hamilton, Jure Leskovec, and Dan Jurafsky. 2016. Diachronic Word Embeddings Reveal Statistical Laws of Semantic Change. In *Proceedings of the 54th Annual Meeting of the Association for Computational Linguistics (Volume 1: Long Papers)*, pages 1489–1501, Berlin, Germany. Association for Computational Linguistics.

M Honnibal and I Montani. 2017. spacy 2: Natural language understanding with bloom embeddings, convolutional neural networks and incremental parsing. neural machine translation. In *Proceedings of the Association for Computational Linguistics (ACL)*, pages 688–697.

Mathilde Josserand, Marc Allassonnière-Tang, François Pellegrino, and Dan Dediu. 2021. Interindividual Variation Refuses to Go Away: A Bayesian Computer Model of Language Change in Communicative Networks. *Frontiers in Psychology*, 12:626118.

Ying Li and Cynthia S. Q. Siew. 2022. Diachronic semantic change in language is constrained by how people use and learn language. *Memory & Cognition*, 50(6):1284–1298.

Christopher D. Manning, Kevin Clark, John Hewitt, Urvashi Khandelwal, and Omer Levy. 2020. Emergent linguistic structure in artificial neural networks trained by self-supervision. *Proceedings of the National Academy of Sciences*, 117(48):30046–30054.

Jean-Baptiste Michel, Yuan Kui Shen, Aviva Presser Aiden, Adrian Veres, Matthew K. Gray, The Google Books Team, Joseph P. Pickett, Dale Hoiberg, Dan Clancy, Peter Norvig, Jon Orwant, Steven Pinker, Martin A. Nowak, and Erez Lieberman Aiden. 2011. Quantitative Analysis of Culture Using Millions of Digitized Books. *Science*, 331(6014):176–182.

Michael Ramscar, Peter Hendrix, Cyrus Shaoul, Petar Milin, and Harald Baayen. 2014. The Myth of Cognitive Decline: Non-Linear Dynamics of Lifelong Learning. *Topics in Cognitive Science*, 6(1):5–42.

Rachel A. Ryskin, Zhenghan Qi, Melissa C. Duff, and Sarah Brown-Schmidt. 2017. Verb biases are shaped through lifelong learning. *Journal of Experimental Psychology: Learning, Memory, and Cognition*, 43(5):781–794.

Jesse Snedeker and John C. Trueswell. 2004. The developing constraints on parsing decisions: The role of lexical-biases and referential scenes in child and adult sentence processing. *Cognitive Psychology*, 49(3):238–299.

Mahesh Srinivasan and Hugh Rabagliati. 2015. How concepts and conventions structure the lexicon: Cross-linguistic evidence from polysemy. *Lingua*, 157:124–152.

Bill Thompson, Simon Kirby, and Kenny Smith. 2016. Culture shapes the evolution of cognition. *Proceedings of the National Academy of Sciences*, 113(16):4530–4535.

Christoph Wolk, Joan Bresnan, Anette Rosenbach, and Benedikt Szmrecsanyi. 2013. Dative and genitive variability in late modern english: Exploring cross-constructional variation and change. *Diachronica*, 30(3):382–419.

Dirk U. Wulff, Simon De Deyne, Samuel Aeschbach, and Rui Mata. 2021. Understanding the aging lexicon by linking individuals' experience, semantic networks, and cognitive performance. Preprint, PsyArXiv.

How Useful is Context, *Actually*? Comparing LLMs and Humans on Discourse Marker Prediction

Emily Sadlier-Brown[a] **Millie Lou**[b] **Miikka Silfverberg**[b] **Carla L. Hudson Kam**[a]
[a]University of British Columbia [b]Independent
emily.sadlier-brown@ubc.ca

Abstract

This paper investigates the adverbial discourse particle *actually*. We compare LLM and human performance on cloze tests involving *actually* on examples sourced from the Providence Corpus of speech around children. We explore the impact of utterance context on cloze test performance. We find that context is always helpful, though the extent to which additional context is helpful, and what relative placement of context (i.e. before or after the masked word) is most helpful differs for individual models and humans. The best-performing LLM, GPT-4, narrowly outperforms humans. In an additional experiment, we explore cloze performance on synthetic LLM-generated examples, and find that several models vastly outperform humans.

1 Introduction

Natural human language utterances can be described as containing different levels of information. The most obvious is the main message or topic of the utterance, but speakers often also aim to convey information that is *about* the main message, e.g., reflecting their beliefs about or stance on the message, and its relation to other utterances in the discourse (Clark, 1996). This *pragmatic* information is an essential component of human linguistic interactions. With the recent advent of highly capable large language models (LLMs), it is also becoming a key focus in research on computational language generation.

In this paper we focus on the English adverbial discourse marker *actually*, a word with pragmatic functions. *Actually* serves to 1) highlight unexpectedness by conveying contrast and contradiction (Oh, 2000; Halliday and Hasan, 1976; Lenk, 1998; Aijmer, 2002), and 2) express reality, truth, certainty, and evidentiality (Quirk et al., 1985; Biber and Finegan, 1988; Glougie, 2016). We expect these functions to result in statistically robust properties in the surrounding linguistic context that could potentially allow an LLM to correctly predict a missing *actually*. Our experiments examine how the relative placement of contextual information affects prediction success of a variety of LLMs. Here we provide models context in the form of preceding and following utterances. We also compare the LLMs' performance to that of humans on the same task.

To evaluate prediction success, we utilize standard cloze tests, which consist of masking a word in an utterance or sequence of utterances and asking a model/human to predict the missing word. Our cloze test items are drawn from the Providence Corpus (Demuth et al., 2006) of transcribed everyday conversational speech around children, which represents an under-explored text-type in computational studies. We recruit human participants through the mTurk platform (Crowston, 2012) and compare their performance to artificial language models: GPT-3.5 and GPT-4 (Achiam et al., 2023; Brown et al., 2020), BERT (Devlin et al., 2018), RoBERTa (Liu et al., 2019) and ELECTRA (Clark et al., 2020).

Humans' guessing accuracy on cloze-type tasks has been shown to improve with increased surrounding context and to depend on the placement of that context (Rubin, 1976). We, therefore, vary the amount and type of context available in the cloze examples. Our results show that GPT-4 prediction performance is on par with (in fact higher than) human subjects' performance, echoing very recent findings (Sravanthi et al., 2024) on other pragmatic language processing tasks. Performance depends crucially on surrounding utterance context. Some amount of context is always helpful though different models and humans benefit from different placement of context. For humans and the highest-performing model, GPT-4, preceding context is more helpful than following context.

In an additional experiment, we compare cloze performance on examples sourced from the Provi-

Proceedings of the Workshop on Cognitive Modeling and Computational Linguistics, pages 231–241
August 15, 2024

dence corpus to synthetic examples generated by GPT-3.5. Surprisingly, while human and model performance is quite similar for the corpus-sourced examples, three of the models vastly outperform human subjects on the synthetic examples. This result corroborates earlier findings that LLM-generated data differs in crucial ways from natural data (Das et al., 2024) and that LLMs demonstrate a preference for synthetic text (Panickssery et al., 2024).

Related Work Pragmatic LLM language use is an active research area. Hu et al. (2023) investigate LLM capacity for pragmatically motivated interpretations, finding that humans and models utilize similar cues for pragmatic language use. Sravanthi et al. (2024) present a benchmark of ten pragmatic language use tasks, showing that LLMs achieve near comparable performance with human subjects on many tasks. Our findings lend additional support for this result. Lake and Murphy (2023) raise two important points: 1. current models are strongly linked to text-based patterns and 2. if the aim is human-like language capacity, models should benefit from context in similar ways to humans. We address these observations by targeting (transcribed) spoken language and investigating the impact of context.

Several studies investigate LLM cloze test performance. Lai et al. (2020) compare cloze test performance of BERT and LSTM language models (Hochreiter and Schmidhuber, 1997). Pezzelle et al. (2018) compare LSTMs to human subjects on quantifier prediction in context, observing that humans benefit from broad context, while models do not. Our findings do not agree with this observation because we found that models also benefit from broad context. This possibly reflects differences between LSTMs and LLMs.

Closely related to our approach, Pandia et al. (2021) investigate LLM cloze performance on discourse markers, finding that model performance does not mirror humans on causal connectives. However, in contrast to our approach, they force models to choose a completion from among a set of 66 discourse particles. We instead allow models and humans to freely generate the masked word. We believe our approach to be preferable because artificially restricting the pool of answers makes the task substantially easier. This complicates interpretation of the experimental results and risks inflating performance for models and/or humans.

2 Methods

Data We use both corpus and synthetic data in our experiment. Our corpus data consist of 295 naturally-produced spoken utterances containing the discourse marker *actually* along with a preceding and following context utterance. Utterances are drawn from the Providence corpus (Demuth et al., 2006) of the PhonBank database (Rose and MacWhinney, 2014)[1] which consists of videotaped interactions between six children, family members and other adults in natural situations, usually in the home. All utterances in the corpus are orthographically transcribed and time-aligned with the video.

All *actually*-containing utterances in our dataset are spoken by adults, but many context utterances are child speech, and children are always present or nearby. 70% of target utterances (utterances containing *actually*) are directed at children while the remaining 30% are adult-directed, with the result that the speech style is best described as "speech around children". Preceding and following utterances could be spoken by the same speaker as the target utterance or by a different speaker. In addition to the *actually* examples, 37 distractor examples containing one of three other words, drawn from the same corpus, are included in the dataset. See Appendix A for additional details.

In our experiment with human participants (conducted using Amazon Mechanical Turk (Crowston, 2012), participants control how many cloze items they complete. Because *actually* is always a possible answer, there is a risk that participants will realize that it is the intended completion regardless of the example. To counteract this possibility, we generated 295 *synthetic examples* using GPT-3.5. These are engineered to resemble the *actually* examples, but target a variety of other words (selected based on which word in the synthetic target utterance was predicted with the lowest confidence by BERT). See Appendix A for additional details.

Cloze test To investigate the effect of surrounding context, we created four examples for every *actually* utterance, each accompanied by some combination of the preceding and following context utterance as demonstrated in Figure 1. The four conditions were: T (target utterance only); T+N (target plus next utterance); P+T (preceding utter-

[1]Publicly available at `https://sla.talkbank.org/TBB/phon/Eng-NA/Providence`

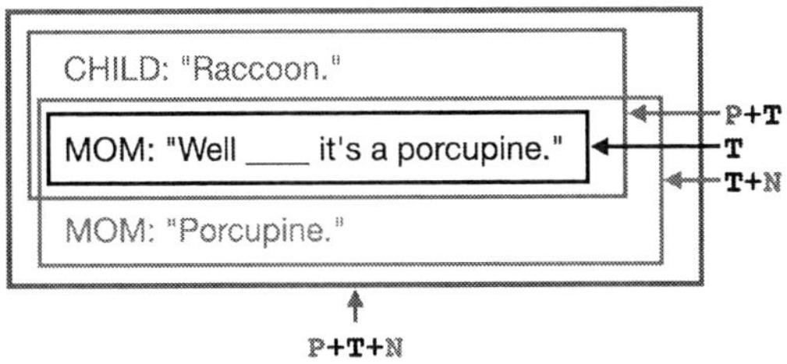

Figure 1: Cloze test (correct answer = *actually*). We investigate different degrees of contextual supervision, asking human participants and models to fill in the missing word given different combinations of: the target utterance (**T**), the following utterance (**N**) and the preceding utterance (**P**).

ance plus target); and P+T+N (preceding, target and next). In total, this results in 2360 examples of which 1180 are *actually* examples and the rest synthetic.

We asked human subjects to fill in the "5 most likely English words" for the target utterance. We chose to ask for five answers because there are normally several reasonable answers for any given example, and overly limiting the number of responses (say, to one or two) would mean our dataset would fail to include words that participants might believe are equally likely. On the other hand, asking for more than five responses could make the task too difficult and time-consuming. All examples and all conditions were randomized such that any given participant received a random mix of *actually* and synthetic examples across a random distribution of conditions. Each example was only completed by one participant (although participants were free to complete as many items as they wanted). In order to ensure the validity of the results, we limited participants to those completing the task in an English-speaking country, and we removed responses which contained high proportions of repeated answers or answers that occurred in the prompt. In total, there were 255 mTurk participants. Given that there were 2360 examples in total, each annotator annotated 8.1 examples on average. See Appendix C for additional details.

We experiment with two types of LLMs: 1) Encoder-only large language models: BERT, RoBERTa and ELECTRA, and 2) Generative large language models: GPT-3.5 and GPT-4. For encoder-only models, which are trained on a masked language modeling objective, we can straightforwardly frame the cloze task as masked prediction. We extracted the five most probable

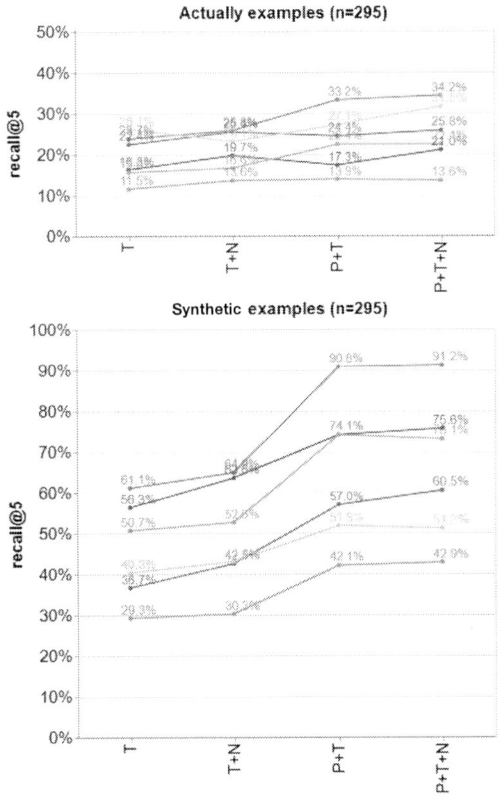

Figure 2: Results (recall@5) on cloze tests for: ● BERT, ● ELECTRA ● RoBERTa, ● GPT-3.5, ● GPT-4 and ○ mTurk. We present results for *actually* examples in the top panel and synthetic examples in the bottom panel. Results are presented for all context types: T, T+N, P+T and P+T+N.

words in the given context. For generative models (GPT-3.5 and GPT-4), we cannot directly frame the cloze task as masked prediction. Instead, we prepared a prompt which asks the model to predict the missing word in the example (see Appendix B for details on the prompts and generation process).

For both models and humans, we evaluate recall@5, i.e., we computed how often the correct word is found among the five completions.

3 Results

Experimental results for human subjects and LLMs are presented in Figure 2. The information is shown in tabular format in Table 1.

***Actually* examples** Across all settings, humans do well in comparison to most models on *actually* prediction but GPT-4 outperforms humans in all settings apart from T, where only the target utterance is provided as context. In general, context is

Model	T	T+N	P+T	P+T+N
ACTUALLY EXAMPLES				
Human	26.1	23.1	27.1	**31.5**
GPT-3.5	16.0	16.6	**22.4**	**22.4**
GPT-4	23.7	25.8	33.2	**34.2**
BERT	16.3	19.7	17.3	**21.0**
ELECTRA	11.5	13.6	**13.9**	13.6
RoBERTa	22.4	25.4	24.4	**25.8**

Model	T	T+N	P+T	P+T+N
SYNTHETIC EXAMPLES				
Human	40.3	42.6	**51.9**	51.2
GPT-3.5	50.7	52.6	**74.1**	73.1
GPT-4	61.1	64.9	90.8	**91.2**
BERT	56.3	63.6	74.1	**75.6**
ELECTRA	29.3	30.3	42.1	**42.9**
RoBERTa	36.7	42.5	57.0	**60.5**

Table 1: Cloze test results (recall@5) for *actually* and synthetic data.

helpful for both models and humans, but the effect of quantity and placement differs across humans and different models. Purely based on the target utterance (T), human recall@5 (0.291) narrowly beats both GPT-4 (0.237) and RoBERTa (0.224), while BERT, GPT-3.5 and ELECTRA deliver substantially lower performance. In the presence of additional supervision in the form of the following utterance (T+N), the general picture remains largely unchanged, although RoBERTa and GPT-4 now narrowly outperform human annotators. Providing the previous utterance as context instead of the following one (P+T), results in a substantial boost in recall for GPT-4 (+0.08) and GPT-3.5 (+0.06), while changes for humans and other models remain small. In this setting, GPT-4 clearly outperforms all other models and humans. Finally, full context (P+T+N) delivers the best performance for GPT-4. In this context, humans' recall@5 gains +0.04 and ends up close to, though still slightly below, GPT-4.

Synthetic examples Performance for all models and human participants is higher on synthetic examples than *actually* examples. In the baseline setting, seeing only the target utterance (T), human participants do 14%-points better on synthetic examples and GPT-4 does 37%-points better. Overall, three of the models– GPT-4, BERT and GPT-3.5– very clearly outperform human participants on the synthetic examples. Given additional context, we see the same overall trend as for *actually* examples: providing the next utterance (T+N) marginally improves performance whereas the preceding utterance (P+T) leads to large improvements for all model types and humans. Providing both context utterances (P+T+N) delivers small additional improvements for RoBERTa and GPT-4 and results in minor degradation for humans and GPT-3.5 compared to P+T. Overall, model performance is extremely high, with GPT-4 achieving 91% recall in the P+T+N setting, which is a whole 40%-points higher than human performance. At the same time, RoBERTa seems to deliver the most humanlike performance. BERT surprisingly delivers far stronger performance than RoBERTa even though the model architectures are very similar.

4 Discussion

Both models and humans achieved moderate success in the cloze task for *actually* and notably higher rates of success on the synthetic examples. Humans' ability to predict *actually* in a variety of contexts generally fell within the range of accuracy of the best-performing models. This suggests that the models were able to generalize to the type of speech from which we drew our examples (largely comprising child-directed speech). GPT-4, in particular, outperformed humans. This is not wholly unexpected given that it is one of the largest LLMs to date.

Context is generally helpful. The preceding context utterance seems to be crucial—the best performance is always achieved either in the condition P+T or P+T+N. For the *actually* examples, the generative models GPT-3.5 and GPT-4, along with humans, derive the largest gains in accuracy from added context, while other models saw smaller improvements. This might indicate that a generative training objective better helps models condition on contextual information in a human-like way compared to a masked language modeling objective. On the other hand, GPT-4 outperforms humans, so it is in fact using context more effectively than our human subjects. Interestingly, although RoBERTa sees little improvement with context, it nevertheless outperforms GPT-3.5 in all conditions.

Models massively outperform humans on synthetic data. Our natural examples proved much more difficult than the synthetic ones. GPT-4, in particular, achieved a stunning 91.2% recall@5 in the synthetic P+T+N condition. As evidenced by far lower human performance at 51.2%, this is unrealistically high. In fact, on synthetic data, humans were outperformed by all models apart from ELECTRA, a pattern of results which stands in stark contrast with the results from the natural data. We hypothesize that synthetically produced examples, unlike real ones, strongly reflect the distribution learned by GPT-3.5 which was used to generate those examples. This makes a cloze task less of a test of generalizability and more of a test of overfitting to training data. Therefore, models in fact benefit from a narrow understanding of language on synthetic data, which makes it less surprising that they outperform humans. The effects of context in the synthetic examples are also much more pronounced and in this setting both humans and all models improve with added context in contrast to the harder *actually* examples.

5 Conclusion and Future Work

In our data, the performance of models and humans fell within the same range. This suggests that models, especially those performing closest to humans, are able to predict the occurrence of the pragmatically-sensitive item *actually*, possibly based on similar aspects of the surrounding context as humans. However, important differences emerged between models and humans in overall accuracy, use of context, and the effect of context location, suggesting differences in how, and how effectively, models and humans utilize context. Our work raises some important questions: where models outperform humans, are they picking up on contextual cues that humans are not sensitive to? If so, what are these cues? Is outperforming humans a desirable goal, or is emulating human behavior—interpreting contextual cues in a human-like way, including failing to make use of certain cues even if they might be useful—more aligned with the goals of language modeling? Finally, our experiments on synthetic examples demonstrate a stark contrast between LLM performance on natural and synthetic data. Consequently, we urge caution when using synthetic data in experiments, especially when comparing human and LLM performance.

6 Limitations

Limitations of working with human subjects There are several limitations related to the human cloze experiment. Although we limited mTurk participants to those performing the task in English-speaking countries, we do not know whether participants are native English speakers, nor do we know their level of English proficiency. In fact, we expect many participants will have been second language speakers, meaning that the results might not carry over to a native English-speaking population. The presumed language background variability of the human participants also reduces comparability between our human results and model results, since the models are trained only on English. Furthermore, as in all experiments involving human subjects, participants' understanding of the task, attention to the task and motivation to follow the instructions cannot be controlled. To mitigate these potential issues as much as possible, we limited participants by experience and approval rating and we automatically filtered out responses that bore the hallmarks of inattention: those that exceeded a pre-determined proportion of repeated answers or answers copied directly from the prompt (see **Appendix C** for details).

Limitations of the experimental design Given that our human participants were allowed to complete as many examples as they wanted, there was a risk that participants who completed more examples would figure out that *actually* is often a possible answer. In an ideal world, each human subject would complete a single example, which would entirely eliminate the effect of seeing multiple *actually* examples, but unfortunately, limiting the task to one example per participant would make it not worthwhile for most participants. We attempted to mitigate the potential effect of seeing multiple *actually* examples by adding the synthetic examples as described in **Methods** and **Appendix A**. In addition, we performed a post-hoc analysis evaluating whether participants who completed more examples in fact guessed *actually* more often. Figure 3 shows the number of *actually* answers as a function of the total number of cloze test items completed by the participant. As the regression line in the plot demonstrates, participants who completed more examples did tend to guess *actually* more frequently than others. However, the effect is moderate. Moreover, as Figure 4 demonstrates, most of our answers

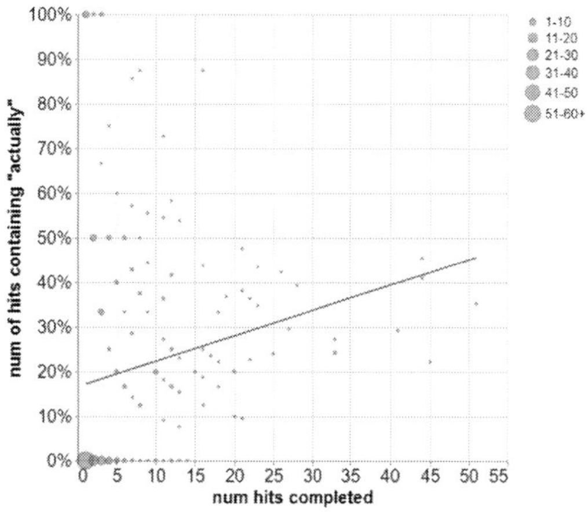

Figure 3: The proportion of correctly identified *actually* answers as a function the number of examples completed. The regression line shows that the proportion of *actually* guesses does tend to increase as the number of completed examples increases.

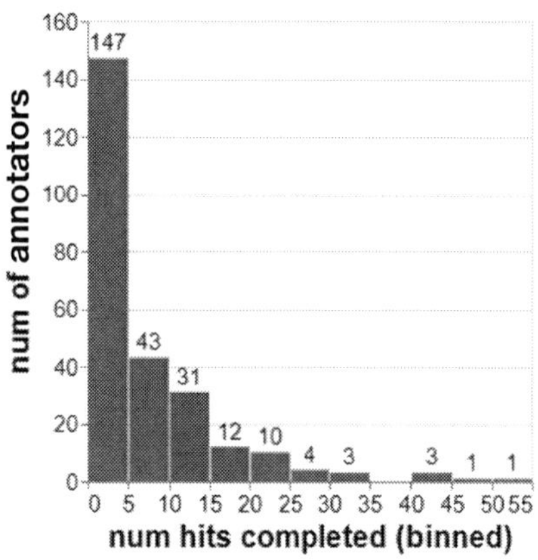

Figure 4: The distribution of the number of completed examples among participants. 58% of participants completed maximally five examples and 87% completed maximally fifteen.

come from participants who completed very few examples. Consequently, most of our correct *actually* responses come from participants who completed very few examples simply because there are far more such participants. This means that the data is unlikely to be very biased on the whole.

Caveat concerning LLMs Finally, there is one major limitation related to the LLMs: while we do not believe that the LLMs would have been exposed to the Providence corpus during their training process, we were only able to check this for BERT, RoBERTa and ELECTRA. For the GPT models it is impossible to know for certain. If these were exposed to the Providence corpus, this might inflate their performance on the *actually* cloze tests.

Acknowledgements

The authors would like to thank Vered Shwartz for suggesting the mturk experiment and for her valuable input in the experiment design phase. The present work was supported by UBC Language Sciences Seed Funding. In addition, we acknowledge the following grant support for PhonBank: NIH-NICHHD RO1-HD051698.

References

Josh Achiam, Steven Adler, Sandhini Agarwal, Lama Ahmad, Ilge Akkaya, Florencia Leoni Aleman, Diogo Almeida, Janko Altenschmidt, Sam Altman, Shyamal Anadkat, et al. 2023. Gpt-4 technical report. *arXiv preprint arXiv:2303.08774*.

Karin Aijmer. 2002. English discourse particles. *English Discourse Particles*, pages 1–315.

Douglas Biber and Edward Finegan. 1988. Adverbial stance types in english. *Discourse Processes*, 11(1):1–34.

Tom Brown, Benjamin Mann, Nick Ryder, Melanie Subbiah, Jared D Kaplan, Prafulla Dhariwal, Arvind Neelakantan, Pranav Shyam, Girish Sastry, Amanda Askell, et al. 2020. Language models are few-shot learners. *Advances in neural information processing systems*, 33:1877–1901.

H. Clark. 1996. Using language. *Cambridge*.

Kevin Clark, Minh-Thang Luong, Quoc V Le, and Christopher D Manning. 2020. Electra: Pre-training text encoders as discriminators rather than generators. *arXiv preprint arXiv:2003.10555*.

Kevin Crowston. 2012. Amazon mechanical turk: A research tool for organizations and information systems scholars. In *Shaping the Future of ICT Research. Methods and Approaches: IFIP WG 8.2, Working Conference, Tampa, FL, USA, December 13-14, 2012. Proceedings*, pages 210–221. Springer.

Debarati Das, Karin De Langis, Anna Martin, Jaehyung Kim, Minhwa Lee, Zae Myung Kim, Shirley Hayati, Risako Owan, Bin Hu, Ritik Parkar, et al. 2024. Under the surface: Tracking the artifactuality of llm-generated data. *arXiv preprint arXiv:2401.14698*.

Katherine Demuth, Jennifer Culbertson, and Jennifer Alter. 2006. Word-minimality, epenthesis and coda licensing in the early acquisition of english. *Language and Speech*, 49(2):137–173.

Jacob Devlin, Ming-Wei Chang, Kenton Lee, and Kristina Toutanova. 2018. Bert: Pre-training of deep bidirectional transformers for language understanding. *arXiv preprint arXiv:1810.04805*.

Jennifer Robin Sarah Glougie. 2016. *The semantics and pragmatics of English evidential expressions: the expression of evidentiality in police interviews*. Ph.D. thesis, University of British Columbia.

M. A. K. Halliday and R. Hasan. 1976. *Cohesion in English*. Longman, London.

Sepp Hochreiter and Jürgen Schmidhuber. 1997. Long short-term memory. *Neural computation*, 9(8):1735–1780.

Jennifer Hu, Sammy Floyd, Olessia Jouravlev, Evelina Fedorenko, and Edward Gibson. 2023. A fine-grained comparison of pragmatic language understanding in humans and language models. In *Proceedings of the 61st Annual Meeting of the Association for Computational Linguistics (Volume 1: Long Papers)*, pages 4194–4213, Toronto, Canada. Association for Computational Linguistics.

Yi-An Lai, Garima Lalwani, and Yi Zhang. 2020. Context analysis for pre-trained masked language models. In *Findings of the Association for Computational Linguistics: EMNLP 2020*, pages 3789–3804.

Brenden M Lake and Gregory L Murphy. 2023. Word meaning in minds and machines. *Psychological review*, 130(2):401.

Uta Lenk. 1998. *Marking discourse coherence: Functions of discourse markers in spoken English*, volume 15. Gunter Narr Verlag.

Yinhan Liu, Myle Ott, Naman Goyal, Jingfei Du, Mandar Joshi, Danqi Chen, Omer Levy, Mike Lewis, Luke Zettlemoyer, and Veselin Stoyanov. 2019. Roberta: A robustly optimized bert pretraining approach. *arXiv preprint arXiv:1907.11692*.

Sun-Young Oh. 2000. Actually and in fact in american english: a data-based analysis. *English Language & Linguistics*, 4(2):243–268.

L Pandia, Y Cong, and A Ettinger. 2021. Pragmatic competence of pre-trained language models through the lens of discourse connectives. In *Proceedings of the 25th Conference on Computational Natural Language Learning (CoNLL)*.

Arjun Panickssery, Samuel R Bowman, and Shi Feng. 2024. Llm evaluators recognize and favor their own generations. *arXiv preprint arXiv:2404.13076*.

Sandro Pezzelle, Steinert-Threlkeld Shane, Raffaella Bernardi, Szymanik Jakub, et al. 2018. Some of them can be guessed! exploring the effect of linguistic context in predicting quantifiers. In *ACL 2018: The 56th Annual Meeting of theAssociation for Computational Linguistics Proceedings of the Conference Vol. 2 (Short Papers)*, pages 114–119. Association for Computational Linguistics.

Randolph Quirk, Sidney Greenbaum, Geoffrey Leech, and Jan Svartvik. 1985. *A Comprehensive Grammar of the English Language*. Longman, London.

Y. Rose and B. MacWhinney. 2014. The phonbank project: Data and software-assisted methods for the study of phonology and phonological development. In J. Durand, U. Gut, and G. Kristoffersen, editors, *Handbook of corpus phonology*, pages 380–401. Oxford University Press, Oxford.

David C Rubin. 1976. The effectiveness of context before, after, and around a missing word. *Perception & Psychophysics*, 19:214–216.

Settaluri Lakshmi Sravanthi, Meet Doshi, Tankala Pavan Kalyan, Rudra Murthy, Pushpak Bhattacharyya, and Raj Dabre. 2024. Pub: A pragmatics understanding benchmark for assessing llms' pragmatics capabilities. *arXiv preprint arXiv:2401.07078*.

A Test Item Creation

Actually items *Actually* examples are drawn from the publicly-available Providence corpus (Demuth et al., 2006), which consists of video-taped spoken English interactions between children (n=6) and their parents and sometimes others. The children ranged in age from 1 year to 4 years. The data was collected in the form of one hour video recordings, collected across an average of 61 sessions per child over the years 2002-2005. The corpus is transcribed in written English, and these transcriptions are time-aligned with the videos. The mean(sd) lengths of example utterances (in number of words) were: for target utterances, 11.1(7.1); for preceding utterance, 5.3(4.8); for following utterance, 5.9(4.9).

We located all utterances containing tokens of *actually* (n=844). As part of a larger project, the *actually*-containing utterance, the utterance before and the utterance after were annotated for a suite of linguistic and other behavioural features (e.g. activity). For the present analysis, the example set was filtered to exclude examples in which the child spoke the target (*actually*-containing) utterance, examples in which there was no behavioural information (e.g. due to speakers being off-camera) and examples in which the utterance before and/or after was missing. Three examples of *actually* test items can be seen in Figure 5.

Synthetic items The synthetic examples were generated by GPT-3.5-turbo-1106 with temperature set to 0.7. The GPT-3.5 prompt is given in Figure 6. To generate a set of synthetic examples that resembled the *actually* examples, we provided GPT with the following variables and populated them with randomly selected values from distributions similar to those of the *actually* dataset:

```
MOM: "Hee hee hee."
MOM: "I think it'd  be a great idea if we
      ____ went to sleep tonight and stayed
      asleep all night."
MOM: "Wouldn't that be great?"
******
CHILD: "More there and there."
MOM: "Nope we ____ don't need more there."
MOM: "The secret to good wrapping is not to
      use too much tape I think."
******
OTHER ADULT: "You have more of the last
              paper?"
MOM: "It's ____ in my car."
MOM: "Let me get it out."
```

Figure 5: Example test items

- 2 speakers (e.g., MOM, DAD, CHILD)
- emotion of speaker2 (e.g., neutral, happy)
- activity of speaker2 (e.g., playing, conversing)
- location in the house (e.g., living room, kitchen)
- age of the CHILD if CHILD was selected as a speaker (e.g., 15 months, 2 years old)
- "do" or "do not" add a discourse marker to the utterance

Out of 295 examples, 50 had to be manually edited so that the format was correct. A common error was that GPT-3.5-turbo added a fourth utterance in the synthetic example when the instructions only asked for three. After this light editing process, the mean(sd) lengths of the synthetic example utterances (in number of words) were: for target utterances, 8.7(3.1); for preceding utterance, 6.0(2.1); for following utterance, 6.5(2.8).

Once synthetic examples were finalized, we simulated masking each word in the utterance and used BERT to make one word predictions for all masked instances. The word with the the lowest probability among BERT's predictions was masked for the cloze test. In Figure 7, we give three examples of synthetic items (the masked words are *Um*, *I'm* and *bedtime*, respectively).

B LLM Prompt Details

LLMs were asked to predict one example at a time to ensure their responses were not influenced by any text from other examples. A synthetic example was provided so that the LLM responded in the correct json format. The prompt is shown in Figure 8.

C mTurk Experiment Details

We recruited human participants via Amazon Mechanical Turk (Crowston, 2012). Each participant was paid \$0.10 per HIT (which consisted of one test question). mTurk participants qualified for the task if they:

- had a HIT approval rate over 95%
- had a number of HITs approved > 500
- were located in one of the 35 most populous countries in which English is an official or predominant language, according to `https://en.wikipedia.org/wiki/List_of_countries_and_territories_where_English_is_an_official_language`

In addition to the above qualifications, mTurk participants were required to pass a qualification test consisting of three fill-in-the-blank questions of the form given in Figure 9.

The instructions in the HIT were: "Fill in the blank with the 5 most likely English words. No duplicates."

To limit the number of examples a participant could complete, and to prevent participants from completing the same example in more than one condition, we implemented the following:

- examples were released in 100-example batches and participants who completed HITs in one batch were unable to complete the task in another batch
- in one batch, there was only one type of context per example (e.g., if T+N of example1 is in Batch1, then T, P+T, P+T+N of example1 will be in a different batch)
- only one set of responses was collected per example

Once answers were collected, a quality check was conducted to filter out poor responses:

- no responses consisting of repeated answers (e.g., "fun", "fun", "fun", "fun", "fun")
- no one-character answers (e.g., "r", "e", "a", "l", "y")

````
You are a screenwriter who is writing a conversation between two people. Speaker1
and Speaker2 are {location} and Speaker2 {act_cat}.{child_msg} Create a three turn
conversation, make up an action for Speaker2 before the Speaker2 utterance and
{discourse_marker_msg} add a discourse marker frequently found in conversations in
Speaker2's utterance. Follow the specified FORMAT. In the FORMAT, more detailed
instructions will be provided between the delimiter triple backticks, ```.

###FORMAT START###
Speaker2 ```The scene will be provided and should be printed exactly the same in
the output```.
Speaker1: "```Says something brief to Speaker2 that fits the scene.```"
Speaker2 ```Make up an action Speaker2 is doing before the next utterance.```
Speaker2: "```Says something brief to Speaker1.```"
Speaker1: "```Responds to Speaker2.```"
###FORMAT END###

###EXAMPLE START###
INSTRUCTIONS:
- Speaker1 = MOM
- Speaker2 = DAD
- Scene = DAD is changing diaper.
- Emotion = DAD is feeling panicked.
- Location = living room
- Do add a discourse marker frequently found in conversations in Speaker2's
utterance

OUTPUT:
DAD is changing diaper.
MOM: "Did you remember to use baby powder?"
DAD looks up quickly.
DAD: "Huh, what do you mean baby powder? I didn't know she needs it. Is she sick?"
MOM: "No calm down. She's fine."
###EXAMPLE END###

Now it's your turn.

INSTRUCTIONS:
- Speaker1 = {s1}
- Speaker2 = {s2}
- Scene = {s2} {act_cat}.
- Emotion = {s2} is feeling {emotion}.
- Location = {location}
- {discourse_marker_msg} add a discourse marker frequently found in conversations in
Speaker2's utterance

OUTPUT:
````

Figure 6: LLM prompt template for generation of synthetic cloze examples. The LLM generates its answer after OUTPUT:.

```
OTHER ADULT: "Hey, do you have the car
              keys?"
MOM: "_____, let me see... Oh, here they
     are."
OTHER ADULT: "Great, let's head out."
******
DAD: "Smells delicious in here, what's for
     dinner?"
MOM: "_____ making your favorite, spaghetti
     and meatballs."
DAD: "That sounds amazing, I can't wait to
     eat!"
******
OTHER ADULT: "I didn't expect to see you
             here."
MOM: "Yeah, I wanted to tidy up a bit
     before _____."
OTHER ADULT: "Well, that's nice of you to
             do."
```

Figure 7: Example synthetic items.

- type-to-token ratio (TTR) was =<0.5
- answer-to-sample-ratio (ATSR) was =>0.1

TTR and ATSR were calculated by participant. We found that low TTR indicates the participant did not meaningfully complete the task due to having repeated a high proportion of words across different HITs. High ATSR indicates that the participant repeatedly used words found in the example utterances as responses, rather than choosing words that fit the context as per task instructions. Examples with rejected answers were put in new batches for another round of mTurk completions. In total, we completed three rounds before all examples received accepted answers.

```
You are a fluent English-speaker. In a conversation between two people, there will
be a blank denoted by _____.

TASK:
  1. Read the text between the characters ```
  2. Determine the 5 most likely English words in place of the blank _____; NO
     DUPLICATES IN THE LIST
  3. Create a JSON object like the following: {"word1": "one_word_only",
     "word2":"one_word_only", "word3": "one_word_only", "word4": "one_word_only",
     "word5":"one_word_only"}
  4. Your response should only contain the JSON object.

EXAMPLE:
```MOM likes to _____ cookies.``` A good response is {"word1": "eat", "word2": "make",
"word3": "buy", "word4": "decorate", "word5": "bake"}

TEXT:
```
{example}
```

OUTPUT:
```

Figure 8: LLM Prompt template for Recall@5. The variable {example} is replaced by a cloze test example. The LLM generates its answer after OUTPUT:.

```
DAD is cooking.

MOM: "Did you add salt?"

DAD is standing.

DAD: "Yeah, _____ course."

MOM: "Oh good."
```

Figure 9: One of our qualification questions for mTurk annotators. The correct answer here is *of*.
```

LLMs' morphological analyses of complex FST-generated Finnish words

Anssi Moisio[1], **Mathias Creutz**[2], and **Mikko Kurimo**[1]
[1]Department of Information and Communications Engineering, Aalto University, Finland
[2]Department of Digital Humanities, University of Helsinki, Finland
anssi.moisio@aalto.fi, mathias.creutz@helsinki.fi, mikko.kurimo@aalto.fi

Abstract

Rule-based language processing systems have been overshadowed by neural systems in terms of utility, but it remains unclear whether neural NLP systems, in practice, learn the grammar rules that humans use. This work aims to shed light on the issue by evaluating state-of-the-art LLMs in a task of morphological analysis of complex Finnish noun forms. We generate the forms using an FST tool, and they are unlikely to have occurred in the training sets of the LLMs, therefore requiring morphological generalisation capacity. We find that GPT-4-turbo has some difficulties in the task while GPT-3.5-turbo struggles and smaller models Llama2-70B and Poro-34B fail nearly completely.

1 Do neural networks learn grammar?

The debate on whether neural networks (NNs) can be accurate models of human language often revolves around the question whether NNs learn similar grammar rules as children do. In a famous instance of the debate, Rumelhart and McClelland (1986) argued that a NN can capture the implicit rules that govern how English verbs are inflected in the past tense. In a response, Pinker and Prince (1988) counter that explicit rules are indispensable to explain how children learn past tenses, and more generally to explain the psychology of language.

Neural methods have gradually become more capable of modelling varied aspects of language, which could be viewed as supporting the implicit rules argument. (For updates on the past-tense debate see Kirov and Cotterell (2018); Corkery et al. (2019); Fukatsu et al. (2024).) The most recent instances of the debate are over large language models (LLMs), whose language-generation and task-solving capabilities have surprised many. The recent debate consequently concerns modelling human language more generally instead of focusing on specific phenomena such as verb inflection. Considering the success of LLMs, it is clear that they learn some implicit rule-abiding behaviour that enables them to process and generate language competently, but it is still not clear if they learn grammar similarly to humans, or if they learn and employ some other set of rules.

Assessing grammatical knowledge learned by NNs is not straightforward, but there are at least two popular approaches. Training a classifier (called a 'probe' (Alain and Bengio, 2016) or a 'diagnostic classifier' (Hupkes et al., 2018), first developed by Shi et al. (2016); Adi et al. (2017)) to classify the internal representations of NNs has been used to inspect what aspects of grammar are encoded in them. Probing studies have found various syntactical information encoded in neural NLP systems (Jawahar et al., 2019; Tenney et al., 2018; Papadimitriou et al., 2021), but interpreting the results remains contentious (Voita and Titov, 2020; Immer et al., 2022).

The other popular method is to directly inspect a neural LM's next-unit predictions, or to train a classifier NN to predict which word is most acceptable, given sequence of previous words. In an influential work by Linzen et al. (2016), knowledge of subject-verb agreement in LSTM networks was assessed this way, and it was concluded that 'LSTMs can learn to approximate structure-sensitive dependencies fairly well'. Similar *targeted syntactic evaluation* methods, inspired by methods in psycholinguistics (e.g. Crain and Fodor (1985); Stowe (1986)), have subsequently been employed to assess the knowledge of many different grammatical phenomena in NNs, for example anaphora or negative polarity items (Marvin and Linzen, 2018; Futrell et al., 2019; Jumelet and Hupkes, 2018; Hu et al., 2020). Larger test suites such as BLiMP (Warstadt et al., 2020) or SyntaxGym (Gauthier et al., 2020) are used as benchmarks to track advances in the field.

The general conclusion has not changed much since that of Linzen et al.'s: the networks are *fairly*

Proceedings of the Workshop on Cognitive Modeling and Computational Linguistics, pages 242–254
August 15, 2024 ©2024 Association for Computational Linguistics

good at acquiring the grammar rules. Sometimes results of a single study are interpreted as evidence that the NNs have acquired a syntactical rule completely (e.g. Wilcox et al. (2023)), but a closer inspection often proves such an interpretation premature (e.g. Lan et al. (2024)). Since there is no conclusive evidence that NNs learn from text the same grammar that people use, it remains an important task to delineate the instances where NNs, and LLMs in particular, adhere to and utilise grammar, and the instances where they do not.

Designing targeted syntactic evaluation tests requires careful formulation of the sequences. For example, Wilcox et al. (2023) examined the understanding of filler-gap effects by comparing the probabilities of acceptable and unacceptable continuations for sentence pairs such as 'I know *what* the lion devoured' and 'I know *that* the lion devoured'. The continuation 'yesterday' is assumed to be acceptable for the former but not the latter sequence. However, 'yesterday' could be an acceptable next word even for the latter sequence: consider the sentence 'I know that the lion devoured yesterday's leftovers.' This example highlights the difficulty of designing test sentences of this sort.

Instead of inspecting the next-unit predictions or training diagnostic classifiers, in this work we ask LLMs explicitly to perform a classification task, which is possible due to the flexible text generation capacity of the LLMs. This makes the evaluation relatively unambiguous. For example, asking an LLM directly 'Is the verb "devour" transitive or intransitive?' does not leave much room for confounding factors. The apparent limitation of this method is that even if a model fails in an explicit classification task like this, we cannot rule out the possibility that the model nevertheless encodes perfect *implicit* knowledge of the verb and how to use it in any context. However, we make the assumption in this work that if the LLMs had learned a grammar rule as perfectly as humans, they would be able to answer the explicit questions as competently as humans. This seems justified considering the type and difficulty of, and LLMs' performance in, other tasks used to evaluate LLMs, such as academic and professional exams (OpenAI, 2023).

This approach was also taken by Weissweiler et al. (2023), who assessed the morphological competence of GPT-3.5-turbo by asking it directly to fill in past tenses of words in a sentence, and concluded that it 'massively underperforms purpose-built systems'. Similarly, Weller-Di Marco and Fraser (2024) took a morphologically complex word W and asked GPT-3.5-turbo questions such as 'What is the head noun of W?'.

In this work we present LLMs directly and explicitly with a classification task to investigate the knowledge of Finnish morphology in LLMs. Although Finnish has relatively few speakers worldwide (<10 million), it is not a low-resource language, having about 32B tokens of available training texts (Luukkonen et al., 2023, 2024). Consequently, the state-of-the-art (SOTA) multilingual LLMs such as GPT-4 are fluent in Finnish, and could be expected to have a good grasp of the grammar, if the LLMs are in fact good at learning grammar from text.

2 Data and methods

Previous datasets of inflected Finnish words include the MorphyNet (Batsuren et al., 2021) and UniMorph (Kirov et al., 2016; Batsuren et al., 2022) corpora. We chose not to use data from these datasets for two reasons. Firstly, complex words comprising unusually many morphemes make it possible to assess if the systems can generalise to many types of possible inflections instead of learning only the most common inflection types. The previous datasets do not include many extremely complex word forms, but these can be generated using a finite-state transducer (FST). Secondly, since the SOTA LLMs have been trained on very large datasets harvested from the Internet, it is likely that the previously published datasets are included in their training data, which would preclude fair assessment.

We use the Omorfi tools (Pirinen, 2015; Pirinen et al., 2017) that are based on finite-state morphology (Koskenniemi, 1984; Beesley and Karttunen, 2003) to generate inflected forms of Finnish nouns. The Omorfi library includes some 500k lexemes, of which about 140k are nouns. We inflect the nouns in all possible combinations of number, grammatical case, and possessive suffix (see Table 1 for examples, and Appendix A for further details), which

BASE	+PL	+INE	+SG2 / +PL1
		laitteissa	*laitteissasi / laitteissamme*
laite	*laitteet*	+TRA	
		laitteiksi	*laitteiksesi / laitteiksemme*

Table 1: Examples of inflections of the word 'laite' ('device'). PL means plural, INE and TRA are case classes, and SG2/PL1 are possessive suffixes. Inflections in each column include also those in the columns to their left.

creates about 25M word forms. A random sample of 2000 inflected nouns is used as a test set in our experiments. We are unaware of any assessment of the generation accuracy of Omorfi, so we performed manual evaluation of the first 200 words in the sample and found 6 incorrectly inflected words. We therefore estimate the generation accuracy to be around 97%, which creates an upper bound for the classification accuracy of the test set. We publish the test set and all code to reproduce the results at `https://github.com/aalto-speech/llm-morph-tests`. We note, however, that once the data is published, it is subject to the same data contamination issue as the previous datasets mentioned above—the good thing is that one can always draw a new random sample from the full set of 25M forms.

Uniform sampling of lexemes creates a bias towards low-frequency types that are correlated with regularity of the inflection (Kodner et al., 2023). We note that this is the case in our data, as we took a random sample of the lexemes, and this should be kept in mind when interpreting the results; there are probably not many irregularly inflected words, which makes the task easier. This is not an issue, however, given our research question of whether the LLMs have picked up even the most *systematic* inflection types from textual data.

Prompt:
Jäsennä taivutetut substantiivit tällä tavalla: taivutusmuoto – perusmuoto, luku, sijamuoto, omistusliite vedessämme – vesi, yksikkö, inessiivi, 1. persoonan monikko kinoksiksensa – kinos, monikko, translatiivi, 3. persoona peukalostanne – peukalo, yksikkö, elatiivi, 2. persoonan monikko huurteenani – huurre, yksikkö, essiivi, 1. persoonan yksikkö sängiltäsi – sänki, monikko, ablatiivi, 2. persoonan yksikkö koivuumme – koivu, yksikkö, illatiivi, 1. persoonan monikko kaistojaan – kaista, monikko, partitiivi, 3. persoona rehtiyksiesi – rehtiys, monikko, genetiivi, 2. persoonan yksikkö laaksoillani – laakso, monikko, adessiivi, 1. persoonan yksikkö talollenne – talo, yksikkö, allatiivi, 2. persoonan monikko kansoiltanne – kansa,

Correct answer:
monikko, ablatiivi, 2. persoonan monikko

Table 2: An example 10-shot prompt. An English translation of the first two rows is: *Parse the inflected nouns in this manner: inflected form – base form, number, grammatical case, possessive suffix.* The following rows are the examples. We use n-shot prompts with $n \in \{0, 1, 5, 10\}$, and for all n we use the same n first examples. For instance, the 5-shot prompts have the *vedessämme, kinoksiksensa, peukalostanne, huurteenani,* and *sängiltäsi* example rows.

LLMs are prompted to give a morphological analysis given an inflected form and the base form. That is, the models should give the correct number, case, and possessive suffix classes of the inflected noun. The prompt, shown in Table 2, comprises a short description of the task and the desired format, after which there are 0, 1, 5, or 10 examples of the task before the test word.

We test **GPT-4-turbo**-1106-preview (Achiam et al., 2023) (which outperformed GPT-4-0613 in preliminary experiments), **GPT-3.5-turbo**-1106, **Llama2-70B** (Touvron et al., 2023) (outperformed smaller Llama2 models and chat versions), and **Poro-34B** (Luukkonen et al., 2024), which is trained on Finnish, English, and programming code.

For Poro and Llama2, we performed a coarse tuning of the temperature parameter on a validation set, and found no large differences but 0.5 to be marginally better than the others, so we used this value in the experiments with these models. For the GPT models we found a temperature of 0.0 to yield the best results, so this value is used for GPT-4-turbo and GPT-3.5-turbo. We did not tune the top_p parameter (of *nucleus sampling*) but used the default value 1.0.

Additionally, we trained simple recurrent neural network (RNN) models to also classify words (one RNN for each category: number, case, and possessive suffix), using random samples of the FST-generated word forms as training data (excluding the test set). The aim of this comparison is to give some indication of the difficulty of the task, and to see if NNs can handle the task if they are specifically trained on this small subset of Finnish morphology. We took the RNN off the shelf of the Pytorch library[1] without tuning any of its hyperparameters. It consists of three layers of size 128.

3 Results

The rightmost plot in Figure 1 shows that besides GPT-4-turbo, the models perform poorly in the task. GPT-4-turbo is not close to perfect accuracy either, and the combined 10-shot result does not reach the result achieved by simple RNNs trained with 80k words. With training set sizes of 800, 4k, 8k, 40k, and 80k words, the RNNs achieved accuracies of 0.380, 0.765, 0.774, 0.821, and 0.840, respectively.

[1]From the tutorial at `https://pytorch.org/tutorials/intermediate/char_rnn_classification_tutorial`

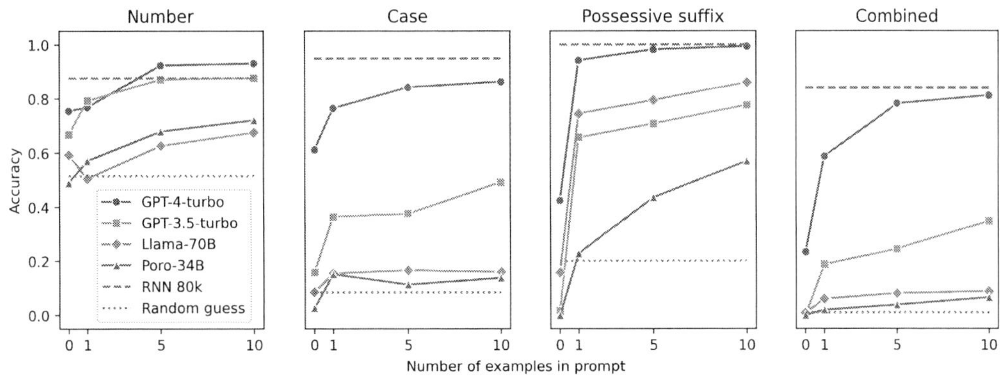

Figure 1: Results in the morphological analysis task.

The first three plots from left in Figure 1 break down the classification task into the three component classification tasks: number, case, and possessive suffix. There are some differences in the strengths of the models: Llama outperforms GPT-3.5 in the possessive suffix classification task, while GPT-3.5 performs better for other classification tasks. In number classification, Poro outperforms Llama, although Llama performs better in other tasks.

Figure 2 shows the confusion matrices for GPT-4-turbo classifications of cases for the 0-shot and 10-shot setups. From the 0-shot confusion matrix we can see that the model does predict all classes even though we did not provide it with the names of the classes we expected it to recognise. This is not surprising, since GPT-4-turbo has no difficulties if asked to inflect a Finnish word in all cases and to provide the names of the cases. It is obvious that GPT-4-turbo has a fair amount of both declarative knowledge (metalinguistic knowledge; it knows the classes) and procedural knowledge (knows how to inflect the words) of the Finnish morphology. Therefore, the challenge in this task comes presumably from the need to generalise to infrequently used, morphologically complex word forms.

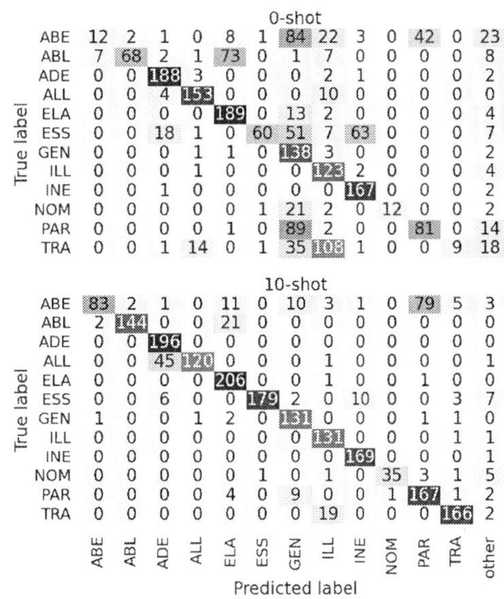

Figure 2: Case label confusions of GPT-4-turbo in the 0-shot and 10-shot setups. See Appendix B for all confusion matrices.

4 Discussion

4.1 Reasons behind the errors

Most current SOTA LLMs use subword tokenisation methods such as BPE (Sennrich et al., 2016) that break down infrequent character sequences into multiple shorter tokens while keeping frequent sequences as single tokens. Intuitively, having long tokens that combine multiple morphemes into a single token could hinder the capacity to model morphology, since multiple embeddings would have to be learned for a single morpheme. Of the three model families, Poro uses the longest tokens, having an average of 3.55 characters per token in our test words, while the Llama average is 2.16 and the GPT average is 2.26. Furthermore, the average length of the last token of a word is even longer: 4.42 for Poro, 2.41 for Llama, and 2.78 for GPT. For example, the first two test words whose possessive suffix Poro classifies incorrectly and differences in the tokenisations of the different models are shown in Table 3. Both of these words have the

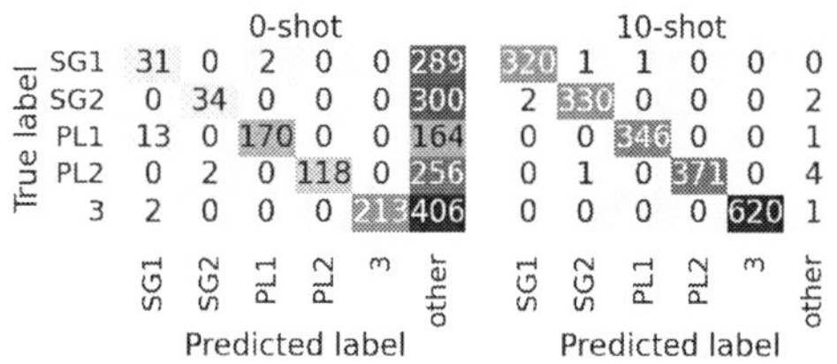

Figure 3: Possessive suffix label confusions of GPT-4-turbo in the 0-shot and 10-shot setups. See Appendix B for all confusion matrices.

Base form	*lyhty (lantern)*	*tarttuma (infection)*
Test word	*lyhtyjämme*	*tarttumassamme*
Poro tokens	ly hty jämme	t art t um assamme
Llama tokens	ly ht yj äm me	tart t um ass am me
GPT tokens	ly ht y j äm me	t art t um ass am me

Table 3: BPE tokenisations of different models.

first person plural possessive suffix, which always ends in 'me'. The possessive suffix 'me' is combined with the case morpheme (partitive 'jä' in 'lyhtyjämme' and inessive 'ssa' in 'tarttumassamme') by Poro but not by GPT or Llama. This might be one reason Poro misclassifies these words, while GPT and Llama do not, and in general why Poro lags behind the other models in the possessive suffix classification task as seen in Figure 1. The possessive suffix is simple to recognise, *if* the tokenisation is conducive to the task: a rule that checks the last two letters of the word and assigns `'ni'->SG1; 'si'->SG2; 'me'->PL1; 'ne'->PL2; else->3` would achieve 100% accuracy on our test set. Admittedly, the rule would have to be more complicated if there were also words without any possessive suffix, since these words could end in virtually any two letters: for instance, 'vesi' ('water') ends in 'si' but does not have any possessive suffix (SG2 form would be 'vetesi') as does the translative case 'vedeksi' without a possessive suffix (the translative case with SG2 suffix becomes 'vedeksesi').

Class frequencies could also explain some of the confusions. For example, GPT-4 often confuses abessive cases as partitive, seen in Figure 2. In addition to partitive being often quite similar to abessive, for example the inflected forms 'kättä' and 'kädettä' of the base 'käsi' ('hand'), partitive is also much more common than abessive: 16.2% versus 0.1% of occurrences in Kettunen (2005).

4.2 Interpretations and implications

The results suggest that despite the versatile language generation capacity of GPT-4-turbo it has not acquired the rules of Finnish morphology as completely as could be expected based on its language generation capacity. Instead, GPT-4 employs some other set of heuristics to decide the next token, although these undoubtedly overlap somewhat with grammar rules. This is hardly a surprise given the literature reviewed in Section 1, where the general conclusion tends to be that NNs rarely use grammar rules systematically, although usually fairly well.

The ineptitude of neural nets to follow grammar rules is related to systematic compositionality and inefficiency w.r.t training data set size, which are said to be weaknesses of neural nets compared to rule-based systems. Learning grammar enables *systematic compositional generalisation* (Fodor and Pylyshyn, 1988): learning a concise grammar rule such as '`the suffix -nne indicates 2nd person plural possessive form`' would enable generalising to all possible 2nd person plural forms in Finnish, obviating the need to learn word-specific associations and therefore reducing the required training corpus size. GPT-4 reaches close to 100% accuracy in this simple task of classifying possessive suffixes (RNN reaches 100%, and it is obvious that Finnish speakers would also reach 100%). However, the fact that it still sometimes classifies words ending in 'nne' as 2nd person singular instead of plural (see Figure 3) betrays its incomplete grasp of the systematic possessive suffixes in Finnish. Similar arguments apply to the other two classification tasks and the combined classification task.

5 Conclusion

We conclude that even a SOTA LLM, GPT-4-turbo, does not model Finnish morphology thoroughly enough to allow it to provide morphological analyses of rare and complex word forms with a high accuracy. Contrasting this with its impressive text generation capacity suggests that it utilises some other language processing heuristics, which clearly overlap somewhat with morphological rules since it rarely produces incorrect forms, but which preclude human-level systematic generalisation on our test set. GPT-4-turbo outperforms models such as GPT-3.5-turbo and Llama2-70B, however, by a large margin.

6 Limitations

Our experiments are limited to only one language and only four LLMs, which of course means we cannot be certain how the models perform on different languages, or how other models perform in Finnish, even though we suggest our results shed some light on general questions of grammar represented in LLMs. We also have not optimised the prompt beyond trying out a few different phrasings, so we assume some other prompt could elicit better performance especially in the 0- and 1-shot setups.

As noted in the introduction, we assess LLMs using explicit, metalinguistic questions about Finnish morphology. It is in principle possible that even if the models fail in this task, having a limited grasp of the morphological labels, they could succeed in using the words correctly in sentences and representing their meanings correctly.

7 Acknowledgements

We thank the anonymous reviewers for their insightful comments and feedback. The work was supported by the Finnish Cultural Foundation grant 00240853 and the Academy of Finland grant 337073. The computational resources were provided by Aalto ScienceIT. The use of the GPT-3.5 and GPT-4 systems via the Azure OpenAI API was provided by Aalto IT Services.

References

Josh Achiam, Steven Adler, Sandhini Agarwal, Lama Ahmad, Ilge Akkaya, Florencia Leoni Aleman, Diogo Almeida, Janko Altenschmidt, Sam Altman, Shyamal Anadkat, et al. 2023. Gpt-4 technical report. *arXiv preprint arXiv:2303.08774*.

Yossi Adi, Einat Kermany, Yonatan Belinkov, Ofer Lavi, and Yoav Goldberg. 2017. Fine-grained analysis of sentence embeddings using auxiliary prediction tasks. In *International Conference on Learning Representations*.

Guillaume Alain and Yoshua Bengio. 2016. Understanding intermediate layers using linear classifier probes. *arXiv preprint arXiv:1610.01644*.

Khuyagbaatar Batsuren, Gábor Bella, and Fausto Giunchiglia. 2021. MorphyNet: a large multilingual database of derivational and inflectional morphology. In *Proceedings of the 18th SIGMORPHON Workshop on Computational Research in Phonetics, Phonology, and Morphology*, pages 39–48, Online. Association for Computational Linguistics.

Khuyagbaatar Batsuren, Omer Goldman, Salam Khalifa, Nizar Habash, Witold Kieraś, Gábor Bella, Brian Leonard, Garrett Nicolai, Kyle Gorman, Ryan Cotterell, Reut Tsarfaty, Ekaterina Vylomova, et al. 2022. UniMorph 4.0: Universal Morphology. In *Proceedings of the Thirteenth Language Resources and Evaluation Conference*, pages 840–855, Marseille, France. European Language Resources Association.

Kenneth R Beesley and Lauri Karttunen. 2003. Finite-state morphology: Xerox tools and techniques. *CSLI, Stanford*, pages 359–375.

Maria Corkery, Yevgen Matusevych, and Sharon Goldwater. 2019. Are we there yet? encoder-decoder neural networks as cognitive models of English past tense inflection. In *Proceedings of the 57th Annual Meeting of the Association for Computational Linguistics*, pages 3868–3877, Florence, Italy. Association for Computational Linguistics.

Stephen Crain and Janet Dean Fodor. 1985. How can grammars help parsers? In *Natural Language Parsing Psychological, Computational, and Theoretical Perspectives*, pages 94–128. Cambridge University Press.

Jerry A Fodor and Zenon W Pylyshyn. 1988. Connectionism and cognitive architecture: A critical analysis. *Cognition*, 28(1-2):3–71.

Akiyo Fukatsu, Yuto Harada, and Yohei Oseki. 2024. Learning bidirectional morphological inflection like humans. In *Proceedings of the 2024 Joint International Conference on Computational Linguistics, Language Resources and Evaluation (LREC-COLING 2024)*, pages 10249–10262, Torino, Italy. ELRA and ICCL.

Richard Futrell, Ethan Wilcox, Takashi Morita, Peng Qian, Miguel Ballesteros, and Roger Levy. 2019. Neural language models as psycholinguistic subjects: Representations of syntactic state. In *Proceedings of the 2019 Conference of the North American Chapter of the Association for Computational Linguistics: Human Language Technologies, Volume 1 (Long and Short Papers)*, pages 32–42, Minneapolis, Minnesota. Association for Computational Linguistics.

Jon Gauthier, Jennifer Hu, Ethan Wilcox, Peng Qian, and Roger Levy. 2020. SyntaxGym: An online platform for targeted evaluation of language models. In *Proceedings of the 58th Annual Meeting of the Association for Computational Linguistics: System Demonstrations*, pages 70–76, Online. Association for Computational Linguistics.

Jennifer Hu, Jon Gauthier, Peng Qian, Ethan Wilcox, and Roger Levy. 2020. A systematic assessment of syntactic generalization in neural language models. In *Proceedings of the 58th Annual Meeting of the Association for Computational Linguistics*, pages 1725–1744, Online. Association for Computational Linguistics.

Dieuwke Hupkes, Sara Veldhoen, and Willem Zuidema. 2018. Visualisation and 'diagnostic classifiers' reveal how recurrent and recursive neural networks process hierarchical structure. *Journal of Artificial Intelligence Research*, 61:907–926.

Alexander Immer, Lucas Torroba Hennigen, Vincent Fortuin, and Ryan Cotterell. 2022. Probing as quantifying inductive bias. In *Proceedings of the 60th Annual Meeting of the Association for Computational Linguistics (Volume 1: Long Papers)*, pages 1839–1851, Dublin, Ireland. Association for Computational Linguistics.

Ganesh Jawahar, Benoît Sagot, and Djamé Seddah. 2019. What does BERT learn about the structure of language? In *Proceedings of the 57th Annual Meeting of the Association for Computational Linguistics*, pages 3651–3657, Florence, Italy. Association for Computational Linguistics.

Jaap Jumelet and Dieuwke Hupkes. 2018. Do language models understand anything? on the ability of LSTMs to understand negative polarity items. In *Proceedings of the 2018 EMNLP Workshop BlackboxNLP: Analyzing and Interpreting Neural Networks for NLP*, pages 222–231, Brussels, Belgium. Association for Computational Linguistics.

Kimmo Kettunen. 2005. Sijamuodot haussa-tarvitseeko kaikkea hakutermien morfologista vaihtelua kattaa? Master's thesis.

Christo Kirov and Ryan Cotterell. 2018. Recurrent neural networks in linguistic theory: Revisiting pinker and prince (1988) and the past tense debate. *Transactions of the Association for Computational Linguistics*, 6:651–665.

Christo Kirov, John Sylak-Glassman, Roger Que, and David Yarowsky. 2016. Very-large scale parsing and normalization of Wiktionary morphological paradigms. In *Proceedings of the Tenth International Conference on Language Resources and Evaluation (LREC'16)*, pages 3121–3126, Portorož, Slovenia. European Language Resources Association (ELRA).

Jordan Kodner, Sarah Payne, Salam Khalifa, and Zoey Liu. 2023. Morphological inflection: A reality check. In *Proceedings of the 61st Annual Meeting of the Association for Computational Linguistics (Volume 1: Long Papers)*, pages 6082–6101, Toronto, Canada. Association for Computational Linguistics.

Kimmo Koskenniemi. 1984. A general computational model for word-form recognition and production. In *10th International Conference on Computational Linguistics and 22nd Annual Meeting of the Association for Computational Linguistics*, pages 178–181.

Nur Lan, Emmanuel Chemla, and Roni Katzir. 2024. Large language models and the argument from the poverty of the stimulus. *Linguistic Inquiry*, pages 1–56.

Tal Linzen, Emmanuel Dupoux, and Yoav Goldberg. 2016. Assessing the ability of LSTMs to learn syntax-sensitive dependencies. *Transactions of the Association for Computational Linguistics*, 4:521–535.

Risto Luukkonen, Jonathan Burdge, Elaine Zosa, Aarne Talman, Ville Komulainen, Väinö Hatanpää, Peter Sarlin, and Sampo Pyysalo. 2024. Poro 34b and the blessing of multilinguality. *arXiv preprint arXiv:2404.01856*.

Risto Luukkonen, Ville Komulainen, Jouni Luoma, Anni Eskelinen, Jenna Kanerva, Hanna-Mari Kupari, Filip Ginter, Veronika Laippala, Niklas Muennighoff, Aleksandra Piktus, Thomas Wang, Nouamane Tazi, Teven Scao, Thomas Wolf, Osma Suominen, Samuli Sairanen, Mikko Merioksa, Jyrki Heinonen, Aija Vahtola, Samuel Antao, and Sampo Pyysalo. 2023. FinGPT: Large generative models for a small language. In *Proceedings of the 2023 Conference on Empirical Methods in Natural Language Processing*, pages 2710–2726, Singapore. Association for Computational Linguistics.

Rebecca Marvin and Tal Linzen. 2018. Targeted syntactic evaluation of language models. In *Proceedings of the 2018 Conference on Empirical Methods in Natural Language Processing*, pages 1192–1202, Brussels, Belgium. Association for Computational Linguistics.

OpenAI. 2023. GPT-4 technical report. *arxiv 2303.08774*.

Isabel Papadimitriou, Ethan A. Chi, Richard Futrell, and Kyle Mahowald. 2021. Deep subjecthood: Higher-order grammatical features in multilingual BERT. In *Proceedings of the 16th Conference of the European Chapter of the Association for Computational Linguistics: Main Volume*, pages 2522–2532, Online. Association for Computational Linguistics.

Steven Pinker and Alan Prince. 1988. On language and connectionism: Analysis of a parallel distributed processing model of language acquisition. *Cognition*, 28(1-2):73–193.

Tommi A Pirinen. 2015. Development and use of computational morphology of finnish in the open source and open science era: Notes on experiences with omorfi development. *SKY Journal of Linguistics*, 28:381–393.

Tommi A Pirinen, Inari Listenmaa, Ryan Johnson, Francis M. Tyers, and Juha Kuokkala. 2017. Open morphology of finnish. LINDAT/CLARIN digital library at the Institute of Formal and Applied Linguistics, Charles University.

David E Rumelhart and James L McClelland. 1986. On learning the past tenses of English verbs. In *Parallel distributed processing: explorations in the microstructure of cognition, vol. 2: psychological and biological models*, pages 216–271. MIT Press.

Rico Sennrich, Barry Haddow, and Alexandra Birch. 2016. Neural machine translation of rare words with subword units. In *Proceedings of the 54th Annual Meeting of the Association for Computational Linguistics (Volume 1: Long Papers)*, pages 1715–1725, Berlin, Germany. Association for Computational Linguistics.

Xing Shi, Inkit Padhi, and Kevin Knight. 2016. Does string-based neural MT learn source syntax? In *Proceedings of the 2016 Conference on Empirical Methods in Natural Language Processing*, pages 1526–1534, Austin, Texas. Association for Computational Linguistics.

Laurie A Stowe. 1986. Parsing wh-constructions: Evidence for on-line gap location. *Language and cognitive processes*, 1(3):227–245.

Ian Tenney, Patrick Xia, Berlin Chen, Alex Wang, Adam Poliak, R Thomas McCoy, Najoung Kim, Benjamin Van Durme, Samuel R Bowman, Dipanjan Das, et al. 2018. What do you learn from context? probing for sentence structure in contextualized word representations. In *International Conference on Learning Representations*.

Hugo Touvron, Louis Martin, Kevin Stone, Peter Albert, Amjad Almahairi, Yasmine Babaei, Nikolay Bashlykov, Soumya Batra, Prajjwal Bhargava, Shruti Bhosale, et al. 2023. Llama 2: Open foundation and fine-tuned chat models. *arXiv preprint arXiv:2307.09288*.

Elena Voita and Ivan Titov. 2020. Information-theoretic probing with minimum description length. In *Proceedings of the 2020 Conference on Empirical Methods in Natural Language Processing (EMNLP)*, pages 183–196, Online. Association for Computational Linguistics.

Alex Warstadt, Alicia Parrish, Haokun Liu, Anhad Mohananey, Wei Peng, Sheng-Fu Wang, and Samuel R. Bowman. 2020. BLiMP: A benchmark of linguistic minimal pairs for English. In *Proceedings of the Society for Computation in Linguistics 2020*, pages 409–410, New York, New York. Association for Computational Linguistics.

Leonie Weissweiler, Valentin Hofmann, Anjali Kantharuban, Anna Cai, Ritam Dutt, Amey Hengle, Anubha Kabra, Atharva Kulkarni, Abhishek Vijayakumar, Haofei Yu, Hinrich Schuetze, Kemal Oflazer, and David Mortensen. 2023. Counting the bugs in ChatGPT's wugs: A multilingual investigation into the morphological capabilities of a large language model. In *Proceedings of the 2023 Conference on Empirical Methods in Natural Language Processing*, pages 6508–6524, Singapore. Association for Computational Linguistics.

Marion Weller-Di Marco and Alexander Fraser. 2024. Analyzing the understanding of morphologically complex words in large language models. In *Proceedings of the 2024 Joint International Conference on Computational Linguistics, Language Resources and Evaluation (LREC-COLING 2024)*, pages 1009–1020, Torino, Italy. ELRA and ICCL.

Ethan Gotlieb Wilcox, Richard Futrell, and Roger Levy. 2023. Using computational models to test syntactic learnability. *Linguistic Inquiry*, pages 1–44.

A Details of the classification task

We inflect Finnish nouns in all possible combinations of number, grammatical case, and possessive suffix. Tables 4 and 5 list the classes of case and possessive suffix with examples of both singular and plural forms. We include a possessive suffix in all the forms in our test set.

Short	Name	SG e.g.	PL e.g.
ABE	abessive	talotta	taloitta
ABL	ablative	talolta	taloilta
ADE	adessive	talolla	taloilla
ALL	allative	talolle	taloille
ELA	elative	talosta	taloista
ESS	essive	talona	taloina
GEN	genitive	talon	talojen
ILL	illative	taloon	taloihin
INE	inessive	talossa	taloissa
NOM	nominative	talo	talot
PAR	partitive	taloa	taloja
TRA	translative	taloksi	taloiksi

Table 4: Finnish grammatical cases used in the experiments, with example inflections of the word 'talo' ('house'). There are three more grammatical cases in Finnish (totalling 15), but comitative and instructive are not supported by Omorfi, and accusative does not have its own unambiguous surface form, so these three are not included in our data.

Class	SG e.g. (ELA)	PL e.g. (ELA)
-	talosta	taloista
SG1	talostani	taloistani
SG2	talostasi	taloistasi
PL1	talostamme	taloistamme
PL2	talostanne	taloistanne
3	talostaan, talostansa	taloistaan, taloistansa

Table 5: Possessive suffixes in Finnish, with example inflections of the word 'talo' ('house') with the elative grammatical case 'talosta'. SG1 is 'first person singular', SG2 is 'second person singular' etc. The third person has the same forms in singular and plural, but there are synonyms such as 'talostaan' and 'talostansa'.

B Detailed results

Figures 4 through 13 show the confusion matrices of all models and in all classification tasks. Not all rows sum up to exactly to the same number: for example, in Figure 5 1-shot matrices, the SG row for Llama2 adds up to 964, whereas for Poro it adds up to 962. This is because of ambiguity in the task: for example the form 'taloni' could be singular or plural (if the case is nominative). If the a system gives one of the correct classes, the 'true label' is also assigned to that class in these confusion matrices. If the system predicts incorrectly, the 'true label' could be any of the correct classes (whichever happens to be listed last in our data).

One notable thing in the confusion matrices is that Llama2-70B does not give many nonsense answers: when one or more examples are given in the prompt, the Llama2-70B almost always gives class names, correct or incorrect, which are actual classes, leaving the 'other' column empty in Figures 5, 8, and 12. One reason that this is not the case for the GPT models is probably that GPT-4-turbo and GPT-3.5-turbo have been tuned for chat. In Microsoft Azure docs it is stated that 'Like GPT-3.5 Turbo, and older GPT-4 models, GPT-4 Turbo is optimized for chat and works well for traditional completions tasks.'[2]. GPT-4-turbo therefore often asks for clarification if it doesn't recognise the word, leading to nonsense classifications. Poro, on the other hand, is not tuned for chat, but still gives a lot of 'other' answers. This seems to be more about Poro not grasping the format that the answer should be given in, or simply not knowing which classes are possible answers.

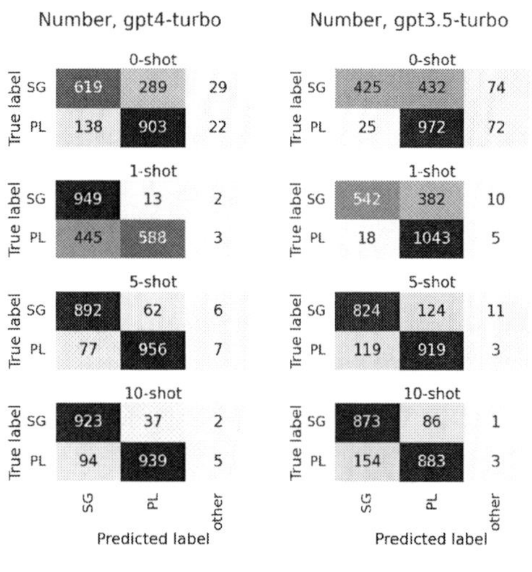

Figure 4: Confusions in the GPT-4-turbo and GPT-3.5-turbo number classification task.

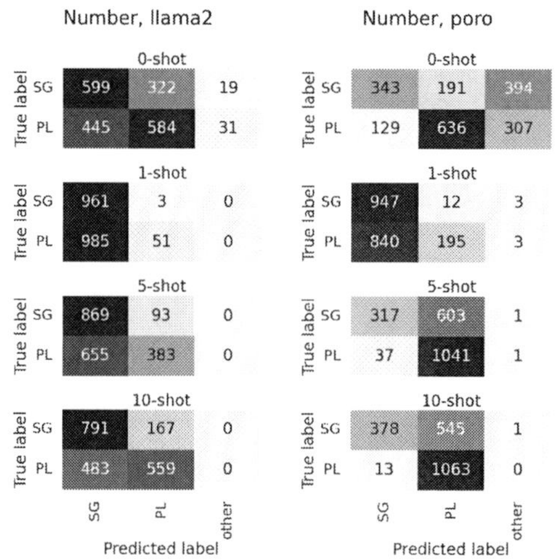

Figure 5: Confusions in the Llama2-70B and Poro-34B number classification task.

[2]https://learn.microsoft.com/en-us/azure/ai-services/openai/concepts/models

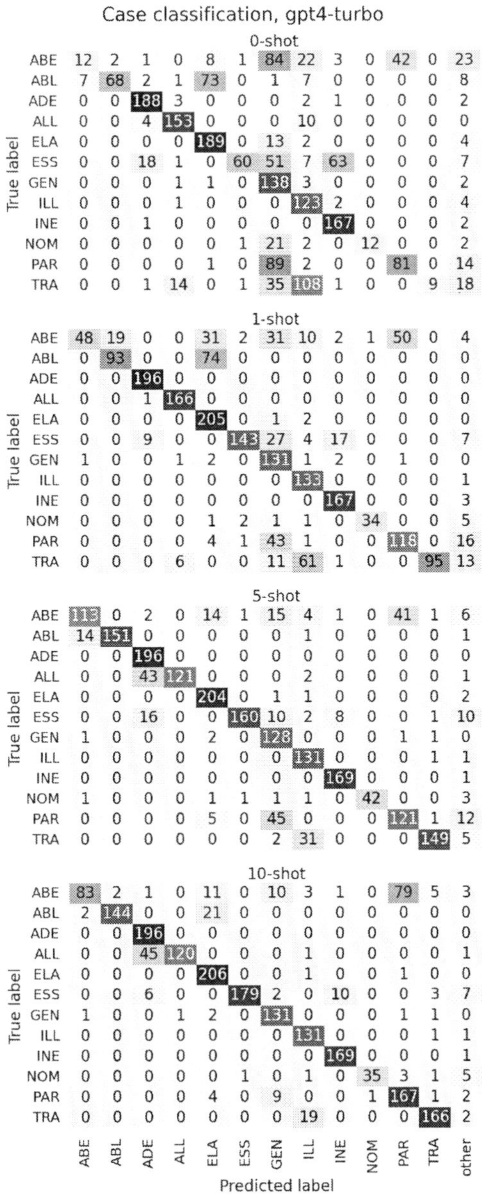

Figure 6: Confusions of GPT-4-turbo in the case classification task.

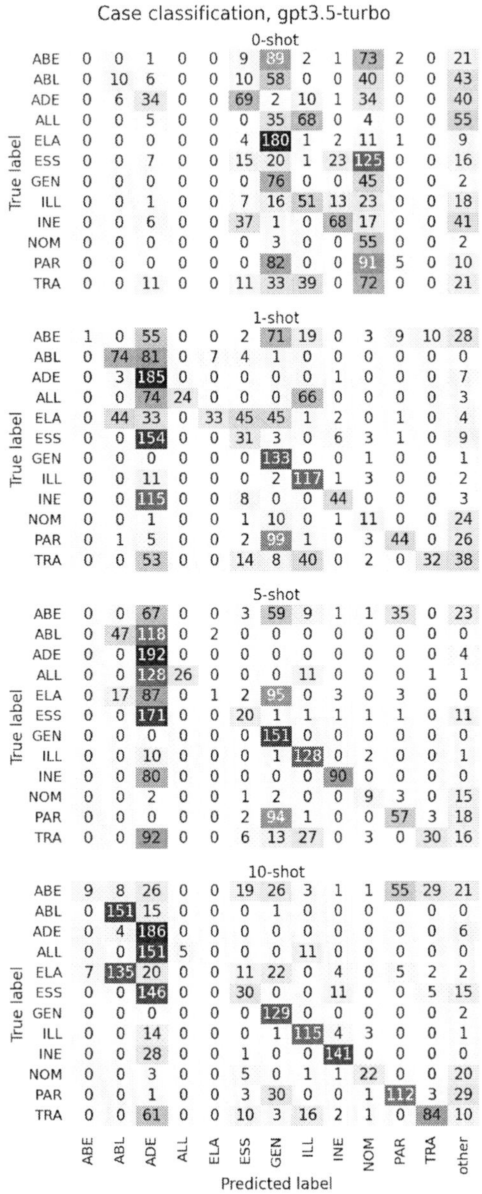

Figure 7: Confusions of GPT-3.5-turbo in the case classification task.

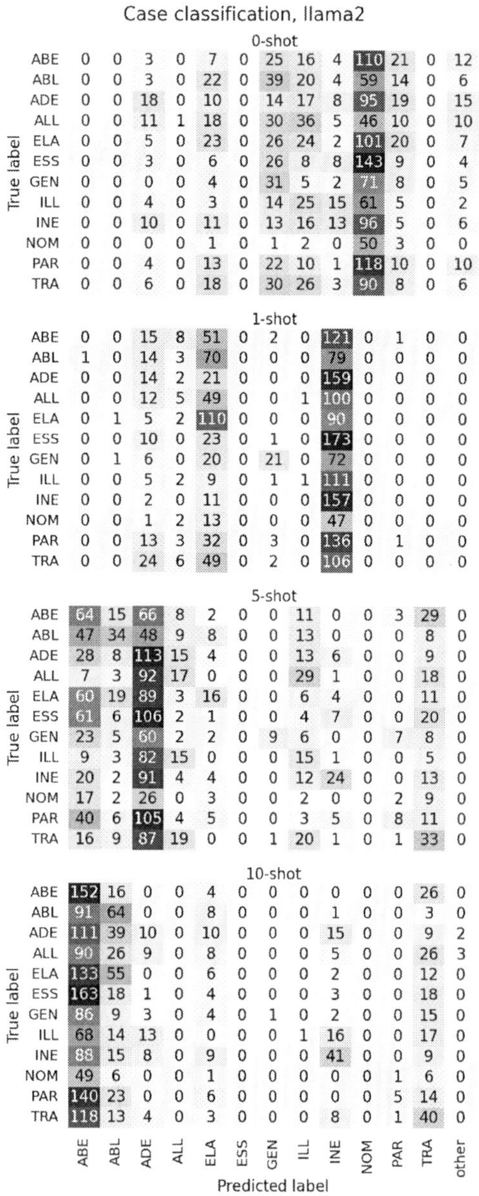

Figure 8: Confusions of Llama2-70B in the case classification task.

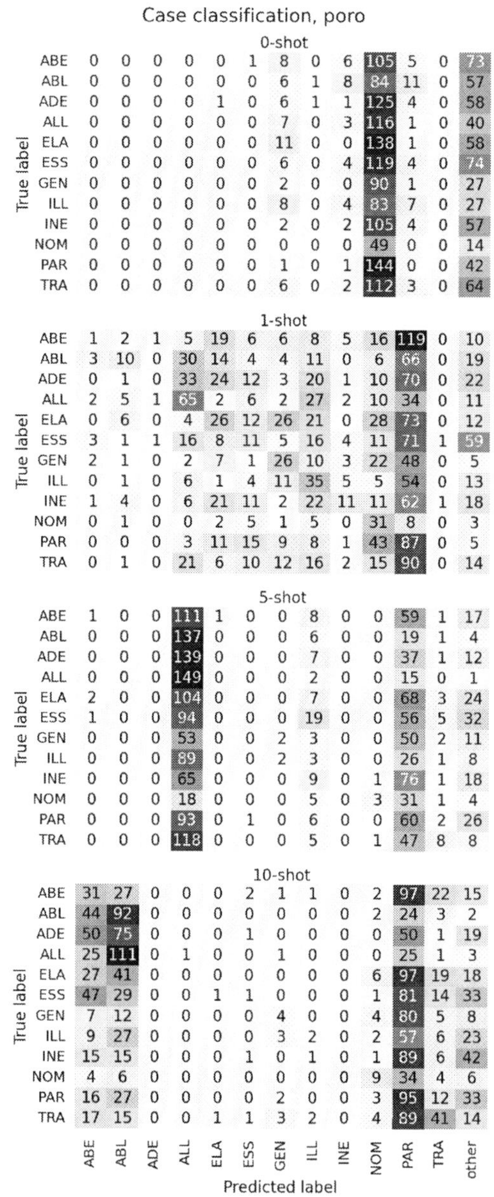

Figure 9: Confusions of Poro-34B in the case classification task.

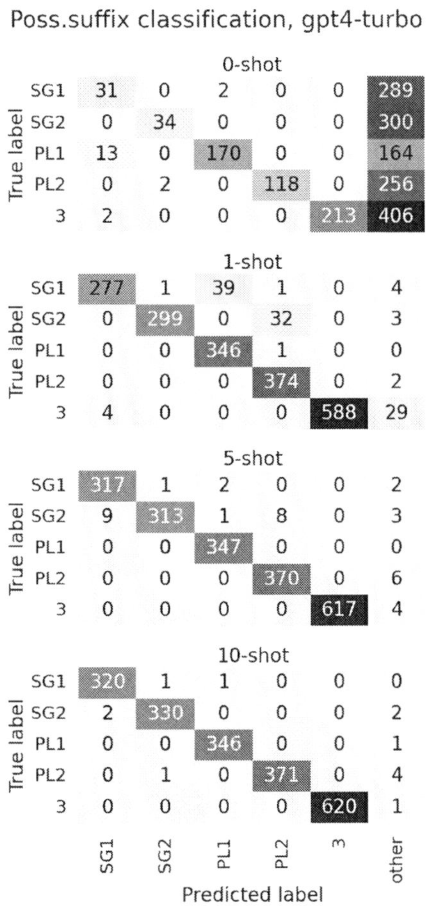

Figure 10: Confusions of GPT-4-turbo in the possessive suffix classification task.

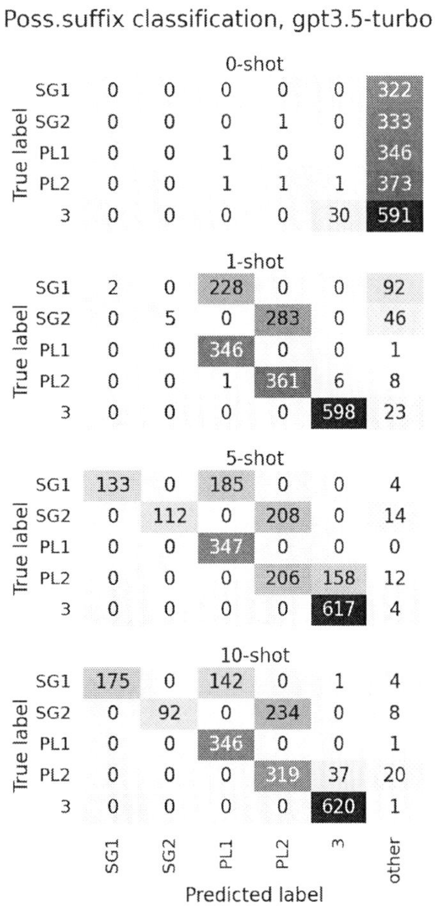

Figure 11: Confusions of GPT-3.5-turbo in the possessive suffix classification task.

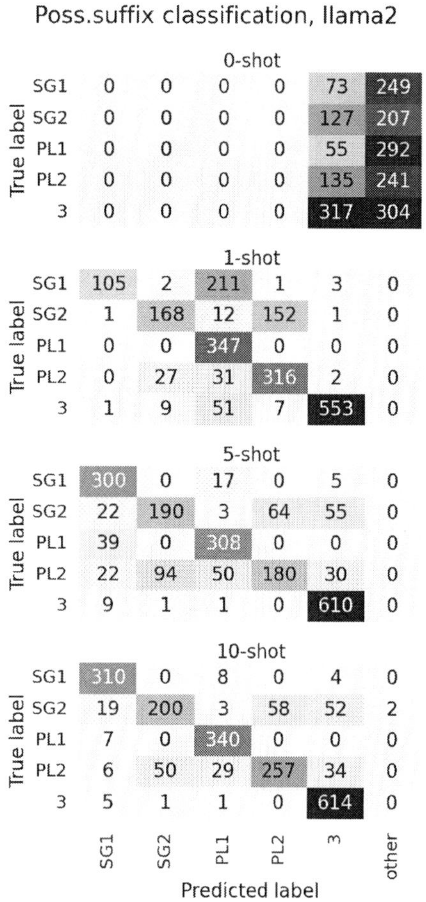

Figure 12: Confusions of Llama2-70B in the possessive suffix classification task.

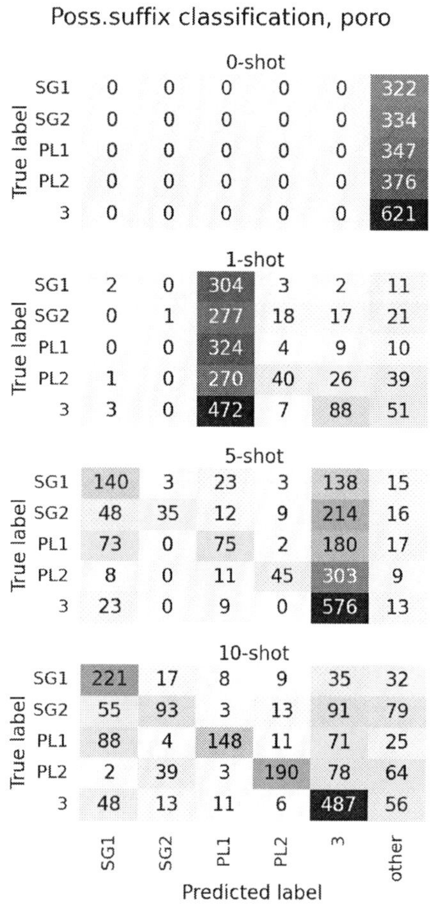

Figure 13: Confusions of Poro-34B in the possessive suffix classification task.

An Eye Opener Regarding Task-Based Text Gradient Saliency

Guojun Wu[1], **Lena S. Bolliger**[1], **David R. Reich**[2,1], **Lena A. Jäger**[1,2]
[1]Department of Computational Linguistics, University of Zurich, Switzerland
[2]Department of Computer Science, University of Potsdam, Germany
guojun.wu@uzh.ch, {bolliger,jaeger}@cl.uzh.ch, david.reich@uni-postdam.de

Abstract

Eye movements in reading reveal humans' cognitive processes involved in language understanding. The duration a reader's eyes fixate on a word has been used as a measure of the visual attention given to that word or its significance to the reader. This study investigates the correlation between the importance attributed to input tokens by language models (LMs) on the one hand and humans, in the form of fixation durations, on the other hand. While previous research on the internal processes of LMs have employed the models' attention weights, recent studies have argued in favor of gradient-based methods. Moreover, previous approaches to interpret LMs' internals with human gaze have neglected the tasks readers performed during reading, even though psycholinguistic research underlines that reading patterns are task-dependent. We therefore employ a gradient-based saliency method to measure the importance of input tokens when LMs are targeted on specific tasks, and we find that task specificity plays a crucial role in the correlation between human- and model-assigned importance. Our implementation is available at `https://github.com/gjwubyron/Scan`.

1 Introduction

Human eye movements during reading reflect cognitive processes involved in language processing (Just and Carpenter, 1980; Rayner, 1998): the fixation duration on a word correlates with reading comprehension (Rayner, 1977; Malmaud et al., 2020a). As such, fixation duration has been employed as proxy of the relative importance of a word to a reader (Hollenstein and Beinborn, 2021).

The introduction of neural attention mechanisms (Bahdanau et al., 2014) and the Transformer architecture (Vaswani et al., 2017), which relies on self-attention to compute input and output representations, has given fresh impetus to research into how language models (LMs) process language. Attention mechanisms assign dynamic weights to input tokens, offering a method to understand a model's internal functioning and decision-making processes (Wang et al., 2016; Ghaeini et al., 2018).

Recent research has compared model and human language comprehension by aligning model attention weights with human reading metrics, such as fixation durations (Sood et al., 2020; Eberle et al., 2022; Bensemann et al., 2022), presuming model attention effectively signifies the relative importance of input tokens. However, the findings are mixed (cf Section 2). While some studies (Sood et al., 2020) observed significant differences between transformer LMs' attention patterns and human fixation patterns, other studies (Eberle et al., 2022; Bensemann et al., 2022) found strong correlations. Besides, research on attention (Jain and Wallace, 2019; Serrano and Smith, 2019; Brunner et al., 2019) has questioned the reliability of attention weights in accurately reflecting token significance.

In contrast, Hollenstein and Beinborn (2021) utilized gradient-based saliency (Simonyan et al., 2014; Li et al., 2016) to approximate relative importance in LMs through iterative token masking and discovered strong correlation between LMs gradient-based saliency and human fixation durations. However, the output space of this approach comprises tens of thousands of tokens, which could make gradient-based saliency uninformative (Yin and Neubig, 2022). Moreover, their work focused on natural reading. Since psycholinguistic studies show that human reading strategies vary with the task and differ from normal reading (Malmaud et al., 2020b; Shubi and Berzak, 2023; Mézière et al., 2023), it is crucial to take task specificity into account.

In this work, we align the LMs with the same tasks performed by human participants during task-specific reading and measure the importance of

Proceedings of the Workshop on Cognitive Modeling and Computational Linguistics, pages 255–263
August 15, 2024

input tokens using gradient-based saliency. Additionally, we expand our analysis to include decoder-based LMs, which, due to their auto-regressive nature, more closely mirror the incremental nature of human processing. We find strong correlations between LMs and humans in this task-specific setting, and further fine-tuning on the task can enhance these correlations.

2 Related Work

Model attention and human attention Research comparing model attention to human visual attention, using fixation locations and durations as proxies, has produced mixed findings. Sood et al. (2020) observed distinct differences between transformer LM attention patterns and human fixation patterns. Conversely, studies by Eberle et al. (2022) and Bensemann et al. (2022) found strong correlations between early transformer layer attention weights, like those in BERT (Devlin et al., 2019), and human visual attention, contrasting with earlier results. This discrepancy can be attributed to methodological differences in processing attention weights: Sood et al. (2020) analyzed maximum attention values from the last layer's sub-word tokens, while Bensemann et al. (2022) averaged attention across sub-word tokens in the first layer.

Limitations of attention-based interpretation The inconsistent results outlined above challenge the usefulness of methods based on model attention to investigate the internals of LMs. Indeed, Brunner et al. (2019) emphasize the lack of token identifiability as one moves to higher layers of a model, and Abnar and Zuidema (2020) show that distinct attention patterns are only found in earlier layers, while in higher layers the attention weights approximate a uniform distribution. Moreover, Jain and Wallace (2019) question whether attention weights can reliably identify the relative importance of inputs to the entire model, showing that different attention distributions yield equivalent model predictions. Similarly, Serrano and Smith (2019) find attention weights to be very noisy indicators of importance. Finally, an analysis of BERT's (Devlin et al., 2019) attention (Clark et al., 2019) reveals a significant focus on the [SEP] token, which does not affect model outputs when its attention is altered, suggesting a"no-op" operation. Similarly, research on attention heads (Voita et al., 2019; Michel et al., 2019) finds that many of them can be pruned with minimal impact, further indicating the potential redundancy or non-operational nature of certain attention mechanisms.

Saliency-based methods for analyzing LMs with human gaze As saliency-based methods are arguably more suited than methods based on attention (Bastings and Filippova, 2020) for model analysis, Hollenstein and Beinborn (2021) extract token importance by iteratively masking each input token, computing the L2 norm of the gradient for the correct output with respect to each token, and then summing all saliency scores for each input token. However, while they do emulate the LM's pre-training objective, this does does not necessarily align with human processing: whereas the model "sees" the input only partially, and as many times as there are tokens, the readers see the input fully and only once. Moreover, the gaze data used in their study was, in parts, recorded while participants were completing a task, such as sentiment analysis and relation extraction (i.e., task-specific reading). In our approach, we thus compute gradients by having the model perform the same kind of classification task that humans performed during reading. Thereby the token importance attributed by both humans and the model refers to the importance within the constraint of a specific task, and the model sees the input only once, and fully.

3 Method

Consider an input sentence, formalized as $\mathbf{x} = \langle x_1, \ldots, x_N \rangle$ of N tokens, where x_j is the jth token (word) in the sentence, and two corresponding token importance vectors of the same length: the *human importance* vector $\mathbf{h} = \langle h_1, \ldots, h_N \rangle$ and the *model importance* vector $\mathbf{m} = \langle m_1, \ldots, m_N \rangle$, where h_j and m_j are the human and model importance attributed to token x_j. We obtain the mean Spearman correlation between model and human importance by computing the by-token Spearman correlations between the vectors $\mathbf{m}$ and $\mathbf{h}$ for all sentences $\mathbf{x}$, then dividing the sum of these correlations by the number of sentences $\mathbf{x}$.

Extracting model importance: gradient-based saliency The *model importance* vector $\mathbf{m}$ consists of gradient saliency values m_j for each input token x_j of the sentence $\mathbf{x}$. "Saliency" refers to neural network interpretation methods that assign an importance distribution over the input in order to analyze a network's prediction (Ding and Koehn, 2021). In other words, saliency methods aim at ex-

	BERT *base*	BERT *large*	RoBERTa	DistilBERT	GPT-2 *base*	GPT-2 *large*	OPT
			Sentiment Analysis (SA)				
fine-tuned	$0.61_{0.010}$	*$0.57_{0.011}$*	*$0.47_{0.012}$*	*$0.53_{0.011}$*	$0.49_{0.011}$	$0.55_{0.010}$	*$0.43_{0.012}$*
pre-trained (0-shot)	$0.55_{0.011}$	$0.59_{0.010}$	$0.45_{0.012}$	$0.52_{0.012}$	$0.4_{0.014}$	$0.48_{0.012}$	$0.42_{0.013}$
random init. (0-shot)	$0.24_{0.013}$	$0.22_{0.013}$	$0.04_{0.014}$	$0.21_{0.013}$	$0.2_{0.014}$	$0.19_{0.014}$	$0.15_{0.015}$
			Relation Extraction (RE)				
fine-tuned	*$0.53_{0.010}$*	$0.52_{0.009}$	$0.42_{0.010}$	$0.45_{0.010}$	$0.46_{0.010}$	$0.52_{0.009}$	$0.5_{0.011}$
pre-trained (0-shot)	$0.51_{0.010}$	$0.47_{0.011}$	$0.37_{0.011}$	$0.49_{0.010}$	$0.37_{0.011}$	$0.45_{0.011}$	$0.42_{0.011}$
random init. (0-shot)	$0.08_{0.011}$	$0.07_{0.011}$	$0.04_{0.012}$	$0.09_{0.011}$	$0.16_{0.013}$	$0.16_{0.013}$	$0.14_{0.014}$

Table 1: We report mean Spearman correlations and standard errors between model and human importance for all models in their *fine-tuned*, *pre-trained (0-shot)*, and *randomly initialized (0-shot)* version, for both tasks SA and RE. The difference in correlations is significant in all cases except for the ones indicated in italic.

plaining how sensitive the decision of a model is to changes in the input. The most common method of assigning this importance distribution is by means of the gradient (Simonyan et al., 2014). Given a parametrized language model f_θ, we compute the gradient g with respect to an input token $x_j \in \mathbf{x}$ as

$$g(x_j) := \frac{\partial f_\theta^c}{\partial x_j}(\mathbf{x}), \tag{1}$$

where c indexes the true class y in the model's output, and f_θ^c refers to the predicted output logit for the true class y. We then follow Li et al. (2016) by defining the gradient saliency m_j of token x_j as the L1 norm of its gradient $m_j := |g(x_j)|$. Since different LMs employ different tokenization methods which split tokens into sub-word tokens (Sennrich et al., 2016; Song et al., 2021), we pool gradients back to token level by summing up the sub-word token-level gradient norms. We then normalize the token-level saliencies by dividing them by the sum of all saliency values in the sentence.

Extracting human importance: relative fixation duration To obtain the *human importance* vector $\mathbf{h}$, we first extract raw total fixation durations $t_{j,r}$ for each token $x_j \in \mathbf{x}$, which is the sum of the durations of all fixations on that token by a reader r. However, due to variations in reading speed across readers and sentences, these raw durations can vary significantly between instances. We thus normalize them by dividing them by the sum of durations across all tokens within a sentence, resulting in *relative fixation durations* $d_{j,r} = t_{j,r} / \sum_j t_{j,r}$ for each token x_j. These relative durations are then averaged across all readers to bypass individual differences and to obtain a more robust signal, resulting in aggregated relative fixation durations $h_j = \sum_r d_{j,r} / |\text{readers}|$ for each token x_j.

4 Experiments

Datasets The eye-tracking part of the *Zurich Cognitive Language Processing Corpus* (ZuCo; Hollenstein et al., 2018) comprises two task-specific readings: in the sentiment analysis (SA) reading, participants were presented with a subset from the *Stanford Sentiment Treebank* (SST; Socher et al., 2013) that consists of movie reviews, based on which they had to rate the movies; in the relation extraction (RE) reading, they performed relation extraction on a subset of sentences from the *Wikipedia relation extraction corpus* (Culotta et al., 2006).

Models and fine-tuning We include both encoder models and decoder models, as well as models from the same family but different in size. Encoders include BERT (Devlin et al., 2019) *base* and *large*, RoBERTa (Liu et al., 2019), and DistilBERT (Sanh et al., 2019); decoders include GPT-2 (Radford et al., 2019) *base* and *large*, and OPT (Zhang et al., 2022). As the models perform classification — ternary for SA, and 9-class for RE —, we utilize the architecture variants implemented for sequence classification in Huggingface (Wolf et al., 2019). For SA, we fine-tune the models on the SST dataset and for RE on the *Wikipedia* dataset (Culotta et al., 2006) , excluding the sentences used for ZuCo SA and RE, respectively.[1]

Baselines. We include two sets of baseline models: the above-mentioned models randomly initialized (*random (0-shot)*), and the models pre-trained but not fine-tuned (*pre-trained (0-shot)*).

Results As depicted in Table 1, the more similar the model's training is to the human task, the more aligned are the model and human importance vectors. There exist medium to strong correlations between the fine-tuned *model importance* and *human*

[1]For training and implementation details as well as classification test results, see Appendix A.

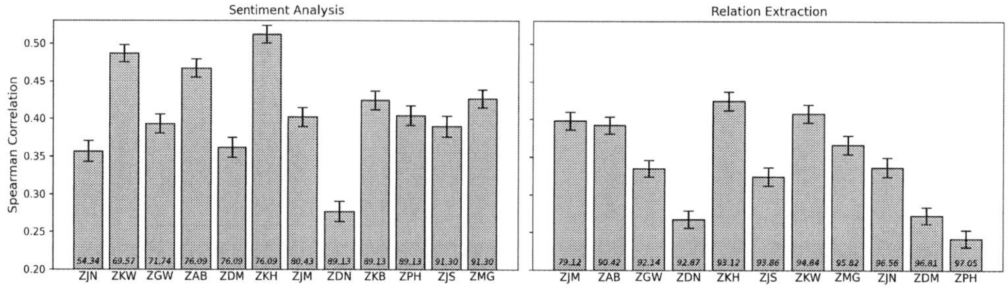

Figure 1: Mean Spearman correlations between relative fixation durations and gradient saliencies for fine-tuned BERT *base* are depicted at the participant level, with error bars denoting the standard error. Participants are arranged according to task accuracy, with their average task accuracies presented at the bottom of each bar.

importance vectors, exemplified by correlations of 0.61 by BERT *base* or 0.55 by GPT-2 *large* for SA. Additionally, most *fine-tuned* models produce significantly higher correlations than the *pre-trained* baselines, and the pre-trained models all have significantly higher correlations than their randomly initialized counterparts. Encoder models, on average, achieve higher correlations than decoders, despite variability within both types. Additionally, SA task model importance correlates more strongly on average than for RE.

5 Participant-level analysis

To investigate whether the models correlate more with certain participants, we perform an additional participant-level analysis in which we compute correlations between the model-extracted saliency values and relative fixation durations for each participant individually. We also extract the participants' response accuracies for both their SA and RE, averaged over sentences. The underlying intuition is that the models possibly correlate more with participants that have a higher task accuracy.

Results The juxtaposition of correlations on participant level and participants' accuracies reveals no discernible pattern, as exemplified by BERT *base* in Figure 1. The correlation coefficients between participants exhibit great variability in both tasks. Participants' task accuracies are distributed across a wide range for SA but exhibit a ceiling effect for RE. Moreover, averaging the participant-level correlations yields lower correlation values than using the aggregate relative fixation durations, e.g., the group-level correlation with BERT *base* is 0.61 and the average on participant-level is 0.41.[2]

[2]An overview of all by-participant accuracies and correlations, for all models can be found in Table 3 in Appendix B.

6 Discussion and Conclusion

The experimental results find medium to strong correlations between model importance vectors, derived from gradient saliencies, and human importance vectors, indicated by relative fixation durations, particularly when language models (LMs) are fine-tuned for tasks mirroring those undertaken by readers: task-specific fine-tuned models demonstrate notably stronger correlations than pre-trained zero-shot baselines. The discrepancy between the pre-trained and randomly initialized models suggests an initial understanding for human importance attribution acquired during pre-training. These findings underline the importance of matching tasks between models and humans for accurate gaze analysis, with task-specificity influencing reading behavior but remaining largely ignored in NLP (Shubi and Berzak, 2023). We further find that SA tasks show consistently higher correlations than RE, possibly due to the complexity introduced by more output classes affecting model predictions. Moreover, initial observations suggest encoders outperform decoders in correlation, potentially due to decoders' unsuitability for classification tasks. Yet, this distinction may be incidental, influenced by factors like pre-training data or model architecture. Surprisingly, BERT *base* yields the highest correlation, while BERT *large* and RoBERTa, who achieve higher test accuracies than BERT, produce lower correlations. This indicates that emulating human importance attribution is neither a function of model parameters nor does it necessarily imply better model performance. The participant-level analysis reveals no distinct pattern, indicating that the models do not mirror the token importance attribution of more proficient humans. Moreover, averaging correlations across individual participants results in a lower correlation value compared to when participant fixation durations are aggregated across sentences. This implies both that by-participant aggregation of relative fixation durations produces a more robust signal, and that models correlate more with average human language processing than with subject-level idiosyncracies.

In conclusion, we have developed a gradient saliency-based method to analyze LMs with human gaze that does not neglect task-specificity and found that mirroring tasks yields higher correlations.

Limitations

First of all, the number of sentences in the eye gaze dataset is quite low, as is the number of readers (which are all L1 English readers based in Zurich, and are not experts in sentiment analysis or relation extraction), which does not make for a representative sample of the population at large.

Relatedly, for a more extensive evaluation of our task-specific approach, one would have to apply it to the same sentences that contain eye movements from natural reading instead of task-specific reading. We leave it to future work to extend the data from ZuCo with eye movements from natural reading.

Moreover, while the studies outlined in Section 2 underline the superiority of gradient-based over attention-based methods, they might still not be the state-of-the-art for explainability methods and one might employ methods such as Integrated Gradients or Layer-wise Relevance Propagation.

Ethics Statement

Working with human data requires careful ethical considerations. The eye-tracking dataset utilized in this study follows ethical standards and has been approved by the responsible ethics committees. It is licensed under the Creative Commons Attribution 4.0 International Public License (CC BY 4.0).

Acknowledgements

We thank the anonymous reviewers for their comments. This work was partially funded by the Swiss National Science Foundation (SNSF) under grant IZCOZ0_220330/1 (EyeNLG), and by the German Federal Ministry of Education and Research under grant 01| S20043 (AEye), and is supported by COST Action MultiplEYE, CA21131, supported by COST (European Cooperation in Science and Technology).

References

Samira Abnar and Willem Zuidema. 2020. Quantifying attention flow in transformers. *arXiv preprint arXiv:2005.00928*.

Dzmitry Bahdanau, Kyunghyun Cho, and Yoshua Bengio. 2014. Neural machine translation by jointly learning to align and translate. *arXiv preprint arXiv:1409.0473*.

Jasmijn Bastings and Katja Filippova. 2020. The elephant in the interpretability room: Why use attention as explanation when we have saliency methods? In *Proceedings of the Third BlackboxNLP Workshop on Analyzing and Interpreting Neural Networks for NLP*, pages 149–155, Online. Association for Computational Linguistics.

Joshua Bensemann, Alex Peng, Diana Benavides-Prado, Yang Chen, Neset Tan, Paul Michael Corballis, Patricia Riddle, and Michael Witbrock. 2022. Eye gaze and self-attention: How humans and transformers attend words in sentences. In *Proceedings of the Workshop on Cognitive Modeling and Computational Linguistics*, pages 75–87, Dublin, Ireland. Association for Computational Linguistics.

Gino Brunner, Yang Liu, Damian Pascual, Oliver Richter, Massimiliano Ciaramita, and Roger Wattenhofer. 2019. On identifiability in transformers. *arXiv preprint arXiv:1908.04211*.

Kevin Clark, Urvashi Khandelwal, Omer Levy, and Christopher D. Manning. 2019. What does BERT look at? an analysis of BERT's attention. In *Proceedings of the 2019 ACL Workshop BlackboxNLP: Analyzing and Interpreting Neural Networks for NLP*, pages 276–286, Florence, Italy. Association for Computational Linguistics.

Aron Culotta, Andrew McCallum, and Jonathan Betz. 2006. Integrating probabilistic extraction models and data mining to discover relations and patterns in text. In *Proceedings of the Human Language Technology Conference of the NAACL, Main Conference*, pages 296–303.

Jacob Devlin, Ming-Wei Chang, Kenton Lee, and Kristina Toutanova. 2019. Bert: Pre-training of deep bidirectional transformers for language understanding.

Shuoyang Ding and Philipp Koehn. 2021. Evaluating saliency methods for neural language models. In *Proceedings of the 2021 Conference of the North American Chapter of the Association for Computational Linguistics: Human Language Technologies*, pages 5034–5052, Online. Association for Computational Linguistics.

Oliver Eberle, Stephanie Brandl, Jonas Pilot, and Anders Søgaard. 2022. Do transformer models show similar attention patterns to task-specific human gaze? In *Proceedings of the 60th Annual Meeting of the Association for Computational Linguistics (Volume 1: Long Papers)*, pages 4295–4309, Dublin, Ireland. Association for Computational Linguistics.

Reza Ghaeini, Xiaoli Fern, and Prasad Tadepalli. 2018. Interpreting recurrent and attention-based neural models: a case study on natural language inference. In *Proceedings of the 2018 Conference on Empirical Methods in Natural Language Processing*, pages 4952–4957, Brussels, Belgium. Association for Computational Linguistics.

Nora Hollenstein and Lisa Beinborn. 2021. Relative importance in sentence processing. In *Proceedings of the 59th Annual Meeting of the Association for Computational Linguistics and the 11th International Joint Conference on Natural Language Processing (Volume 2: Short Papers)*, pages 141–150, Online. Association for Computational Linguistics.

Nora Hollenstein, Jonathan Rotsztejn, Marius Troendle, Andreas Pedroni, Ce Zhang, and Nicolas Langer. 2018. ZuCo, a simultaneous EEG and eye-tracking resource for natural sentence reading. *Scientific Data*, 5:180291.

Sarthak Jain and Byron C. Wallace. 2019. Attention is not explanation.

Marcel A Just and Patricia A Carpenter. 1980. A theory of reading: From eye fixations to comprehension. *Psychological Review*, 87(4):329.

Jiwei Li, Xinlei Chen, Eduard Hovy, and Dan Jurafsky. 2016. Visualizing and understanding neural models in NLP. In *Proceedings of the 2016 Conference of the North American Chapter of the Association for Computational Linguistics: Human Language Technologies*, pages 681–691, San Diego, California. Association for Computational Linguistics.

Yinhan Liu, Myle Ott, Naman Goyal, Jingfei Du, Mandar Joshi, Danqi Chen, Omer Levy, Mike Lewis, Luke Zettlemoyer, and Veselin Stoyanov. 2019. Roberta: A robustly optimized bert pretraining approach. *arXiv preprint arXiv:1907.11692*.

Ilya Loshchilov and Frank Hutter. 2019. Decoupled weight decay regularization. In *International Conference on Learning Representations*.

Jonathan Malmaud, Roger Levy, and Yevgeni Berzak. 2020a. Bridging information-seeking human gaze and machine reading comprehension. *arXiv preprint arXiv:2009.14780*.

Jonathan Malmaud, Roger Levy, and Yevgeni Berzak. 2020b. Bridging information-seeking human gaze and machine reading comprehension. In *Proceedings of the 24th Conference on Computational Natural Language Learning*, pages 142–152, Online. Association for Computational Linguistics.

Diane C Mézière, Lili Yu, Erik D Reichle, Titus Von Der Malsburg, and Genevieve McArthur. 2023. Using eye-tracking measures to predict reading comprehension. *Reading Research Quarterly*, 58(3):425–449.

Paul Michel, Omer Levy, and Graham Neubig. 2019. Are sixteen heads really better than one?

Adam Paszke, Sam Gross, Francisco Massa, Adam Lerer, James Bradbury, Gregory Chanan, Trevor Killeen, Zeming Lin, Natalia Gimelshein, Luca Antiga, Alban Desmaison, Andreas Kopf, Edward Yang, Zachary DeVito, Martin Raison, Alykhan Tejani, Sasank Chilamkurthy, Benoit Steiner, Lu Fang, Junjie Bai, and Soumith Chintala. 2019. Pytorch: An imperative style, high-performance deep learning library. In *Advances in Neural Information Processing Systems*, volume 32, pages 8024–8035. Curran Associates, Inc.

Alec Radford, Jeffrey Wu, Rewon Child, David Luan, Dario Amodei, Ilya Sutskever, et al. 2019. Language models are unsupervised multitask learners. *OpenAI blog*, 1(8):9.

Keith Rayner. 1977. Visual attention in reading: Eye movements reflect cognitive processes. *Memory & cognition*, 5(4):443–448.

Keith Rayner. 1998. Eye movements in reading and information processing: 20 years of research. *Psychological Bulletin*, 124(3):372–422.

Victor Sanh, Lysandre Debut, Julien Chaumond, and Thomas Wolf. 2019. Distilbert, a distilled version of bert: smaller, faster, cheaper and lighter. *arXiv preprint arXiv:1910.01108*.

Rico Sennrich, Barry Haddow, and Alexandra Birch. 2016. Neural machine translation of rare words with subword units. In *Proceedings of the 54th Annual Meeting of the Association for Computational Linguistics (Volume 1: Long Papers)*, pages 1715–1725, Berlin, Germany. Association for Computational Linguistics.

Sofia Serrano and Noah A. Smith. 2019. Is attention interpretable? In *Proceedings of the 57th Annual Meeting of the Association for Computational Linguistics*, pages 2931–2951, Florence, Italy. Association for Computational Linguistics.

Omer Shubi and Yevgeni Berzak. 2023. Eye movements in information-seeking reading. In *Proceedings of the Annual Meeting of the Cognitive Science Society*, volume 45.

Karen Simonyan, Andrea Vedaldi, and Andrew Zisserman. 2014. Deep inside convolutional networks: Visualising image classification models and saliency maps.

Richard Socher, Alex Perelygin, Jean Wu, Jason Chuang, Christopher D Manning, Andrew Y Ng, and Christopher Potts. 2013. Recursive deep models for semantic compositionality over a sentiment treebank. In *Proceedings of the 2013 conference on empirical methods in natural language processing*, pages 1631–1642.

Xinying Song, Alex Salcianu, Yang Song, Dave Dopson, and Denny Zhou. 2021. Fast WordPiece tokenization. In *Proceedings of the 2021 Conference on Empirical Methods in Natural Language Processing*, pages 2089–2103, Online and Punta Cana, Dominican Republic. Association for Computational Linguistics.

Ekta Sood, Simon Tannert, Diego Frassinelli, Andreas Bulling, and Ngoc Thang Vu. 2020. Interpreting attention models with human visual attention in machine reading comprehension.

Ashish Vaswani, Noam Shazeer, Niki Parmar, Jakob Uszkoreit, Llion Jones, Aidan N Gomez, Ł ukasz Kaiser, and Illia Polosukhin. 2017. Attention is all you need. In *Advances in Neural Information Processing Systems*, volume 30. Curran Associates,

Inc.

Elena Voita, David Talbot, Fedor Moiseev, Rico Sennrich, and Ivan Titov. 2019. Analyzing multi-head self-attention: Specialized heads do the heavy lifting, the rest can be pruned. In *Proceedings of the 57th Annual Meeting of the Association for Computational Linguistics*, pages 5797–5808, Florence, Italy. Association for Computational Linguistics.

Yequan Wang, Minlie Huang, Xiaoyan Zhu, and Li Zhao. 2016. Attention-based LSTM for aspect-level sentiment classification. In *Proceedings of the 2016 Conference on Empirical Methods in Natural Language Processing*, pages 606–615, Austin, Texas. Association for Computational Linguistics.

Thomas Wolf, Lysandre Debut, Victor Sanh, Julien Chaumond, Clement Delangue, Anthony Moi, Pierric Cistac, Tim Rault, Rémi Louf, Morgan Funtowicz, et al. 2019. Huggingface's transformers: State-of-the-art natural language processing. *arXiv preprint arXiv:1910.03771*.

Kayo Yin and Graham Neubig. 2022. Interpreting language models with contrastive explanations.

Susan Zhang, Stephen Roller, Naman Goyal, Mikel Artetxe, Moya Chen, Shuohui Chen, Christopher Dewan, Mona Diab, Xian Li, Xi Victoria Lin, et al. 2022. Opt: Open pre-trained transformer language models. *arXiv preprint arXiv:2205.01068*.

Appendices

A Fine-Tuning Details

We fine-tune the models outlined in Section 3 on the SST (Socher et al., 2013) dataset for ternary sentiment classification, excluding the sentences used for ZuCo SA, and on the *Wikipedia* dataset (Culotta et al., 2006) for 9-class relation classification, excluding the sentences used for ZuCo RE. After excluding sentences from ZuCo SA and RE, we are left with 5211 sentences allocated for SA and 889 sentences allocated for RE. Subsequently, we implement an 80/20 split for training and validation. For testing, there are 400 sentences from ZuCo SA and 335 sentences from ZuCo RE [3]. We train the models for 10 epochs, with an early stopping patience of 3 epochs, using the AdamW (Loshchilov and Hutter, 2019) optimizer, a learning rate of $2 * 10^{-5}$, and a batch size of 16. All models are implemented in PyTorch (Paszke et al., 2019).

	BERT *base*	BERT *large*	RoBERTa	DistilBERT	GPT-2 *base*	GPT-2 *large*	OPT
SA	75.3	76.5	82.8	75.0	71.8	77.8	73.8
RE	57.9	61.2	57.9	60.9	53.1	56.1	55.2

Table 2: We report the accuracy of fine-tuning the models on the SST (Socher et al., 2013) for sentiment analysis (SA) and on the *Wikipedia* dataset (Culotta et al., 2006) for relation extraction (RE). In both cases, the ZuCo SA and RE sentences are excluded from the training data; the models are tested on the ZuCo sentences for SA and RE.

B Participant-Level Analysis

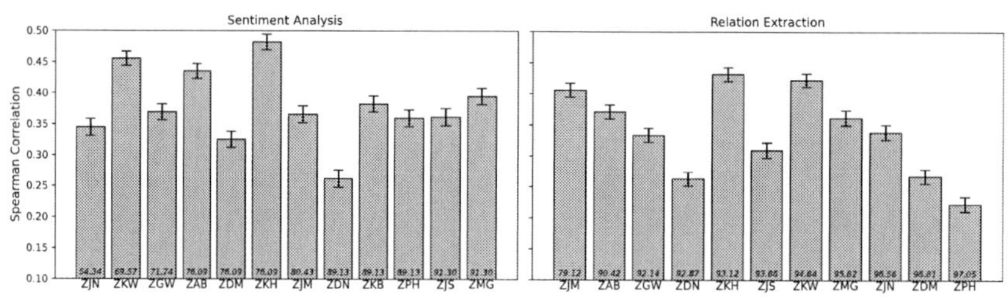

(a) BERT *large*

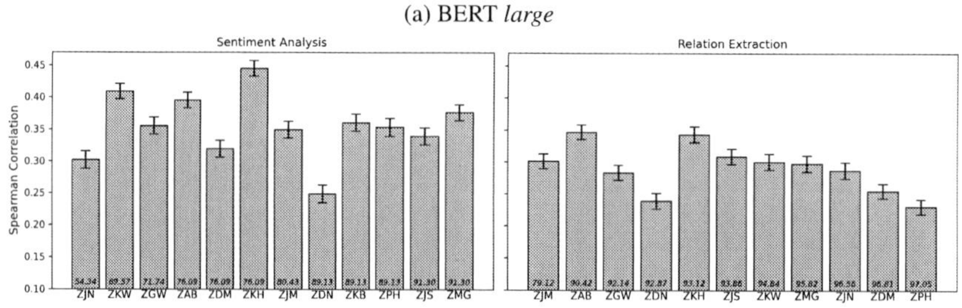

(b) DistilBERT

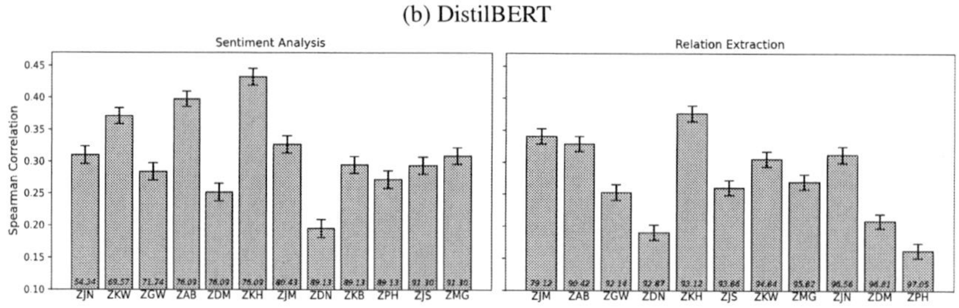

(c) RoBERTa

[3]Out of the original 407 sentences in ZuCo RE, we retain only 335 sentences that contain a specific relation.

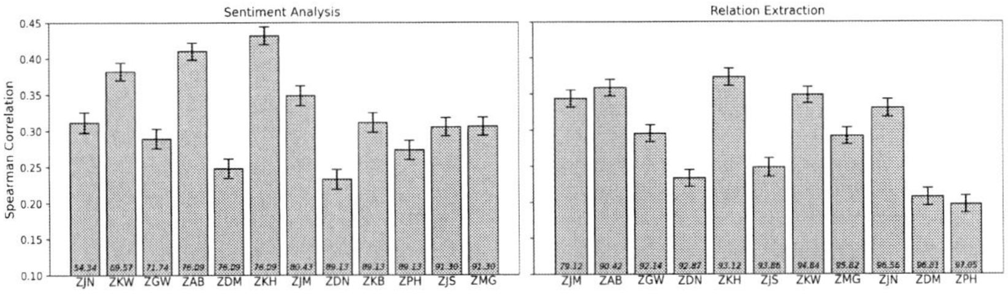

(d) GPT-2 *base*

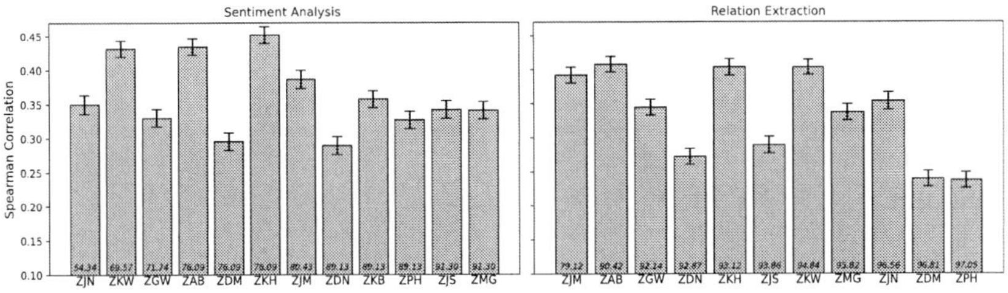

(e) GPT-2 *large*

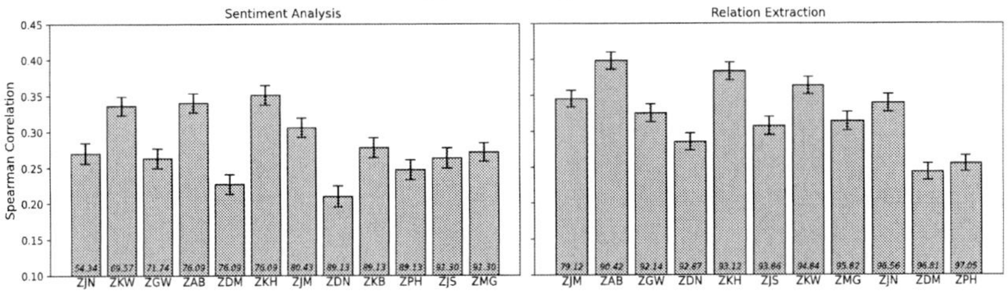

(f) OPT

Figure 2: Spearman correlations between relative fixation durations and gradient saliencies for various models are depicted at the participant level, including standard error. Participants are arranged according to task accuracy, with their accuracy values presented at the bottom of each bar.

	ZAB	ZDM	ZDN	ZGW	ZJM	ZJN	ZJS	ZKB	ZKH	ZKW	ZMG	ZPH	avg
						Sentiment Analysis (SA)							
Task acc	76.09	76.09	89.13	71.74	80.43	54.34	91.3	89.13	76.09	69.57	91.3	89.13	79.53
BERT *base*	0.47	0.36	0.28	0.39	0.40	0.36	0.39	0.42	0.51	0.49	0.43	0.40	0.41
BERT *large*	0.44	0.33	0.26	0.37	0.37	0.34	0.36	0.38	0.48	0.46	0.39	0.36	0.38
DistilBERT	0.40	0.32	0.25	0.36	0.35	0.30	0.34	0.36	0.44	0.41	0.38	0.35	0.35
RoBERTa	0.4	0.25	0.2	0.28	0.33	0.31	0.29	0.3	0.43	0.37	0.31	0.27	0.31
GPT-2 *base*	0.41	0.25	0.23	0.29	0.35	0.31	0.31	0.31	0.43	0.38	0.31	0.27	0.32
GPT-2 *large*	0.43	0.3	0.29	0.33	0.39	0.35	0.34	0.36	0.45	0.43	0.34	0.33	0.36
OPT	0.34	0.23	0.21	0.26	0.31	0.27	0.26	0.28	0.35	0.34	0.27	0.25	0.28
						Relation Extraction (RE)							
Task acc	90.42	96.81	92.87	92.14	79.12	96.56	93.86	95.33	93.12	94.84	95.82	97.05	93.16
BERT *base*	0.39	0.27	0.27	0.34	0.40	0.34	0.32	–	0.42	0.41	0.37	0.24	0.34
BERT *large*	0.37	0.27	0.26	0.33	0.41	0.34	0.31	–	0.43	0.42	0.36	0.22	0.34
DistilBERT	0.35	0.25	0.24	0.28	0.30	0.29	0.31	–	0.34	0.30	0.30	0.23	0.29
RoBERTa	0.33	0.21	0.19	0.25	0.34	0.31	0.26	–	0.38	0.31	0.27	0.16	0.27
GPT-2 *base*	0.36	0.21	0.23	0.30	0.34	0.33	0.25	–	0.37	0.35	0.29	0.20	0.29
GPT-2 *large*	0.41	0.24	0.27	0.34	0.39	0.35	0.29	–	0.4	0.4	0.34	0.24	0.33
OPT	0.4	0.24	0.29	0.33	0.35	0.34	0.31	–	0.38	0.36	0.31	0.25	0.32

Table 3: The participants' task accuracy and their Spearman correlations with the LMs are reported. There is a lack of correlations for one participant in the RE task because of a pre-processing issue with the eye-tracking data.

Improving Language Models for Emotion Analysis: Insights from Cognitive Science

Constant Bonard
University of Bern, Institute of Philosophy, Hochschulstrasse 4, 3012 Berne, Suisse
constant.bonard@gmail.com

Gustave Cortal
Université Paris-Saclay, ENS Paris-Saclay, CNRS, LMF, 91190, Gif-sur-Yvette, France
Université Paris-Saclay, CNRS, LISN, 91400, Orsay, France
gcortal@ens-paris-saclay.fr

Abstract

We propose leveraging cognitive science research on emotions and communication to improve language models for emotion analysis. First, we present the main emotion theories in psychology and cognitive science. Then, we introduce the main methods of emotion annotation in natural language processing and their connections to psychological theories. We also present the two main types of analyses of emotional communication in cognitive pragmatics. Finally, based on the cognitive science research presented, we propose directions for improving language models for emotion analysis. We suggest that these research efforts pave the way for constructing new annotation schemes, methods, and a possible benchmark for emotional understanding, considering different facets of human emotion and communication.

1 Introduction

Emotion analysis in natural language processing aims to develop computational models capable of discerning human emotions in text. Recently, language models have been widely used to solve various tasks in natural language processing, including emotion analysis (Devlin et al., 2019; Brown et al., 2020). This field of research faces several limitations. First, different ways of conceptualizing emotions lead to different annotation schemes and datasets (Klinger, 2023). As a result, the generalization ability of models is limited, and it is often impossible to compare studies. To address these limitations, it has been proposed to unify some annotation schemes based on the semantic proximity of emotion categories (Bostan and Klinger, 2018), to automatically find emotion categories from data (De Bruyne et al., 2020), or to obtain emotion embeddings independent of annotation schemes (Buechel et al., 2021). Inspired by psychology and cognitive science research, we believe building an annotation scheme unifying different perspectives on the emotional phenomenon would be possible and desirable.

In addition, existing benchmarks evaluate certain aspects of emotional understanding but do not consider its full complexity (Campagnano et al., 2022; Zhang et al., 2023a; Paech, 2024). For example, Paech (2024) proposes to evaluate the emotional understanding of language models by predicting the intensity of emotions in conflict scenes. This type of evaluation is too limited: benchmarks should reflect as much as possible the richness of emotional understanding in humans, a richness documented in different branches of affective sciences (Green, 2007; Wharton, 2016; Scarantino, 2017; Barrett et al., 2019; Bonard and Deonna, 2023).

Another related research area focuses on the theory of mind of language models, *i.e.*, their ability to correctly attribute mental states to others. In our view, this literature is promising in that it links recent developments in language models to theories and empirical methods in cognitive science (for a review, see Bonard (2024, section 5)). Notably, several tasks and benchmarks have been developed to measure the ability of language models to succeed at different versions of the False Belief Task (Trott et al., 2022; Aru et al., 2023; Gandhi et al., 2023; Holterman and van Deemter, 2023; Kosinski, 2023; Mitchell and Krakauer, 2023; Shapira et al., 2023; Stojnić et al., 2023; Ullman, 2023). However, theory of mind and, more generally, social reasoning abilities go beyond the ability to succeed at the False Belief Task (Apperly and Butterfill, 2009; Langley et al., 2022; Ma et al., 2023). The ability to correctly interpret expressed emotions cannot be reduced to it. The degree to which language models possess this emotional competence is worth studying in its own right.

Generally speaking, research on language mod-

[*] The authors contributed equally and are listed in alphabetical order.

Proceedings of the Workshop on Cognitive Modeling and Computational Linguistics, pages 264–277
August 15, 2024

els for emotion analysis would benefit from cognitive science research on emotion and communication. In particular, we believe this approach can lead to better ways of annotating emotions expressed in text. Additionally, it can improve the evaluation of the emotional understanding of language models by developing new benchmarks. In what follows, we present an overview of psychological theories of emotion (section 2) and ways of annotating emotions in natural language processing (section 3). Then, inspired by specific psychological and linguistic theories (section 4), we propose research directions to address some of the current limitations of emotion analysis (section 5).

Contributions. We propose integrating different cognitive science theories on emotion with NLP research. We explain why and how emotion analysis should use research from cognitive pragmatics, specifically what we call "the detective analysis", to improve automatic emotion analysis. We suggest that these points lead both to devising a new annotation scheme and improving how language models should be evaluated for emotion analysis.

2 Emotion Theories in Cognitive Science

This section will present the three main emotion theories in psychology to provide a background for connecting emotion analysis in natural language processing with cognitive science.

Basic emotion theory. Basic emotion theory is certainly the most influential today. Inspired by Darwin's research on emotions (Darwin, 1872), it postulates a certain number of discrete, basic emotions that are universal and innate among humans due to their evolutionary origins. Emotions are understood as psycho-physiological "programs" that were naturally selected to help overcome recurrent evolutionary challenges (Cosmides and Tooby, 2000). A prominent version is that of Paul Ekman (Ekman, 1999), who sought to show, as Darwin envisaged, that some emotions are expressed with the same facial expressions across cultures – Ekman used Darwin's (Darwin, 1872) list of six "core" expressions of emotions: anger, fear, surprise, disgust, happiness, and sadness. He notably conducted studies with individuals having no exposure to Western culture, indicating that they could accurately identify facial expressions for these six emotions (Ekman and Friesen, 1971). It should be noted that Ekman left it open how many basic emotions there are. Besides the six emotions listed, candidates include amusement, contempt, embarrassment, guilt, pride, and shame (Ekman, 1999). Other versions of basic emotion theory have different lists (Tomkins, 1962; Izard, 1992; Panksepp, 1998; Plutchik, 2001). For a discussion of the evidence supportive of basic emotion theory, notably the potential physiological and neurological signatures of basic emotions, see Moors (2022, 129—131).

Psychological constructivism. Psychological constructivism is the most influential alternative to basic emotion theory today. It rejects that there are discrete, basic emotions universally shared by humans and posits instead that emotion kinds such as anger, fear, and joy are constructed through the interplay of biological, psychological, and sociocultural factors. Early proponents include Schachter and Singer (1962), but its main representatives are James Russell and Lisa Feldman Barrett (Russell and Barrett, 1999). Psychological constructivists focus on the feeling component of emotions that they interpret as a continuum with no categorical barriers. Feelings are typically represented in a two-dimensional space with a valence axis (pleasant–unpleasant feelings) and an arousal axis (feelings of activation–deactivation). The impression that there are discrete emotions is seen as a social construct: different forms of enculturation yield different ways to conceptualize or label our bodily feelings into discrete emotional kinds. For a discussion of the evidence supportive of psychological constructivism, see Moors (2022, 261—265). Some evidence comes from so-called "arousal misattribution" studies, i.e. cases where subjects misinterpret the source of their arousal and where that seems to influence what emotions they undergo.

Appraisal theory. The third major psychological theory of emotion is appraisal theory, whose empirical version was pioneered by Magda Arnold (Arnold, 1960). It was developed to explain the absence of a bijective, one–to–one correspondence between kinds of emotions and emotional stimuli, *i.e.*, the fact that the same kind of stimuli triggers different emotions and that different kinds of stimuli trigger the same kind of emotion. To explain this fact, appraisals are postulated as mediators between stimuli and emotional reactions. Appraisals are cognitive evaluations (unconscious, fast, and error-prone) of the relevance of stimuli given one's concerns and how one should react. Appraisal theory hypothesizes that, for instance, Sam is fearful of the mouse in the kitchen because he appraises it as an imminent threat to his safety, while Maria, on the other, is angry that there is a mouse in the kitchen because she appraises it as an intruder to be kicked out. Thus, each emotion kind can be analyzed by the associated appraisal. For instance, Lazarus (1991) proposes *imminent danger* for fear, *demeaning offense* for anger, *irrevocable loss* for sadness, and *progress towards a goal* for happiness.

In the 1980s, appraisal theorists started to analyze appraisals as regions in a multi-dimensional space (Moors et al., 2013). Appraisal dimensions typically include (a) the goal-conduciveness of the stimulus, (b) the coping potential of the individual in the situation, (c) the urgency of the needed response, (d) the cause of the eliciting event (me, others, intentional or not), and (e) the compatibility with one's normative standards. For instance, fear is triggered by an appraisal of a stimulus as (a) highly inconducive, (b) hard to cope with, and (c) requiring an urgent response. For a discussion of the evidence supportive of appraisal theory, see Moors (2022, 190—196). Most evidence comes from self-report studies where participants are asked to recall instances of emotions and to rate these in terms of appraisal variables. Other evidence comes from manipulating appraisal dimensions and measuring associated emotions (*e.g.*, in a video-game setting) or from neurological predictions about correlations between brain activations and appraisal dimensions.

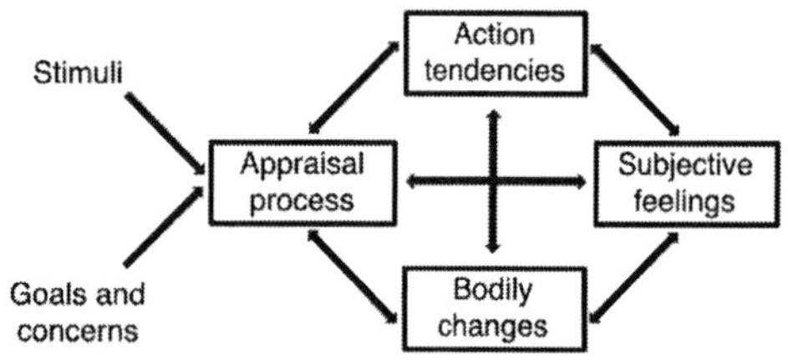

Figure 1: The integrated framework for emotion theories. Rectangles represent the four components constituting an emotional episode, and arrows represent causation. Adapted from Scherer and Moors (2019).

An integrated framework for emotion theories. Though the three theories reviewed are usually considered rivals, some have argued for their integration (Scherer and Moors, 2019; Bonard, 2021b; Scherer, 2022). Arguably, the three theories differ mainly in their focus. Basic emotion theory focuses on the universal traits inherited from evolution, particularly their physiological and bodily expressions. Psychological constructivism focuses on the dimensions of feeling and how individuals categorize them. Appraisal theory focuses on emotional elicitation and action tendencies. We believe that a framework integrating the various elements studied by these theories is possible and desirable. What we call "the integrated framework for emotion theories" proposes to do so by postulating that paradigmatic emotional episodes are made of synchronized and causally interconnected changes in four components: appraisal process, action tendencies, bodily changes (motor expressions and physiological responses), and subjective feelings. For a discussion of this integrated framework, see Scherer (2022).

3 Emotion Analysis in Text

3.1 How is emotion annotated in text?

Emotion is a category. Textual emotion analysis relies on basic emotion theories to define different emotion categories to associate with textual units (a textual span, a sentence, or a document). For instance, the sentence "I love philosophy." could automatically be associated with the discrete emotion *happiness*. Several annotation schemes focus on subsets of categories while others encompass a broader set, reaching over 28 different categories (Demszky et al., 2020; Bostan and Klinger, 2018).

Emotion is a continuous value with affective meaning. Instead of representing emotion as a category, some annotation schemes consider emotion as a point in a multidimensional space, associating continuous values with textual units (Buechel and Hahn, 2017). These dimensions carry an affective meaning. Two dimensions dominate the literature and stem from psychological constructivism, which considers, as we have seen, that an emotion can be characterized by its degree of *pleasantness* and its degree of *arousal*. Thus, the sentence "His voice soothes me." could be automatically associated with two continuous values: a degree of *pleasantness* of 4 out of 5 and a degree of *arousal* of 1 out of 5.

Emotion is a continuous value with cognitive meaning. These dimensions can also carry a cognitive meaning. Recently, a new line of research proposes incorporating appraisal theories into emotion analysis models (Hofmann et al., 2020; Troiano et al., 2022; Zhan et al., 2023). From this perspective, emotions are caused by events evaluated according to several cognitive dimensions. For example, the sentence "I received a surprise gift." could be automatically associated with several continuous values: the event is *sudden* (4 out of 5), *contrary to social norms* (0 out of 5), and the person has *control* over the event (0 out of 5).

Emotion consists of semantic roles. An emotion cannot be reduced to a category or continuous values with affective or cognitive meaning. To better understand an emotional event, several approaches associate spans of text with semantic roles, such as *cause*, *target*, *experiencer*, and *cue* of the emotion (Lee et al., 2010; Kim and Klinger, 2018; Bostan et al., 2020; Oberländer et al., 2020; Campagnano et al., 2022; Wegge et al., 2023; Cortal, 2024). Thus, instead of considering emotion as caused by an event, semantic role labeling of emotions considers that emotion *is* an event (Klinger, 2023) that must be reconstructed by answering the question: "Who (*experiencer*) feels what (*cue*) towards whom (*target*) and why (*cause*)?". In this example, each text span can be associated with a semantic role: "Louise (*experiencer*) was angry (*cue*) at Paul (*target*) because he did not warn her (*cause*)."

Emotion is a refined feeling. Sentiment analysis, a fundamental task in natural language processing, is sometimes considered a simplified version of emotion analysis. In its most basic form, sentiment analysis associates textual units with a category indicating a polarity (*positive* or *negative*) (Poria et al., 2020). A finer-grained task identifies aspects of a product or topic and determines the sentiment expressed about each of these aspects (Zhang et al., 2022). For example, in the sentence "The battery life of this phone is amazing, but its camera quality is disappointing.", the sentiment is *positive* for the aspect "battery life" and is *negative* for the aspect "camera quality."

3.2 Limitations

No unified annotation scheme. Divergences in the psychological definition of emotion lead to divergences in how emotion is annotated in the text. Psychological theories of emotions represent different perspectives on the emotional phenomenon. However, these perspectives are not as contradictory as they seem and may even tend towards unification (section 2). We believe this is also the case for annotation schemes in emotion analysis. In section 5, we provide directions for constructing a unified annotation scheme inspired by recent debates in psychology (Scherer, 2022).

Emotion verbalization is overlooked. Emotion analysis rarely considers the process of emotion verbalization. As a result, it is difficult to obtain annotation guides that clearly define the linguistic markers to annotate in text. We want to highlight the linguistic theory of Raphael Micheli, which categorizes a broad panel of linguistic markers into three emotion expression modes (Micheli, 2014): *labeled*, *displayed*, and *suggested* emotion. Emotion can be expressed explicitly with an emotional label ("I am *happy* today"), be displayed with linguistic characteristics of an utterance such as interjections and punctuations ("*Ah!* That's great *!*"), or be suggested with the description of a situation that, in a given sociocultural context, leads to an emotion ("*She gave me a gift*"). Most annotation schemes have implicitly focused on the *labeled* emotion, overlooking the other two expression modes. Recently, annotation schemes based on appraisal theories implicitly concern themselves with the *suggested* emotion (Troiano et al., 2023). Micheli's theory thus analyzes the different types of verbal signs humans use to infer expressed emotions. In a complementary manner, theories of cognitive pragmatics are interested in the psychological mechanisms used to infer what is communicated, especially the emotions expressed by these different types of signs. In the next section, we will hypothesize that the sign categories distinguished by Micheli correspond to different sources of inferences postulated by cognitive pragmatics.

4 Cognitive Pragmatics and Emotional Communication

Two analyses of communication. Cognitive pragmatics is the branch of cognitive science concerned with how agents use and interpret signs in communication. In this and related branches, it is common to distinguish between two broad ways to analyze communication: the "dictionary analysis" (a.k.a. the "code", "semiotic", or "semantic" model) and the "detective analysis" (a.k.a. the "Gricean", "inferential", or "pragmatic" model) (Sperber and Wilson, 1995; Schlenker, 2016; Heintz and Scott-Phillips, 2023).

Dictionary analysis. The dictionary analysis depicts communication as a sender who intentionally or unintentionally encodes information into a signal that the receiver decodes. Vitally, prior to the communicative exchange, the sender and the receiver must share the same code. A code here is understood as a pre-established pairing between kinds of stimuli (symbolized by "<...>") and sets of information (symbolized by "[...]"). For instance, the Morse code consists of a pairing between <combinations of short and long signals> and [letters] that senders and receivers must share to communicate with it. Codes can be conventional, as the Morse code is and as is the formal semantics of a language: a code made of syntactical and lexical rules that pairs <strings of words> with [sentential meanings] (Heim and Kratzer, 1998). Codes can also be non-conventional or "natural" (Wharton, 2003; Bonard, 2023a). For instance, bees are thought to use a code pairing their <dances> with the [location of nectar]. As mentioned in section 2, humans are thought to use a code pairing types of <facial expressions> with types of [emotions expressed].

The main limitation of the dictionary analysis is that codes sometimes *underdetermine meaning*: The pre-established pairings between <types of stimuli> and [sets of information] are sometimes insufficient to account for the information communicated. Paradigmatically, in *conversational implicatures* (Grice, 1975), the utterer implicitly communicates information beyond what is linguistically encoded, beyond what is determined by syntactical and lexical rules. For instance (Wilson and Sperber, 2006), if Peter asks, "Did John pay back the money he owed you?" and Mary answers, "He forgot to go to the bank.", Peter will readily understand that Mary means "no". However, the relevant code – the rules pairing <English grammar and lexicon> with [sentential meaning] – is insufficient to account for this since the code only tells you that John forgot to go to the bank.

Codes underdetermine the meaning of verbal expressions of emotions as well. To illustrate, let us go back to Micheli's typology: *labeled*, *displayed*, and *suggested* emotions (Micheli, 2013). As far as *labeled* emotions are concerned, the dictionary analysis does quite well thanks to the pairing between <emotion words> (*e.g.*, happy, amazing, sadly) with the [emotion kinds] they refer to. However, even *labeled* emotions sometimes do not encode all that is communicated. For instance, "I am happy now" is explicit about the kind of emotion expressed but does not encode what the emotion is about. Nevertheless, we often correctly infer such information in the relevant context. The dictionary analysis fairs even less well with *displayed* emotions because these are often ambiguous. For instance, interjections such as "Wow!", "Damn!", "Fuck!", "Shit!", "Ah!", and "Oh!" though they readily display that the utterer undergoes an emotion, can express various positive and negative emotions. Furthermore, these interjections don't encode what emotions are about. However, receivers usually correctly infer these pieces of information. The dictionary analysis regarding *suggested* emotions is even more limited. Depending on what the person expressing their emotion believes or desires, a phrase that only suggests emotions can communicate pretty much any kind of emotion. Imagine, for instance, that someone says, "The ship has black sails.". In a certain context, this apparently vapid sentence may poignantly convey intense emotion – because, say, it means that the son of the utterer died, as in the story of Aegeus and Theseus. Note that, beyond verbal expression, most, if not all, types of emotional expressions also underdetermine what emotions are expressed. Facial expressions or acoustic cues (*e.g.*, screams, laughter, sighs) also communicate different emotions given different contexts (Aviezer et al., 2008; Teigen, 2008; Vlemincx et al., 2009; Barrett et al., 2011, 2019; Bonard, 2023b). The dictionary analysis is thus also insufficient for these kinds of emotional expressions.

So, how do humans disambiguate emotional expressions in cases where codes underdetermine what is communicated? If we trust contemporary cognitive pragmatics, the answer should be found in the detective analysis of communication.

Detective analysis. What we call "the detective analysis" is constituted by a family of theories developed by Paul Grice (Grice, 1957, 1989) and his heirs (for reviews, see Bonard (2021a), chapter one and appendix). Note that although our presentation aims to remain balanced, no universally accepted version of this analysis exists.

As mentioned, the detective analysis was developed to account for conversational implicatures, cases where what is communicated goes beyond what is conveyed through conventional meaning, as in Peter and Mary's example above. To do so, the detective analysis conceptualizes linguistic interpretation as a type of abductive reasoning – *i.e.*, as an inference that seeks the simplest and most likely conclusion given the evidence available. The analysis spells out three main sources of evidence:

1. *Codes*, *i.e.*, pre-established pairings between types of stimuli and sets of information, *e.g.*, English syntactical and lexical rules; the codes for verbal and nonverbal emotional expressions. As we saw, expressions using labeled (*e.g.*, "I'm happy") and displayed emotions (*e.g.*, "Damn!") are partially understood through such codes, though they are too ambiguous to account for all that is communicated.

2. *Pragmatic expectations*, *i.e.*, how people are expected to behave in given contexts, particularly the kind of signal they receive. For instance, in conversations, people are expected to say things relevant to the question under discussion (see Grice (1975)'s maxims of conversation). For this reason, although what is literally encoded in Mary's reply is that John forgot to go to the bank, Peter will nevertheless expect this to be relevant to the question he asked. Similarly, we expect someone's emotional expressions to be about something relevant to their concerns (Wharton et al., 2021; Bonard, 2022). For instance, if someone says "Damn!" after receiving a surprisingly nice compliment, we expect the compliment to be particularly relevant to the person and will interpret the interjection accordingly.

3. *Common ground*, *i.e.*, the information presumed to be shared by the participants in the exchange (Stalnaker, 2002). For instance, Mary and Peter both presume that a bank is a place where one can withdraw money. Similarly, we usually presume that receiving a compliment is something that one seeks, especially if it is surprisingly nice – though this is not always part of the common ground, *e.g.*, if the complimenter is the complimentee's archenemy. The common ground also allows us to understand that Aegeus can express deep despair with the sentence « The ship has black sails. ».

Based on these three sources of evidence, the detective analysis further postulates that the interpreter uses *mindreading* abilities (*i.e.*, theory of mind, mentalizing, or social cognition) to infer what is the most likely piece of information that is implicitly communicated – *e.g.*, Peter infers that Mary meant "no" and we infer that the person saying "Damn!" is probably pleased. Finally, the detective analysis specifies that the information so inferred is added to the common ground shared by participants in the exchange so that it may be a new source of evidence in the upcoming exchanges.

Let us note that the detective analysis predicts that the ability to correctly infer what is communicated by emotional expressions heavily depends on one's mind-reading capacities. Corroborating this prediction, children or people on the autistic spectrum may struggle to infer implicit meaning correctly, *e.g.*, conversational implicatures (Foppolo and Mazzaggio, 2024) or in expressions using suggested emotions (Blanc and Quenette, 2017).

5 Research Directions for Emotion Analysis

5.1 Towards a Unified Annotation Scheme

Training models on data annotated with a scheme that reflects the multifaceted nature of emotions is desirable to improve the capacity of language models to understand emotions. Such a scheme would need to integrate different perspectives on the emotional phenomena to allow for better study comparisons. This would also increase the performance and generalization of models.

Attempts at unification. Several recent studies attempt to unify different ways of annotating emotion in text. Campagnano et al. (2022) propose a new annotation scheme that unifies various schemes on emotion semantic roles. To choose a set of shared categories, the different discrete emotions from the schemes were converted to the basic emotions of Plutchik's theory (Plutchik, 2001). Klinger (2023) explores the divergences and commonalities between semantic role labeling of emotions and approaches based on appraisal theories. The study identifies several research directions, such as using appraisal variables to improve the task of detecting emotion causes, or analyzing experiencer-specific appraisals (Wegge et al., 2023). These studies show that combining schemes allows knowledge transfer between tasks, increasing performance and generalization.

In search of a common framework. What we have previously referred to as "the integrated framework for emotion theories" (section 2) aims to reconcile the main emotion theories in psychology (Scherer, 2022). In our view, it represents a strong candidate to provide a common framework for annotation schemes. As mentioned in section 2, this model considers that emotion consists of synchronized changes in different components: the appraisal process, action tendencies, bodily changes (motor expressions and physiological responses), and subjective feelings. Research in emotion analysis must draw from the recent debates in the psychology of emotions to bring existing annotation schemes into dialogue on a solid theoretical basis and, ideally, construct a unified annotation scheme.

Emotion comprises several interacting components. A unified annotation scheme could clarify some gray areas in emotion analysis, such as the lack of clear definitions for emotion semantic roles (*e.g.*, experiencer, cause, and target). It could also better situate existing schemes. For example, annotating discrete emotions and affective dimensions emphasizes subjective feeling, whereas annotating cognitive dimensions emphasizes appraisals. Few schemes account for physiological responses, motor expressions, and action tendencies. More generally, few schemes consider all components. Kim and Klinger (2019) analyze the communication of emotions in fiction through descriptions of subjective sensations, postures, facial expressions, and spatial relations between characters. Casel et al. (2021) associate text spans with categories corresponding to Scherer's emotional components. Cortal et al. (2022, 2023) structure emotional narratives according to components similar to Scherer's. Each text span corresponds to observable behaviors, thoughts, physical feelings, or appraisals. To our knowledge, no annotation schemes attempt to capture the interaction between components. Generally, emotion analysis pays little attention to the dynamic nature of emotion and the synchronization of its various components.

Improving the clarity of annotation guides. We note that few studies psychologically justify the choice of different objects to detect in the text. Emotion analysis needs to develop a systematic approach to compare annotation guides with one another, thereby precisely understanding how different annotation schemes capture emotion. Thus, these schemes must draw from psychological theories (section 2) but also from linguistic theories (sections 3.2 and 4) to identify linguistic markers that verbalize emotion. With clear annotation guides, it would be easier for research teams to focus on points of convergence between schemes.

5.2 Better Knowledge Use and Environmental Interaction

In natural language processing, *prompting* refers to supplying a tailored input to a language model, aiming to direct its generation process towards a desired response (Brown et al., 2020). Numerous prompting methods draw inspiration from human cognition to improve the performance of language models (Zhang et al., 2023b). These methods propose generating reasoning steps (Wei et al., 2023; Kojima et al., 2023), reasoning through multiple generated responses (Wang et al., 2023b; Yoran et al., 2023), facilitating communication by rephrasing questions (Deng et al., 2023), and self-improving with its own generated feedback (Madaan et al., 2023; Yuan et al., 2024).

Prompting methods for emotional understanding. Most methods have been explored to improve model performance on tasks requiring formal reasoning (Zhang et al., 2023b). We believe it is possible to adapt these methods or even create new ones to improve model performance on tasks requiring social reasoning, such as emotional understanding. It would be interesting to rely on the ability of language models to act as character simulators (Shanahan et al., 2023; Lu et al., 2024), capable of adopting multiple perspectives to change style (Deshpande et al., 2023), solve tasks requiring expert knowledge (Xu et al., 2023), or simulate discussions to encourage exploration (Wang et al., 2023c; Liang et al., 2023). Zhou et al. (2023) enhance the ability of language models to make relevant inferences for solving theory of mind tasks. They propose a reasoning structure that anticipates future challenges and reasons about potential actions. More globally, a major challenge in natural language processing is finding suitable reasoning structures to effectively use the internal knowledge of models (Kojima et al., 2023; Zhou et al., 2023, 2024). The contribution of the detective analysis (section 4) could prove valuable here: prompts that explicitly ask models to seek evidence from the three sources highlighted by this analysis could lead to better performance and explainability. Finally, the integrated framework for emotion theories (section 3) can serve as inspiration for prompts that aim to exploit all the different facets of emotions rather than focusing on just one of them (*e.g.*, subjective feeling).

Interaction with the environment. Current language models, trained solely on predicting missing words, have essentially mastered linguistic codes, *i.e.*, lexical and syntactic rules (section 4), which Mahowald et al. (2023) call "formal linguistic competence". However, they struggle to perform well on tasks relying on what Mahowald et al. (2023) call "functional linguistic competence", *i.e.* the skills required to use language in real-world situations. These skills centrally involve the mechanisms postulated by the detective analysis – in particular, sharing a common ground and having sensible pragmatic expectations (section 4). To address this limitation, studies augment language models with external modules like a mathematical calculator (Schick et al., 2023), a web browser (Gur et al., 2023), or a virtual environment (Park et al., 2023). Through tool manipulation, language models intertwine reasoning with action and can thus effectively combine internal with external knowledge (Yao et al., 2023). This point is crucial to develop models that exhibit human-like social behaviors. For example, Park et al. (2023) show that observation, planning, and reflection are important components for increasing the credibility of behaviors in a virtual environment. Research on human communication can help highlight relevant abilities to augment language models (*e.g.*, with external modules). This surely applies to emotional communication as well: models could be complemented with modules encapsulating, for instance, our knowledge of codes for emotional expressions, of how kinds of appraisals relate to kinds of emotions, and of how we expect people undergoing emotions to behave, along the lines sketched in sections 2 and 4 above.

5.3 Better Benchmarks for Emotional Understanding

Recent benchmarks evaluate language models on specific aspects of emotional understanding (Wang et al., 2023a; Paech, 2024), but they don't consider its full richness (Scherer, 2007; Mayer et al., 2008; O'Connor et al., 2019). For example, Paech (2024) assesses emotional understanding by predicting the intensity of multiple emotions in conflict scenes. Some benchmarks evaluate models on related tasks, such as sentiment analysis (Zhang et al., 2023a) and theory of mind (Zhou et al., 2023; Ma et al., 2023; Kim et al., 2023; Gandhi et al., 2023). However, no benchmark specifically proposes to evaluate the multiple facets of emotions that affective sciences reveal (section 2). Therefore, it is difficult to know whether current models are efficient for emotional understanding.

This limitation is compounded by the fact that it is difficult to clearly determine which properties of emotional understanding are to be evaluated. We believe that evaluating language models should be grounded in research on human emotional communication, especially psycholinguistics. For example, before the age of ten, basic emotions (e.g., joy or sadness) are better remembered than complex emotions (e.g., pride or guilt) (Davidson et al., 2001; Creissen and Blanc, 2017). From six to ten years old, *labeled* emotions are better understood than *suggested* emotions (Blanc, 2010; Creissen and Blanc, 2017). Another example of relevant studies concerns the difficulty that autistic people have in understanding different types of emotional expressions (Foppolo and Mazzaggio, 2024). These studies suggest that, for humans, different types of emotions and different modes of emotional expression are more or less difficult to interpret. It would be desirable for benchmarks to evaluate language models in ways that reflect the relative difficulty of tasks for humans. Such a project would certainly benefit from research in cognitive pragmatics (section 4), knowing, for example, that people with communication disorders have difficulty understanding conversational implicatures (Foppolo and Mazzaggio, 2024), which indicates that the different sources of evidence distinguished by the detective analysis are associated with different levels of difficulty.

We believe the concept of emotion should be addressed through its relationship with text understanding, i.e., the ability of a reader to construct a mental representation of a situation in a text (Zwaan and Radvansky, 1998). Thus, we would need to go beyond current conceptualizations of emotion in natural language processing (section 3.1) to consider the diversity of linguistic markers used to verbalize emotion (section 3.2) as well as the different types of emotion (basic or complex) from psycholinguistic research (section 2). Inspired by previous studies, Etienne et al. (2022) propose an annotation scheme that considers emotion expression modes and types of emotion. Future benchmarks assessing the ability of language models to analyze emotions should consider such annotation schemes, which, as we have recommended, seek to be solidly based on relevant research in cognitive science.

6 Conclusion

Emotion analysis has several limitations that, we believe, are partially due to a lack of communication with other disciplines and, in particular, cognitive science. We propose exploiting cognitive science research on emotions and communication to address some limitations, especially what we called "the integrated framework" in emotion theories and "the detective analysis" in cognitive pragmatics. We suggest that this opens the way for constructing new annotation schemes, methods, and benchmarks for emotional understanding that consider the multiple facets of human emotion and communication.

Limitations

We propose a theoretical perspective on emotion analysis in natural language processing. We believe it would benefit the emotion analysis community to adopt an interdisciplinary approach by drawing from cognitive science theories to address certain existing limitations in the research field. In practice, this is a challenging task. Although we focus on concrete actions that could be undertaken soon (for example, clarifying annotation guidelines), we recognize that our contribution involves speculative research directions. In future research, it would be desirable to complement these speculative aspects with more concrete proposals, notably with empirically testable hypotheses and implementable algorithms.

Ethics Statement

We have not conducted any experimentation or published any data or models in this paper. The present research aims to better understand human emotional communication, not to develop tools for automatically detecting individuals' private subjective states. While we believe our paper does not present direct ethical concerns, the research directions it raises could indirectly harm individuals and societal structures. Although we have highlighted the potential benefits of natural language processing applications (such as emotion regulation tools), it is crucial to ensure that the development and use of such tools do not have any adverse effects in the future.

Acknowledgements

Thanks to the AI-PHI group[*] for making our collaboration possible and for insightful discussions. Thanks also to the ACL ARR 2024 February reviewers for useful and constructive feedback.

References

Ian A. Apperly and Stephen A. Butterfill. 2009. Do humans have two systems to track beliefs and belief-like states? *Psychological review*, 116(4):953. Publisher: American Psychological Association.

Magda B. Arnold. 1960. *Emotion and Personality*. Columbia University Press, New York.

Jaan Aru, Aqeel Labash, Oriol Corcoll, and Raul Vicente. 2023. Mind the gap: challenges of deep learning approaches to Theory of Mind. *Artificial Intelligence Review*, 56(9):9141–9156.

Hillel Aviezer, Ran R. Hassin, Jennifer Ryan, Cheryl Grady, Josh Susskind, Adam Anderson, Morris Moscovitch, and Shlomo Bentin. 2008. Angry, disgusted, or afraid? Studies on the malleability of emotion perception. *Psychological science*, 19(7):724–732. Publisher: SAGE Publications Sage CA: Los Angeles, CA.

Lisa Feldman Barrett, Ralph Adolphs, Stacy Marsella, Aleix M. Martinez, and Seth D. Pollak. 2019. Emotional expressions reconsidered: Challenges to inferring emotion from human facial movements. *Psychological Science in the Public Interest*. Publisher: SAGE PublicationsSage CA: Los Angeles, CA.

Lisa Feldman Barrett, Batja Mesquita, and Maria Gendron. 2011. Context in emotion perception. *Current Directions in Psychological Science*, 20(5):286–290. Publisher: Sage Publications Sage CA: Los Angeles, CA.

Nathalie Blanc. 2010. La compréhension des contes entre 5 et 7 ans: Quelle représentation des informations émotionnelles? [The comprehension of the tales between 5 and 7 year-olds: Which representation of emotional information?]. *Canadian Journal of Experimental Psychology / Revue canadienne de psychologie expérimentale*, 64(4):256–265.

Nathalie Blanc and Guy Quenette. 2017. La production d'inférences émotionnelles entre 8 et 10 ans: quelle méthodologie pour quels résultats? *Enfance*, 4(4):503–511. Publisher: NecPlus.

Constant Bonard. 2021a. *Meaning and emotion: The extended Gricean model and what emotional signs mean*. Doctoral dissertation, University of Geneva and University of Antwerp.

[*]https://ai-phi.github.io/

Constant Bonard. 2021b. Émotions et sensibilité aux valeurs : quatre conceptions philosophiques contemporaines. *Revue de métaphysique et de morale*, 110(2):209–229. Place: Paris cedex 14 Publisher: Presses Universitaires de France.

Constant Bonard. 2022. Beyond ostension: Introducing the expressive principle of relevance. *Journal of Pragmatics*, 187:13–23.

Constant Bonard. 2023a. Natural meaning, probabilistic meaning, and the interpretation of emotional signs. *Synthese*, 201(5):167. Publisher: Springer.

Constant Bonard. 2023b. Underdeterminacy without ostension: A blind spot in the prevailing models of communication. *Mind & Language*.

Constant Bonard. 2024. Can AI and humans genuinely communicate? In Anna Strasser, editor, *Anna's AI Anthology. How to live with smart machines?* Xenemoi, Berlin.

Constant Bonard and Julien Deonna. 2023. Emotion and language in philosophy. In Gesine Lenore Schiewer, Jeanette Altarriba, and Bee Chin Ng, editors, *Language and emotion: An international handbook*, volume 1, pages 54–72. de Gruyter, Berlin.

Laura Ana Maria Bostan, Evgeny Kim, and Roman Klinger. 2020. GoodNewsEveryone: A corpus of news headlines annotated with emotions, semantic roles, and reader perception. In *Proceedings of the Twelfth Language Resources and Evaluation Conference*, pages 1554–1566, Marseille, France. European Language Resources Association.

Laura-Ana-Maria Bostan and Roman Klinger. 2018. An analysis of annotated corpora for emotion classification in text. In *Proceedings of the 27th International Conference on Computational Linguistics*, pages 2104–2119, Santa Fe, New Mexico, USA. Association for Computational Linguistics.

Tom Brown, Benjamin Mann, Nick Ryder, Melanie Subbiah, Jared D Kaplan, Prafulla Dhariwal, Arvind Neelakantan, Pranav Shyam, Girish Sastry, Amanda Askell, Sandhini Agarwal, Ariel Herbert-Voss, Gretchen Krueger, Tom Henighan, Rewon Child, Aditya Ramesh, Daniel Ziegler, Jeffrey Wu, Clemens Winter, Chris Hesse, Mark Chen, Eric Sigler, Mateusz Litwin, Scott Gray, Benjamin Chess, Jack Clark, Christopher Berner, Sam McCandlish, Alec Radford, Ilya Sutskever, and Dario Amodei. 2020. Language Models are Few-Shot Learners. In *Advances in Neural Information Processing Systems*, volume 33, pages 1877–1901. Curran Associates, Inc.

Sven Buechel and Udo Hahn. 2017. EmoBank: Studying the impact of annotation perspective and representation format on dimensional emotion analysis. In *Proceedings of the 15th Conference of the European Chapter of the Association for Computational Linguistics: Volume 2, Short Papers*, pages 578–585, Valencia, Spain. Association for Computational Linguistics.

Sven Buechel, Luise Modersohn, and Udo Hahn. 2021. Towards label-agnostic emotion embeddings. In *Proceedings of the 2021 Conference on Empirical Methods in Natural Language Processing*, pages 9231–9249, Online and Punta Cana, Dominican Republic. Association for Computational Linguistics.

Cesare Campagnano, Simone Conia, and Roberto Navigli. 2022. SRL4E – Semantic Role Labeling for Emotions: A unified evaluation framework. In *Proceedings of the 60th Annual Meeting of the Association for Computational Linguistics (Volume 1: Long Papers)*, pages 4586–4601, Dublin, Ireland. Association for Computational Linguistics.

Felix Casel, Amelie Heindl, and Roman Klinger. 2021. Emotion recognition under consideration of the emotion component process model. In *Proceedings of the 17th Conference on Natural Language Processing (KONVENS 2021)*, pages 49–61, Düsseldorf, Germany. KONVENS 2021 Organizers.

Gustave Cortal. 2024. Sequence-to-sequence language models for character and emotion detection in dream narratives. In *Proceedings of the 2024 Joint International Conference on Computational Linguistics, Language Resources and Evaluation (LREC-COLING 2024)*, pages 14717–14728, Torino, Italia. ELRA and ICCL.

Gustave Cortal, Alain Finkel, Patrick Paroubek, and Lina Ye. 2022. Natural language processing for cognitive analysis of emotions. In *Semantics, Memory, and Emotion 2022*, Paris, France.

Gustave Cortal, Alain Finkel, Patrick Paroubek, and Lina Ye. 2023. Emotion recognition based on psychological components in guided narratives for emotion regulation. In *Proceedings of the 7th Joint SIGHUM Workshop on Computational Linguistics for Cultural Heritage, Social Sciences, Humanities and Literature*, pages 72–81, Dubrovnik, Croatia. Association for Computational Linguistics.

Leda Cosmides and John Tooby. 2000. Evolutionary psychology and the emotions. In Michael Lewis and Jeannette M. Haviland-Jones, editors, *Handbook of emotions*, 2nd edition, pages 91–115. Guilford Press, New York. Publisher: Citeseer.

S. Creissen and N. Blanc. 2017. Quelle représentation des différentes facettes de la dimension émotionnelle d'une histoire entre l'âge de 6 et 10 ans ? Apports d'une étude multimédia. *Psychologie Française*, 62(3):263–277.

Charles Darwin. 1872. *The expression of the emotions in man and animals.* John Murray, London.

Denise Davidson, Zupei Luo, and Matthew J. Burden. 2001. Children's recall of emotional behaviours, emotional labels, and nonemotional behaviours: Does emotion enhance memory? *Cognition and Emotion*, 15(1):1–26.

Luna De Bruyne, Orphee De Clercq, and Veronique Hoste. 2020. An emotional mess! deciding on a framework for building a Dutch emotion-annotated corpus. In *Proceedings of the Twelfth Language Resources and Evaluation Conference*, pages 1643–1651, Marseille, France. European Language Resources Association.

Dorottya Demszky, Dana Movshovitz-Attias, Jeongwoo Ko, Alan Cowen, Gaurav Nemade, and Sujith Ravi. 2020. GoEmotions: A dataset of fine-grained emotions. In *Proceedings of the 58th Annual Meeting of the Association for Computational Linguistics*, pages 4040–4054, Online. Association for Computational Linguistics.

Yihe Deng, Weitong Zhang, Zixiang Chen, and Quanquan Gu. 2023. Rephrase and Respond: Let Large Language Models Ask Better Questions for Themselves.

Ameet Deshpande, Vishvak Murahari, Tanmay Rajpurohit, Ashwin Kalyan, and Karthik Narasimhan. 2023. Toxicity in ChatGPT: Analyzing Persona-assigned Language Models.

Jacob Devlin, Ming-Wei Chang, Kenton Lee, and Kristina Toutanova. 2019. BERT: Pre-training of deep bidirectional transformers for language understanding. In *Proceedings of the 2019 Conference of the North American Chapter of the Association for Computational Linguistics: Human Language Technologies, Volume 1 (Long and Short Papers)*, pages 4171–4186, Minneapolis, Minnesota. Association for Computational Linguistics.

Paul Ekman. 1999. Basic emotions. In Tim Dalgleish and Mike J. Power, editors, *Handbook of cognition and emotion*, pages 45–60. John Wiley & Sons Ltd, Chichester.

Paul Ekman and W V Friesen. 1971. Constants across cultures in the face and emotion. *Journal of personality and social psychology*, 17 2:124–9.

Aline Etienne, Delphine Battistelli, and Gwénolé Lecorvé. 2022. A (psycho-)linguistically motivated scheme for annotating and exploring emotions in a genre-diverse corpus. In *Proceedings of the Thirteenth Language Resources and Evaluation Conference*, pages 603–612, Marseille, France. European Language Resources Association.

Francesca Foppolo and Greta Mazzaggio. 2024. Conversational Implicature and Communication Disorders. In Martin J. Ball, Nicole Müller, and Elizabeth Spencer, editors, *The Handbook of Clinical Linguistics, Second Edition*, 1 edition, pages 15–27. Wiley.

Kanishk Gandhi, Jan-Philipp Fränken, Tobias Gerstenberg, and Noah D. Goodman. 2023. Understanding Social Reasoning in Language Models with Language Models.

Mitchell Green. 2007. *Self-expression*. Oxford University Press, Oxford.

H. Paul Grice. 1957. Meaning. *The Philosophical Review*, 66(3):377–388.

H. Paul Grice. 1975. Logic and conversation. In *Speech acts*, pages 41–58. Brill, Leiden.

H. Paul Grice. 1989. *Studies in the way of words*. Harvard University Press, Cambridge (MA).

Izzeddin Gur, Hiroki Furuta, Austin Huang, Mustafa Safdari, Yutaka Matsuo, Douglas Eck, and Aleksandra Faust. 2023. A Real-World WebAgent with Planning, Long Context Understanding, and Program Synthesis.

Irene Heim and Angelika Kratzer. 1998. *Semantics in generative grammar*. Wiley, Hoboken. Google-Books-ID: jAvR2DB3pPIC.

Christophe Heintz and Thom Scott-Phillips. 2023. Expression unleashed: The evolutionary & cognitive foundations of human communication. *Behavioral and Brain Sciences*, 46:E1. Type: article.

Jan Hofmann, Enrica Troiano, Kai Sassenberg, and Roman Klinger. 2020. Appraisal theories for emotion classification in text. In *Proceedings of the 28th International Conference on Computational Linguistics*, pages 125–138, Barcelona, Spain (Online). International Committee on Computational Linguistics.

Bart Holterman and Kees van Deemter. 2023. Does ChatGPT have Theory of Mind? ArXiv:2305.14020 [cs].

Carroll E. Izard. 1992. Basic Emotions, Relations Among Emotions, and Emotion-Cognition Relations. *Psychological Review*, 99(3):561–565.

Evgeny Kim and Roman Klinger. 2018. Who Feels What and Why? Annotation of a Literature Corpus with Semantic Roles of Emotions. In *Proceedings of the 27th International Conference on Computational Linguistics*, pages 1345–1359, Santa Fe, New Mexico, USA. Association for Computational Linguistics.

Evgeny Kim and Roman Klinger. 2019. An analysis of emotion communication channels in fan-fiction: Towards emotional storytelling. In *Proceedings of the Second Workshop on Storytelling*, pages 56–64, Florence, Italy. Association for Computational Linguistics.

Hyunwoo Kim, Melanie Sclar, Xuhui Zhou, Ronan Le Bras, Gunhee Kim, Yejin Choi, and Maarten Sap. 2023. FANToM: A Benchmark for Stress-testing Machine Theory of Mind in Interactions.

Roman Klinger. 2023. Where are We in Event-centric Emotion Analysis? Bridging Emotion Role Labeling and Appraisal-based Approaches. In *Proceedings of the Big Picture Workshop*, pages 1–17, Singapore. Association for Computational Linguistics.

Takeshi Kojima, Shixiang Shane Gu, Machel Reid, Yutaka Matsuo, and Yusuke Iwasawa. 2023. Large Language Models are Zero-Shot Reasoners.

Michal Kosinski. 2023. Theory of Mind Might Have Spontaneously Emerged in Large Language Models. ArXiv:2302.02083 [cs].

Christelle Langley, Bogdan Ionut Cirstea, Fabio Cuzzolin, and Barbara J. Sahakian. 2022. Theory of Mind and Preference Learning at the Interface of Cognitive Science, Neuroscience, and AI: A Review. *Frontiers in Artificial Intelligence*, 5.

Richard S. Lazarus. 1991. Progress on a cognitive-motivational-relational theory of emotion. *American psychologist*, 46(8):819.

Sophia Yat Mei Lee, Ying Chen, and Chu-Ren Huang. 2010. A text-driven rule-based system for emotion cause detection. In *Proceedings of the NAACL HLT 2010 Workshop on Computational Approaches to Analysis and Generation of Emotion in Text*, pages 45–53, Los Angeles, CA. Association for Computational Linguistics.

Tian Liang, Zhiwei He, Wenxiang Jiao, Xing Wang, Yan Wang, Rui Wang, Yujiu Yang, Zhaopeng Tu, and Shuming Shi. 2023. Encouraging Divergent Thinking in Large Language Models through Multi-Agent Debate.

Keming Lu, Bowen Yu, Chang Zhou, and Jingren Zhou. 2024. Large Language Models are Superpositions of All Characters: Attaining Arbitrary Role-play via Self-Alignment.

Ziqiao Ma, Jacob Sansom, Run Peng, and Joyce Chai. 2023. Towards A Holistic Landscape of Situated Theory of Mind in Large Language Models.

Aman Madaan, Niket Tandon, Prakhar Gupta, Skyler Hallinan, Luyu Gao, Sarah Wiegreffe, Uri Alon, Nouha Dziri, Shrimai Prabhumoye, Yiming Yang, Shashank Gupta, Bodhisattwa Prasad Majumder, Katherine Hermann, Sean Welleck, Amir Yazdanbakhsh, and Peter Clark. 2023. Self-Refine: Iterative Refinement with Self-Feedback.

Kyle Mahowald, Anna A. Ivanova, Idan A. Blank, Nancy Kanwisher, Joshua B. Tenenbaum, and Evelina Fedorenko. 2023. Dissociating language and thought in large language models.

John D. Mayer, Richard D. Roberts, and Sigal G. Barsade. 2008. Human Abilities: Emotional Intelligence. *Annual Review of Psychology*, 59(1):507–536.

Raphaël Micheli. 2013. Esquisse d'une typologie des différents modes de sémiotisation verbale de l'émotion. *Semen*, (35).

Raphaël Micheli. 2014. *Les émotions dans les discours*. De Boeck Supérieur.

Melanie Mitchell and David C. Krakauer. 2023. The debate over understanding in AI's large language models. *Proceedings of the National Academy of Sciences*, 120(13):e2215907120. Publisher: Proceedings of the National Academy of Sciences.

Agnes Moors. 2022. *Demystifying emotions: A Typology of theories in psychology and philosophy*, cambridge university press edition. Cambridge.

Agnes Moors, Phoebe C. Ellsworth, Klaus R. Scherer, and Nico H. Frijda. 2013. Appraisal theories of emotion: state of the art and future development. *Emotion Review*, 5(2):119–124. Publisher: Sage Publications Sage UK: London, England.

Laura Oberländer, Kevin Reich, and Roman Klinger. 2020. Experiencers, Stimuli, or Targets: Which Semantic Roles Enable Machine Learning to Infer the Emotions? *arXiv:2011.01599 [cs]*.

Peter J. O'Connor, Andrew Hill, Maria Kaya, and Brett Martin. 2019. The measurement of emotional intelligence: A critical review of the literature and recommendations for researchers and practitioners. *Frontiers in psychology*, 10:1116. Publisher: Frontiers.

Samuel J. Paech. 2024. EQ-Bench: An Emotional Intelligence Benchmark for Large Language Models.

Jaak Panksepp. 1998. *Affective neuroscience: the foundations of human and animal emotions*. Oxford University Press, New York.

Joon Sung Park, Joseph C. O'Brien, Carrie J. Cai, Meredith Ringel Morris, Percy Liang, and Michael S. Bernstein. 2023. Generative Agents: Interactive Simulacra of Human Behavior.

Robert Plutchik. 2001. The Nature of Emotions: Human emotions have deep evolutionary roots, a fact that may explain their complexity and provide tools for clinical practice. *American Scientist*, 89(4):344–350.

Soujanya Poria, Devamanyu Hazarika, Navonil Majumder, and Rada Mihalcea. 2020. Beneath the Tip of the Iceberg: Current Challenges and New Directions in Sentiment Analysis Research.

James A. Russell and Lisa Barrett. 1999. Core affect, prototypical emotional episodes, and other things called emotion: Dissecting the elephant. *Journal of personality and social psychology*, 76:805–19.

Andrea Scarantino. 2017. How to do things with emotional expressions: The theory of affective pragmatics. *Psychological Inquiry*, 28(2-3):165–185. Publisher: Taylor & Francis.

Stanley Schachter and Jerome Singer. 1962. Cognitive, social, and physiological determinants of emotional state. *Psychological review*, 69(5):379. Publisher: American Psychological Association.

Klaus R. Scherer. 2007. Componential emotion theory can inform models of emotional competence. Publisher: Oxford University Press.

Klaus R. Scherer. 2022. Theory convergence in emotion science is timely and realistic. *Cognition and Emotion*, 36(2):154–170.

Klaus R. Scherer and Agnes Moors. 2019. The emotion process: event appraisal and component differentiation. *Annual Review of Psychology*, 70:719–745. Publisher: Annual Reviews.

Timo Schick, Jane Dwivedi-Yu, Roberto Dessì, Roberta Raileanu, Maria Lomeli, Luke Zettlemoyer, Nicola Cancedda, and Thomas Scialom. 2023. Toolformer: Language Models Can Teach Themselves to Use Tools.

Philippe Schlenker. 2016. The semantics-pragmatics interface. In Maria Aloni and Paul Dekker, editors, *The Cambridge Handbook of Formal Semantics*, pages 664–727. Cambridge University Press, Cambridge.

Murray Shanahan, Kyle McDonell, and Laria Reynolds. 2023. Role play with large language models. *Nature*, 623(7987):493–498.

Natalie Shapira, Mosh Levy, Seyed Hossein Alavi, Xuhui Zhou, Yejin Choi, Yoav Goldberg, Maarten Sap, and Vered Shwartz. 2023. Clever Hans or Neural Theory of Mind? Stress Testing Social Reasoning in Large Language Models. ArXiv:2305.14763 [cs].

Dan Sperber and Deirdre Wilson. 1995. *Relevance: Communication and cognition*, 2nd edition edition. Blackwell, Oxford and Cambridge (MA).

Robert Stalnaker. 2002. Common ground. *Linguistics and philosophy*, 25(5/6):701–721.

Gala Stojnić, Kanishk Gandhi, Shannon Yasuda, Brenden M. Lake, and Moira R. Dillon. 2023. Commonsense psychology in human infants and machines. *Cognition*, 235:105406.

Karl Halvor Teigen. 2008. Is a sigh "just a sigh"? Sighs as emotional signals and responses to a difficult task. *Scandinavian journal of Psychology*, 49(1):49–57. Publisher: Wiley Online Library.

Silvan Tomkins. 1962. *Affect imagery consciousness*, volume Volume I: The positive affects. Springer, New York.

Enrica Troiano, Laura Oberländer, and Roman Klinger. 2022. Dimensional Modeling of Emotions in Text with Appraisal Theories: Corpus Creation, Annotation Reliability, and Prediction. *Computational Linguistics*, pages 1–71.

Enrica Troiano, Laura Oberländer, and Roman Klinger. 2023. Dimensional modeling of emotions in text with appraisal theories: Corpus creation, annotation reliability, and prediction. *Computational Linguistics*, 49(1):1–72.

Sean Trott, Cameron Jones, Tyler Chang, James Michaelov, and Benjamin Bergen. 2022. Do Large Language Models know what humans know? *arXiv preprint arXiv:2209.01515*.

Tomer Ullman. 2023. Large Language Models Fail on Trivial Alterations to Theory-of-Mind Tasks. ArXiv:2302.08399 [cs].

Elke Vlemincx, Ilse Van Diest, Steven De Peuter, Johan Bresseleers, Katleen Bogaerts, Stien Fannes, Wan Li, and Omer Van Den Bergh. 2009. Why do you sigh? Sigh rate during induced stress and relief. *Psychophysiology*, 46(5):1005–1013. Publisher: Wiley Online Library.

Xuena Wang, Xueting Li, Zi Yin, Yue Wu, and Jia Liu. 2023a. Emotional intelligence of Large Language Models. *Journal of Pacific Rim Psychology*, 17:18344909231213958.

Xuezhi Wang, Jason Wei, Dale Schuurmans, Quoc Le, Ed Chi, Sharan Narang, Aakanksha Chowdhery, and Denny Zhou. 2023b. Self-Consistency Improves Chain of Thought Reasoning in Language Models.

Zhenhailong Wang, Shaoguang Mao, Wenshan Wu, Tao Ge, Furu Wei, and Heng Ji. 2023c. Unleashing Cognitive Synergy in Large Language Models: A Task-Solving Agent through Multi-Persona Self-Collaboration.

Maximilian Wegge, Enrica Troiano, Laura Oberländer, and Roman Klinger. 2023. Experiencer-Specific Emotion and Appraisal Prediction.

Jason Wei, Xuezhi Wang, Dale Schuurmans, Maarten Bosma, Brian Ichter, Fei Xia, Ed Chi, Quoc Le, and Denny Zhou. 2023. Chain-of-Thought Prompting Elicits Reasoning in Large Language Models.

Tim Wharton. 2003. Natural pragmatics and natural codes. *Mind & language*, 18(5):447–477. Publisher: Wiley Online Library.

Tim Wharton. 2016. That bloody so-and-so has retired: Expressives revisited. *Lingua*, 175:20–35. Publisher: Elsevier.

Tim Wharton, Constant Bonard, Daniel Dukes, David Sander, and Steve Oswald. 2021. Relevance and emotion. *Journal of Pragmatics*, 181:259–269.

Deirdre Wilson and Dan Sperber. 2006. Relevance theory. In Laurence Horn, editor, *The Handbook of pragmatics*. Blackwell, Oxford.

Benfeng Xu, An Yang, Junyang Lin, Quan Wang, Chang Zhou, Yongdong Zhang, and Zhendong Mao. 2023. ExpertPrompting: Instructing Large Language Models to be Distinguished Experts.

Shunyu Yao, Jeffrey Zhao, Dian Yu, Nan Du, Izhak Shafran, Karthik Narasimhan, and Yuan Cao. 2023. ReAct: Synergizing Reasoning and Acting in Language Models.

Ori Yoran, Tomer Wolfson, Ben Bogin, Uri Katz, Daniel Deutch, and Jonathan Berant. 2023. Answering Questions by Meta-Reasoning over Multiple Chains of Thought. In *Proceedings of the 2023 Conference on Empirical Methods in Natural Language Processing*, pages 5942–5966, Singapore. Association for Computational Linguistics.

Weizhe Yuan, Richard Yuanzhe Pang, Kyunghyun Cho, Sainbayar Sukhbaatar, Jing Xu, and Jason Weston. 2024. Self-Rewarding Language Models.

Hongli Zhan, Desmond Ong, and Junyi Jessy Li. 2023. Evaluating Subjective Cognitive Appraisals of Emotions from Large Language Models. In *Findings of the Association for Computational Linguistics: EMNLP 2023*, pages 14418–14446, Singapore. Association for Computational Linguistics.

Wenxuan Zhang, Yue Deng, Bing Liu, Sinno Jialin Pan, and Lidong Bing. 2023a. Sentiment Analysis in the Era of Large Language Models: A Reality Check.

Wenxuan Zhang, Xin Li, Yang Deng, Lidong Bing, and Wai Lam. 2022. A Survey on Aspect-Based Sentiment Analysis: Tasks, Methods, and Challenges. *arXiv:2203.01054 [cs]*.

Zhuosheng Zhang, Yao Yao, Aston Zhang, Xiangru Tang, Xinbei Ma, Zhiwei He, Yiming Wang, Mark Gerstein, Rui Wang, Gongshen Liu, and Hai Zhao. 2023b. Igniting Language Intelligence: The Hitchhiker's Guide From Chain-of-Thought Reasoning to Language Agents.

Pei Zhou, Aman Madaan, Srividya Pranavi Potharaju, Aditya Gupta, Kevin R. McKee, Ari Holtzman, Jay Pujara, Xiang Ren, Swaroop Mishra, Aida Nematzadeh, Shyam Upadhyay, and Manaal Faruqui. 2023. How FaR Are Large Language Models From Agents with Theory-of-Mind?

Pei Zhou, Jay Pujara, Xiang Ren, Xinyun Chen, Heng-Tze Cheng, Quoc V. Le, Ed H. Chi, Denny Zhou, Swaroop Mishra, and Huaixiu Steven Zheng. 2024. Self-Discover: Large Language Models Self-Compose Reasoning Structures.

R. A. Zwaan and G. A. Radvansky. 1998. Situation models in language comprehension and memory. *Psychological Bulletin*, 123(2):162–185.

Author Index

Association for Computational Linguistics
209 N. Eighth Street
Stroudsburg, Pennsylvania 18360

ISBN 979-8-3313-0160-6

CURRAN ASSOCIATES INC.
proceedings.com